The Complete Plays
of
William Congreve

Curtain Playwrights

GENERAL EDITOR:

R. C. Bald

The Complete Plays
of
William Congreve

Edited by

Herbert Davis

The University of Chicago Press
Chicago and London

Library of Congress Catalog Card Number: 66–20598

THE UNIVERSITY OF CHICAGO PRESS, CHICAGO & LONDON
The University of Toronto Press, Toronto 5, Canada

Published 1967. Composed and printed by William Clowes and Sons, Limited, London and Beccles, England

Preface

This edition of the plays of William Congreve provides a text based on the first printed quartos of the single plays, which takes us as near as we can get to the plays as his audience first heard them in the theater, and shows on what his reputation was founded. It seemed more appropriate for a series of playbooks to reproduce the plays as they belonged to the theater rather than the later, altered versions that Congreve himself prepared for the collected edition of his *Works*, published in 1710. For some of his later alterations were due to his concession to the changing tastes as well as to the royal proclamations for reforming the abuses of the theater. Some were due to his desire to provide a "reading edition" of his whole work, which led him for example to divide his plays into acts and scenes in accordance with the classical and the French tradition, and to rewrite much of the verse of *The Mourning Bride* in a more regular fashion. Although these changes are not here incorporated into the text, they are recorded in the collations of all the later editions printed in Congreve's lifetime, which have been placed at the end of the volume together with the lists of the corrections and emendations made in the copytext of the plays, with the source of those emendations.

The general introduction is concerned only with Congreve's work as a dramatist and with the early part of his life before 1700 when he was writing for the theater. A short account of the composition and sources, the first performances and subsequent reputation of each play precedes the text; and the footnotes are intended to supply such glosses, explanations, or illustrations as may be required by the modern reader.

I began this work some time ago in Oxford, where in the Bodleian Library I was able to examine copies of all the early printed editions of the plays and to collate them with copies from Worcester College and with the Bute copies temporarily on loan from the National Library of Scotland. I have also examined copies in the British Museum and in the Brotherton Library at the University of Leeds. Since then I have been granted fellowships that enabled me to work for nine months at the Huntington Library and for three months at the Folger Library. To their directors and trustees, I am much indebted for the privilege of sharing in the life of those delightful academies and centers of research, so splendidly served by the devoted and expert staffs of the libraries. I am also indebted to the Houghton Library of Harvard University for the machine copies of the plays from which this text has been printed and for others of later editions, which I have used for collation.

I was invited to undertake this edition by my old friend Cecil Bald, whose wide learning and rigorous scholarship I had learned to admire from the time when we were colleagues at Cornell University in 1938. I have had the benefit of his encouragement and his help throughout, and had the satisfaction of placing the completed manuscript in his hands a few months before his sudden death, which meant so great a loss to all concerned with English studies in the seventeenth century. I am also indebted to Fredson Bowers for his advice on matters concerned with the text and for the use of some of his notes of variant copies of Congreve's plays.

Earlier editions have been consulted: *The Complete Works of William Congreve* edited for the Nonesuch Press, London, in 1923 by the Reverend Montagu Summers; *Congreve, Complete Works*, 2 vols., World's Classics, edited in 1925 and 1928 by Bonamy Dobrée; *The Works of Congreve*, in one volume, edited in 1930 by F. W. Bateson, who very kindly gave me his collations of all the Harvard copies of the plays. Finally, I should like to acknowledge the particular generosity of John Hodges, who offered me the use of everything in his large collection, and whose volumes on the life, the library and the letters of Congreve have been constantly at my elbow.

The sharpest criticism and the ablest support have come from my wife, whose devotion to the theater has been of longer standing than mine.

HERBERT DAVIS

Contents

I

Introduction

When Congreve's first play was printed in 1693, he was hailed as Dryden's successor:

> The Darling, and last Comfort of his Years:
>
> . . . .
>
> Heir to his Merit, be in Fame his Son.
> What thou hast done, shews all is in thy Power.[1]

Congreve was then a young man of twenty-three, with less than four years' experience of the town, who had written enough to show that he was a better poet than lawyer and had just brought off his first great popular success in the theater.

> What mayn't we then, great Youth, of thee presage,
> Whose Art and Wit so much transcend thy Age?
> How wilt thou shine at thy Meridian height?
> Who, at thy rising, give so vast a Light.[2]

This may be said to be simply the enthusiasm of his young friends, fellow students at Trinity College, Dublin, or at the Middle Temple; but it was another matter when Dryden himself, in the following year, addressed some lines "To my Dear Friend Mr. Congreve" to be printed as prefatory verses to his second comedy, *The Double-Dealer*. In these, he greets him as the heir to all wealth of English comedy. "o'er-matching in wit" both Jonson and Fletcher, combining all the beauties of his predecessors such as Etherege and Wycherley and Southerne—and finally sets him at the side of Shakespeare:

> Heav'n, that but once was Prodigal before,
> To Shakespeare gave as much; she cou'd not give him
> more.

But, then, as if to protect him from any animosity that such extravagant praise might well call forth, he adds these charming lines:

> All this in blooming Youth you have Atchiev'd;
> Nor are your foil'd Contemporaries griev'd;

[1] See p. 31.
[2] See p. 33.

So much the sweetness of your manners move,
We cannot envy you because we Love.[3]

Even this was true. For at the very same moment, one of these "foil'd Contemporaries," a student a few years senior to Congreve at Trinity College, with no less wit but not yet the chance to prove it, was also addressing Congreve in verses probably intended to be printed before his next play. Already he had hopes that Congreve would "reform the stage":

For never did poetic mine before
Produce a richer vein or cleaner ore;
The bullion stampt in your refining mind
Serves by retail to furnish half mankind.[4]

The imagery that Swift uses—the wealth of bullion, the clean fresh-minted coinage—probably reflects the kind of reputation that Congreve had already gained for the perfection of his art, in which from the first there had never been anything hesitant, groping, experimental, or lacking in taste and judgment.

Swift may even have remembered Congreve from 1681, when he had first arrived at Kilkenny School, a boy of eleven, the son of an English officer who had come to join the Duke of Ormonde's regiment after serving several years in garrisons in different parts of Ireland. He had been born in Yorkshire, in 1670, four years before his father had been sent to Ireland; and his family, like Swift's, was proud of their Royalist tradition. In 1686, he followed Swift to Trinity College, Dublin, where they had the same tutor, St. George Ashe. Congreve had matriculated in April of that year, and certainly spent most of the remaining months in residence. But changes were soon to take place in the Irish regiments, and officers who were English Protestants like his father were being removed. Exactly when the family left Ireland is not known, but they seem to have been settled in London in 1689, when his father is described as living "in and about the town"[5]. Later, Congreve tells us himself that it was in that year, when he was nineteen and was recovering from an illness, that he wrote the first draft of the play that was to be called *The Old Batchelour.* Although he suggests that he wrote only for his own amusement during his convalescence, it is

[3] See p. 123.

[4] *Lines to Mr. Congreve*, vv. 51–54. See *The Poems of Jonathan Swift*, ed. Harold Williams (Oxford: The Clarendon Press, 1937), I, 45.

[5] For this and other biographical details, see John C. Hodges, *William Congreve, the Man* (1941), pp. 30–31.

clear that he already felt himself to have some talent as a writer.

He was soon to give evidence of his taste and his wide interests in literature; and although he was entered at the Middle Temple in the spring of 1691, he does not seem to have allowed the study of law to interfere with his other pursuits. He must then have been at work on a romance, *Incognita*, which was published anonymously in 1692; it shows the quality of his craftsmanship and the sharpness of his wit. He was also trying his hand at translations in verse of Homer and Juvenal, as well as at imitations of some of the odes of Horace. When Dryden's *Satires of Juvenal and Persius* appeared in October, 1692, he chose Congreve's version of the Ninth Satire, and printed also the verses that Congreve had addressed to him *On his Translation of Persius*. Before the end of 1692, he had been accepted among the group of those who sought Dryden's company at Will's Coffee House, where he was soon to be known as the favorite of the master. When he showed them the manuscript of his play, they were astonished at its brilliance, offered him their assistance, and procured for him the freedom of the theater, which gave him an opportunity to become familiar with the company and with the stage conditions at Drury Lane.

He would have seen there in that winter season of 1692 a considerable variety of plays, since most of them ran only for a few days. There were revivals of Dryden and Etherege and Sedley, a good deal of Shadwell, and new plays by Tom Durfey and Captain Thomas Southerne—an Irishman, also from Trinity College, Dublin, and the Middle Temple. These new comedies were all contemporary in their theme and setting, plays of intrigue and cuckoldry in the Restoration tradition, and spiced with sufficient bawdy jokes to meet the taste of the town. Besides the theater, there were the regular weekly concerts at which he would have heard the music of Purcell; and he would probably have seen the magnificent spectacle of the performance of *The Fairy Queen*. He came to know Purcell well enough during the last months of the composer's short life to have all the songs that he wrote at this time set to music by Purcell, who also provided the dramatic music that served as a framework for the acts of the play.

What good use he made of these opportunities is shown by the extraordinary success of his first play, when it was finally produced at Drury Lane on March 9, 1693. Even the Earl of Burlington was impressed, and in a letter written two days later to Congreve's father, his agent in Ireland, he reported:

> Your sons Play was Acted on Thursday last & was by all the hearers applauded to bee the best that has been Acted for many yeares, Monday is to bee his day which will bring him in a better sume of money than the writters of late have had, for the house will bee so full that very many persons of Quality cannot have a Seate all the places having been bespoken many days since.[6]

Many have expressed astonishment that a writer so young and inexperienced could have done so well in comedy, which is concerned with contemporary life and manners. Dr. Johnson offered the explanation that if *The Old Batchelour* be "more nearly examined, it will be found to be one of those comedies which may be made by a mind vigorous and acute, and furnished with comick characters by the perusal of other poets."[7]

Such a familiarity with other poets and dramatists Congreve undoubtedly possessed. He had read Plautus and Terence, Corneille and Molière, Shakespeare and Jonson. He seems to have been familiar with the critics of drama, and to have studied carefully such books as *The Whole Art of the Stage* by François Hédelin, who had been nominated by Richelieu to be the superintendent of the theatre in France. Congreve had a copy of the original French edition of 1657, and also of the English translation of 1684,[8] and he may well have found some of Hédelin's practical hints about the construction of a play both useful and enlightening, as he sat there in the theater watching the actors at their job and eagerly noting how the comedies of his rivals were put together.

There are certainly one or two points that Hédelin is very insistent on, which are not overlooked in *The Old Batchelour*, such as the careful arrangement of the time scheme to fit the action that takes place offstage between the acts, "for the actors are not idle while they are absent, but are acting something of their part, though one sees them not."[9] There is the matter, important to the plot, of Lucy's forged letter, which we first hear about at the end of Act III, and which therefore has to be delivered before the action of the next Act begins;

[6] From the Lismore Papers; MSS in National Library, Dublin; microfilm in the Huntington Library, San Marino, California.

[7] See Samuel Johnson, *Lives of the English Poets*, ed. G. B. Hill (Oxford: The Clarendon Press, 1905), ii. 216.

[8] See John C. Hodges (ed.), *The Library of William Congreve* (New York: New York Public Library, 1955), nos. 10, 469.

[9] François Hédelin, *The Whole Art of the Stage* (London, 1684), Bk. II, p. 91.

earlier, we are told of a meeting between Vainlove and Araminta that must have taken place during the period of time supposed to elapse between Acts II and III, when Vainlove had "snatch'd a Kiss from Araminta," and she had made a quarrel about it. And in the fourth act, Belinda, meeting Araminta in the park, describes her visit to Mrs. Snipwell's shop and reveals her own character as she talks about the strange creatures that she met there, the squire and his wife and daughters "so bedeck'd, you wou'd have taken 'em for *Friezland*-Hens."

We may note also that Congreve is very careful to follow Hédelin's instructions (whether learned from him or not) to put into the dialogue "all the Decorations, Clothes, or necessary motions for the understanding of the play," even "any ornament or part of the stage architecture."[10] Thus Bellmour draws attention to the particulars of his disguise—"This Cloak my Sanctity, and trusty *Scarron's* Novels my Prayer-Book"—the book which is to give him away a little later. The movements of the actors and the precise details of place are not left to stage directions, but are mentioned in the dialogue, so that we cannot overlook them. We remember the frequent references to characters seen "coming round the corner" as they approach or turn and go off another way, to the portals of Fondlewife's house or to the "two white posts" at Silvia's door:

> *Sharper*. 'Tis but to yond' Corner-House?
> *Heartwell*. Whither? Whither? Which Corner-House?
> *Sharper*. Why, there: The Two white Posts.[11]

But the miracle that had astonished Dryden and led him to praise it extravagantly as "the best first play" that had ever been, lay in the brilliance of the talk, and the liveliness and the convincing reality of these gay and amusing interchanges, which showed the new young playwright as a more skillful and more gifted artist than any of his practiced contemporaries. He must have had an ear that caught the accent of the time and enabled him to give to every phrase its fitting shape, although none knew better than he, already, that the playwright could not achieve verisimilitude by reproducing the actual reality:

> I believe if a Poet should steal a Dialogue of any length from the *Extempore* Discourse of the two Wittiest Men

[10] *Ibid.*, Bk. I., p. 53.
[11] See p. 104.

> upon Earth, he would find the Scene but coldly receiv'd by the Town.[12]

He knew, apparently by instinct, that the dialogue must not be lacking in "Spirit, Grace and Noble Raillery"—those virtues that Dennis tells him were inseparable from a finished comedy. He could somehow place himself in the mood or the humor of his character, and lend him the grace and delicacy and liveliness of his own conversation: "Come come, leave Business to Idlers, and Wisdom to Fools; they have need of 'em: Wit, be my Faculty; and Pleasure, my Occupation"—.[13] All the dull, serious values of the pillars of society—merchants, lawyers, tradesmen—are swept aside, and we are smilingly invited into a world of comedy to enjoy ourselves. It is irresistible. We are lured into the game and find ourselves in a minute or two introduced to some of the players, and eagerly listening to details of the plots that are to enmesh them.

But perhaps there is something more—and again something we might not expect to find in a piece which he said he wrote to amuse himself during convalescence. The theme of the play is the exposing of the Old Bachelor, the surly Heartwell, "pretending to slight women," one experienced in the ways of the world, honest: "I am for having every body be what they pretend to be;—My Talent is chiefly that of speaking Truth, which I don't expect should ever recommend me to People of Quality"— and moreover delighting in every opportunity to rail bitterly at all the hypocrisies and nauseous cant of his friends, "snarling odious Truths, and entertaining Company like a Physician, with discourse of their diseases and infirmities."[14] In the conversation of Vainlove and Bellmour there is a good deal of sparring just for the pleasure of it; we remain in a world of light comedy, where it may be necessary to make a fuss of the lady's lapdog to win her favor, or even read her a play to entertain her on a wet afternoon; a place where jealous old husbands are brought in only to be made fun of and country squires are taken in by braggarts and sharpers. These characters play their accustomed parts and contribute to the surprising intrigues with which we are to be kept amused. But in the scene where Heartwell is first introduced—the part was, of course, originally played by Betterton—he is allowed to become almost a real character.

[12] Letter to Dennis; see John C. Hodges (ed.), *William Congreve, Letters and Documents* (New York: Harcourt, Brace, and World, 1964), p. 181. (Hereafter referred to as *Letters and Documents*.)

[13] See p. 37.

[14] See p. 42.

He enters from another world; he convinces us that he is not like these foolish creatures; his values are different. He is allowed time to make an impression upon us, to disturb us a little by some of his plain speaking—before his pride leads him to boast of his safety, and immediately we know that he is doomed: "I think I have baited too many of those Traps, to be caught in one my self."[15] Later, in the love scene with Silvia, he is largely occupied in lamenting his sad condition: "Oh Manhood, where art thou! What am I come to? A Woman's Toy; at these years! Death, a bearded Baby for a Girl to dandle."[16] We may wonder where that strange astringency comes from, which makes the very tone so convincing, without spoiling the comedy of the situation. When at last they all turn upon him to make fun of him in his misery, this tone jars a little with the last trick of the farce that we know is just about to take place. Congreve himself is evidently not unaware of this and cleverly turns it to account when the situation is in danger of becoming too serious for comedy. Vainlove restrains them: "*Bellmour*, Give it over; you vex him too much; 'tis all serious to him." Even Belinda says she is beginning to pity him. But this only goads him to express all his bitterness:

> Damn your pity.—But let me be calm a little.—How have I deserv'd this of you? Any of ye? Sir, have I impair'd the Honour of your House, promis'd your Sister Marriage, and whor'd her?...Madam, have I had an Opportunity with you and bauk'd it?[17]

Was this harsh roughness learned from Ben Jonson, or borrowed from Juvenal and Horace, whose epistles and satires he had just been translating; or was it already, even in this first play, that uncanny gift which certainly developed later to provide the experienced actors of the Theatre Royal with just the right situations and dialogue to bring out all their powers, to provide here, for example, even in this comedy of intrigue, scope for a Betterton to move his audience by words of intensity and passion? Certainly in his dedication of the play, written in 1693, he is willing to allow that he can no longer plead ignorance of the town and of the stage, of which he could now claim to have had some years' experience. And he is also very careful to acknowledge how much he owed to the skill and care of the players.

[15] See p. 45.
[16] See p. 72.
[17] See p. 109.

His second play, *The Double-Dealer*, was intended to show that he could use the theater to satirize the follies and vices of society. He was not content to play with and manipulate characters and situations, prompted mainly by his reading or his recollection of the theater, merely to try to meet the tastes of his audience; here he would make a play with an original plot of his own to fit the kind of situation he wanted to exploit. He had become interested in the current discussion of dramatic theory, the arguments about what constituted a good plot for a comedy, who were the right kind of characters to introduce, what treatment of time and place could best strengthen the dramatic illusion and increase the tension. He was willing to make use of some of these ideas, deliberately and consciously to plan a play of perfect regularity according to the rules, or, as he put it in the dedication:

> ... the Mechanical part of it is perfect. That, I may say with as little vanity, as a Builder may say he has built a House according to the Model laid down before him; or a Gardiner that he has set his Flowers in a knot of such or such a Figure. I design'd the Moral first, and to that Moral I invented the Fable, and do not know that I have borrow'd one hint of it any where. I made the Plot as strong as I could, because it was single, and I made it single, because I would avoid confusion, and was resolved to preserve the three Unities of the Drama.[18]

It is a good plot, which through all its involutions keeps up the suspense from the outset until the very last scene. It is a web of intrigue spun by one central character for his own ends, involving nearly everybody except two or three minor characters who provide some comedy and carry further the satire of contemporary society. For greater concentration and tension, and perhaps also to give it a familiar convincing setting, the action is centered in one place, the long gallery that was the main room for entertaining guests in the houses of the gentry. Only twice did he use the inner stage for a room off the gallery. He restricted the time of the action to a few hours of one evening, accelerating the pace until the very minutes counted.

It is a play of great intensity and power, but for all that it is a set piece; all the characters tend to fit into the plot—with one exception, Lady Touchwood—rather than create it. They seem to move round the central figure, the Double-Dealer, and are entirely under his control as he tricks them

[18] See pp. 118–19.

one after another to further his ambition, his love, and his greed for wealth and power. But we know little enough of him, except that he finds it "such a pleasure, to angle for fair-faced Fools," even though he is allowed so many soliloquies. These serve rather to further the plot than to provide the means of revealing his character. When he is made to utter such generalizations as "Love cancels all the Bonds of Friendship, and sets Men right upon their first Foundations,"[19] we feel that this is addressed to the audience with the purpose of removing any unwillingness they might well feel to believe in the possibility of such a role of persistent, unhesitating treachery. It is, in fact, not the fascination of being shown what can happen to the human soul, of probing the villany of an Iago, but the trickery of Maskwell—his "invention upon the Rack," his easy triumphs almost to the last—that is the central pivot of the play.

Similarly even the character of the lovers is shaped and determined by the demands of the plot. Cynthia and Mellefont are a convincing as well as a diverting pair. She is a cool, eminently sensible person, well aware of the silly fatuousness of her father. She is a little dubious about marriage in that world of fools and rogues: "Tis an odd Game we're going to Play at." This is not a passionate romance, but they are undoubtedly in love:

> *Cynthia.* You know we Marry for Love.
> *Mellefont.* Love, Love, down right very Villanous Love.[20]

Yet she vows to give him up and remain single for life, unless he can demonstrate his wit by outwitting his aunt. Perhaps we are too much aware, to borrow that figure Congreve used in his dedication, that the "Gardiner . . . has set his Flowers in a knot of such or such a Figure."

The minor characters, some of them his "Follies", both male and female, are all enmeshed in a network of intrigue, involved in the pursuit of sex. But here he could make full use of the company of Drury Lane actors he had now come to know well. Dogget was given even fuller scope in the role of the uxorious old knight, Sir Paul Plyant, to repeat the great success he had achieved as Fondlewife. Mrs. Mountfort, according to Cibber their favourite coquette, could play the wanton with that pert coxcomb Brisk, whose facile wit so cleverly escaped banality; and Bowman, who could write a dull song and sing it too, would do admirably as Lord Froth.

[19] See p. 150.
[20] See p. 168.

But perhaps sometimes he used them a little dangerously to caricature the pseudo-intelligentsia of the town, a game not as popular with the mixed London audience as with Molière's audience in Paris.

In spite of the brilliance of the performance, the mechanical perfection, the excitement of the plot, the pleasant fooling, the play did not take. It was perhaps felt that he had strained the limits of comedy to the utmost in those scenes where Mrs. Barry made Lady Touchwood a character of almost tragic intensity. He doubtless realized the danger of this and tried to counteract it with gay music and songs, and the verse trimmings at the end of each act that help to preserve it as a play of artifice within the domain of the comic muse. But the last scenes leave a curious impression for all that. Lady Touchwood rushes out "affrighted," with a cry of real anguish: "O I'm betray'd,—Save me, help me." Then she makes her exit, with just the right words: "Stand off, let me go"; followed by the curse of her outraged lord: "Go, and thy own Infamy pursue thee." These are genuine strokes of passion, and Congreve has to make a masterly effort to re-establish the world of comedy. But Mr. Brisk is there and can be trusted to make the appropriate remark. "This is all very surprizing, let me perish."[21] And then there is the final coupling of hands and Lord Touchwood's happy benediction on the lucky lovers, but no dance and no gay music. We are forced instead to listen to six lines of measured verse, declaring sharply enough the moral of the whole piece, and leaving us with that horrid image of base treachery, "Like Vipers in the Womb, . . . Still gnawing that, whence first it did arise." It is really not surprising that an audience delighted by the gaiety and wit of *The Old Batchelour*, and enjoying its theme of cuckoldry treated in the Ovidean manner to which they had become accustomed in the songs and plays of Suckling, Rochester, Dryden, and Southerne, should now be shocked at the harsh discordances with which this same brilliant young man had dared to entertain them. But for his main defense he falls back upon Aristotle's definition of comedy. Comedy is an imitation of the worse sort of people, worse in respect to their manners: ". . . they must be exposed after a ridiculous manner: For Men are to be laugh'd out of their Vices in Comedy."[22] He almost goes so far as to say that it is the business of comedy to instruct vicious people, who "are made

[21] See p. 203.

[22] See Montagu Summers (ed.), *The Complete Works of William Congreve* (London: Nonesuch Press, 1923), III, 173. (Hereafter this will be referred to as the Nonesuch ed.)

asham'd of their Follies or Faults, by seeing them expos'd in a ridiculous manner"; and to delight good People who are at once both warn'd and diverted at the expense of the Vicious. This might well lead to all comedies with a serious moral proving rather unpopular with the majority of any theater audience, since those who shared the follies or the faults of people like Maskwell and Lady Touchwood, or thought themselves suspected of being like them, might well resent the instruction offered them.

He is still much concerned with this problem when he writes the prologue to his next play, *Love for Love*. It was a gala occasion, the opening of the new theater at Lincoln's Inn Fields, and he has tried to please everyone—by providing variety at least:

> There's Humour, which for chearful Friends we got,
> And for the thinking Party there's a Plot.
> We've something too, to gratifie ill Nature,
> (If there be any here) and that is Satire.
> Though Satire scarce dares grin, 'tis grown so mild
> Or only shews its Teeth as if it smil'd.

But even now he cannot bear to think that the Wycherley tradition is dead, and that no one should dare "to lash this crying age."

> This time, the Poet owns the bold Essay,
> Yet hopes there's no ill-manners in his Play.[23]

With *Love for Love* he hit the taste of the town and provided excellent comic parts in traditional figures—almost Jonsonian humors—like Foresight, the superstitious old astrologer, and Ben the hearty sailor home from the sea; the folly of Miss Prue and the scheming of Mrs. Frail still belong to a world of laughter, and only Sir Sampson, the old father who has never been allowed to win any sympathy, is left to make his exit after being tricked so that the rest can remain on stage and join in the dance. But we are not quite let off. Angelica is entrusted with the moral of the play, which Congreve is always careful to set down plainly. When Scandal compliments her for punishing an inhuman father and rewarding the faithful lover, and converting him who had always been an infidel to her sex, she retorts:

> Men are generally Hypocrites and Infidels, they pretend to Worship, but have neither Zeal nor Faith: How few,

[23] See pp. 213–14.

like Valentine, would persevere even to Martyrdom, and sacrifice their Interest to their Constancy!

> The Miracle to Day is, that we find
> A Lover true: Not that a Woman's Kind.[24]

Here, as in his first play, he had set out to please his audience, and had been content, almost like Terence, to borrow his characters and his themes from earlier English comedies that had proved themselves successful in the theater. He had not confined himself quite so strictly to the rules, although the action is carefully contrived, and we are very cleverly introduced to the characters and let into the situation with remarkable skill; Sir Sampson and Miss Prue are given exactly the right words and mannerisms, just as well fitted to their parts as the admirable conversations between Valentine and his very intelligent servant Jeremy. And the assumed madness of Valentine provides plenty of satire in the Juvenalian mode at the expense of the court and the city: he poses the question "whether the Bible saves more Souls in *Westminster Abby*, or dams more in *Westminster*-Hall?" He asks them what they are for, Religion or Politicks.

> There's a couple of Topicks for you, no more like one another than Oyl and Vinegar; and yet those two beaten together by a State-Cook, make Sauce for the whole Nation.

He can prophesy as well as Foresight.

> Dost thou know what will happen tomorrow?—Answer me not—for I will tell thee. Tomorrow Knaves will thrive thro' craft, and Fools thro' Fortune; and Honesty will go as it did, Frost-nipt in a Summer Suit.[25]

But this kind of general satire is always safe enough with an audience, who will naturally find itself adopting the attitude of the speaker and sharing his contempt for the ways of the world. There is even something of the romantic tradition in the final reconciliation between the two lovers; and they are allowed to speak in a tone very rarely heard in this kind of satirical comedy:

> Had I the World to give you, it cou'd not make me worthy of so generous and faithful a Passion; Here's my Hand, my Heart was always yours, and struggl'd very hard to make this utmost Tryal of your Virtue.

[24] See p. 314.
[25] See pp. 282, 288.

Valentine. Between Pleasure and Amazement, I am lost. —But on my Knees I take the Blessing.

Then, as if once started he could not have enough of this theme, they turn to one another a little later, while waiting for the fiddles to appear, and Angelica says:

I have done dissembling now, *Valentine*; and if that Coldness which I have always worn before you, should turn to an extream Fondness, you must not suspect it.

Valentine. I'll prevent that suspicion:—for I intend to doat on at that immoderate rate, that your Fondness shall never distinguish it self enough to be, taken notice of.[26]

Congreve had now established his reputation as a writer of comedy with three plays of considerable variety, two of which had been so popular in the theater that they continued to be reprinted and read. In his dedications of the printed quartos, he had given some ideas of his aims and his conception of comedy. But in June, 1695, John Dennis attempted to draw him further by sending him some remarks on the comedies of Ben Jonson, and submitting them to him for his better judgment: "For you who, after Mr. *Wicherly*, are incomparably the best Writer of it living; ought to be allowed to be the best Judge, too."[27]

Congreve replied in a long letter of July 10, and directed himself particularly to a discussion of "that which is generally call'd *Humour* in Comedy." He is inclined to accept the current notion from Ben Jonson to Sir William Temple that there is more of humor in our English comic writers than in any others, but feels that it is necessary to refine the general conception of humor, to distinguish it from wit and folly, and also to show that the representation of real humor has nothing to do with ridiculing natural deformities and infirmities, or the singularity of manners and speech peculiar to a certain trade or profession, or mere affectations. He tries his hand at a positive statement of what he takes humor to be:

A singular and unavoidable manner of doing, or saying any thing, Peculiar and Natural to one Man only; by which his Speech and Actions are distinguish'd from those of other Men.

[26] See p. 313.
[27] See Hodges, *Letters and Documents*, p. 176.

And he makes what seems to me an extraordinary admission:

> But I must confess I have never made any observation of what I Apprehend to be true Humor in Women....
>
> For if ever any thing does appear Comical or Ridiculous in a Woman, I think it is little more than an acquir'd Folly, or an Affectation.

But he adds a charming compliment, with that candor and generosity that made him so delightful a companion:

> We may call them the weaker Sex, but I think the true Reason is, because our Follies are Stronger, and our Faults are more prevailing.[28]

We may wonder why, after his late success and after these considerations on the matter of comedy, it was at this moment that Congreve began to write his one tragedy, *The Mourning Bride*, first heard of in a letter from Walter Moyle, dated October 7, 1695, which ends with an inquiry about "what Progress you have made in your Tragedy."[29] Was it perhaps that after the death of Queen Mary, who had been a patron of the arts and the theater and had been present at a court performance of the *Double-Dealer*, Congreve had decided to write a play that could be fittingly dedicated to the Princess Anne, who had now returned to take her place at court. And had he recognized that her tastes were not for comedy? It was clearly intended, as he put it in the dedication, "to convince Your Royal Highness, that a Play may be with Industry so dispos'd (in spight of the licentious Practice of the Modern Theatre) as to become sometimes an innocent, and no unprofitable Entertainment." But it was also to be noted that in choosing a tragic theme, "which distinguishes it self from the Vulgar Poetry, by the Dignity of its Characters," he had hoped to offer to his audience "some small Sketches and Imagings of the Virtues" of her Royal Highness, "abstracted and represented in the Theatre."[30]

In the virtue of Almeria and in her sufferings caused by the conflict between her constancy to her husband and her filial duty, there is indeed, "abstracted and represented in the Theatre," a situation not altogether unlike that of the Princess Anne at the time when her father had been dispossessed of the crown of England, and she was left to take her place at

[28] *Ibid.*, pp. 182–83.
[29] *Ibid.*, p. 192.
[30] See p. 321.

the usurper's court and was required to shift her loyalty to her sister, the new queen. Now after the death of the queen, she had been recalled to court to take her place as the next heir to the throne. Although she did not share her sister's love for the theater, and was thought to be concerned about the need to reform the manners of society, Congreve may well have felt that a serious play on such a theme would be a fit offering, and that at least the strict morality of this tragedy would make it acceptable to her. But this does not explain the extraordinary success of *The Mourning Bride*, or account for the fact that it brought him greater fame among his contemporaries than any of his comedies. Perhaps it is not so difficult to see why. For what he did was to take a strange obsession of that age—that sport of fancy which Charles II had introduced, the heroic play—and turn it into a dramatic symphonic poem, something beginning to develop in the direction of opera. He succeeded because of the quality of the verse, the dignity of the rhetoric, and because of the dramatic gifts that enabled him to provide full scope for the different abilities of his two leading actresses, Mrs. Barry and Mrs. Bracegirdle. The play has two main themes—the devoted loves of Almeria and Alphonso, and the wild exotic passions of Zara—that run counter to one another; but from the outset lesser strands of ambition and jealousy are woven in, and the whole action is involved in a larger pattern of a popular struggle to overthrow the power of a successful usurper and tyrant.

The tragedy begins with music, fitted to Almeria's mood, as she sits in her dress of mourning black, and tells of her sad fate and her griefs, not to be calmed by harmony, "by Magick Numbers and persuasive Sound." The music changes to other tones when Gonzalez enters and announces the coming of the tyrant and the barbaric splendor of his triumph, as he approaches the palace amidst his captives and his troops. Here Congreve shows his ability to break through the narrow limits of the stage and by the power of his rhetoric to open to our imaginations the scene outside—the precipitous streets approaching the Alhambra, their "lifted stones" teeming with the shouting populace welcoming the victors. The contrast between the two themes is given deliberate play throughout. It is symbolized by the two striking figures of the princess, passive and withdrawn in her bereavement, and Zara, the captive queen, seen in all the barbaric splendor of her power to turn the infatuation of the king or the devotion of her slaves to serve her untamable desire for Osmyn, who could not but admit "this Woman has a Soul, Of God-like

Mould."[31] All the extravagancies of the heroic play can be made use of to add to the effect—the silent, terrifying figures of Zara's mutes, the savagery of Selim's death at her hands, the cups of poison, even the horror of the severed head in the inmost prison, all culminating in the death scene that provided a final test and a superb opportunity for Mrs. Barry and all the tragic actresses who succeeded her throughout the century.

Even the princess, the gentle Almeria, is drawn into the violence of the action, flung into the extremes of joy and utter despair in her discovery of Alphonso, in her horror at the king's plans for her marriage, in her mad ravings and betrayal of her husband, who only at the last moment saves her by dashing the poisoned cup from her hand. Here was a more difficult role, more passive and therefore providing less opportunity for movement and action, and almost requiring the conventions of opera, where we have to be content to wait and listen, and allow the movement of the passions and emotions to be translated into music and expressed in lyric shapes. Congreve knew that he could rely upon the lyrical quality of Mrs. Bracegirdle's voice, could trust to her gifts as a singer to bring out all the music of his verse from those most familiar opening lines, which must have been deliberately intended as a sort of invocation to music, to that scene in the prison with her manacled and fettered lover, where they sing together of their joys and woes:

Must I meet thee thus, *Almeria*?

Almeria. Thus, thus; we parted, thus to meet again.
Thou told'st me thou would'st think how we might meet
To part no more—Now we will part no more, . . .
No, no, 'tis better thus, . . .
Thus, better, than for any Cause to part.[32]

And finally in that scene in the last act, when she thinks Alphonso lies dead at her feet, and has determined to drink the poison:

Yet I will take a cold and parting Leave,
From his pale Lips; Ill kiss him e'er I drink,
Lest the rank Juice should blister on my Mouth,
And stain the Colour of my last Adieu.

This, it may be said, is artifice rather than lyricism, if we

[31] See p. 355.
[32] See pp. 355–56.

remember those words written for a less pallid world than that of an heroic play:

I will kiss thy lips;
Haply some poison yet doth hang on them,
To make me die with a restorative.
Thy lips are warm![33]

Yet, at the end, even with the expected denouement of a happy ending, there are some lines that are not pure theater:

...my Arms alone shall hold her up:
Warm her to Life...

And her reply recalls those familiar notes, turned and repeated before, sounding again in the quiet close:

This is my Lord, my Life, my only Husband;
I have him now, and we no more will part.[34]

The Epilogue brings us back firmly to the theater world of the 1690's, when it had become the fashion for the actors to come and speak directly to the audience, chaffing and bantering them, especially the critics. It was a custom as old as the plays of Plautus and Terence that the Restoration dramatists had imitated, the author taking this opportunity to deal with his critics, flattering or deriding them according to the fluctuations of the unending conflict in which they both engaged. It may be said that there is something eminently reasonable in this unromantic attitude toward the play, this recognition that it is nothing more than theater, and that when the play is finished, whether tragedy or comedy, and the actors come forward at the end to receive their due applause, they immediately resume their own personalities as the familiar members of the company and can be used by the author to argue about his play or make fun of his critics. They certainly managed very frequently to get a good deal of wit and satire into these neatly turned rhyming couplets.

The Mourning Bride seems to have served the further purpose of giving Her Majesty enough confidence in Congreve's uprightness and morality that later, in 1704, he was granted, together with Vanbrugh, a license for a new company of comedians. In her proclamation of January 17, 1704, the queen gave orders

> that Nothing be Acted in either of the Theatres contrary to Religion or Good Manners, upon Pain of our High

[33] *Romeo and Juliet*, V. iii. 164–65.
[34] See p. 383.

> Displeasure and of being Silenc'd from further Acting; And being further desirous to reform all other Indecencies, and Abuses of the Stage.... We do hereby strictly Command, That no Person of what Quality soever, Presume to go Behind the Scenes, or come upon the Stage, either before, or during the Acting of any Play.[35]

This attempt to control the theater may be regarded not so much as the result of Jeremy Collier's attack on the stage as part of the increasing concern with the reformation of manners, which marked the opening years of Queen Anne's reign. But even earlier, by the turn of the century, a change was taking place and in the Prologue to his next play, his final and greatest comedy, *The Way of the World*, Congreve rallies his audience on their better behavior:

> Satire, he thinks, you ought not to expect,
> For so Reform'd a Town, who dares Correct?
> To please, this time, has been his sole Pretence,
> He'll not instruct, lest it shou'd give Offence.

He acknowledges that he has had their favors. His last two plays had both been very successful. But he will not presume upon past favors, and he rather warns them that this is something different:

> He owns, with Toil, he wrought the following Scenes,
> But if they're naught ne're spare him for his Pains:
> Damn him the more; have no Commiseration
> For Dulness on mature Deliberation.[36]

That was really his dilemma. He accepts the obligation to please his audience, but he could not be content to do it the easy and the obvious way by giving them the sort of farce and jokes that would guarantee the popularity of a play. He wanted to write a regular classical play and to use for the dialogue only the perfection of the language of his day. In his dedication to the Earl of Montagu, he frankly states that he has Terence and his friends in mind. And although he does not seem to have borrowed his plots and his characters, as Terence did from Menander, he doubtless felt that he owed something to the tradition of comedy that Terence had established, and to earlier dramatists such as Jonson and Corneille who had followed it. But he stresses most

[35] Quoted in J. Ashton, *Social Life in the Reign of Queen Anne*, Vol. II (London, 1882), p. 10.

[36] See p. 393.

the further Advantage which *Terence* possess'd, towards giving his Plays the due Ornaments of Purity of Stile, and Justness of Manners, . . . from the freedom of Conversation, which was permitted him with *Lelius* and *Scipio*, two of the greatest and most polite Men of his Age. And indeed, the Privilege of such a Conversation, is the only certain Means of attaining to the Perfection of Dialogue.

He seems to want to give the impression that he is strictly observing the rules, by setting below the list of Dramatis Personae

SCENE, LONDON:
The Time equal to that of the Presentation.

But in fact he compromises. The first act takes place in a chocolate house; the second in St. James's Park, the rest in a room in Lady Wishfort's house. There is also variety in the action, although it must be allowed that all the separate concerns of Fainall and Mrs. Marwood, of Sir Wilful and Foible and Waitwell are involved in working out the main intrigue. The general idea of the play is suggested, in the quotations on the title page from Horace's *Second Satire of the First Book* which are concerned with the ways of adulterers and with all the evil things that can happen to them, such as losing their marriage portions. And the moral is tagged on at the end as usual:

From hence let those be warn'd, who mean to wed;
Lest mutual Falshood stain the Bridal-Bed:
For each Deceiver to his Cost may find,
That Marriage Frauds too oft are paid in kind.[37]

None of the characters are to be drawn from contemporary figures, for it is not the business of the comic poet to deal in libel or even in caricature. We must be taught to know

That *Satire* scorns to stoop so meanly low,
As any *one abstracted* Fop to shew,
For, as when Painters form a matchless Face,
They from each *Fair One* catch some different Grace;
And shining Features in one Portrait blend,
To which no single Beauty must pretend:
So Poets oft, do in one Piece expose
Whole *Belles Assemblées* of *Cocquetts* and *Beaux*.[38]

[37] See p. 478.
[38] See p. 479.

He can make use of the most familiar scenes—the game of cards in the chocolate house, the gallants and their ladies walking in the park, the country squire calling on his embarrassed sophisticated brother, the cabal nights when the ladies meet together at one another's apartments, where they come together like the coroner's inquest, to sit upon the murdered reputations of the week.

But familiar scenes are dull; and it is only by the perfection of his art that Congreve was able to create perhaps the most perfect opening of any comedy of manners out of the moment when two gentlemen, seated at a card table in the chocolate house, come to the end of their game and agree they have had enough. The whole of the first masterly scene consists in the natural continuation of their conversation, as they rise from their cards. There is of course no time in a comedy for the idle and pointless remarks that make up so much of the conversation of ordinary life; they must tell us who they are, make us aware of their feelings towards one another, arouse our interest in those friends who are going to appear in the following scenes.

All these considerations are only the mere preliminaries, however, a choice of the material to be used, the rough stuff that has to be fashioned into shape. It is the final form of the dialogue that gives it its beauty—that perfection of delight which satisfies us completely as we listen to the phrases so poised and balanced, as finely wrought as a perfect heroic couplet:

> The Coldness of a losing Gamester
> lessens the Pleasure of the Winner.

> I'd no more play with a Man
> that slighted his ill Fortune
> than I'd make Love to a Woman
> who undervalu'd the Loss of her Reputation.

> Not at all;
> I happen to be grave today;
> and you are gay;
> that's all.[39]

It is not enough for the dialogue to please us in itself, however. It must also perform its dramatic purpose, getting us ready, putting us into the right mood, stirring our affections for those whom we are intended to admire and delight in,

[39] See p. 395.

and thus helping to prepare us for a brilliant entertainment when at last these characters make their appearance. Notice the care with which we are introduced to Millamant, the heroine of the play, before her first superb entrance. Before a dozen lines have been spoken, her name comes up. Fainall is her cousin and knows something of her trying ways: "my fair Cousin has some Humours, that wou'd tempt the patience of a Stoick. What, some Coxcomb came in, and was well receiv'd by her while you were by." Mirabell then confesses that he had been annoyed when she had joined her aunt in hints that long visits were a bore; and later, when he reveals how well and critically he has observed her, Fainall remarks: "For a passionate Lover, methinks you are a Man somewhat too discerning in the Failings of your Mistress." This prompts that marvelous confession, which prepares the audience to accept her and love her on her own terms.

> *Mirabell.* I like her with all her Faults; nay like her for her Faults. Her Follies are so natural, or so artful, that they become her; and those Affectations which in another Woman wou'd be odious, serve but to make her more agreeable.... she once us'd me with that Insolence, that in Revenge I took her to pieces; sifted her, and separated her Failings; I study'd 'em and got 'em by rote. The Catalogue was so large, that I was not without hopes, one Day or other, to hate her heartily: To which end, I so us'd my self to think of 'em, that at length, contrary to my Design and Expectation, they gave me every Hour less disturbance[12]; till in a few Days it became habitual to me, to remember 'em without being displeas'd. They are now grown as familiar to me as my own Frailties; and in all probability in a little time longer I shall like 'em as well.[40]

Our curiosity is further aroused when we meet her hangers-on, Petulant and Witwoud. The latter confesses that he shall never break his heart for her: "She's handsome; but she's a sort of an uncertain Woman." When he is reminded that she has wit, he immediately retorts: "'Tis what she will hardly allow any Body else; Now, Demme, I shou'd hate her, if she were as handsome as Cleopatra." Finally he admits that he can't tell what she might be capable of: "she's a Woman and a kind of a Humorist."[41] She does not actually appear until the middle of the second act, but when her

[40] See p. 399.
[41] See p. 408.

entrance is announced, and Mirabell watches her approach, we are full of expectant curiosity: "Here she comes i'faith, full sail, with her Fan spread and Streamers out," and after all the little sparks that fly about her dazzling entry the two duelists are drawn into the encounter. First she taunts Mirabell with her pleasure in having given him pain and boasts of her cruelty as her power. But he parries this by warning her that her cruelty would destroy her lover, and that would be the death of her beauty, for beauty is the lover's gift. She retorts:

> O the Vanity of these Men! *Fainall*, dee hear him? If they did not commend us, we were not handsome! Now you must know, they could not commend one, if one was not handsome. Beauty the Lover's Gift—Lord, what is a Lover, that it can give? Why one makes Lovers as fast as one pleases, and they live as long as one pleases, and they die as soon as one pleases: And then if one pleases, one makes more.[42]

Here we may be for the moment reminded of the pretty wit of some of the clever girls in Shakespeare's comedies, who succeed so well in making fun of their lovers. But there is a bright, almost boyish quality about them, especially when these boy actors are dressed up as pert pages. In Millamant, we are presented with a much more sophisticated woman who has learned to hold her own in this dangerous company of the wits of the Restoration. She is always in complete command; she is allowed to make a fool of her lover.

> I shan't endure to be reprimanded, nor instructed; 'tis so dull to act always by Advice, and so tedious to be told of ones Faults—I can't bear it. Well, I won't have you, *Mirabell*—I'm resolv'd—I think—You may go—Ha, ha, ha. What wou'd you give, that you cou'd help loving me?

After teasing Mirabell and making fun of him she challenges him to woo her, then turns and leaves him, bidding him think of her.

> Think of you! To think of a Whirlwind, tho' 'twere in a Whirlwind, were the Case of more steady Contemplation; a very tranquility of Mind and Mansion. A Fellow that lives in a Windmill, has not a more whimsical Dwelling than the Heart of a Man that is lodg'd in a Woman. There is no point of the Compass to which they cannot

[42] See p. 420.

turn, and by which they are not turn'd; and by one as well as another; for Motion not Method is their Occupation.[43]

In this comedy, written and first played in 1700, the conversation achieves a perfection of English, a purity and elegance that reveals its peculiar idiom and quality, setting a standard for the language of the modern world:

For never did poetic mine before
Produce a richer vein or cleaner ore;
The Bullion stampt in your refining mind
Serves by retail to furnish half mankind.[44]

It has remained there for more than two centuries ready for use and has served the purpose of comedy at least as far as Wilde and Shaw. Congreve has, in fact, triumphantly succeeded in doing just what Terence had done in catching the quality of the perfection of his native tongue.

Whatever the public might think he knew that in *The Way of the World* he had succeeded in doing what he had set himself to do in the writing of comedy; perhaps we ought not to be surprised that after that he wrote no more plays. He seems to have withdrawn into a quiet, modest life among a few friends, choosing rather to be alone "than to conform myself to the manners of my court or chocolate-house acquaintance"[45]; turning to poetry, especially to the composition of masques and odes, such as could be set to music and publicly performed in the concert rooms and in the theater.

The five plays contained in this volume, which are Congreve's most remarkable achievement, were written for the theater in its most flourishing days in the last decade of the seventeenth century, when the art of acting had reached great perfection and the music for the songs and airs and dances was written by Purcell and Eccles; and perhaps it is not the least glory of them that they were the work of a young man in the freshness of his youth, whose genius had come to its full flowering before he reached the age of thirty.

[43] See p. 423.
[44] See n. 4, p. 2.
[45] Letter to Keally, quoted by Hodges in *William Congreve, The Man*, p. 83.

2

The Old Batchelour

INTRODUCTORY NOTE

In his reply to Jeremy Collier's "dreadful comment" on *The Old Batchelour,* Congreve asks us to remember

> How young a beginner and how very much a Boy I was when that Comedy was written; which several know was some years before it was Acted; When I wrote it I had little thoughts of the Stage; but did it to amuse my self in a slow Recovery from a Fit of Sickness.

In his dedication of the play, he had also spoken of it as his "first Offence . . . in any kind of Poetry," written "almost four years earlier," which would place it in the summer of 1689, when he had just returned to England. Although he may have had some acquaintance with the Dublin theater while he was an undergraduate at Trinity College, he probably owed more to his reading of the plays of Plautus and Terence, of Ben Jonson, Dryden, Wycherley, and Sedley and, we might add, to his study of the Roman satirists. There is indeed a hint of the central theme of the play in Juvenal's Sixth Satire:

> That he to Wedlock, dotingly betrayd,
> Should hope, in this lewd Town, to find a Maid!
> The Man's grown Mad:

and it remains an interesting possibility that he may have found his title in Dryden's translation of the preceding lines in which Ursidius is described as "the rich Old Batchelour." This translation was probably done in 1691, and would certainly have been available to Congreve, who was later to translate the Eleventh Satire for Dryden. On the other hand, Dryden may himself have suggested this very apt title; for we know that Dryden helped him prepare his play for the theater. Thomas Southerne, ten years ahead of Congreve at Trinity College and at the Middle Temple, now established as a successful dramatist in London, and a recent collaborator with Dryden, has left his own account of how he, the experienced man of the world, took charge of the young unknown genius, and was able to be

> very usefull to him in the whole course of his play. He engagd Mr. Dryden in its favour, who upon reading it sayd he never saw such a first play in his life, but the Author not being acquainted with the stage or the town, it would be pity to have it miscarry for want of a little Assistance: the stuff was rich indeed, it wanted only the fashionable cutt of the town. To help that Mr Dryden, Mr Arthur Manwayring, and Mr Southerne red it with great care, and Mr Dryden putt it in the order it was playd.[1]

Dryden recognized and was amazed by the rich quality of the material this boy had used for his dialogue, drawing so lightly and confidently upon his reading of Greek, Latin, French and English poets and dramatists, and also doubtless upon his early vivid impressions as a young gentleman of the Temple and as one of the company at Will's, getting a taste of the town.

What trimming or rearranging Dryden did is impossible to say; but we may detect some striking echoes, both in words and images, from his *Amphitryon*, played in 1691, which must have come into *The Old Batchelour* after that date, whether introduced by Congreve or by Dryden. There seems to be an insertion into the dialogue, in the early part of Act II, bringing Bluffe's talk up to date by referring to the campaign in Flanders during the summer of 1692. There are, of course, other touches that may remind us of Jonson and Wycherley: Heartwell in his talk and character occasionally resembles a Surly or a Horner; and Congreve's rakes and fops belong to the same world we have seen in the plays of Sedley and Etheredge. But there was a freshness and originality, a masterly ease and confidence astonishing in a first play, that promised a successful performance. To show that he does not forget the warning of Horace, however, he is careful to place on the title page of the printed play those lines from the First Epistle of the Second Book, thus paraphrased by Pope:

> O you! whom Vanity's light bark conveys
> On Fame's mad voyage by the wind of Praise,
> With what a shifting gale your course you ply,
> For ever sunk too low, or born too high!
> Who pants for glory finds but short repose,
> A breath revives him, or a breath o'erthrows.

[1] See Hodges, *Letters and Documents*, p. 151; cf. also *PMLA*, LXVIII, 971.

The first performance of this and other plays had been much delayed by the grievous losses suffered by the Drury Lane Company—first Mountfort, treacherously murdered by Captain Hill and Lord Mohun on December 9, 1692; then Leigh, a close friend, who died a few days later after a sudden illness. Nevertheless, Congreve acknowledged how much he owed to the excellence of the actors, whose talents he had come to appreciate during the recent months when he had been given the freedom of the theater. Henry Purcell provided the music for the play—not only the airs and accompaniments for the two songs and the music for the dances, but also the airs and dances performed before the play began and during the intervals between the acts.[2]

The play was dedicated to Charles Boyle, the son of the Earl of Cork and Burlington, to whom the Congreve family had many obligations (the father of the dramatist, Colonel Congreve, was at this time living in the College of Youghall, in charge of the earl's estate there). Boyle had taken his seat in the House of Lords as Lord Clifford of Lanesborough in 1689, at the age of fifty. The dedication is followed by three poems addressed to Congreve: the first is by Southerne who, having recommended him to Dryden, now publicly acclaims him as Dryden's successor; the second by Jerry Marsh, son of the Archbishop of Dublin, and grandson of Jeremy Taylor—later to become himself the Dean of Kilmore—who indicates the risk he is taking in proclaiming his friendship for Congreve and his enthusiasm for such a comedy:

> Expos'd to Censure for my weak Applause,
> I'm pleas'd to suffer in so just a Cause:

the third by Bevil Higgons, the nephew of George Granville, Lord Lansdowne, and likewise a Jacobite, who had only just returned to England, but had found a place among the circle of poets at Will's. A Prologue had been sent to the author by an Unknown Hand, and this was printed before his own Prologue written to be spoken by Mrs. Bracegirdle. The anonymous author was Antony Carey, the fifth Viscount Falkland, who died of smallpox in 1694, shortly after he had been made First Lord of the Admiralty.

Thus splendidly acclaimed, the printed play ran into several editions within the month. The first was advertised in the *Gazette* (no. 2852) for March 9–13, 1693; and the third in the *Gazette* for March 23–27. It was noticed in the *Gentleman's*

[2] *Dramatic Music Part III* ("The Works of Henry Purcell" [London: The Purcell Society, 1917]) XXI, iii–v, 19–37.

Journal, dated February 1693 (but not appearing until the end of March):

> The success of Mr. Congreve's *Old Batchelour* has been so extraordinary, that I can tell you nothing new of that Comedy; you have doubtless read it before this, since it has been already printed thrice. And indeed the Wit which is diffus'd through it, makes it lose but few of those Charms in the Perusal, which yield such Pleasure in the Representation. Mr. Congreve will in some time give us another Play; you may judge by this how acceptable it will be.[3]

Some of his rivals, however, attributed its popularity to other reasons.[4] His fellow templar, Henry Higden, whose first play, *The Wary Widdow: or Sir Noisy Parrat*, followed at the Theatre Royal, comments in his Preface on

> the surprising success of the Baudy Batchelour [which] has touch'd upon the true string, to please and tickle.... What though the Plots are old, and stale, they are so prettily jumbled and blended together they can never fail of being well receiv'd.

He writes with envy and malice, complaining of the disadvantages under which his play had suffered in the performance, in contrast to the care that had been lavished on *The Old Batchelour*.

For an account of later performances, see Cibber's amusing story[5] of the occasion in 1695 when he set himself to imitate in the part of Fondlewife the dress, gestures, and speech of the famous Dogget; and for the subsequent history of *The Old Batchelour* on the stage, see Emmet Avery's *Congreve's Plays on the Eighteenth-century Stage*.[6]

[3] *Gentleman's Journal* (February, 1693), p. 61.

[4] See Dave F. Smith, *The Critics in the Audience of the London Theatres from Buckingham to Sheridan* (Albuquerque: University of New Mexico Press, 1953), pp. 37–38.

[5] Colley Cibber, *An Apology for the Life of Colley Cibber*, ed. R. W. Lowe (London, 1889), i, 205–9. (Hereafter referred to as *Apology*.)

[6] *M.L.A. Monograph Ser.* 18 (New York: 1951).

THE

Old Batchelour,

A

COMEDY.

As it is ACTED at the

Theatre Royal,

BY

Their MAJESTIES Servants.

Written by Mr. *Congreve.*

Quem tulit ad Scenam ventoso gloria Curru,
Exanimat lentus Spectator; sedulus inflat.
Sic leve, sic parvum est, animum quod laudis avarum
Subruit, aut reficit———

Horat. Epist. I. Lib. II.

LONDON,

Printed for *Peter Buck,* at the Sign of the *Temple* near the *Temple-gate* in *Fleet-street,* 1693.

Quem tulit—O you! whom Vanity's light bark conveys
On Fame's mad voyage by the wind of praise,
With a shifting gale your course you ply,
For ever sunk too low, or born too high!
Who pants for glory finds but short repose,
A breath revives him, or a breath o'erthrows.
(Pope's *Imitation,* II. 296 ff.)

To the Right Honourable, Charles *Lord* Clifford *of* Lanesborough, *&c.*

My Lord,

It is with a great deal of Pleasure, that I lay hold on this first Occasion, which, the Accidents of my Life have given me of writing to your Lordship: For since at the same time I write to all the World, it will be a means of publishing, (what I would have every Body know) the Respect and Duty which I owe and pay to you. I have so much Inclination to be yours, that I need no other Engagement: But the particular Ties, by which I am bound to your Lordship and Family, have put it out of my power to make you any Complement; since all Offers of my self, will amount to no more than an honest Acknowledgment, and only shew a willingness in me to be grateful.

I am very near wishing, That it were not so much my Interest to be your Lordships Servant, that it might be more my Merit; not that I would avoid being obliged to you, but I would have my own Choice to run me into the Debt; that I might have it to boast, I had distinguished a Man, to whom I would be glad to be obliged, even without the hopes of having it in my Power, ever to make him a return.

It is impossible for me to come near your Lordship, in any kind, and not to receive some Favour; and while in appearance I am only making an Acknowledgment (with the usual underhand dealing of the World) I am at the same time, insinuating my own Interest. I cannot give your Lordship your due, without tacking a Bill of my own Priviledges. 'Tis true, if a Man never committed a Folly, he would never stand in need of a Protection: But then Power would have nothing to do, and good Nature no occasion to shew itself; and where those Vertues are, 'tis pity they should want Objects to shine upon. I must confess this is no reason, why a Man should do an idle thing, nor indeed any good Excuse for it, when done; yet it reconciles the uses of such Authority and Goodness, to the necessities of our Follies; and is a sort of Poetical Logick, which, at this time I would make use of, to argue your Lordship into a Protection of this Play. It is the first Offence I have committed in this kind, or indeed, in any kind of Poetry, tho' not the first made publick; and, therefore, I hope will the more easily be pardoned: But had it been Acted, when it was first written, more might have been said in its behalf; Ignorance of the Town and Stage, would then, have been Excuses in a young Writer, which now, almost four Years experience, will scarce allow of. Yet I must declare my self sensible of the good Nature of the Town, in receiving this Play so kindly, with all its Faults, which I must own were, for the most part, very industriously covered by the care of the Players; for, I think, scarce a Character but receiv'd all the Advantage it would admit of, from the justness of Action.

As for the Criticks, my Lord, I have nothing to say, to, or against any of them of any kind; from those who make just Exceptions, to those who find fault in the wrong place. I will only make this general Answer in behalf of my Play (an Answer, which *Epictetus* advises every Man to make for himself, to his Censurers) viz. *That if they who find some Faults in it, were as intimate with it as I am, they would find a great many more.* This is a Confession, which I need not to have made; but however, I can draw this use from it, to my own Advantage, that I think there are no Faults in it, but what I do know; which, as I take it, is the first step to an amendment.

Thus I may live in hopes (sometime or other) of making the Town amends; but you, my Lord, I never can, tho' I am ever

Your Lordships
most obedient and
most humble Servant,

Will. Congreve.

To Mr. *CONGREVE.*

When Vertue in pursuit of Fame appears,
And forward shoots the growth beyond the Years:
We timely court the rising Hero's Cause;
And on his side, the Poet wisely draws;
Bespeaking him hereafter, by Applause.
The days will come, when we shall all receive,
Returning Interest from what now we give:
Instructed, and supported by that Praise,
And Reputation, which we strive to raise.
Nature so coy, so hardly to be Woo'd
Flies, like a Mistress, but to be pursu'd.
O *CONGREVE!* boldly follow on the Chase;
She looks behind, and wants thy strong Embrace:
She yields, she yields, surrenders all her Charms,
Do you but force her gently to your Arms:
Such Nerves, such Graces, in your Lines appear,
As you were made to be her Ravisher.
DRYDEN has long extended his Command,
By Right-divine, quite through the Muses Land,
Absolute Lord; and holding now from none,
But great *Apollo*, his undoubted Crown:
(That Empire settled, and grown old in Pow'r)
Can wish for nothing, but a Successor:
Not to enlarge his Limits, but maintain
Those Provinces, which he alone could gain.
His eldest *Wicherly*, in wise Retreat,
Thought it not worth his quiet to be great.
Loose, wandring, *Etherege*, in wild Pleasures tost,
And foreign Int'rests, to his hopes long lost:
Poor *Lee* and *Otway* dead! *CONGREVE* appears,
The Darling, and last Comfort of his Years:
May'st thou live long in thy great Masters smiles,
And growing under him, adorn these Isles:
But when—when part of him (be that but late)
His body yielding must submit to Fate,
Leaving his deathless Works, and thee behind,
(The natural Successor of his Mind)
Then may'st thou finish what he has begun:
Heir to his Merit, be in Fame his Son.
What thou hast done, shews all is in thy Power;
And to Write better, only must Write more.
'Tis something to be willing to commend;
But my best Praise, is, that I am your Friend.

THO. SOUTHERNE.

To Mr. CONGREVE

The Danger's great in these censorious days,
When Criticks are so rife, to venture Praise:
When the infectious and ill-natured Brood
Behold, and damn the Work, because 'tis good;
And with a proud, ungenerous Spight would try
To pass an Ostracism on Poetry.
But you, my Friend, your Worth does safely bear
Above their Spleen; you have no cause for fear;
Like a well-metled Hawk, you took your flight
Quite out of reach, and almost out of sight.
As the strong Sun, in a fair Summers day,
You rise, and drive the Mists and Clowds away,
The Owls and Bats, and all the Birds of Prey.
Each Line of yours, like polisht Steel's so hard,
In Beauty safe, it wants no other guard.
Nature her self's beholden to your Dress,
Which tho' still like, much fairer you express.
Some vainly striving Honour to obtain,
Leave to their Heirs the Traffick of their Brain;
Like *China* under Ground, the ripening Ware,
In a long time, perhaps grows worth our Care:
But you now reap the Fame, so well you've sown;
The Planter tastes his Fruit to ripeness grown.
As a fair Orange-tree at once is seen,
Big with what's ripe, yet springing still with Green:
So at one time, my worthy Friend appears,
With all the sap of Youth, and weight of Years.
  Accept my pious Love, as forward Zeal,
Which tho' it ruins me I can't conceal:
Expos'd to Censure for my weak Applause,
I'm pleas'd to suffer in so just a Cause:
And tho' my Offering may unworthy prove,
Take as a Friend the Wishes of my Love.

J. MARSH.

To Mr. *CONGREVE,* on his PLAY, called, The *OLD BATCHELOR.*

Wit, like true Gold, refin'd from all Allay,
Immortal is, and never can decay:
'Tis in all Times and Languages the same;
Nor can an ill Translation quench the Flame:
For, tho' the Form and Fashion don't remain,
Th' intrinsick value still it will retain.
Then let each studied Scene be writ with Art;
And Judgment sweat to form the labour'd Part:
Each Character be just, and Nature seem;
Without th' Ingredient, Wit, 'tis all but Phlegm:
For that's the Soul, which all the Mass must move,
And wake our Passions into Grief, or Love.
But you, too Bounteous, sow your Wit so thick,
We are surpriz'd, and know not where to pick:
And while our Clapping does you Justice do,
Our selves we injure, and lose something new.
What may'nt we then, great Youth, of thee presage,
Whose Art and Wit so much transcend thy Age?
How wilt thou shine at thy Meridian height?
Who, at thy rising, give so vast a Light.
When *DRYDEN* dying, shall the World deceive,
Whom we Immortal, as his Works, believe;
Thou shalt succeed, the Glory of the Stage,
Adorn and entertain the coming Age.

BEVIL HIGGONS.

PROLOGUE Intended for The *OLD BATCHELOUR.* Written by the Lord *FALKLAND*

Most Authors on the Stage at first appear
Like Widows-Bridegrooms, full of doubt and fear:
They judge from the experience of the Dame,
How hard a Task it is to quench her Flame:
And who falls short of furnishing a course,
Up to his brawny Predecessors force:
With utmost rage from her Embraces thrown,
Remains convicted, as an empty Drone.
Thus often, to his Shame, a pert Beginner
Proves in the end, a miserable Sinner.
    As for our Youngster, I am apt to doubt him,
With all the vigour of his Youth about him:
But he, more Sanguine, trusts in one and twenty,
And impudently hopes he shall content you:
For tho' his Batchelour be worn and cold:
He thinks the Young may club to help the Old:
And what alone can be atchieved by neither,
Is often brought about by both together.
The briskest of you all have felt Allarms
Finding the fair One prostitute her Charms
With broken Sighs, in her old Fumblers Arms
But for our Spark, he Swears he'll ne're be jealous
Of any Rivals, but young lusty Fellows.
Faith let him try his Chance, and if the Slave,
After his bragging prove a washy Knave;
May he be banish'd to some lonely Den,
And never more have leave to dip his Pen:
But if he be the Champion he pretends,
Both Sexes sure will join to be his Friends;
For all agree, where all can have their ends.
And you must own him for a Man of Might,
If he holds out to please you the third Night.

Prologue

Spoken by Mrs. *Bracegirdle*

How this vile World is chang'd! In former days,
Prologues, were serious Speeches, before Plays;
Grave solemn Things, as Graces are to Feasts;
Where, Poets beg'd a Blessing, from their Guests.
But now, no more like Suppliants, we come;
A Play makes War, and Prologue is the Drum:
Arm'd with keen Satyr, and with pointed Wit,
We threaten you who do for Judges sit,
To save our Plays, or else we'll damn your Pit.
But for your Comfort, it falls out to day,
We've a young Author and his first born Play;
So, standing only on his good Behaviour,
He's very civil, and entreats your Favour.
Not but the Man has Malice, would he show it,
But on my Conscience he's a bashful Poet;
You think that strange—no matter, he'll out grow it.
Well, I'm his Advocate—by me he prays you,
(I don't know whether I shall speak to please you)
He prays—O bless me! what shall I do now!
Hang me if I know what he prays, or how!
And 'twas the prettiest Prologue, as he wrote it!
Well, the Deuce take me, if I han't forgot it.
O Lord, for Heavens sake excuse the Play,
Because, you know, if it be damn'd to day,
I shall be hang'd for wanting what to say.
For my sake then—but I'm in such Confusion,
I cannot stay to hear your Resolution.

Runs off.

Dramatis Personæ

MEN

Heartwell, a surly old Batchelour, pretending to slight Women; secretly in Love with *Silvia*	Mr. Betterton
Bellmour, in Love with *Belinda*	Mr. Powel
Vainlove, capricious in his Love; in Love with *Araminta*	Mr. Williams
Sharper	Mr. Alexander [*later*, Mr. Verbruggen]
Sir Joseph Wittoll	Mr. Bowen
Capt. Bluffe	Mr. Hains
Fondlewife, a Banker	Mr. Dogget
Setter, a Pimp	Mr. Underhill
Servant to Fondlewife	

WOMEN

Araminta, in Love with *Vainlove*	Mrs. Bracegirdle
Belinda, her Cousin and affected Lady, in Love with *Bellmour*	Mrs. Mountfort
Lætitia, Wife to *Fondlewife*	Mrs. Barry
Silvia, *Vainlove's* forsaken Mistress	Mrs. Bowman
Lucy, her Maid	Mrs. Leigh
Betty	

Boy and Footmen.

The Scene, *LONDON.*

THE

Old Batchelour.

ACT I. Scene I. The Street.

Bellmour *and* Vainlove *Meeting.*

Bellmour. *Vainlove,* and abroad so early! good Morrow; I thought a Contemplative Lover could no more have parted with his Bed in a Morning, than a' could have slept in't.

Vainlove. *Bellmour,* good Morrow—Why truth on't is, these early Sallies are not usual to me; but Business as you see Sir———(*Shewing Letters.*) And Business must be follow'd, or be lost.

Bellmour. Pox o' Business———And so must Time, my Friend, be close pursued, or lost. Business is the rub of Life, perverts our Aim, casts off the Bias, and leaves us wide and short of the intended Mark.

Vainlove. Pleasure, I guess you mean.

Bellmour. Ay, what else has meaning?

Vainlove. Oh the Wise will tell you———

Bellmour. More than they believe———Or understand.

Vainlove. How how, *Ned,* a wise Man say more than he understands?

Bellmour. Ay ay, pox Wisdom's nothing but a pretending to know and believe more than really we do. You read of but one wise Man, and all that he knew was, that he knew nothing. Come come, leave Business to Idlers, and Wisdom to Fools; they have need of 'em: Wit, be my Faculty; and Pleasure, my Occupation; and let Father Time shake his Glass. Let low and earthy Souls grovel till they have

rub of Life—The fashionable Epicurean philosophy gaily expressed in the terms of a game of bowls, business being the obstruction which diverts from the true aim and highest good, pleasure.

one wise Man—Socrates invoked in support of scepticism.

work'd themselves six foot deep into a Grave——— Business is not my Element———I rowl in a higher Orb and dwell———

Vainlove. In Castles ith' Air of thy own building: That's thy Element *Ned*———Well as high as a Flyer as you are, I have a Lure may make you stoop. *Flings a Letter.*

Bellmour. I marry Sir, I have a Hawks Eye at a Womans hand ———There's more Elegancy in the false Spelling of this Superscription (*Takes up the Letter.*) than in all *Cicero*——— Let me see———How now! Dear perfidious *Vainlove*. *Reads.*

Vainlove. Hold hold, 'slife that's the wrong.

Bellmour. Nay let's see the Name (*Silvia!*) how can'st thou be ungrateful to that Creature? She's extreamly pretty and loves thee intirely—I have heard her breath such Raptures about thee———

Vainlove. Ay, or any Body that she's about———

Bellmour. No faith *Frank* you wrong her; she has been just to you.

Vainlove. That's pleasant, by my troth from thee, who hast enjoy'd her.

Bellmour. Never———Her Affections, 'tis true by Heaven, she own'd it to my Face; and blushing like the Virgin Morn when it disclosed the Cheat, which, that trusty Bawd of Nature, Night, had hid, confess'd her Soul was true to you; tho' I by treachery had stoll'n the Bliss—

Vainlove. So was true as Turtle———in imagination *Ned*, ha? Preach this Doctrin to Husbands, and the married Women will adore thee.

Bellmour. Why faith I think it will do well enough———If the Husband be out of the way, for the Wife to shew her Fondness and Impatience of his Absence, by choosing a Lover as like him as she can, and what is unlike she may help out with her own Fancy.

Vainlove. But is it not an Abuse to the Lover to be made a Blind of? For she only stalks under him to take aim at her Husband.

Lure—An artificial bird, baited with flesh to lure back a hawk.

Bawd of Nature—an echo from Dryden's adaptation of Plautus' *Amphitryon*, recently played in October, 1690; *Mercury to Night*: "Thou hast been a Bawd . . . from the first Hour of thy Creation" (I, i, end).

Turtle—Turtledove, noted for its faithfulness to its mate.

Blind—A place of concealment in war or hunting.

Bellmour. As you say the Abuse is to the Lover, not the Husband: For 'tis an Argument of her great Zeal towards him, that she will enjoy him in Effigie.

Vainlove. It must be a very superstitious Country, where such Zeal passes for true Devotion. I doubt it will be damn'd by all our Protestant Husbands for flat Idolatry———But if you can make Alderman *Fondlewife* of your Perswasion, this Letter will be needless.

Bellmour. What, the old Banker with the handsome Wife?

Vainlove. Ay.

Bellmour. Let me see, *Lætitia*! Oh 'tis a delicious Morsel. Dear *Frank* thou art the truest Friend in the World.

Vainlove. Ay, am I not? To be continually starting of Hares for you to Course. We were certainly cut out for one another; for my Temper quits an Amour, just where thine takes it up———But read that, it is an Appointment for me, this Evening; when *Fondlewife* will be gone out of Town, to meet the Master of a Ship about the return of a Venture which he's in danger of losing. Read, read.

Bellmour (*Reads*). Hum, Hum—*Out of Town this Evening, and talks of sending for* Mr. Spintext *to keep me Company; but I'le take care, he shall not be at home.* Good! *Spintext!* Oh the Fanatick one-ey'd Parson!

Vainlove. Ay.

Bellmour (*Reads*). Hum, Hum—*That your Conversation will be much more agreeable, if you can counterfeit his Habit to blind the Servants.* Very good! Then I must be disguised—With all My Heart—It adds a Gusto to an Amour; gives it the greater resemblance of Theft; and among us lewd Mortals, the deeper the Sin the sweeter. *Frank* I'm amaz'd at thy good Nature—

Vainlove. Faith I hate Love when 'tis forced upon a Man; as I do Wine—And this Business is none of my seeking; I only hapned to be once or twice, where, *Lætitia* was the handsomest Woman in Company, so consequently apply'd my self to her—And it seems she has taken me at my word—Had you been there or any Body 'thad been the same.

Bellmour. I wish I may succeed as the same.

Venture—A cargo or ship risked at sea.
Fanatick—A reproachful title for Quakers and other dissenters.

Vainlove. Never doubt it; for if the Spirit of Cuckoldom be once raised up in a Woman, the Devil can't lay it, till she has don't.

Bellmour. Prithee, what sort of Fellow is *Fondlewife*?

Vainlove. A kind of Mungril Zealot, sometimes very precise and peevish: But I have seen him pleasant enough in his way; much addicted to Jealousie, but more to Fondness: So that as he is often Jealous without a Cause, he's as often satisfied without Reason.

Bellmour. A very even Temper and fit for my purpose. I must get your Man *Setter* to provide my Disguise.

Vainlove. Ay, you may take him for good-and-all if you will, for you have made him fit for no Body else—Well—

Bellmour. You're going to visit in return of *Silvia's* Letter—Poor Rogue. Any hour of the day or night will serve her—But do you know nothing of a new Rival there?

Vainlove. Yes, *Heartwell*, that surly, old, pretended Woman-hater thinks her Vertuous; that's one reason why I fail her: I would have her fret her self out of conceit with me, that she may entertain some Thoughts of him. I know he visits her ev'ry day.

Bellmour. Yet rails on still, and thinks his Love unknown to us; a little time will swell him so, he must be forc'd to give it birth, and the discovery must needs be very pleasant from himself, to see what pains he will take, and how he will strein to be deliver'd of a Secret, when he has miscarried on't already.

Vainlove. Well good Morrow, let's dine together, I'l meet at the old place.

Bellmour. With all my Heart, it lies convenient for us, to pay our Afternoon Service to our Mistresses; I find I am damnably in Love; I'm so uneasie for not seeing *Belinda* yesterday.

Vainlove. But I saw my *Araminta*, yet am as impatient.

Exit.

Bellmour. Why what a Cormorant in Love am I! who not contented with the slavery of honourable Love in one

Mungril Zealot—"A great Stickler or party-man in matters of religion." (Phillips, *New World of Words* [1706]).

Cormorant—"Used to catch fish, thus doing other people's business for them" (Dobrée).

place, and the pleasure of enjoying some half a score Mistresses of my own acquiring; must yet take *Vainlove's* Business upon my hands, because it lay too heavy upon his: So am not only forc'd to lie with other Mens Wives for 'em, but must also undertake the harder Task, of obliging their Mistresses—I must take up, or I shall never hold out; Flesh and Blood cannot bear it always.

Enter Sharper.

Sharper. I'm sorry to see this, *Ned*: Once a Man comes to his Soliloques I give him for gone.

Bellmour. *Sharper*, I'm glad to see thee.

Sharper. What, is *Belinda* cruel, that you are so thoughtful?

Bellmour. No faith, not for that—But there's a Business of Consequence fall'n out to day that requires some Consideration.

Sharper. Prithee what mighty Business of Consequence canst thou have?

Bellmour. Why you must know, 'tis a piece of Work toward the finishing of an Alderman; it seems I must put the last hand to it, and dub him Cuckold, that he may be of equal Dignity with the rest of his Brethren. So I must beg *Belinda's* Pardon———

Sharper. Faith e'en give her over for good-and-all; you can have no hopes of getting her for a Mistress, and she is too Proud, too Inconstant, too Affected and too Witty, and too handsome for a Wife.

Bellmour. But she can't have too much Mony—There's twelve thousand Pound *Tom*—'Tis true she is excessively foppish and affected, but in my Conscience I believe the Baggage loves me, for she never speaks well of me her self, nor suffers any Body else to rail at me. Then as I told you there's twelve thousand Pound—Hum—Why faith upon second Thoughts, she does not appear to be so very affected neither—Give her her due, I think the Woman's a Woman, and that's all. As such I'm sure I shall like her; for the Devil take me if I don't love all the Sex.

Sharper. And here comes one who Swears as heartily he hates all the Sex.

Enter Heartwell.

Bellmour. Who *Heartwell!* Ay, but he knows better things—How now *George*, where hast thou been snarling odious Truths, and entertaining company like a Physician, with discourse of their diseases and infirmities? What fine Lady hast thou been putting out of conceit with her self, and perswading that the Face she had been making all the morning was none of her own? for I know thou art as unmannerly and as unwelcome to a Woman, as a Looking glass after the Small-pox.

Heartwell. I confess I have not been sneering fulsome Lies and nauseous Flattery, fawning upon a little tawdry Whore, that will fawn upon me again, and entertain any Puppy that comes; like a Tumbler with the same tricks over and over. For such I guess may have been your late employment.

Bellmour. Would thou hadst come a little sooner, *Vainlove* would have wrought thy Conversion and been a Champion for the Cause.

Heartwell. What, has he been here? that's one of Loves April-fools, is always upon some errand that's to no purpose, ever embarking in Adventures, yet never comes to harbour.

Sharper. That's because he always sets out in foul Weather, loves to buffet with the Winds, meet the Tide and sail in the Teeth of opposition.

Heartwell. What has he not drop't Anchor at *Araminta*?

Bellmour. Truth on't is she fits his temper best, is a kind of floating Island; sometimes seems in reach, then vanishes and keeps him busied in the search.

Sharper. She had need have a good share of sense, to manage so *Capricious* a Lover.

Bellmour. Faith I don't know, he's of a temper the most easie to himself in the World; he takes as much always of an Amour as he cares for, and quits it when it grows stale, or unpleasant.

Sharper. An argument of very little Passion, very good Understanding, and very ill Nature.

Heartwell. And proves that *Vainlove* plays the Fool with Discretion.

Sharper. You *Bellmour* are bound in gratitude to stickle for him; you with pleasure reap that fruit, which he takes pains to sow: he does the drudgery in the Mine, and you stamp your image on the Gold.

Bellmour. He's of another opinion, and says I do the drudgery in the Mine; well, we have each our share of sport, and each that which he likes best; 'tis his diversion to Set, 'tis mine to Cover the Partridge.

Heartwell. And it should be mine to let 'em go again.

Sharper. Not till you had Mouth'd a little *George*, I think that's all thou art fit for now.

Heartwell. Good Mr. Young-fellow, you're mistaken; as able as your self and as nimble too, though I mayn't have so much Mercury in my Limbs; 'tis true indeed, I don't force Appetite, but wait the natural call of my Lust, and think it time enough to be lew'd, after I have had the temptation.

Bellmour. Time enough, ay too soon, I should rather have expected, from a person of your gravity.

Heartwell. Yet it is oftentimes too late with some of you young, termagant flashy sinners—you have all the guilt of the intention, and none of the pleasure of the practice—'tis true you are so eager in pursuit of the temptation, that you save the Devil the trouble of leading you into it: Nor is it out of discretion, that you don't swallow that very Hook your selves have baited, but you are cloy'd with the preparative, and what you mean for a Whet, turns the edge of your puny Stomacks. Your love is like your courage, which you shew for the first year or two upon all occasions; till in a little time, being disabled or disarm'd, you abate of your vigor; and that daring Blade which was so often drawn, is bound to the Peace for ever after.

Bellmour. Thou art an old Fornicator of a singular good principle indeed! and art for encouraging Youth, that they may be as wicked as thou art at thy years.

Heartwell. I am for having every body be what they pretend to be; a Whoremaster be a Whoremaster; and not like *Vainlove*, kiss a Lap-Dog with passion, when it would disgust him from the Lady's own Lips.

stickle—To stand up for.

260

265

270

275

280

285

295

Bellmour. That only happens sometimes, where the Dog has the sweeter Breath, for the more cleanly conveyance. But George, you must not quarrel with little Gallantries of this nature; Women are often won by 'em: who would refuse to kiss a Lap-Dog, if it were preliminary to the Lips of his Lady?

Sharper. Or omit playing with her Fan, and cooling her if she were hot, when it might entitle him to the office of warming her when she should be cold?

Bellmour. What is it to read a Play in a rainy day, when it may be the means of getting into a fair Lady's Books? Though you should be now and then interrupted in a witty Scene, and she perhaps preserve her Laughter, till the Jest were over; even this may be born with, considering the reward in prospect.

Heartwell. I confess you that are Women's Asses bear greater burdens, are forced to undergo Dressing, Dancing, Singing, Sighing, Whining, Rhyming, Flattering, Lying, Grinning, Cringing, and the drudgery of loving to boot.

Bellmour. O Brute, the drudgery of loving!

Heartwell. Ay, why to come to Love through all these incumbrances is like coming to an Estate overcharg'd with Debts, which by the time you have pay'd, yields no further profit than what the bare tillage and manuring of the Land will produce at the expense of your own Sweat.

Bellmour. Prithee how dost thou love?

Sharper. He! he hates the Sex.

Heartwell. So I hate Physick too—yet I may love to take it for my health.

Bellmour. Well come off George, if at any time you should be taken straying.

Sharper. He has need of such an excuse, considering the present state of his Body.

290 Heartwell. How d'ee mean?

Sharper. Why if whoring be purging (as you call it) then I may say Marriage is entring into a Course of Physick.

Bellmour. How George, do's the Wind blow there?

Heartwell. It will as soon blow North and by South—marry quotha! I hope in Heaven I have a greater portion of Grace, and I think I have baited too many of those Traps, to be caught in one my self.

Bellmour. Who the Devil would have thee? unless 'twere an Oyster-woman, to propagate young Fry for *Bilingsgate*—thy Talent will never recommend thee to any thing of better quality.

Heartwell. My Talent is chiefly that of speaking truth, which I don't expect should ever recommend me to People of Quality—I thank Heaven, I have very honestly purchas'd the hatred of all the great Families in Town.

Sharper. And you in return of Spleen hate them: But could you hope to be receiv'd into the Alliance of a noble Family—

Heartwell. No, I hope I shall never merit that affliction—to be punish'd with a Wife of Birth—be a Stag of the first Head and bear my Horns aloft, like one of the supporters of my Wives Coat. S'death I would not be a Cuckold to ere an illustrious Whore in *England.*

Bellmour. What not to make your family Man! and provide for your Children!

Sharper. For her Children you mean.

Heartwell. Ay there you've nick't it—there's the Devil upon Devil—Oh the Pride and Joy of Heart 'twould be to me, to have my Son and heir resemble such a Duke—to have a fleering Coxcomb scoff and cry, Mr. your Son's mighty like his Grace, has just his smile and air of's Face. Then replies another—methink he has more of the Marquess of such a place, about his Nose and Eyes; though a' has my Lord what d'ee-cals Mouth to a Tittle—Then I to put it off as unconcern'd, come chuck the Infant under the chin, force a smile and cry, ay, the Boy takes after his Mothers relations—when the Devil and she knows, 'tis a little Compound of the whole Body of Nobility.

Bellmour
Sharper } Ha, ha, ha.

Bellmour. Well but *George* I have one Question to ask you—

Stag of the first Head—The first growth of antlers.
my Wives Coat—The animals supporting her coat of arms.
fleering—Looking disdainfully.

Heartwell. Pox I have pratled away my time—I hope you are in no hast for an Answer—for I shan't stay now.

Looking on his Watch.

Bellmour. Nay prithee *George*—

Heartwell. No, besides by Business, I see a Fool coming this way. Adieu.

Exit.

Bellmour. What do's he mean? Oh here he comes, stand close let 'em pass.

Sir Joseph Wittoll and *Capt. Bluffe*, cross the Stage.

Sharper. What in the name of wonder is it?

Bellmour. Why a Fool.

Sharper. 'Tis a tawdry Outside.

Bellmour. And a very beggarly Lining———yet he may be worth your acquaintance—a little of thy Chymistry *Tom*, may extract Gold from that Dirt.

Sharper. Say you so? faith I am as poor as a Chymist and would be as industrious. But what was he that follow'd him? is not he a Draggon that watches those Golden Pippins?

Bellmour. Hang him, no, he a Draggon! if he be 'tis a very peacefull one, I can ensure his Anger dormant; or should he seem to rouse, 'tis but well lashing him, and he will sleep like a Top.

Sharper. Ay, Is he of that kidney?

Bellmour. Yet is ador'd by that Biggot *Sr. Joseph Wittoll*, as the image of Valour. He calls him his Back, and indeed they are never asunder—yet last night, I know not by what mischance, the Knight was alone, and had fallen into the hands of some Nightwalkers, who I suppose would have pillag'd him. But I chanc'd to come by and rescued him, though I believe he was heartily frightned, for as soon as ever he was loose, he ran away, without staying to see who help'd him.

Sharper. Is that Bully of his in the Army?

Bellmour. No, But is a pretender, and wears the habit of a Soldier, which now a'days as often cloaks Cowardice, as a

Golden Pippins—In the Garden of the Hesperides.

Black Gown does Atheism—You must know he has been abroad—went purely to run away from a Campagne; enrich'd himself with the plunder of a few Oaths;—and here vents 'em against the General, who slighting Men of Merit, and preferring only those of interest, has made him quit the Service.

Sharper. Wherein no doubt he magnifies his own performance.

Bellmour. Speaks Miracles, is the Drum to his own praise—the only implement of a Soldier he resembles, like that, being full of blustring noise and emptiness———

Sharper. And like that, of no use but to be beaten.

Bellmour. Right, but then the comparison breaks, for he will take a drubbing with as little noise as a Pulpit Cushion.

Sharper. His name, and I have done.

Bellmour. Why that, to pass it current too, he has guilded with a Title; he is call'd, *Capt. Bluffe.*

Sharper. Well, Ile endeavour his acquaintance—you steer another Course, are bound,

For Love's Island: I, for the Golden Coast.
May each succeed in what he wishes most.

Exeunt.

ACT II. Scene I.

Sir Joseph Wittoll, Sharper *following.*

Sharper. Sure that's he and alone.

Sir Joseph. Um—Ay this, this is the very damn'd place; the inhumane Cannibals, the bloody-minded Villains would have Butcher'd me last night: No doubt, they would have flead me alive, have sold my Skin, and devour'd my Members.

Sharper. How's this!

Sir Joseph. An it hadn't been for a civil Gentleman as came by and frightn'd 'em away—but agad I durst not stay to give him thanks.

Sharper. This must be *Bellmour* he means—ha! I have a thought—

Sir Joseph. Zooks, would the Captain would come; the very remembrance makes me quake; agad I shall never be reconciled to this place heartily.

Sharper. 'Tis but trying, and being where I am at worst, now luck!— curs'd fortune! this must be the place, this damn'd unlucky place—

Sir Joseph. Agad and so 'tis—why here has been more mischief done I perceive.

Sharper. No, 'tis gone, 'tis lost—ten thousand Devils on that chance which drew me hither; ay here, just here, this spot to me is Hell; nothing to be found, but the despair of what I've lost. *Looking about as in search.*

Sir Joseph. Poor Gentleman—by the Lord *Harry* I'le stay no longer, for I have found too—

Sharper. Ha! who's that has found? what have you found? restore it quickly, or by—

Sir Joseph. Not I Sir, not I, as I've a Soul to be sav'd, I have found nothing but what has been to my loss, as I may say, and as you were saying Sir.

Sharper. O your Servant Sir, you are safe then it seems; 'tis an ill Wind that blows no body good: well, you may rejoyce over my ill fortune, since it pay'd the price of your ransome.

Sir Joseph. I rejoyce! agad not I Sir; I'me sorry for your loss, with all my Heart, Blood and Guts Sir; and if you did but know me, you'd nere say I were so ill natur'd.

Sharper. Know you! why can you be so ungrateful, to forget me!

Sir Joseph. O Lord forget him! No no Sir, I don't forget you—because I never saw your face before, agad. Ha, ha, ha.

Sharper. How! *Angrily.*

Sir Joseph. Stay, stay Sir, let me recollect—(*aside*) he's a damn'd angry Fellow—I believe I had better remember him, till I can get out of his sight; but out o'sight out o'mind agad.

Sharper. Methought the service I did you last night Sir, in preserving you from those Ruffians, might have taken better root in your shallow memory.

Sir Joseph. Gads-Daggers-Belts-Blades-and Scabbards, this is the very Gentleman! how shall I make him a return suitable to the greatness of his merit—I had a pretty thing to that Purpose, if he han't frighted it out of my memory. Hem! hem! Sir, I must submissively implore your pardon for my transgression of ingratitude and omission; having my intire dependance Sir, upon the superfluity of your goodness, which, like an innundation will I hope totally immerge the recollection of my errour, and leave me floating in your sight, upon the full blown Bladders of repentance—by the help of which, I shall once more hope to swim into your favour. *Bows.*

Sharper. So—h, O Sir I am easily pacify'd, the acknowledgment of a Gentleman—

Sir Joseph. Acknowledgment! Sir I am all over acknowledgment, and will not stick to shew it in the greatest extremity, by night, or by day, in sickness, or in health, Winter, or Summer, all Seasons and occasions shall testify the reality and gratitude of your superabundant humble Servant Sir *Joseph Wittoll* Knight. Hem! hem!

Sharper. Sir *Joseph Wittoll!*

Sir Joseph. The same Sir, of *Wittoll-hall* in *Comitatu Bucks.*

Sharper. Is it possible! Then I am happy to have obliged the Mirrour of Knighthood and Pink of Courtesie in the Age, let me embrace you.

Sir Joseph. O Lord Sir!

Sharper. My loss, I esteem as a trifle repay'd with interest, since it has purchas'd me the friendship and acquaintance of the person in the World, whose Character I admire.

Sir Joseph. You are only pleas'd to say so Sir—But pray if I may be so bold, what is that loss you mention?

Sharper. O term it no longer so Sir. In the Scuffle last Night I only dropt a Bill of a hundred Pound, which I confess, I came half despairing to recover; but thanks to my better Fortune—

Sir Joseph. You have found it Sir then it seems; I profess I'me heartily glad—

Sharper. Sir your humble Servant—I don't question but you are; that you have so cheap an opportunity of expressing

Comitatu Bucks—In the county of Buckingham.

your gratitude and generosity. Since the refunding so trivial a Sum, will wholly acquit you and doubly engage me.

Sir Joseph (*aside*). What a dickens do's he mean by a trivial Sum—But han't you found it Sir!

Sharper. No otherwise I vow to Gad but in my hopes in you Sir.

Sir Joseph. Humph.

Sharper. But that's sufficient—'Twere injustice to doubt the honour of Sir *Joseph Wittoll.*

Sir Joseph. O Lord Sir.

Sharper. You are above (I'me sure) a thought so low, to suffer me to lose what was ventur'd in your service; Nay'twas in a manner—Pay'd down for your deliverance; 'twas so much lent you—And you scorn, 'Ile say that for you———

Sir Joseph. Nay 'Ile say that for my self (with your leave Sir) I do scorn a dirty thing. But agad 'Ime a little out of pocket at present.

Sharper. Pshaw you can't want a hundred Pound. Your Word is sufficient any where: 'Tis but borrowing so much Dirt, you have large Acres and can soon repay it——— Mony is but Dirt Sir *Joseph*—Mere Dirt.

Sir Joseph. But I profess, 'tis a Dirt I have wash'd my Hands of at present; I have lay'd it all out upon my Back.

Sharper. Are you so extravagant in Cloaths Sir *Joseph*?

Sir Joseph. Ha, ha, ha, a very good Jest I Profess, ha, ha, ha, a very good Jest, and I did not know that I had say'd it, and that's a better Jest than tother. 'Tis a sign you and I ha'n't been long acquainted; you have lost a good Jest for want of knowing me—I only mean a Friend of mine whom I call my Back; he sticks as close to me, and follows me through all dangers—he is indeed Back, Breast and Head-piece as it were to me—agad he's a brave Fellow—Pauh, I am quite another thing, when I am with him: I don't fear the Devil (God bless us) almost if he be by. Ah—had he been with me last night—

Sharper. If he had Sir, what then? he could have done no more, nor perhaps have suffer'd so much———had he a hundred Pound to lose? *Angrily.*

Sir Joseph. O Lord Sir by no means (but I might have sav'd a hundred Pound) I meant innocently as I hope to be sav'd Sir (a damn'd hot Fellow) only as I was saying, I let him have all my ready Mony to redeem his great Sword from Limbo———But Sir I have a Letter of Credit to Alderman *Fondlewife*, as far as two hundred Pound, and this Afternoon you shall see I am a Person, such a one as you would wish to have met with.

Sharper (*aside*). That you are Ile be sworn. Why that's great and like your self.

Enter Bluffe.

Sir Joseph. Oh here a' comes—Ah my Hector of *Troy*, welcome my Bully, my Back; agad my heart has gone a pit pat for thee.

Bluffe. How how, my young Knight? Not for fear I hope; he that knows me must be a stranger to fear.

Sir Joseph. Nay agad I hate fear ever since I had like to have dy'd of a fright. But—

Bluffe. But? Look you here Boy, here's your antidote, here's your Jesuits Powder for a shaking fit—But who hast thou got with thee, is he of mettle?

Laying his Hand upon his Sword.

Sir Joseph. Ay Bully, a Devilish smart Fellow, 'a will fight like a Cock.

Bluffe. Say you so? then I honour him—But has he been abroad? for every Cock will fight upon his own Dunghil.

Sir Joseph. I don't know, but I'le present you—

Bluffe. I'le recommend my self—Sir I honour you; I understand you love Fighting, I reverence a Man that loves Fighting, Sir I Kiss your Hilts.

Sharper. Sir your Servant, but you are misinform'd, for unless it be to serve my particular Friend, as Sir *Joseph* here, my Country, or my Religion, or in some very Justifiable Cause, I'me not for it.

Bluffe. O Lord I beg your pardon Sir, I find you are not of of my Pallat, you can't relish a Dish of Fighting without

from Limbo—Out of pawn.

Jesuits Powder—Quinine, which the Jesuit missions in South America had found in use as a cure for the ague.

Sweet Sawce. Now I think—Fighting, for Fighting sake's sufficient Cause; Fighting, to me's Religion and the Laws.

Sir Joseph. Ah, well said my *Hero*; was not that great Sir? by the Lord *Harry* he says true; Fighting, is Meat, Drink and Cloth to him. But Back, this Gentleman is one of the best Friends I have in the World and saved my Life last Night———You know I told you.

Bluffe. Ay! Then I honour him again—Sir may I crave your name?

Sharper. Ay Sir, my name's *Sharper.*

Sir Joseph. Pray Mr. *Sharper* Embrace my Back———very well———By the Lord *Harry* Mr. *Sharper* he's as brave a Fellow as Cannibal, are not you Bully—Back?

Sharper. Hannibal I believe you mean Sir *Joseph.*

Bluffe. Undoubtedly he did Sir; faith *Hannibal* was a very pretty Fellow—but Sir *Joseph*, comparisons are odious—*Hannibal* was a very pretty Fellow in those Days, it must be granted—But Alas Sir! were he alive now, he would be nothing, Nothing in the Earth.

Sharper. How Sir! I make a doubt, if there be at this Day a greater General breathing.

Bluffe. Oh excuse me Sir; have you serv'd abroad Sir?

Sharper. Not I really Sir.

Bluffe. Oh I thought so—Why then you can know nothing Sir: I'me afraid you scarce know the History of the Late War in *Flanders*, with all its particulars.

Sharper. Not I, Sir, no more than publick Letters, or *Gazettes* tell us.

Bluffe. Gazette! Why there again now—Why, Sir, there are not three words of Truth, the Year round, put into the *Gazette*—I'll tell you a strange thing now as to that———You must know, Sir, I was resident in *Flanders* the last Campagn, had a small Post there; but no matter for that—Perhaps, Sir, there was a scarce any thing of moment done but an humble Servant of yours, that shall be nameless, was an Eye-witness of—I won't say had the greatest

Gazette—The London newspaper, then published twice a week.

the last Campagn—During the summer of 1692, when William had lost Namur and had been defeated at Steenkirk.

share in't. Tho' I might say that too, since I am no Body you know—Well, Mr. *Sharper*, would you think it? In all this time—as I hope for a Truncheon—this rascally *Gazette*-writer never so much as once mention'd me—Not once by the Wars—Took no more notice, than as if *Nol. Bluffe* had not been in the Land of the Living.

Sharper. Strange!

Sir Joseph. Yet by the Lord *Harry* 'tis true Mr. *Sharper*, for I went every day to Coffee-houses to read the *Gazette* my self.

Bluffe. Ay, ay, no matter———You see Mr. *Sharper* after all I am content to retire———Live a private Person——— *Scipio* and others have done it.

Sharper (*aside*). Impudent Rogue.

Sir Joseph. Ay, this damn'd Modesty of yours———Agad if he would put in for't he might be made General himself yet.

Bluffe. Oh fy no Sir *Joseph*—You know I hate this.

Sir Joseph. Let me but tell Mr. *Sharper* a little, how you eat fire once out of the mouth of a Canon—agad he did; those impenetrable Whiskers of his have confronted Flames———

Bluffe. Death, what do you mean Sir *Joseph*?

Sir Joseph. Look you now, I tell you he's so modest he'l own nothing.

Bluffe. Pish you have put me out, I have forgot what I was about, Pray hold your Tongue, and give me leave. *Angrily*.

Sir Joseph. I am dumb.

Bluffe. This Sword I think I was telling you of Mr. *Sharper* ———This Sword I'l maintain to be the best Divine, Anatomist, Lawyer or Casuist in *Europe*; it shall decide a Controversie or split a Cause—

Sir Joseph. Nay, now I must speak; it will split a Hair by the Lord *Harry*, I have seen it.

Bluffe. Zoons Sir, it's a Lie, you have not seen it, nor shant see it; Sir I say you can't see; what de'e say to that now?

Sir Joseph. I am blind.

Scipio—The Roman general who conquered Hannibal.

Bluffe. Death, had any other Man interrupted me———

Sir Joseph. Good Mr. *Sharper* speak to him; I dare not look that way.

Sharper. Captain, Sir *Joseph's* penitent.

Bluffe. O I am calm Sir, calm as a discharg'd Culverin—But 'twas indiscreet, when you know what will provoke me—Nay come Sir *Joseph*, you know my Heat's soon over.

Sir Joseph. Well I am a Fool sometimes—But I'm sorry.

Bluffe. Enough.

Sir Joseph. Come we'll go take a Glass to drown Animosities. Mr. *Sharper* will you partake?

Sharper. I wait on you Sir; nay pray Captain———You are Sir *Joseph's* Back.

Exeunt.

[SCENE II]

SCENE *Changes to Lodgings*

Enter Araminta, Belinda.

Belinda. Ay! nay Dear—prithee good, dear sweet Cousin no more. Oh Gad, I swear you'd make one sick to hear you.

Araminta. Bless me! what have I said to move you thus?

Belinda. Oh you have raved, talked idly, and all in Commendation of that filthy, awkard, two-leg'd Creature, Man—you don't know what you said, your Fever has transported you.

Araminta. If Love be the Fever which you mean; kind Heav'n avert the cure: Let me have Oil to feed that Flame and never let it be extinct, till I my self am Ashes.

Belinda. There was a Whine—O Gad I hate your horrid Fancy———This Love is the Devil, and sure to be in Love is to be possess'd———Tis in the Head, the Heart, the Blood, the———All over———O Gad you are quite

Culverin—A cannon, requiring a charge of sixteen pounds.

spoil'd———I shall loath the sight of Mankind for your sake.

Araminta. Fie, this is gross Affectation—A little of *Bellmour's* Company would change the Scene.

Belinda. Filthy Fellow! I wonder Cousin———

Araminta. I wonder Cousin you should imagine, I don't perceive you love him.

Belinda. O I love your hideous Fancy! Ha, ha, ha, love a Man!

Araminta. Love a Man! yes, you would not love a Beast.

Belinda. Of all Beasts not an Ass———Which is so like your *Vainlove*———Lard I have seen an Ass look so Chagrin, Ha, ha, ha, (you must pardon me I can't help Laughing) that an absolute Lover would have concluded the poor Creature to have had Darts, and Flames, and Altars, and all that in his Breast. *Araminta*, come I'll talk seriously to you now; could you but see with my Eyes, the buffoonry of one Scene of Address, a Lover, set out with all his Equipage and Appurtenances; O Gad! sure you would—But you play the Game, and consequently can't see the Miscarriages obvious to every Stander by.

Araminta. Yes, yes, I can see something near it when you and *Bellmour* meet. You don't know that you dreamt of *Bellmour* last Night, and call'd him aloud in your sleep.

Belinda. Pish, I can't help dreaming of the Devil sometimes; would you from thence infer I love him?

Araminta. But that's not all; you caught me in your Arms when you named him, and press'd me to your Bosom ———Sure if I had not pinch'd you till you wak'd, you had stifled me with Kisses.

Belinda. O barbarous Aspersion!

Araminta. No Aspersion, Cousin, we are alone———Nay, I can tell you more.

Belinda. I deny it all.

Araminta. What, before you hear it?

Belinda. My Denyal is premeditated like your Malice—Lard, Cousin, you talk odly———What ever the Matter is, O my Sol, I'm afraid you'l follow evil Courses.

Sol—Apollo, the sun.

Araminta. Ha, ha, ha, this is pleasant.

Belinda. You may laugh, but———

Araminta. Ha, ha, ha.

Belinda. You think the malicious Grinn becomes you—The Devil take *Bellmour*———Why do you tell me of him?

Araminta. Oh is it come out—Now you are angry, I am sure you love him. I tell no Body else Cousin—I have not betray'd you yet.

Belinda. Prithee tell it all the World, it's false. Betty. *Calls*

Araminta. Come then, Kiss and Friends.

Belinda. Pish.

Araminta. Prithee don't be so Peevish.

Belinda. Prithee don't be so Impertinent.

Araminta. Ha, ha, ha.

Enter Betty.

Betty. Did your Ladyship call, Madam?

Belinda. Get my Hoods and Tippet, and bid the Footman call a Chair.

Exit Betty.

Araminta. I hope you are not going out in dudgeon, Cousin.

Enter Footman.

Footman. Madam, there are—

Belinda. Is there a Chair?

Footman. No, Madam, there are Mr. *Bellmour* and Mr. *Vainlove* to wait upon your Ladyship.

Araminta. Are they below?

Footman. No, Madam, they sent before, to know if you were at home.

Belinda. The Visit's to you, Cousin, I suppose I am at my liberty.

Chair—sedan-chair, said to have been introduced from Italy during the reign of Charles I.

Araminta. Be ready to shew 'em up.

Exit Footman.

I can't tell, Cousin, I believe we are equally concern'd: But if you continue your Humour, it won't be very entertaining—(*aside*) I know she'd fain be persuaded to stay.

Belinda. I shall oblige you, in leaving you to the full and free enjoyment of that Conversation you admire.

Enter Betty, *with Hoods and Looking-glass.*

Belinda. Let me see; hold the Glass———Lard I look wretchedly to day.

Araminta. Betty, why don't you help my Cousin?

Putting on her Hoods.

Belinda. Hold off your Fists, and see that he gets a Chair with a high Roof, or a very low Seat—Stay, Come back here you Mrs. Fidget———You are so ready to go to the Footman———Here, take 'em all again, my Mind's chang'd, I won't go.

Exit Betty *with the Things.*

Araminta. So, this I expected———You won't oblige me then, Cousin, and let me have all the Company to my self?

Belinda. No; upon deliberation, I have too much Charity to trust you to your self. The Devil watches all opportunities; and in this favourable disposition of your Mind, Heav'n knows how far you may be tempted: I am tender of your Reputation.

Araminta. I am oblig'd to you—But who's malicious now, *Belinda*?

Belinda. Not I; witness my Heart I stay out of pure Affection.

Araminta. In my Conscience I believe you.

Enter Bellmour, Vainlove.

Bellmour. So Fortune be prais'd! To find you both within, Ladies, is———

Araminta. No Miracle, I hope.

Bellmour. Not o' your side, Madam, I confess———But my Tyrant there and I, are two Buckets that can never come together.

Belinda. Nor are ever like———Yet we often meet and clash.

Bellmour. How never like! marry *Hymen* forbid. But this it is to run so extravagantly in Debt; I have laid out such a world of Love in your Service, that you think you can never be able to pay me all: So shun me for the same reason that you would a Dun.

Belinda. Ay, on my Conscience, and the most impertinent and troublesome of Duns———A Dun for Mony will be quiet, when he sees his Debtor has not wherewithal——— But a Dun for Love is an eternal Torment that never rests———

Bellmour. Till he has created Love where there was none, and then gets it for his pains. For importunity in Love, like importunity at Court; first creates its own Interest, and then pursues it for the Favour.

Araminta. Favours that are got by Impudence and Importunity, are like Discoveries from the Rack, when the afflicted Person, for his ease, sometimes confesses Secrets his Heart knows nothing of.

Vainlove. I should rather think Favours, so gain'd, to be due Rewards to indefatigable Devotion———For as Love is a Deity, he must be serv'd by Prayer.

Belinda. O Gad, would you would all pray to Love then, and let us alone.

Vainlove. You are the Temples of Love, and 'tis through you, our Devotion must be convey'd.

Araminta. Rather poor silly Idols of your own making, which, upon the least displeasure you forsake, and set up new ———Every Man, now, changes his Mistress and his Religion, as his Humour varies or his Interest.

Vainlove. O Madam———

Araminta. Nay come, I find we are growing serious, and then we are in great danger of being dull—If my Musick-master be not gone, I'll entertain you with a new Song, which comes pretty near my own Opinion of Love and your Sex—Who's there? *Calls.*

Enter Footman.

Is Mr. *Gavot* gone?

Footman. Only to the next door, Madam; I'll call him.
Exit.

Bellmour. Why, you wont hear me with Patience.

Araminta. What's the Matter, Cousin.

Bellmour. Nothing, Madam, only———

Belinda. Prithee hold thy Tongue———Lard, he has so pester'd me with Flames and Stuff———I think I shan't endure the sight of a Fire this Twelvemonth.

Bellmour. Yet all can't melt that cruel frozen Heart.

Belinda. O Gad I hate your hideous Fancy—You said that once before—If you must talk impertinently, for Heav'ns sake let it be with variety; don't come always, like the Devil, wrapt in Flames———I'll not hear a Sentence more, that begins with an, I burn——— Or an, I beseech you, Madam.

Bellmour. But tell me how you would be Ador'd—I am very tractable.

Belinda. Then know, I would be Ador'd in Silence.

Bellmour. Humph, I thought so, that you might have all the Talk to your self—You had better let me speak; for if my Thoughts fly to any pitch, I shall make villainous Signs.

Belinda. What will you get by that? To make such Signs as I won't understand.

Bellmour. Ay, but if I'm Tongue-ty'd, I must have all my Actions free to—Quicken your Apprehension—And I-gad let me tell you, my standing Argument is depress'd in dumb shew.

Enter Musick master.

Araminta. O I am glad we shall have a Song to divert the Discourse—Pray oblige us with the last new Song.

SONG.

I.

Thus, to a ripe, consenting Maid,
Poor, old, repenting *Delia* said,
Would you long preserve your Lover?
Would you still his Goddess reign?
Never let him all discover,
Never let him much obtain.

new song—Congreve's words, set to music by Henry Purcell.

II.

Men will admire, adore and die,
While wishing at your Feet they lie:
But admitting their Embraces,
  Wakes 'em from the golden Dream;
Nothing's new besides our Faces,
  Every Woman is the same.

Araminta. So, how de'e like the Song, Gentlemen?

Bellmour. O very well perform'd——But I don't much admire the Words.

Araminta. I expected it——there's too much Truth in 'em: If Mr. *Gavot* will walk with us in the Garden, we'll have it once again——You may like it better at second hearing. You'l bring my Cousin.

Bellmour. Faith, Madam, I dare not speak to her, but I'll make Signs. *Addresses* Belinda *in dumb shew.*

Belinda. O fogh, your dumb Rhetorick is more ridiculous, than your talking Impertinence; as an Ape is a much more troublesome Animal than a Parrot.

Araminta. Ay, Cousin, and 'tis a sign the Creatures mimick Nature well, for there are few Men, but do more silly things, than they say.

Bellmour. Well, I find my Apishness has paid the Ransome for my Speech, and set it at liberty——Tho', I confess, I could be well enough pleas'd to drive on a Love-bargain, in that silent manner——'Twould save a Man a World of Lying and Swearing at the Years end. Besides, I have had a little Experience, that brings to my mind——

When Wit and Reason, both, have fail'd to move;
Kind Looks and Actions (from Success) do prove,
Ev'n Silence may be Eloquent in Love.

Exeunt Omnes.

ACT III. Scene I. The Street.

Silvia *and* Lucy.

Silvia. Will a' not come then?

Lucy. Yes Yes, come, I warrant him, if you will go in and be ready to receive him.

Silvia. Why did you not tell me?———Whom mean you?

Lucy. Whom you should mean, *Heartwell.*

Silvia. Senseless Creature, I meant my *Vainlove.*

Lucy. You may as soon hope, to recover your own Maidenhead, as his Love. Therefore e'n set your Heart at rest, and in the name of opportunity mind your own Business. Strike *Heartwell* home, before the Bait's worn off the Hook, Age will come; he nibbled fairly yesterday, and no doubt will be eager enough to day, to swallow the Temptation.

Silvia. Well, since there's no remedy———Yet tell me——— For I would know, though to the anguish of my Soul; how did he refuse? Tell me—how did he receive my letter, in Anger or in Scorn?

Lucy. Neither; but what was ten times worse, with damn'd, senseless indifference. By this Light I could have spit in his Face—Receive it! why he receiv'd it, as I would one of your Lovers that should come empty-handed; as a Court Lord does his Mercers Bill, or a begging Dedication; ———a' receiv'd it, as if 'thad been a Letter from his Wife.

Silvia. What did he not read it?

Lucy. Hum'd it over, gave you his Respects, and said, he would take time to peruse it—But then he was in haste.

Silvia. Respects, and peruse it! He's gone, and *Araminta* has bewitch'd him from me———Oh how the name of Rival fires my Blood—I could curse 'em both; eternal Jealousie attend her Love; and Disappointment meet his Lust. Oh that I could revenge the Torment he has caus'd—Methinks I feel the Woman strong within me, and Vengeance itches in the room of Love.

Lucy. I have that in my Head may make Mischief.

Silvia. How, dear *Lucy.*

Lucy. You know *Aramintas* dissembled Coyness has won, and keeps him hers———

Silvia. Could we perswade him, that she Loves another———

By this light—(Good or God's light) an expression from current usage very common in seventeenth-century plays.

Lucy. No, you're out; could we perswade him, that she doats on him, himself———Contrive a kind Letter as from her, 'twould disgust his nicety, and take away his Stomach.

Silvia. Impossible, 'twill never take.

Lucy. Trouble not your Head. Let me alone———I will inform my self of what past between 'em to Day, and about it streight———Hold, I'me mistaken, or that's *Heartwell*, who stands talking at the Corner———'tis he—Go get you in Madam, receive him pleasantly, dress up your Face in Innocence and Smiles; and dissemble the very want of Dissimulation———You know what will take him.

Silvia. 'Tis as hard to Counterfeit Love, as it is to conceal it: but I'le do my weak endeavour, though I fear I have not Art.

Lucy. Hang Art, Madam, and trust to Nature for Dissembling.

Man, was by Nature Womans Cully made:
We, never are but by our selves betray'd.

Exeunt.

Enter Heartwell, Vainlove *and* Bellmour *following.*

Bellmour. Hist hist, is not that *Heartwell* going to *Silvia*?

Vainlove. He's talking to himself, I think; Prithee lets try if we can hear him.

Heartwell. Why whither in the Devils name am I going now? Hum—Let me think———Is not this *Silvia's* House, the Cave of that Enchantress and which consequently I ought to shun as I would infection? To enter here, is to put on the envenom'd Shirt, to run into the Embraces of a Fever, and in some raving fit, be led to plunge my self into that more Consuming Fire, a Womans Arms. Ha! well recollected, I will recover my reason and be gone.

Bellmour. Now *Venus* forbid!

Vainlove. Hust———

Heartwell. Well, Why do you not move? Feet do your Office———Not one Inch; no, Foregod I'me caught———

envenom'd shirt—left by Nessus, one of the Centaurs who had been killed by Hercules, to bring him to an agonizing death; see Ovid. *Metamorphoses*, Bk. IX.

There stands my North, and thither my Needle points ———Now could I curse my self, yet cannot repent. O thou Delicious, Damn'd, Dear, destructive Woman! S'death how the young Fellows will hoot me! I shall be the Jest of the Town: Nay in two Days, I expect to be Chronicled in Ditty, and sung in woful Ballad, to the Tune of the Superanuated Maidens Comfort, or the Batchelors Fall; and upon the third, I shall be hang'd in Effigie, pasted up for the exemplary Ornament of necessary Houses and Coblers Stalls———Death, I can't think on't———I'le run into the danger to lose the apprehension.

Goes in.

Bellmour. A very certain remedy, *probatum est*—Ha, ha, ha, poor *George*, thou art i'th right, thou hast sold thy self to Laughter; the ill-natur'd Town will find the Jest just where thou hast lost it. Ha, ha, how a' strugled, like an Old Lawyer, between two Fees.

Vainlove. Or a young Wench, betwixt pleasure and reputation.

Bellmour. Or as you did to day, when half afraid you snatch'd a kiss from *Araminta.*

Vainlove. She has made a quarrel on't.

Bellmour. Pauh, Women are only angry at such offences, to have the pleasure of forgiving 'em.

Vainlove. And I love to have the pleasure of making my peace—I should not esteem a Pardon if too easie won.

Bellmour. Thou dost not know what thou would'st be at; whether thou wouldst have her angry or pleas'd. Couldst thou be content to marry *Araminta*?

Vainlove. Could you be content to go to Heaven?

Bellmour. Hum, not immediately, in my conscience not heartily? I'de do a little more good in my generation first, in order to deserve it.

Vainlove. Nor I to marry *Araminta* till I merit her.

Bellmour. But how the Devil dost thou expect to get her if she never yield?

Vainlove. That's true; but I would———

Bellmour. Marry her without her Consent; thou'rt a Riddle beyond Woman———

Enter Setter.

Trusty *Setter* what tidings? How goes the project?

Setter. As all lew'd projects do Sir, where the Devil prevents our endeavours with success.

Bellmour. A good hearing, *Setter.*

Vainlove. Well, I'le leave you with your Engineer.

Exit.

Bellmour. And hast thou provided necessaries?

Setter. All, all Sir; the large sanctified Hat, and the little precise Band, with a swinging long Spiritual Cloak, to Cover Carnal Knavery—not forgetting the Black Patch, which Tribulation Spintext wears as I'm inform'd, upon one Eye, as a penal Mourning for the ogling Offences of his Youth; and some say, with that Eye, he first discover'd the frailty of his Wife.

Bellmour. Well in this Fanatick Fathers habit, will I confess *Lætitia.*

Setter. Rather prepare her for Confession, Sir by helping her to Sin.

Bellmour. Be at your Masters Lodging in the Evening———I shall use the Robes.

Exit Bellmour.

Setter. I shall Sir———I wonder to which of these two Gentlemen I do most properly appertain———The one uses me as his Attendant; the other (being the better acquainted with my parts) employs me as a Pimp: why that's much the more honourable employment———by all means———I follow one as my Master, but the tother follows me as his Conductor.

Enter Lucy.

Lucy. Ther's the Hang-Dog his Man———I had a power over him in the Reign of my Mistress; but he is too true a *Valet-de-chambre* not to affect his Masters faults; and consequently is revolted from his Allegiance.

prevents—With the Devil, not God, going before us and making our efforts futile by providing success.

Setter. Undoubtedly 'tis impossible to be a Pimp and not a Man of parts. That is without being politick, diligent, secret, wary and soforth———And to all this valiant as Hercules ———That is, passively valiant and actively obedient. Ah! *Setter* what a treasure is here lost for want of being known.

Lucy. Here's some Villany a Foot he's so thoughtful; may be I may discover something in my Masque—Worthy Sir, a word with you.

Puts on her Masque.

Setter. Why if I were known, I might come to be a great Man.—

Lucy. Not to interrupt your meditation—

Setter. And I should not be the first that has procur'd his greatness by Pimping.

Lucy. Now Poverty and the Pox light upon thee, for a Contemplative Pimp.

Setter. Ha! what art, who thus maliciously hast awakned me, from my Dream of Glory? speak thou vile Disturber———

Lucy. Of thy most vile Cogitations———Thou poor, Conceited Wretch, how, wer't thou valuing thy self, upon thy Masters employment. For he's the head Pimp to Mr. *Bellmour*.

Setter. Good Words, Damsel, or I shall———But how dost thou know my Master or me?

Lucy. Yes, I know both Master and Man to be———

Setter. To be Men perhaps; nay faith like enough; I often march in the rear of my Master, and enter the Breaches which he was made.

Lucy. Ay, the Breach of Faith, which he has begun: Thou Traytor to thy lawful Princess.

Setter. Why how now! prithee who art? lay by that Worldly Face and produce your natural Vizor.

Lucy. No Sirrah, I'le keep it on to abuse thee and leave thee without hopes of revenge.

Setter. Oh! I begin to smoak ye, thou art some forsaken *Abigail*, we have dallied with heretofore———And art come to tickle thy Imagination with remembrance of iniquity past.

Lucy. No thou pitiful Flatterer of thy Masters imperfections; thou Maukin made up of the Shreds and Pairings of his superfluous Fopperies.

Setter. Thou are thy Mistresses foul self, Composed of her sully'd iniquities and Cloathing.

Lucy. Hang thee———Beggars Curr———Thy Master is but a Mumper in Love, lies Canting at the Gate; but never dare presume to enter the House.

Setter. Thou art the Wicket to thy Mistresses Gate, to be opened for all Comers. In Fine thou art the high Road to thy Mistress, as a Clap is to the Pox.

Lucy. Beast, filthy Toad, I can hold no longer, look and tremble.

Unmasques.

Setter. How, Mrs. *Lucy!*

Lucy. I wonder thou hast the impudence to look me in the Face.

Setter. Adsbud who's in fault, Mistress Mine? who flung the first Stone? who undervalued my Function? and who the Devil could know you by instinct?

Lucy. You could know my Office by instinct, and be hang'd, which you have slander'd most abominably. It vexes me not what you said of my Person; but that my innocent Calling should be expos'd and scandaliz'd—I cannot bear it. *Cries*

Setter. Nay faith *Lucy* I'me sorry, I'le own my self to blame, though we were both in fault as to our Offices——— Come I'le make you any reparation.

Lucy. Swear.

Setter. I do swear to the utmost of my power.

Lucy. To be brief then; what is the reason your Master did not appear to Day according to the Summons I brought him?

Setter. To answer you as briefly—He has a cause to be try'd in another Court.

Lucy. Come tell me in plain Terms, how forward he is with *Araminta.*

Maukin—A scarecrow.
Mumper—A beggar (in the jargon of beggars and gypsies); see *Dictionary of the Canting Crew* (1700).

Setter. Too forward to be turn'd back—Though he's a little in disgrace at present about a Kiss which he forced. You and I can Kiss *Lucy* without all that.

Lucy. Stand off———He's a precious Jewel.

Setter. And therefore you'd have him to set in your Ladies Locket.

Lucy. Where is he now?

Setter. He'l be in the *Piaza* presently.

Lucy. Remember to Days behaviour—Let me see you with a penitent Face.

Setter. What no Token of amity *Lucy*? you and I don't use to part with dry Lips.

Lucy. No no, avaunt———I'le not be slabber'd and kiss'd now———I'me not 'ith humour. *Exit.*

Setter. I'le not quit you so———I'le Follow and put you into the humour.

Exit after her.

Enter Sir Joseph Wittoll, Bluffe.

Bluffe. And so out of your unwonted Generosity———

Sir Joseph. And good Nature, Back; I am good Natur'd and I can't help it.

Bluffe. You have given him a note upon *Fondlewife* for a hundred Pound.

Sir Joseph. Ay ay, poor Fellow, he ventur'd fair fort.

Bluffe. You have disoblig'd me in it———for I have occasion for the Mony, and if you would look me in the Face again and live, go, and force him, to redeliver you the Note—go—and bring it me hither. I'le stay here for you.

Sir Joseph. You may stay till the day of Judgment then, by the Lord-*Harry*. I know better things than to be run through the Guts for a hundred Pound———Why I gave that hundred Pound for being saved, and d'ee think, an there were no danger, I'le be so ungrateful to take it from the Gentleman again?

Piaza—The Inigo Jones arcades in Covent Garden, which were a fashionable resort.

Bluffe. Well, go to him from me———Tell him, I say, he must refund—or Bilbo's the Word, and Slaughter will ensue—If he refuse, tell him—But whisper that———Tell him———I'll pink his Soul———but whisper that softly to him.

Sir Joseph. So softly, that he shall never hear on't I warrant you———Why what a Devil's the Matter, Bully, are you mad? Or de'e think I'm mad? Agad for my part, I don't love to be the Messenger of ill News; 'tis an ungrateful Office—So tell him your self.

Bluffe. By these Hilts I believe he frightned you into this Composition; I believe you gave it him out of fear, pure paultry fear—confess.

Sir Joseph. No, no, hang't I was not afraid neither—Tho' I confess he did in a manner snap me up—Yet I can't say that it was altogether out of fear, but partly to prevent mischief—For he was a devilish cholerick Fellow: And if my Choller had been up too, agad there would have been mischief done, that's flat. And yet I believe if you had been by, I would as soon have let him a' had a hundred of my Teeth. Adsheart if he should come just now when I'm angry, I'd tell him———Mum.

Enter Sharper, Bellmour.

Bellmour. Thou'rt a lucky Rogue; there's your Benefactor, you ought to return him Thanks now you have receiv'd the Favour.

Sharper. Sir *Joseph*———Your Note was accepted, and the Mony paid at sight: I'm come to return my Thanks———

Sir Joseph. They won't be accepted, so readily as the Bill, Sir.

Bellmour. I doubt the Knight repents, *Tom*—He looks like the Knight of the sorrowful Face.

Sharper. This is a double Generosity———Do me a Kindness and refuse my Thanks—But I hope you are not offended that I offer'd 'em.

Sir Joseph. May be I am Sir, may be I am not Sir, may be I am both Sir; what then? I hope I may be offended, without any offence to you Sir.

Bilbo's—Sword from Bilbao, used by all the bullies in the plays.
Adsheart—Ads, a variant of Ods; for Gods.
Knight of the sorrowful Face—A title Don Quixote assumes, see I, 3, v.

Sharper. Hey day! Captain, what's the matter? You can tell.

Bluffe. Mr. *Sharper*, the matter is plain—Sir *Joseph* has found out your Trick, and does not care to be put upon; being a Man of Honour.

Sharper. Trick, Sir.

Sir Joseph. Ay Trick, Sir, and won't be put upon Sir, being a Man of Honour Sir, and so Sir—

Sharper. Hearkee, Sir *Joseph*, a word with ye—In consideration of some favours lately receiv'd; I would not have you draw your self into a Premunire, by trusting to that sign of a Man there—That Pot-gun charg'd with Wind.

Sir Joseph. O Lord, O Lord, Captain, come justifie your self—I'll give him the Lie if you'll stand to it.

Sharper. Nay then I'll be beforehand with you, take that—Oafe.

Cuffs him.

Sir Joseph. Captain, will you see this? Won't you pink his Soul?

Bluffe. Husht, 'tis not so convenient now———I shall find a time.

Sharper. What do you mutter about a time, Rascal—You were the Incendiary———There's to put you in mind of your time———A Memorandum.

Kicks him.

Bluffe. O this is your time Sir, you had best make use on't.

Sharper. I Gad and so I will: There's again for you.

Kicks him.

Bluffe. You are obliging Sir, but this is too publick a Place to thank you in: But in your Ear, you are to be seen again.

Sharper. Ay thou inimitable Coward and to be felt———As for Example.

Kicks him.

Bellmour. Ha, ha, ha, prithee come away, 'tis scandalous to

Premunire—Legal jargon for a bad predicament, such as that of a person subject to the penalties of a *praemunire*. See Thomas Blount, *Law Dictionary* (1670).

kick this Puppy without a Man were cold, and had no other way to get himself a heat.

Exit Bellmour, Sharper.

Bluffe. Very well—Very fine———But 'tis no matter——— Is not this fine, Sir *Joseph*?

Sir Joseph. Indifferent, agad in my opinion very indifferent ———I'd rather go plain all my Life, than wear such Finery.

Bluffe. Death and Hell to be affronted thus! I'll die before I'll suffer it.

Draws.

Sir Joseph. O Lord his Anger was not raised before———Nay, dear Captain, don't be in Passion now, he's gone——— Put up, put up, dear Back, 'tis your Sir *Joseph* begs, come let me kiss thee, so so, put up, put up.

Bluffe. By Heav'n 'tis not to be put up.

Sir Joseph. What, Bully?

Bluff. Th' Affront.

Sir Joseph. No agad no more 'tis, for that's put up already; thy Sword I mean.

Bluffe. Well, Sir *Joseph*, at your entreaty———But were not you my Friend; Abus'd and Cuff'd and Kick'd.

Putting up his Sword.

Sir Joseph. Ay, ay, so were you too; no matter, 'tis past.

Bluffe. By the immortal Thunder of great Guns, 'tis false ———He sucks not vital Air who dares affirm it to this Face.

Looks big.

Sir Joseph. To that Face I grant you Captain———No, no, I grant you———Not to that Face by the Lord *Harry*—If you had put on your fighting Face before, you had done his Business—He durst as soon have kiss'd you, as kick'd you to your Face—But a Man can no more help what's done behind his Back, than what's said—Come wee'l think no more of what's past.

Bluffe. I'll call a Council of War within to consider of my Revenge to come.

Exeunt.

10

15

20

25

[Scene II]

SCENE Changes to Silvia's Lodgings.

Enter Heartwell, Silvia.

SONG.

I.

As Amoret and Thyrsis, lay
Melting the Hours, in gentle Play;
Joining Faces, mingling Kisses,
And exchanging harmless Blisses:
He trembling, cry'd, with eager haste,
O let me feed as well as taste,
I die, if I'm not wholly blest.

II

The fearful Nymph reply'd—Forbear; I cannot, dare not, must not hear:
Dearest Thyrsis, do not move me,
Do not—do not—if you Love me
O let me—still the Shepherd said;
But while she fond Resistance made,
The hasty Joy, in strugling fled.

III.

Vex'd at the Pleasure she had miss'd,
She frown'd and blush'd, then sigh'd and kiss'd,
And seem'd to moan, in sullen Cooing,
The sad miscarriage of their Wooing:
But vain alas! were all her Charms;
For Thyrsis deaf to Loves allarms,
Baffled and senseless, tir'd her Arms.

After the Song, a Dance of Antick.

Silvia. Indeed it is very fine———I could look upon 'em all day.

Heartwell. Well, has this prevail'd for me, and will you look upon me?

Antick—Dancers grotesquely dressed.

Silvia. If you could Sing and Dance so, I should love to look upon you too.

Heartwell. Why 'twas I Sung and Danc'd; I gave Musick to the Voice, and Life to their Measures———Look you here *Silvia*, here are Songs and Dances, Poetry and Musick ———hark! (*pulling out a Purse and chinking it*) how sweetly one Guinea rhymes to another———And how they dance to the Musick of their own Chink. This buys all the 'tother ———And this thou shalt have; this, and all that I am worth for the purchase of thy Love—Say, is it mine then, ha? Speak Syren———Oons why do I look on her! Yet I must—Speak dear Angel, Devil, Saint, Witch; do not rack me in suspence.

Silvia. Nay don't stare at me so———You make me blush ———I cannot look.

Heartwell. Oh Manhood, where art thou! What am I come to? A Womans Toy; at these years! Death, a bearded Baby for a Girl to dandle. O dotage, dotage! That ever that noble passion, *Lust*, should ebb to this degree—No reflux of vigorous Blood: But milky Love, supplies the empty Channels; and prompts me to the softness of a Child———A meer Infant and would suck. Can you love me *Silvia*? speak.

Silvia. I dare not speak till I believe you, and indeed I'm afraid to believe you yet.

Heartwell. Pox, how her Innocence torments and pleases me! Lying, Child, is indeed the Art of Love; and Men are generally Masters in it: But I'm so newly entred, you cannot distrust me of any skill in the treacherous Mystery— Now by my Soul, I cannot lie, though it were to serve a Friend or gain a Mistress.

Silvia. Must you lie then, if you say you Love me?

Heartwell. No, no, dear ignorance, thou beauteous Change-l'ng———I tell thee I do love thee, and tell it for a Truth, a naked Truth, which I'm ashamed to discover.

Silvia. But Love, they say, is a tender thing, that will smooth Frowns, and make calm an angry Face; will soften a rugged Temper, and make ill-humoured People good: You look ready to fright one, and talk as if your Passion were not Love, but Anger.

Heartwell. 'Tis both; for I am angry with my self, when I am pleased with you—And a Pox upon me for loving thee so well———Yet I must on———'Tis a bearded Arrow, and will more easily be thrust forward than drawn back.

Silvia. Indeed if I were well assur'd you lov'd; but how can I be well assur'd?

Heartwell. Take the Symptoms———And ask all the Tyrants of thy Sex, if their Fools are not known by this Party-coloured Livery—I am Melancholy when thou art absent; look like an Ass when thou art present; Wake for you, when I should Sleep, and even Dream of you, when I am Awake; Sigh much, Drink little, Eat less, court Solitude, am grown very entertaining to my self, and (as I am informed) very troublesome to everybody else. If this be not Love, it is Madness, and then it is pardonable—Nay yet a more certain Sign than all this; I give thee my Mony.

Silvia. Ay, but that is no Sign, for they say, Gentlemen will give Mony to any naughty Woman to come to Bed to them—O *Gemini*, I hope you don't mean so———For I won't be a Whore.

Heartwell. The more is the pity.

Aside.

Silvia. Nay if you would Marry me, you should not come to Bed to me—You have such a Beard and would so prickle one. But do you intend to Marry me?

Heartwell (*aside*). That a Fool should ask such a malicious Question! Death, I shall be drawn in, before I know where I am—However, I find I am pretty sure of her consent, if I am put to it.
Marry you? no, no, I'll love you.

Silvia. Nay, but if you love me, you must Marry me; what dont I know my Father lov'd my Mother, and was married to her?

Heartwell. Ay, ay, in old days People married where they lov'd; but that fashion is chang'd, Child.

Silvia. Never tell me that, I know it is not chang'd by my self; for I love you, and would Marry you.

Heartwell. I'll have my Beard shav'd, it shan't hurt thee, and we'l go to Bed—

Silvia. No, no, I'm not such a Fool neither but I can keep my self—honest—Here, I won't keep any thing that's yours,

(*Throws the Purse*) I hate you now, and I'll never see you again, 'cause you'd have me be naught.

Going.

Heartwell. Damn her let her go, and a good riddance—Yet so much Tenderness and Beauty———and Honesty together is a Jewel———Stay *Silvia*———But then to Marry——— Why every Man plays the Fool once in his Life: But to Marry, is playing the Fool all ones Life long.

Silvia. What did you call me for?

Heartwell. I'll give thee all I have: And thou shalt live with me in every thing, so like my Wife, the World shall believe it: Nay, thou shalt think so thy self—Only let me not think so.

Silvia. No, I'll die before I'll be your Whore—as well as I love you.

Heartwell (*aside*). A Woman, and Ignorant, may be honest, when 'tis out of Obstinacy and Contradiction—But S'death it is but a may be, and upon scurvy Terms——— Well, farewell then———if I can get out of her sight I may get the better of my self.

Silvia. Well———good by.

Turns and Weeps.

Heartwell. Ha! Nay come, we'll kiss at parting (*kisses her*) by Heaven she kisses sweeter than Liberty—I will Marry thee—There thou hast don't, all my Resolve melted in that Kiss—one more.

Silvia. But when?

Heartwell. I'm impatient till it be done; I will not give my self liberty to think, lest I should cool—I will about a Licence streight—in the Evening expect me—One Kiss more to confirm me mad; so.

Exit.

Silvia. Ha, ha, ha, an old Fox trapt—

Enter Lucy.

Bless me! you frighted me, I thought he had been come again, and had heard me.

Lucy. Lord, Madam, I met your Lover in as much haste, as if he had been going for a Midwife.

Silvia. He's going for a Parson, Girl, the forerunner of a Midwife, some nine Months hence—Well, I find dissembling, to our Sex is as natural as swimming to a *Negro*; we may depend upon our skill to save us at a plunge, though till then we never make the experiment—But how hast thou succeeded?

Lucy. As you would wish—Since there is no reclaiming *Vainlove*, I have found out a picque she has taken at him; and have fram'd a Letter, that makes her sue for Reconciliation first. I know that will do—walk in and I'le shew it you. Come Madam, you're like to have a happy time on't, both your Love and Anger satisfied!—All that can charm our Sex conspire to please you.

That Woman sure enjoys a blessed Night,
Whom Love and Vengeance do at once delight.

Exeunt.

ACT IV. Scene I. The Street

Enter Bellmour *in Fanatick habit,* Setter.

Bellmour. 'Tis pretty near the Hour—

Looking on his Watch.

Well and how *Setter* hæ, does my Hypocrisy fit me hæ? Does it sit easy on me?

Setter. O most religously well Sir.

Bellmour. I wonder why all our young Fellows should glory in an opinion of Atheism; when they may be so much more conveniently lewd, under the Coverlet of Religion.

Setter. S'bud Sir, away quickly, there's *Fondlewife* just turn'd the Corner, and's coming this way.

Bellmour. Gads so there he is, he must not see me.

Exeunt.

Enter Fondlewife *and* Barnaby.

Fondlewife. I say I will tarry at home.

Barnaby. But Sir.

Fondlewife. Good lack! I profess the Spirit of contradiction hath possess'd the Lad—I say I will tarry at home—*Varlet.*

Barnaby. I have done Sir, then farewell 500 Pound.

Fondlewife. Ha, how's that? Stay stay, did you leave word say you with his Wife? With *Comfort* her self.

Barnaby. I did; and *Comfort* will send *Tribulation* hither as soon as ever he comes home—I could have brought young Mr. *Prig*, to have kept my Mistress Company in the mean time: but you say—

Fondlewife. How how, say *Varlet*! I say let him not come near my Doors. I say, he is a wanton young *Levite* and pampereth himself up with Dainties, that he may look lovely in the Eyes of Women—Sincerely I am afraid he hath already defiled the Tabernacle of our Sister *Comfort*; while her good Husband is deluded by his Godly appearance———I say, that even Lust doth sparkle in his Eyes, and glow upon his Cheeks, and that I would as soon trust my Wife, with a Lords high-fed Chaplain.

Barnaby. Sir, the Hour draws nigh—And nothing will be done there till you come.

Fondlewife. And nothing can be done here till I go—So that I'le tarry, d'ee see.

Barnaby. And run the hazard to lose your affair so!

Fondlewife. Good lack, good lack—I profess it is a very sufficient vexation, for a Man to have a handsome Wife.

Barnaby. Never Sir, but when the Man is an insufficient Husband. 'Tis then indeed, like the vanity of taking a fine House, and yet be forced to let Lodgings, to help pay the Rent.

Fondlewife. I profess a very apt Comparison, *Varlet*. Go in and bid my Cocky come out to me, I will give her some instructions, I will reason with her before I go.

Exit Barnaby.

And in the mean time, I will reason with my self——— Tell me *Isaac*, why art thee Jealous? Why art thee distrustful of the Wife of thy Bosom?—Because she is young and vigorous, and I am Old and impotent—Then why didst thee marry *Isaac*?—Because she was beautiful and tempting, and because I was obstinate and doating; so that my inclination was (and is still) greater than my power——— And will not that which tempted thee, also tempt others, who will tempt her *Isaac*?———I fear it much—But

Levite—A term of contempt for a domestic chaplain.

does not thy Wife love thee, nay doat upon thee?——— Yes—Why then!—Ay, but to say truth, She's fonder of me, than she has reason to be; and in the way of Trade, we still suspect the smoothest Dealers of the deepest designs—And that she has some designs deeper than thou canst reach, th' hast experimented *Isaac*—But Mum.

Enter Lætitia

Lætitia. I hope my dearest Jewel, is not going to leave me— Are you *Nykin*?

Fondlewife. Wife—Have you throughly consider'd how detestable, how hainous, and how Crying a Sin, the Sin of Adultery is? have you weigh'd it I say? For it is a very weighty Sin; and although it may lie heavy upon thee, yet thy Husband must also bear his part: For thy iniquity will fall upon his Head.

Lætitia. Bless me, what means my Dear!

Fondlewife (*aside*). I profess she has an alluring Eye; I am doubtfull, whether I shall trust her, even with *Tribulation* himself—

Speak I say, have you consider'd, what it is to Cuckold your Husband?

Lætitia (*aside*). I'me amaz'd; sure he has discover'd nothing— Who has wrong'd me to my Dearest? I hope my Jewel does not think, that ever I had any such thing in my Head, or ever will have.

Fondlewife. No no, I tell you I shall have it in my Head—You will have it some where else.

Lætitia (*aside*). I know not what to think. But I'me resolv'd to find the meaning of it———

Unkind Dear! Was it for this, you sent to call me? is it not affliction enough that you are to leave me, but you must study to encrease it by unjust suspicions? (*Crying*) Well—Well—You know my Fondness, and you love to Tyrannize———Go on cruel Man, do, Triumph over my poor Heart, while it holds; which cannot be long, with this usage of yours—But that's what you want—Well— You will have your ends soon—You will—You will——— Yes it will break to oblige you.

Sighs.

Fondlewife (*aside*). Verily I fear I have carry'd the Jest, too far

—Nay look you now if she does not weep—'tis the fondest Fool—

Nay Cocky Cocky, nay dear Cocky, don't cry, I was but in Jest, I was not ifeck.

Lætitia (*aside*). Oh then alls safe. I was terrible frighted—

My affliction is always your Jest, barbarous Man! Oh that I should love to this degree! yet—

Fondlewife. Nay Cocky.

Lætitia. No no, you are weary of me, that's it—That's all, you would get another Wife—Another fond Fool, to break her Heart—Well, be as cruel as you can to me, I'le pray for you; and when I am dead with grief, may you have one that will love you as well as I have done: I shall be contented to lie at peace in my cold Grave—Since it will please you.

Sighs.

Fondlewife. Good lack, good lack, she would melt a Heart of Oak—I profess I can hold no longer—Nay dear Cocky—Ifeck you'l break my Heart—Ifeck you will—See you have made me weep—made poor *Nykin* weep—Nay come Kiss, buss poor *Nykin*—And I wont leave thee—I'le lose all first.

Lætitia (*aside*). How! Heav'n forbid! that will be carrying the Jest too far indeed.

Fondlewife. Wont you Kiss *Nykin*?

Lætitia. Go naughty *Nykin*, you don't love me.

Fondlewife. Kiss kiss, ifeck I do.

Lætitia. No you dont.

She Kisses him.

Fondlewife. What not love Cocky!

Lætitia. No—h

Sighs

Fondlewife. I profess I do love thee better, than 500 Pound—And so thou shalt say, for I'le leave it to stay with thee.

Lætitia. No you shan't neglect your business for me—No indeed you sant. *Nykin*———if you don't go, I'le think you been dealous of me still.

ifeck—An oath (i'faith) innocuous enough for Puritans to favor. Summers quotes "I'fac's no oath" from Jonson's *The Alchemist*, I, ii (see Nonesuch ed., I, 252).

Fondlewife. He, he, he, wilt thou poor Fool? Then I will go, I wont be dealous———Poor Cocky, Kiss *Nykin*, Kiss *Nykin*, ee, ee, ee,—Here will be the good Man anon, to talk to Cocky and teach her how a Wife ought to behave her self.

Lætitia (*aside*). I hope to have one that will shew me how a Husband ought to behave himself———I shall be glad to learn, to please my Jewel.

Kiss.

Fondlewife. That's my good Dear—Come Kiss *Nykin* once more, and then get you in———So———Get you in, get you in, By, by.

Lætitia. By *Nykin*.

Fondlewife. By Cocky.

Lætitia. By *Nykin*.

She goes in.

Fondlewife. By Cocky, by, by.

Exit.

Enter Vainlove, Sharper.

Sharper. How! *Araminta* lost!

Vainlove. To confirm what I have said read this

Gives a letter.

Sharper (reads). *Hum hum———And what then appear'd a fault, upon reflection, seems only an effect of a too powerful passion. I'me afraid I give too great a Proof of my own at this time——— I am in disorder for what I have written. But something, I know not what, forced me. I only beg a favourable Censure of this and your*

Araminta.

Sharper. Lost! Pray Heaven thou hast not lost thy Wits. Here, here, she's thy own Man, sign'd and seal'd too——— To her Man———A delicious Mellon pure and consenting ripe, and only waits thy Cutting up———She has been breeding Love to thee all this while, and just now she is deliver'd of it.

Vainlove. 'Tis an untimely Fruit, and she has miscarried of her Love.

Sharper. Never leave this damn'd illnatur'd whimsey *Frank*?

Censure—Opinion.

Thou hast a sickly peevish Appetite; only chew Love and cannot digest it.

Vainlove. Yes, when I feed my self—But I hate to be cram'd —By Heav'n there's not a Woman, will give a Man the pleasure of a chase: My sport is always balkt or cut short ———I stumble ore the Game I would pursue.———'Tis dull and unnatural to have a Hare run full in the Hounds Mouth; and would distaste the keenest Hunter———I would have overtaken, not have met my Game.

Sharper. However I hope you don't mean to forsake it, that will be but a kind of a Mungril Curs trick. Well, are you for the Mall?

Vainlove. No, she will be there this evening———Yes I will go too———And she shall see her error in———

Sharper. In her choice I gad———But thou canst not be so great a Brute as to slight her.

Vainlove. I should disappoint her if I did not—By her management I should think she expects it.

All Naturally fly what does pursue:
'Tis fit Men should be coy, when Women woo.

Exeunt.

[Scene II]

SCENE *changes to a chamber in* Fondlewife's *House.*

A Servant introducing Bellmour *in Fanatick Habit, with a Patch upon one Eye, and a Book in his Hand.*

Servant. Here's a Chair, Sir, if you please to repose your self. I'll call my Mistress.

Exit Servant.

Bellmour. Secure in my Disguise, I have out-fac'd Suspicion, and even dar'd Discovery———This Cloak my Sanctity, and trusty *Scarron's* Novels my Prayer-Book.——— Methinks I am the very Picture of *Montufar* in the *Hypocrites.*—Oh! she comes.

Montufar in the Hypocrites—Scarron's novel—English translation, 1682—frequently reprinted, in which Montufar is dressed in a cassock and black cloak.

Enter Lætitia.

So breaks Aurora *through the Veil of Night;*
Thus fly the Clouds, divided by her Light,
And ev'ry Eye receives a new-born Sight.

Throwing off his Cloak, Patch, &c.

Lætitia. Thus strew'd with Blushes, like———
Ah! Heav'n defend me! Who's this?

(*discovering him, starts*)

Bellmour. Your Lover.

Lætitia (*aside*). *Vainlove's* Friend! I know his Face, and he has betrayed me to him.

Bellmour. You are surprised. Did you not expect a Lover, Madam? Those Eyes shone kindly on my first Appearance, tho' now they are o'er-cast.

Lætitia. I may well be surpriz'd at your Person and Impudence; they are both new to me.—You are not what your first Appearance promised: The Piety of your Habit was welcome, but not the Hypocrisie.

Bellmour (*aside*). Rather the Hypocrisie was welcome, but not the Hypocrite.

Lætitia. Who are you, Sir? You have mistaken the House sure.

Bellmour. I have Directions in my Pocket, which agree with every thing but your Unkindness.

Pulls out the letter.

Lætitia (*aside*). My Letter! Base *Vainlove*! Then 'tis too late to dissemble. 'Tis plain then you have mistaken the Person.

Going.

Bellmour. If we part so I'm mistaken.———Hold, hold, Madam;—I confess I have run into an Errour:—I beg your Pardon a thousand times.—What an eternal Block-head am I! Can you forgive me the Disorder I have put you into; —But it is a Mistake which any Body might have made.

Lætitia (*aside*). What can this mean! 'Tis impossible he should be mistaken after all this.—A handsom Fellow if he had not surpriz'd me: Methinks, now I look on him again, I would not have him mistaken.
We are all liable to Mistakes, Sir: If you own it to be so, there needs no farther Apology.

Aurora . . . *Blushes*—See Dryden, *Amphitryon*, II, ii, 20–22.

Bellmour. Nay, 'Faith, Madam, 'tis a pleasant one; and worth your hearing. Expecting a Friend, last Night, at his Lodgings, till 'twas late; my Intimacy with him gave me the Freedom of his Bed: He not coming home all Night, a Letter was deliver'd to me by a Servant, in the Morning: Upon the Perusal I found the Contents so charming, that I cou'd think of nothing all Day but putting 'em in practice —'till just now, (the first time I ever look'd upon the Superscription,) I am the most surpriz'd in the World to find it directed to Mr. *Vainlove*. Gad, Madam, I ask you a Million of Pardons, and will make you any Satisfaction.

Lætitia (*aside*). I am discover'd:———And either *Vainlove* is not guilty, or he has handsomly excused him.

Bellmour. You appear concern'd, Madam.

Lætitia. I hope you are a Gentleman;———and since you are privy to a weak Woman's Failing, won't turn it to the prejudice of her Reputation—You look as if you had more Honour.———

Bellmour. And more Love; or my Face is a False-Witness, and deserves to be pillory'd.——— No, by Heaven, I swear———

Lætitia. Nay, don't swear if you'd have me believe you; but promise.—

Bellmour. Well, I promise.———A promise is so cold.——— Give me leave to swear—by those Eyes, those killing Eyes; by those healing Lips.———Oh! press the soft Charm close to mine,—and seal 'em up for ever.

He kisses her.

Lætitia. Upon that Condition.

Bellmour. Eternity was in that Moment.—One more, upon any Condition.

Lætitia. Nay, now.—(*aside*) I never saw any thing so agreeably Impudent. Won't you censure me for this, now;—but 'tis to buy your Silence.

Kiss.

Oh, but what am I doing!

Bellmour. Doing! No Tongue can express it,—not thy own; nor any thing, but thy Lips. I am faint with the Excess of Bliss:—Oh, for Love-sake, lead me any whither, where I may lie down;—quickly, for I'm afraid I shall have a Fit.

Lætitia. Bless me! What Fit?

Bellmour. Oh, a Convulsion.———I feel the Symptoms.

Lætitia. Does it hold you long? I'm afraid to carry you into my Chamber.

Bellmour. Oh, No: Let me lie down upon the Bed;———the Fit will be soon over.

Exeunt.

[SCENE III]

SCENE *changes to* St. James's Park.

Araminta *and* Belinda *meeting.*

Belinda. Lard, my Dear! I am glad I have met you:———I have been at the *Exchange* since, and am so tir'd———

Araminta. Why, What's the matter?

Belinda. Oh the most inhumane, barbarous Hackney-Coach! I am jolted to a Jelly.—Am I not horridly touz'd?

Pulls out a Pocket-Glass.

Araminta. Your Head's a little out of Order.

Belinda. A little! O frightful! What a furious Fiz I have! O most rueful! Ha, ha, ha: O Gad, I hope no-body will come this Way, till I put my self a little in Repair,—Ah! my Dear,—I have seen such unhewn Creatures since,—Ha, ha, ha, I can't for my Soul help thinking that I look just like one of 'em:—Good Dear, pin this, and I'll tell you. ———Very well.———So, thank you my Dear.———But as I was telling you———Pish, this is the untoward'st Lock———So, as I was telling you———How d'ye like me now? Hideous, ha? Frightful still? Or how?

Araminta. No, no; you're very well as can be.

Belinda. And so—But where did I leave off, my Dear? I was telling you—

Araminta. You were about to tell me something, Child,—but you left off before you began.

Exchange—Shops on south side of the Strand, famous for millinery and trinkets.

Belinda. Oh; a most Comical Sight: A Country-Squire, with the Equipage of a Wife and two Daughters, came to Mrs. *Snipwel's* Shop while I was there.———But, Oh Gad! Two such unlick'd Cubs!———

Araminta. I warrant, plump, Cherry-cheek'd Country-Girls.

Belinda. Ay, O my Conscience; fat as Barn-door-Fowl: But so bedeck'd, you wou'd have taken 'em for *Friezland*-Hens, with their Feathers growing the wrong way.—O such Out-landish Creatures! Such *Tramontanæ*, and Foreigners to the Fashion, or any thing in practice! I had not patience to behold.———I undertook the modelling of one of their Fronts, the more modern Structure.———

Araminta. Bless me, Cousin! Why wou'd you affront any body so? They might be Gentlewomen of a very good Family.———

Belinda. Of a very ancient one, I dare swear, by their Dress. ———Affront! Pshaw, how you're mistaken! The poor Creature, I warrant, was as full of Courtesies, as if I had been her Godmother: The Truth on't is, I did endeavour to make her look like a Christian,———and she was sensible of it; for she thank'd me, and gave me two Apples, piping hot, out of her Under-Petticoat-Pocket,———Ha, ha, ha: And t'other did so stare and gape,—I fansied her like the Front of her Father's Hall; her Eyes were the two Jut-Windows, and her Mouth the great Door, most hospitably kept open, for the Entertainment of travelling Flies.

Araminta. So then; you have been diverted. What did they buy?

Belinda. Why, the Father bought a Powder-Horn, and an Almanack, and a Comb-Case; the Mother, a great Fruz-Towr, and a Fat-Amber-Necklace; the Daughters only tore two Pair of Kid-Gloves, with trying 'em on.——— Oh Gad, here comes the Fool that din'd at my Lady *Free-love's* t'other Day.

Enter Sir Joseph *and* Bluffe.

Araminta. May be he may not know us again.

Belinda. We'll put on our Masks to secure his Ignorance.

They put on their Masks.

Tramontanæ—Uncouth folk from beyond the mountains.

Fruz-Towr—A very high headdress for "her who has no hair, or has but some"; cf. Congreve's translation of *Art of Love*, III, 306.

Sir Joseph. Nay, gad, I'll pick up; I'm resolv'd to make a Night on't.—I'll go to Alderman *Fondlewife* by-and-by, and get 50 Pieces more from him. Adslidikins, *Bully*, we'll wallow in Wine and Women. Why, this same *Madera*-Wine has made me as light as a Grasshopper.—Hist, hist, *Bully*, dost thou see those Tearers? (*Sings.*) *Look you what here is,—Look you what here is:—Toll—loll—dera—toll—loll.* —A-Gad, t'other Glass of *Madera*, and I durst have attack'd 'em in my own proper Person, without your help.

Bluffe. Come on then, Knight.———But d'ye know what to say to 'em?

Sir Joseph. Say: Pooh, Pox, I've enough to say,———never fear it;———that is, if I can but think on't: Truth is, I have but a treacherous Memory.

Belinda. O frightful! Cousin, What shall we do? These things come toward us.

Araminta. No matter,———I see *Vainlove* coming this way,—and, to confess my Failing, I am willing to give him an Opportunity of making his Peace with me;———and to rid me of these Coxcombs, when I seem oppress'd with 'em, will be a fair one.

Bluffe. Ladies, by these Hilts you are well met.

Araminta. We are afraid not.

Bluffe. What says my pretty little Knapsack-Carrier? *To* Belinda.

Belinda. O monstrous filthy Fellow! Good slovenly Captain *Huffe*, *Bluffe*, (What's your hideous Name?) be gone: You stink of Brandy and Tobacco, most Soldier-like. Foh. *Spits.*

Sir Joseph (*aside*). Now am I slap-dash down in the Mouth, and have not one Word to say.

Araminta (*aside*). I hope my Fool has not Confidence enough to be troublesom.

Sir Joseph. Hem! Pray Madam, Which Way's the Wind?

Araminta. A pithy Question.———Have you sent your Wits for a Venture, Sir, that you enquire?

Sir Joseph (*aside*). Nay, now I'm in—I can prattle like a Magpye.

Tearers—Swaggerers.

Enter Sharper *and* Vainlove, *at a Distance.*

Belinda. Dear *Araminta*, I'm tir'd.

Araminta. 'Tis but pulling off our Masks, and obliging *Vainlove* to know us, I'll be rid of my Fool by fair means ———Well, Sir *Joseph*, you shall see my Face.———But, be gone immediately.———I see one that will be Jealous, to find me in discourse with you.———Be discreet.——— No reply; but away.

Unmasks.

Sir Joseph (*aside*). The great Fortune, that dined at my Lady *Free-loves*! Sir *Joseph*, thou art a Mad-man. Agad, I'm in Love, up to the Ears. But I'll be discreet, and husht.

Bluffe. Nay, by the World, I'll see your face.

Belinda. You shall.

Unmasks.

Sharper. Ladies, your humble Servant.———We were afraid, you would not have given us leave to know you.

Araminta. We thought to have been private.———But we find fools, have the same advantage, over a Face in a Mask; that a Coward has, while the Sword is in the Scabbard ———So were forced to draw, in our own defence.

Bluffe. My Blood rises at that Fellow: I can't stay where he is; and I must not draw in the Park.

To Sir Joseph.

Sir Joseph. I wish I durst stay to let her know my Lodging.———

Exeunt Sir Joseph *and* Bluffe.

Sharper. There is in true Beauty, as in Courage, somewhat, which narrow Souls cannot dare to admire.———And see, the Owls are fled, as at the break of Day.

Belinda. Very courtly.———I believe, Mr. *Vainlove* has not rubb'd his Eyes, since break of Day neither, he looks as if he durst not approach.———Nay, come Cousin, be friends with him.———I swear, he looks so very simply, ha, ha, ha.—Well, a Lover in the state of separation from his Mistriss, is like a Body without a Soul. Mr. *Vainlove*, shall I be bound for your good Behaviour for the future?

draw in the Park—St. James's, the royal precincts, where dueling was forbidden.

Vainlove. Now must I pretend ignorance equal to hers, of what she knows as well as I. (*Aside*). Men are apt to offend ('tis true) where they find most Goodness to forgive.——— But, Madam, I hope I shall prove of a Temper, not to abuse Mercy, by committing new Offences.

Araminta (*aside*). So cold!

Belinda. I have broke the ice for you, Mr. *Vainlove*, and so I leave you. Come, Mr. *Sharper*, you and I will take a turn, and laugh at the Vulgar.—Both the great Vulgar and the small.———Oh Gad! I have a great Passion for *Cowley*. ———Don't you admire him?

Sharper. Oh Madam! He was our English *Horace*.

Belinda. Ah so fine! So extreamly fine! So every thing in the World that I like.———Oh Lord, walk this way.———I see a couple, I'll give you their History.

Exeunt Belinda *and* Sharper.

Vainlove. I find, Madam, the Formality of the Law must be observ'd tho' the Penalty of it be dispens'd with; and an Offender must Plead to his Arraignment, tho' he have his Pardon in his pocket.

Araminta. I'm amaz'd! This Insolence exceeds the t'other;— whoever has encourag'd you to this assurance—presuming upon the easiness of my Temper, has much deceiv'd you, and so you shall find.

Vainlove (*aside*). Hey day! Which way now? Here's fine doubling.

Araminta. Base Man! Was it not enough to affront me with your sawcy Passion?

Vainlove. You have given that Passion a much kinder Epithet than Sawcy, in another place.

Araminta. Another place! Some villainous Design to blast my Honour.———But tho' thou hadst all the Treachery and Malice of thy Sex, thou canst not lay a Blemish on my Fame.———No, I have not err'd in one favourable Thought of Mankind.———How time might have deceiv'd me in you, I know not; my Opinion was but young, and your early baseness has prevented its growing to a wrong Belief.———Unworthy, and ungrateful! Be gone, and never see me more.

the great Vulgar and the small—Cowley's imitation of Horace, *Odes*, III, i. in his *Essay on Greatness*.

Vainlove. Did I dream? Or do I dream? Shall I believe my Eyes, or Ears? The Vision is here still.———Your Passion, Madam, will admit of no farther reasoning.———But here is a silent Witness of your acquaintance.———

Takes out the Letter, and offers it: She snatches it, and throws it away.

Araminta. There's poison in every thing you touch.——— Blisters will follow———

Vainlove. That Tongue, which denies what the Hands have done.

Araminta. Still mystically senceless and impudent.———I find I must leave the place.

Vainlove. No, Madam, I'm gone.———She knows her Name's to it, which she will be unwilling to expose to the Censure of the first finder.

Exit.

Araminta. Woman's Obstinacy made me blind to what Woman's Curiosity now tempts me to see.

Takes up the Letter, and Exit.

Enter Belinda, Sharper.

Belinda. Nay, we have spared No-body, I swear. Mr. *Sharper*, you're a pure Man; Where did you get this excellent Talent of Railing?

Sharper. Faith, Madam, the Talent was born with me:—I confess, I have taken care to improve it; to qualify me for the society of Ladies.

Belinda. Nay, sure Railing is the best qualification in a Woman's Man.

Sharper. The second-best;—indeed I think.

Enter Footman.

Belinda. How now, *Pace*? Where's my Cousin?

Footman. She's not very well, Madam, and has sent to know, if your Ladiship would have the Coach come again for you?

Belinda. O Lord, No, I'll go along with her. Come, Mr. *Sharper*.

Exeunt.

mystically—Incomprehensibly.

[Scene IV]

SCENE *changes to a Chamber in* Fondlewife's *House.*

Enter Lætitia *and* Bellmour, *his Cloak, Hat, &c. lying loose about the Chamber.*

Bellmour. Here's no body, nor no noise;———'twas nothing but your fears.

Lætitia. I durst have sworn, I had heard my Monster's Voice. —I swear, I was heartily frightned.———Feel how my heart beats.

Bellmour. 'Tis an alarm to love.———Come in again, and let us———

Fondlewife without. Cocky, Cocky, Where are you, Cocky? I'm come home.

Lætitia. Ah! There he is. Make haste, gather up your things.

Fondlewife. Cocky, Cocky, open the door

Bellmour. Pox choak him, would his Horns were in his Throat. My Patch, my Patch.

Looking about, and gathering up his things.

Lætitia. My Jewel, Art thou there? No matter for your Patch.—You s'an't tum in, *Nykin.*———Run into my Chamber, quickly, quickly. You s'an't tum in.

Bellmour *goes in.*

Fondlewife. Nay, prithee, Dear, Ifeck I'm in haste.

Lætitia. Then, I'll let you in.

Opens the Door.

Enter Fondlewife, *and* Sir Joseph.

Fondlewife. Kiss, Dear,———I met the Master of the Ship by the way,———and I must have my Papers of Accounts out of your Cabinet.

Lætitia (*aside*). Oh, I'm undone!

Sir Joseph. Pray, first let me have 50 Pounds, good Alderman, for I'm in haste.

Fondlewife. A Hundred has already been paid, by your Order, Fifty? I have the Summ ready in Gold, in my Closet.

Goes into his Closet.

Sir Joseph. Agad, it's a curious, fine, pretty Rogue; I'll speak to her,———Pray, Madam, what News d'ye hear?

Lætitia. Sir, I seldom stir abroad.

Walks about in disorder.

Sir Joseph. I wonder at that, Madam, for 'tis most curious fine Weather.

Lætitia. Methinks, 't has been very ill Weather.

Sir Joseph. As you say, Madam, 'tis pretty bad Weather, and has been so a great while.

Enter Fondlewife.

Fondlewife. Here are fifty Pieces in this Purse, Sir *Joseph*——— If you will tarry a Moment, till I fetch my Papers, I'll wait upon you down stairs.

Lætitia (*aside*). Ruin'd, past redemption! What shall I do?— Ha! This fool may be of use. Stand off, rude Ruffian. Help me, my Dear,—O bless me! Why will you leave me alone with such a Satyr?

As Fondlewife *is going into the Chamber, she runs to* Sir Joseph, *almost pushes him down, and Cries out.*

Fondlewife. Bless us! What's the matter? What's the matter?

Lætitia. Your back was no sooner turn'd, but like a Lion, he came open mouth'd upon me, and would have ravished a kiss from me by main force.

Sir Joseph. O Lord! Oh terrible! Ha, ha, ha, Is your Wife mad, Alderman?

Lætitia. Oh! I am sick with the fright; won't you take him out of my sight?

Fondlewife. Oh Traytor! I'm astonished. Oh bloody-minded Traytor!

Sir Joseph. Hey-day! Traytor yourself.———By the Lord-*Harry*, I was in most danger of being ravish'd, if you go to that.

Fondlewife. Oh, how the blasphemous Wretch swears! Out of my house, thou Son of the Whore of *Babylon*; Off-spring of *Bell* and the *Dragon*.—Bless us! Ravish my Wife! My *Dinah*! Oh *Schechemite!* Begone, I say.

Bell and the Dragon—The false gods destroyed by Daniel; see the Apocrypha.

Dinah . . . Schechemite—Dinah, the daughter of Leah and Jacob, ravished by Schechem; see Gen. 34:2.

Sir Joseph. Why, the Devil's in the People, I think.

Exit.

Lætitia. Oh! Won't you follow, and see him out of Doors, my Dear?

Fondlewife. I'll shut this door, to secure him from coming back.—Give me the Key of your Cabinet, Cocky——Ravish my Wife before my face! I warrant he's a Papist in his heart, at least, if not a *French*-man.

Lætitia (*aside*). What can I do now! Oh! my Dear, I have been in such a fright, that I forgot to tell you, poor Mr. *Spin-text*, has a sad Fit of the Cholick, and is forced to lie down upon our bed.———You'll disturb him; I can tread softlier.

Fondlewife. Alack poor Man.—No, no,—you don't know the Papers.—I won't disturb him; Give me the Key.

She gives him the Key, goes to the Chamber-door, and speaks aloud.

Lætitia. 'Tis no body but Mr. *Fondlewife*, Mr. *Spin-text*, lie still on your Stomach; lying on your Stomach, will ease you of the Cholick.

Fondlewife. Ay, ay, lie still, lie still; don't let me disturb you.

Goes in.

Lætitia. Sure, when he does not see his face, he won't discover him. Dear Fortune, help me but this once, and I'll never run in thy debt again. But this Opportunity is the Devil.

Fondlewife *returns with Papers.*

Fondlewife. Good Lack! Good Lack!———I profess, the poor Man is in great torment, he lies as flat———Dear, you should heat a Trencher, or a Napkin.—Where's *Deborah*? Let her clap a warm thing to his Stomach, or chafe it with a warm-hand, rather than fail. What Book's this?

Sees the Book that Bellmour *forgot.*

Lætitia. Mr. *Spintext's* Prayer-Book, Dear.———(*aside*) Pray Heav'n it be a Prayer-Book.

Fondlewife. Good Man! I warrant he dropp'd it on purpose, that you might take it up, and read some of the pious Ejaculations.

Taking up the Book.

O bless me! O monstrous! A Prayer-Book? Ay, this is the Devil's *Pater-noster*. Hold, let me see: *The Innocent Adultery*.

Lætitia (*aside*). Misfortune! Now all's ruin'd again.

Bellmour (*peeping*). Damn'd Chance! If I had gone a-Whoring with the *Practice of Piety* in my Pocket, I had never been discover'd.

Fondlewife. Adultery, and innocent! O Lord! Here's Doctrine! Ay, here's Discipline!

Lætitia. Dear Husband, I'm amaz'd:——Sure it's a good Book, and only tends to the Speculation of Sin.

Fondlewife. Speculation! No, no; something went farther than Speculation when I was not to be let in.——Where is this Apocryphal Elder? I'll ferret him.

Lætitia (*aside*). I'm so distracted, I can't think of a Lye.

Fondlewife *haling out* Bellmour.

Fondlewife. Come out here, thou *Ananias* incarnate.——Who, how now! Who have we here?

Lætitia. Ha!

Shrieks, as surpriz'd.

Fondlewife. Oh, thou salacious Woman! Am I then brutified? Ay, I feel it here; I sprout, I bud, I blossom, I am ripe-horn-mad. But who, in the Devil's name, are you? Mercy on me for swearing. But——

Lætitia. Oh, Goodness keep us! Who's this? Who are you? What are you?

Bellmour. Soh.

Lætitia. In the Name of the——Oh! Good, my Dear, don't come near it, I'm afraid 'tis the Devil; indeed it has hoofs, Deare.

Fondlewife. Indeed, and I have Horns, Deare. The Devil, no. I'm afraid, 'tis the Flesh, thou Harlot. Deare, with the Pox. Come *Syren*, speak, confess, who is this reverend, brawny Pastor?

The Innocent Adultery—the third of Scarron's novels, in the English translation of 1683.

The Practice of Piety—Written by Lewis Bayly, Bishop of Bangor, 1612; it had recently reached its forty-first edition.

Lætitia. Indeed, and indeed, now my dear *Nykin*———I never saw this wicked Man before.

Fondlewife. Oh, it is a Man then, it seems.

Lætitia. Rather, sure it is a Wolf in the cloathing of a Sheep.

Fondlewife. Thou art a Devil in his proper Cloathing, Womans-flesh. What, you know nothing of him, but his Fleece here!—You don't love Mutton?—you *Magdalen* unconverted.

Bellmour (*aside*). Well, now I know my Cue.———That is very honourably, to excuse her, and very impudently accuse my self.

Lætitia. Why then, I wish I may never enter into the Heaven of your Embraces again, my Dear, if ever I saw his face before.

Fondlewife. O Lord! O strange! I am in admiration of your impudence. Look at him a little better; he is more modest, I warrant you, than to deny it. Come, Were you two never face to face before? Speak.

Bellmour. Since all Artifice is vain—and I think my self obliged to speak the truth in justice to your Wife.—No.

Fondlewife. Humph.

Lætitia. No, indeed Dear.

Fondlewife. Nay, I find you are both in a Story; that, I must confess. But, what—not to be cured of the Cholick? Don't you know your Patient, Mrs. *Quack*? Oh, lie upon your Stomach; lying upon your Stomach will cure you of the Cholick. Ah! I wish he has lain upon no bodies stomach but his own. Answer me that, *Jezabel*?

Lætitia. Let the wicked Man answer for himself; does he think that I have nothing to do but excuse him; 'tis enough, if I can clear my own innocence to my own Deare.

Bellmour. By my troth, and so 'tis.———(*aside*) I have been a little too backward, that's the truth on't.

Fondlewife. Come, Sir, Who are you, in the first place? And what are you?

Bellmour. A Whore-master.

Fondlewife. Very Concise.

Lætitia. O beastly, impudent Creature.

Fondlewife. Well Sir, And what came you hither for?

Bellmour. To lie with your Wife.

Fondlewife. Good again—A very civil Person this, and, I believe speaks truth.

Lætitia. Oh, insupportable Impudence!

Fondlewife. Well, Sir,—Pray be cover'd———and you have ———Heh! You have finish'd the matter, Heh? And I am, as I should be, a sort of a civil Perquisite to a Whore-master, called *a Cuckold*, Heh. Is it not so? Come, I'm inclining to believe every word you say.

Bellmour. Why, Faith I must confess, so I design'd you.——— But, you were a little unlucky in coming so soon, and hindred the making of your own Fortune.

Fondlewife. Humph, Nay, if you mince the matter once, and go back of your word; you are not the Person I took you for. Come, come, go on boldly—What, don't be asham'd of your Profession.———Confess, confess, I shall love thee the better for't.———I shall, Ifeck———What, dost think I don't know how to behave my self in the Employment of a Cuckold, and have been 3 Years Apprentice to Matrimony? Come, come, plain-dealing is a Jewel.

Bellmour. Well, since I see thou art a good honest Fellow, I'll confess the whole matter to thee.

Fondlewife. Oh, I am a very honest Fellow———You never lay with an honester Man's Wife in your life.

Lætitia (*aside*). How my heart akes! All my comfort lies in his impudence, and Heaven be praised, he has a considerable Portion.

Bellmour. In short then, I was informed of the opportunity of your absence, by my Spy, (for Faith, honest *Isaac*, I have a long time designed thee this favour) I knew *Spintext* was to come by your direction.———But I laid a trap for him, and procured his Habit; in which, I pass'd upon your Servants, and was conducted hither. I pretended a Fit of the Cholick, to excuse my lying down upon your Bed, hoping that when she heard of it, her good Nature

plain-dealing is a Jewel—Proverbial, and perhaps also an echo of Wycherley's *Plain Dealer*, I, i.

would bring her to administer Remedies for my Distemper.———You know what might have follow'd.———But like an uncivil Person, you knock'd at the Door, before your Wife was come to me.

Fondlewife. Ha! This is Apocryphal; I may chuse whether I will believe it or no.

Bellmour. That you may, Faith, and I hope you won't believe a word on't.—But I can't help telling the truth, for my life.

Fondlewife. How! Would not you have me believe you, say you?

Bellmour. No, for then you must of consequence part with your Wife, and there will be some hopes of having her upon the Publick; then the encouragement of a separate maintenance.———

Fondlewife. No, no, for that matter———when she and I part, she'll carry her separate-maintenance about her.

Lætitia. Ah cruel Dear, how can you be so barbarous? You'll break my heart, if you talk of parting.

Cries.

Fondlewife. Ah, dissembling Vermin!

Bellmour. How canst thou be so cruel, *Isaac*? Thou hast the Heart of a Mountain-Tyger. By the faith of a sincere Sinner, she's innocent, for me. Go to him, Madam, fling your snowy Arms about his stubborn Neck; bathe his relentless face in your salt trickling Tears.—So, a few soft Words, and a Kiss; and the good Man melts. See, how kind Nature works, and boils over in him.

She goes and hangs upon his neck, and kisses him. Bellmour *kisses her hand, behind* Fondlewife's *back.*

Lætitia. Indeed, my Dear, I was but just coming down stairs, when you knock'd at the door; and the Maid told me, Mr. *Spin-text* was ill of the Cholick, upon our bed. And won't you speak to me, cruel *Nykin*? Indeed, I'll die, if you don't.

Fondlewife. Ah! No, no, I cannot speak; my heart's so full—I have been a tender Husband, a tender Yoke-fellow; you know I have—But thou hast been a faithless *Dallilah*, and the *Philistines* have been upon thee. Heh! Art thou not vile and unclean, Heh? Speak.

Weeping.

Lætitia. No-h. *Sighing.*

Fondlewife. Oh, that I could believe thee!

Lætitia. Oh, my heart will break! *Seeming to faint.*

Fondlewife. Heh. How? No, stay, stay, I will believe thee, I will———Pray, bend her forward, Sir.

Lætitia. Oh! Oh! Where is my Dear.

Fondlewife. Here, here, I do believe thee.———I won't believe my own Eyes.

Bellmour. For my part, I am so charm'd with the Love of your Turtle to you, that I'll go and sollicite Matrimony with all my might and main.

Fondlewife. Well, well, Sir, as long as I believe it, 'tis well enough. No thanks to you Sir, for her Vertue.———But, I'll show you the way out of my house, if you please. Come, my Dear. Nay, I will believe thee, I do, Ifeck.

Bellmour. See the great Blessing of an easy Faith; Opinion cannot err.

No Husband, by his Wife, can be deceiv'd:
She still is Vertuous, if she's so believ'd.

Exeunt.

ACT V. Scene I. The Street

Enter Bellmour *in Fanatick Habit, and* Setter.

Bellmour. Setter! Well encounter'd.

Setter. Joy of your Return, Sir. Have you made a good Voyage. Or have you brought your own Lading back?

Bellmour. No, I have brought nothing but Ballast back,——— made a delicious Voyage, *Setter*; and might have rode at Anchor in the Port till this time, but the Enemy surpriz'd us.———I wou'd unrig.

Setter. I attend you, Sir.

Heartwell *and* Lucy *appear at* Sylvia' *Door.*

Bellmour. Ha! Is not that *Heartwell* at *Sylvia's* Door; be gone quickly, I'll follow you:———I wou'd not be known. (*Exit* Setter.) Pox take 'em, they stand just in my Way.

Heartwell. I'm impatient till it be done.

Lucy That may be, without troubling your self to go again for your Brother's Chaplain. Don't you see that stalking Form of Godliness?

Heartwell. O Pox; He's a Fanatick.

Lucy. An Executioner qualified to do your Business. He has been lawfully ordain'd.

Heartwell. I'll pay him well, if you'll break the Matter to him.

Lucy. I warrant you—Do you go and prepare your Bride.

Exit Heartwell.

Bellmour. Humph, Sits the Wind there?———What a lucky Rogue am I! Oh, what Sport will be here, if I can persuade this Wench to Secresie!

Lucy. Sir: Reverend Sir.

Bellmour. Madam.

Discovers himself.

Lucy. Now, Goodness have Mercy upon me! Mr. *Bellmour!* Is it you?

Bellmour. Even I. What dost think?

Lucy. Think: That I shou'd not believe my Eyes, and that you are not what you seem to be.

Bellmour. True. But to convince thee who I am, thou know'st my old Token.

Kisses her.

Lucy. Nay, Mr. *Bellmour*: O Lard! I believe you are a Parson in good earnest, you kiss so devoutly.

Bellmour. Well, Your Business with me, *Lucy*?

Lucy. I had none, but through Mistake.

Bellmour. Which Mistake you must go thorough with, *Lucy.*—Come, I know the Intrigue between *Heartwell* and your Mistress; and you mistook me for Tribulation-*Spin-text*, to marry 'em.———Ha? Are not Matters in this posture?———Confess.———Come, I'll be faithful: I will I-faith.———What Diffide in me, *Lucy*?

Diffide—Have no confidence.

Lucy. Alas-a-day! You and Mr. *Vainlove*, between you, have ruin'd my poor Mistress: You have made a Gap in her Reputation; And can you blame her if she stop it up with a Husband?

Bellmour. Well, It is as I say?

Lucy. Well, It is then: But you'll be secret?

Bellmour. Phuh, Secret, ay.—And to be out of thy Debt, I'll trust thee with another Secret. Your Mistress must not marry *Heartwell, Lucy*.

Lucy. How! O Lord!———

Bellmour. Nay, don't be in Passion, *Lucy*:—I'll provide a fitter Husband for her.—Come, Here's Earnest of my good Intentions for thee too: Let this mollifie.—(*Gives her Money*). Look you, *Heartwell* is my Friend; and tho' he be blind, I must not see him fall into the Snare, and unwittingly marry a Whore.

Lucy. Whore! I'd have you know, my Mistress scorns———

Bellmour. Nay, nay: Look you, *Lucy*; there are Whores of as good Quality.———But to the purpose, if you will give me Leave to acquaint you with it.———Do you carry on the Mistake of me: I'll marry 'em.———Nay, don't pause: ———If you do, I'll spoil all.———I have some private Reasons for what I do, which I'll tell you within.———In the mean time, I promise,———and rely upon me,———to help your Mistress to a Husband.———Nay, and thee too, *Lucy*.———Here's my Hand, I will; with a fresh Assurance.

Gives her more Money.

Lucy. Ah, the Devil is not so cunning.———You know my easie Nature.———Well, For once I'll venture to serve you; but if you do deceive me, the Curse of all kind, tender-hearted Women light upon you.

Bellmour. That's as much as to say, *The Pox take me*.—Well lead on.

Exeunt.

Enter Vainlove, Sharper *and* Setter.

Sharper. Just now, say you, gone in with *Lucy*?

Setter. I saw him, Sir; and stood at the Corner where you found me, and over-heard all they said. Mr. *Bellmour* is to marry 'em.

Sharper. Ha, ha; 'Twill be a pleasant Cheat.——I'll plague *Heartwell* when I see him. Prithee, *Frank*, let's teaze him; make him fret till he foam at the Mouth, and disgorge his Matrimonial Oath with Interest.—Come, thou'rt so musty.——

Setter (*to* Sharper). Sir, A Word with you.

Whispers him.

Vainlove. Sharper swears, she has forsworn the Letter.——I'm sure he tells me Truth;——but I am not sure she told him Truth:——Yet she was unaffectedly concern'd, he says; and often blush'd with Anger and Surprize:——And so I remember in the Park.—She had reason, if I wrong her.——I begin to doubt.

Sharper. Say'st thou so!

Setter. This afternoon, Sir, about an Hour before my Master received the Letter.

Sharper. In my Conscience, like enough.

Setter. Ay, I know her, Sir: At least, I'm sure I can fish it out of her. She's the very Sluce to her Lady's Secrets:——'Tis but setting her Mill a-going, and I can drein her of 'em all.

Sharper. Here, *Frank*; your Blood-Hound has made out the Fault: This Letter, that so sticks in thy Maw, is Counterfeit; only a Trick of *Sylvia* in Revenge; contriv'd by *Lucy*.

Vainlove. Ha! It has a Colour.——But how do you know it, Sirrah?

Setter. I do suspect as much;——because why, Sir:——She was pumping me about how your Worship's Affairs stood towards Madam *Araminta*. As, When you had seen her last; When you were to see her next; And, Where you were to be found at that time: And such like.

Vainlove. And where did you tell her?

Setter. In the *Piazza*.

Vainlove. There I receiv'd the Letter——It must be so. ——And why did you not find me out, to tell me this before, Sot?

Setter. Sir, I was Pimping for Mr. *Bellmour*.

Sharper. You were well employ'd.——I think there is no Objection to the Excuse.

Vainlove. Pox o' my sawcy Credulity.——If I have lost her, I deserve it. But if Confession and Repentance be of force, I'll win her, or weary her into a Forgiveness.
Exit.

Sharper. Methinks I long to see *Bellmour* come forth.

Enter Bellmour.

Setter. Talk of the Devil——See where he comes.

Sharper. Hugging himself in his prosperous Mischief——No real Fanatick can look better pleas'd after a successful Sermon of Sedition.

Bellmour. Sharper! Fortifie thy Spleen: Such a Jest! Speak when thou art ready.

Sharper. Now, were I ill-natur'd, wou'd I utterly disappoint thy Mirth: Hear thee tell thy mighty Jest, with as much Gravity as a Bishop hears Venereal Causes in the Spiritual Court: Not so much as wrinkle my Face with one Smile; but let thee look simply, and laugh by thy self.

Bellmour. Pshaw, No: I have a better Opinion of thy Wit. ——Gad, I defie thee.—

Sharper. Were it not Loss of Time, you should make the Experiment. But honest *Setter*, here, over-heard you with *Lucy*, and has told me all.

Bellmour. Nay, then I thank thee for not putting me out of Countenance. But, to tell you something you don't know. ——I got an Opportunity (after I had marry'd 'em) of discovering the Cheat to *Sylvia*. She took it at first, as another Woman would the like Disappointment; but my Promise to make her Amends quickly with another Husband, somewhat pacify'd her.

Sharper. But how the Devil do you think to acquit your self of your Promise? Will you marry her your self?

Bellmour. I have no such Intentions at present.——Prithee, wilt thou think a little for me? I am sure the ingenious Mr. *Setter* will assist——

Setter. O Lord, Sir!

Bellmour. I'll leave him with you, and go shift my Habit.
Exit.

Enter Sir Joseph *and* Bluffe.

Sharper. Heh! Sure, Fortune has sent this Fool hither on purpose. *Setter*, stand close; seem not to observe 'em; and, Hark-ye.

Whispers.

Bluffe. Fear him not,—I am prepar'd for him now; and he shall find he might have safer rous'd a sleeping Lion.

Sir Joseph. Hush, hush: Don't you see him?

Bluffe. Shew him to me. Where is he?

Sir Joseph. Nay, Don't speak so loud.———I don't jest, as I did a little while ago.———Look yonder.———A-gad, if he shou'd hear the Lion roar, he'd cudgel him into an Ass, and his primitive Braying. Don't you remember the Story in *Æsop's Fables*, *Bully*? A-Gad there are good Morals to be pick'd out of *Æsop's Fables*, let me tell you that; and *Reynard the Fox* too.

Bluffe. Damn your Morals.

Sir Joseph. Prithee, don't speak so loud.

Bluffe. Damn your Morals: I must revenge th'Affront done to my Honour.

In a low Voice.

Sir Joseph. Ay; Do, do, Captain, if you think fit.———You may dispose of your own Flesh as you think fitting, d'ye see:—But, by the Lord *Harry*, I'll leave you.

Stealing away upon his Tip-toes.

Bluffe. Prodigious! What, will you forsake your Friend in his extremity! You can't, in honour, refuse to carry him a Challenge.

Almost whispering, and treading softly after him.

Sir Joseph. Prithee, What do you see in my face, that looks as if I would carry a Challenge? Honour is your Province, Captain: Take it—All the World know me to be a Knight, and a Man of Worship.

Setter. I warrant you, Sir, I'm instructed.

Story in Æsop's Fables—"Of the Ass and the Lion's skin" in Sir Roger L'Estrange's translation of *Fables of Æsop* (1692), CCXXIV, p. 196.

good Morals etc.—Cf. Bayes remark in Prior's parody of Dryden, *The Hind and the Panther Transvers'd* (1687), pp. 14–15: "there is good Morality . . . in the delectable *History of Reynard the Fox*," etc.

Sharper. Impossible! *Araminta* take a liking to a Fool!

Aloud.

Setter. Her head runs on nothing else, nor she can talk of nothing else.

Sharper. I know, she commended him all the while we were in the Park; but I thought it had been only to make *Vainlove* jealous.—

Sir Joseph. How's this! Good Bully, hold your breath, and let's hearken. A-gad, this must be I.———

Sharper. Death, it can't be———An Oaf, an Ideot, a Wittal.

Sir Joseph. Ay, now it's out; 'tis I, my own individual Person.

Sharper. A Wretch, that has flown for shelter to the lowest shrub of Mankind, and seeks Protection from a blasted Coward.

Sir Joseph. That's you, *Bully* Back.

Bluffe *frowns upon* Sir Joseph.

Sharper. She has given *Vainlove* her Promise, to marry him before to Morrow Morning.———Has she not?

To Setter.

Setter. She has, Sir;———And I have it in Charge to attend her all this Evening, in order to conduct her to the Place appointed.

Sharper. Well, I'll go and inform your Master; and do you press her to make all the haste imaginable.

Exit.

Setter. Were I a Rogue now, what a noble Prize could I dispose of! A goodly Pinnace, richly laden, and to launch forth under my Auspicious Convoy. Twelve Thousand Pounds, and all her Rigging; besides what lies conceal'd under Hatches.———Ha! All this committed to my Care! —Avaunt Temptation.———*Setter*, shew thy self a Person of Worth; be true to thy Trust, and be reputed honest. Reputed honest! Hum: Is that all? Ay: For, to be honest is nothing; the Reputation of it is all. Reputation! What have such poor Rogues as I to do with Reputation? —'Tis above us:———And, for Men of Quality, they are above it. So that Reputation is e'en as foolish as Honesty. ———And, for my part, if I meet Sir *Joseph* with a Purse of Gold in his Hand, I'll dispose of mine to the best Advantage.

Pinnace—Small boat carried on a man-of-war; *figuratively*, a mistress.

Sir Joseph. Heh, heh, heh: Here 'tis for you, i'Faith, Mr. *Setter*. Nay, I'll take you at your Word.

Chinking a Purse.

Setter. Sir *Joseph* and the Captain too! undone, undone! I'm undone, my Master's undone, my Lady's undone, and all the Business is undone.

Sir Joseph. No, no, Never fear, Man, the Lady's business shall be done. What—Come, Mr. *Setter*, I have over-heard all, and to speak, is but loss of time; but if there be occasion, let these worthy Gentlemen intercede for me.

Gives him Gold.

Setter. O Lord, Sir, What d'ye mean? Corrupt my honesty. —They have indeed, very perswading faces. But———

Sir Joseph. 'Tis too little, there's more, Man. There, take all— Now—

Setter. Well, Sir *Joseph*, you have such a winning way with you.—

Sir Joseph. And how, and how, good *Setter*, did the little Rogue look, when she talk'd of Sir *Joseph*? Did not her Eyes twinkle, and her Mouth water? Did not she pull up her little Bubbies? And—A-gad, I'm so over-joy'd—And stroke down her Belly; and then step aside to tie her Garter, when she was thinking of her Love. Heh, *Setter*.

Setter. Oh, Yes, Sir.

Sir Joseph. How now, Bully? What, melancholy because I'm in the Ladies favours?—No matter, I'll make your peace.—I know, they were a little smart upon you—But, I warrant, I'll bring you into the Ladies good Graces.

Bluffe. Pshaw, I have Petitions to show, from other-guess-toys than she. Look here: These were sent me this Morning— There, read. (*Shows Letters.*) That—That's a Scrawl of Quality. Here, here's from a Countess too. Hum—No hold—That's from a Knight's Wife, she sent it me by her Husband—But here, both these are from Persons of great Quality.

Sir Joseph. They are either from Persons of great Quality, or no Quality at all, 'tis such a Damn'd ugly Hand.

While Sir Joseph *reads*, Bluffe *whispers* Setter.

other-guess-toys—Lovers of another kind.

Setter. Captain, I wou'd do any thing to serve you; but this is so difficult———

Bluffe. Not at all. Don't I know him?

Setter. You'll remember the Conditions?———

Bluffe. I'll give't you under my Hand.———In the mean time, here's Earnest. (*Gives him Money*). Come, Knight; ———I'm capitulating with Mr. *Setter* for you.

Sir Joseph. Ah, honest *Setter*.———Sirrah, I'll give thee any thing but a Night's Lodging.

Enter Sharper, *tugging in* Heartwell.

Sharper. Nay, Prithee, leave Railing, and come along with me: May be she mayn't be within. 'Tis but to yond' Corner-house.

Heartwell. Whither? Whither? Which Corner-House?

Sharper. Why, there: The Two white Posts.

Heartwell. And who wou'd you visit there, say you? (O'ons, How my Heart akes.)

Sharper. Pshaw: Thou'rt so troublesom and inquisitive.——— Why, I'll tell you: 'Tis a young Creature that *Vainlove* debauch'd, and has forsaken. Did you never hear *Bellmour* chide him about *Sylvia*.

Heartwell (*aside*). Death, and Hell, and Marriage! My Wife!

Sharper. Why, thou art as musty as a New-married Man, that had found his Wife Knowing the first Night.

Heartwell (*aside*). Hell, and the Devil! Does he know it? But, hold:———If he shou'd not, I were a Fool to discover it.— I'll dissemble, and try him.—Ha, ha, ha. Why, *Tom*; Is that such an Occasion of Melancholy? Is it such an uncommon Mischief?

Sharper. No, Faith; I believe not.———Few Women, but have their Year of Probation, before they are cloister'd in the narrow Joys of Wedlock. But prithee come along with me, or I'll go and have the Lady to my self. B'w'y' *George*. *Going*.

Heartwell. O Torture! How he racks and tears me!——— Death! Shall I own my Shame, or wittingly let him go and whore my Wife? No, That's insupportable.——— Oh, *Sharper*.

Sharper. How now?

Heartwell. Oh, I am—married.

Sharper. (Now hold Spleen.) Married!

Heartwell. Certainly, irrecoverably married.

Sharper. Heav'n forbid, Man. How long?

Heartwell. Oh, an Age, an Age: I have been married these two Hours.

Sharper. My old Batchelor married! That were a Jest. Ha, ha, ha.

Heartwell. Death: D'ye mock me? Heark-ye: If either you esteem my Friendship, or your own Safety,———come not near that House,———that Corner-house,———that hot Brothel. Ask no Questions.

Exit.

Sharper. Mad, by this Light.
Thus Grief still treads upon the Heels of Pleasure:
Marry'd in haste, we may repent at leisure.

Setter *Entering*.

Setter. Some by Experience find those Words misplac'd:
At leisure marry'd, they repent in haste.
As I suppose my Master *Heartwell*.

Sharper. Here again, my *Mercury*!

Setter. Sublimate, if you please, Sir: I think my Atchievments do deserve the Epithet.———*Mercury* was a Pimp too; but, tho' I blush to own it at this time, I must confess I am somewhat fall'n from the Dignity of my Function; and do condescend to be scandalously employ'd in the Promotion of Vulgar Matrimony.

Sharper. As how, dear dexterous Pimp?

Setter. Why, to be brief, for I have weighty Affairs depending:———Our Stratagem succeeding as you intended, ———*Bluffe* turns errant Traytor; bribes me to make a private Conveyance of the Lady to him, and put a Sham-Settlement upon Sir *Joseph*.

Sharper. O Rogue! Well, but I hope———

Mercury—From *Amphitryon* again; and then this awful pun on "mercury sublimate" and his sublime performance.

Setter. No, no; never fear me, Sir.———I privately inform'd the Knight of the Treachery; who has agreed, seemingly to be cheated, that the Captain may be so in reality.

Sharper. Where's the Bride?

Setter. Shifting Cloaths for the purpose at a Friend's House of mine. Here's Company coming, if you'll walk this way, Sir, I'll tell you.

Exeunt.

Enter Bellmour, Belinda, Araminta *and* Vainlove.

Vainlove (*to* Araminta). Oh, 'twas Frenzy all: Cannot you forgive it?———Men in Madness have a Title to your Pity.

Araminta. ———Which they forfeit when they are restor'd to their Senses.

Vainlove. I am not presuming beyond a Pardon.

Araminta. You who cou'd reproach me with one Counterfeit, how insolent wou'd a real Pardon make you? But there's no need to forgive what is not worth my Anger.

Belinda (*to* Bellmour). O my Conscience, I cou'd find in my Heart to marry thee, purely to be rid of thee.———At least, Thou art so troublesome a Lover, there's Hopes thou'lt make a more than ordinary quiet Husband.

Bellmour. Say you so?———Is that a Maxim among ye?

Belinda. Yes: You flattering Men of the Mode have made Marriage a mere *French* Dish.

Bellmour (*aside*). I hope there's no *French* Sawce.

Belinda. You are so curious in the Preparation, that is, your Courtship, one wou'd think you meant a noble Entertainment:———But when we come to feed, 'tis all Froth, and poor, but in show. Nay, often, only Remains, which have been I know not how many times warm'd for other Company, and at last serv'd up cold to the Wife.

Bellmour. That were a miserable Wretch indeed, who cou'd not afford one warm Dish for the Wife of his Bosom. ———But you timorous Virgins, form a dreadful Chimæra of a Husband, as of a Creature contrary to that soft, humble, pliant, easie thing, a Lover, so guess at Plagues in

French Dish—a mere show; French *Sawce*, the French disease, the pox.

Matrimony, in Opposition to the Pleasures of Courtship. Alas! Courtship to Marriage, is but as the Musick in the Play-house, till the Curtain's drawn; but that once up, then opens the Scene of Pleasure.

Belinda. Oh, foh,———no: Rather, Courtship to Marriage, as a very witty Prologue to a very dull Play.

Enter Sharper.

Sharper. Hist,———*Bellmour*: If you'll bring the Ladies, make haste to *Silvia's* Lodgings, before *Heartwell* has fretted himself out of breath.———I'm in haste now, but I'll come in at the Catastrophe.

Exit.

Bellmour. You have an Opportunity now, Madam, to revenge your self upon *Heartwell*, for affronting your Squirrel.

To Belinda.

Belinda. O the filthy rude Beast!

Araminta. 'Tis a lasting Quarrel: I think he has never been at our House since.

Bellmour. But give your selves the trouble to walk to that Corner-House, and I'll tell you by the way what may divert and surprize you.

Exeunt.

[Scene II]

SCENE *changes to* Silvia's *Lodgings.*

Enter Heartwell *and* Boy.

Heartwell. Gone forth, say you, with her Maid!

Boy. There was a Man too that fetch'd 'em out:———*Setter*, I think they call'd him.

Heartwell. So-h,——— That precious Pimp too.——— Damn'd, damn'd Strumpet! Cou'd she not contain her self on her Wedding-Day! Not hold out till Night! Leave me.

Exit Boy.

O cursed State! How wide we err, when apprehensive of the Load of Life! ——We hope to find
That Help which Nature meant in Woman-kind,
To Man that Supplemental Self design'd;
But proves a burning Caustick when apply'd.
And *Adam*, sure, cou'd with more Ease abide
The Bone when broken, than when made a Bride.

Enter Bellmour, Belinda, Vainlove, Araminta.

Bellmour. Now *George*, What Rhyming! I thought the Chimes of Verse were past, when once the doleful Marriage-knell was rung.

Heartwell. Shame and Confusion. I am exposed.

Vainlove *and* Araminta *talk a-part.*

Belinda. Joy, Joy Mr. *Bride-groom*; I give you Joy, Sir.

Heartwell. 'Tis not in thy Nature to give me Joy——A Woman can as soon give Immortality.

Belinda. Ha, ha, ha, O Gad, Men grow such Clowns when they are married.

Bellmour. That they are fit for no Company but their Wives.

Belinda. Nor for them neither, in a little time——I swear, at the Month's End, you shall hardly find a Married-man, that will do a civil thing to his Wife, or say a civil thing to any body else. *Jesus*! how he looks already. Ha, ha, ha.

Bellmour. Ha, ha, ha.

Heartwell. Death, Am I made your Laughing-stock? For you, Sir, I shall find a time; but take off your Wasp here, or the Clown may grow boistrous, I have a Fly-flap.

Belinda. You have occasion for't, your Wife has been blown upon.

Bellmour. That's home.

Heartwell. Not Fiends or Furies could have added to my vexation, or any thing, but another Woman.——You've wrack'd my patience; begon, or By——

Bellmour. Hold, hold. What the Devil, thou wilt not draw upon a Woman?

Vainlove. What's the matter?

Araminta. Bless me! What have you done to him?

Belinda. Only touch'd a gall'd-beast till he winch'd.

Vainlove. Bellmour, Give it over; you vex him too much; 'tis all serious to him.

Belinda. Nay, I swear, I begin to pity him, my self.

Heartwell. Damn your pity. But let me be calm a little.——— How have I deserv'd this of you? Any of ye? Sir, have I impair'd the Honour of your House, promis'd your Sister Marriage, and whor'd her? Wherein have I injured you? Did I bring a Physician to your Father when he lay expiring, and endeavour to prolong his life, and you One-and-twenty? Madam, have I had an Opportunity with you and bauk'd it? Did you ever offer me the Favour that I refus'd it? Or———

Belinda. Oh foh! What does the filthy-fellow mean? Lard, let me begone.

Araminta. Hang me, if I pity you; you are right enough serv'd.

Bellmour. This is a little scurrilous tho'.

Vainlove. Nay, 'tis a Sore of your own scratching.—Well *George*,—

Heartwell. You are the principal Cause of all my present Ills. If *Sylvia* had not been your Whore, my Wife might have been honest.

Vainlove. And if *Sylvia* had not been your Wife, my Whore might have been just.———There, we are even.——— But have a good heart, I heard of your Misfortune, and come to your relief.

Heartwell. When Execution's over, you offer a Reprieve.

Vainlove. What would you give?

Heartwell. Oh! Any thing, every thing, a Leg or two, or an Arm; nay, I would be divorced from my Virility, to be divorced from my Wife.

Enter Sharper.

Vainlove. Faith, that's a sure way.———But here's one can sell you freedom better cheap.

Sharper. Vainlove, I have been a kind of a God-father to you, yonder. I have promised and vow'd some things in your Name, which I think you are bound to perform.

Vainlove. No signing to a Blank, friend.

Sharper. No, I'll deal fairly with you.———'Tis a full and free Discharge to Sir *Joseph Wittoll* and Captain *Bluffe*; for all Injuries whatsoever, done unto you by them; until the present Date hereof.—How say you?

Vainlove. Agreed.

Sharper. Then, let me beg these Ladies to wear their Masks, a Moment.

Exit.

Heartwell. What the Devil's all this to me.

Vainlove. Patience.

Re-enter Sharper, *with* Sir Joseph, Bluffe, Sylvia, Lucy, Setter.

Bluffe. All Injuries whatsoever, Mr. *Sharper.*

Sir Joseph. Ay, ay, whatsoever, Captain, stick to that; whatsoever.

Sharper. 'Tis done, those Gentlemen are witnesses to the general Release.

Vainlove. Ay, ay, to this instant Moment.———I have past an Act of Oblivion.

Bluffe. 'Tis very generous, Sir, since I needs must own———

Sir Joseph. No, no, Captain, you need not own, Heh, heh, heh. 'Tis I must own———

Bluffe. ———That you are over-reach'd too, ha, ha, ha, only a little Art military, used———only undermined, or so, as shall appear by the fair *Araminta*, my Wife's permission. Oh, the Devil, cheated at last!

Lucy *unmasks.*

Sir Joseph. Only a little Art-military Trick, Captain, only countermin'd, or so—Mr. *Vainlove*, I suppose you know whom I have got———now, but all's forgiven.

Vainlove. I know whom you have not got; pray Ladies convince him.

Araminta *and* Belinda *unmask.*

Sir Joseph. Ah! O Lord, my heart akes———Ah! *Setter*, a Rogue of all sides.

Sharper. Sir *Joseph*, you had better have pre-engag'd this Gentleman's Pardon: For though *Vainlove* be so generous to forgive the loss of his Mistress.———I know not how *Heartwell* may take the loss of his Wife.

Sylvia *unmasks*.

Heartwell. My Wife! By this Light 'tis she, the very Cockatrice—Oh *Sharper*! Let me embrace thee.———But art thou sure she is really married to him?

Setter. Really and lawfully married, I am witness.

Sharper. *Bellmour* will unriddle to you.

Heartwell *goes to* Bellmour.

Sir Joseph. Pray, Madam, Who are you? For I find, you and I are like to be better acquainted.

Sylvia. The worst of me, is, that I am your Wife———

Sharper. Come, Sir *Joseph*, your Fortune is not so bad as you fear.———A fine Lady, and a Lady of very good Quality.

Sir Joseph. Thanks to my Knight-hood, she's a Lady———

Vainlove. —That deserves a Fool with a better Title.——— Pray use her as my Relation, or you shall hear on't.

Bluffe. What, Are you a Woman of Quality too, Spouse?

Setter. And my Relation; pray let her be respected accordingly.———Well, honest *Lucy*, Fare-thee-well.———I think, you and I have been Play-fellows off-and-on, any time this Seven Years.

Lucy. Hold your prating.———I'm thinking what Vocation I shall follow, while my Spouse is planting Laurels in the Wars.

Bluffe. No more Wars, Spouse, no more Wars.———While I plant Laurels for my Head abroad, I may find the Branches sprout at home.

Heartwell. *Bellmour*, I approve thy mirth, and thank thee. ———And I cannot in gratitude (for I see which way thou art going) see thee fall into the same snare, out of which thou hast deliver'd me.

Bellmour. I thank thee, *George*, for thy good intention.——— But there is a fatality in Marriage.———For I find I'm resolute.

Heartwell. Then good Councel will be thrown away upon you.———For my part, I have once escap'd———And when I wed again, may she be———Ugly, as an old Bawd.———

Vainlove. ———Ill-natur'd, as an old Maid.———

Bellmour. Wanton, as a Young-widow.———

Sharper. And jealous as a barren Wife.

Heartwell. Agreed.

Bellmour. Well; 'Midst of these dreadful Denunciations, and notwithstanding the Warning and Example before me, I commit my self to lasting Durance.

Belinda. Prisoner, make much of your Fetters.

Giving her Hand.

Bellmour. Frank, Will you keep us in Countenance.

Vainlove. May I presume to hope so great a Blessing?

To Araminta.

Araminta. We had better take the Advantage of a little of our Friends Experience first.

Bellmour. O my Conscience she dares not consent, for fear he shou'd recant. (*Aside.*) Well, we shall have your Company to Church in the Morning?———May be it may get you an Appetite to see us fall to before ye. *Setter*, Did not you tell me?———

Setter. They're at the Door: I'll call 'em in.

A Dance.

Bellmour. Now set we forward on a Journey for Life:——— Come, take your Fellow-Travellers. Old *George*, I'm sorry to see thee still plod on alone.

Heartwell.

With gawdy Plumes and gingling Bells made proud,
The youthful Beast sets forth, and neighs aloud.
A Morning-Sun his Tinsell'd Harness gilds,
And the first Stage a Down-hill Green-sword yields.
But, Oh,———
What rugged Ways attend the Noon of Life!
(Our Sun declines,) and with what anxious Strife,
What Pain we tug that galling Load, a Wife.
All Coursers the first Heat with Vigour run;
But 'tis with Whip and Spur the Race is won.

Exeunt Omnes.

Epilogue,

Spoken by Mrs. *Barry*.

As a rash Girl, who will all Hazards run,
And be enjoy'd, tho' sure to be undone;
Soon as her Curiosity is over,
Would give the World she could her Toy recover:
So fares it with our Poet; and I'm sent
To tell you, he already does repent:
Would you were all as forward, to keep Lent.
Now the Deed's done, the Giddy-thing has leasure
To think oth' Sting, that's in the tail of Pleasure.
Methinks I hear him in Consideration!
What will the World say? Where's my Reputation?
Now that's at stake—No fool, 'tis out o'fashion.
If loss of that should follow want of Wit,
How many Undone Men were in the Pit!
Why that's some Comfort, to an Author's fears,
If he's an Ass, he will be Try'd by's Peers.
But hold—I am exceeding my Commission;
My Business here, was humbly to petition:
But we're so us'd to Rail on these Occasions,
I could not help one tryal of your Patience:
For 'tis our way (you know) for fear o'th' worst,
To be before-hand still, and cry Fool first.
How say you, Sparks? How do you stand affected?
I swear, young *Bays* within, is so dejected,
'Twould grieve your hearts to see him; shall I call him?
But then you cruel Criticks would so maul him!
Yet, may be, you'll encourage a beginner;
But how?—Just as the Devil does a Sinner.
Women and Wits are used e'en much at one;
You gain your End, and damn 'em when you've done.

FINIS.

to keep Lent—By fasting and repentance; the season had just begun when the play opened.

Bays—Perhaps to recall the name under which Dryden had been made fun of in the *Rehearsal*, now here proudly assumed by his youngest protégé.

3

The Double-Dealer

INTRODUCTORY NOTE

It has already been noted that, immediately after the success of *The Old Batchelour*, Congreve was reported to be at work on another play (see p. 27). This was *The Double-Dealer*, first performed in November, 1693, according to the *Gentleman's Journal*[1] for that date.

> I need not say anything of Mr. Congreve's *Double-Dealer*, (the only new Play since my last) after the Character which Mr. Dryden has given of it: Yet my Respect for its Author will not suffer me to omit the following Lines.
>
> To Mr. *Congreve*: by Mr. *William Dove*.
>
> Since Inspiration's ceas'd, I fain would know
> To whom thy wondrous store of Wit we owe?
> 'Tis more than e'er Philosophy could teach,
> How Imperfection should Perfection reach;
> Yet while thy Works with native Glory shine,
> And sprightly Phrazes render them divine,
> We think thou'rt sprung from the Prophetic Line.
> How smooth the Current of thy Fancy glides!
> It never ebbs, and knows no boist'rous Tides;
> No lofty nonsense in thy Play appears,
> With shew of Wit to please unskilful Ears, etc.[1]

Yet in spite of these compliments and the approval of those friends who had read the play, it was not well received at first by the theater audience. Congreve was surprised and angered at the criticism it provoked; and when, early in December, it was published by Jacob Tonson,[2] he took occasion in his dedication to Charles Montagu, one of the Lords of the Treasury, to abuse those critics who had expressed their dislike of the performance, arrogantly denouncing them as illiterate and only fit to be treated cheaply.

[1] *Gentleman's Journal*, II (November, 1693), 374.
[2] See *London Gazette*, December 4–7, 1693.

Nevertheless, in spite of opposition, and perhaps helped by the difference of opinion it had evoked, the play continued to be performed. For, in a letter to Walsh, dated December 12, accompanying a copy of the play sent to him by the author, Dryden reports:

> His Double Dealer is much censurd by the greater part of the Town: and is defended onely by the best Judges, who, you know, are commonly the fewest. Yet it gets ground daily, and has already been acted Eight times. The women thinke he has exposd their Bitchery too much and the Gentlemen are offended with him; for the discovery of their follyes: & the way of their Intrigues, under the notion of Friendship to their Ladyes Husbands. My verses, which you will find before it, were written before the play was acted, but I neither altered them nor do I alter my opinion of the play.

Indeed the verdict of "the best Judges" remained unshaken, and Congreve was to benefit considerably from the patronage of Charles Montagu, later Earl of Halifax, who provided him with several minor offices. In 1704, Congreve dedicated to him *The Birth of the Muse*; and in 1710, he prefaced the volume of his *Collected Poems* with "An Epistle to the Right Honourable Charles, Lord Halifax":

> To you, on whose Indulgence she depends,
> Her few collected Lays she now commends.

Dryden seems to have tolerated generously this friendship of his young protégé with the man who had, not many years before, collaborated with Prior in a parody attacking *The Hind and the Panther*. But he may well have thought that Congreve's extravagant compliments in his dedication, where Halifax is described as "a Lover of Poetry to whom the Muse has been fruitful in a most beautiful Issue," were hardly warranted by anything he had written up to that time, or indeed by anything in that slim volume that appeared in 1715 after Halifax's death.

In defending his play, Congreve was content to claim that "the mechanical part of it is perfect" and that it was all his own invention. Nevertheless, there were at least two plays fresh in his mind when he wrote it. One was Wycherley's *Plain Dealer*, to which he has occasion to refer in his dedication; the other was Terence's *Heautontimoroumenos*, from which he seems willing to admit that he had taken some suggestions for the character of Maskwell. At any rate, in the later edition of 1706, he added to the title page those few lines from Terence's play in which Syrus so adequately describes his particular method of double-dealing.

Davies has also suggested[3] that Maskwell and Lady Touchwood both owe something to Fletcher's *Cupid's Revenge*. For his satire on *Les Femmes Savantes* and *Les Précieuses Ridicules* he did not need to go, as Summers rightly reminds us, to Molière. He may well have been more concerned to create parts that would provide suitable scope for Mrs. Barry and Mrs. Mountfort, and for Betterton and Powell, than to draw upon his memory of other plays; although his memory of these actors playing other roles must have provided him with hints and suggestions in the creation of his own characters.

The play was performed before Queen Mary on January 13, 1694, when young Cibber was called upon at short notice to play the part of Lord Touchwood in place of Kynaston, who had fallen ill.[4] Another performance on March 4, 1699 is of particular interest, because, as Dryden pointed out in a letter to Mrs. Steward, "in the playbill was printed 'Written by Mr. Congreve; with several Expressions omitted:' What kind of Expressions those were you may easily ghess; if you have seen the Monday's Gazette, wherein is the King's Order, for the Reformation of the Stage."[5] The play received full recognition in *A Comparison between the two Stages*, 1702: "I do take the *Double Dealer* to be among the most correct and regular Comedies: Mr. *C.* intended it so, and it cost him unusual Labour to do't."[6] For a further account of subsequent performances, see Emmet Avery's *Congreve's Plays on the Eighteenth-century Stage* (1951).

[3] Thomas Davies, *Dramatic Miscellanies* (London, 1785), III, 320.

[4] See Cibber, *Apology*, 1889, I, 185.

[5] Dryden, *Letters*, Chas. E. Ward (Duke, 1942), p. 113.

[6] [Charles Gildon] *A Comparison between the two Stages*, ed. S. B. Wells, (Princeton, 1942), p. 38.

THE

Double-Dealer,

A

COMEDY.

Acted at the

THEATRE ROYAL,

By Their Majesties Servants.

Written by Mr. *CONGREVE*.

Interdum tamen, vocem Comœdia tollit.
Hor. Ar. Po.

LONDON,

Printed for *Jacob Tonson*, at the *Judges-Head* near the *Inner-Temple-Gate* in *Fleet-street*. 1694.

Interdum tamen,—Yet, sometime doth the Comedy excite Her Voice,
(Ben Jonson's translation, *Ars Poetica*, l.93)

To the Right Honourable

Charles Mountague,

ONE OF THE

Lords of the *TREASURY.*

SIR,

I heartily wish this Play were as perfect as I intended it, that it might be more worthy your acceptance; and that my Dedication of it to you, might be more becoming that Honour and Esteem which I, with every Body, who are so fortunate as to know you, have for you. It had your Countenance when yet unknown; and now it is made publick, it wants your Protection.

And give me leave, without any Flattery to you, or Vanity in my self, to tell my Illiterate Criticks, as an answer to their Impotent Objections, that they have found fault with that, which has been pleasing to you. This Play in relation to my concern for its Reputation, succeeded before it was Acted, for thro' your early Patronage it had an audience of several Persons of the first Rank both in Wit and Quality; and their allowance of it, was a Consequence of your approbation. Therefore if I really wish it might have had a more popular reception; it is not at all in consideration of my self; but because I wish well, and would gladly contribute to the benefit of the Stage, and diversion of the Town. They were (not long since) so kind to a very imperfect Comedy of mine, that I thought my self justly indebted to them all my endeavours for an entertainment that might merit some little of that Applause, which they were so lavish of, when I thought I had no Title to it. But I find they are to be treated cheaply, and I have been at an unnecessary expense.

I would not have any Body imagine, that I think this Play without its Faults, for I am Conscious of several, (and ready to own 'em; but it shall be to those who are able to find 'em out.) I confess I design'd (whatever Vanity or Ambition occasion'd that design) to have written a true and regular Comedy, but I found it an undertaking which put me in mind of—*Sudet multum, frustraque laboret ausus idem.* And now to make amends for the vanity of such a design, I do confess both the attempt, and the imperfect performance. Yet I must take the boldness to say, I have not miscarried in the whole; for the Mechanical part of it is perfect. That, I may say with as little vanity, as a Builder may say he has built a House according to the Model laid down before him; or a Gardiner that he has set his Flowers in a knot of such or such a Figure. I design'd the Moral first, and to that Moral I invented the Fable, and do not know that I have borrow'd one hint of it any where. I made the Plot as strong as I could, because it was single, and I made it single, because I would avoid confusion and was resolved to preserve the three Unities of the Drama, which I have visibly done to the utmost severity. This is what I ought not to observe upon my self; but the Ignorance and Malice of the greater part of the Audience is such, that they would make a Man turn Herauld to his own Play, and Blazon every Character. However, Sir, this Discourse is very impertinent to you, whose Judgment, much better can discern the Faults, than I can excuse them; and whose good Nature, like that of a Lover, will find out those hidden Beauties (if there are any such) which it would be great immodesty in me to discover. I think I don't speak improperly when I call you a Lover of Poetry; for it is very well known she has been a kind Mistress to you; she has not deny'd you the last Favour; you have injoy'd her, and she has been fruitful in a most Beautiful Issue—If I break off abruptly here, I hope every Body will understand that it is to avoid a Commendation, which, as it is your due, would be most easie for me to pay, and too troublesome for you to receive.

I have since the Acting of this Play hearkned after the Objections which have been made to it; for I was Conscious where a true Critick might have put me upon my defence. I was prepared for their Attack; and am pretty confident I could have vindicated some parts, and excused others; and where there were any plain Miscarriages, I would most ingenuously have confess'd 'em. But I have not heard any thing said sufficient to provoke an Answer. Some little snarling and barking there has been, but I don't know one well-mouth'd Curr that has opened at all. That, which looks most like an Objection, does not relate in particular to this Play, but to all or most that ever have been written; and that is Soliloquy. Therefore I will answer it, not only for my own sake, but to save others the trouble, to whom it may hereafter be Objected.

I grant, that for a Man to Talk to himself, appears absurd and unnatural; and indeed it is so in most Cases; but the circumstances which may attend the occasion, make great alteration. It oftentimes happens to a Man, to have designs which require him to himself, and in their Nature, cannot admit of a Confident. Such, for certain, is all Villany; and other less mischievous intentions may be very improper to be Communicated to a second Person. In such a case therefore the Audience must observe, whether the Person upon the Stage takes any notice of them at all, or no. For if he supposes any one to be by, when he talks to himself, it is monstrous and ridiculous to the last degree. Nay, not only in this case, but in any part of a Play, if there is expressed any knowledge of an Audience, it is insufferable. But otherwise when a Man in Soliloquy reasons with himself, and *Pro's* and *Con's*, and weighs all his Designs: We ought not to imagine that this Man either talks to us, or to himself; he is only thinking, and thinking such Matter, as were inexcusable Folly in him to speak. But because we are conceal'd Spectators of the Plot in agitation, and the Poet finds it necessary to let us know the whole Mystery of his Contrivance he is willing to inform us of this Person's Thoughts; and to that end is forced to make use of the expedient of Speech, no other better way being yet invented for the Communication of Thought.

Another very wrong Objection has been made by some who have not taken leisure to distinguish the Characters. The Hero of the Play, as they are pleas'd to call him, (meaning *Mellefont*) is a Gull, and made a Fool and cheated. Is every Man a Gull and a Fool that is deceiv'd? At that rate I'm afraid the two Classes of Men, will be reduc'd to one, and the Knaves themselves be at a loss to justifie their Title: But if an Open-hearted Honest Man, who has an entire Confidence in one whom he takes to be his Friend, and whom he has obliged to be so; and who (to confirm him in his Opinion) in all appearance, and upon several tryals has been so: If this Man be deceived by the Treachery of the other; must he of necessity commence Fool immediately, only because the other has proved a Villain? Ay, but there was Caution given to *Mellefont* in the first Act by his Friend *Careless*. Of what Nature was that Caution? Only to give the Audience some light into the Character of *Maskwell*, before his appearance; and not to convince *Mellefont* of his Treachery; for that was more than *Careless* was then able to do: He never knew *Maskwell* guilty of any Villany; he was only a sort of Man which he did not like. As for his suspecting his Familiarity with my Lady *Touchwood*: Let 'em examine the Answer that *Mellefont* makes him, and compare it with the Conduct of *Maskwell's* Character through the Play.

I would have 'em again look into the Character of *Maskwell*, before they accuse any Body of weakness for being deceiv'd by him. For upon summing up the enquiry into this Objection, [I] find they have only mistaken Cunning in one Character, for Folly in another.

But there is one thing at which I am more concerned than all the false Criticisms that are made upon me; and that is, some of the Ladies are offended: I am heartily sorry for it, for I declare I would rather disoblige all the Criticks in the World, than one of the Fair Sex. They are concerned that I have represented some Women Vicious and Affected: How can I help it? It is the Business of a Comick Poet to paint the Vices and Follies of Humane kind; and there are but two Sexes that I know, *viz. Men* and *Women*, which have a Title to Humanity: And if I leave one half of them out, the Work will be imperfect. I should be very glad of an opportunity to make my Complement to those Ladies who are offended: But they can no more expect it in a Comedy, than to be Tickled by a Surgeon, when he's letting 'em Blood. They who are Virtuous or Discreet, I'm sure cannot be offended, for such Characters as these distinguish them, and make their Beauties more shining and observ'd: And they who are of the other kind, may nevertheless pass for such, by seeming not to be displeased, or touched with the Satyr of this *Comedy*. Thus have they also wrongfully accused me of doing them a prejudice, when I have in reality done them a Service.

I have heard some whispering, as if they intended to accuse this Play of Smuttiness and Bawdy: But I declare I took a particular care to avoid it, and if they find any in it, it is of their own making, for I did not design it to be so understood. But to avoid my saying any thing upon a Subject, which has been so admirably handled before, and for their better instruction, I earnestly recommend to their perusal, the Epistle Dedicatory before the *Plain-Dealer*.

You will pardon me, Sir, for the freedom I take of making Answers to other People, in an Epistle which ought wholly to be sacred to you: But since I intend the Play to be so too, I hope I may take the more liberty of Justifying it, where it is in the right. I hear a great many of the Fools are angry at me, and I am glad of it; for I Writ at them, not to 'em. This is a bold confession, and yet I don't think I shall disoblige one Person by it; for no Body can take it to himself, without owning the *Character*.

I must now, Sir, declare to the World, how kind you have been to my Endeavours; for in regard of what was well meant, you have excused what was ill perform'd. I beg you would continue the same Method in your acceptance of this Dedication. I know no other way of making a return to that *Charity* you shew'd, in protecting an Infant, but by

Enrolling it in your Service, now that it is of Age and come into the World. Therefore be pleased to accept of this as an Acknowledgement of the Favour you have shewn me, and an earnest of the real Service and Gratitude of,

SIR,
Your Most Obliged
Humble Servant

William Congreve.

To my Dear Friend

Mr. Congreve,

On His COMEDY, call'd,

The Double-Dealer.

Well then; the promis'd hour is come at last;
The present Age of Wit obscures the past:
Strong were our Syres; and as they Fought they Writ,
Conqu'ring with force of Arms, and dint of Wit;
Theirs was the Gyant Race, before the Flood;
And thus, when *Charles* Return'd, our Empire stood.
Like *Janus* he the stubborn Soil manur'd,
With Rules of Husbandry the rankness cur'd:
Tam'd us to manners, when the Stage was rude;
And boistrous *English* Wit, with Art indu'd.
Our Age was cultivated thus at length;
But what we gain'd in skill we lost in strength.
Our Builders were, with want of Genius, curst;
The second Temple was not like the first:
Till You, the best *Vitruvius*, come at length;
Our Beauties equal; but excel our strength.
Firm *Dorique* Pillars found Your solid Base:
The Fair *Corinthian* Crowns the higher Space;
Thus all below is Strength, and all above is Grace.
In easie Dialogue is *Fletcher*'s Praise:
He mov'd the mind, but had not power to raise.
Great *Johnson* did by strength of Judgment please:
Yet doubling *Fletcher*'s Force, he wants his Ease.
In differing Tallents both adorn'd their Age;
One for the Study, t'other for the Stage.
But both to *Congreve* justly shall submit,
One match'd in Judgment, both o'er-match'd in Wit.
In Him all Beauties of this Age we see;
Etherege his Courtship, *Southern*'s Purity;
The Satire, Wit, and Strength of Manly *Witcherly*.
All this in blooming Youth you have Atchiev'd;
Nor are your foil'd Contemporaries griev'd;
So much the sweetness of your manners move,
We cannot envy you because we Love.
Fabius might joy in *Scipio*, when he saw
A Beardless Consul made against the Law,
And joyn his Suffrage to the Votes of *Rome*;

Though He with *Hannibal* was overcome.
Thus old *Romano* bow'd to *Raphel's* Fame;
And Scholar to the Youth he taught, became.

Oh that your Brows my Lawrel had sustain'd,
Well had I been Depos'd, if You had reign'd!
The Father had descended for the Son;
For only You are lineal to the Throne.
Thus when the State one *Edward* did depose;
A Greater *Edward* in his room arose.
But now, not I, but Poetry is curs'd;
For *Tom* the Second reigns like *Tom* the first.
But let 'em not mistake my Patron's part;
Nor call his Charity their own desert.
Yet this I Prophecy; Thou shalt be seen,
(Tho' with some short Parenthesis between:)
High on the Throne of Wit; and seated there,
Not mine (that's little) but thy Lawrel wear.
Thy first attempt an early promise made;
That early promise this has more than paid.
So bold, yet so judiciously you dare,
That Your least Praise, is to be Regular.
Time, Place, and Action, may with pains be wrought,
But Genius must be born; and never can be taught.
This is Your Portion; this Your Native Store;
Heav'n that but once was Prodigal before,
To *Shakespeare* gave as much; she cou'd not give him more.

Maintain Your Post: That's all the Fame You need;
For 'tis impossible you shou'd proceed.
Already I am worn with Cares and Age;
And just abandoning th'Ungrateful Stage:
Unprofitably kept at Heav'ns expence,
I live a Rent-charge on his Providence:
But You, whom ev'ry Muse and Grace adorn,
Whom I foresee to better Fortune born,
Be kind to my Remains; and oh defend,
Against Your Judgment Your departed Friend!
Let not the Insulting Foe my Fame pursue;
But shade those Lawrels which descend to You:
And take for Tribute what these Lines express:
You merit more; nor cou'd my Love do less.

John Dryden.

Prologue

Spoken by Mrs. *Bracegirdle*

Moors, have this way (as Story tells) to know
Whether their Brats are truly got, or no;
Into the Sea, the New-born Babe is thrown,
There, as instinct directs, to Swim, or Drown.
A Barbarous Device, to try if Spouse,
Have kept Religiously her Nuptial Vows!

Such are the Tryals, Poets make of Plays:
Only they trust to more inconstant Seas;
So, does our Author, this his Child commit
To the Tempestuous Mercy of the Pit,
To know, if it be truly born of Wit.

Criticks avaunt; for you are Fish of Prey,
And feed like Sharks, upon an Infant Play.
Be ev'ry Monster of the Deep away;
Let's have a fair Tryal, and a clear Sea.

Let Nature work, and do not Damn too soon,
For Life will struggle long, 'ere it sink down:
Let it at least rise thrice, before it Drown.
Let us consider, had it been our Fate,
Thus hardly to be prov'd Legitimate!
I will not say, we'd all in danger been,
Were each to suffer for his Mothers Sin:
But by my Troth I cannot avoid thinking,
How nearly some Good Men might have scap'd Sinking.
But Heav'n be prais'd, this Custom is confin'd
Alone to the Offspring of the Muses kind:
Our Christian Cuckolds are more bent to pity;
I know not one *Moor*-Husband in the City.
I'th' Good Man's Arms, the Chopping Bastard thrives,
For he thinks all his own, that is his Wives.

Whatever Fate is for this Play design'd,
The Poet's sure he shall some comfort find:
For if his Muse has play'd him false, the worst
That can befal him, is, to be Divorc'd;
You Husbands Judge, if that, be to be Curs'd.

Dramatis Personæ

MEN

Maskwell, A Villain; pretended Friend to *Mellefont*, Gallant to Lady *Touchwood*, and in Love with *Cynthia*	Mr. Betterton.
Lord Touchwood, Uncle to *Mellefont*	Mr. Kynaston.
Mellefont, Promised to, and in Love with *Cynthia*	Mr. Williams.
Careless, His Friend	Mr. Alexander.
Lord Froth, A Solemn Coxcomb	Mr. Bowman.
Brisk, A Pert Coxcomb	Mr. Powell.
Sir Paul Plyant, An Uxorius, Foolish, old Knight; Brother to *Lady Touchwood*, and Father to *Cynthia*	Mr. Dogget.

WOMEN

Lady Touchwood, In Love with *Mellefont*	Mrs. Barry.
Cynthia, Daughter to *Sir Paul* by a former Wife, promised to *Mellefont*	Mrs. Bracegirdle.
Lady Froth, A great Cocquet; pretender to Poetry, Wit, and Learning	Mrs. Mountfort.
Lady Plyant, Insolent to her Husband, and easie to any Pretender	Mrs. Leigh.

Chaplain, *Boy*, *Footmen*, and *Attendants*.

The SCENE, A Gallery in the *Lord Touchwood's* House

The Time, from Five a Clock to Eight in the Evening

The Double-Dealer. A Comedy.

ACT I. SCENE I.

A Gallery in the Lord Touchwood's *House, with Chambers adjoyning.*

Enter Careless, *Crossing the Stage, with his Hat, Gloves, and Sword in his Hands; as just risen from Table:* Mellefont *following him.*

Mellefont. Ned, Ned, whither so fast? What, turn'd flincher! Why, you wo' not leave us?

Careless. Where are the Women? Pox I'm weary of guzling, and begin to think them the better Company.

Mellefont. Then thy Reason staggers, and thou'rt almost drunk.

Careless. No faith, but your Fools grow noisy———and if a man must endure the noise of words without Sence, I think the Women have the more Musical Voices, and become Nonsence better.

Mellefont. Why, they are at that end of the Gallery; retired to their Tea, and Scandal; according to their Antient Custome, after Dinner.———But I made a pretence of following you, because I had something to say to you in private, and I am not like to have many opportunities this Evening.

A Gallery—a large, long room for entertaining on an upper floor characteristic of English houses in the seventeenth century.

Careless. And here's this Cox-Comb most Critically come to interrupt you.

Enter Brisk.

Brisk. Boys, Boys, Lads, where are you? What, do you give ground? Mortgage for a Bottle, ha? *Careless*, this is your trick; you're always spoiling Company by leaving it.

Careless. And thou art always spoiling Company by coming into 't.

Brisk. Pooh, ha, ha, ha, I know you envy me. Spite, proud spite, by the Gods! and burning envy.———I'le be judged by *Mellefont* here, who gives and takes Raillery better, you or I. Pox, Man, when I say you spoil Company by leaving it, I mean you leave No body for the Company to Laugh at. I think there I was with you, ha? *Mellefont.*

Mellefont. O' my word, *Brisk*, that was a home thrust; you have silenc'd him.

Brisk. Oh, my dear *Mellefont*, let me perish, if thou art not the Soul of Conversation, the very Essence of Wit, and Spirit of Wine,—the Deuce take me if there were three good things said; or one, understood, since thy Amputation from the body of our Society.———He, I think that's pretty and Metaphorical enough: I' Gad I could not have said it out of thy Company.———*Careless*, ha?

Careless. Hum, ay, what is't?

Brisk. O, *Mon Cœur*! What is't! nay gad I'll punish you for want of Apprehension: The Deuce take me if I tell you.

Mellefont. No, no, hang him, he has no tast.—but dear *Brisk* excuse me, I have a little business.

Careless. Prithee get thee gone; thou seest we are serious.

Mellefont. We'll come immediately, if you'll but go in, and keep up good Humour and Sense in the Company, prithee do, they'll fall asleep else.

Brisk. I'gad so they will———well I will, I will, Gad you shall Command me from the *Zenith* to the *Nadir.*——— But the Deuce take me if I say a good thing till you come.— But prithee dear Rogue, make haste, prithee make haste, I shall burst else.———And yonder your Uncle my Lord *Touchwood* swears, he'll Disinherit you, and Sir *Paul Pliant* threatens to disclaim you for a Son-in-Law, and my Lord

Froth won't Dance at your Wedding to Morrow; nor the Deuce take me, I won't Write your Epithalamium ———and see what a condition you're like to be brought to.

Mellefont. Well, I'll speak but three words, and follow you.

Brisk. Enough, enough; *Careless*, bring your Apprehension along with you.

Exit.

Careless. Pert Cox-Comb.

Mellefont. Faith 'tis a good natur'd Cox-Comb, and has very Entertaining follies—you must be more humane to him; at this Juncture it will do me Service.———I'll tell you, I would have mirth continued this day at any rate; tho' Patience purchase folly, and Attention be paid with noise: There are times when Sense may be unseasonable, as well as Truth. Prithee do thou wear none to day; but allow *Brisk* to have Wit, that thou may'st seem a Fool.

Careless. Why, how now, why this extravagant proposition?

Mellefont. O, I would have no room for serious design; for I am Jealous of a Plot. I would have Noise and Impertinence keep my Lady *Touchwood's* Head from Working: For Hell is not more busie than her Brain, nor contains more Devils, than that Imaginations.

Careless. I thought your fear of her had been over———is not to Morrow appointed for your Marriage with *Cynthia*, and her Father Sir *Paul Plyant*, come to settle the Writings, this day, on purpose?

Mellefont. True, but you shall judge whether I have not reason to be allarm'd. None besides you, and *Maskwell*, are acquainted with the Secret of my Aunt *Touchwood's* violent Passion for me. Since my first refusal of her Addresses, she has endeavour'd to do me all ill Offices with my Uncle; yet has managed 'em with that subtilty, that to him they have born the face of kindness; while her Malice, like a Dark Lanthorn, onely shone upon me, where it was directed. Still it gave me less perplexity to prevent the success of her displeasure, than to avoid the importunities of her Love; and of two evils, I thought my self favour'd in her aversion: But whether urged by her despair, and the short prospect of time she saw, to accomplish her designs; whether the hopes of her revenge, or of her Love, terminated in the view of this my Marriage with *Cynthia*, I know not; but this Morning she surpriz'd me in my Bed.———

Careless. Was there ever such a Fury! 'tis well Nature has not put it into her Sexes power to Ravish.———Well, bless us! Proceed. What follow'd?

Mellefont. What at first amaz'd me; for I look'd to have seen her in all the Transports of a slighted and revengful Woman: But when I expected Thunder from her Voice, and Lightning in her Eyes; I saw her melted into Tears, and hush'd into a Sigh. It was long before either of us spoke, Passion had ty'd her Tongue, and Amazement mine.——— In short, the Consequence was thus, she omitted nothing, that the most violent Love could urge, or tender words express; which when she saw had no effect; but still I pleaded Honour and nearness of Blood to my Uncle; then came the Storm I fear'd at first: For starting from my Bed-side like a Fury, she flew to my Sword, and with much ado I prevented her doing me or her self a mischief: having disarm'd her; in a gust of Passion she left me, and in a resolution, confirm'd by a Thousand Curses, not to close her Eyes, till she had seen my ruin.

Careless. Exquisite Woman! But what the Devil, does she think thou hast no more Sense, than to get an Heir upon her Body to Disinherit thy self: for as I take it this Settlement upon you, is, with a Proviso, that your Uncle have no Children.

Mellefont. It is so. Well, the Service that you are to do me, will be a Pleasure to your self; I must get you to engage my Lady *Plyant* all this Evening, that my Pious Aunt may not work her to her Interest. And if you chance to secure her to your self, you may incline her to mine. She's handsome, and knows it; is very silly, and thinks she has Sense, and has an old fond Husband.

Careless. I confess a very fair Foundation, for a Lover to build upon.

Mellefont. For my Lord *Froth*, he and his Wife will be sufficiently taken up, with admiring one another, and *Brisk's* Gallantry, as they call it. I'le observe my Uncle my self; and *Jack Maskwell* has promised me, to watch my Aunt narrowly, and give me notice upon any Suspicion. As for Sir *Paul*, my wise Father-in-Law that is to be, my Dear *Cynthia* has such a share in his Fatherly fondness, he would scarce make her a Moment uneasy, to have her happy hereafter.

Careless. So, you have Mann'd your Works: But I wish you may not have the weakest Guard, where the Enemy is strongest.

Mellefont. Maskwell, you mean; prithee why should you suspect him?

Careless. Faith I cannot help it, you know I never lik'd him; I am a little Superstitious in Physiognomy.

Mellefont. He has Obligations of Gratitude, to bind him to me; his Dependance upon my Uncle is through my means.

Careless. Upon your Aunt, you mean.

Mellefont. My Aunt!

Careless. I'm mistaken if there be not a Familiarity between them, you do not suspect: For all her Passion for you.

Mellefont. Pooh, pooh, nothing in the World but his design to do me Service; and he endeavours to be well in her esteem, that he may be able to effect it.

Careless. Well, I shall be glad to be mistaken; but, your Aunts Aversion in her Revenge, cannot be any way so effectually shown, as in bringing forth a Child to Disinherit you. She is Handsome and cunning, and naturally wanton. *Maskwell* is Flesh and Blood at best, and opportunities between them are frequent. His Affection to you, you have confessed, is grounded upon his Interest, that, you have transplanted; and should it take Root in my Lady, I don't see what you can expect from the Fruit.

Mellefont. I confess the Consequence is visible, were your suspicions just,——but see the Company is broke up, let's meet 'em.

Enter Lord Touchwood, Lord Froth, Sir Paul Plyant, *and* Brisk.

Lord Touchwood. Out upon't, Nephew——leave your Father-in-Law, and me, to maintain our ground against Young People.

Mellefont. I beg your Lordships Pardon——We were just returning.——

Sir Paul. Were you, Son? Gadsbud much better as it is——good, strange! I swear I'm almost Tipsy——t'other

Bottle would have been too powerful for me,——as sure as can be it would.——we wanted your Company, but Mr. *Brisk*——where is he? I swear and vow, he's a most facetious Person.——and the best Company.—— And, my Lord *Froth*, your Lordship is so merry a Man, he, he, he.

Lord Froth. O foy, Sir *Paul*, what do you mean? Merry! O Barbarous! I'd as lieve you call'd me Fool.

Sir Paul. Nay, I protest and vow now, 'tis true; when Mr. *Brisk* Jokes, your Lordships Laugh does so become you, he, he, he.

Lord Froth. Ridiculous! Sir *Paul* you're strangely mistaken, I find Champagne is powerful. I assure you, Sir *Paul*, I Laugh at no bodies Jest but my own, or a Lady's; I assure you, Sir *Paul*.

Brisk. How? how, my Lord? What, affront my Wit! Let me perish, do I never say any thing worthy to be Laugh'd at?

Lord Froth. O foy, don't misapprehend me, I don't say so, for I often smile at your Conceptions. But there is nothing more unbecoming a Man of Quality, than to Laugh; Jesu, 'tis such a Vulgar Expression of the Passion! every body can Laugh. Then especially to Laugh at the Jest of an Inferiour Person, or when any body else of the same Quality does not Laugh with him. Ridiculous! To be pleased with what pleases the Croud! Now when I Laugh, I always Laugh alone.

Brisk. I suppose that's because you Laugh at your own Jests, I'gad, ha, ha, ha.

Lord Froth. He, he, I swear tho', your Raillery provokes me to a smile.

Brisk. Ay, my Lord, it's a sign I hit you in the Teeth, if you show 'em.

Lord Froth. He, he, he, I swear that's so very pretty, I can't forbear.

Careless. I find a Quibble bears more sway in your Lordships Face, than a Jest.

Lord Touchwood. Sir *Paul*, if you please we'll retire to the Ladys, and Drink a Dish of Tea, to settle our Heads.

Sir Paul. With all my heart.———Mr. *Brisk* you'll come to us,—or call me when you're going to Joke, I'll be ready to Laugh incontinently.

Exit Lord Touchwood *and* Sir Paul.

Mellefont. But does your Lordship never see Comedies?

Lord Froth. O yes, sometimes,—but I never Laugh.

Mellefont. No?

Lord Froth. Oh, no.———Never Laugh indeed, Sir.

Careless. No, why what d'ee go there for?

Lord Froth. To distinguish my self from the Commonalty, and mortify the Poets; the Fellows grow so Conceited, when any of their foolish Wit prevails upon the side Boxes.———I swear,———he, he, he, I have often constrained my Inclinations to Laugh.———He, he, he, to avoid giving them encouragement.

Mellefont. You are Cruel to your self, my Lord, as well as Malicious to them.

Lord Froth. I confess, I did my self some violence at first, but now I think I have Conquer'd it.

Brisk. Let me perish, my Lord, but there is something very particular and novel in the Humour; 'tis true, it makes against Wit, and I'm sorry for some Friends of mine that Write, but———I'gad, I love to be malicious.———Nay, Deuce take me, there's Wit in't too———and Wit must be foil'd by Wit; cut a Diamond with a Diamond; no other way, I'gad.

Lord Froth. Oh, I thought you would not be long, before you found out the Wit.

Careless. Wit, In what? Where the Devil's the Wit, in not Laughing when a Man has a mind to't.

Brisk. O Lord, why can't you find it out?———Why there 'tis, in the not Laughing———don't you Apprehend me? ———My Lord, *Careless*, is a very honest Fellow, but harkee,———you understand me. Somewhat heavy, a little shallow, or so.———Why I'll tell you now, suppose now, you come up to me———nay, prithee *Careless* be

side Boxes—The better places to sit, in tiers on either side of the theater, but not on the stage at this period.

instructed. Suppose, as I was saying, you come up to me, holding your sides, and Laughing as if you would bepiss your self———I look grave, and ask the cause of this Immoderate Mirth.—You Laugh on still, and are not able to tell me———still I look grave, not so much as smile.———

Careless. Smile, no, what the Devil should you smile at, when you suppose I can't tell you?

Brisk. Pshaw, pshaw, prithee don't interrupt me.———But I tell you, you shall tell me———at last.———But it shall be a great while first.

Careless. Well, but prithee don't let it be a great while, because I long to have it over.

Brisk. Well then, you tell me, some good Jest, or very Witty thing, Laughing all the while as if you were ready to die ———and I hear it, and look thus.———Would not you be disappointed?

Careless. No; for if it were a witty thing, I should not expect you to understand it.

Lord Froth. O foy, Mr. *Careless,* all the World allow Mr. *Brisk* to have Wit; my Wife says, he has a great deal. I hope you think her a Judge?

Brisk. Pooh, my Lord, his Voice goes for nothing.———I can't tell how to make him Apprehend,———take it t'other way. Suppose I say a witty thing to you?

Careless. Then I shall be disappointed indeed.

Mellefont. Let him alone, *Brisk,* he is obstinately bent not to be instructed.

Brisk. I'm sorry for him, Deuce take me.

Mellefont. Shall we go to the Ladies, my Lord?

Lord Froth. With all my heart, methinks we are a Solitude without 'em.

Mellefont. Or, what say you, to another Bottle of Champaign?

Lord Froth. O, for the Universe, not a drop more I beseech you, O Intemperate! I have a flushing in my Face already.
Takes out a Pocket-Glass, and looks in it.

Brisk. Let me see, let me see, my Lord, I broke my Glass that was in the Lid of my Snuff-Box. Hum! Deuce take me, I have encourag'd a Pimple here too.

Takes the Glass and looks.

Lord Froth. Then you must mortifie him, with a Patch; my Wife shall supply you. Come, Gentlemen, *allons.*

Exeunt.

Enter Lady Touchwood, *and* Maskwell.

Lady Touchwood. I'll hear no more.———Y' are False and Ungrateful; come, I know you false.

Maskwell. I have been frail, I confess, Madam, for your Ladyships Service.

Lady Touchwood. That I should trust a Man, whom I had known betray his Friend!

Maskwell. What Friend have I betray'd? Or to Whom?

Lady Touchwood. Your fond Friend *Mellefont,* and to me; can you deny it?

Maskwell. I do not.

Lady Touchwood. Have you not wrong'd my Lord, who has been a Father to you in your wants, and given you being? have you not wrong'd him in the highest manner, in his Bed?

Maskwell. With your Ladyships help, and for your Service, as I told you before. I can't deny that neither.———Any thing more, Madam?

Lady Touchwood. More! Audacious Villain. O what's more, is most my Shame,———have you not Dishonoured me?

Maskwell. No, that I deny; for I never told in all my Life: So that Accusation's Answer'd; on to the next.

Lady Touchwood. Death, do you dally with my Passion? Insolent Devil! But have a care,———provoke me not; For, by the Eternal Fire, you shall not scape my Vengance. ———Calm Villain! How unconcern'd he stands, Confessing Treachery and Ingratitude! Is there Vice more black!—O I have Excuses, Thousands for my Faults; Fire in my Temper, Passions in my Soul, apt to every provocation; oppressed at once with Love, and with Despair. But a sedate, a thinking Villain, whose Black Blood runs temperately bad, what excuse can clear? one, who is no more moved with the reflection of his Crimes, than of his Face; but walks unstartled from the Mirrour, and streight forgets the hideous form.

She Walks about Disorder'd.

Maskwell. Will you be in Temper, Madam? I would not talk, not to be heard. I have been a very great Rogue for your sake, and you reproach me with it; I am ready to be a Rogue still, to do you Service; and you are flinging Conscience and Honour in my Face, to rebate my Inclinations. How am I to behave my self? You know I am your Creature, my Life and Fortune in your power; to disoblige you, brings me certain Ruin. Allow it, I would betray you, I would not be a Traytor to my self: I don't pretend to Honesty, because you know I am a Rascal: But I would convince you, from the necessity of my being firm to you.

Lady Touchwood. Necessity, Impudence! Can no Gratitude incline you, no Obligations touch you? Have not my Fortune, and my Person, been subjected to your Pleasure? Were you not in the nature of a Servant, and have not I in effect made you Lord of all, of me, and of my Lord? Where is that humble Love, the Languishing, that Adoration, which once was paid me, and everlastingly engaged?

Maskwell. Fix'd, Rooted in my Heart, whence nothing can remove 'em, yet you———

Lady Touchwood. Yet, what yet?

Maskwell. Nay, Misconceive me not, Madam, when I say I have had a Generous, and a Faithful Passion, which you had never favour'd, but through Revenge and Policy.

Lady Touchwood. Ha!

Maskwell. Look you, Madam, we are alone,———pray contain your self, and hear me. You know you Lov'd your Nephew, when I first Sigh'd for you; I quickly found it an Argument that I Lov'd; for with that Art you veil'd your Passion, 'twas imperceptible to all but Jealous Eyes. This discovery made me bold; I confess it; for by it, I thought you in my Power. Your Nephew's Scorn of you, added to my hopes; I watch'd the Occasion, and took you, just Repulsed by him, warm at once with Love and Indignation; your Disposition, my Arguments, and happy Opportunity, accomplish'd my Design; I prest the yielding

in Temper—Composed, moderate.

Minute, and was blest. How I have Lov'd you since, Words have not shown, then how should Words express.

Lady Touchwood. Well, mollifying Devil!———And have I not met your Love with forward Fire?

Maskwell. Your Zeal I grant was Ardent, but misplac'd; there was Revenge in view; that Womans Idol had defil'd the Temple of the God, and Love was made a Mock-Worship,———a Son and Heir, would have edg'd Young *Mellefont* upon the brink of Ruin, and left him nought but you to catch at for Prevention.

Lady Touchwood. Again, provoke me! Do you wind me like a Larum, only to rouse my own still'd Soul for your Diversion? Confusion!

Maskwell. Na, Madam, I'm gone, if you Relapse,———what needs this? I say nothing but what your self, in open hours of Love, have told me. Why should you deny it? Nay, how can you? Is not all this present Heat owing to the same Fire? Do you not Love him still? How have I this day Offended you, but in not breaking off his Match with *Cynthia*? Which e're to Morrow shall be done,———had you but Patience.

Lady Touchwood. How, what said you *Maskwell*——— another Caprice, to unwind my temper.

Maskwell. By heaven, no; I am your Slave, the Slave of all your Pleasures; and will not rest till I have given you peace, would you suffer me.

Lady Touchwood. O' *Maskwell*, in Vain I do disguise me from thee, thou know'st me, know'st the very inmost Windings and Recesses of my Soul.———Oh *Mellefont*! I burn; Married to Morrow! Despair strikes me. Yet my Soul knows I hate him too: Let him but once be mine, and next immediate Ruin seize him.

Maskwell. Compose your self, You shall Enjoy and Ruin him too,———Will that please you?

Lady Touchwood. How, how? Thou Dear, thou precious Villain, how?

Maskwell. You have already been tampering with my Lady *Plyant*?

Lady Touchwood. I have: She is ready for any Impression I think fit.

Maskwell. She must be throughly perswaded, that *Mellefont* Loves her.

Lady Touchwood. She is so Credulous that way naturally, and likes him so well, that she will believe it faster than I can perswade her. But I don't see what you can propose from such a trifling design; for her first Conversing with *Mellefont,* will convince her of the contrary.

Maskwell. I know it.———I don't depend upon it.——— But it will prepare some thing else; and gain us leasure to lay a stronger Plot: if I gain a little time, I shall not want Contrivance.

One Minute, gives Invention to Destroy,
What, to Rebuild, will a whole Age Employ.

Exeunt.

End of the first Act.

ACT II. Scene I.

Enter Lady Froth *and* Cynthia.

Cynthia. Indeed, Madam! Is it Possible your Ladyship could have been so much in Love?

Lady Froth. I could not sleep; I did not sleep one wink for Three Weeks together.

Cynthia. Prodigious! I wonder, want of sleep, and so much Love, and so much Wit as your Ladyship has, did not turn your Brain.

Lady Froth. O my Dear *Cynthia,* you must not rally your Friend,———but really, as you say, I wonder too,—but then I had a way.———For between you and I, I had Whymsies and Vapours, but I gave them vent.

Cynthia. How pray, Madam?

Lady Froth. O I Writ, Writ abundantly,———do you never Write?

Cynthia. Write, what?

Lady Froth. Songs, Elegies, Satyrs, Encomiums, Panegyricks, Lampoons, Plays, or Heroick Poems.

Cynthia. O Lord, not I, Madam; I'm content to be a Courteous Reader.

Lady Froth. O Inconsistent! In Love, and not Write! if my Lord and I had been both of your Temper, we had never come together,———O bless me! What a sad thing would that have been, if my Lord and I should never have met!

Cynthia. Then neither my Lord nor you would ever have met with your Match, on my Conscience.

Lady Froth. O' my Conscience no more we should; thou say'st right———for sure my Lord *Froth* is as fine a Gentleman, and as much a Man of Quality! Ah! Nothing at all of the Common Air,———I think I may say he wants nothing, but a Blue Ribbon and a Star, to make him Shine, the very Phosphorus of our Hemisphere. Do you understand those Two hard Words? If you don't, I'll explain 'em to you.

Cynthia. Yes, yes, Madam, I'm not so Ignorant.——— (*aside*). At least I won't own it, to be troubled with your Instructions.

Lady Froth. Nay, I beg your Pardon; but being Derived from the *Greek*, I thought you might have escap'd the Etymology.———But I'm the more amazed, to find you a Woman of Letters, and not Write! Bless me! how can *Mellefont* believe you Love him?

Cynthia. Why Faith, Madam, he that won't take my Word, shall never have it under my Hand.

Lady Froth. I Vow *Mellefont's* a pretty Gentleman, but Methinks he wants a Manner.

Cynthia. A Manner! what's that, Madam?

Lady Froth. Some distinguishing Quality, as for example, the *Belle-air* or *Brillant* of Mr. *Brisk*; the Solemnity, yet Complaisance of my Lord, or something of his own, that should look a little *Je-ne-scay quoysh*; he is too much a Mediocrity, in my mind.

Cynthia. He does not indeed affect either pertness, or formality; for which I like him: Here he comes.

Lady Froth. And my Lord with him: pray observe the difference.

Enter Lord Froth, Mellefont, Brisk.

Cynthia (*aside*). Impertinent Creature, I could almost be angry with her now.

Lady Froth. My Lord, I have been telling my dear *Cynthia*, how much I have been in Love with you; I swear I have; I'm not asham'd to own it now; ah! it makes my heart leap, I vow I sigh when I think on't: my dear Lord! ha, ha, ha, do you remember, my Lord?

Squeezes him by the hand, looks kindly on him, sighs, and then laughs out.

Lord Froth. Pleasant Creature! perfectly well, ah! that look, ay, there it is; who could resist! 'twas so my heart was made a Captive first, and ever since 't has been in Love with happy Slavery.

Lady Froth. O that Tongue, that dear deceitful Tongue! that Charming Softness in your Mien and your Expression, and then your Bow! Good my Lord, bow as you did when I gave you my Picture, here suppose this my Picture——

Gives him a Pocket-glass.

Pray mind, my Lord; ah! he bows Charmingly; nay, my Lord, you sha'n't kiss it so much; I shall grow jealous, I vow now.

He bows profoundly low, then kisses the Glass.

Lord Froth. I saw my self there, and kissed it for your sake.

Lady Froth. Ah! Gallantry to the last degree——Mr. *Brisk*, you're a Judge; was ever any thing so well-bred as my Lord?

Brisk. Never any thing; but your Ladyship, let me perish.

Lady Froth. O prettily turn'd again; let me die, but you have a great deal of Wit: Mr. *Mellefont*, don't you think Mr. *Brisk* has a World of Wit?

Mellefont. O, yes, Madam.

Brisk. O Lord, Madam—

Lady Froth. An infinite deal!

Brisk. O Jesu, Madam—

Lady Froth. More Wit than any Body.

Brisk. I'm everlastingly your humble Servant, Deuce take me, Madam.

Lord Froth. Don't you think us a happy Couple?

Cynthia. I vow, my Lord, I think you the happiest Couple in the World, for you are not only happy in one another, and when you are together, but happy in your selves, and by your selves.

Lord Froth. I hope *Mellefont* will make a good Husband too.

Cynthia. 'Tis my Interest to believe he will, my Lord.

Lord Froth. D'e think he'll Love you as well as I do my Wife? I'm afraid not.

Cynthia. I believe he'll Love me better.

Lord Froth. Heavens! that can never be; but why do you think so?

Cynthia. Because he has not so much reason to be fond of himself.

Lord Froth. O your humble Servant for that, dear Madam; well, *Mellefont*, you'll be a happy Creature.

Mellefont. Ay, my Lord, I shall have the same reason for my happiness that your Lordship has, I shall think my self happy.

Lord Froth. Ah, that's all.

Brisk (*to Lady* Froth). Your Ladyship is in the right; but I'gad I'm wholly turn'd into Satyr. I confess I Write but seldom, but when I do———keen *Iambicks* I'gad. But my Lord was telling me, your Ladyship has made an Essay toward an Heroick Poem.

Lady Froth. Did my Lord tell you? Yes I vow, and the Subject is my Lord's Love to me. And what do you think I call it? I dare Swear you won't guesse———*The Sillibub*, ha, ha, ha.

Brisk. Because my Lord's Title's *Froth*, I'gad, ha, ha, ha, Deuce take me very *a Propos* and Surprizing, ha, ha, ha.

Lady Froth. He, Ay, is not it?———and then I call my Lord *Spumoso*; and my self, what d'e think I call my self?

Brisk. *Lactilla* may be,———'gad I cannot tell.

Lady Froth. *Biddy*, that's all; just my own Name.

keen Iambicks—Summers notes Horace, *Odes*, I, xvi, 24, "in celeres iambos."

the Sillibub—A drink of milk or cream, clotted with wine.

Brisk. Biddy! I'gad very pretty——Deuce take me if your Ladyship has not the Art of Surprizing the most Naturally in the World,——I hope you'll make me happy in Communicating the Poem.

Lady Froth. O, you must be my Confident, I must ask your Advice.

Brisk. I'm your Humble Servant, let me perish.——I presume your Ladyship has Read *Bossu*?

Lady Froth. O yes, and *Rapine*, and *Dacier* upon *Aristotle* and *Horace*.——My Lord you must not be Jealous, I'm Communicating all to Mr. *Brisk*.

Lord Froth. No, no, I'll allow Mr. *Brisk*; have you nothing about you to shew him, my Dear?

Lady Froth. Yes, I believe I have.——Mr. *Brisk*, come will you go into the next Room? and there I'll shew you all I have.

Exit Lady Froth *and* Brisk.

Lord Froth. I'll walk a turn in the Garden, and come to you. *Exit.*

Mellefont. You're thoughtful, *Cynthia*?

Cynthia. I'm thinking, that tho' Marriage makes Man and Wife One Flesh, it leaves 'em still Two Fools; and they become more Conspicuous by setting off one another.

Mellefont. That's only when Two Fools meet, and their follies are oppos'd.

Cynthia. Nay, I have known Two Wits meet, and by the opposition of their Wits, render themselves as ridiculous as Fools. 'Tis an odd Game we're going to Play at: What think you of drawing Stakes, and giving over in time?

Mellefont. No, hang't, that's not endeavouring to Win, because it's possible we may lose; since we have Shuffled and Cutt, let's e'en turn up Trump now.

Cynthia. Then I find its like Cards, if either of us have a good Hand, it is an Accident of Fortune.

Bossu, Rapine, Dacier—The fashionable names among the critics. Le Bossu's *Treatise on the Epic Poem* was being translated; Rapin's *Reflections on Aristotle's Art of Poetry* had been published in English by Tho. Rhymer, 1674; André Dacier's translation of Aristotle's *Art of Poetry* was printed in Amsterdam, 1692, and his essay on satire, in English translation, in Gildon's *Miscellany*, 1692, where Congreve's earliest poems first appeared.

Mellefont. No, Marriage is rather like a Game at Bowls, Fortune indeed makes the match, and the Two nearest, and sometimes the Two farthest are together, but the Game depends entirely upon Judgment.

Cynthia. Still it is a Game, and Consequently one of us must be a Loser.

Mellefont. Not at all; only a Friendly Tryal of Skill, and the Winnings to be Shared between us.———What's here, the Musick!—Oh, my Lord has promised the Company a New Song, we'll get 'em to give it us by the way.

Musicians crossing the Stage.

Pray let us have the Favour of you, to practice the Song, before the Company hear it.

SONG.

I.

Cynthia frowns when e're I Woo her,
Yet she's vext if I give over;
Much she fears I should undo her,
But much more, to lose her Lover:
Thus, in doubting, she refuses;
And not Winning, thus she loses.

II.

Prithee *Cynthia* look behind you,
Age and Wrinckles will o'retake you;
Then too late, desire will find you,
When the power does forsake you:
Think, O think o'th' sad Condition,
To be past, yet wish Fruition.

Mellefont. You shall have my thanks below.

To the Musick, they go out.

Enter Sir Paul Plyant *and* Lady Plyant.

Sir Paul. Gads bud! I am provoked into a Fermentation, as my Lady *Froth* says; was ever the like read of in Story?

Lady Plyant. Sir *Paul* have patience, let me alone to rattle him up.

Song—Sung by Mrs. Ayliff to Purcell's setting.

Sir Paul. Pray your Ladyship give me leave to be Angry—I'll rattle him up I Warrant you, I'll firk him with a *Certiorari.*

Lady Plyant. You firk him, I'll firk him my self; pray Sir *Paul* hold you Contented.

Cynthia. Bless me, what makes my Father in such a Passion!—I never saw him thus before.

Sir Paul. Hold your self Contented, my Lady *Plyant,*———I find Passion coming upon me by inspiration, and I cannot submit as formerly, therefore give way.

Lady Plyant. How now! will you be pleased to retire, and———

Sir Paul. No marry will I not be pleased, I am pleased to be angry, that's my pleasure at this time.

Mellefont. What can this mean!

Lady Plyant. Gads my life, the man's Distracted, why how now, who are you? What am I? 'Slidikins can't I govern you? What did I Marry you for? Am I not to be absolute and uncontroulable? Is it fit a Woman of my Spirit, and Conduct, should be contradicted in a matter of this Concern?

Sir Paul. It concerns me, and only me;—besides, I'm not to be govern'd at all times. When I am in Tranquility, my Lady *Plyant* shall Command Sir *Paul*; but when I am provoked to fury, I cannot incorporate with Patience and Reason,—as soon may Tygers Match with Tygers, Lambs with Lambs, and every Creature couple with its Foe, as the Poet says.—

Lady Plyant. He's hot-headed still! 'Tis in vain to talk to you; but remember I have a Curtain-Lecture for you, you disobedient, headstrong Brute.

Sir Paul. No, 'tis because I won't be headstrong, because I won't be a Brute, and have my Head fortifi'd, that I am thus exasperated,—but I will protect my Honour, and yonder is the Violater of my Fame.

Lady Plyant. 'Tis my Honour that is concern'd, and the violation was intended to me. Your Honour! You have none,

firk—whip.
certiorari—"A Chancery writ to an inferior court to call up the records of a cause," *Glossographia* (1666).

but what is in my keeping, and I can dispose of it when I please—therefore don't provoke me.

Sir Paul. Hum, gads bud she says true,———well, my Lady, March on, I will fight under you then: I am convinced, as far as Passion will permit.

Lady Plyant *and* Sir Paul *come up to* Mellefont.

Lady Plyant. Inhuman and Treacherous.

Sir Paul. Thou Serpent and first Tempter of Womankind.—

Cynthia. Bless me! Sir; Madam; what mean you?

Sir Paul. Thy, Thy, come away *Thy,* touch him not, come hither Girl, go not near him, there's nothing but deceit about him; Snakes are in his Peruke, and the Crocodile of *Nilus* in his Belly, he will eat thee up alive.

Lady Plyant. Dishonourable, impudent Creature!

Mellefont. For Heaven's sake, Madam, to whom do you direct this Language!

Lady Plyant. Have I behaved my self with all the decorum, and nicety, befitting the Person of Sir *Paul's* Wife? Have I preserved my Honour as it were in a Snow-House for this three year past? Have I been white and unsulli'd even by Sir *Paul* himself?

Sir Paul. Nay, she has been an impenetrable Wife, even to me, that's the truth on't.

Lady Plyant. Have I, I say, preserv'd my self, like a fair Sheet of Paper, for you to make a Blot upon———

Sir Paul. And she shall make a Simile with any Woman in *England.*

Mellefont. I am so amazed, I know not what to speak.

Sir Paul. Do you think my Daughter, this pretty Creature; gads bud she's a Wife for a Cherubin! Do you think her fit for nothing but to be a Stalking-Horse, to stand before you, while you take aim at my Wife? Gads bud I was never angry before in my Life, and I'll never be appeased again.

Mellefont (*aside*). Hell and Damnation! this is my Aunt; such malice can be engendred no where else.

Lady Plyant. Sir *Paul*, take *Cynthia* from his sight; leave me to strike him with the remorse of his intended Crime.

Cynthia. Pray, Sir, stay, hear him, I dare affirm he's innocent.

Sir Paul. Innocent! why heark'ee, come hither *Thy*, heark'ee, I had it from his Aunt, my Sister *Touchwood*, ———gadsbud he does not care a Farthing for any thing of thee, but thy Portion, why he's in Love with my Wife; he would have tantalized thee, and made a Cuckold of thy poor Father,—and that would certainly have broke my Heart———I'm sure if ever I should have Horns, they would kill me; they would never come kindly, I should dye of 'em, like any Child, that were cutting his Teeth—I should, indeed, *Thy*———therefore come away; but providence has prevented all, therefore come away, when I bid you.

Cynthia. I must obey.

Exit Sir Paul, *and* Cynthia.

Lady Plyant. O, such a thing! the Impiety of it startles me———to wrong so good, so fair a Creature, and one that lov'd you tenderly———'tis a barbarity of barbarities, and nothing could be guilty of it———

Mellefont. But the greatest Villain imagination can form, I grant it; and next to the Villany of such a fact, is the Villany of aspersing me with the guilt. How? which way was I to wrong her? for yet I understand you not.

Lady Plyant. Why, gads my life, Cousin *Mellefont*, you cannot be so peremptory as to deny it; when I tax you with it to your face; for now Sir *Paul's* gone, you are *Corum Nobus*.

Mellefont. By Heaven, I love her more than life, or—

Lady Plyant. Fiddle, faddle, don't tell me of this and that, and every thing in the World, but give me Mathemacular Demonstration, answer me directly———but I have not patience———oh! the Impiety of it, as I was saying, and the unparallel'd wickedness! O merciful Father! how could you think to reverse Nature so, to make the Daughter the means of procuring the Mother?

Mellefont. The Daughter procure the Mother!

Lady Plyant. Ay, for tho' I am not *Cynthia's* own Mother, I am her Father's Wife; and that's near enough to make it Incest.

Mellefont (*aside*). Incest! O my precious Aunt, and the Devil in Conjunction.

Corum Nobus—Mispronunciation of *coram nobis*, in our Court.

Lady Plyant. O reflect upon the horror of that, and then the guilt of deceiving every body; Marrying the Daughter, only to make a Cuckold of the Father; and then seducing me, debauching my purity, and perverting me from the road of Virtue, in which I have trod thus long, and never made one Trip, not one *faux pas*; O consider it, what would you have to answer for, if you should provoke me to frailty? Alas! Humanity is feeble, Heaven knows! very feeble, and unable to support it self.

Mellefont. Where am I? sure, is it day? and am I awake, Madam?———

Lady Plyant. And no body knows how Circumstances may happen together,———to my thinking, now I could resist the strongest Temptation,———but yet I know, 'tis impossible for me to know whether I could or not, there is no certainty in the things of this life.

Mellefont. Madam, pray give me leave to ask you one question.———

Lady Plyant. O Lord, ask me the question, I'll swear I'll refuse it; I swear I'll deny it,———therefore don't ask me, nay you shan't ask me, I swear I'll deny it. O Gemini, you have brought all the Blood into my face; I warrant, I am as red as a Turky-Cock; O fie, Cousin *Mellefont*!

Mellefont. Nay, Madam, hear me; I mean—

Lady Plyant. Hear you, no, no; I'll deny you first, and hear you afterwards: For one does not know how ones mind may change upon hearing———hearing is one of the Senses, and all the Senses are fallible; I won't trust my Honour, I assure you; my Honour is infallible and uncomatible.

Mellefont. For Heaven's sake, Madam.—

Lady Plyant. O name it no more———bless me, how can you talk of Heaven! and have so much wickedness in your Heart? May be you don't think it a sin,———they say some of you Gentlemen don't think it a sin,———may be it is no sin to them that don't think it so;———indeed, If I did not think it a sin,———but still my honour, if it were no sin,———but then, to Marry my Daughter, for the Conveniency of frequent Opportunities,———I'll never consent to that, as sure as can be, I'll break the Match.

Mellefont. Death and amazement,—Madam, upon my knees.—

Lady Plyant. Nay, nay, rise up, come you shall see my good Nature. I know Love is powerful, and no body can help his passion: 'Tis not your fault; nor I swear it is not mine,—how can I help it, if I have Charms? And how can you help it, if you are made a Captive? I swear it's pity it should be a fault,———but my honour———well, but your honour too———but the sin!———well but the necessity———O Lord, here's some body coming, I dare not stay. Well, you must consider of your Crime; and strive as much as can be against it,—strive be sure———but don't be melancholly, don't despair,———but never think that I'll grant you any thing; O Lord, no,———but be sure you lay aside all thoughts of the Marriage, for tho' I know you don't Love *Cynthia*, only as a blind for your Passion to me; yet it will make me jealous,—O Lord, what did I say? Jealous! no, no, I can't be jealous, for I must not Love you,—therefore don't hope,—but don't despair neither,—O, they're coming, I must fly.

Exit.

Mellefont (*after a pause*). So then,—spight of my care and foresight, I am caught, caught in my security,—yet this was but a shallow artifice, unworthy of my Matchiavilian Aunt: There must be more behind, this is but the first flash, the priming of her Engine; destruction follows hard, if not most presently prevented.

Enter Maskwell.

Maskwell, welcome, thy presence is a view of Land, appearing to my Shipwrack'd hopes: The Witch has rais'd the Storm, and her Ministers have done their Work; you see the Vessels are parted.

Maskwell. I know it; I met Sir *Paul* towing away *Cynthia*: Come, trouble not your head, I'll joyn you together e're to Morrow Morning, or drown between you in the attempt.

Mellefont. There's comfort in a hand stretch'd out, to one that's sinking; tho' ne'er so far off.

Maskwell. No sinking, nor no danger,———come, cheer up; why you don't know, that while I plead for you, your Aunt has given me a retaining Fee;—nay, I am your greatest Enemy, and she does but Journey-Work under me.

Mellefont. Ha! how's this?

Maskwell. What d'e think of my being employ'd in the execution of all her Plots? Ha, ha, ha, by Heaven it's true; I have undertaken to break the Match, I have undertaken to make your Uncle Disinherit you, to get you turn'd out of Doors; and to—ha, ha, ha, I can't tell you for Laughing, —oh she has open'd her heart to me,—I am to turn you a Grazing, and to—ha, ha, ha, Marry *Cynthia* my self; there's a Plot for you.

Mellefont. Ha! O I see, I see my Rising Sun! Light breaks thro' Clouds upon me, and I shall live in Day—O my *Maskwell*! how shall I thank or praise thee; Thou hast outwitted Woman.—But tell me, how could'st thou thus get into her Confidence.—Ha! How? But was it her Contrivance to perswade my Lady *Plyant* to this extravagant belief?

Maskwell. It was, and to tell you the truth, I encouraged it for your diversion: Tho it made you a little uneasy for the present, yet the reflection of it must needs be entertaining. —I warrant she was very Violent at first.

Mellefont. Ha, ha, ha, ay, a very Fury; but I was most afraid of her violence at last,—if you had not come as you did; I don't know what she might have attempted.

Maskwell. Ha, ha, ha, I know her temper,—well, you must know then, that all my Contrivances were but Bubbles; till at last I pretended to have been long Secretly in Love with *Cynthia*; that did my business; that convinced your Aunt, I might be trusted; since it was as much my interest as hers to break the Match: Then she thought my Jealousie might qualifie me to assist her in her Revenge. And, in short, in that belief, told me the Secrets of her heart. At length we made this agreement, if I accomplish her designs (as I told you before) she has ingaged to put *Cynthia* with all her Fortune into my Power.

Mellefont. She is most gracious in her Favour,—well, and dear *Jack*, how hast thou Contrived?

Maskwell. I would not have you stay to hear it now; for I don't know, but she may come this way; I am to meet her anon, after that I'll tell you the whole matter; be here in this Gallery an hour hence, by that time I imagine our Consultation may be over.

Mellefont. I will; till then, success attend thee.

Exit.

Bubbles—Cheats.

Maskwell. Till then, Success will attend me; for when I meet you, I meet the only Obstacle to my Fortune. *Cynthia*, let thy Beauty gild my Crimes; and whatsoever I commit of Treachery or Deceit, shall be imputed to me as a Merit ———Treachery, what Treachery? Love cancels all the Bonds of Friendship, and sets Men right upon their first Foundations.

Duty to Kings, Piety to Parents, Gratitude to Benefactors, and Fidelity to Friends, are different and particular Ties: But the Name of Rival cuts 'em all asunder, and is a general acquittance—Rival is equal, and Love like Death an universal Leveller of Mankind. Ha! but is there not such a thing as Honesty? Yes, and whosoever has it about him, bears an Enemy in his Breast: For your honest man, as I take it, is that nice, scrupulous, conscientious Person, who will cheat no body but himself; such another Coxcomb, as your wise man, who is too hard for all the World, and will be made a Fool of by no body, but himself: Ha, ha, ha. Well for Wisdom and Honesty, give me Cunning and Hypocrisie; oh 'tis such a pleasure, to angle for fair-faced Fools! then that hungry Gudgeon Credulity, will bite at any thing———Why, let me see, I have the same Face, the same Words and Accents, when I speak what I do think; and when I speak what I do not think—the very same—and dear dissimulation is the only Art, not to be known from Nature.

Why will Mankind be Fools, and be deceiv'd?
And why are Friends and Lovers Oaths believ'd;
When each, who searches strictly his own mind,
May so much Fraud and Power of Baseness find?

The End of the Second ACT.

ACT III. Scene I.

Enter Lord Touchwood, *and* Lady Touchwood.

Lady Touchwood. My Lord, can you blame my Brother *Plyant*, if he refuse his Daughter upon this Provocation? The Contract's void by this unheard of Impiety.

Lord Touchwood. I don't believe it true; he has better Principles—Pho, 'tis nonsense. Come, come; I know my Lady

Plyant has a large Eye, and wou'd centre every thing in her own Circle; 'tis not the first time she has mistaken Respect for Love, and made Sir *Paul* jealous of the Civility of an undesigning person, the better to bespeak his security in her unfeigned Pleasures.

Lady Touchwood. You censure hardly, my Lord; my Sister's Honour is very well known.

Lord Touchwood. Yes, I believe I know some that have been familiarly acquainted with it. This is a little Trick wrought by some pitiful Contriver, envious of my Nephew's Merit.

Lady Touchwood. Nay, my Lord, it may be so, and I hope it will be found so: but that will require some time; for in such a Case as this, demonstration is necessary.

Lord Touchwood. There should have been demonstration of the contrary too, before it had been believ'd—

Lady Touchwood. So I suppose there was.

Lord Touchwood. How! Where? When?

Lady Touchwood. That I can't tell: nay, I don't say there was— I am willing to believe as favourably of my Nephew as I can.

Lord Touchwood (*half aside*). I don't know that.

Lady Touchwood. How? Don't you believe that, say you, my Lord?

Lord Touchwood. No, I don't say so—I confess I am troubled to find you so cold in his Defence.

Lady Touchwood. His Defence! bless me, wou'd you have me defend an ill thing?

Lord Touchwood. You believe it then?

Lady Touchwood. I don't know; I am very unwilling to speak my Thoughts in any thing that may be to my Cousin's disadvantage; besides, I find, my Lord, you are prepared to receive an ill impression from any opinion of mine which is not consenting with your own: But since I am like to be suspected in the end, and 'tis a pain any longer to dissemble: I own it to you; in short I do believe it, nay, and can believe any thing worse, if it were laid to his charge ———Don't ask me my Reasons, my Lord, for they are not fit to be told you.

Lord Touchwood (*aside*). I'm amaz'd, here must be something more than ordinary in this.

Not fit to be told me, Madam? You can have no Interests, wherein I am not concern'd, and consequently the same Reasons ought to be convincing to me, which create your satisfaction or disquiet.

Lady Touchwood. But those which cause my disquiet, I am willing to have remote from your hearing. Good my Lord, don't press me.

Lord Touchwood. Don't oblige me to press you.

Lady Touchwood. Whatever it was, 'tis past: And that is better to be unknown which cannot be prevented; therefore let me beg you rest satisfied—

Lord Touchwood. When you have told me, I will—

Lady Touchwood. You won't.

Lord Touchwood. By my Life, my Dear, I will.

Lady Touchwood. What if you can't.

Lord Touchwood. How? Then I must know, nay I will: No more trifling———I charge you tell me———by all our mutual Peace to come; upon your Duty—

Lady Touchwood. Nay, my Lord, you need say no more, to make me lay my heart before you, but don't be thus transported; compose your self: It is not of Concern, to make you lose one minutes temper. 'Tis not indeed, my Dear. Nay, by this kiss you shan't be angry. O Lord, I wish I had not told you any thing.———Indeed, my Lord, you have frighted me. Nay, look pleas'd, I'll tell you.

Lord Touchwood. Well, well.

Lady Touchwood. Nay, but will you be calm—indeed it's nothing but—

Lord Touchwood. But what?

Lady Touchwood. But will you promise me not to be angry ———nay you must———not to be angry with *Mellefont* —I dare swear he's sorry—and were it to do again, would not—

Lord Touchwood. Sorry, for what? 'Death you rack me with delay.

Lady Touchwood. Nay, no great matter, only—well I have your promise—Pho, why nothing, only your Nephew had a mind to amuse himself, sometimes with a little Gallantry towards me. Nay, I can't think he meant any thing seriously, but methought it look'd odly.

Lord Touchwood. Confusion and Hell, what do I hear!

Lady Touchwood. Or, may be, he thought he was not enough a-kin to me, upon your account, and had a mind to create a nearer relation on his own; a Lover you know, my Lord—Ha, ha, ha. Well but that's all———now you have it; well remember your promise, my Lord, and don't take any notice of it to him.

Lord Touchwood. No, no, no———Damnation!

Lady Touchwood. Nay, I swear you must not———a little harmless mirth———only misplac'd that's all—but if it were more, 'tis over now, and all's well. For my part I have forgot it; and so has he, I hope———for I have not heard any thing from him these two days.

Lord Touchwood. These two days! Is it so fresh? Unnatural Villain! 'Death I'll have him stripp'd and turn'd naked out of my doors this moment, and let him rot and perish, incestuous Brute!

Lady Touchwood. O for Heaven's sake, my Lord, you'll ruine me if you take such publick notice of it, it will be a Town-talk: Consider your own and my Honour—nay, I told you you would not be satisfied when you knew it.

Lord Touchwood. Before I've done, I will be satisfied. Ungrateful Monster, how long?—

Lady Touchwood. Lord, I don't know: I wish my Lips had grown together when I told you———almost a Twelve-month—nay, I won't tell you any more, till you are your self. Pray, my Lord, don't let the Company see you in this disorder—Yet, I confess, I can't blame you; for I think I was never so surpriz'd in my Life—Who would have thought my Nephew could have so misconstrued my Kindness—but will you go into your Closet, and recover your Temper. I'll make an excuse of sudden Business to the Company, and come to you. Pray, good dear my Lord, let me beg you do now: I'll come immediately, and tell you all; will you, my Lord?

Lord Touchwood. I will———I am mute with wonder.

Lady Touchwood. Well but go now, here's some body coming.

Lord Touchwood. Well I go———you won't stay, for I would hear more of this.

Exit Lord Touchwood.

Lady Touchwood. I follow instantly———So.

Enter Maskwell.

Maskwell. This was a Master-piece, and did not need my help———tho' I stood ready for a Cue to come in and confirm all, had there been occasion.

Lady Touchwood. Have you seen *Mellefont*?

Maskwell. I have; and am to meet him here about this time.

Lady Touchwood. How does he bear his Disappointment?

Maskwell. Secure in my Assistance, he seem'd not much afflicted, but rather laugh'd at the shallow Artifice, which so little time must of necessity discover. Yet he is apprehensive of some farther design of yours, and has engaged me to watch you. I believe he will hardly be able to prevent your Plot, yet I would have you use Caution and Expedition.

Lady Touchwood. Expedition indeed; for all we do, must be perform'd in the remaining part of this Evening, and before the Company break up; lest my Lord should cool, and have an opportunity to talk with him privately———my Lord must not see him again.

Maskwell. By no means; therefore you must aggravate my Lord's Displeasure to a degree that will admit of no Conference with him.—What think you of mentioning me?

Lady Touchwood. How?

Maskwell. To my Lord, as having been privy to *Mellefont's* design upon you, but still using my utmost Endeavours to dissuade him: Tho' my Friendship and Love to him has made me conceal it; yet you may say, I threatned the next time he attempted any thing of that kind, to discover it to my Lord.

Lady Touchwood. To what end is this?

Maskwell. It will confirm my Lord's opinion of my Honour and Honesty, and create in him a new Confidence in me, which (should this design miscarry) will be necessary to the forming of another Plot that I have in my head—(*aside*) to cheat you, as well as the rest.

Lady Touchwood. I'll do it———I'll tell him you hindred him once from forcing me.

Maskwell. Excellent! your Ladyship has a most improving Fancy. You had best go to my Lord, keep him as long as you can in his Closet, and I doubt not but you will mould him to what you please; your Guests are so engaged in their own Follies and Intrigues, they'll miss neither of you.

Lady Touchwood. When shall we meet?———at eight this Evening in my Chamber; there rejoice at our success, and toy away an hour in mirth.

Maskwell. I will not fail.

Exit Lady Touchwood.

I know what she means by toying away an hour well enough. Pox I have lost all Appetite to her; yet she's a fine Woman, and I lov'd her once. But I don't know, since I have been in a great measure kept by her, the case is alter'd; what was my Pleasure is become my Duty: And I have as little stomach to her now as if I were her Husband. Should she smoke my design upon *Cynthia*, I were in a fine pickle. She has a damn'd penetrating head, and knows how to interpret a Coldness the right way; therefore I must dissemble Ardour and Ecstasie, that's resolv'd: How easily and pleasantly is that dissembled before Fruition! Pox on't that a Man can't drink without quenching his Thirst. Ha! yonder comes *Mellefont* thoughtful. Let me think: Meet her at eight———hum———ha! by Heaven I have it———' if I can speak to my Lord before———Was it my Brain or Providence? No Matter which———I will deceive 'em all, and yet secure my self, 'twas a lucky thought! Well this Double-Dealing is a Jewel.

Maskwell *pretending not to see him, walks by him, and speaks as it were to himself.*

Here he comes, now for me—

Enter Mellefont *musing.*

Mercy on us, What will the Wickedness of this World come to?

Mellefont. How now, *Jack*? What, so full of Contemplation that you run over!

Double-Dealing is a Jewel—A proverbial form; cf. "Learning is a Jewel," Thomas Nashe, *Works*, III, 388, 11.

Maskwell. I'm glad you're come, for I could not contain my self any longer: and was just going to give vent to a Secret, which no body but you ought to drink down. Your Aunt's just gone from hence.

Mellefont. And having trusted thee with the Secrets of her Soul, thou art villainously bent to discover all to me, ha?

Maskwell. I'm afraid my frailty leans that way—but I don't know whether I can in honour discover all.

Mellefont. All, all man, what you may in honour betray her as far as she betrays her self. No tragical design upon my Person I hope.

Maskwell. No, but it's a Comical design upon mine.

Mellefont. What dost thou mean?

Maskwell. Listen, and be dumb, we have been bargaining about the rate of your ruine—

Mellefont. Like any two Guardians to an Orphan Heiress—well.

Maskwell. And whereas pleasure is generally paid with mischief, what mischief I shall do, is to be paid with Pleasure.

Mellefont. So when you've swallow'd the Potion, you sweeten your mouth with a plumb.

Maskwell. You are merry, Sir, but I shall probe your Constitution. In short, the price of your Banishment is to be paid with the Person of—

Mellefont. Of *Cynthia*, and her Fortune———Why you forget you told me this before.

Maskwell. No, no———so far you are right, and I am, as an earnest of that Bargain, to have full and free possession of the person of—your Aunt.

Mellefont. Ha!———Pho, you trifle.

Maskwell. By this Light, I'm serious; all raillery apart——— I knew 'twould stun you: This Evening at eight she will receive me in her Bed-Chamber.

Mellefont. Hell and the Devil, is she abandon'd of all Grace—Why the Woman is possess'd—

Maskwell. Well, will you go in my stead?

Mellefont. By Heav'n into a hot Furnace sooner.

Maskwell. No, you would not—it would not be so convenient, as I can order Matters.

Mellefont. What d'ye mean?

Maskwell. Mean? Not to disappoint the Lady I assure you—Ha, ha, ha, how gravely he looks———Come, come, I won't perplex you. 'Tis the only thing that Providence could have contriv'd to make me capable of serving you, either to my Inclination or your own necessity—

Mellefont. How, how, for Heaven's sake, dear *Maskwell*?

Maskwell. Why thus———I'll go according to Appointment; you shall have notice at the critical minute to come and surprize your Aunt and me together: Counterfeit a rage against me, and I'll make my escape through the private passage from her Chamber, which I'll take care to leave open: 'twill be hard, if then you can't bring her to any Conditions. For this Discovery will disarm her of all Defence, and leave her entirely at your Mercy: nay, she must ever after be in awe of you.

Mellefont. Let me adore thee, my better *Genius*! By Heav'n I think it is not in the power of Fate to disappoint my hopes—my hopes, my certainty!

Maskwell. Well, I'll meet you here, within a quarter of eight, and give you notice.

Mellefont. Good Fortune ever go along with thee.

Enter to him Careless.

Careless. Mellefont, get out o'th' way, my Lady *Plyant's* coming, and I shall never succeed while thou art in sight—tho' she begins to tack about; but I made Love a great while to no purpose.

Mellefont. Why, what's the Matter? She's convinc'd that I don't care for her.

Careless. 'Pox I can't get an Answer from her, that does not begin with her Honour, or her Vertue, her Religion, or some such Cant. Then she has told me the whole History of Sir *Paul's* nine years Courtship; how he has lain for whole nights together upon the Stairs, before her Chamber-door; and that the first Favour he receiv'd from her, was a piece of an old Scarlet Petticoat for a Stomacher; which, since the day of his Marriage, he has, out of a piece of Gallantry, converted into a Night-Cap, and wears it still with much Solemnity on his anniversary Wedding-night.

Mellefont. That I have seen, with the Ceremony thereunto belonging—for on that night he creeps in at the Bed's Feet like a gull'd Bassa that has married a Relation of the *Grand Signior's*, and that night he has his arms at liberty. Did not she tell you at what a distance she keeps him. He has confess'd to me that but at some certain times, that is I suppose when she apprehends being with Child, he never has the privilege of using the familiarity of a Husband with his Wife. He was once given to scrambling with his hands and sprawling in his Sleep; and ever since she has him swaddled up in Blankets, and his hands and feet swath'd down, and so put to bed; and there he lies with a great Beard, like a *Russian* Bear upon a drift of Snow. You are very great with him, I wonder he never told you his Grievances, he will I warrant you.

Careless. Excessively foolish—But that which gives me most hopes of her, is her telling me of the many Temptations she has resisted.

Mellefont. Nay, then you have her; for a woman's bragging to a man that she has overcome Temptations, is an argument that they were weakly offered, and a challenge to him to engage her more irresistably. 'Tis only an inhancing the price of the Commodity, by telling you how many Customers have underbid her.

Careless. Nay, I don't despair—but still she has a grudging to you—I talk'd to her t'other night at my Lord *Froth's* Masquerade, when I'm satisfied she knew me, and I had no reason to complain of my Reception; but I find women are not the same bare-faced and in Masks,—and a Vizor disguises their Inclinations as much as their Faces.

Mellefont. 'Tis a mistake, for women may most properly be said to be unmask'd when they wear Vizors; for that secures them from blushing, and being out of Countenance, and next to being in the dark, or alone, they are most truly themselves in a Vizor Mask. Here they come, I'll leave you. Ply her close, and by and by clap a *Billet doux* into her

gull'd Bassa . . . Signior—The story of the marriage of a Pashaw with a Soltana—when the Grand Signior fears he is growing too powerful, and so subjects him to the humiliation and spoliations of a marriage with one of the Signior's kindred—is told in Rycaut's *History of the Ottoman Empire*, 5th ed. (1682), pp. 132–33.

hand: For a woman never thinks a man truly in love with her, till he has been fool enough to think of her out of her sight, and to lose so much time as to write to her.

Exit.

Enter Sir Paul *and* Lady Plyant.

Sir Paul. Shan't we disturb your Meditation, Mr. *Careless*: you wou'd be private?

Careless. You bring that along with you, Sir *Paul*, that shall be always welcome to my privacy.

Sir Paul. O, sweet Sir, you load your humble Servants, both me and my Wife, with continual Favours.

Lady Plyant. Jesu, Sir *Paul*, what a Phrase was there? You will be making Answers, and taking that upon you, which ought to lie upon me: That you should have so little breeding to think Mr. *Careless* did not apply himself to me. Pray what have you about you to entertain any bodies privacy? I swear and declare in the face of the World I'm ready to blush for your Ignorance.

Sir Paul (*aside to her*). I acquiesce, my Lady; but don't snub so loud.

Lady Plyant. Mr. *Careless*, If a person that is wholly illiterate might be supposed to be capable of being qualified to make a suitable return to those Obligations which you are pleased to conferr upon one that is wholly incapable of being qualified in all those Circumstances, I'm sure I should rather attempt it than any thing in the World, (*Curtesies*) for I'm sure there's nothing in the World that I would rather. (*Curtesies*). But I know Mr. *Careless* is so great a Critick and so fine a Gentleman, that it is impossible for me—

Careless. O Heavens! Madam, you confound me.

Sir Paul. Gad's bud, she's a fine person—

Lady Plyant. O Lord! Sir, pardon me, we women have not those Advantages: I know my own Imperfections———but at the same time you must give me leave to declare in the face of the World that no body is more sensible of Favours and Things; for with the Reserve of my Honour, I assure you, Mr. *Careless* I don't know any thing in the World I would refuse to a person so meritorious———you'll pardon my want of Expression———

Careless. O your Ladyship is abounding in all Excellence, particularly that of Phrase.

Lady Plyant. You are so obliging, Sir.

Careless. Your Ladyship is so charming.

Sir Paul. So, now, now; now my Lady.

Lady Plyant. So well bred.

Careless. So surprizing.

Lady Plyant. So well drest, so boon mein, so eloquent, so unaffected, so easie, so free, so particular, so agreeable—

Sir Paul. Ay, so so, there.

Careless. O Lord, I beseech you, Madam, don't—

Lady Plyant. So gay, so graceful, so good teeth, so fine shape, so fine limbs, so fine linen, and I don't doubt but you have a very good skin, Sir.

Careless. For Heaven's sake, Madam—I'm quite out of Countenance.

Sir Paul. And my Lady's quite out of Breath; or else you should hear———Gad's bud, you may talk of my Lady *Froth*.

Careless. O fie, fie, not to be named of a day—my Lady *Froth* is very well in her Accomplishments—but it is when my Lady *Plyant* is not thought of—if that can ever be.

Lady Plyant. O you overcome me—that is so excessive—

Sir Paul. Nay, I swear and vow that was pretty.

Careless. O, Sir *Paul*, you are the happiest man alive. Such a Lady! that is the envy of her Sex, and the admiration of ours.

Sir Paul. Your humble Servant, I am I thank Heaven in a fine way of living, as I may say, peacefully and happily, and I think need not envy any of my Neighbours, blessed be Providence—ay, truly, Mr. *Careless*, my Lady is a great Blessing, a fine, discreet, well-spoken woman as you shall see—if it becomes me to say so; and we live very comfortably together; she's a little hasty sometimes, and so am I; but mine's soon over, and then I'm so sorry—O, Mr. *Careless*, if it were not for one thing—

Enter Boy with a Letter, carries it to Sir Paul.

Lady Plyant. How often have you been told of that you Jack-a-napes?

Sir Paul. Gad so, gad's bud—*Tim*, carry it to my Lady, you should have carry'd it to my Lady first.

Boy. 'Tis directed to your Worship.

Sir Paul. Well, well, my Lady reads all Letters first—Child, do so no more; d'ye hear, *Tim*?

Boy. No, an please you.

Carries the Letter to my Lady and Exit.

Sir Paul. A humour of my wife's, you know women have little fancies—But as I was telling you, Mr. *Careless*, if it were not for one thing, I should think my self the happiest man in the World; indeed that touches me near, very near.

Careless. What can that be, Sir *Paul*?

Sir Paul. Why, I have, I thank Heaven, a very plentiful Fortune, a good Estate in the Country, some houses in Town, and some money, a pretty tolerable personal Estate; and it is a great grief to me, indeed it is Mr. *Careless*, that I have not a Son to inherit this———'Tis true I have a Daughter, and a fine dutiful Child she is, though I say it, blessed be Providence I may say; for indeed, Mr. *Careless*, I am mightily beholding to Providence———a poor unworthy Sinner———But if I had a Son, ah, that's my affliction, and my only affliction; indeed I cannot refrain Tears when it comes in my mind.

Cries.

Careless. Why, methinks that might be easily remedied—my Lady's a fine likely Woman—

Sir Paul. Oh, a fine likely Woman as you shall see in a Summers-day———indeed she is, Mr. *Careless*, in all respects.

Careless. And I should not have taken you to have been so old—

Sir Paul. Alas, that's not it, Mr. *Careless*; ah! that's not it; no, no, you shoot wide of the mark a mile; indeed you do, that's not it, Mr. *Careless*; no, no, that's not it.

Careless. No, what can be the matter then?

Sir Paul. You'll scarcely believe me, when I shall tell you—my Lady is so nice———it's very strange, but it's true: too true—she's so very nice, that I don't believe she would touch a Man for the World—at least not above once a year; I'm sure I have found it so; and alas, what's once a year to an Old Man, who would do good in his Generation? indeed it's true, Mr. *Careless*, it breaks my heart—I am her Husband, as I may say, though far unworthy of that honour, yet I am her Husband; but alas-a-day, I have no more familiarity with her Person—as to that matter—than with my own Mother—no indeed.

Careless. Alas-a-day, this is a lamentable story; my Lady must be told on't; she must i'faith, Sir *Paul*; 'tis an injury to the World.

Sir Paul. Ah! would to Heav'n you would, Mr. *Careless*; you are mightily in her favour.

Careless. I warrant you, what we must have a Son some way or other.

Sir Paul. Indeed, I should be mightily bound to you, if you could bring it about, Mr. *Careless*....

Lady Plyant. Here, Sir *Paul*, it's from your Steward, here's a return of 600 Pounds; you may take fifty of it for your next half year.

Gives him the Letter.

Enter Lord Froth, Cynthia.

Sir Paul. How does my Girl? come hither to thy Father, poor Lamb, thou'rt melancholy.

Lord Froth. Heav'n, Sir *Paul*, you amaze me, of all things in the World—you are never pleased but when we are all upon the broad grin, all laugh and no Company; ah, then 'tis such a sight to see some teeth—sure you're a great admirer of my Lady *Whifler*, Mr. *Sneer*, and Sir *Laurence Loud*, and that gang.

Sir Paul. I vow and swear she's a very merry Woman, but I think she laughs a little too much.

Lord Froth. Merry! O Lord, what a character that is of a Woman of Quality—you have been at my Lady *Whifler*'s upon her day, Madam?

Cynthia. Yes, my Lord—(*aside*) I must humour this Fool.

Lord Froth. Well and how? hee! what is your sense of the Conversation there?

Cynthia. O most ridiculous, a perpetual consort of laughing without any harmony; for sure, my Lord, to laugh out of time, is as disagreeable as to sing out of time or out of tune.

Lord Froth. Hee, hee, hee, right; and then my Lady *Whifler* is so ready—she always comes in three bars too soon—and then, what do they laugh at? For you know laughing without a jest is as impertinent; hee! as, as—

Cynthia. As dancing without a Fiddle.

Lord Froth. Just 'ifaith, that was at my tongues end.

Cynthia. But that cannot be properly said of them, for I think they are all in good nature with the World, and only laugh at one another; and you must allow they have all jests in their Persons, though they have none in their Conversation.

Lord Froth. True, as I'm a Person of Honour—for Heaven's sake let us sacrifice 'em to mirth a little.

Enter Boy *and whispers* Sir Paul.

Sir Paul. 'Gads so—Wife, Wife, my Lady *Plyant*, I have a word.

Lady Plyant. I'm busie, Sir *Paul*, I wonder at your impertinence—

Careless. Sir *Paul*, harkee, I'm reasoning the matter you know; Madam,—if your Ladyship please, we'll discourse of this in the next Room.

Exit Careless *and* Lady Plyant.

Sir Paul. O ho, I wish you good success, I wish you good success. Boy, tell my Lady, when she has done, I would speak with her below.

Exit Sir Paul.

Enter Lady Froth *and* Brisk.

Lady Froth. Then you think that *Episode* between *Susan*, the Dairymaid, and our Coach-man is not amiss; you know, I may suppose the Dairy in Town, as well as in the Country.

Brisk. Incomparable, let me perish—but then being an Heroick Poem, had not you better call him a *Charioteer*? *Charioteer* sounds great; besides your Ladyship's Coach-man having a

consort—A group of instruments or singers.

red face, and you comparing him to the Sun—and you know the Sun is call'd *Heav'ns Charioteer.*

Lady Froth. Oh, infinitely better; I'm extremely beholding to you for the hint, stay we'll read over those half a score lines again (*pulls out a Paper.*) Let me see here, you know what goes before, the comparison, you know.

Reads.

For as the Sun shines every day,
So of our Coach-man I may say.

Brisk. I'm afraid that simile wont do in wet Weather—because you say the Sun shines every day.

Lady Froth. No, for the Sun it wont, but it will do for the Coachman, for you know there's most occasion for a Coach in wet Weather.

Brisk. Right, right, that saves all.

Lady Froth. Then I don't say the Sun shines all the day, but, that he peeps now and then, yet he does shine all the day too, you know, tho' we don't see him.

Brisk. Right, but the vulgar will never comprehend that.

Lady Froth. Well you shall hear—let me see.

Reads.

For as the Sun shines every day,
So, of our Coach-man I may say,
He shows his drunken fiery Face,
Just as the Sun does, more or less.

Brisk. That's right, all's well, all's well.

Lady Froth (*reads*).

And when at night his labour's done,
Then too like Heav'ns Charioteer, the Sun:

Ay, *Charioteer* does better.

Into the Dairy he descends,
And there his whipping and his driving ends;
There he's secure from danger of a bilk,
His fare is paid him, and he sets in Milk.

For *Susan*, you know, is *Thetis*, and so—

Brisk. Incomparable well and proper, Igad—but I have one exception to make.———don't you think *bilk* (I know its

Thetis—A Nereid, who was given by the gods to Peleus, and who bore him a son, Achilles.

good Rhime) but don't you think *bilk* and *fare* too like a Hackney Coach-man?

Lady Froth. I swear and vow I'm afraid so——And yet our *Jehu* was a Hackney Coach-man, when my Lord took him.

Brisk. Was that he then, I'm answered, if *Jehu* was a Hackney Coach-man—you may put that into the marginal Notes, tho' to prevent Criticisms—only mark it with a small asterism, and say,—*Jehu* was formerly a Hackney Coach-man.

Lady Froth. I will; you'd oblige me extremely to write Notes to the whole Poem.

Brisk. With all my Heart and Soul, and proud of the vast honour, let me perish.

Lord Froth. Hee, hee, hee, my Dear, have you done——wont you joyn with us, we were laughing at my Lady *Whifler*, and Mr. *Sneer*.

Lady Froth.—Ay my Dear—were you? Oh filthy Mr. *Sneer*; he's a nauseous figure, a most fulsamick Fop, Foh—he spent two days together in going about *Covent-Garden* to suit the lining of his Coach with his complexion.

Lord Froth. O silly! yet his Aunt is as fond of him, as if she had brought the Ape into the World her self.

Brisk. Who, my Lady *Toothless*; O, she's a mortifying Spectacle; she's always chewing the Cud like an old *Yew*.

Cynthia. Fie Mr. *Brisk*, 'tis *Eringo's* for her Cough.

Lady Froth. I have seen her take 'em half chew'd out of her Mouth, to Laugh, and then put 'em in again—Foh.

Lord Froth. Foh.

Lady Froth. Then she's always ready to Laugh when *Sneer* offers to speak—And sits in expectation of his no Jest, with her Gums bare, and her Mouth open.—

Brisk. Like an Oyster at low Ebb, I'gad——ha, ha, ha.

Cynthia (*aside*). Well, I find there are no Fools so inconsiderable in themselves, but they can render other People contemptible in exposing their Infirmities.

fulsamick—Wearisome or in bad taste.
Eringo—An aphrodisiac, made from a herb of that name which grows by the sea.

Lady Froth. Then that t'other great strapping Lady———I can't hit of her Name; the old fat Fool that Paints so exorbitantly.

Brisk. I know whom you mean———But Deuce take me, I can't hit of her Name neither———Paints de'e say? Why she lays it on with a Trowel———Then she has a great Beard that bristles through it, and makes her look as if she were plaistred with Lime and Hair, let me perish.

Lady Froth. Oh you made a Song upon her, Mr. *Brisk.*

Brisk. He? e'gad, so I did———My Lord can sing it.

Cynthia. O good my Lord let's hear it.

Brisk. 'Tis not a Song neither—it's a sort of an Epigram, or rather an Epigrammatick Sonnet; I don't know what to call it, but it's Satyr.—Sing it my Lord.

SONG.

Lord Froth (*sings*).

Ancient *Phillis* has young Graces,
'Tis a strange thing, but a true one;
Shall I tell you now?
She her self makes her own Faces,
And each Morning wears a new one;
Where's the Wonder now?

Brisk. Short, but there's Salt in't, my way of writing I'gad.

Enter Footman.

Lady Froth. How now?

Footman. Your Ladiships Chair is come.

Lady Froth. Is Nurse and the Child in it?

Footman. Yes, Madam.

Lady Froth. O the dear Creature! Let's go see it.

Lord Froth. I swear, my Dear, you'll spoil that Child, with sending it to and again so often, this is the seventh time the Chair has gone for her to Day.

Lady Froth. O-law, I swear it's but the sixth,—and I han't seen her these two hours.———The poor dear Creature

Song—Set and sung by John Bowman, a good singer, who played the part of Lord Froth.

———I swear, my Lord, you don't Love poor little *Sapho* ———Come, my dear *Cynthia*, Mr. *Brisk*, we'll go see *Sapho*, tho' my Lord wont.

Cynthia. I'll wait upon your Ladiship.

Brisk. Pray, Madam, how old is Lady *Sapho*?

Lady Froth. Three Quarters, but I swear she has a World of Wit, and can sing a Tune already. My Lord wont you go? Wont you? What not to see *Saph*? Pray, My Lord, come see little *Saph*. I knew you cou'd not stay.

Exeunt.

Cynthia. 'Tis not so hard to counterfeit Joy in the depth of Affliction, as to dissemble Mirth in Company of Fools— Why should I call 'em Fools? The World thinks better of 'em; for these have Quality and Education, Wit and fine Conversation are receiv'd and admir'd by the World——— If not, they like and admire themselves———And why is not that true Wisdom, for 'tis Happiness: And for ought I know, we have misapply'd the Name all this while, and mistaken the thing: Since

If Happiness in Self-content is plac'd,
The Wise are Wretched, and Fools only Bless'd.

Exit.

The End of the Third ACT.

ACT IV. SCENE I.

Enter Mellefont *and* Cynthia.

Cynthia. I heard him loud as I came by the Closet-Door, and my Lady with him, but she seem'd to moderate his Passion.

Mellefont. Ay, Hell thank her, as gentle breezes moderate a fire; but I shall counter-work her Spells, and ride the Witch in her own Bridle.

Cynthia. It's impossible; she'll cast beyond you still———I'll lay my Life it will never be a Match.

Mellefont. What?

ride the Witch—Mall Spencer, the witch in Shadwell's *Lancashire Witches*—a very popular play revived with music by Eccles in 1691—puts a bridle on Clod and rides him off the stage.

Cynthia. Between you and me.

Mellefont. Why so?

Cynthia. My Mind gives me it wont———because we are both so willing; we each of us strive to reach the Gole, and hinder one another in the Race; I swear it never do's well when the Parties are so agreed———for when People walk hand in hand, there's neither overtaking nor meeting: We Hunt in Couples where we both pursue the same Game, but forget one another; and 'tis because we are so near that we don't think of coming together.

Mellefont. Hum, 'gad I believe there's something in't;——— Marriage is the Game that we Hunt, and while we think that we only have it in view, I don't see but we have it in our power.

Cynthia. Within reach; for example, give me your hand; why have you look'd through the wrong end of the Perspective all this while; for nothing has been between us but our fears.

Mellefont. I don't know why we should not steal out of the House this moment and Marry one another, without Consideration or the fear of Repentance. Pox o'Fortune, Portion, Settlements and Joyntures.

Cynthia. Ay, ay, what have we to do with 'em; you know we Marry for Love.

Mellefont. Love, Love, down right very Villanous Love.

Cynthia. And he that can't live upon Love, deserves to die in a Ditch—Here then, I give you my promise, in spight of Duty, any temptation of Wealth, your inconstancy, or my own inclination to change—

Mellefont. To run most wilfully and unreasonably away with me this moment and be Married.

Cynthia. Hold———Never to Marry any Body else.

Mellefont. That's but a kind of Negative Consent.———Why, you wont baulk the Frollick?

Cynthia. If you had not been so assured of your own Conduct I would not———But 'tis but reasonable that since I consent to like a Man without the vile Consideration of Money, He should give me a very evident demonstration of his Wit: Therefore let me see you undermine my Lady

Touchwood, as you boasted, and force her to give her Consent, and then—

Mellefont. I'll do't.

Cynthia. And I'll do't.

Mellefont. This very next ensuing hour of Eight a Clock, is the last Minute of her Reign, unless the Devil assist her in *propria persona*.

Cynthia. Well, if the Devil should assist her, and your Plot miscarry—

Mellefont. Ay, what am I to trust to then?

Cynthia. Why if you give me very clear demonstration that it was the Devil, I'll allow for irresistable odds. But if I find it to be only chance, or destiny, or unlucky Stars, or any thing but the very Devil, I'm inexorable: Only still I'll keep my word, and live a Maid for your sake.

Mellefont. And you won't die one, for your own, so still there's hope.

Cynthia. Here's my Mother-in-Law, and your Friend *Careless*, I would not have 'em see us together yet.

Exeunt.

Enter Careless *and* Lady Plyant.

Lady Plyant. I swear, Mr. *Careless*, you are very alluring— And say so many fine things, and nothing is so moving to me as a fine thing. Well, I must do you this justice, and declare in the face of the World, never any body gain'd so far upon me as your self, with Blushes I must own it, you have shaken, as I may say, the very foundation of my Honour———Well, sure if I escape your Importunities, I shall value my self as long as I live, I swear.

Careless (*Sighing*). And Despise me.

Lady Plyant. The last of any Man in the World, by my purity; now you make me swear———O Gratitude forbid, that I should ever be wanting in a respectful acknowledgment of an intire resignation of all my best Wishes, for the Person and Parts of so accomplish'd a Person, whose Merit challenges much more, I'm sure, than my illiterate Praises can description.

Careless (*in a Whining Tone*). Ah Heavens, Madam, you ruine me with Kindness; your Charming Tongue pursues the Victory of your Eyes, while at your Feet your poor Adorer dies.

Lady Plyant. Ah! Very fine.

Careless (*Still Whining*). Ah why are you so Fair, so bewitching Fair? O let me grow to the ground here, and feast upon that hand; O let me press it to my heart, my aking trembling heart, the nimble movement shall instruct your Pulse, and teach it to allarm Desire. (*Aside.*) Zoons I'm almost at the end of my Cant, if she does not yield quickly.

Lady Plyant. O that's so passionate and fine, I cannot hear it —I am not safe if I stay, and must leave you.

Careless. And must you leave me! Rather let me Languish out a Wretched Life, and breath my Soul beneath your Feet. (*Aside.*) I must say the same thing over again, and can't help it.

Lady Plyant. I swear I am ready to Languish too———O my Honour! Whither is it going? I protest you have given me the Palpitation of the Heart.

Careless. Can you be so cruel.—

Lady Plyant. O rise I beseech you, say no more till you rise ———Why did you kneel so long? I swear I was so transported, I did not see it.———Well, to shew you how far you have gain'd upon me; I assure you if Sir *Paul* should die, of all Mankind there's none I'd sooner make my second choice.

Careless. O Heaven! I can't out-live this Night without your favour———I feel my Spirits faint, a general dampness overspreads my face, a cold deadly dew already vents through all my Pores, and will to Morrow wash me for ever from your sight, and drown me in my Tomb.

Lady Plyant. O you have Conquered, sweet, melting, moving Sir, you have Conquered———What heart of Marble can refrain to weep and yield to such sad Sayings.—

Cries.

Careless. I thank Heav'n, they are the saddest that I ever said—Oh! (*Aside.*) I shall never contain Laughter.

Lady Plyant. Oh, I yield my self all up to your uncontroulable Embraces———Say, thou dear dying Man, when, where, and how———Ah, there's Sir *Paul.*

Enter Sir Paul *and* Cynthia.

Careless. 'Slife yonder's Sir *Paul*, but if he were not come, I'm so transported I cannot speak———This Note will inform you. (*Gives her a Note*)

Exit.

Sir Paul. Thou art my tender Lambkin, and shalt do what thou wilt—But endeavour to forget this *Mellefont*.

Cynthia. I would obey you to my power, Sir; but if I have not him, I have sworn never to Marry.

Sir Paul. Never to Marry! Heaven forbid; must I neither have Sons nor Grandsons? Must the Family of the *Plyants* be utterly extinct for want of Issue Male. Oh Impiety! But did you swear, did that sweet Creature swear! ha? How durst you swear without my Consent, ha? Gads-bud, who am I?

Cynthia. Pray don't be angry, Sir, when I swore, I had your Consent; and therefore I swore.

Sir Paul. Why then the revoking my Consent does annul, or make of none effect your Oath: So you may unswear it again———The Law will allow it.

Cynthia. Ay, but my Conscience never will.

Sir Paul. Gads-bud no matter for that, Conscience and Law never go together; you must not expect that.

Lady Plyant. Ay, but *Sir Paul*, I conceive if she has sworn, d'ye mark me, if she has once sworn: It is most unchristian inhumane, and obscene that she should break it. (*Aside.*) I'll make up this Match again, because Mr. *Careless* said it would oblige him.

Sir Paul. Does your Ladiship conceive so—Why I was of that Opinion once too—Nay if your Ladiship conceives so, I'm of that Opinion again; but I can neither find my Lord nor my Lady to know what they intend.

Lady Plyant. I'm satisfied that my Cousin *Mellefont* has been much wrong'd.

Cynthia (*aside*). I'm amazed to find her of our side, for I'm sure she lov'd him.

Lady Plyant. I know my Lady *Touchwood* has no kindness for him; and besides, I have been inform'd by Mr. *Careless*, that *Mellefont* had never any thing more than a profound respect——That he has own'd himself to be my Admirer 'tis true, but he never was so presumptuous to entertain any dishonourable Notions of things; so that if this be made plain——I don't see how my Daughter can in Conscience, or Honour, or any thing in the World.——

Sir Paul. Indeed if this be made plain, as my Lady your Mother says Child—

Lady Plyant. Plain! I was inform'd of it by Mr. *Careless*—— And I assure you Mr. *Careless* is a Person——that has a most extraordinary respect and honour for you, Sir *Paul.*

Cynthia (*aside*). And for your Ladiship too, I believe, or else you had not chang'd sides so soon; now I begin to find it.

Sir Paul. I am much obliged to Mr. *Careless* really, he is a Person that I have a great value for not only for that, but because he has a great veneration for your Ladiship.

Lady Plyant. O las, no indeed, Sir *Paul,* 'tis upon your account.

Sir Paul. No I protest and vow, I have no title to his esteem, but in having the honour, to appertain in some measure, to your Ladyship, that's all.

Lady Plyant. O law now, I swear and declare, it shan't be so, you'r too modest, Sir *Paul.*

Sir Paul. It becomes me, when there is any comparison made, between—

Lady Plyant. O fy, fy, Sir *Paul,* you'l put me out of Countenance—Your very obedient and affectionate Wife; that's all—and highly honoured in that Title.

Sir Paul. Gads bud, I am transported! give me leave to kiss your Ladiships Hand.

Cynthia (*aside*). That my poor Father, should be so very silly.

Lady Plyant. My Lip indeed, Sir *Paul,* I swear you shall.

He kisses her, and bows very low.

Sir Paul. I humbly thank your Ladiship——I don't know whether I fly on Ground, or walk in Air—Gads bud, she was never thus before——Well, I must own my self the most beholden to Mr. *Careless*——As sure as can be this is all his doings——something that he has said; Well, 'tis a rare thing to have an ingenious Friend. Well, your Ladiship is of opinion that the Match may go forward.

Lady Plyant. By all means—Mr. *Careless* has satisfied me of the matter.

Sir Paul. Well, why then Lamb you may keep your Oath, but have a care of making rash Vows; Come hither to me, and kiss *Papa.*

Lady Plyant. I swear and declare, I am in such a twitter to read Mr. *Careless* his Letter, that I can't forbear any longer —but though I may read all Letters first by Prerogative, yet I'll be sure to be unsuspected this time.—Sir *Paul.*

Sir Paul. Did your Ladiship call?

Lady Plyant. Nay, not to interrupt you my Dear———only lend me your Letter, which you had from your Steward to day: I would look upon the Account again; and may be increase your Allowance.

Sir Plyant. There it is, Madam; Do you want a Pen and Ink?
Bows and gives the Letter.

Lady Plyant. No, no, nothing else I thank you, Sir *Paul,*— (*Aside.*) So now I can read my own Letter under the cover of his.

Sir Paul. He? And wilt thou bring a Grandson at 9 Months end—He? A brave Chopping Boy.—I'll settle a Thousand pound a Year upon the Rogue as soon as ever he looks me in the Face, I will Gads-bud. I'm overjoy'd to think I have any of my Family that will bring Children into the World. For I would fain have some resemblance of my self in my Posterity, he *Thy*? Can't you contrive that affair Girl? Do gads-bud, think on thy old Father; Heh? Make the young Rogue as like as you can.

Cynthia. I'm glad to see you so merry, Sir.

Sir Paul. Merry, Gads-bud I'm serious, I'll give thee 500*l.* for every inch of him that resembles me; ah this Eye, this Left Eye! A 1000 *l.* for this Left Eye. This has done Execution in its time Girl; why thou hast my Leer Hussey, just thy Father's Leer.———Let it be transmitted to the young Rogue by the help of imagination; why, 'tis the mark of our Family *Thy*; our House is distinguished by a Languishing Eye, as the House of *Austria* is by a thick Lip.

House of Austria . . . by a thick Lip—Cf. Jonson's jokes in the *Alchemist*, IV, i, 56. Simpson quotes Howell, *Familiar Letters*, I, 3, ix: "held a Beauty, rather than a Blemish, or any excess, in the Austrian Family; it being a thing incident to most of the Race."

———Ah! when I was of your Age Hussy, I would have held fifty to one, I could have drawn my own Picture ———Gads-bud I could have done—not so much as you neither,—but—Nay, don't Blush———

Cynthia. I don't Blush Sir, for I vow I don't understand.—

Sir Paul. Pshaw, Pshaw, you fib you Baggage, you do understand, and you shall understand, come don't be so nice, Gads-bud don't learn after your Mother-in-Law my Lady here: Marry Heaven forbid that you should follow her Example, that would spoil all indeed. Bless us, if you should take a Vagarie and make a rash Resolution on your Wedding Night, to die a Maid; as she did; all were ruin'd, all my hopes lost———My Heart would break, and my Estate would be left to the wide World, he? I hope you are a better Christian than to think of being a Nun; he? Answer me?

Cynthia. I'm all Obedience, Sir, to your Commands.

Lady Plyant (*Having read the Letter*). O dear Mr. *Careless*, I swear he writes charmingly, and he talks charmingly, and he looks charmingly, and he has charm'd me, as much as I have charm'd him; and so I'll tell him in the Wardrobe when 'tis Dark. O Crimine! I hope, Sir *Paul* has not seen both Letters.—(*Puts the wrong Letter hastily up, and gives him her own*), Sir *Paul*, here's your Letter, to Morrow Morning I'll settle the Accounts to your Advantage.

Enter Brisk.

Brisk. Sir *Paul*, Gads-bud you're an uncivil Person, let me tell you, and all that; and I did not think it had been in you.

Sir Paul. O Law, what's the matter now? I hope you are not angry, Mr. *Brisk*.

Brisk. Deuce take me I believe you intend to Marry your Daughter your self; you're always brooding over her like an Old Hen, as if she were not well hatch'd, I'gad, he?

Sir Paul. Good strange! Mr. *Brisk* is such a Merry Facetious Person, he, he, he. No, No, I have done with her. I have done with her now.

Brisk. The Fiddles have stay'd this hour in the Hall; and my Lord *Froth* wants a Partner, we can never begin without her.

Sir Paul. Go, go Child, go, get you gone and Dance and be Merry, I'll come and look at you by and by———Where's my Son *Mellefont*?

Exit Cynthia.

Lady Plyant. I'll send him to them, I know where he is—

Exit.

Brisk. Sir *Paul*, will you send *Careless* into the Hall if you meet him.

Sir Paul. I will, I will, I'll go and look for him on purpose.

Exit.

Brisk. So now they are all gone, and I have an opportunity to practice.———Ah! My dear Lady *Froth*! She's a most engaging Creature, if she were not so fond of that damn'd coxcomly Lord of hers; and yet I am forced to allow him Wit too, to keep in with him———No matter, she's a Woman of parts, and I'gad parts will carry her. She said she would follow me into the Gallery———Now to make my Approaches———Hem Hem! (*Bows.*) Ah Madam! ———Pox on't, why should I disparage my parts by thinking what to say? None but dull Rogues *think*; witty Men like rich Fellows, are always ready for all Expences; while your Blockheads, like poor needy Scoundrels, are forced to examine their Stock, and forecast the Charges of the Day. Here she comes, I'll seem not to see her, and try to win her with a new airy invention of my own, hem!

Enter Lady Froth.

Brisk (*sings*). *I'm sick with Love*, ha ha ha, *prithee come walking about. Cure me.*

I'm sick with, &c.

O ye Powers! O my Lady *Froth*, my Lady *Froth*! My Lady *Froth*! Heigho! Break Heart; God's I thank you.

Stands musing with his Arms a-cross.

Lady Froth. O Heavens Mr. *Brisk*! What's the matter?

Brisk. My Lady *Froth*! Your Ladyships most humble Servant; ———The matter Madam? Nothing, Madam, nothing at all I'gad. I was fallen into the most agreeable amusement in the whole Province of Contemplation: That's all——— (*Aside.*) I'll seem to conceal my Passion, and that will look like Respect.

Lady Froth. Bless me, why did you call out upon me so loud?—

Brisk. O Lord I Madam! I beseech your Ladyship——— when?

Lady Froth. Just now as I came in, bless me, why don't you know it?

Brisk. Not I, let me perish———But did I! Strange! I confess your Ladyship was in my Thoughts; and I was in a sort of Dream that did in a manner represent a very pleasing Object to my imagination, but—But did I indeed?—To see how Love and Murder will out. But did I really name my Lady *Froth*?

Lady Froth. Three times aloud, as I love Letters———But did you talk of Love? O *Parnassus*! Who would have thought Mr. *Brisk* could have been in Love, ha ha ha. O Heaven's I thought you cou'd have no Mistress but the Nine Muses.

Brisk. No more I have I'gad, for I adore 'em all in your Ladiship———Let me perish, I don't know whether to be splenatick, or airy upon't; the Deuce take me if I can tell whether I am glad or sorry that your Ladiship has made the Discovery.

Lady Froth. O be merry by all means———Prince *Volscius* in Love! Ha ha ha.

Brisk. O barbarous, to turn me into ridicule! Yet, ha ha ha. The Deuce take me, I can't help laughing my self neither, ha ha ha; yet by Heavens I have a violent passion for your Ladiship, seriously.

Lady Froth. Seriously? Ha ha ha.

Brisk. Seriously, ha ha ha. Gad, I have, for all I Laugh.

Lady Froth. Ha ha ha! What d'e think I Laugh at? Ha ha ha.

Brisk. Me I'gad, ha ha.

Lady Froth. No the Deuce take me if I don't Laugh at my self; for hang me if I have not a violent Passion for Mr. *Brisk*, ha ha ha.

Brisk. Seriously?

Lady Froth. Seriously, ha ha ha.

Prince Volscius in Love!—The absurd lover in Buckingham's *Rehearsal*, III, ii, "born/To sudden love, and to more sudden scorn."

Brisk. That's well enough; let me perish, ha ha ha. O Miraculous, what a happy Discovery. Ah my dear charming Lady *Froth.*

Lady Froth. Oh my adored Mr. *Brisk*!

Embrace.

Enter Lord Froth.

Lord Froth. The Company are all ready———How now!

Brisk. Zoons, Madam, there's my Lord.

Softly to her.

Lady Froth. Take no notice———But observe me—Now cast off, and meet me at the lower end of the Room, and then joyn hands again; I could teach my Lord this Dance purely, but I vow Mr. *Brisk*, I can't tell how to come so near any other Man. Oh here's my Lord, now you shall see me do it with him.

They pretend to practice part of a Country-Dance.

Lord Froth (*aside*). —Oh I see there's no harm yet—But I don't like this familiarity.

Lady Froth. —Shall you and I do our close Dance to show Mr. *Brisk*?

Lord Froth. —No, my Dear, do it with him.

Lady Froth. —I'll do it with him, my Lord, when you are out of the way.

Brisk (*aside*). That's good I'gad, that's good, Deuce take me I can hardly hold Laughing in his Face.

Lord Froth. Any other time, my Dear, or we'll Dance it below.

Lady Froth. With all my heart.

Brisk. Come my Lord, I'll wait on you—(*To her*) My charming witty Angel!

Lady Froth. We shall have whispering time enough, you know, since we are Partners.

Exeunt.

Enter Lady Plyant, *and* Careless.

Lady Plyant. O Mr. *Careless*, Mr. *Careless*, I'm ruin'd, I'm undone.

Careless. What's the matter, Madam?

Lady Plyant. O the unlucki'st Accident, I'm afraid I shan't live to tell it you.

Careless. Heav'n forbid! What is it?

Lady Plyant. I'm in such a fright; the strangest Quandary and Premunire! I'm all over in a Universal Agitation, I dare swear every Circumstance of me trembles.—O your Letter, your Letter! By an Unfortunate Mistake, I have given Sir *Paul* your Letter instead of his own.

Careless. That was unlucky.—

Lady Plyant. O yonder he comes reading of it, for Heavens sake step in here and advise me quickly, before he sees.

Exeunt.

Enter Sir Paul *with the Letter.*

Sir Plyant. ———O Providence, what a Conspiracy have I discover'd———But let me see to make an end on't.——— (*Reads*) Hum———*After Supper in the Wardrobe by the Gallery. If Sir* Paul *should surprize us, I have a Commission from him to treat with you about the very matter of Fact.*——— Matter of Fact! Very pretty; it seems than I am conducing to my own Cuckoldom; why this is the very traiterous Position of taking up Arms by my Authority, against my Person! Well, let me see———*Till then I Languish in expectation of my Adored Charmer.*

Dying Ned. Careless.

Gads-bud, would that were Matter of Fact too. Die and be Damn'd for a *Judas Maccabeus,* and *Iscariot* both. O friendship! What art thou but a Name! Henceforward, let no Man make a Friend that would not be a Cuckold: For whomsoever he receives into his bosom, will find the way to his Bed, and there return his Caresses with interest to his Wife. Have I for this been pinion'd Night after Night for three Years past? Have I been swath'd in Blankets till I have even been depriv'd of motion, and render'd uncapable of using the common benefits of Nature? Have I approach'd the Marriage Bed with reverence as to a sacred shrine, and

Quandary—"In study, or doubt what to do or whether to go."

Premunire—In danger of "the same punishment, which is inflicted on those that transgress the Statute of Praemunire" (Thomas Blount, *Law Dictionary*).

Judas Maccabeus and Iscariot both—The great leader who was killed at the height of his success, and the other Judas who betrayed his master.

deny'd my self the enjoyment of lawful Domestick Pleasures to preserve its Purity, and must I now find it polluted by Foreign Iniquity? O my Lady *Plyant*, you were Chaste as Ice, but you are melted now, and false as Water. —But Providence has been constant to me in discovering this Conspiracy; still I am beholden to Providence, if it were not for Providence, sure poor Sir *Paul* thy Heart would break.

Enter Lady Plyant.

Lady Plyant. So Sir, I see you have read the Letter,—well now, Sir *Paul*, what do you think of your Friend *Careless*? Has he been Treacherous, or did you give his insolence a License to make trial of your Wifes suspected Vertue? De'e see here? Look, read it? (*Snatches the Letter as in anger.*) Gad's my Life if I thought it were so, I would this moment renounce all Communication with you. Ungrateful Monster! He? Is it so? Ay, I see it, a Plot upon my Honour; your guilty Cheeks confess it; Oh where shall wrong'd Vertue fly for Reparation! I'll be Divorced this instant.

Sir Paul. Gads-bud, what shall I say? This is the strangest Surprize! Why I don't know any thing at all, nor I don't know whether there be any thing at all in the World, or no.

Lady Plyant. I thought I should try you, false Man. I that never dissembled in my Life. Yet to make tryal of you, pretended to like that Monster of Iniquity, *Careless*, and found out that contrivance to let you see this Letter; which now I find was of your own inditing———I do Heathen, I do, see my Face no more; there has hardly been Consummation between us, and I'll be Divorced presently.

Sir Plyant. O strange, what will become of me!———I'm so amazed, and so overjoy'd, so afraid, and so sorry.—But did you give me this Letter on purpose he? Did you?

Lady Plyant. Did I? Do you doubt me, Turk, Sarazen? I have a Cousin that's a Proctor in the Commons, I'll go to him instantly.—

Sir Paul. Hold, stay, I beseech your Ladiship———I'm so overjoy'd, stay I'll confess all.

Proctor in the Commons—Officer to whom papers were sent in every case of a dissolution of marriage.

Lady Plyant. What will you confess, Jew?

Sir Paul. Why now as I hope to be saved, I had no hand in this Letter———Nay hear me, I beseech your Ladiship: The Devil take me now if he did not go beyond my Commission———If I desired him to do any more than speak a good word only just for me, Gads-bud only for poor Sir *Paul*, I'm an Anabaptist, or a Jew, or what you please to call me.

Lady Plyant. Why is not here Matter of Fact?

Sir Paul. Ay, but by your own Vertue and Continency that matter of Fact is all his own doing.———I confess I had a great desire to have some Honours Conferr'd upon me, which lie all in your Ladiships Breast, and he being a well spoken Man, I desired him to intercede for me.—

Lady Plyant. Did you so, Presumption! Well, remember for this, your Right Hand shall be swathed down again to Night———and I thought to have always allow'd you that Liberty—

Sir Paul. Nay but Madam, I shall offend again if you don't allow me that to reach—

Lady Plyant. Drink the less you Sot, and do't before you come to Bed.

Exit.

Enter Careless.

Careless. Sir *Paul*, I'm glad I've met with you, 'gad I have said all I could, but can't prevail———Then my Friendship to you has carried me a little farther in this matter—

Sir Plyant. Indeed—Well Sir—(*aside*) I'll dissemble with him a little.

Careless. Why faith I have in my time known Honest Gentlemen abused by a pretended Coyness in their Wives, and I had a mind to try my Ladies Vertue—And when I could not prevail for you, 'gad I pretended to be in Love my self —but all in vain, she would not hear a word upon that Subject: Then I writ a Letter to her; I don't know what effects that will have, but I'll be sure to tell you when I do, tho' by this Light I believe her Virtue is impregnable.

Sir Paul. O Providence! Providence! What Discoveries are here made? Why, this is better and more Miraculous than the rest.

Careless. What do you mean?

Sir Paul. I can't tell you I'm so overjoy'd; come along with me to my Lady, I can't contain my self; come my dear Friend. *Exeunt.*

Careless (aside). So, so, so, this difficulty's over.

Enter Mellefont *and* Maskwell *severally.*

Mellefont. Maskwell! I have been looking for you———'tis within a Quarter of Eight.

Maskwell. My Lady is just gone down from my Lords Closet, you had best steal into her Chamber before she comes, and lie conceal'd there; otherwise she may Lock the Door when we are together, and you not easily get in to surprize us.

Mellefont. He? you say true.

Maskwell. You had best make haste, for she's but gone to make some Apology to the Company for her own, and my Lords absence all this while, and will to her Chamber instantly.

Mellefont. I go this moment: Now Fortune I defie thee. *Exit.*

Maskwell. I confess you may be allow'd to be secure in your own Opinion; the appearance is very fair, but I have an After-Game to play that shall turn the Tables, and here comes the Man that I must Manage.

Enter Lord Touchwood.

Lord Touchwood. Maskwell, you are the Man I wish'd to meet.

Maskwell. I am happy to be in the way of your Lordships Commands.

Lord Touchwood. I have always found you prudent and careful in any thing that has concern'd me or my Family.

Maskwell. I were a Villain else———I am bound by Duty and Gratitude, and my own Inclination, to be ever your Lordship's Servant.

Lord Touchwood. Enough———You are my Friend; I know it: Yet there has been a thing in your Knowledge, which has concern'd me nearly, that you have conceal'd from me.

Maskwell. My Lord!

Lord Touchwood. Nay, I excuse your Friendship to my unnatural Nephew thus far———but I know you have been Privy to his impious Designs upon my Wife. This Evening she has told me all: Her good Nature conceal'd it as long as was possible; but he perseveres so in Villany, that she has told me even you were weary of disswading him, though you have once actually hindered him from forcing her.

Maskwell. I am sorry, my Lord, I can make you no Answer; this is an Occasion in which I would not willingly be so silent.

Lord Touchwood. I know you would excuse him———and I know as well that you can't.

Maskwell. Indeed I was in hopes 'thad been a youthful Heat that might have soon boil'd over; but—

Lord Touchwood. Say on.

Maskwell. I have nothing more to say, my Lord———but to express my Concern; for I think his Frenzy increases daily.

Lord Touchwood. How! give me but Proof of it, Ocular Proof, that I may justifie my Dealing with him to the World, and share my Fortunes.

Maskwell. O my Lord! consider that is hard: besides, time may work upon him: then, for me to do it! I have profess'd an everlasting Friendship to him.

Lord Touchwood. He is your Friend, and what am I?

Maskwell. I am answered.

Lord Touchwood. Fear not his Displeasure; I will put you out of his, and Fortune's Power, and for that thou art scrupulously honest, I will secure thy Fidelity to him, and give my Honour never to own any Discovery that you shall make me. Can you give me a demonstrative Proof? Speak.

Maskwell. I wish I could not———To be plain, my Lord, I intended this Evening to have try'd all Arguments to disswade him from a Design, which I suspect; and if I had not succeeded, to have informed your Lordship of what I knew.

Lord Touchwood. I thank you. What is the Villains Purpose?

Maskwell. He has own'd nothing to me of late, and what I mean now, is only a bare Suspicion of my own. If your Lordship will meet me a quarter of an Hour hence there, in that Lobby by my Lady's Bed-Chamber, I shall be able to tell you more.

Lord Touchwood. I will.

Maskwell. My Duty to your Lordship, makes me do a severe Piece of Justice—

Lord Touchwood. I will be secret, and reward your Honesty beyond your Hopes.

Exeunt, severally.

[Scene II]

SCENE opening, shews Lady Touchwood's *Chamber.*

Mellefont, *Solus.*

Mellefont. Pray Heaven my Aunt keep touch with her Assignation—Oh that her Lord were but sweating behind this Hanging, with the Expectation of what I shall see—Hist, she comes—Little does she think what a Mine is just ready to spring under her Feet. But to my Post.

Goes behind the Hanging.

Enter Lady Touchwood.

Lady Touchwood. 'Tis Eight a Clock: Methinks I should have found him here. Who does not prevent the Hour of Love; outstays the Time; for to be dully punctual, is too slow. —I was accusing you of Neglect.

Enter Maskwell.

Maskwell. I confess you do Reproach me when I see you here before me; but 'tis fit I should be still behind hand, still to be more and more indebted to your goodness.

Lady Touchwood. You can excuse a fault too well, not to have been to blame———a ready Answer shews you were prepar'd.

Maskwell. Guilt is ever at a loss and confusion waits upon it, when Innocence and bold Truth are always ready for expression—

Lady Touchwood. Not in Love, Words are the weak support of Cold indifference; Love has no Language to be heard.

Maskwell. Excess of Joy had made me stupid! Thus may my Lips be ever clos'd. (*Kisses her.*) And thus———Oh who would not lose his Speech, upon condition to have Joys above it?

Lady Touchwood. Hold, let me Lock the Door first.

Goes to the door.

Maskwell (*aside*). That I believ'd; 'twas well I left the private passage open.

Lady Touchwood. So, that's safe.

Maskwell. And so may all your Pleasures be, and secret as this kiss—

Mellefont. And may all Treachery be thus discovered.

Leaps out.

Lady Touchwood. Ah! (*Shrieks.*)

Mellefont. Villain! (*Offers to Draw.*)

Maskwell. Nay then, there's but one way.

Runs out.

Mellefont. Say you so, were you provided for an Escape? Hold, Madam, you have no more holes to your Burrough, I'll stand between you and this Sally-Port.

Lady Touchwood. Thunder strike thee Dead for this Deceit, immediate Lightning blast thee, me and the whole World —Oh! I could rack my self, play the Vulture to my own Heart, and gnaw it piece-meal, for not boding to me this misfortune.

Mellefont. Be Patient.—

Lady Touchwood. Be Damn'd.

Mellefont. Consider I have you on the hook; you will but flounder your self a weary, and be nevertheless my Prisoner.

Lady Touchwood. I'le hold my breath and die, but I'le be free.

Mellefont. O Madam, have a care of dying unprepared, I doubt you have some unrepented Sins that may hang heavy and retard your flight.

Lady Touchwood. O. What shall I do? say? whither shall I turn? has Hell no remedy?

Mellefont. None, Hell has served you even as Heaven has done, left you to your self.—You're in a kind of *Erasmus* Paradice; yet if you please you may make it a Purgatory; and with a little Pennance and my Absolution all this may turn to good account.

Lady Touchwood (*aside*). Hold in my passion, and fall, fall, a little thou swelling Heart; let me have some intermission of this rage, and one minutes coolness to dissemble.

She Weeps.

Mellefont. You have been to blame———I like those Tears, and hope they are of the purest kind—Penitential Tears.

Lady Touchwood. O the Scene was shifted quick before me—I had not time to think—I was surprised to see a Monster in the Glass, and now I find it is my self; Can you have mercy to forgive the faults I have imagined, but never put in practice———O Consider, Consider, how fatal you have been to me, you have already killed the quiet of this Life, the love of you, was the first wandring fire that e're misled my steps, and while I had only that in view, I was betray'd into unthought of ways of ruine.

Mellefont. May I believe this true?

Lady Touchwood. O be not cruelly incredulous———How can you doubt these streaming Eyes? Keep the severest Eye o're all my future Conduct; and if I once relapse, let me not hope forgiveness, 'twill ever be in your power to ruin me—My Lord shall sign to your desires; I will my self create your Happiness, and *Cynthia* shall be this night your Bride———Do but conceal my failings, and forgive—

Mellefont. Upon such terms I will be ever yours in every honest way.

Enter Lord Touchwood, Maskwell *softly behind him.*

Maskwell. I have kept my word, he's here, but I must not be seen.

Exit.

Lord Touchwood. Hell and Amazement, she's in Tears.

Erasmus Paradice—Summers notes Roger L'Estrange's Introduction to his translation of Erasmus' *Colloquies* (1689): "the Translator . . . is crush'd betwixt two Extremes, as they hang up Erasmus himself, between Heaven and Hell."

Lady Touchwood (*kneeling*). Eternal Blessings thank you——— (*Aside.*) Ha! my Lord listning! O Fortune has o'repaid me all, all! all's my own!

Mellefont. Nay, I beseech you rise.

Lady Touchwood (*aloud*). Never, never! I'le grow to the Ground, be buried quick beneath it, e're I be consenting to so damn'd a Sin as Incest! unnatural Incest!

Mellefont. Ha!

Lady Touchwood. O cruel Man, will you not let me go—I'le forgive all that's past———O Heaven, you will not ravish me!

Mellefont. Damnation!

Lord Touchwood. Monster, Dog! your Life shall answer this—

Draws, and runs at Mellefont, *is held by* Lady Touchwood.

Lady Touchwood. O Heavens my Lord! hold, hold, for Heavens sake.

Mellefont. Confusion, my Uncle! O the damn'd Sorceress.

Lady Touchwood. Moderate your rage good my Lord! he's mad, alas he's mad—indeed he is my Lord, and knows not what he does—see how wild he looks.

Mellefont. By Heaven 'twere senceless not to be mad, and see such Witchcraft.

Lady Touchwood. My Lord, you hear him—he talks Idly.

Lord Touchwood. Hence from my sight, thou living infamy to my Name; when next I see that Face, I'le write Villain in't with my Swords point.

Mellefont. Now, by my Soul, I will not go till I have made known my wrongs—Nay, till I have made known yours, which (if possible) are greater—Though she has all the Host of Hell her Servants; Though she can wear more shapes in shining day, then fear shews Cowards in the dark———

Lady Touchwood. Alas he raves! talks very Poetry! for Heavens sake away my Lord, he'll either tempt you to extravagance, or commit some himself.

Mellefont. Death and Furies, will you not hear me—Why by Heaven she laughs, grins, points to your Back, she forks out Cuckoldom with her Fingers, and you're running Horn mad after your Fortune.

As she is going she turns back and smiles at him.

Lord Touchwood. I fear he's mad indeed—Let's send *Maskwell* to him—

Mellefont. Send him, to her.

Lady Touchwood. Come, come, good my Lord, my Heart akes so, I shall faint if I stay.

Exeunt.

Mellefont. O I could curse my Stars, Fate, and Chance; all Causes and Accidents of Fortune in this Life! but to what purpose? yet, 'sdeath, for a Man to have the fruit of all his Industry grown full and ripe, ready to drop into his mouth, and just when he holds out his hand to gather it, to have a sudden Whirlwind come, tear up Tree and all, and bear away the very root and foundation of his hopes; What temper can contain? They talk of sending *Maskwell* to me; I never had more need of him—But what can he do? Imagination cannot form a fairer and more plausible design than this of his which has miscarried.—O my Pretious Aunt, I shall never thrive without I deal with the Devil, or another Woman.

Women like flames have a destroying pow'r,
Ne'er to be quench'd, till they themselves devour.

Exit.

SCENE shuts.

End of the Fourth ACT.

ACT V. Scene I.

Enter Lady Touchwood *and* Maskwell.

Lady Touchwood. Wast not Lucky?

Maskwell. Lucky! Fortune is your own, and 'tis her interest so to be; By Heaven I believe you can controul her power, and she fears it; though chance brought my Lord, 'twas your own art that turned it to advantage.

Lady Touchwood. 'Tis true it might have been my ruine—but yonders my Lord, I believe he's coming to find you, I'le not be seen.

Exit.

Maskwell. So; I durst not own my introducing my Lord, though it succeeded well for her, for she would have suspected a design which I should have been puzled to excuse. My Lord is thoughtful—I'le be so too; yet he shall know my thoughts; or think he does—

Enter Lord Touchwood.

Maskwell. What have I done?

Lord Touchwood. Talking to himself!

Maskwell. 'Twas honest—And shall I be rewarded for it? No, 'twas honest, therefore I shan't;—Nay, rather, therefore I ought not; for it rewards it self.

Lord Touchwood (*aside*). Unequall'd Virtue!

Maskwell. But should it be known! then I have lost a Friend! He was an ill Man, and I have gain'd; for half my self I lent him, and that, I have recall'd; so I have served my self, and what is yet better, I have served a worthy Lord to whom I owe my self.

Lord Touchwood (*aside*). Excellent Man!

Maskwell. Yet I am wretched———O there is a secret burns within this Breast, which should it once blaze forth, would ruine all, consume my honest Character, and brand me with the name of Villain.

Lord Touchwood. Ha!

Maskwell. Why do I love! yet Heaven and my waking Conscience are my Witnesses, I never gave one working thought a vent; which might discover that I lov'd, nor ever must; no, let it prey upon my Heart; for I would rather die, than seem once, barely seem, dishonest:——— O, should it once be known I love fair *Cynthia*, all this that I have done, would look like Rivals Malice, false Friendship to my Lord, and base Self-interest. Let me perish first, and from this hour avoid all sight and speech, and, if I can, all thought of that pernicious Beauty. Ha! but what is my distraction doing? I am wildly talking to my self, and some ill Chance might have directed malicious Ears this way.

Seems to start, seeing my Lord.

Lord Touchwood. Start not—let guilty and dishonest Souls start at the revelation of their thoughts, but be thou fix'd, as is thy Vertue.

Maskwell. I am confounded, and beg your Lordship's pardon for those free discourses which I have had with my self.

Lord Touchwood. Come, I beg your pardon that I over-heard you, and yet it shall not need———Honest *Maskwell*! thy and my good Genius led me hither———mine, in that I have discovered so much Manly Vertue; thine, in that thou shalt have due reward of all thy worth. Give me thy hand ———my Nephew is the alone remaining Branch of all our ancient Family; him I thus blow away, and constitute thee in his room to be my Heir—

Maskwell. Now Heaven forbid—

Lord Touchwood. No more———I have resolv'd———The Writings are ready drawn, and wanted nothing but to be sign'd, and have his name inserted———yours will fill the Blank as well———I will have no reply———Let me command this time; for 'tis the last, in which I will assume Authority—hereafter, you shall rule where I have Power.

Maskwell. I humbly would petition—

Maskwell *pauses.*

Lord Touchwood. Is't for your self?—I'll hear of nought for any body else.

Maskwell. Then witness Heaven for me, this Wealth and Honour was not of my seeking, nor would I build my Fortune on another's ruine: I had but one desire—

Lord Touchwood. Thou shalt enjoy it———if all I'm worth in Wealth or Interest can purchase *Cynthia*, she is thine.— I'm sure Sir *Paul's* Consent will follow Fortune; I'll quickly show him which way that is going.

Maskwell. You oppress me with Bounty; my Gratitude is weak, and shrinks beneath the weight, and cannot rise to thank you———What, enjoy my Love! Forgive the Transports of a Blessing so unexpected, so unhop'd for, so unthought of!

Lord Touchwood. I will confirm it, and rejoyce with thee.

Exit.

Maskwell. This is prosperous indeed———Why let him find me out a Villain, settled in possession of a fair Estate, and full fruition of my Love, I'll bear the railings of a losing Gamester—but shou'd he find me out before! 'tis dangerous to delay———let me think———shou'd my Lord proceed to treat openly of my Marriage with *Cynthia*, all must be discover'd, and *Mellefont* can be no longer blinded.——— It must not be; nay, shou'd my Lady know it———ay, then were fine work indeed! her fury wou'd spare nothing, tho' she involv'd her self in ruine. No, it must be by Stratagem———I must deceive *Mellefont* once more, and get my Lord to consent to my private management. He comes opportunely———now will I, in my old way, discover the whole and real truth of the matter to him, that he may not suspect one word on't.

No Mask like open Truth to cover Lies,
As to go naked is the best disguise.

Enter Mellefont.

Mellefont. O *Maskwell*, what hopes? I am confounded in a maze of thoughts, each leading into one another, and all ending in perplexity. My uncle will not see, nor hear me.

Maskwell. No matter, Sir, don't trouble your head, all's in my power.

Mellefont. How? for Heaven's sake?

Maskwell. Little do you think that your Aunt has kept her word,———how the Devil she wrought my Lord into this dotage, I know not; but he's gone to Sir *Paul* about my Marriage with *Cynthia*, and has appointed me his Heir.

Mellefont. The Devil he has! what's to be done?

Maskwell. I have it, it must be by Stratagem; for it's in vain to make Application to him. I think I have that in my head that cannot fail: Where's *Cynthia*?

Mellefont. In the Garden.

Maskwell. Let us go and consult her, my life for yours, I cheat my Lord.

Exeunt.

Enter Lord Touchwood, Lady Touchwood.

in my old way—Like Syrus, "to cheat both of them, by telling the truth" (see Introductory Note, p. 116).

Lady Touchwood. Maskwell your Heir, and Marry *Cynthia*!

Lord Touchwood. I cannot do too much, for so much merit.

Lady Touchwood. But this is a thing of too great moment, to be so suddenly resolv'd. Why, *Cynthia*? Why must he be Married? Is there not reward enough in raising his low Fortune, but he must mix his Blood with mine, and Wed my Niece? how know you that my Brother will consent, or she? nay, he himself perhaps may have Affections otherwhere.

Lord Touchwood. No, I am convinced he loves her.

Lady Touchwood. Maskwell love *Cynthia*, impossible!

Lord Touchwood. I told you, he confess'd it to me.

Lady Touchwood (*aside*). Confusion! how's this!

Lord Touchwood. His humility long stifled his Passion: And his Love of *Mellefont* would have made him still conceal it,—but, by Encouragement, I wrung the secret from him; and know he's no way to be rewarded but in her. I'll defer my farther proceedings in it, till you have consider'd it, but remember how we are both indebted to him.

Exit.

Lady Touchwood. Both indebted to him! yes, we are both indebted to him, if you knew all, damn'd Villain! oh, I am wild with this surprize of Treachery: Hell and Fire, it is impossible, it cannot be,———he Love *Cynthia*! what have I been Bawd to his designs? his Property only, a baiting place to stay his stomach in the road to her; now I see what made him false to *Mellefont*,———Shame and Destruction! I cannot bear it, oh! what Woman can bear to be a Property? To be kindled to a flame, only to light him to anothers Arms; oh! that I were Fire indeed, that I might burn the vile Traytor to a Hell of Torments,———but he's Damnation proof, a Devil already, and Fire is his Element. What shall I do? how shall I think? I cannot think,—all my designs are lost, my Love unsated, my Revenge unfinished, and fresh cause of fury from unthought of Plagues.

Enter Sir Paul.

Sir Paul. Madam, Sister, my Lady Sister, did you see my Lady my Wife?

Property—Cf. *Julius Caesar*, IV, i, 40: "Do not talk of him but as a property." Dobrée refers also to *Way of the World*, V, i.

Lady Touchwood. Oh! Torture!

Sir Paul. Gad'sbud, I can't find her high nor low; where can she be, think you?

Lady Touchwood. Where she's serving you, as all your Sex ought to be served; making you a Beast. Don't you know that you're a Fool, Brother?

Sir Paul. A Fool; he, he, he, you're merry———no, no, not I, I know no such matter.

Lady Touchwood. Why then you don't know half your happyness?

Sir Paul. That's a jest with all my heart, faith and troth,——— but hearkee, my Lord told me something of a Revolution of things; I don't know what to make on't,———gad'sbud I must consult my Wife,———he talks of disinheriting his Nephew; and I don't know what,———look you, Sister, I must know what my Girl has to trust to; or not a syllable of a Wedding, gad'sbud———to shew you that I am not a Fool.

Lady Touchwood. Hear me; consent to the breaking off this Marriage, and the promoting any other, without consulting me, and I'll renounce all Blood, all relation and concern with you for ever,———nay, I'll be your Enemy, and pursue you to Destruction, I'll tear your Eyes out, and tread you under my feet.—

Sir Paul. Why, what's the matter now? Good Lord, what's all this for? Pooh, here's a joke, indeed———why, where's my Wife?

Lady Touchwood. With *Careless*, in the close Arbour, he may want you by this time, as much as you want her.

Sir Paul. O, if she be with Mr. *Careless*, 'tis well enough.

Lady Touchwood. Fool, Sot, insensible Ox! but remember what I said to you, or you had better eat your own Horns, and Pimp for your living, by this light you had.

Exit.

Sir Paul. She's a passionate Woman, gad'sbud,———but to say truth, all our Family are Cholerick; I am the only peaceable Person amongst 'em.

Exit.

Enter Mellefont, Maskwell, *and* Cynthia.

Mellefont. I know no other way but this he has proposed; If you have Love enough to run the venture.

Cynthia. I don't know whether I have Love enough,——— but I find I have obstinacy enough to pursue whatever I have once resolved; and a true Female courage to oppose any thing that resists my will, tho' 'twere reason it self.

Maskwell. That's right,———well, I'll secure the Writings; and run the hazard along with you.

Cynthia. But how can the Coach and six Horses be got ready without suspicion?

Maskwell. Leave it to my care; that shall be so far from being suspected, that it shall be got ready by my Lord's own order.

Mellefont. How?

Maskwell. Why, I intend to tell my Lord the whole matter of our Contrivance, that's my way.

Mellefont. I don't understand you.

Maskwell. Why, I'll tell my Lord, I laid this Plot with you, on purpose to betray you; and that which put me upon it, was, the finding it impossible to gain the Lady any other way, but in the hopes of her Marrying you.—

Mellefont. So.—

Maskwell. So, why so, while you are busied in making your self ready, I'll wheedle her into the Coach; and instead of you, Borrow my Lords Chaplain, and so run away with her my self.

Mellefont. O I conceive you, you'll tell him so?

Maskwell. Tell him so! Ay, why you don't think I mean to do so?

Mellefont. No, no; ha, ha, I dare swear thou wilt not.

Maskwell (*aside*). You may be deceiv'd———Therefore, for our farther Security, I would have you Disguis'd like a Parson, that if my Lord should have Curiosity to peep, he may not discover you in the Coach, but think the Cheat is carried on as he would have it.

Mellefont. Excellent *Maskwell*, thou wer't certainly meant for a Statesman or a Jesuite, but that thou'rt too honest for one, and too pious for the other.

Maskwell. Well, get your selves ready, and meet me in half an hour, yonder in my Lady's Dressing-Room; go by the back Stairs, and so we may slip down without being observ'd.—I'll send the Chaplain to you with his Robes; I have made him my own,———and ordered him to meet us to Morrow Morning at St. *Albans*; there we will Sum up this Account, to all our satisfactions.

Mellefont. Should I begin to thank or praise thee, I should waste the little time we have.

Exit.

Maskwell. Madam you will be ready?

Cynthia. I will be punctual to the Minute.

Going.

Maskwell. Stay, I have a doubt———upon second thoughts, we had better meet in the Chaplain's Chamber, here, the corner Chamber at this end of the Gallery, there is a back way into it, so that you need not come thro' this Door ———and a Pair of private Stairs leads down to the Stables———it will be more convenient.

Cynthia. I am guided by you,———but *Mellefont* will mistake.

Maskwell. No, no, I'll after him immediately, and tell him.

Cynthia. I will not fail.

Exit.

Maskwell. Why, *qui vult decipi decipiatur.*———'Tis no fault of mine, I have told 'em in plain terms, how easie 'tis for me to cheat 'em; and if they will not hear the Serpent's hiss, they must be stung into experience, and future caution,—Now to prepare my Lord to consent to this.——— But first I must instruct my little Levite, there is no Plot, publick or private, that can expect to prosper without one of 'em have a finger in't, he promised me to be within at this hour,—Mr. *Saygrace*, Mr. *Saygrace.*

Goes to the Chamber Door and knocks.

Saygrace (*looking out*). Sweet Sir, I will but pen the last Line of an Acrostick, and be with you in the twinckling of an Ejaculation, in the pronouncing of an *Amen*, or before you can—

Maskwell, Nay, good Mr. *Saygrace* do not prolong the time, by describing to me the shortness of your stay; rather if you please, defer the finishing of your Wit, and let us talk about our business, it shall be Tithes in your way.

Saygrace (*enters*). You shall prevail, I would break off in the middle of a Sermon to do you pleasure.

Maskwell. You could not do me a greater,———except——— the business in hand———have you provided a Habit for *Mellefont*?

Saygrace. I have, they are ready in my Chamber, together with a clean starch'd Band and Cuffs.

Maskwell. Good, let them be carried to him,———have you stitch'd the Gown Sleeve, that he may be puzzled, and waste time in putting it on?

Saygrace. I have; the Gown will not be indued without perplexity.

Maskwell. Meet me in half an Hour, here in your own Chamber. When *Cynthia* comes, let there be no Light, and do not speak, that she may not distinguish you from *Mellefont*. I'll urge haste, to excuse your silence.

Saygrace. You have no more Commands?

Maskwell. None, your Text is short.

Saygrace. But pithy, and I will handle it with Discretion. *Exit.*

Maskwell. It will be the first you have so serv'd.

Enter Lord Touchwood.

Lord Touchwood. Sure I was born to be controuled by those I should Command: my very Slaves will shortly give me Rules how I shall govern them.

Maskwell. I am concern'd to see your Lordship discomposed—

Lord Touchwood. Have you seen my Wife lately, or disobliged her?

Maskwell. No, my Lord. (*Aside.*) What can this mean?

Lord Touchwood. Then *Mellefont* has urg'd some body to incense her—something she has heard of you which carries her beyond the bounds of Patience.

Maskwell (*aside*). This I fear'd. Did not your Lordship tell her of the Honours you designed me?

Lord Touchwood. Yes.

Maskwell. 'Tis that; you know my Lady has a high Spirit, she thinks I am unworthy.

Lord Touchwood. Unworthy! 'tis an ignorant Pride in her to think so—Honesty to me is true Nobility. However, 'tis my Will it should be so, and that shou'd be convincing to her as much as reason—by Heav'n, I'll not be Wife-ridden; were it possible it shou'd be done this night.

Maskwell (*aside*). By Heav'n, he meets my wishes. Few things are impossible to willing minds.

Lord Touchwood. Instruct me how this may be done, you shall see I want no inclination.

Maskwell. I had laid a small design for to morrow (as Love will be inventing) which I thought to communicate to your Lordship—but it may be as well done to night.

Lord Touchwood. Here's Company—come this way and tell me.

Exeunt.

Enter Careless *and* Cynthia.

Careless. Is not that he, now gone out with my Lord?

Cynthia. Yes.

Careless. By Heaven there's Treachery———the Confusion that I saw your Father in, my Lady *Touchwood's* Passion, with what imperfectly I over-heard between my Lord and her, confirm me in my fears. Where's *Mellefont*?

Cynthia. Here he comes.

Enter Mellefont.

Did *Maskwell* tell you any thing of the Chaplain's Chamber?

Mellefont. No; my Dear, will you get ready———the things are all in my Chamber; I want nothing but the Habit.

Careless. You are betray'd, and *Maskwell* is the Villain that I always thought him.

Cynthia. When you were gone, he said his mind was chang'd, and bid me meet him in the Chaplain's Room, pretending immediately to follow you, and give you notice.

Mellefont. How!

Careless. There's *Saygrace* tripping by with a bundle under his Arm———he cannot be ignorant that *Maskwell* means to use his Chamber; let's follow and examine him.

Mellefont. 'Tis loss of time———I cannot think him false.

Exeunt Mellefont *and* Careless.

Cynthia. My Lord musing!

Enter Lord Touchwood.

Lord Touchwood. He has a quick invention, if this were suddenly design'd———yet he says he had prepar'd my Chaplain already.

Cynthia. How's this! now I fear indeed.

Lord Touchwood. Cynthia here; alone, fair Cousin, and melancholly?

Cynthia. Your Lordship was thoughtful.

Lord Touchwood. My thoughts were on serious business, not worth your hearing.

Cynthia. Mine were on Treachery concerning you, and may be worth your hearing.

Lord Touchwood. Treachery concerning me! pray be plain ———hark! what noise!

Maskwell (*within*). Will you not hear me?

Lady Touchwood (*within*). No, Monster! Hellish Traitor! no.

Cynthia. My Lady and *Maskwell*! this may be lucky——— My Lord, let me entreat you to stand behind this Skreen, and listen; perhaps this chance may give you proof of what you ne're could have believ'd from my suspicions.

They abscond.

Enter Lady Touchwood *with a Dagger*, Maskwell.

Lady Touchwood. You want but leasure to invent fresh falshood, and sooth me to a fond belief of all your fictions; but I will stab the Lie that's forming in your heart, and save a Sin, in pity to your Soul.

Maskwell. Strike then———Since you will have it so.

Lady Touchwood. Ha! a steady Villain to the last!

Maskwell. Come, why do you dally with me thus?

Lady Touchwood. Thy stubborn temper shocks me, and you knew it would———by Heav'n, this is Cunning all, and not Courage; no, I know thee well: but thou shalt miss thy aim.

Maskwell. Ha, ha, ha.

Lady Touchwood. Ha! do you mock my Rage? then this shall punish your fond, rash Contempt! Again smile!

Goes to strike.

And such a smile as speaks in Ambiguity! Ten thousand meanings lurk in each corner of that various face. O! that they were written in thy heart, That I, with this, might lay thee open to my sight! But then 'twill be too late to know— Thou hast, thou hast found the only way to turn my Rage; Too well thou know'st my jealous Soul cou'd never bear Uncertainty. Speak then, and tell me———yet are you silent? Oh, I am wilder'd in all Passions! but thus my Anger melts. (*weeps*) Here, take this Ponyard, for my very Spirits faint, and I want strength to hold it, thou hast disarm'd my Soul.

Gives the Dagger.

Lord Touchwood. Amazement shakes me———where will this end?

Maskwell. So, 'tis well———let your wild fury have a vent; and when you have temper, tell me.

Lady Touchwood. Now, now, now I am calm, and can hear you.

Maskwell (*aside*). Thanks, my invention; and now I have it for you.———First tell me what urg'd you to this violence? for your Passion broke in such imperfect terms, that yet I am to learn the cause.

Lady Touchwood. My Lord himself surpriz'd me with the News, You were to marry *Cynthia*———that you had own'd your Love to him, and his indulgence would assist you to attain your ends.

Cynthia. How, my Lord!

Lord Touchwood. Pray forbear all Resentments for a while, and let us hear the rest.

Maskwell. I grant you in appearance all is true; I seem'd consenting to my Lord; nay, transported with the Blessing —but could you think that I who had been happy in your lov'd Embraces, could e're be fond of an inferiour Slavery.

Lord Touchwood. Ha! O poison to my Ears! what do I hear!

Cynthia. Nay, good my Lord, forbear Resentment, let us hear it out.

Lord Touchwood. Yes, I will contain, tho' I cou'd burst.

Maskwell. I that had wanton'd in the wide Circle of your World of Love, cou'd be confin'd within the puny Province of a Girl. No———yet tho' I doat on each last Favour more than all the rest; though I would give a Limb for every look you cheaply throw away on any other Object of your Love; yet so far I prize your Pleasures o're my own, that all this seeming Plot that I have laid, has been to gratifie your taste, and cheat the World, to prove a faithful Rogue to you.

Lady Touchwood. If this were true———but how can it be?

Maskwell. I have so contriv'd, that *Mellefont* will presently, in the Chaplain's habit, wait for *Cynthia* in your Dressing-Room: but I have put the change upon her, that she may be otherwhere employ'd—do you procure her Night-Gown, and with your Hoods tied over your face, meet him in her stead, you may go privately by the back Stairs, and, unperceiv'd, there you may propose to reinstate him in his Uncle's favour, if he'll comply with your desires; his Case is desperate, and I believe he'll yield to any Conditions,—if not, here take this; you may employ it better, than in the Death of one who is nothing when not yours.

Gives the Dagger.

Lady Touchwood. Thou can'st deceive every body,———nay, thou hast deceiv'd me; but 'tis as I would wish,——— trusty Villain! I could worship thee.—

Maskwell. No more,———there want but a few Minutes of the time; and *Mellefont's* Love will carry him there before his hour.

Lady Touchwood. I go, I fly, incomparable *Maskwell.*

Exit.

Maskwell. So, this was a pinch indeed, my invention was upon the Rack; and made discov'ry of her last Plot: I hope *Cynthia,* and my Chaplain will be ready, I'll prepare for the Expedition.

Exit.

Cynthia, *and* Lord Touchwood, *come forward.*

Cynthia. Now, my Lord?

Lord Touchwood. Astonishment binds up my rage! Villany upon Villany! Heavens, what a long track of dark deceit has this discover'd! I am confounded when I look back, and want a Clue to guide me through the various mazes of unheard of Treachery. My Wife! Damnation! my Hell.

Cynthia. My Lord, have patience, and be sensible how great our happiness is, that this discovery was not made too late.

Lord Touchwood. I thank you, yet it may be still too late, if we don't presently prevent the Execution of their plots;—ha, I'll do't, where's *Mellefont*, my poor injured Nephew,—how shall I make him ample satisfaction?—

Cynthia. I dare answer for him.

Lord Touchwood. I do him fresh wrong to question his forgivness; for I know him to be all goodness,—yet my Wife! Dam her,———she'll think to meet him in that Dressing-Room,———was't not so? And *Maskwell* will expect you in the Chaplain's Chamber,———for once, I'll add to my Plot too,———let us haste to find out, and inform my Nephew, and do you quickly as you can, bring all the Company into this Gallery,—I'll expose the Strumpet, and the Villain.

Exeunt.

Enter Lord Froth, *and* Sir Paul.

Lord Froth. By Heaven's, I have slept an Age,———Sir *Paul*, what a Clock is't? past Eight, on my Conscience; my Lady's is the most inviting Couch; and a slumber there, is the prettiest amusement! but where's all the Company?

Sir Paul. The Company, gad'sbud, I don't know, my Lord, but here's the strangest Revolution, all turn'd topsie turvy; as I hope for Providence.

Lord Froth. O Heaven's, what's the matter? Where's my Wife?

Sir Paul. All turn'd topsie turvey, as sure as a Gun.

Lord Froth. How do you mean? My Wife!

Sir Paul. The strangest posture of Affairs!

Lord Froth. What, my Wife?

Sir Paul. No, no, I mean the Family,———your Lady's Affairs may be in a very good posture; I saw her go into the Garden with Mr. *Brisk*.

as sure as a Gun—Cock-sure, *Dictionary of the Canting Crew* (1700).

Lord Froth. How? where, when, what to do?

Sir Paul. I suppose they have been laying their heads together.

Lord Froth. How?

Sir Paul. Nay, only about Poetry, I suppose, my Lord; making Couplets.

Lord Froth. Couplets.

Sir Paul. O, here they come.

Enter Lady Froth, Brisk.

Brisk. My Lord, your humble Servant; Sir *Paul* yours,——the finest night!

Lord Froth. My dear, Mr. *Brisk* and I have been Star-gazing, I don't know how long.

Sir Paul. Does it not tire your Ladyship? are not you weary with looking up?

Lady Froth. Oh, no, I love it violently,——my dear you're melancholly.

Lord Froth. No, my dear; I'm but just awake.——

Lady Froth. Snuff some of my Spirit of Hartshorn.

Lord Froth. I've some of my own, thank you, my dear.

Lady Froth. Well, I swear, Mr. *Brisk*, you understood Astronomy like an old *Egyptian*.

Brisk. Not comparable to your Ladyship; you are the very *Cynthia* of the Skies, and Queen of Stars.

Lady Froth. That's because I've no light, but what's by Reflection from you, who are the Sun.

Brisk. O Jesu! Madam, you have Eclips'd me quite, let me perish,—I can't answer that.

Lady Froth. No matter,——heark'ee, shall you and I make an Almanack together.

Brisk. With all my Soul,——your Ladyship has made me the Man in't already, I'm so full of the Wounds which you have given.

Cynthia—"A poetic name for the moon, personified as a goddess, and said to have been born near Mt. Cynthus," *Ladies Dictionary* (1694).

Almanack . . . Man in't—Picture of the man, frequently found in old almanacs, who is surrounded by the signs of the Zodiac, each sign next to that part of the body it afflicts or cures.

Lady Froth. O finely taken! I swear, now you are even with me, O *Parnassus*, you have an infinite deal of Wit.

Sir Paul. So he has, gad'sbud, and so has your Ladyship.

Enter Lady Plyant, Careless, Cynthia.

Lady Plyant. You tell me most surprizing things; bless me who would ever trust a man? O my heart akes for fear they should be all deceitful alike.

Careless. You need not fear, Madam, you have Charms to fix Inconstancy it self.

Lady Plyant. O dear, you make me blush.

Lord Froth. Come my dear, shall we take leave of my Lord and Lady?

Cynthia. They'll wait upon your Lordship presently.

Lord Froth. Mr. *Brisk*, my Coach shall set you down.

All. What's the matter?

A great shriek from the corner of the Stage. Lady Touchwood *runs out affrighted, my Lord after her, like a Parson.*

Lady Touchwood. O I'm betray'd,———save me, help me.

Lord Touchwood. Now what Evasion, Strumpet?

Lady Touchwood. Stand off, let me go, and Plagues, and Curses seize you all.

Runs out.

Lord Touchwood. Go, and thy own Infamy pursue thee,——— you stare as you were all amazed,—I don't wonder at it,— but too soon you'll know mine, and that Woman's shame.

Enter Mellefont *lugging in* Maskwell *from the other side of the Stage,* Mellefont *like a Parson.*

Mellefont. Nay, by Heaven you shall be seen,———*Careless*, your hand;—do you hold down your head? Yes, I am your Chaplain, look in the Face of your injur'd Friend; thou wonder of all Falsehood.

Lord Touchwood. Are you silent, Monster?

Mellefont. Good Heavens! how I believ'd and Lov'd this Man!—Take him hence, for he's a Disease to my Sight.

Lord Touchwood. Secure that manifold Villain.

Careless. Miracle of Ingratitude!

They carry out Maskwell, *who hangs down his head.*

Brisk. This is all very surprizing, let me perish.

Lady Froth. You know I told you *Saturn* look'd a little more angry than usual.

Lord Touchwood. We'll think of punishment at leasure, but let me hasten to do Justice, in rewarding Virtue and wrong'd Innocence.———Nephew, I hope I have your pardon, and *Cynthia's.*

Mellefont. We are your Lordships Creatures.

Lord Touchwood. And be each others comfort;———let me joyn your hands.———Unwearied Nights, and wishing Days attend you both; mutual Love, lasting Health, and Circling Joys, tread round each happy Year of your long Lives.

Let secret Villany from hence be warn'd;
Howe're in private, Mischiefs are conceiv'd,
Torture and shame attend their open Birth:
Like Vipers in the Womb, base Treach'ry lies,

Still gnawing that, whence first it did arise;
No sooner born, but the Vile Parent dies.

Exeunt Omnes.

FINIS.

Vipers in the Womb—A much-used image from Pliny to Ben Jonson. Dobrée quotes Sir Thomas Browne's *Vulgar Errors*, III, xvi: "Vipers force their way through the bowels of their dam."

Epilogue

Spoken by Mrs. *Mountford.*

Could Poets but forsee how Plays would take,
Then they could tell what Epilogues to make;
Whether to thank, or blame their Audience, most:
But that late knowledge, does much hazard cost,
Till Dice are thrown, there's nothing won, nor lost.
So till the Thief has stoll'n, he cannot know
Whether he shall escape the Law, or no.
But Poets run much greater hazards far,
Than they who stand their Trials at the Barr;
The Law provides a curb for 'its own Fury,
And suffers Judges to direct the Jury.
But in this Court, what difference does appear!
For every one's both Judge and Jury here;
Nay, and what's worse, an Executioner.
All have a Right and Title to some part,
Each chusing that, in which he has most Art.
The dreadful men of Learning, all Confound,
Unless the Fable's good, and Moral sound.
The Vizor-Masks, that are in Pit and Gallery,
Approve, or Damn the Repartee and Rallery.
The Lady Criticks, who are better Read,
Enquire if Characters are nicely bred;
If the soft things are Penn'd and spoke with grace;
They Judge of Action too, and Time, and Place;
In which, we do not doubt but they're discerning,
For that's a kind of *Assignation Learning*.
Beaus Judge of Dress; the Witlings Judge of Songs;
The Cuckoldom, of Ancient Right, to Cits belongs.
Poor Poets thus the Favour are deny'd,
Even to make exceptions, when they're Try'd.
'Tis hard that they must every one admit;
Methinks I see some Faces in the Pit,
Which must of Consequence be Foes to Wit.
You who can Judge, to Sentence may proceed;
But tho' he cannot Write, let him be freed
At least from their Contempt, who cannot Read.

FINIS.

Vizor-masks—OED quotes Tom Brown, *Amusements Serious and Comic*, (1700), "A Whore is known by a Visor mask."

Assignation Learning—"learning picked up from others indirectly, not gained by one's own efforts" (Blount, *Law Dictionary*).

4

Love for Love

INTRODUCTORY NOTE

Love for Love was finished before the end of 1694 when, according to Cibber, it was "read and accepted of at the Theatre Royal."[1] But upon the death of Queen Mary on December 28, the theater was closed. And at the same time

> a difference happening between the Patentees, and the chief Actors . . . the latter complaining of Oppression from the former; they for Redress, Appeal'd to my Lord of Dorset, then Lord Chamberlain, for Justice; who, Espousing the Cause of the Actors, with the assistance of Sir Robert Howard, finding their Complaints just, procur'd from King William a seperate License for Mr. Congreve, Mr. Betterton, Mrs. Bracegirdle, and Mrs. Barry, and others, to set up a new Company, calling it the New Theatre in Lincolns-Inn-Fields.[2]

Congreve naturally withheld his play so that it could be produced by the actors for whom he had written it, and with whom he was now closely associated. It was put on by them at the opening of the new theater, and provided with a special Prologue, to be spoken by Betterton, for this occasion:

> So from your Bounty, we receive this Stage;
> The Freedom Man was born to, you've restor'd, . . .
>
> We who remain, would gratefully repay
> What our Endeavours can, and bring this day,
> The First-Fruit Offering, of a Virgin Play.
>
> And shou'd th'ensuing Scenes not chance to hit,
> He offers but this one Excuse, 'twas writ
> Before your late Encouragement of Wit.

[1] Cibber, *Apology*, i, 197.
[2] John Downes, *Roscius Anglicanus* (1708), p. 43.

It proved to be a tremendous success, offering full scope for the great variety of talent in this splendid company, and Ben the sailor[3] became Dogget's favourite role. He seems to have made it a "very natural" as well as a "very pleasant" role, if it be allowed to modify Dr. Johnson's opinion. He is said to have attempted to acquire the accent and mannerisms of the sailors of Wapping.

Although some of the characters may remind us of Jonsonian humors, and others, like the witty servant and the foolish girl from the country, are traditional in English comedy, they speak and act as persons of their own day and age. Dr. Johnson was evidently aware of this, and he is surely right in maintaining that this play is

> a comedy of nearer alliance to life, . . . exhibiting more real manners than either of the former. The character of Foresight was then common. Dryden calculated nativities; both Cromwell and King William had their lucky days; and Shaftesbury himself, though he had no religion, was said to regard predictions.[4]

The character of Foresight and the use of the jargon of astrology owes something to Ben Jonson's *Alchemist* and perhaps also to Tomkis's *Albumazar*. The latter (adapted in 1615 from an Italian play about the great Arabian astrologer) had been revived in 1668, with a preface by Dryden in which he refers to the tradition in the theater that Jonson's *Subtle* had an Italian parentage:

> *Subtle* was got, by our *Albumazar*,
> That *Alchemist* by this *Astrologer*.

But Congreve had in his own library (no. 359) *England's Propheticall Merline*, by William Lilly, student in Astrologie, dated 1644, where may be found references to Ptolemy, Haly, Merlin, and Albumazar, as well as all the technical terms used by Foresight in Act II, scene 1. Or he could have found such things even more clearly set forth in William Ramesey's *Astrologia Restaurata: Or, Astrologie Restored*: (Being an Introduction to the General and Chief Part of the Language of the Stars,) In four Books, 1653. It is more important, however, to remember that he and his actors and his audience would all be familiar with the monthly almanacs, most of which provided astrological tables as well as prophecies founded on them.

[3] On the authorship of the ballad, "A Soldier and a Sailor," see John C. Hodges, *PMLA*, XLVIII, 953; and A. E. H. Swaen, *Archiv*. CLXVIII, 237.

[4] *Lives of the Poets*, (ed. G. B. Hill, 1905) II, 218.

When the play was printed, it was naturally dedicated to the Earl of Dorset, the Lord Chamberlain, through whom the company had obtained their new license. Himself a poet and a patron of poets and playwrights, Dorset had continued to support Dryden in spite of their differing political views after the Revolution, and he remained a good friend of Congreve. In this printed version, a part of Act III was included that had been cut in the performance, perhaps to leave time for the music and the singing and the dance provided to add to the gaiety of the occasion.

Other editions were soon called for and in the theater "it ran on with such extraordinary Success that they had seldom occasion to act any other Play till the End of the Season."[5] It remained the most popular of Congreve's plays throughout the whole of the eighteenth century. In the very first number of the *Tatler*, April 9, 1709, Steele describes the splendid performance that had just been given for the Benefit of Mr. Betterton:

> Those excellent Players, Mrs. Barry, Mrs. Bracegirdle, and Mr. Dogget, tho' not at present concern'd in the House, acted on that Occasion. There has not been known so great a Concourse of Persons of Distinction, the Stage itself was cover'd with Gentlemen and Ladies, and when the Curtain was drawn, there appear'd also a very splendid Audience.... All the Parts were acted to Perfection, and there seem'd a peculiar Regard had to their Behaviour on this Occasion: No one was guilty of the Affectation to insert Witticisms of his own.

Later with Mrs. Oldfield playing Angelica, it continued to be the most popular of Congreve's plays. It was performed nearly every season throughout the century and even through the first twenty years of the nineteenth.[6]

[5] Cibber, *Apology*, i, 197.

[6] See Avery, *Congreve on the Eighteenth-century Stage*, pp. 187–200.

Love for Love:

A

COMEDY.

Acted at the

THEATRE in *Little Lincolns-Inn Fields*,

BY

His Majesty's Servants.

Written by Mr. *CONGREVE*.

Nudus agris, nudus nummis paternis,
Insanire parat certa ratione modoque. Hor.

LONDON:

Printed for *Jacob Tonson* at the *Judge's-Head*, near the *Inner-Temple-Gate* in *Fleetstreet*, 1695.

Nudus agris, etc.—Thou madman!

When thy Hereditary Lands t'hast sold
And spent thy Father's Silver and his Gold.
. . . .
he is as much a fool,
As if he would be mad by art and rule.

(Horace, Satire II, iii, 184 and 271. From *Odes*, *Satires*, etc. rendered in English verse by several persons, 1666.)

TO THE
RIGHT HONOURABLE
CHARLES
Earl of *Dorset* and *Middlesex*,
Lord Chamberlain of His Majesty's Houshold, and Knight of the Most Noble Order of the Garter, &c.

MY LORD,

A young Poet, is liable to the same Vanity and Indiscretion with a Young Lover; and the Great Man that smiles upon one, and the Fine Woman that looks kindly upon t'other, are each of 'em in Danger of having the Favour publish'd with the first Opportunity.

But there may be a different Motive, which will a little distinguish the Offenders. For tho' one should have a Vanity in ruining another's Reputation, yet the other may only have an Ambition to advance his own. And I beg leave, my Lord, that I may plead the latter, both as the Cause and Excuse of this Dedication.

Whoever is King, is also the Father of his Country; and as no body can dispute Your Lordship's *Monarchy* in *Poetry*; so all that are concern'd, ought to acknowledge Your Universal Patronage: And it is only presuming on the Priviledge of a Loyal Subject, that I have ventur'd to make this my Address of Thanks, to Your Lordship; which at the same time, includes a Prayer for Your Protection.

I am not Ignorant of the Common Form of Poetical Dedications, which are generally made up of Panegyricks, where the Authors endeavour to distinguish their Patrons, by the shining Characters they give them, above other Men. But that, my Lord, is not my business at this time, nor is Your Lordship *now* to be distinguish'd. I am contented with the Honour I do my self in this Epistle; without the Vanity of attempting to add to, or explain Your Lordship's Character.

I confess it is not without some strugling, that I behave my self in this Case, as I ought: For it is very hard to be pleased with a Subject, and yet forbear it. But I chuse rather to follow *Pliny*'s Precept, than his Example, when in his Panegyrick to the Emperour *Trajan*, he says,

Nec minus considerabo quid aures ejus pati possint, Quam quid virtutibus debeatur.

Nec minus considerabo etc.—"Nor shall I less consider what will make him blush to hear, than what the merit of his vertues might claim to be spoke." *An Address of Thanks to a good Prince* (a translation of Pliny's *Panegyrick* by White Kennett [1686], p. 6).

I hope I may be excus'd the Pedantry of a Quotation, when it is so justly apply'd. Here are some Lines in the Print, (and which your Lordship read before this Play was Acted) that were omitted on the Stage; and particularly one whole Scene in the Third Act, which not only helps the Design forward with less Precipitation, but also heightens the ridiculous Character of *Foresight*, which indeed seems to be maim'd without it. But I found my self in great danger of a long Play, and was glad to help it where I could. Tho' notwithstanding my Care, and the kind Reception it had from the Town; I could heartily wish it yet shorter: But the Number of Different Characters represented in it, would have been too much crowded in less room.

This Reflection on Prolixity, (a Fault, for which scarce any one Beauty will attone) warns me not to be tedious now, and detain Your Lordship any longer with the Trifles of,

MY LORD,
Your Lordship's
Most Obedient
and Most Humble
Servant,
WILL. CONGREVE.

A
Prologue
FOR
The opening of the new Play-House, propos'd to be spoken by Mrs. *Bracegirdle* in Man's Cloaths.

Sent from an unknown Hand.

Custom, which everywhere bears mighty Sway,
Brings me to act the Orator to Day:
But Women, you will say, are ill at Speeches,
'Tis true, and therefore I appear in Breeches:
Not for Example to you City-Wives;
That by Prescription's setled for your Lives.
Was it for gain the Husband first consented?
O yes, their Gains are mightily augmented:

Making Horns with her Hands over her Head.

And yet, methinks, it must have cost some Strife:
A Passive Husband, and an Active Wife!
'Tis awkward, very awkward, by my Life.
But to my Speech, Assemblies of all Nations
Still are suppos'd to open with Orations:
Mine shall begin, to shew our Obligations.
To you, our Benefactors, lowly Bowing,
Whose Favours have prevented our undoing;
A long *Egyptian* Bondage we endur'd,
Till Freedom, by your Justice we procur'd:
Our Taskmasters were grown such very *Jews*,
We must at length have Play'd in Wooden Shooes,
Had not your Bounty taught us to refuse.
Freedom's of *English* growth, I think, alone;
What for lost *English* Freedom can attone?
A Free-born Player loaths to be compell'd;
Our Rulers Tyraniz'd, and We Rebell'd.
Freedom! the Wise Man's Wish, the Poor Man's Wealth;
Which you, and I, and most of us enjoy by Stealth;

The Soul of Pleasure, and the Sweet of Life,
The Woman's Charter, Widdow, Maid or Wife,
This they'd have cancell'd, and thence grew the Strife.
But you perhaps, wou'd have me here confess
How we obtain'd the Favour;—Can't you guess?
Why then I'll tell you, (for I hate a Lye)
By Brib'ry, errant Brib'ry, let me dye:
I was their Agent, but by Jove I swear
No honourable Member had a share
Tho' young and able Members bid me Fair:
I chose a wiser way to make you willing,
Which has not cost the House a single Shilling;
Now you suspect at least I went a Billing.
You see I'm Young, and to that Air of Youth,
Some will add Beauty, and a little Truth;
These Pow'rful Charms, improv'd by Pow'rful Arts,
Prevail'd to captivate your op'ning Hearts.
Thus furnish'd, I prefer'd my poor Petition,
And brib'd ye to commiserate our Condition:
I Laugh'd, and Sigh'd, and Sung, and Leer'd upon ye;
With Roguish Loving Looks, and that way won ye:
The Young Men kiss'd me, and the Old I kiss'd,
And luringly, I led them as I list.
The Ladies in meer Pity took our Parts,
Pity's the darling Passion of their Hearts.
Thus Bribing, or thus Brib'd, fear no Disgraces;
For thus you may take Bribes, and keep your Places.

Prologue.

Spoken at the opening of the New House,

By Mr. *Betterton.*

The Husbandman in vain renews his Toil,
To cultivate each Year a hungry Soil;
And fondly hopes for rich and generous Fruit,
When what should feed the Tree, devours the Root:
Th'unladen Boughs, he sees, bode certain Dearth,
Unless transplanted to more kindly Earth.
So, the poor Husbands of the Stage, who found
Their Labours lost upon the ungrateful Ground,
This last and only Remedy have prov'd;
And hope new Fruit from ancient Stocks remov'd.
Well may they hope, when you so kindly aid,
And plant a Soil which you so rich have made.
As Nature gave the World to Man's first Age,
So from your Bounty, we receive this Stage;
The Freedom Man was born to, you've restor'd,
And to our World, such Plenty you afford,
It seems like *Eden*, fruitful of its own accord.
But since in *Paradise* frail Flesh gave way,
And when but two were made, both went astray;
Forbear your Wonder, and the Fault forgive,
If in our larger Family we grieve
One falling *Adam*, and one tempted *Eve*.
We who remain, would gratefully repay
What our Endeavours can, and bring this day,
The First-fruit Offering, of a Virgin Play.
We hope there's something that may please each Taste,
And tho' of Homely Fare we make the Feast,
Yet you will find variety at least.
There's Humour, which for chearful Friends we got,
And for the thinking Party there's a Plot.
We've something too, to gratifie ill Nature,
(If there be any here) and that is Satire.
Tho Satire scarce dares grin, 'tis grown so mild;
Or only shews its Teeth, as if it smil'd.

As Asses Thistles, Poets mumble Wit,
And dare not bite, for fear of being bit.
They hold their Pens, as Swords are held by Fools,
And are afraid to use their own Edge-Tools.
Since the *Plain-Dealers* Scenes of Manly Rage,
Not one has dar'd to lash this Crying Age.
This time, the Poet owns the bold Essay,
Yet hopes there's no ill-manners in his Play:
And he declares by me, he has design'd
Affront to none, but frankly speaks his mind.
And shou'd th' ensuing Scenes not chance to hit,
He offers but this one Excuse, 'twas writ
Before your late Encouragement of Wit.

Dramatis Personæ

MEN.

Sir Sampson Legend, Father to *Valentine* and *Ben*.	Mr. Underhill.
Valentine, Fallen under his Father's Displeasure by his expensive way of living, in love with *Angelica*.	Mr. Betterton.
Scandal, His Friend, a Free Speaker.	Mr. Smith.
Tattle, A half-witted Beau, vain of his Amours, yet valuing himself for Secresie.	Mr. Bowman.
Ben, *Sir Sampson*'s Younger Son, half home-bred, and half-Sea-bred, design'd to marry *Miss Prue*.	Mr. Dogget.
Foresight, An illiterate Old Fellow, peevish and positive, superstitious, and pretending to understand Astrology, Palmistry, Phisiognomy, Omens, Dreams, *&c.* Uncle to *Angelica*.	Mr. Sanford.
Jeremy, Servant to *Valentine*.	Mr. Bowen.
Trapland, A Scrivener.	Mr. Triffusis.
Buckram, A Lawyer.	Mr. Freeman.

WOMEN.

Angelica, Niece to *Foresight*, of a considerable Fortune in her own Hands.	Mrs. Bracegirdle.
Mrs. Foresight, Second Wife to *Foresight*.	Mrs. Bowman.
Mrs. Frail, Sister to *Mrs. Foresight*, a Woman of the Town.	Mrs. Barry.
Miss Prue, Daughter to *Foresight* by a former Wife, a silly, awkard, Country Girl.	Mrs. Ayliff.
Nurse, to *Miss Prue*.	Mrs. Leigh.
Jenny, Maid to *Angelica*.	Mrs. Lawson.

A Steward, Officers, Sailers, and several Servants.

The SCENE in *LONDON*.

Love for Love.

ACT I. Scene I.

Valentine *in his Chamber Reading.* Jeremy *waiting.*

Several Books upon the Table.

Valentine. Jeremy.

Jeremy. Sir.

Valentine. Here, take away; I'll walk a turn, and digest what I have read—

Jeremy. You'll grow Devilish fat upon this Paper-Diet.
Aside and taking away the Books.

Valentine. And d'ye hear, go you to Breakfast—There's a Page doubled down in *Epictetus*, that is a Feast for an Emperour.

Jeremy. Was *Epictetus* a real Cook, or did he only write Receipts?

Valentine. Read, read, Sirrah, and refine your Appetite; learn to live upon Instruction; feast your Mind, and mortifie your Flesh; Read, and take your Nourishment in at your Eyes; shut up your Mouth, and chew the Cud of Understanding. So *Epictetus* advises.

Jeremy. O Lord! I have heard much of him, when I waited upon a Gentleman at *Cambridge*: Pray what was that *Epictetus*?

Valentine. A very rich Man.———Not worth a Groat.

Jeremy. Humph, and so he has made a very fine Feast, where there is nothing to be eaten.

Valentine. Yes.

So Epictetus advises—Cf. Valentine's neat phrases with Ellis Walker's *Poetical Paraphrase of Epictetus* (1692), LXVIII, p. 106.

Besides to be too much inclined to speak
Shews your Minds Constitution to be weak,
Your very love of talking doth declare
How ill your Principles digested are...

Jeremy. Sir, you're a Gentleman, and probably understand this fine Feeding: But if you please, I had rather be at Board-Wages. Does your *Epictetus*, or your *Seneca* here, or any of these poor rich Rogues, teach you how to pay your Debts without Money? Will they shut up the Mouths of your Creditors? Will *Plato* be Bail for you? Or *Diogenes*, because he understands Confinement, and liv'd in a Tub, go to Prison for you? 'Slife, Sir, what do you mean, to mew your self up here with Three or Four musty Books, in commendation of Starving and Poverty?

Valentine. Why, Sirrah, I have no Money, you know it; and therefore resolve to rail at all that have: And in that I but follow the Examples of the wisest and wittiest Men in all Ages; these Poets and Philosophers whom you naturally hate, for just such another Reason; because they abound in Sense, and you are a Fool.

Jeremy. Aye, Sir, I am a Fool, I know it: And yet, Heav'n help me, I'm poor enough to be a Wit———But I was always a Fool, when I told you what your Expences would bring you to; your Coaches and your Liveries; your Treats and your Balls; your being in Love with a Lady, that did not care a Farthing for you in your Prosperity; and keeping Company with Wits, that car'd for nothing but your Prosperity; and now when you are poor, hate you as much as they do one another.

Valentine. Well; and now I am poor, I have an opportunity to be reveng'd on 'em all; I'll pursue *Angelica* with more Love then ever, and appear more notoriously her Admirer in this Restraint, than when I openly rival'd the rich Fops, that made Court to her; so shall my Poverty be a Mortification to her Pride, and perhaps, make her compassionate that Love, which has principally reduc'd me to this Lowness of Fortune. And for the Wits, I'm sure I'm in a Condition to be even with them—

Jeremy. Nay, your Condition is pretty even with theirs, that's the truth on't.

Valentine. I'll take some of their Trade out of their Hands.

Jeremy. Now Heav'n of Mercy continue the Tax upon Paper; you don't mean to write!

Valentine. Yes, I do; I'll write a Play.

Jeremy. Hem!———Sir, if you please to give me a small Certificate of Three Lines———only to certifie those whom it may concern; That the Bearer hereof, *Jeremy Fetch* by Name, has for the space of Sev'n Years truly and faithfully serv'd *Valentine Legend* Esq; and that he is not now turn'd away for any Misdemeanour; but does voluntarily dismiss his Master from any future Authority over him—

Valentine. No, Sirrah, you shall live with me still.

Jeremy. Sir, it's impossible—I may die with you, starve with you, or be damn'd with your Works: But to live even Three days, the Life of a Play, I no more expect it, than to be Canoniz'd for a Muse after my Decease.

Valentine. You are witty, you Rogue, I shall want your Help; ———I'll have you learn to make Couplets, to tag the ends of Acts: d'ye hear, get the Maids to Crambo in an Evening, and learn the knack of Rhiming, you may arrive at the height of a Song, sent by an unknown Hand, or a Chocolate-House Lampoon.

Jeremy. But Sir, Is this the way to recover your Father's Favour? Why Sir *Sampson* will be irreconcilable. If your Younger Brother shou'd come from Sea, he'd never look upon you again. You're undone, Sir; you're ruin'd; you won't have a Friend left in the World, if you turn Poet ———Ah Pox confound that *Will*'s Coffee-House, it has ruin'd more Young Men than the *Royal Oak* Lottery——— Nothing thrives that belongs to't. The Man of the House would have been an Alderman by this time with half the Trade, if he had set up in the City—For my part, I never sit at the Door, that I don't get double the Stomach that I do at a Horse-Race. The Air upon *Banstead-Downs* is nothing to it for a Whetter; yet I never see it, but the Spirit of Famine appears to me; sometimes like a decay'd Porter, worn out with pimping, and carrying *Billet-doux* and Songs; not like other Porters for Hire, but for the Jests sake. Now like a thin Chairman, melted down to half his Proportion, with carrying a Poet upon Tick, to visit some great Fortune; and his Fare to be paid him like the Wages of Sin, either at the Day of Marriage, or the Day of Death.

Three days—Many plays only lasted till the author's Benefit on the third night.

Will's—Where Congreve himself was to be found with Dryden and his friends.

Royal Oak Lottery—Started in 1664, the only lottery not prohibited under James II. Finally suppressed in 1699.

Banstead Downs—Racecourse moved after 1730 to Epsom.

Valentine. Very well, Sir; can you proceed?

Jeremy. Sometimes like a bilk'd Bookseller, with a meagre terrify'd Countenance, that looks as if he had written for himself, or were resolv'd to turn Author, and bring the rest of his Brethren into the same Condition. And Lastly, In the Form of a worn-out Punk, with Verses in her Hand, which her Vanity had preferr'd to Settlements, without a whole Tatter to her Tail, but as ragged as one of the Muses; or as if she were carrying her Linnen to the Paper-Mill, to be converted into Folio Books, of Warning to all Young Maids, not to prefer Poetry to good Sense; or lying in the Arms of a needy Wit, before the Embraces of a wealthy Fool.

Enter Scandal.

Scandal. What, *Jeremy* holding forth?

Valentine. The Rogue has (with all the Wit he could muster up) been declaiming against Wit.

Scandal. Aye? Why then I'm afraid *Jeremy* has Wit: For where-ever it is, it's always contriving it's own Ruine.

Jeremy. Why so I have been telling my Master, Sir: Mr. *Scandal*, for Heaven's sake, Sir, try if you can disswade him from turning Poet.

Scandal. Poet! He shall turn Soldier first, and rather depend upon the outside of his Head, than the Lining. Why, what the Devil has not your Poverty made you Enemies enough? Must you needs shew your Wit to get more?

Jeremy. Ay, more indeed; for who cares for any Body that has more Wit than himself?

Scandal. Jeremy speaks like an Oracle. Don't you see how worthless great Men, and dull rich Rogues, avoid a witty Man of small Fortune? Why, he looks like a Writ of Enquiry into their Titles and Estates; and seems Commission'd by Heav'n to seize the better half.

Valentine. Therefore I would rail in my Writings, and be reveng'd.

Scandal. Rail? At whom? the whole World? Impotent and vain! Who would die a Martyr to Sense in a Country where the Religion is Folly? You may stand at Bay for a while; but when the full Cry is against you, you won't have fair Play for your Life. If you can't be fairly run down by the Hounds, you will be treacherously shot by the Huntsmen.———No, turn Pimp, Flatterer, Quack, Lawyer, Parson, be Chaplain to an Atheist, or Stallion to an Old Woman, any thing but Poet; a Modern Poet is worse, more servile, timorous, and fawning, than any I have nam'd: Without you could retrieve the Ancient Honours of the Name, recall the Stage of *Athens*, and be allow'd the force of open honest Satire.

Valentine. You are as inveterate against our Poets, as if your Character had been lately expos'd upon the Stage.—Nay, I am not violently bent upon the Trade.—

One Knocks.

Jeremy, see who's there.

Exit Jeremy.

But tell me what you would have me do?———What do the World say of me, and of my forc'd Confinement?

Scandal. The World behaves it self, as it used to do on such Occasions; some pity you, and condemn your Father: Others excuse him, and blame you: only the Ladies are merciful, and wish you well, since Love and Pleasurable Expence, have been your greatest faults.

Enter Jeremy.

Valentine. How now?

Jeremy. Nothing new, Sir; I have dispatch'd some half a Dozen Duns with as much Dexterity, as a hungry Judge do's Causes at Dinner time.

Valentine. What answer have you given 'em?

Scandal. Patience, I suppose, the old Receipt.

Jeremy. No, faith Sir; I have put 'em off so long with patience and forbearance, and other fair words; that I was forc'd now to tell 'em in plain downright *English*—

Valentine. What?

Jeremy. That they should be paid.

Valentine. When?

a hungry Judge—A common jibe. See Nahum Tate, *A Duke and no Duke* (1693), II: "What! Justice before I have dined? I tell you it is a dangerous thing . . ."; see also Summers (Nonesuch ed., II, 258), who notes Pope, *Rape of the Lock*, iii, 21: The hungry Judges soon the Sentence sign,/And Wretches hang that Jury-men may Dine.

Jeremy. To morrow.

Valentine. And how the Devil do you mean to keep your word?

Jeremy. Keep it? Not at all; it has been so very much stretch'd, that I reckon it will break of course by to morrow, and no body be surpriz'd at the Matter—(*Knocking*)—Again! Sir, if you don't like my Negotiation, will you be pleas'd to answer these your self.

Valentine. See who they are.

Exit Jeremy.

By this, *Scandal*, you may see what it is to be great; Secretaries of State, Presidents of the Council, and Generals of an Army lead just such a life as I do; have just such Crowds of Visitants in a morning, all soliciting of past promises; which are but a civiller sort of Duns, that lay claim to voluntary Debts.

Scandal. And you, like a true great Man, having engaged their Attendance, and promis'd more than ever you intend to perform; are more perplex'd to find Evasions, than you would be to invent the honest means of keeping your word, and gratifying your Creditors.

Valentine. *Scandal*, learn to spare your Friends, and do not provoke your Enemies; this liberty of your Tongue, will one day bring a Confinement on your Body, my Friend.

Re-enter Jeremy.

Jeremy. O Sir, there's *Trapland* the Scrivener, with two suspicious Fellows like lawful Pads, that wou'd knock a Man down with Pocket-Tipstaves,———And there's your Father's Steward, and the Nurse with one of your Children from *Twitnam*.

Valentine. Pox on her, cou'd she find no other time to fling my Sins in my Face: Here, give her this,

Gives Money.

and bid her trouble me no more; a thoughtless two handed Whore, she knows my Condition well enough, and might have overlaid the Child a Fortnight ago, if she had had any forecast in her.

Scandal. What is it Bouncing *Margery*, and my Godson?

Pads—Footpads, highway robbers.
Pocket-Tipstaves—Staff tipped with metal, badge of office.
Twitnam—Twickenham.

Jeremy. Yes, Sir.

Scandal. My Blessing to the Boy, with this Token

Gives Money.

of my Love. And d'ee hear, bid *Margery* put more Flocks in her Bed, shift twice a Week, and not work so hard, that she may not smell so vigorously.———I shall take the Air shortly.

Valentine. *Scandal*, don't spoil my Boy's Milk.———Bid *Trapland* come in.

Exit Jeremy.

If I can give that *Cerberus* a Sop, I shall be at rest for one day.

Enter Trapland *and* Jeremy.

O Mr. *Trapland*! my old Friend! Welcome. *Jeremy*, a Chair quickly: A Bottle of Sack and a Toast—fly—a Chair first.

Trapland. A good Morning to you Mr. *Valentine*, and to you Mr. *Scandal*.

Scandal. The Morning's a very good Morning, if you don't spoil it.

Valentine. Come sit you down, you know his way.

Trapland (*sits*). There is a Debt, Mr. *Valentine*, of 1500 *l*. of pretty long standing—

Valentine. I cannot talk about Business with a Thirsty Palate.—Sirrah the Sack.—

Trapland. And I desire to know what Course you have taken for the Payment?

Valentine. Faith and Troth, I am heartily glad to see you———my Service to you,———fill, fill, to honest Mr. *Trapland*, fuller.

Trapland. Hold, Sweet-heart.———This is not to our Business:———my Service to you Mr. *Scandal*—(*Drinks*)—I have forborn as long—

Valentine. T'other Glass, and then we'll talk. Fill, *Jeremy*.

Trapland. No more, in truth.———I have forborn, I say—

Valentine. Sirrah, fill when I bid you.———And how do's your handsome Daughter———Come a good Husband to her.

Drinks.

Trapland. Thank you———I have been out of this Money—

Valentine. Drink first. *Scandal,* why do you not Drink?

They Drink.

Trapland. And in short, I can be put off no longer.

Valentine. I was much oblig'd to you for your Supply: It did me Signal Service in my necessity. But you delight in doing good.—*Scandal,* Drink to me, my Friend *Trapland*'s Health. An honester Man lives not, nor one more ready to serve his Friend in Distress, tho' I say it to his face. Come, fill each Man his Glass.

Scandal. What, I know *Trapland* has been a Whoremaster, and loves a Wench still. You never knew a Whoremaster, that was not an honest Fellow.

Trapland. Fie, Mr. *Scandal,* you never knew—

Scandal. What don't I know?———I know the Buxom black Widdow in the *Poultry*———800 *l.* a Year Joynture, and 20000 *l.* in Money. A hah! Old *Trap.*

Valentine. Say you so, I'faith: Come, we'll remember the Widow: I know where abouts you are: Come, to the Widow—

Trapland. No more indeed.

Valentine. What, the Widows Health; give it him———off with it:

They Drink.

A Lovely Girl, I'faith, black sparkling Eyes, soft pouting Ruby-Lips! better sealing there, than a Bond for a Million, hah!

Trapland. No, no, there's no such thing, we'd better mind our business.———You're a Wag.

Valentine. No faith, we'll mind the Widow's business, fill again.—Pretty round heaving Breasts,———a *Barbary* shape, and a Jut with her Bum, would stir an *Anchoret:* And the prettiest Foot! Oh if a Man could but fasten his Eyes to her Feet, as they steal in and out, and play at Bo-peep under her Petticoats, ah! Mr. *Trapland*?

Poultry—The East end of Cheapside, then containing poulterers' shops.
Barbary shape—Perhaps, as beautiful as an Arab mare.
Anchoret—Hermit, monk of the desert.

Trapland. Verily, give me a Glass,———you're a Wag,—and here's to the Widow.

Drinks.

Scandal. He begins to Chuckle;—ply him close, or he'l relapse into a Dun.

Enter Officer.

Officer. By your leave, Gentlemen,———Mr. *Trapland*, if we must do our Office, tell us.———We have half a dozen Gentlemen to Arrest in *Pall-Mall* and *Covent-Garden*; and if we don't make haste, the Chairmen will be abroad, and block up the Chocolate-Houses, and then our labour's lost.

Trapland. 'Udso that's true, Mr. *Valentine* I love Mirth, but business must be done, are you ready to—

Jeremy. Sir, your Father's Steward says he comes to make Proposals concerning your Debts.

Valentine. Bid him come in: Mr. *Trapland*, send away your Officer, You shall have an answer presently.

Trapland. Mr. *Snap* stay within Call.

Exit Officer.

Enter Steward and Whispers Valentine.

Scandal. Here's a Dog now, a Traytor in his Wine, Sirrah refund the Sack: *Jeremy* fetch him some warm water, or I'll rip up his Stomach, and go the shortest way to his Conscience.

Trapland. Mr. *Scandal*, you are Uncivil; I did not value your Sack; but you cannot expect it again, when I have drank it.

Scandal. And how do you expect to have your Money again, when a Gentleman has spent it?

Valentine. You need say no more, I understand the Conditions; they are very hard, but my Necessity is very pressing: I agree to 'em, take Mr. *Trapland* with you, and let him draw the Writing———Mr. *Trapland*, you know this Man, he shall satisfie you.

Trapland. Sincerely, I am loth to be thus pressing, but my necessity.

Valentine. No Apology, good Mr. Scrivener, you shall be paid.

Trapland. I hope you forgive me, my business requires—

Exeunt Steward, Trapland *and* Jeremy.

Scandal. He begs Pardon like a Hangman at an Execution.

Valentine. But I have got a Reprieve.

Scandal. I am surpriz'd; what, do's your Father relent?

Valentine. No; He has sent me the hardest Conditions in the World: You have heard of a Booby-Brother of mine, that was sent to Sea three Years ago? This Brother, my Father hears is Landed; whereupon he very affectionately sends me word; If I will make a Deed of Conveyance of my Right to his Estate after his Death, to my younger Brother, he will immediately furnish me with Four thousand Pound to pay my Debts, and make my Fortune. This was once propos'd before, and I refus'd it; but the present impatience of my Creditors for their Money, and my own impatience of Confinement, and absence from *Angelica*, force me to consent.

Scandal. A very desperate demonstration of your love to *Angelica*: And I think she has never given you any assurance of hers.

Valentine. You know her temper; she never gave me any great reason either for hope or despair.

Scandal. Women of her airy temper, as they seldom think before they act, so they rarely give us any light to guess at what they mean: But you have little reason to believe that a Woman of this Age, who has had an indifference for you in your Prosperity, will fall in love with your ill Fortune; besides, *Angelica* has a great Fortune of her own; and great Fortunes either expect another great Fortune, or a Fool.

Enter Jeremy.

Jeremy. More Misfortunes, Sir.

Valentine. What, another Dun?

Jeremy. No Sir, but Mr. *Tattle* is come to wait upon you.

Valentine. Well, I can't help it,———you must bring him up; He knows I don't go abroad.

Exit Jeremy.

Scandal. Pox on him, I'll be gone.

Valentine. No, prithee stay: *Tattle* and you should never be asunder; you are light and shadow, and shew one another;

he is perfectly thy reverse both in humour and understanding; and as you set up for Defamation, he is a mender of Reputations.

Scandal. A mender of Reputations! aye, just as he is a keeper of secrets, another Vertue that he sets up for in the same manner. For the Rogue will speak aloud in the posture of a Whisper; and deny a Woman's name, while he gives you the marks of her Person: He will forswear receiving a Letter from her, and at the same time, shew you her Hand upon the Superscription: And yet perhaps he has Counterfeited the Hand too; and sworn to a truth; but he hopes not to be believ'd; and refuses the reputation of a Ladies favour, as a Doctor says, No, to a Bishoprick, only that it may be granted him—In short, he is a publick Professor of Secresie, and makes Proclamation that he holds private Intelligence.———He's here.

Enter Tattle.

Tattle. Valentine good Morrow, *Scandal* I am Yours.——— That is, when you speak well of me.

Scandal. That is, when I am yours; for while I am my own, or any body's else, that will never happen.

Tattle. How Inhumane!

Valentine. Why *Tattle*, you need not be much concern'd at any thing that he says: For to converse with *Scandal*, is to play at *Losing Loadum*; you must lose a good Name to him, before you can win it for your self.

Tattle. But how Barbarous that is, and how unfortunate for him, that the World shall think the better of any Person for his Calumniation!—I thank Heav'n, it has always been a part of my Character, to handle the Reputation of others very tenderly.

Scandal. Aye, such rotten Reputations as you have to deal with, are to be handl'd tenderly indeed.

Tattle. Nay, but why rotten? Why should you say rotten, when you know not the persons of whom you speak? How cruel that is?

Scandal. Not know 'em? Why, thou never hadst to do with any body that did not stink to all the Town.

Losing Loadum—A game in which you try to lose tricks.

Tattle. Ha, ha, ha; nay, now you make a Jest of it indeed. For there is nothing more known, than that no body knows any thing of that nature of me: As I hope to be sav'd, *Valentine*, I never expos'd a Woman, since I knew what Woman was.

Valentine. And yet you have convers'd with several.

Tattle. To be free with you, I have———I don't care if I own that—Nay more (I'm going to say a bold Word now) I never could meddle with a Woman that had to do with any body else.

Scandal. How!

Valentine. Nay faith, I'm apt to believe him———Except her Husband, *Tattle.*

Tattle. Oh that—

Scandal. What think you of that Noble Commoner, Mrs. *Drab*?

Tattle. Pooh, I know Madam *Drab* has made her Brags in three or four places, that I said this and that, and writ to her, and did I know not what———But, upon my Reputation, she did me wrong———Well, well, that was Malice———But I know the bottom of it. She was brib'd to that by one that we all know—A Man too. Only to bring me into Disgrace with a certain Woman of Quality—

Scandal. Whom we all know.

Tattle. No matter for that———Yes, yes, every body knows ———No doubt on't, every body knows my Secrets——— But I soon satisfy'd the Lady of my Innocence; for I told her———Madam, says I, there are some Persons who make it their Business to tell Stories, and say this and that of one and t'other, and every thing in the World; and, says I, if your Grace—

Scandal. Grace!

Tattle. O Lord, what have I said? my Unlucky Tongue!

Valentine. Ha, ha, ha.

Scandal. Why, *Tattle*, thou hast more Impudence than one can in reason expect: I shall have an esteem for thee, well, and ha, ha, ha, well, go on, and what did you say to her Grace?

Valentine. I confess this is something extraordinary.

Tattle. Not a word as I hope to be sav'd; an errant *Lapsus Linguæ*———Come, let's talk of something else.

Valentine. Well, but how did you acquit your self?

Tattle. Pooh, pooh, nothing at all, I only rally'd with you ———a Woman of ord'nary Rank was a little jealous of me, and I told her something or other, faith———I know not what———Come, let's talk of something else.

Hums a Song.

Scandal. Hang him, let him alone, he has a mind we should enquire.

Tattle. *Valentine*, I Supp'd last Night with your Mistress, and her Unkle Old *Foresight*: I think your Father lies at *Foresight*'s.

Valentine. Yes.

Tattle. Upon my Soul *Angelica*'s a fine Woman———And so is Mrs. *Foresight*, and her Sister Mrs. *Frail.*

Scandal. Yes, Mrs. *Frail* is a very fine Woman, we all know her.

Tattle. Oh that is not fair.

Scandal. What?

Tattle. To tell.

Scandal. To tell what? Why, what do you know of Mrs. *Frail*?

Tattle. Who I? Upon Honour I don't know whether she be Man or Woman; but by the smoothness of her Chin, and roundness of her Lips.

Scandal. No!

Tattle. No.

Scandal. She says otherwise.

Tattle. Impossible!

Scandal. Yes Faith. Ask *Valentine* else.

Tattle. Why then, as I hope to be sav'd, I believe a Woman only obliges a Man to Secresie, that she may have the pleasure of telling her self.

Scandal. No doubt on't. Well, but has she done you wrong, or no? You have had her? Ha?

Tattle. Tho' I have more Honour than to tell first; I have more Manners than to contradict what a Lady has declar'd.

Scandal. Well, you own it?

Tattle. I am strangely surpriz'd! Yes, yes, I can't deny't, if she taxes me with it.

Scandal. She'll be here by and by, she sees *Valentine* every Morning.

Tattle. How!

Valentine. She does me the favour——I mean of a Visit sometimes. I did not think she had granted more to any body.

Scandal. Nor I faith——But *Tattle* does not use to bely a Lady; it is contrary to his Character——How one may be deceiv'd in a Woman, *Valentine*?

Tattle. Nay, what do you mean, Gentlemen?

Scandal. I'm resolv'd I'll ask her.

Tattle. O Barbarous! why did you not tell me—

Scandal. No, you told us.

Tattle. And bid me ask *Valentine*.

Valentine. What did I say? I hope you won't bring me to confess an Answer, when you never ask'd me the Question.

Tattle. But, Gentlemen, this is the most inhumane Proceeding—

Valentine. Nay, if you have known *Scandal* thus long, and cannot avoid such a palpable Decoy as this was; the Ladies have a fine time, whose Reputations are in your keeping.

Enter Jeremy.

Jeremy. Sir, Mrs. *Frail* has sent to know if you are stirring.

Valentine. Shew her up, when she comes.

Exit Jeremy.

Tattle. I'll be gone.

Valentine. You'll meet her.

Tattle. Have you not a back way?

Valentine. If there were, you have more Discretion, than to give *Scandal* such an Advantage; why, your running away will prove all that he can tell her.

Tattle. Scandal, you will not be so ungenerous———O, I shall lose my Reputation of Secresie for ever———I shall never be receiv'd but upon Publick Days; and my Visits will never be admitted beyond a Drawing-Room: I shall never see a Bed-Chamber again, never be lock't in a Closet, nor run behind a Screen, or under a Table; never be distinguish'd among the Waiting-Women by the Name of Trusty Mr. *Tattle* more———You will not be so cruel.

Valentine. Scandal, have pity on him; he'll yield to any Conditions.

Tattle. Any, any Terms.

Scandal. Come then, sacrifice half a Dozen Women of good Reputation to me presently———Come, where are you familiar—And see that they are Women of Quality too, the first Quality—

Tattle. 'Tis very hard—Won't a Baronet's Lady pass?

Scandal. No, nothing under a Right Honourable.

Tattle. O inhumane! You don't expect their Names.

Scandal. No, their Titles shall serve.

Tattle. Alas, that's the same thing: Pray spare me their Titles; I'll describe their Persons.

Scandal. Well, begin then: But take notice, if you are so ill a Painter, that I cannot know the Person by your Picture of her, you must be condemned, like other bad Painters, to write the Name at the bottom.

Tattle. Well, first then—

Enter Mrs. Frail.

O unfortunate! she's come already; will you have Patience till another time———I'll double the number.

Scandal. Well, on that Condition———Take heed you don't fail me.

Mrs. Frail. Hey day! I shall get a fine Reputation by coming to see Fellows in a Morning. *Scandal,* you Devil, are you here too? Oh Mr. *Tattle,* every thing is safe with you, we know.

Scandal. Tattle.

Tattle. Mum———O Madam, you do me too much Honour.

Valentine. Well Lady Galloper, how does *Angelica*?

Mrs. Frail. Angelica? Manners!

Valentine. What, you will allow an absent Lover—

Mrs. Frail. No, I'll allow a Lover present with his Mistress to be particular———But otherwise I think his Passion ought to give place to his Manners.

Valentine. But what if he have more Passion than Manners?

Mrs. Frail. Then let him Marry and reform.

Valentine. Marriage indeed may qualifie the Fury of his Passion, but it very rarely mends a Man's Manners.

Mrs. Frail. You are the most mistaken in the World; there is no Creature perfectly Civil, but a Husband. For in a little time he grows only rude to his Wife, and that is the highest good Breeding, for it begets his Civility to other People. Well, I'll tell you News; but I suppose you hear your Brother *Benjamin* is landed. And my Brother *Foresight*'s Daughter is come out of the Country———I assure you, there's a Match talk'd of by the Old People———Well, if he be but as great a Sea-Beast, as she is a Land-Monster, we shall have a most Amphibious Breed———The Progeny will be all Otters: he has been bred at Sea, and she has never been out of the Country.

Valentine. Pox take 'em, their Conjunction bodes no good, I'm sure.

Mrs. Frail. Now you talk of Conjunction, my Brother *Foresight* has cast both their Nativities, and prognosticates an Admiral and an eminent Justice of the Peace to be the Issue-Male of their two Bodies; 'tis the most superstitious Old Fool! He would have perswaded me, that this was an Unlucky Day, and wou'd not let me come abroad: But I invented a Dream, and sent him to *Artimedorus* for Interpretation, and so stole out to see you. Well, and what will you give me now? Come, I must have something.

Valentine. Step into the next Room—and I'll give you something.

Scandal. Ay, we'll all give you something.

Artemidorus—A Greek of Ephesus, a great authority on dreams, *c.* A.D. 200.

Mrs. Frail. Well, what will you all give me?

Valentine. Mine's a Secret.

Mrs. Frail. I thought you would give me something, that would be a trouble to you to keep.

Valentine. And *Scandal* shall give you a good Name.

Mrs. Frail. That's more than he has for himself. And what will you give me, Mr. *Tattle*?

Tattle. I? My Soul, Madam.

Mrs. Frail. Pooh, No I thank you, I have enough to do to take care of my own. Well; but I'll come and see you one of these Mornings: I hear you have a great many Pictures.

Tattle. I have a pretty good Collection at your Service, some Originals.

Scandal. Hang him, he has nothing but the *Seasons* and the *Twelve Cæsars*, paultry Copies; and the *Five Senses*, as ill represented as they are in himself: And he himself is the only Original you will see there.

Mrs. Frail. Ay, but I hear he has a Closet of Beauties.

Scandal. Yes, all that have done him Favours, if you will believe him.

Mrs. Frail. Ay, let me see those, Mr. *Tattle.*

Tattle. Oh Madam, those are Sacred to Love and Contemplation. No Man but the Painter and my self was ever blest with the Sight.

Mrs. Frail. Well, but a Woman—

Tattle. Nor Woman, till she consented to have her Picture there too——for then she is obliged to keep the Secret.

Scandal. No, no; come to me if you wou'd see Pictures.

Mrs. Frail. You?

Scandal. Yes Faith, I can shew you your own Picture, and most of your Acquaintance to the Life, and as like as at *Knellers*.

Seasons . . . Five Senses—Prints of the paintings of Pierre Brueghel le Jeune. Summers notes (Nonesuch ed., II, 258) that the Twelve Caesars adorn the walls in Hogarth's *Rake's Progress*, III.

Kneller's—Godfrey Kneller, painter of the Kit-cat portraits for Tonson.

Mrs. Frail. O lying Creature———*Valentine*, does not he lye? —I can't believe a word he says.

Valentine. No indeed, he speaks truth now: For as *Tattle* has Pictures of all that have granted him favours, he has the Pictures of all that have refus'd him: If Satyrs, Descriptions, Characters and Lampoons are Pictures.

Scandal. Yes, mine are most in black and white.—And yet there are some set out in their true Colours, both Men and Women. I can shew you Pride, Folly, Affectation, Wantonness, Inconstancy, Covetousness, Dissimulation, Malice, and Ignorance, all in one Piece. Then I can shew you Lying, Foppery, Vanity, Cowardise, Bragging, Lechery, Impotence and Ugliness in another Piece; and yet one of these is a celebrated Beauty, and t'other a profest Beau. I have Paintings too, some pleasant enough.

Mrs. Frail. Come, let's hear 'em.

Scandal. Why, I have a Beau in a Bagnio, Cupping for a Complexion, and Sweating for a Shape.

Mrs. Frail. So.

Scandal. Then I have a Lady burning of Brandy in a Cellar with a Hackney-Coachman.

Mrs. Frail. O Devil! Well, but that Story is not true.

Scandal. I have some Hieroglyphicks too; I have a Lawyer with a hundred Hands, two Heads, and but one Face; a Divine with two Faces, and one Head; and I have a Soldier with his Brains in his Belly, and his Heart where his Head shou'd be.

Mrs. Frail. And no Head?

Scandal. No Head.

Mrs. Frail. Pooh, this is all Invention. Have you ne're a Poet?

Scandal. Yes, I have a Poet weighing Words, and selling Praise for Praise, and a Critick picking his Pocket. I have another large Piece too, representing a School; where there are huge Proportion'd Criticks, with long Wigs, Lac'd

Cupping for a Complexion—Bleeding by means of a cupping-glass.
Hieroglyphicks—Pictures with symbolical meanings: emblems.

Coats, *Steinkirk* Cravats, and terrible Faces; with Catcalls in their Hands, and Horn-Books about their Necks. I have many more of this kind, very well Painted, as you shall see.

Mrs. Frail. Well, I'll come, if it be only to disprove you.

Enter Jeremy.

Jeremy. Sir, here's the Steward again from your Father.

Valentine. I'll come to him—will you give me leave, I'll wait on you again presently.

Mrs. Frail. No, I'll be gone. Come, who Squires me to the *Exchange*, I must call my Sister *Foresight* there.

Scandal. I will; I have a mind to your Sister.

Mrs. Frail. Civil!

Tattle. I will; because I have a tender for your Ladiship.

Mrs. Frail. That's somewhat the better reason, to my Opinion.

Scandal. Well, if *Tattle* entertains you, I have the better opportunity to engage your Sister.

Valentine. Tell *Angelica*, I am about making hard Conditions to come abroad, and be at Liberty to see her.

Scandal. I'll give an account of you, and your Proceedings. If Indiscretion be a sign of Love, you are the most a Lover of any Body that I know: you fancy that parting with your Estate, will help you to your Mistress.—In my mind he is a thoughtless Adventurer,

Who hopes to purchase Wealth, by selling Land;
Or win a Mistress, with a losing hand.

Exeunt.

Steinkirk cravats—Casually tied muslin neckcloth, named after the battle of Steenkirk, in 1692, where the French officers had no time to tie them properly.

Catcalls—A squeaky instrument (which cost Pepys two groats) used by theater audiences to express their disapproval of the play.

Hornbooks—A child's spelling book.

Exchange—Shops on the south side of the Strand, with covered walks, rebuilt after the Great Fire in 1666.

ACT II. SCENE I.

A Room in Foresight's *House.*

Foresight and Servant.

Foresight. Hey day! What are all the Women of my Family abroad? Is not my Wife come home? Nor my Sister, nor my Daughter?

Servant. No, Sir.

Foresight. Mercy on us, what can be the meaning of it? Sure the Moon is in all her Fortitudes; Is my Neice *Angelica* at home?

Servant. Yes, Sir.

Foresight. I believe you lie, Sir.

Servant. Sir?

Foresight. I say you lie, Sir. It is impossible that any thing should be as I would have it; for I was born, Sir, when the Crab was ascending, and all my Affairs go backward.

Servant. I can't tell indeed, Sir.

Foresight. No, I know you can't, Sir: But I can tell, Sir, and foretell, Sir.

Enter Nurse.

Nurse, Where's your young Mistress?

Nurse. Wee'st heart, I know not, they're none of 'em come home yet: Poor Child, I warrant she's fond o'seeing the Town,—Marry, pray Heav'n they ha' given her any Dinner—good lack-a-day, ha, ha, ha, O strange; I'll vow and swear now, ha, ha, ha, Marry and did you ever see the like!

Foresight. Why how now, what's the matter?

Nurse. Pray Heav'n send your Worship good Luck, Marry and Amen with all my heart, for you have put on one Stocking with the wrong side outward.

Moon in all her Fortitudes—Exerting her full power, and thus causing uncertainty and changeableness.

Crab ascending—The fourth sign of the Zodiac; "the Sun being therein, goeth as it were backward (after the nature of the Crab)." W. Ramesey, *Astrologie Restored* (1660), II, xxiv.

Wee'st heart—(dialect) Woe's my heart.

Foresight. Ha, How? Faith and troth I'm glad of it, and so I have, that may be good Luck in troth, in troth it may, very good Luck: Nay, I have had some Omens; I got out of Bed backwards too this morning, without Premeditation; pretty good that too; but then I stumbl'd coming down Stairs, and met a Weasel; bad Omens those: some bad, some good, our lives are checquer'd, Mirth and Sorrow, Want and Plenty, Night and Day, make up our time,—But in troth I am pleas'd at my Stocking. Very well pleas'd at my Stocking—Oh here's my Neice!—

Enter Angelica.

Sirrah, go tell Sir *Sampson Legend* I'll wait on him, if he's at leisure—'tis now Three a Clock, a very good hour for Business, *Mercury* governs this hour.

Exit Servant.

Angelica. Is not it a good hour for Pleasure too? Uncle, pray lend me your Coach, mine's out of Order.

Foresight. What, wou'd you be gadding too? Sure all Females are mad to day———It is of evil portent, and bodes Mischief to the Master of a Family———I remember an old Prophesie written by *Messehalah* the *Arabian*, and thus translated by a Reverend *Buckinghamshire* Bard.

When Housewifes all the House forsake,
And leave good Man to Brew and Bake,
Withouten Guile, then be it said,
That House doth stond upon its Head;
And when the Head is set in Grond,
Ne marl, if it be fruitful fond.

Fruitful, the Head fruitful, that bodes Horns; the Fruit of the Head is Horns———Dear Neice, stay at home——— For by the Head of the House is meant the Husband; the Prophecy needs no Explanation.

Angelica. Well, but I can neither make you a Cuckold, Uncle,

Mercury governs this hour—"*Mercury, quasi Merces, a merendo,* signifying wages and mercature, being the cause and author thereof." Ramesey, *ibid.*, II, xix.

Messahalah—Wrote in the eighth century on conjunction of the eighth and the fourteenth planets, and on eclipses; translated into Latin in the fourteenth century and was frequently quoted by Ramesey.

Buckinghamshire Bard—John Mason, buried at Water Stratford, Bucks., on May 22, 1694. A hymn writer, convinced of the immediate coming of the millennium, whose followers refused to believe he was dead.

by going abroad; nor secure you from being one, by staying at home.

Foresight. Yes, yes; while there's one Woman left, the Prophesie is not in full Force.

Angelica. But my Inclinations are in force, I have a mind to go abroad; and if you won't lend me your Coach, I'll take a Hackney, or a Chair, and leave you to erect a Scheme, and find who's in Conjunction with your Wife. Why don't you keep her at Home, if you're Jealous when she's abroad? You know my Aunt is a little Retrograde (as you call it) in her Nature. Uncle, I'm afraid you are not Lord of the Ascendant, ha, ha, ha.

Foresight. Well, Jill-flirt, you are very pert——and always ridiculing that Celestial Science.

Angelica. Nay Uncle, don't be angry——If you are, I'll reap up all your false Prophesies, ridiculous Dreams, and idle Divinations. I'll swear you are a Nusance to the Neighbourhood—What a Bustle did you keep against the last Invisible Eclipse, laying in Provision as 'twere for a Siege? What a World of Fire and Candle, Matches and Tinderboxes did you purchase! One would have thought we were ever after to live under Ground, or at least making a Voyage to *Greenland*, to inhabit there all the dark Season.

Foresight. Why, you malapert Slut—

Angelica. Will you lend me your Coach, or I'll go on——Nay, I'll declare how you prophecy'd Popery was coming, only because the Butler had mislaid some of the Apostle's Spoons, and thought they were lost. Away went Religion and Spoon-meat together—Indeed, Uncle, I'll indite you for a Wizard.

Foresight. How Hussie! was there ever such a provoking Minx?

Nurse. O merciful Father, how she talks!

Angelica. Yes, I can make Oath of your unlawful Midnight Practices; you and the old Nurse there—

erect a Scheme . . . Conjunction . . . Retrograde—Astrologers' terms, concerned with setting up a figure of the heavens. Explained in Ramesey, *ibid.*, II, xliii.

the last invisible Eclipse—Two eclipses of the sun during 1695 are given in the almanacs, both "not visible in London."

Spoon-meat—broth, soup.

Nurse. Marry Heav'n defend——I at Midnight Practices ——O Lord, what's here to do?——I in unlawful Doings with my Masters Worship——Why, did you ever hear the like now——Sir, did ever I do any thing of your Midnight Concerns——but warm your Bed, and tuck you up, and set the Candle, and your Tobacco-Box, and your Urinal by you, and now and then rub the Soles of your Feet?——O Lord, I!

Angelica. Yes, I saw you together, through the Key-hole of the Closet, one Night, like *Saul* and the Witch of *Endor*, turning the Sieve and Sheers, and pricking your Thumbs, to write poor innocent Servants Names in Blood, about a little Nutmeg-Grater, which she had forgot in the Caudle-Cup——Nay, I know something worse, if I would speak of it—

Foresight. I defie you, Hussie; but I'll remember this, I'll be reveng'd on you, Cockatrice; I'll hamper you——You have your Fortune in your own Hands——But I'll find a way to make your Lover, your Prodigal Spendthrift Gallant, *Valentine*, pay for all, I will.

Angelica. Will you? I care not, but all shall out then——Look to it, Nurse; I can bring Witness that you have a great unnatural Teat under your Left Arm, and he another; and that you Suckle a Young Devil in the Shape of a Tabby-Cat, by turns, I can.

Nurse. A Teat, a Teat, I an unnatural Teat! O the false slanderous thing; feel, feel here, if I have any thing but like another Christian, (*crying*) or any Teats, but two that han't given Suck this Thirty Years.

Foresight. I will have Patience, since it is the Will of the Stars I should be thus tormented——This is the effect of the malicious Conjunctions and Oppositions in the Third House of my Nativity; there the Curse of Kindred was foretold——But I will have my Doors lock'd up——I'll punish you, not a Man shall enter my House.

Saul and the Witch of Endor—See I. Sam. 28: 3–25.

Sieve and shears—Divination by a balanced sieve between extended points of shears; cf. Samuel Butler, *Hudibras*, II, 3, l. 569–70: "Than th'oracle of sieve and sheers/That turns as certain as the spheres."

Caudle—A warm spiced drink.

Third House of my Nativity—Signifying "The third, how Brethren; fourth how Parents live" (R. Ball, *Introduction to Astrology* (1794), p. 31).

Angelica. Do Uncle, lock 'em up quickly before my Aunt come home———You'll have a Letter for Alimony to morrow morning———But let me be gone first, and then let no Mankind come near the House, but Converse with Spirits and the Celestial Signs, the Bull, and the Ram, and the Goat. Bless me! there are a great many Horn'd Beasts among the Twelve Signs, Uncle. But Cuckolds go to Heav'n.

Foresight. But there's but one Virgin among the Twelve Signs, Spitfire, but one Virgin.

Angelica. Nor there had not been that one, if she had had to do with any thing but Astrologers, Uncle. That makes my Aunt go abroad.

Foresight. How? how? is that the reason? Come, you know something; tell me, and I'll forgive you; do, good Neice ———Come, you shall have my Coach and Horses——— Faith and Troth you shall———Does my Wife complain? Come, I know Women tell one another———She is young and sanguine, has a wanton Hazle Eye, and was born under *Gemini*, which may incline her to Society; she has a Mole upon her Lip, with a moist Palm, and an open Liberality on the Mount of *Venus.*

Angelica. Ha, ha, ha.

Foresight. Do you laugh?———Well Gentlewoman, I'll— But come, be a good Girl, don't perplex your poor Uncle, tell me—won't you speak? Odd I'll—

Enter Servant.

Servant. Sir *Sampson* is coming down to wait upon you—

Angelica. Good bu'y Uncle———Call me a Chair—I'll find out my Aunt, and tell her, she must not come home.

Exit Angelica *and Servant.*

Foresight. I'm so perplex'd and vex'd, I am not fit to receive him; I shall scarce recover my self before the Hour be past: Go Nurse, tell Sir *Sampson* I'm ready to wait on him.

Nurse. Yes, Sir.

Exit.

Foresight. Well———Why, if I was born to be a Cuckold, there's no more to be said—

Gemini—"A sign hot and moist"; humour, "somewhat sanguine . . . a curious hazel eye" (Ball, *ibid.*, p. 34).

Enter Sir Sampson Legend *with a Paper.*

Sir Sampson. Nor no more to be done, Old Boy; that's plain—here 'tis, I have it in my Hand, Old *Ptolomee*; I'll make the ungracious Prodigal know who begat him; I will, old *Nostrodamus.* What, I warrant my Son thought nothing belong'd to a Father, but Forgiveness and Affection; no Authority, no Correction, no Arbitrary Power; nothing to be done, but for him to offend, and me to pardon. I warrant you, if he danc'd till Doomsday, he thought I was to pay the Piper. Well, but here it is under Black and White, *Signatum, Sigillatum,* and *Deliberatum*; that as soon as my Son *Benjamin* is arriv'd, he is to make over to him his Right of Inheritance. Where's my Daughter that is to be———hah! old *Merlin*! body o' me, I'm so glad I'm reveng'd on this undutiful Rogue.

Foresight. Odso, let me see; Let me see the Paper———Ay, faith and troth, here 'tis, if it will but hold———I wish things were done, and the Conveyance made———When was this Sign'd, what Hour? Odso, you should have consulted me for the time. Well, but we'll make haste—

Sir Sampson. Haste, ay, ay; haste enough, my Son *Ben* will be in Town to night———I have order'd my Lawyer to draw up Writings of Settlement and Joynture—All shall be done to Night—No matter for the time; prithee, Brother *Foresight,* leave Superstition———Pox o'th'time; there's no time but the time present, there's no more to be said of what's past, and all that is to come will happen. If the Sun shine by Day, and the Stars by Night, why, we shall know one another's Faces without the help of a Candle, and that's all the Stars are good for.

Foresight. How, how? Sir *Sampson,* that all? Give me leave to contradict you, and tell you, you are ignorant.

Sir Sampson. I tell you I am wise; and *sapiens dominabitur astris*; there's Latin for you to prove it, and an Argument to confound your *Ephemeris*———Ignorant!———I tell

Nostrodamus—Physician to Henri II, who claimed the gift of prophesying.

Merlin—Enchanter and necromancer, in the almanacs, and recently in plays, from Dryden's *King Arthur,* 1691, to D'Urfey's *Don Quixote,* 1694.

sapiens dominabitur astris—"A wise man will be ruled by the stars." A much quoted tag, attributed to Ptolemy.

Ephemeris—The popular monthly almanac.

you, I have travel'd old *Fircu*, and know the Globe. I have seen the *Antipodes*, where the Sun rises at Midnight, and sets at Noon-day.

Foresight. But I tell you, I have travell'd, and travell'd in the Cœlestial *Spheres*, know the *Signs* and the *Planets*, and their Houses. Can judge of Motions Direct and Retrograde, of *Sextiles*, *Quadrates*, *Trines* and *Oppositions*, Fiery *Trigons* and Aquatical *Trigons*. Know whether Life shall be long or short, Happy or Unhappy; whether Diseases are Cureable or Incureable. If Journeys shall be prosperous, Undertakings successful; or Goods stoll'n recover'd, I know—

Sir Sampson. I know the length of the Emperour of *China*'s Foot; have kiss'd the Great *Mogul*'s Slipper, and rid a Hunting upon an Elephant with the Cham of *Tartary*——— Body o' me, I have made a Cuckold of a King, and the present Majesty of *Bantam* is the Issue of these Loyns.

Foresight. I know when Travellers lie or speak Truth, when they don't know it themselves.

Sir Sampson. I have known an Astrologer made a Cuckold in the twinckling of a Star; and seen a Conjurer, that cou'd not keep the Devil out of his Wives Circle.

Foresight. What does he twit me with my Wife too, I must be better inform'd of this—(*Aside*)—Do you mean my Wife, Sir *Sampson*? Tho' you made a Cuckold of the King of *Bantam*, yet by the Body of the Sun—

Sir Sampson. By the Horns of the Moon, you wou'd say, Brother *Capricorn*.

Foresight. Capricorn in your Teeth, thou Modern *Mandevil*; *Ferdinand Mendez Pinto* was but a Type of thee, thou Lyar of the first Magnitude. Take back your Paper of Inheritance; send your Son to Sea again. I'll wed my Daughter to an *Egyptian* Mummy, e're she shall Incorporate with a Contemner of Sciences, and a defamer of Vertue.

Fircu—Perhaps a familiar spirit.

Sextiles, etc.—The positions of the planets as they move through the signs of the Zodiac.

Bantam—See John Evelyn's account of the East Indian ambassador's visit, *Diary*, II, June 20, 1682.

Mandeville . . . Pinto—Pinto's *Travels to the Far East*, translated into English (1663), outdid Mandeville's fourteenth-century stories of "the marvayles of Inde."

Sir Sampson. Body o' me, I have gone too far;—I must not provoke honest *Albumazar*———an *Egyptian* Mummy is an Illustrious Creature, my trusty Hieroglyphick; and may have significations of futurity about him; Odsbud, I wou'd my Son were an *Egyptian* Mummy for thy sake. What, thou art not angry for a Jest, my good *Haly*———I Reverence the Sun, Moon and Stars with all my heart. ———What, I'll make thee a Present of a Mummy: Now I think on't, Body o' me, I have a Shoulder of an *Egyptian* King, that I purloyn'd from one of the Pyramids, powder'd with Hieroglyphicks, thou shalt have it sent home to thy House, and make an Entertainment for all the *Philomaths*, and Students in Physick and Astrology in and about *London*.

Foresight. But what do you know of my Wife, Sir *Sampson*?

Sir Sampson. Thy Wife is a Constellation of Vertues; she's the Moon, and thou art the Man in the Moon: Nay, she is more Illustrious than the Moon; for she has her Chastity without her Inconstancy. 'S'bud I was but in Jest.

Enter Jeremy.

How now, who sent for you? Ha! what wou'd you have?

Foresight. Nay, if you were but in Jest.———Who's that Fellow? I don't like his Physiognomy.

Sir Sampson. My Son, Sir; what Son, Sir? My Son *Benjamin*, hoh?

Jeremy. No, Sir, Mr. *Valentine*, my master,———'tis the first time he has been abroad since his Confinement, and he comes to pay his Duty to you.

Sir Sampson. Well, Sir.

Enter Valentine.

Jeremy. He is here, Sir.

Albumazar—Arabian astrologer, the subject of an Italian play adapted by Tomkis in 1615 and revived in 1668, with a preface by Dryden, referring to what may have been a theatrical tradition: "*Subtle* was got, by our *Albumazar*,/That *Alchemist* by this Astrologer."

Haly—An astrologer whom Ramesey refers to as an authority on predicting the weather, often referred to in the almanacs. Not, I think, the famous contemporary astronomer Edmund Halley.

Philomaths—astrologers.

Valentine. Your Blessing, Sir.

Sir Sampson. You've had it already, Sir, I think I sent it you to day in a Bill of Four thousand Pound: A great deal of Money, Brother *Foresight.*

Foresight. Aye indeed, Sir *Sampson*, a great deal of Money for a young Man, I wonder what he can do with it!

Sir Sampson. Body o' me, so do I.———Heark ye, *Valentine*, if there is too much, refund the Superfluity; Do'st hear Boy?

Valentine. Superfluity, Sir, it will scarce pay my Debts,—I hope you will have more Indulgence, than to oblige me to those hard Conditions, which my necessity Sign'd to.

Sir Sampson. Sir, how, I beseech you, what were you pleas'd to intimate, concerning Indulgence?

Valentine. Why, Sir, that you wou'd not go to the extremity of the Conditions, but release me at least from some part.—

Sir Sampson. Oh Sir, I understand you,———that's all, ha?

Valentine. Yes, Sir, all that I presume to ask.———But what you, out of Fatherly fondness, will be pleas'd to add, shall be doubly welcome.

Sir Sampson. No doubt of it, sweet Sir, but your filial Piety, and my Fatherly fondness wou'd fit like two Tallies.—Here's a Rogue, Brother *Foresight*, makes a Bargain under Hand and Seal in the Morning, and would be releas'd from it in the Afternoon; here's a Rogue, Dog, here's Conscience and Honesty; this is your Wit now, this is the Morality of your Wits! You are a Wit, and have been a Beau, and may be a———Why, Sirrah, is it not here under Hand and Seal———Can you deny it?

Valentine. Sir, I don't deny it.—

Sir Sampson. Sirrah, you'l be hang'd; I shall live to see you go up *Holborn-hill*,—Has he not a Rogues face?—Speak, Brother, you understand Physiognomy, a hanging look to me;———of all my Boys the most unlike me; a has a damn'd *Tyburn* face, without the benefit o' the Clergy.

Foresight. Hum—truly I don't care to discourage a young Man,—he has a violent death in his face; but I hope no danger of Hanging.

Holborn-hill—On the way to the gallows at Tyburn.

Valentine. Sir, is this Usage for your Son?——for that old, Weatherheaded fool, I know how to laugh at him; but you, Sir—

Sir Sampson. You Sir; and you Sir:—Why, who are you Sir?

Valentine. Your Son, Sir.

Sir Sampson. That's more than I know, Sir, and I believe not.

Valentine. Faith, I hope not.

Sir Sampson. What, wou'd you have your Mother a Whore! Did you ever hear the like! Did you ever hear the like! Body o' me—

Valentine. I would have an excuse for your Barbarity and Unnatural Usage.

Sir Sampson. Excuse! Impudence! why Sirrah, mayn't I do what I please? Are not you my Slave? Did not I beget you? And might not I have chosen whether I would have begot you or no? Ouns who are you? Whence came you? What brought you into the World? How came you here, Sir? Here, to stand here, upon those two Leggs, and look erect with that audacious face, hah? Answer me that? Did you come a Voluntier into the World? Or did I beat up for you with the lawful Authority of a Parent, and press you to the service?

Valentine. I know no more why I came, than you do why you call'd me. But here I am, and if you don't mean to provide for me, I desire you wou'd leave me as you found me.

Sir Sampson. With all my heart: Come, Uncase, Strip, and go naked out of the World as you came into't.

Valentine. My Cloaths are soon put off:——But you must also deprive me of Reason, Thought, Passions, Inclinations, Affections, Appetites, Senses, and the huge Train of Attendants that you begot along with me.

Sir Sampson. Body o' me, what a many headed Monster have I propagated?

Valentine I am of my self, a plain easie simple Creature; and to be kept at small expence; but the Retinue that you gave me are craving and invincible; they are so many Devils that you have rais'd, and will have employment.

Sir Sampson. 'Oons, what had I to do to get Children,——— can't a private man be born without all these followers: ———Why nothing under an Emperour should be born with Appetites,———Why at this rate a fellow that has but a Groat in his Pocket, may have a Stomach capable of a Ten Shilling Ordinary.

Jeremy. Nay, that's as clear as the Sun; I'll make Oath of it before any Justice in *Middlesex*.

Sir Sampson. Here's a Cormorant too,———'S'heart this Fellow was not born with you?—I did not beget him, did I?—

Jeremy. By the Provision that's made for me, you might have begot me too:———Nay, and to tell your Worship another truth, I believe you did, for I find I was born with those same Whoreson Appetites too; that my Master speaks of.

Sir Sampson. Why look you there now,———I'll maintain it, that by the rule of right Reason, this fellow ought to have been born without a Palate.—'S'heart, what shou'd he do with a distinguishing taste?—I warrant now he'd rather eat a Pheasant, than a piece of poor *John*; and smell, now, why I warrant he can smell, and loves Perfumes above a stink.—Why there's it; and Musick, don't you love Musick, Scoundrell?

Jeremy. Yes, I have a reasonable good Ear, Sir, as to Jiggs and Country Dances; and the like; I don't much matter your *Sola*'s or *Sonata*'s, they give me the Spleen.

Sir Sampson. The Spleen, ha, ha, ha, a Pox confound you— *Sola*'s and *Sonata*'s? 'Oons whose Son are you? how were you engendred, Muckworm?

Jeremy. I am by my Father, the Son of a Chair-man, my Mother sold Oysters in Winter, and Cucumbers in Summer; and I came up Stairs into the World; for I was born in a Cellar.

Foresight. By your Looks, you shou'd go up Stairs out of the World too, Friend.

Sir Sampson. And if this Rogue were Anatomiz'd now, and dissected, he has his Vessels of Digestion and Concoction, and so forth, large enough for the inside of a Cardinal, this

poor John—Slang for dried, salted fish, i.e. the poorest fare.
matter—(obs.) care for.

Son of a Cucumber.———These things are unaccountable and unreasonable,———Body o' me, why was not I a Bear? that my Cubs might have liv'd upon sucking their Paws; Nature has been provident only to Bears and Spiders; the one has its Nutriment in his own hands; and t'other spins his Habitation out of his Entrails.

Valentine. Fortune was provident enough to supply all the Necessities of my Nature; if I had my right of Inheritance.

Sir Sampson. Again! 'Ouns han't you four thousand Pound ———If I had it again, I wou'd not give thee a Groat, ———What, would'st thou have me turn Pelican, and feed thee out of my own Vitals?———'S'heart, live by your Wits,———You were always fond of the Wits,—Now let's see, if you have Wit enough to keep your self?—Your Brother will be in Town to Night, or to morrow morning, and then look you perform Covenants, and so your Friend and Servant———Come Brother *Foresight.*

Exeunt Sir Sampson *and* Foresight.

Jeremy. I told you what your Visit wou'd come to.

Valentine. 'Tis as much as I expected—I did not come to see him: I came to *Angelica*; but since she was gone abroad, it was easily turn'd another way; and at least look'd well on my side: What's here? Mrs. *Foresight* and Mrs. *Frail,* they are earnest,———I'll avoid 'em,———Come this way, and go and enquire when *Angelica* will return.

Exeunt.

Enter Mrs. Foresight *and* Mrs. Frail.

Mrs. Frail. What have you to do to watch me?—'S'life I'll do what I please.

Mrs. Foresight. You will?

Mrs. Frail. Yes marry will I———A great piece of business to go to *Covent-Garden Square* in a Hackney-Coach, and take a turn with one's Friend.

Mrs. Foresight. Nay, two or three Turns, I'll take my Oath.

Mrs. Frail. Well, what if I took twenty———I warrant if you had been there, it had been only innocent Recreation. —Lord, where's the comfort of this Life, if we can't have the happiness of conversing where we like.

turn Pelican—Tearing its breast to feed its young, a very favorite symbol in art and heraldry.

Mrs. Foresight. But can't you converse at home?———I own it, I think there's no happiness like conversing with an agreeable man; I don't quarrel at that, nor I don't think but your Conversation was very innocent; but the place is publick, and to be seen with a man in a Hackney-Coach is scandalous: What if any Body else shou'd have seen you alight as I did?—How can any Body be happy, while they're in perpetual fear of being seen and censur'd?—Besides, it wou'd not only reflect upon you, Sister, but me.

Mrs. Frail. Pooh, here's a Clutter———why should it reflect upon you?———I don't doubt but you have thought your self happy in a Hackney-Coach before now.—If I had gone to *Knights-bridge*, or to *Chelsey*, or to *Spring-Garden*, or *Barn-Elms* with a man alone———something might have been said.

Mrs. Foresight. Why, was I ever in any of these places? What do you mean Sister?

Mrs. Frail. Was I? what do you mean?

Mrs. Foresight. You have been at a worse place.

Mrs. Frail. I at a worse place, and with a man!

Mrs. Foresight. I suppose you would not go alone to the *World's-End.*

Mrs. Frail. The World's end! What, do you mean to banter me?

Mrs. Foresight. Poor innocent! you don't know that there's a place call'd the *World's-End*? I'll swear you can keep your Countenance purely, you'd make an Admirable Player.

Mrs. Frail. I'll swear you have a great deal of Impudence, and in my mind too much for the Stage.

Mrs. Foresight. Very well, that will appear who has most, You never were at the *World's End*?

Mrs. Frail. No.

Mrs. Foresight. You deny it positively to my Face.

Mrs. Frail. Your Face, what's Your Face?

Mrs. Foresight. No matter for that, it's as good a Face as yours.

Mrs. Frail. Not by a Dozen Years wearing.———But I do deny it positively to Your Face then.

World's-End—In Chelsea. The other places referred to were outer suburbs of dubious resort.

Mrs. Foresight. I'll allow you now to find fault with my Face;—for I'll swear your impudence has put me out of Countenance:—But look you here now,———where did you lose this Gold Bodkin?—Oh Sister, Sister!

Mrs. Frail. My Bodkin!

Mrs. Foresight. Nay, 'tis Yours, look at it.

Mrs. Frail. Well, if you go to that, where did you find this Bodkin?—Oh Sister, Sister!—Sister every way.

Mrs. Foresight (*aside*). O Devil on't, that I cou'd not discover her, without betraying my self.

Mrs. Frail. I have heard Gentlemen say, Sister; that one should take great care when one makes a thrust in Fencing, not to lye open ones self.

Mrs. Foresight. It's very true, Sister: Well since all's out, and as you say, since we are both Wounded, let us do that is often done in Duels, take care of one another, and grow better Friends than before.

Mrs. Frail. With all my heart, ours are but slight Flesh-wounds, and if we keep 'em from Air, not at all dangerous: Well, give me your Hand in token of sisterly secresie and affection.

Mrs. Foresight. Here 'tis with all my heart.

Mrs. Frail. Well, as an earnest of Friendship and Confidence; I'll acquaint you with a design that I have: To tell Truth, and speak openly one to another; I'm afraid the World have observ'd us more than we have observ'd one another. You have a Rich Husband, and are provided for, I am at a loss, and have no great Stock either of Fortune or Reputation; and therefore must look sharply about me. Sir *Sampson* has a Son that is expected to Night; and by the Account I have heard of his Education can be no Conjurer: The Estate You know is to be made over to him:——— Now if I cou'd wheedle him, Sister, ha? You understand me?

Mrs. Foresight. I do; and will help you to the utmost of my power—And I can tell you one thing that falls out luckily enough; my awkard Daughter-in-Law, who you know is design'd for his Wife, is grown fond of Mr. *Tattle*; now if we can improve that, and make her have an Aver-

Bodkin—A long, ornamental hairpin.

sion for the Booby, it may go a great way towards his liking of you. Here they come together; and let us contrive some way or other to leave 'em together.

Enter Tattle, *and* Miss Prue.

Miss Prue. Mother, Mother, Mother, look you here.

Mrs. Foresight. Fie, fie, Miss, how you bawl———besides, I have told you, you must not call me Mother.

Miss Prue. What must I call you then, are not you my Father's Wife?

Mrs. Foresight. Madam; you must say Madam———By my Soul, I shall fancy my self Old indeed, to have this great Girl call me Mother———Well, but Miss, what are you so overjoy'd at?

Miss Prue. Look you here, Madam then, what Mr. *Tattle* has giv'n me———Look you here Cousin, here's a Snuff-box; nay, there's Snuff in't;———here, will you have any——— Oh good! how sweet it is———Mr. *Tattle* is all over sweet, his Perruke is sweet, and his Gloves are sweet.———and his Handkerchief is sweet, pure sweet, sweeter than Roses ———Smell him Mother, Madam, I mean———He gave me this Ring for a kiss.

Tattle. O fie Miss, you must not kiss and tell.

Miss Prue. Yes; I may tell my Mother———And he says he'll give me something to make me smell so———Oh pray lend me your Handkerchief———Smell Cousin; he says, he'll give me something that will make my Smocks smell this way———Is not it pure?———It's better than Lavender mun———I'm resolv'd I won't let Nurse put any more Lavender among my Smocks———ha, Cousin?

Mrs. Frail. Fie, Miss; amongst your Linnen, you must say ———You must never say Smock.

Miss Prue. Why, It is not bawdy, is it Cousin?

Tattle. Oh Madam; you are too severe upon Miss; you must not find fault with her pretty simplicity, it becomes her strangely———pretty Miss, don't let 'em perswade you out of your Innocency.

Mrs. Foresight. Oh, Demm you Toad———I wish you don't perswade her out of her Innocency.

mun—An expletive, used here in addressing Mrs. Frail.

Tattle. Who I, Madam?——Oh Lord, how can your Ladyship have such a thought——sure you don't know me?

Mrs. Frail. Ah Devil, sly Devil——He's as close, Sister, as a Confessor——He thinks we don't observe him.

Mrs. Foresight. A cunning Cur; how soon he cou'd find out a fresh harmless Creature; and left us, Sister, presently.

Tattle. Upon Reputation.—

Mrs. Foresight. They're all so, Sister, these Men——they love to have the spoiling of a Young Thing, they are as fond of it, as of being first in the Fashion, or of seeing a new Play the first day,—I warrant it wou'd break Mr. *Tattle*'s Heart, to think that any body else shou'd be before-hand with him.

Tattle. Oh Lord, I swear I wou'd not for the World—

Mrs. Frail. O hang you; who'll believe you?——You'd be hang'd before you'd confess——we know you——she's very pretty!——Lord, what pure red and white!——she looks so wholsome;——ne're stir, I don't know, but I fancy, if I were a Man—

Miss Prue. How you love to jear one, Cousin.

Mrs. Foresight. Heark'ee, Sister——by my Soul the Girl is spoil'd already——d'ee think shee'll ever endure a great lubberly Tarpawlin——Gad I warrant you, she won't let him come near her, after Mr. *Tattle*.

Mrs. Frail. O' my Soul, I'm afraid not——eh!——filthy Creature, that smells all of Pitch and Tarr——Devil take you, you confounded Toad——why did you see her, before she was Married?

Mrs. Foresight. Nay, why did we let him——my Husband will hang us——He'll think we brought 'em acquainted.

Mrs. Frail. Come, Faith let us be gone——If my Brother *Foresight* shou'd find us with them;——He'd think so, sure enough.

Mrs. Foresight. So he wou'd——but then leaving 'em together is as bad—And he's such a sly Devil, he'll never miss an opportunity.

Mrs. Frail. I don't care; I won't be seen in't.

Mrs. Foresight. Well, if you should, Mr. *Tattle*, you'll have a world to answer for, remember I wash my Hands of it, I'm thoroughly Innocent.

Exeunt Mrs. Foresight *and* Mrs. Frail.

Miss Prue. What makes 'em go away, Mr. *Tattle*? What do they mean, do you know?

Tattle. Yes, my Dear———I think I can guess———But hang me if I know the reason of it.

Miss Prue. Come, must not we go too?

Tattle. No, no, they don't mean that.

Miss Prue. No! what then? what shall you and I do together?

Tattle. I must make Love to you, pretty Miss; will you let me make Love to you?

Miss Prue. Yes, if you please.

Tattle (*aside*). Frank, I Gad at least. What a Pox does Mrs. *Foresight* mean by this Civility? Is it to make a Fool of me? Or does she leave us together out of good Morality, and do as she would be done by———Gad I'll understand it so.

Miss Prue. Well, and how will you make Love to me——— Come, I long to have you begin;———must I make Love too? You must tell me how.

Tattle. You must let me speak Miss, you must not speak first; I must ask you Questions, and you must answer.

Miss Prue. What, is it like the Catechisme?———Come then ask me.

Tattle. De'e you think you can Love me?

Miss Prue. Yes.

Tattle. Pooh, Pox, you must not say yes already; I shan't care a Farthing for you then in a twinckling.

Miss Prue. What must I say then?

Tattle. Why you must say no, or you believe not, or you can't tell—

Miss Prue. Why, must I tell a Lie then?

Tattle. Yes, if you would be well-bred. All well-bred Persons Lie———Besides, you are a Woman, you must never speak what you think: Your words must contradict your thoughts; but your Actions may contradict your words.

So, when I ask you, if you can Love me, you must say no, but you must Love me too——If I tell you you are Handsome, you must deny it, and say I flatter you——But you must think your self more Charming than I speak you:—And like me, for the Beauty which I say you have, as much as if I had it my self—If I ask you to Kiss me, you must be angry, but you must not refuse me. If I ask you for more, you must be more angry,——but more complying; and as soon as ever I make you say you'l cry out, you must be sure to hold your Tongue.

Miss Prue. O Lord, I swear this is pure,—I like it better than our old fashion'd Country way of speaking ones mind;—and must not you lie too?

Tattle. Hum——Yes——But you must believe I speak Truth.

Miss Prue. O *Gemini*! well, I always had a great mind to tell Lies—but they frighted me, and said it was a sin.

Tattle. Well, my pretty Creature; will you make me happy by giving me a Kiss?

Miss Prue. No, indeed; I'm angry at you.—

Runs and Kisses him.

Tattle. Hold, hold, that's pretty well,—but you should not have given it me, but have suffer'd me to take it.

Miss Prue. Well, we'll do it again.

Tattle. With all my heart,—Now then my little Angel.

Kisses her.

Miss Prue. Pish.

Tattle. That's right,——again my Charmer.

Kisses again.

Miss Prue. O fie, now I can't abide you.

Tattle. Admirable! That was as well as if you had been born and bred in *Covent-Garden*, all the days of your Life;——And won't you shew me, pretty *Miss*, where your Bed-Chamber is?

Miss Prue. No, indeed won't I: But I'll run there, and hide my self from you behind the Curtains.

Tattle. I'll follow you.

Miss Prue. Ah, but I'll hold the Door with both Hands, and be angry;—and you shall push me down before you come in.

Tattle. No, I'll come in first, and push you down afterwards.

Miss Prue. Will you? then I'll be more angry, and more complying.

Tattle. Then I'll make you cry out.

Miss Prue. Oh but you sha'nt, for I'll hold my Tongue.—

Tattle. Oh my Dear, apt Scholar.

Miss Prue. Well, now I'll run and make more haste than you.

Exit Miss Prue.

Tattle. You shall not fly so fast, as I'll pursue.

Exit after her.

The End of the Second Act.

ACT III. Scene I.

Enter Nurse.

Nurse. Miss, Miss, Miss *Prue*———Mercy on me, marry and Amen: Why, what's become of the Child?—Why Miss, Miss *Foresight*———Sure she has not lock'd her self up in her Chamber, and gone to sleep, or to Prayers; Miss, Miss, I hear her———Come to your Father, Child: Open the Door—Open the Door Miss———I hear you cry husht———O Lord, who's there? (*peeps*) What's here to do?———O the Father! a Man with her!———Why, Miss I say, God's my Life, here's fine doings towards——— O Lord, We're all undone———O you young Harlotry (*knocks*) Ods my Life, won't you open the Door? I'll come in the back way.

Exit.

Tattle *and* Miss Prue *at the Door.*

Miss Prue. O Lord, she's coming———and she'll tell my Father, what shall I do now?

Tattle. Pox take her; if she had staid two Minutes longer, I shou'd have wish'd for her coming.

Miss Prue. O Dear, what shall I say? Tell me, Mr. *Tattle*, tell me a Lie.

Tattle. There's no occasion for a Lie; I cou'd never tell a Lie to no purpose—But since we have done nothing, we must say nothing, I think. I hear her———I'll leave you together, and come off as you can.

Thrusts her in, and shuts the Door.

Enter Valentine, Scandal, *and* Angelica.

Angelica. You can't accuse me of Inconstancy; I never told you, that I lov'd you.

Valentine. But I can accuse you of Uncertainty, for not telling me whether you did or no.

Angelica. You mistake Indifference for Uncertainty; I never had Concern enough to ask my self the Question.

Scandal. Nor good Nature enough to answer him that did ask you: I'll say that for you, Madam.

Angelica. What, are you setting up for good Nature?

Scandal. Only for the affectation of it, as the Women do for ill Nature.

Angelica. Perswade your Friend, that it is all Affectation.

Valentine. I shall receive no Benefit from the Opinion: For I know no effectual Difference between continued Affectation and Reality.

Tattle (*coming up*). *Scandal*, are you in private Discourse, any thing of Secresie?

Aside to Scandal.

Scandal. Yes, but I dare trust you; We were talking of *Angelica*'s Love for *Valentine*; you won't speak of it.

Tattle. No, no, not a Syllable———I know that's a Secret, for it's whisper'd every where.

Scandal. Ha, ha, ha.

Angelica. What is, Mr. *Tattle*? I heard you say something was whisper'd every where.

Scandal. Your Love of *Valentine*.

Angelica. How!

Tattle. No, Madam, his Love for your Ladyship———Gad take me, I beg your Pardon———for I never heard a Word of your Ladyships Passion, till this instant.

Angelica. My Passion! And who told you of my Passion, pray Sir?

Scandal. Why, is the Devil in you? Did not I tell it you for a Secret?

Tattle. Gadso; but I thought she might have been trusted with her own Affairs.

Scandal. Is that your Discretion? trust a Woman with her self?

Tattle. You say true, I beg your Pardon;—I'll bring all off—It was impossible, Madam, for me to imagine, that a Person of your Ladyship's Wit and Gallantry, could have so long receiv'd the passionate Addresses of the accomplisht *Valentine*, and yet remain insensible; therefore you will pardon me, if from a just weight of his Merit, with your Ladyship's good Judgment, I form'd the Ballance of a reciprocal Affection.

Valentine. O the Devil, what damn'd Costive Poet has given thee this Lesson of Fustian to get by Rote?

Angelica. I dare swear you wrong him, it is his own—And Mr. *Tattle* only judges of the Success of others, from the Effects of his own Merit. For certainly Mr. *Tattle* was never deny'd any thing in his Life.

Tattle. O Lord! yes indeed, Madam, several times.

Angelica. I swear I don't think 'tis possible.

Tattle. Yes, I vow and swear I have: Lord, Madam, I'm the most unfortunate Man in the World, and the most cruelly us'd by the Ladies.

Angelica. Nay, now you're ungrateful.

Tattle. No, I hope not———'tis as much Ingratitude to own some Favours, as to conceal others.

Valentine. There, now it's out.

Angelica. I don't understand you now. I thought you had never ask'd any thing, but what a Lady might modestly grant, and you confess.

Scandal. So faith, your Business is done here; now you may go brag somewhere else.

Tattle. Brag! O Heav'ns! Why, did I name any body?

Angelica. No; I suppose that is not in your Power; but you wou'd if you cou'd, no doubt on't.

Tattle. Not in my Power, Madam! What does your Ladyship mean, that I have no Womans Reputation in my Power?

Scandal (*aside*). Ouns, why you won't own it, will you?

Tattle. Faith, Madam, you're in the right; no more I have, as I hope to be sav'd; I never had it in my Power to say any thing to a Lady's Prejudice in my Life———For as I was telling you Madam, I have been the most unsuccessful Creature living, in things of that nature; and never had the good Fortune to be trusted once with a Lady's Secret, not once.

Angelica. No.

Valentine. Not once, I dare answer for him.

Scandal. And I'll answer for him; for I'm sure if he had, he wou'd have told me; I find, Madam, you don't know Mr. *Tattle*.

Tattle. No indeed, Madam, you don't know me at all, I find: For sure my intimate Friends wou'd have known—

Angelica. Then it seems you would have told, if you had been trusted.

Tattle. O pox, *Scandal*, that was too far put———Never have told Particulars, Madam. Perhaps I might have talk'd as of a Third Person———or have introduc'd an Amour of my own, in Conversation, by way of Novel: but never have explain'd Particulars.

Angelica. But whence comes the Reputation of Mr. *Tattle*'s Secresie, if he was never trusted?

Scandal. Why thence it arises———The thing is proverbially spoken; but may be apply'd to him———As if we shou'd say in general Terms, He only is Secret who never was trusted; a Satyrical Proverb upon our Sex———There's another upon yours—As she is chaste, who was never ask'd the Question. That's all.

Valentine. A couple of very civil Proverbs, truly: 'Tis hard to tell whether the Lady or Mr. *Tattle* be the more obliged to you. For you found her Vertue, upon the Backwardness of the Men; and his Secresie, upon the mistrust of the Women.

Satyrical Proverb—Summers quotes Ovid, *Amores*, I, viii, 43: *casta est, quam nemo rogavit.*

Tattle. Gad, it's very true, Madam, I think we are oblig'd to acquit our selves———And for my part———But your Ladyship is to speak first—

Angelica. Am I? Well, I freely confess I have resisted a great deal of Temptation.

Tattle. And I Gad, I have given some Temptation that has not been resisted.

Valentine. Good.

Angelica. I cite *Valentine* here, to declare to the Court, how fruitless he has found his Endeavours, and to confess all his Solicitations and my Denials.

Valentine. I am ready to plead, Not guilty for you; and Guilty, for my self.

Scandal. So, why this is fair, here's Demonstration with a Witness.

Tattle. Well, my Witnesses are not present———But I confess I have had Favours from Persons———But as the Favours are numberless, so the Persons are nameless.

Scandal. Pooh, pox, this proves nothing.

Tattle. No? I can shew Letters, Locketts, Pictures, and Rings, and if there be occasion for Witnesses, I can summon the Maids at the Chocolate-Houses, all the Porters of *Pall-Mall* and *Covent-Garden*, the Door-keepers at the Play-House, the Drawers at *Locket*'s, *Pontack*'s, the *Rummer*, *Spring Garden*; my own Landlady and *Valet de Chambre*; all who shall make Oath, that I receive more Letters than the Secretary's Office; and that I have more Vizor-Masks to enquire for me, than ever went to see the Hermaphrodite, or the Naked Prince. And it is notorious, that in a Country Church, once, an Enquiry being made, who I was, it was answer'd, I was the famous *Tattle*, who had ruin'd so many Women.

Valentine. It was there, I suppose, you got the Nick-Name of the *Great Turk*.

Locket's etc.—Eating houses constantly mentioned in the plays.

Hermaphrodite—Still living in London in Moorfields, in 1693, mentioned as an attraction for visitors in F. Colsoni's *Guide de Londres*, Cambridge, 1951, p. 5.

Naked Prince—Summers quotes from a broadside, c. 1694: "Prince Giolo, son of King of Moangis . . . will be expos'd to public View every day from the 16th of this instant June at his Lodgings . . . in Fleet Street, near Water Lane" (Nonesuch ed., II, 263).

Tattle. True; I was call'd *Turk-Tattle* all over the Parish——— The next *Sunday* all the Old Women kept their Daughters at home, and the Parson had not half his Congregation. He wou'd have brought me into the Spiritual Court, but I was reveng'd upon him, for he had a handsom Daughter whom I initiated into the Science. But I repented it afterwards, for it was talk'd of in Town———And a Lady of Quality that shall be nameless, in a raging Fit of Jealousie, came down in her Coach and Six Horses, and expos'd her self upon my Account; Gad, I was sorry for it with all my Heart———You know whom I mean———You know where we raffl'd—

Scandal. Mum, *Tattle.*

Valentine. 'Sdeath, are not you asham'd?

Angelica. O barbarous! I never heard so insolent a piece of Vanity———Fie, Mr. *Tattle*———I'll swear I could not have believ'd it———Is this your Secresie?

Tattle. Gad so, the Heat of my Story carry'd me beyond my Discretion, as the Heat of the Lady's Passion hurry'd her beyond her Reputation———But I hope you don't know whom I mean; for there were a great many Ladies raffled —Pox on't, now could I bite off my Tongue.

Scandal. No don't; for then you'l tell us no more—Come, I'll recommend a Song to you upon the Hint of my two Proverbs, and I see one in the next Room that will sing it. *Goes to the Door.*

Tattle. For Heaven's sake, if you do guess, say nothing; Gad, I'm very unfortunate.

Re-enter Scandal, *with one to Sing.*

Scandal. Pray sing the first Song in the last new Play.

SONG.

Set by Mr. *John Eccles.*

A Nymph and a Swain to *Apollo* once pray'd,
The Swain had been Jilted, the Nymph been Betray'd;
Their Intent was to try if his Oracle knew
E're a Nymph that was Chaste, or a Swain that was True.

in the last new Play—In fact written by Congreve for this play on the theme of Scandal's two proverbs, see ll. 125–28. Eccles had written the music; sung by Mr. Pate; see *Thesaurus Musicus* (1695), IV, 27–28.

2.

Apollo was mute, and had like t' have been pos'd,
But sagely at length he this Secret disclos'd:
He alone won't Betray in whom none will Confide,
And the Nymph may be Chaste that has never been Try'd.

Enter Sir Sampson, Mrs. Frail, Miss Prue, *and* Servant.

Sir Sampson. Is *Ben* come? Odso, my Son *Ben* come? Odd, I'm glad on't: Where is he? I long to see him. Now, Mrs. *Frail,* you shall see my Son *Ben*———Body o'me, he's the Hopes of my Family———I han't seen him these Three Years———I warrant he's grown———Call him in, bid him make haste———I'm ready to cry for Joy.

Exit Servant.

Mrs. Frail. Now Miss, you shall see your Husband.

Miss Prue (*aside to* Mrs. Frail). Pish, he shall be none of my Husband.

Mrs. Frail. Hush: Well he shan't, leave that to me———I'll beckon Mr. *Tattle* to us.

Angelica. Won't you stay and see your Brother?

Valentine. We are the Twin-Stars, and cannot shine in one Sphere: when he Rises I must set—Besides, if I shou'd stay, I don't know but my Father in good Nature may press me to the immediate Signing the Deed of Conveyance of my Estate, and I'll defer it as long as I can—Well, you'll come to a Resolution.

Angelica. I can't. Resolution must come to me, or I shall never have one.

Scandal. Come, *Valentine*, I'll go with you; I've something in my Head to communicate to you.

Exit Valentine *and* Scandal.

Sir Sampson. What, is my Son *Valentine* gone? What, is he sneak'd off, and would not see his Brother? There's an Unnatural Whelp! There's an ill-natur'd Dog! What, were you here too, Madam, and could not keep him! Cou'd neither Love, nor Duty, nor Natural Affection oblige him. Odsbud, Madam, have no more to say to him; he is not worth your Consideration. The Rogue has

Twin Stars—The Gemini; Castor and Pollux, yet never in the heavens at the same time.

not a Drachm of Generous Love about him: All Interest, all Interest; he's an undone Scoundrel, and courts your Estate: Body o' me, he does not care a Doit for your Person.

Angelica. I'm pretty even with him, Sir *Sampson*; for if ever I cou'd have lik'd any thing in him, it shou'd have been his Estate too: But since that's gone, the Bait's off, and the naked Hook appears.

Sir Sampson. Odsbud, well spoken; and you are a Wiser Woman than I thought you were: For most young Women now-a-days are to be tempted with a naked Hook.

Angelica. If I marry, Sir *Sampson*, I'm for a good Estate with any Man, and for any Man with a good Estate: Therefore if I were obliged to make a Choice, I declare I'd rather have you than your Son.

Sir Sampson. Faith and Troth you're a wise Woman, and I'm glad to hear you say so; I was afraid you were in Love with the Reprobate; Odd, I was sorry for you with all my Heart: Hang him, Mungrel; cast him off; you shall see the Rogue shew himself, and make Love to some desponding *Cadua* of Fourscore for Sustenance. Odd, I love to see a young Spendthrift forc'd to cling to an Old Woman for Support, like Ivy round a dead Oak: Faith I do; I love to see 'em hug and cotten together, like Down upon a Thistle.

Enter Ben. Legend *and Servant.*

Ben. Where's Father?

Servant. There, Sir, his back's toward you.

Sir Sampson. My Son *Ben*! bless thee my dear Boy; body o' me, thou art heartily welcome.

Ben. Thank you Father, and I'm glad to see you.

Sir Sampson. Odsbud, and I'm glad to see thee, kiss me Boy, kiss me again and again, dear *Ben*.

Kisses him.

Ben. So, so, enough Father—Mess, I'de rather kiss these Gentlewomen.

Doit—Smallest Dutch coin.
Cadua—Perhaps caduac, a windfall, i.e., a rich old woman.

Sir Sampson. And so thou shalt,———Mrs. *Angelica*, my Son *Ben.*

Ben. Forsooth an you please—(*Salutes her.*) Nay Mistress, I'm not for dropping Anchor here; About Ship i' faith—

Kisses Mrs. Frail.

Nay, and you too, my little Cock-boat—so—

Kisses Miss Prue.

Tattle. Sir, you're welcome a-shore.

Ben. Thank you, thank you Friend.

Sir Sampson. Thou hast been many a weary League *Ben*, since I saw thee.

Ben. Ey, ey, been! Been far enough, an that be all———well Father, and how do all at home? How do's Brother *Dick*, and Brother *Val*?

Sir Sampson. Dick, body o' me, *Dick* has been dead these two Years; I writ you word, when you were at *Legorne.*

Ben. Mess, and that's true: marry I had forgot. *Dick*'s dead as you say———well, and how? I have a many Questions to ask you; well, you be'nt Marry'd again, Father, be you?

Sir Sampson. No, I intend you shall Marry, *Ben*; I would not Marry for thy sake.

Ben. Nay, what do's that signifie?—an you Marry again—Why then, I'll go to Sea again, so there's one for t'other, an that be all—Pray don't let me be your hindrance; e'en Marry a God's Name an the wind sit that way. As for my part, may-hap I have no mind to Marry.

Mrs. Frail. That wou'd be pity, such a Handsome Young Gentleman.

Ben. Handsome! he, he, he, nay forsooth, an you be for Joking, I'll Joke with you, for I love my jest, an the Ship were sinking, as we sayn at Sea. But I'll tell you why I don't much stand towards Matrimonie. I love to roam about from Port to Port, and from Land to Land: I could never abide to be Portbound as we call it: Now a man that is marry'd, has as it were, d'ee see, his feet in the Bilboes, and may hap may'nt get 'em out again when he wou'd.

Sir Sampson. Ben's a Wagg.

Bilboes—Ship's irons.

Ben. A man that is marri'd, d'ee see, is no more like another man, than a Galley-slave is like one of us free Sailors, he is chain'd to an Oar all his life; and may-hap forc'd to tug a leaky Vessel into the Bargain.

Sir Sampson. A very Wag, *Ben*'s a very Wag; only a little rough, he wants a little Polishing.

Mrs. Frail. Not at all; I like his humour mightily, it's plain and honest, I shou'd like such a humour in a Husband extreamly.

Ben. Say'n you so forsooth: Marry and I shou'd like such a handsome Gentlewoman for a Bed-fellow hugely, how say you Mistress, wou'd you like going to Sea? Mess you're a tight Vessel, and well rigg'd, an you were but as well Mann'd.

Mrs. Frail. I shou'd not doubt that, if you were Master of me.

Ben. But I'll tell you one thing, an you come to Sea in a high Wind, or that Lady.———You mayn't carry so much Sail o' your Head———Top and Top-gallant by the Mess.

Mrs. Frail. No, why so?

Ben. Why an you do, You may run the risk to be overset, and then you'll carry your Keels above Water, he, he, he.

Angelica. I swear, Mr. *Benjamin* is the verriest Wag in nature; an absolute Sea-wit.

Sir Sampson. Nay, *Ben* has Parts, but as I told you before, they want a little Polishing: You must not take any thing ill, Madam.

Ben. No, I hope the Gentlewoman is not angry; I mean all in good part: For if I give a Jest, I'll take a Jest: And so forsooth you may be as free with me.

Angelica. I thank you, Sir, I am not at all offended;———but methinks Sir *Sampson*, You shou'd leave him alone with his Mistress. Mr. *Tattle*, we must not hinder Lovers.

Tattle. Well *Miss*, I have your promise.

Aside to Miss Prue.

Sir Sampson. Body o' me, Madam, you say true:———Look you *Ben*; this is your Mistress,———Come *Miss*, you must not be shame-fac'd, we'll leave you together.

Miss Prue. I can't abide to be left alone, mayn't my Cousin stay with me?

Sir Sampson. No, no. Come, let's away.

Ben. Look you Father, may-hap the young Woman mayn't take a liking to me.—

Sir Sampson. I warrant thee Boy, Come, come, we'll be gone; I'll venture that.

Exeunt all but Ben *and* Miss Prue.

Ben. Come Mistress, will you please to sit down, for an you stand a stern a that'n, we shall never grapple together,— Come, I'll haule a Chair; there, an you please to sit, I'll sit by you.

Miss Prue. You need not sit so near one, if you have any thing to say, I can hear you farther off, I an't deaf.

Ben. Why that's true as you say, nor I an't dumb, I can be heard as far as another, —I'll heave off to please you.

Sits further off.

An we were a League asunder, I'de undertake to hold Discourse with you, an 'twere not a main high Wind indeed, and full in my Teeth. Look you forsooth, I am as it were, bound for the Land of Matrimony; 'tis a Voyage d'ee see that was none of my seeking, I was commanded by Father, and if you like of it, may-hap I may steer into your Harbour. How say you Mistress? the short of the thing is this, that if you like me, and I like you, we may chance to swing in a Hammock together.

Miss Prue. I don't know what to say to you, nor I don't care to speak with you at all.

Ben. No, I'm sorry for that.———But pray why are you so scornful?

Miss Prue. As long as one must not speak one's mind, one had better not speak at all, I think, and truly I won't tell a lie for the matter.

Ben. Nay, You say true in that, it's but a folly to lie: For to speak one thing, and to think just the contrary way; is as it were, to look one way, and to row another. Now, for my part d'ee see, I'm for carrying things above Board, I'm not for keeping any thing under Hatches,—so that if you ben't as willing as I, say so a God's name, there's no harm done; may-hap you may be shame-fac'd, some Maidens tho'f they love a man well enough, yet they don't care to tell'n so to's face: If that's the Case, why silence gives consent.

Miss Prue. But I'm sure it is not so, for I'll speak sooner than you should believe that; and I'll speak truth, tho' one should always tell a lie to a man; and I don't care, let my Father do what he will; I'm too big to be whipt, so I'll tell you plainly, I don't like you, nor love you at all, nor never will, that's more: So, there's your answer for you; and don't trouble me no more, you ugly thing.

Ben. Look you Young Woman, You may learn to give good words however. I spoke you fair d'ee see, and civil.—As for your Love or your liking, I don't value it of a Rope's end;—And may-hap I like you as little as you do me:—What I said was in Obedience to Father; Gad I fear a Whipping no more than you do. But I tell you one thing, if you shou'd give such Language at Sea, you'd have a Cat o' Nine-tails laid cross your Shoulders. Flesh! who are you? You heard t'other handsome Young Woman speak civilly to me, of her own accord: Whatever you think of your self, Gad I don't think you are any more to compare to her, than a Cann of Small-beer to a Bowl of Punch.

Miss Prue. Well, and there's a handsome Gentleman, and a fine Gentleman, and a sweet Gentleman, that was here that loves me, and I love him; and if he sees you speak to me any more, he'll thrash your Jacket for you, he will, you great Sea-calf.

Ben. What, do you mean that fair-Weather Spark that was here just now? Will he thrash my Jacket?—Let'n, let'n,—But an he comes near me, may-hap I may giv'n a Salt Eel for's Supper, for all that. What do's Father mean to leave me alone as soon as I come home, with such a dirty dowdy.—Sea-calf? I an't Calf enough to lick your Chalk'd face, You Cheese-curd you,—Marry thee! Oons I'll Marry a *Lapland*-Witch as soon, and live upon selling of contrary Winds, and Wrack'd Vessels.

Miss Prue. I won't be call'd Names, nor I won't be abus'd thus, so I won't.—If I were a man,—(*Crys.*)—You durst not talk at this rate——No you durst not, you stinking Tar-barrel.

Enter Mrs. Foresight, *and* Mrs. Frail.

Mrs. Foresight. They have quarrel'd just as we cou'd wish.

Ben. Tar-barrel? Let your Sweet-heart there call me so, if he'll

Lapland Witch—noted for raising winds and tempests.

take your part, Your *Tom Essence*, and I'll say something to him; Gad I'll lace his Musk-Doublet for him, I'll make him stink; he shall smell more like a Weasel than a Civet-Cat, afore I ha' done with 'en.

Mrs. Foresight. Bless me, what's the matter? *Miss*, what do's she cry?—Mr. *Benjamin*, what have you done to her?

Ben. Let her cry: The more she cries, the less she'll———she has been gathering foul weather in her Mouth, and now it rains out at her Eyes.

Mrs. Foresight. Come, *Miss*, come along with me, and tell me, poor Child.

Mrs. Frail. Lord, what shall we do, there's my Brother *Foresight*, and Sir *Sampson* coming. Sister, do you take *Miss* down into the Parlour, and I'll carry Mr. *Benjamin* into my Chamber, for they must not know that they are fall'n out.———Come, Sir, will you venture your self with me?

Looks kindly on him.

Ben. Venture, *Mess*, and that I will, tho' 'twere to Sea in a Storm.

Exeunt.

Enter Sir Sampson *and* Foresight.

Sir Sampson. I left 'em together here; What are they gone? *Ben*'s a brisk Boy: He has got her into a Corner, Father's own Son, faith, he'll touzle her, and mouzle her: The Rogue's sharp set, coming from Sea, if he should not stay for saying Grace, old *Foresight*, but fall too without the help of a Parson, ha? Odd if he should I cou'd not be angry with him; twould be but like me, *A Chip of the Old Block*. Ha! thou'rt melancholly old Prognostication; As melancholly as if thou hadst spilt the Salt, or par'd thy Nails of a Sunday:———Come, Cheer up, look about thee: Look up old Star-Gazer. Now is he poring upon the Ground for a crooked Pin, or an old Horse-nail, with the head towards him.

Foresight. Sir *Sampson*, we'll have the Wedding to morrow morning.

Sir Sampson. With all my Heart.

Foresight. At Ten a Clock, punctually at Ten.

Tom Essence—A character in Thomas Rawlins' *Tom Essence: or, The Modish Wife*, 1676.

Sir Sampson. To a Minute, to a Second; thou shall set thy Watch, and the Bridegroom shall observe it's Motions; they shall be married to a Minute, go to Bed to a Minute; and when the Alarm strikes, they shall keep time like the Figures of St. *Dunstan*'s Clock, and *Consummatum est* shall ring all over the Parish.

Enter Scandal.

Scandal. Sir *Sampson*, sad News.

Foresight. Bless us!

Sir Sampson. Why, what's the matter?

Scandal. Can't you guess at what ought to afflict you and him, and all of us, more than any thing else?

Sir Sampson. Body o' me, I don't know any universal Grievance, but a new Tax, and the loss of the Canary Fleet. Without Popery shou'd be landed in the *West*, or the *French* Fleet were at Anchor at *Blackwall.*

Scandal. No. Undoubtedly Mr. *Foresight* knew all this, and might have prevented it.

Foresight. 'Tis no Earthquake!

Scandal. No, not yet; nor Whirlwind. But we don't know what it may come to—But it has had a Consequence already that touches us all.

Sir Sampson. Why, body o' me, out with't.

Scandal. Something has appear'd to your Son *Valentine*——— He's gone to Bed upon't, and very ill———He speaks little, yet says he has a World to say. Asks for his Father and the Wise *Foresight*; talks of *Raymond Lully*, and the Ghost of *Lilly*. He has Secrets to impart I suppose to you two. I can get nothing out of him but Sighs. He desires he may see you in the Morning, but would not be disturb'd to Night, because he has some Business to do in a Dream.

Figures in St. Dunstan's Clock—Painted wooden figures that appear and strike the quarters.

Blackwall—On the north bank of the river, below Greenwich—"ship yards, with fine store houses ... and good docks"; Pepys, *Diary*, July 12, 1664.

Lully—The great Franciscan, Raymond Lully, philosopher and missionary to the Arabs, who had encouraged the study of Greek and semitic languages in the thirteenth century.

Ghost of Lilly—William, one of the most popular of the almanac-makers.

Sir Sampson. Hoity toity, What have I to do with his Dreams or his Divination———Body o' me, this is a Trick to defer Signing the Conveyance. I warrant the Devil will tell him in a Dream, that he must not part with his Estate: But I'll bring him a Parson to tell him, that the Devil's a Liar———Or if that won't do, I'll bring a Lawyer that shall out-lie the Devil. And so I'll try whether my Black-Guard or his shall get the better of the Day.

Exit.

Scandal. Alas, Mr. *Foresight*, I'm afraid all is not right——— You are a Wise Man, and a Conscientious Man; a Searcher into Obscurity and Futurity; and if you commit an Error, it is with a great deal of Consideration, and Discretion, and Caution—

Foresight. Ah, good Mr. *Scandal*—

Scandal. Nay, nay, 'tis manifest; I do not flatter you———But Sir *Sampson* is hasty, very hasty;—I'm afraid he is not scrupulous enough, Mr. *Foresight*———He has been wicked, and Heav'n grant he may mean well in his Affair with you———But my Mind gives me, these things cannot be wholly insignificant. You are wise, and shou'd not be over-reach'd, methinks you shou'd not—

Foresight. Alas Mr. *Scandal*———*Humanum est errare.*

Scandal. You say true, Man will err; meer Man will err——— but you are something more———There have been wise Men; but they were such as you———Men who consulted the Stars, and were Observers of Omens—*Solomon* was wise, but how?———by his Judgment in Astrology——— So says *Pineda* in his Third Book and Eighth Chapter—

Foresight. You are learn'd, Mr. *Scandal*—

Scandal. A Trifler———but a Lover of Art———And the Wise Men of the *East* ow'd their Instruction to a Star, which is rightly observ'd by *Gregory* the Great in favour of Astrology! And *Albertus Magnus* makes it the most valuable Science, Because, says he, it teaches us to consider the Causation of Causes, in the Causes of things.

Foresight. I protest I honour you, Mr. *Scandal*—I did not think you had been read in these matters—Few Young Men are inclin'd—

Pineda—A Spanish Jesuit, who wrote a commentary on Solomon, 1609.

Albertus Magnus—An Aristotelian who taught Thomas Aquinas, but lent his authority to a belief in the value of alchemy and astrology.

Scandal. I thank my Stars that have inclin'd me—But I fear this Marriage and making over this Estate, this transferring of a rightful Inheritance, will bring Judgments upon us. I prophesie it, and I wou'd not have the Fate of *Cassandra*, not to be believ'd. *Valentine* is disturb'd, what can be the Cause of that? And Sir *Sampson* is hurry'd on by an unusual Violence——I fear he does not act wholly from himself; methinks he does not look as he used to do.

Foresight. He was always of an impetuous Nature——But as to this marriage I have consulted the Stars; and all Appearances are prosperous—

Scandal. Come, come, Mr. *Foresight*, let not the Prospect of Worldly Lucre carry you beyond your Judgment, nor against your Conscience—You are not satisfy'd that you act justly.

Foresight. How!

Scandal. You are not satisfy'd, I say——I am loath to discourage you—But it is palpable that you are not satisfy'd.

Foresight. How does it appear, Mr. *Scandal*? I think I am very well satisfy'd.

Scandal. Either you suffer your self to deceive your self; or you do not know your self.

Foresight. Pray explain your self.

Scandal. Do you sleep well o'nights?

Foresight. Very well.

Scandal. Are you certain? You do not look so.

Foresight. I am in Health, I think.

Scandal. So was *Valentine* this Morning; and look'd just so.

Foresight. How! Am I alter'd any way? I don't perceive it.

Scandal. That may be, but your Beard is longer than it was two Hours ago.

Foresight. Indeed! bless me.

Enter Mrs. Foresight.

Mrs. Foresight. Husband, will you go to Bed? It's Ten a Clock. Mr. *Scandal*, your Servant—

Scandal. Pox on her, she has interrupted my Design———But I must work her into the Project. You keep early Hours, Madam.

Mrs. Foresight. Mr. *Foresight* is punctual, we sit up after him.

Foresight. My Dear, pray lend me your Glass, your little Looking-glass.

Scandal. Pray lend it him, Madam———I'll tell you the reason. (*She gives him the Glass:* Scandal *and she whisper.*) My Passion for you is grown so violent—that I am no longer Master of my self—I was interrupted in the morning, when you had Charity enough to give me your Attention, and I had Hopes of finding another opportunity of explaining my self to you—but was disappointed all this day; and the Uneasiness that has attended me ever since, brings me now hither at this unseasonable hour—

Mrs. Foresight. Was there ever such Impudence, to make Love to me before my Husband's Face? I'll Swear I'll tell him.

Scandal. Do, I'll dye a Martyr, rather than disclaim my Passion. But come a little farther this way, and I'll tell you what Project I had to get him out of the way; that I might have an opportunity of waiting upon you.

Whisper.

Foresight (*looking in the Glass*). I do not see any Revolution here;———Methinks I look with a serene and benign aspect———pale, a little pale—but the Roses of these Cheeks have been gather'd many Years;—ha! I do not like that suddain flushing———gone already!—hem, hem, hem! faintish. My Heart is pretty good; yet it beats; and my Pulses ha!—I have none—Mercy on me—hum—Yes, here they are—Gallop, gallop, gallop, gallop, gallop, gallop, hey! Whither will they hurry me?—Now they're gone again—And now I'm faint again; and pale again, and hem! and my hem!—breath, hem!—grows short; hem! hem! he, he, hem!

Scandal. It takes, pursue it in the name of Love and Pleasure.

Mrs. Foresight. How do you do, Mr. *Foresight*?

Foresight. Hum, not so well as I thought I was. Lend me your Hand.

Scandal. Look you there now———Your Lady says your Sleep has been unquiet of late.

Foresight. Very likely.

Mrs. Foresight. O, mighty restless, but I was afraid to tell him so—He has been subject to Talking and Starting.

Scandal. And did not use to be so.

Mrs. Foresight. Never, never; till within these three Nights; I cannot say that he has once broken my Rest, since we have been Marry'd.

Foresight. I will go to Bed.

Scandal. Do so, Mr. *Foresight*, and say your Pray'rs;———He looks better than he did.

Mrs. Foresight. Nurse, Nurse!

Calls.

Foresight. Do you think so, Mr. *Scandal*?

Scandal. Yes, yes, I hope this will be gone by Morning, taking it in time—

Foresight. I hope so.

Enter Nurse.

Mrs. Foresight. Nurse; your Master is not well; put him to Bed.

Scandal. I hope you will be able to see *Valentine* in the Morning,—you had best take a little Diacodion and Cowslip water, and lye upon your back, may be you may dream.

Foresight. I thank you Mr. *Scandal*, I will—Nurse, let me have a Watch-light, and lay the Crums of Comfort by me.—

Nurse. Yes, Sir.

Foresight. And—hem, hem! I am very faint.—

Scandal. No, no, you look much better.

Foresight. Do I? And d'ye hear—bring me, let me see—within a quarter of Twelve—hem—he, hem!—just upon the turning of the Tide, bring me the Urinal;—And I hope, neither the Lord of my Ascendant, nor the Moon will be combust; and then I may do well.

Diacodion—An opiate.
Lord of my Ascendant—"Let the Lord of the ascendant and the Moon . . . be free from Impediment" when giving physic (Ramesey, *Astrologie Restored*, III, ii, 163).

Scandal. I hope so—Leave that to me; I will erect a Scheme; and I hope I shall find both *Sol* and *Venus* in the sixth House.

Foresight. I thank you, Mr. *Scandal*, indeed that wou'd be a great Comfort to me. Hem, hem! good Night.

Exit.

Scandal. Good Night, good Mr. *Foresight*;—and I hope *Mars* and *Venus* will be in Conjunction;—while your Wife and I are together.

Mrs. Foresight. Well; and what use do you hope to make of this Project? You don't think, that you are ever like to succeed in your design upon me?

Scandal. Yes, Faith I do; I have a better Opinion both of you and my self, than to despair.

Mrs. Foresight. Did you ever hear such a Toad—heark'ee Devil; do you think any Woman Honest?

Scandal. Yes, several, very honest;—they'll cheat a little at Cards, sometimes, but that's nothing.

Mrs. Foresight. Pshaw! but Vertuous, I mean.

Scandal. Yes, Faith, I believe some Women are Vertuous too; but 'tis as I believe some Men are Valiant, thro' fear—For why shou'd a Man court Danger, or a Woman shun Pleasure?

Mrs. Foresight. O Monstrous! What are Conscience and Honour?

Scandal. Why, Honour is a publick Enemy; and Conscience a Domestick Thief; and he that wou'd secure his Pleasure, must pay a Tribute to one, and go halves with the t'other. As for Honour, that you have secur'd, for you have purchas'd a perpetual opportunity for Pleasure.

Mrs. Foresight. An Opportunity for Pleasure!

Scandal. Aye, your Husband, a Husband is an opportunity for Pleasure, so you have taken care of Honour, and 'tis the least I can do to take care of Conscience.

Venus in the sixth house—A good sign, free from sickness, and for this Foresight thanks him; but he had also other things in mind.

Mrs. Foresight. And so you think we are free for one another?

Scandal. Yes Faith, I think so; I love to speak my mind.

Mrs. Foresight. Why then I'll speak my mind. Now as to this Affair between you and me. Here you make love to me; why, I'll confess it does not displease me. Your Person is well enough, and your Understanding is not a-miss.

Scandal. I have no great Opinion of my self; yet I think, I'm neither Deform'd, nor a Fool.

Mrs. Foresight. But you have a Villanous Character; you are a Libertine in Speech, as well as Practice.

Scandal. Come, I know what you wou'd say,———you think it more dangerous to be seen in Conversation with me, than to allow some other Men the last Favour; you mistake, the liberty I take in Talking, is purely affected, for the Service of your Sex. He that first cries out stop Thief, is often he that has stolen the Treasure. I am a Jugler, that act by Confederacy; and if you please, we'll put a Trick upon the world.

Mrs. Foresight. Aye; but you are such an universal Jugler, ———that I'm afraid you have a great many Confederates.

Scandal. Faith, I'm sound.

Mrs. Foresight. O, fie———I'll Swear you're Impudent.

Scandal. I'll Swear you're Handsome.

Mrs. Foresight. Pish, you'd tell me so, tho' you did not think so.

Scandal. And you'd think so, tho' I should not tell you so: And now I think we know one another pretty well.

Mrs. Foresight. O Lord, who's here?

Enter Mrs. Frail, *and* Ben.

Ben. Mess, I love to speak my mind———Father has nothing to do with me———Nay, I can't say that neither; he has something to do with me. But what do's that signifie? If so be, that I ben't minded to be steer'd by him; 'tis as tho'f he should strive against Wind and Tyde.

Mrs. Frail. Aye, but my Dear, we must keep it secret, till the Estate be setled; for you know, Marrying without an Estate, is like Sailing in a Ship without Ballast.

Ben. He, he, he; why that's true; just so for all the World it is indeed, as like as two Cable Ropes.

Mrs. Frail. And tho' I have a good Portion; you know one wou'd not venture all in one Bottom.

Ben. Why that's true again; for may-hap one Bottom may spring a Leak. You have hit it indeed, Mess you've nick'd the Channel.

Mrs. Frail. Well, but if you shou'd forsake me after all, you'd break my Heart.

Ben. Break your Heart? I'de rather the *Mary-gold* shou'd break her Cable in a storm, as well as I love her. Flesh, you don't think I'm false-hearted, like a Land-man. A Sailer will be honest, tho'f may-hap he has never a Penny of Mony in his Pocket——May-hap I may not have so fair a Face, as a Citizen or a Courtier; but for all that, I've as good Blood in my Veins, and a Heart as sound as a Bisket.

Mrs. Frail. And will you love me always?

Ben. Nay, an I love once, I'll stick like pitch; I'll tell you that. Come, I'll sing you a Song of a Sailor.

Mrs. Frail. Hold, there's my Sister, I'll call her to hear it.

Mrs. Foresight. Well; I won't go to Bed to my Husband to Night; because I'll retire to my own Chamber, and think of what you have said.

Scandal. Well; You'll give me leave to wait upon you to your Chamber-door; and leave you my last Instructions?

Mrs. Foresight. Hold, here's my Sister coming toward us.

Mrs. Frail. If it won't interrupt you, I'll entertain you with a Song.

Ben. The Song was made upon one of our Ships-Crew's Wife; our Boat-swain made the Song, may-hap you may know her, Sir. Before she was Marry'd, she was call'd buxom *Joan* of *Deptford.*

Scandal. I have heard of her.

Ben *Sings.*

BALLAD.

Set by Mr. *John Eccles.*

A Souldier and a Sailor,
A Tinker, and a Tailor,
Had once a doubtful strife, Sir,
To make a Maid a Wife, Sir,
  Whose Name was Buxom *Joan.*
For now the time was ended,
When she no more intended,
To lick her Lips at Men, Sir,
And gnaw the Sheets in vain, Sir,
  And lie o' Nights alone.

2.

The Souldier Swore like Thunder,
He lov'd her more than Plunder;
And shew'd her many a Scar, Sir,
That he had brought from far, Sir.
  With Fighting for her sake.
The Tailor thought to please her,
With off'ring her his Measure.
The Tinker too with Mettle,
Said he could mend her Kettle,
  And stop up ev'ry leak.

3.

But while these three were prating,
The Sailor slily waiting,
Thought if it came about, Sir,
That they should all fall out, Sir:
  He then might play his part.
And just e'en as he meant, Sir,
To Loggerheads they went, Sir,
And then he let fly at her,
A shot 'twixt wind and water,
  That won this Fair Maids Heart.

Ben. If some of our Crew that came to see me, are not gone; you shall see, that we Sailors can Dance sometimes, as well as other Folks.

Whistles.

I warrant that brings 'em, an' they be within hearing.

The Ballad—Sung with great success by Dogget, it became very popular and was reprinted with additional stanzas, not by Congreve. There may have been an older ballad with a traditional tune, Eccles' music being described as "a new play house tune."

Enter Seamen.

Oh here they be———And Fiddles along with 'em; come, my Lads, let's have a round, and I'll make one.

Dance.

We're merry Folk, we Sailors, we han't much to care for. Thus we live at Sea; eat Bisket, and drink Flip; put on a clean Shirt once a Quarter———Come home and lie with our Landladies once a Year, get rid of a little Mony; and then put off with the next fair wind. How de'e like us?

Mrs. Frail. O' you are the happiest, merriest Men alive.

Mrs. Foresight. We're beholding to Mr. *Benjamin* for this Entertainment. I believe it's late.

Ben. Why, forsooth, an you think so, you had best go to Bed. For my part, I mean to toss a Can, and remember my Sweet-Heart, a-fore I turn in; may-hap I may dream of her.

Mrs. Foresight. Mr. *Scandal*, you had best go to Bed and Dream too.

Scandal. Why Faith, I have a good lively Imagination; and can Dream as much to the purpose as another, if I set about it: But Dreaming is the poor retreat of a lazy, hopeless, and imperfect Lover; 'tis the last glimpse of Love to worn-out Sinners, and the faint dawning of a Bliss to wishing Girls, and growing Boys.

There's nought but willing, waking Love, that can
Make Blest the Ripen'd Maid, and Finish'd Man.

Exeunt.

The End of the Third Act.

ACT IV. Scene I.

Valentine's *Lodging.*

Enter Scandal, *and* Jeremy.

Scandal. Well, Is your Master ready; do's he look madly, and talk madly?

Flip—"A sea-drink of small beer and brandy, sweetened and spiced" (*Dictionary of the Canting Crew*).

Jeremy. Yes, Sir; you need make no great doubt of that; he that was so near turning Poet yesterday morning, can't be much to seek in playing the Madman to day.

Scandal. Would he have *Angelica* acquainted with the Reason of his design?

Jeremy. No, Sir, not yet;—He has a mind to try, whether his playing the Madman, won't make her play the Fool, and fall in Love with him; or at least own that she has lov'd him all this while, and conceal'd it.

Scandal. I saw her take Coach just now with her Maid; and think I heard her bid the Coach-man drive hither.

Jeremy. Like enough, Sir, for I told her Maid this morning, my Master was run stark mad only for Love of her Mistress; I hear a Coach stop; if it should be she, Sir, I believe he would not see her, till he hears how she takes it.

Scandal. Well, I'll try her———'tis she, here she comes.

Enter Angelica *with* Jenny.

Angelica. Mr. *Scandal*, I suppose you don't think it a Novelty, to see a Woman visit a Man at his own Lodgings in a morning.

Scandal. Not upon a kind occasion, Madam. But when a Lady comes Tyrannically to insult a ruin'd Lover, and make manifest the cruel Triumphs of her Beauty; the barbarity of it, something surprizes me.

Angelica. I don't like Raillery from a serious Face———pray tell me what is the matter.

Jeremy. No strange matter, Madam; my Master's mad, that's all: I suppose your Ladyship has thought him so a great while.

Angelica. How d'ye mean, mad?

Jeremy. Why faith, Madam, he's mad for want of his Wits, just as he was poor for want of Money; his Head is e'en as light as his Pockets; and any body that has a mind to a bad Bargain, can't do better than to beg him for his Estate.

Angelica. If you speak Truth, your endeavouring at Wit is very unseasonable—

Scandal. She's concern'd, and loves him. *Aside*.

Angelica. Mr. *Scandal*, you can't think me guilty of so much Inhumanity, as not to be concern'd for a Man I must own my self oblig'd to———pray tell me truth.

Scandal. Faith, Madam, I wish telling a Lie would mend the matter. But this is no new effect of an unsuccessful Passion.

Angelica (*aside*). I know not what to think———Yet I shou'd be vext to have a trick put upon me———May I not see him?

Scandal. I'm afraid the Physician is not willing you shou'd see him yet———*Jeremy*, go in and enquire.

Exit Jeremy.

Angelica. Ha! I saw him wink and smile———I fancy 'tis a trick—I'll try———I would disguise to all the World a Failing, which I must own to you———I fear my Happiness depends upon the recovery of *Valentine*. Therefore I conjure you, as you are his Friend, and as you have Compassion upon one fearful of Affliction, to tell me what I am to hope for—I cannot speak—But you may tell me, tell me, for you know what I wou'd ask?

Scandal. So, this is pretty plain———Be not too much concern'd, Madam; I hope his Condition is not desperate: An Acknowledgment of Love from you, perhaps, may work a Cure; as the fear of your Aversion occasion'd his Distemper.

Angelica (*aside*). Say you so; nay, then I'm convinc'd: And if I don't play Trick for Trick, may I never taste the Pleasure of Revenge———Acknowledgment of Love! I find you have mistaken my Compassion, and think me guilty of a Weakness I am a Stranger to. But I have too much Sincerity to deceive you, and too much Charity to suffer him to be deluded with vain Hopes. Good Nature and Humanity oblige me to be concern'd for him; but to Love is neither in my Power nor Inclination; and if he can't be cur'd without I suck the Poyson from his Wounds, I'm afraid he won't recover his Senses till I lose mine.

Scandal. Hey, brave Woman, i' faith———Won't you see him then, if he desire it?

Angelica. What signifie a Madman's Desires? Besides, 'twou'd make me uneasie———If I don't see him, perhaps my Concern for him may lessen———If I forget him, 'tis no more than he has done by himself: and now the Surprize is over, methinks I am not half so sorry for him as I was—

Scandal. So, faith good Nature works a-pace; you were confessing just now an Obligation to his Love.

Angelica. But I have consider'd that Passions are unreasonable and involuntary; if he loves, he can't help it; and if I don't love, I can't help it; no more than he can help his being a Man, or I my being a Woman; or no more than I can help my want of Inclination to stay longer here—Come, *Jenny.*

Exit Angelica *and* Jenny.

Scandal. Humh!———An admirable Composition, faith, this same Womankind.

Enter Jeremy.

Jeremy. What, is she gone, Sir?

Scandal. Gone; why she was never here, nor any where else; nor I don't know her if I see her; nor you neither.

Jeremy. Good lack! What's the matter now? Are any more of us to be mad? Why, Sir, my Master longs to see her; and is almost mad in good earnest, with the Joyful News of her being here.

Scandal. We are all under a mistake———Ask no Questions, for I can't resolve you; but I'll inform your Master. In the mean time, if our Project succeed no better with his Father, than it does with his Mistress, he may descend from his Exaltation of madness into the road of common Sense, and be content only to be made a Fool with other reasonable People. I hear Sir *Sampson*, you know your Cue; I'll to your Master.

Exit.

Enter Sir Sampson Legend *with a Lawyer.*

Sir Sampson. D'ye see, Mr. *Buckram*, here's the Paper sign'd with his own Hand.

Buckram. Good, Sir. And the Conveyance is ready drawn in this Box, if he be ready to sign and seal.

Sir Sampson. Ready, body o' me, he must be ready; his Sham-sickness shan't excuse him———O, here's his Scoundrel. Sirrah, where's your Master?

Jeremy. Ah, Sir, he's quite gone.

Sir Sampson. Gone! What, he is not dead?

Jeremy. No, Sir, not dead.

Sir Sampson. What, is he gone out of Town, run away, ha! has he trick't me? speak, Varlet.

Jeremy. No, no, Sir; he's safe enough, Sir, an he were but as sound, poor Gentleman. He is indeed here, Sir, and not here, Sir.

Sir Sampson. Hey day, Rascal, do you banter me? Sirrah, d'ye banter me———Speak Sirrah, where is he, for I will find him.

Jeremy. Would you could, Sir; for he has lost himself. Indeed, Sir, I have a most broke my Heart about him———I can't refrain Tears when I think of him, Sir; I'm as melancholy for him as a Passing-Bell, Sir; or a Horse in a Pound.

Sir Sampson. A Pox confound your Similitudes, Sir——— Speak to be understood, and tell me in plain Terms what the matter is with him, or I'll crack your Fools Skull.

Jeremy. Ah, you've hit it, Sir; that's the matter with him, Sir; his Skull's crack'd, poor Gentleman; he's stark mad, Sir.

Sir Sampson. Mad!

Buckram. What, is he *Non Compos*?

Jeremy. Quite *Non Compos*, Sir.

Buckram. Why then all's obliterated, Sir *Sampson*, if he be *Non Compos mentis*, his Act and Deed will be of no effect, it is not good in Law.

Sir Sampson. Oons, I won't believe it; let me see him, Sir ———Mad, I'll make him find his Senses.

Jeremy. Mr. *Scandal* is with him, Sir; I'll knock at the Door.

Goes to the Scene, which opens and discovers Valentine *upon a Couch disorderly dress'd,* Scandal *by him.*

Sir Sampson. How now, what's here to do?—

Valentine (*starting*). Ha! who's that?

Scandal. For Heav'ns sake softly, Sir, and gently; don't provoke him.

Valentine. Answer me; Who is that? and that?

Sir Sampson. Gads bobs, does he not know me? Is he mischievous? I'll speak gently———*Val, Val,* do'st thou not know me, Boy? Not know thy own Father, *Val*! I am thy own Father, and this is honest *Brief Buckram* the Lawyer.

Valentine. It may be so———I did not know you—the World is full———There are People that we do know, and People that we do not know; and yet the Sun shines upon all alike—There are Fathers that have many Children; and there are Children that have many Fathers———'tis strange! But I am Truth, and come to give the World the Lie.

Sir Sampson. Body o' me, I know not what to say to him.

Valentine. Why does that Lawyer wear black?—Does he carry his Conscience withoutside?———Lawyer, what art thou? Dost thou know me?

Buckram. O Lord, what must I say?———Yes, Sir.

Valentine. Thou liest, for I am Truth. 'Tis hard I cannot get a Livelyhood amongst you. I have been sworn out of *Westminster-Hall* the first Day of every Term———Let me see ———No matter how long———But I'll tell you one thing; it's a Question that would puzzle an Arithmetician, if you should ask him, whether the Bible saves more Souls in *Westminster-Abby*, or damns more in *Westminster-Hall*: For my part, I am Truth, and can't tell; I have very few Acquaintance.

Sir Sampson. Body o' me, he talks sensibly in his madness—Has he no Intervals?

Jeremy. Very short, Sir.

Buckram. Sir, I can do you no Service while he's in this Condition: Here's your Paper, Sir———He may do me a mischief if I stay———The Conveyance is ready, Sir. If he recover his Senses.

Exit.

Sir Sampson. Hold, hold, don't you go yet.

Scandal. You'd better let him go, Sir; and send for him if there be occasion; for I fancy his Presence provokes him more.

Valentine. Is the Lawyer gone? 'tis well, then we may drink about without going together by the Ears—heigh ho! What a Clock is't? My Father here! Your Blessing, Sir?

I am Truth—Collier remarked: "A poet that had not been smitten with the pleasure of Blasphemy, would not have furnish'd Frenzy with Inspiration." Congreve replied that he had in fact originally written "Tom-tell-troth"; "but the sound and meanness of the Expression displeas'd me" (Nonesuch ed., III, 187).

Westminster-Hall—Opposite the Abbey, then used as the law courts.

Sir Sampson. He recovers———bless thee, *Val*—How do'st thou do, Boy?

Valentine. Thank you, Sir, pretty well———I have been a little out of Order; won't you please to sit, Sir?

Sir Sampson. Ay boy———Come, thou shalt sit down by me.

Valentine. Sir, 'tis my Duty to wait.

Sir Sampson. No, no, come, come, sit you down, honest *Val*: How do'st thou do? let me feel thy Pulse—Oh, pretty well now, *Val*: Body o' me, I was sorry to see thee indisposed: But I'm glad thou'rt better, honest *Val*.

Valentine. I thank you, Sir.

Scandal (*aside*). Miracle! the Monster grows loving.

Sir Sampson. Let me feel thy Hand again, *Val*: it does not shake—I believe thou can'st write, *Val*: Ha, boy? Thou can'st write thy Name, *Val*?———*Jeremy*, step and overtake Mr. *Buckram*, bid him make haste back with the Conveyance———quick—quick (*In Whisper to* Jeremy.) *Exit* Jeremy.

Scandal (*aside*). That ever I shou'd suspect such a Heathen of any Remorse!

Sir Sampson. Do'st thou know this Paper, *Val*: I know thou'rt honest, and wilt perform Articles.
Shews him the Paper, but holds it out of his reach.

Valentine. Pray let me see it, Sir. You hold it so far off, that I can't tell whether I know it or no.

Sir Sampson. See it, boy? Aye, aye, why thou do'st see it—'tis thy own Hand, *Val*. Why, let me see, I can read it as plain as can be: Look you here (*reads*) *The Condition of this Obligation*—Look you, as plain as can be, so it begins—And then at the bottom———*As witness my Hand*, VALENTINE LEGEND, in great Letters. Why, 'tis as plain as the Nose in one's Face: What, are my Eyes better than thine? I believe I can read it farther off yet—let me see.
Stretches his Arm as far as he can.

Valentine. Will you please to let me hold it, Sir?

Sir Sampson. Let thee hold it, say'st thou———Aye, with all my Heart———What matter is it who holds it? What need any body hold it?———I'll put it up in my Pocket, *Val*: And then no body need hold it (*puts the Paper in his*

Pocket.) There *Val*: it's safe enough, Boy———But thou shalt have it as soon as thou hast set thy Hand to another Paper, little *Val.*

Re-enter Jeremy *with* Buckram.

Valentine. What, is my bad Genius here again! Oh no, 'tis the Lawyer with an itching Palm; and he's come to be scratch'd———My Nails are not long enough———Let me have a Pair of Red hot Tongues quickly, quickly, and you shall see me act St. *Dunstan*, and lead the Devil by the Nose.

Buckram. O Lord, let me be gone; I'll not venture my self with a Madman.

Exit Buckram.

Valentine. Ha, ha, ha; you need not run so fast, Honesty will not overtake you———Ha, ha, ha, the Rogue found me out to be in *Forma Pauperis* presently.

Sir Sampson. Oons! What a Vexation is here! I know not what to do, or say, nor which way to go.

Valentine. Who's that, that's out of his Way?—I am Truth, and can set him right———Hearkee, Friend, the straight Road is the worst way you can go———He that follows his Nose always, will very often be led into a Stink. *Probatum est.* But what are you for? Religion or Politicks? There's a couple of Topicks for you, no more like one another than Oyl and Vinegar; and yet those two beaten together by a State-Cook, make Sauce for the whole Nation.

Sir Sampson. What the Devil had I to do, ever to beget Sons? Why did I ever marry?

Valentine. Because thou wer't a Monster; old Boy:———The two greatest Monsters in the World are a Man and a Woman; what's thy Opinion?

Sir Sampson. Why, my Opinion is, that those two Monsters join'd together, make yet a greater, that's a Man and his Wife.

Valentine. A ha! Old Truepenny, say'st thou so? thou hast nick'd it—But its wonderful strange, *Jeremy*!

St. Dunstan—Near the church the "young Devil Tavern" had as its sign the saint taking the devil by the nose with a pair of tongs.

Forma Pauperis—Relieved of costs in the law courts on account of poverty.

Jeremy. What is, Sir?

Valentine. That Gray Hairs shou'd cover a Green Head—and I make a Fool of my Father.

Enter Foresight, Mrs. Foresight, *and* Mrs. Frail.

Valentine. What's here! *Erra Pater?* or a bearded Sybil? If Prophecy comes, Truth must give place.

Exit with Jeremy.

Foresight. What says he? What, did he prophesie? Ha, Sir *Sampson*, bless us! How are we?

Sir Sampson. Are we? A Pox o' your Prognostication—Why, we are Fools as we use to be———Oons, that you cou'd not foresee that the Moon wou'd predominate, and my Son be mad—Where's your Oppositions, your Trines, and your Quadrates?—What did your *Cardan* and your *Ptolomee* tell you? Your *Messahalah* and your *Longomontanus*, your Harmony of Chiromancy with Astrology. Ah! pox on't, that I that know the World, and Men and Manners, that don't believe a Syllable in the Sky and Stars, and Sun and Almanacks, and Trash, should be directed by a Dreamer, an Omen-hunter, and defer Business in Expectation of a lucky Hour. When, body o' me, there never was a lucky Hour after the first opportunity.

Exit Sir Sampson.

Foresight. Ah, Sir *Sampson*, Heav'n help your Head——— This is none of your lucky Hour; *Nemo omnibus horis sapit*. What, is he gone, and in contempt of Science! Ill Stars and unconvertible Ignorance attend him.

Scandal. You must excuse his Passion, Mr. *Foresight*; for he has been heartily vex'd—His Son is *Non compos mentis*, and thereby incapable of making any Conveyance in Law; so that all his measures are disappointed.

Foresight. Ha! say you so?

Mrs. Frail. What, has my Sea-Lover lost his Anchor of Hope then?

Aside to Mrs. Foresight.

Mrs. Foresight. Oh Sister, what will you do with him?

Erra Pater—A term for an astrologer or his almanac.

Cardan and Longomontanus—Great mathematicians who lent their authority to astrology and divination.

Nemo omnibus horis sapit—Summers refers to Pliny, *Nat. Hist.* VII, xl. "no man is at all times wise and in his perfect wits."

Mrs. Frail. Do with him, send him to Sea again in the next foul Weather——He's us'd to an inconstant Element, and won't be surpriz'd to see the Tide turn'd.

Foresight. Wherein was I mistaken, not to foresee this? *Considers.*

Scandal. Madam, you and I can tell him something else, that he did not foresee, and more particularly relating to his own Fortune.

Aside to Mrs. Foresight.

Mrs. Foresight. What do you mean? I don't understand you.

Scandal. Hush, softly——the Pleasures of last Night, my Dear, too considerable to be forgot so soon.

Mrs. Foresight. Last Night! and what wou'd your Impudence infer from last night? last Night was like the Night before, I think.

Scandal. 'S'death do you make no difference between me and your Husband?

Mrs. Foresight. Not much,——he's superstitious; and you are mad in my opinion.

Scandal. You make me mad——You are not serious——Pray recollect your self.

Mrs. Foresight. O yes, now I remember, you were very impertinent and impudent,—and would have come to Bed to me.

Scandal. And did not?

Mrs. Foresight. Did not! with that face can you ask the Question?

Scandal. This I have heard of before, but never believ'd. I have been told she had that admirable quality of forgetting to a man's face in the morning, that she had layn with him all night, and denying favours with more impudence, than she cou'd grant 'em.—Madam, I'm your humble Servant, and honour you.—You look pretty well, Mr. *Foresight*;—How did you rest last night?

Foresight. Truly Mr. *Scandal*, I was so taken up with broken Dreams and distracted Visions, that I remember little.

Scandal. 'Twas a very forgetting Night.—But would you not talk with *Valentine*, perhaps you may understand him;

I'm apt to believe there is something mysterious in his Discourses, and sometimes rather think him inspir'd than mad.

Foresight. You speak with singular good Judgment, Mr. *Scandal*, truly,———I am inclining to your *Turkish* opinion in this matter, and do reverence a man whom the vulgar think mad. Let us go in to him.

Mrs. Frail. Sister, do you stay with them; I'll find out my Lover, and give him his discharge, and come to you. O' my Conscience, here he comes.

Exeunt Foresight, Mrs. Foresight *and* Scandal.

Enter Ben.

Ben. All mad, I think—Flesh, I believe all the *Calentures* of the Sea are come ashore, for my part.

Mrs. Frail. Mr. *Benjamin* in Choler!

Ben. No, I'm pleas'd well enough, now I have found you,—Mess, I've had such a Hurricane upon your account yonder.—

Mrs. Frail. My account, pray what's the matter?

Ben. Why, Father came and found me squabling with yon chitty fac'd thing, as he would have me marry,—so he ask'd what was the matter.—He ask'd in a surly sort of a way—(It seems Brother *Val* is gone mad, and so that put'n into a passion; but what did I know that, what's that to me?)———So he ask'd in a surly sort of manner,———and Gad I answer'd 'n as surlily,———What tho'f he be my Father, I an't bound Prentice to 'en:———so faith I told 'n in plain terms, if I were minded to marry, I'de marry to please my self, not him; and for the Young Woman that he provided for me, I thought it more fitting for her to learn her Sampler, and make Dirt-pies, than to look after a Husband; for my part I was none of her man.———I had another Voyage to make, let him take it as he will.

Mrs. Frail. So then you intend to go to Sea again?

Ben. Nay, nay, my mind run upon you,———but I wou'd not tell him so much.—So he said he'd make my heart ake;

Turkish opinion—Used here of the mystical school that is contrasted in astrology and medicine with the new experimental scientists.

Calentures—A tropical fever, causing delirium.

and if so be that he cou'd get a Woman to his mind, he'd marry himself. Gad, says I, an you play the fool and marry at these years, there's more danger of your head's aking than my heart.———He was woundy angry when I gav'n that wipe—He had 'nt a word to say, and so I left 'n, and the Green Girl together;—May hap the Bee may bite, and he'll marry her himself, with all my heart.

Mrs. Frail. And were you this undutiful and graceless Wretch to your Father?

Ben. Then why was he graceless first,—if I am undutiful and Graceless, why did he beget me so? I did not get my self.

Mrs. Frail. O Impiety! how have I been mistaken! what an inhumane merciless Creature have I set my heart upon? O I am happy to have discover'd the Shelves and Quicksands that lurk beneath that faithless smiling face.

Ben. Hey toss! what's the matter now? why you ben't angry, be you?

Mrs. Frail. O see me no more,—for thou wert born amongst Rocks, suckl'd by Whales, Cradled in a Tempest, and whistled to by Winds; and thou art come forth with Finns and Scales, and three rows of Teeth, a most outragious Fish of prey.

Ben. O Lord, O Lord, she's mad, poor Young Woman, Love has turn'd her senses, her Brain is quite overset. Well-a-day, how shall I do to set her to rights.

Mrs. Frail. No, no, I am not mad, Monster, I am wise enough to find you out.———Had'st thou the Impudence to aspire at being a Husband with that stubborn and disobedient temper?—You that know not how to submit to a Father, presume to have a sufficient stock of Duty to undergo a Wife? I should have been finely fobb'd indeed, very finely fobb'd.

Ben. Hearkee forsooth; If so be that you are in your right senses, d'ee see; for ought as I perceive I'm like to be finely fobb'd,———if I have got anger here upon your account, and you are tack'd about already.———What d'ee mean, after all your fair speeches, and stroaking my Cheeks, and Kissing and Hugging, what wou'd you sheer off so? wou'd you, and leave me aground?

Mrs. Frail. No, I'll leave you a-drift, and go which way you will.

Ben. What, are you false hearted then?

Mrs. Frail. Only the Wind's chang'd.

Ben. More shame for you,———the Wind's chang'd?——— it's an ill Wind blows no body good,———may-hap I have good riddance on you, if these be your Tricks,———What d'ee mean all this while, to make a fool of me?

Mrs. Frail. Any fool, but a Husband.

Ben. Husband! Gad I wou'd not be your Husband, if you wou'd have me; now I know your mind, tho'f you had your weight in Gold and Jewels, and tho'f I lov'd you never so well.

Mrs. Frail. Why canst thou love, Porpoise?

Ben. No matter what I can do? don't call Names,———I don't love You so well as to bear that, whatever I did, ———I'm glad you shew your self, Mistress:———Let them marry you, as don't know you:———Gad I know you too well, by sad experience;—I believe he that marries you will go to Sea in a Hen-peck'd Frigat.—I believe that, Young Woman———and may-hap may come to an Anchor at *Cuckolds-point*; so there's a dash for you, take it as you will, may-hap you may holla after me when I won't come too.

Exit.

Mrs. Frail. Ha, ha, ha, no doubt on't.—

Sings.

My true Love is gone to Sea.—

Enter Mrs. Foresight.

O Sister, had you come a minute sooner, you would have seen the Resolution of a Lover,———Honest *Tarr* and I are parted;—and with the same indifference that we met. ———O' my life I am half vex'd at the insensibility of a Brute that I despis'd.

Mrs. Foresight. What then, he bore it most Heroically?

Mrs. Frail. Most Tyranically,———for you see he has got the start of me; and I the poor forsaken Maid am left complaining on the Shore. But I'll tell you a hint that he has given me; Sir *Sampson* is enrag'd, and talks desperately of committing Matrimony himself.———If he has a mind to throw himself away, he can't do it more effectually than upon me, if we could bring it about.

Mrs. Foresight. Oh hang him old Fox, he's too cunning, besides he hates both you and me.———But I have a project in my head for you, and I have gone a good way towards it. I have almost made a Bargain with *Jeremy*, *Valentine*'s man, to sell his Master to us.

Mrs. Frail. Sell him, how?

Mrs. Foresight. Valentine raves upon *Angelica*, and took me for her, and *Jeremy* says will take any body for her that he imposes on him.—Now I have promis'd him Mountains; if in one of his mad fits he will bring you to him in her stead, and get you married together, and put to Bed together; and after Consummation, Girl, there's no revoking. And if he should recover his Senses, he'll be glad at least to make you a good Settlement.—Here they come, stand aside a little, and tell me how you like the design.

Enter Valentine, Scandal, Foresight, *and* Jeremy.

Scandal. And have you given your Master a hint of their Plot upon him?

To Jeremy.

Jeremy. Yes, Sir; he says he'll favour it, and mistake her for *Angelica.*

Scandal. It may make sport.

Foresight. Mercy on us!

Valentine. Husht———Interrupt me not———I'll whisper Prediction to thee, and thou shalt Prophesie;———I am Truth, and can teach thy Tongue a new Trick,———I have told thee what's past,———Now I tell what's to come;———Dost thou know what will happen to morrow?———Answer me not—for I will tell thee. To morrow, Knaves will thrive thro' craft, and Fools thro' Fortune; and Honesty will go as it did, Frost-nip't in a Summer suit. Ask me Questions concerning to morrow?

Scandal. Ask him, Mr. *Foresight.*

Foresight. Pray what will be done at Court?

Valentine. Scandal will tell you;———I am Truth, I never come there.

Foresight. In the City?

Valentine. Oh, Prayers will be said in empty Churches, at the usual Hours. Yet you will see such Zealous Faces behind Counters, as if Religion were to be sold in every Shop. Oh things will go methodically in the City, the Clocks will strike Twelve at Noon, and the Horn'd Herd Buz in the Exchange at Two. Wives and Husbands will drive distinct Trades, and Care and Pleasure separately Occupy the Family. Coffee-Houses will be full of Smoak and Stratagem. And the cropt Prentice, that sweeps his Master's Shop in the morning, may ten to one, dirty his Sheets before Night. But there are two things that you will see very strange; which are Wanton Wives, with their Legs at liberty, and Tame Cuckolds, with Chains about their Necks. But hold, I must examine you before I go further; You look suspiciously. Are you a Husband?

Foresight. I am Married.

Valentine. Poor Creature! Is your Wife of *Covent-Garden* Parish?

Foresight. No; St. *Martins* in the Fields.

Valentine. Alas, poor Man; his Eyes are sunk, and his Hands shrivell'd; his Legs dwindl'd, and his back bow'd, Pray, pray, for a Metamorphosis——Change thy Shape, and shake off Age; get thee *Medea*'s Kettle, and be boil'd a-new, come forth with lab'ring *Callous* Hands, a Chine of Steel, and *Atlas*' Shoulders. Let *Taliacotius* trim the Calves of Twenty Chairmen, and make thee Pedestals to stand erect upon, and look Matrimony in the face. Ha, ha, ha! That a Man shou'd have a Stomach to a Wedding Supper, when the Pidgeons ought rather to be laid to his feet, ha, ha, ha.

Foresight. His Frenzy is very high now, Mr. *Scandal.*

Scandal. I believe it is a Spring Tide.

Foresight. Very likely truly; You understand these Matters ——Mr. *Scandal*, I shall be very glad to confer with you about these things which he has utter'd.——His Sayings are very Mysterious and Hieroglyphical.

Valentine. Oh, why would *Angelica* be absent from my Eyes so long?

Jeremy. She's here, Sir.

Medea's Kettle—To restore youth; see Ovid, *Metamorphoses*, vii, 251.
Taliacotius—Famous sixteenth-century surgeon from Bologna.
Pidgeons . . . laid to his feet—Current remedy for the plague.

Mrs. Foresight. Now, Sister.

Mrs. Frail. O Lord, what must I say?

Scandal. Humour him, Madam, by all means.

Valentine. Where is she? Oh I see her—she comes, like Riches, Health, and Liberty at once, to a despairing, starving, and abandon'd Wretch.
Oh welcome, welcome.

Mrs. Frail. How de'e you, Sir? Can I serve you?

Valentine. Heark'ee;—I have a Secret to tell you——— *Endymion* and the Moon shall meet us upon Mount *Latmos*, and we'll be Marry'd in the dead of Night.———But say not a word. *Hymen* shall put his Torch into a dark Lanthorn, that it may be secret; and *Juno* shall give her *Peacock* Poppy-water, that he may fold his Ogling Tail, and *Argos*'s hundred Eyes be shut, ha? No body shall know, but *Jeremy*.

Mrs. Frail. No, no, we'll keep is secret, it shall be done presently.

Valentine. The sooner the better—*Jeremy*, come hither—closer—that none may over-hear us;—*Jeremy*, I can tell you News;—*Angelica* is turn'd Nun; and I am turning Fryar, and yet we'll Marry one another in spite of the Pope——— Get me a Coul and Beads, that I may play my part,——— For she'll meet me Two Hours hence in black and white, and a long Veil to cover the Project, and we won't see one anothers Faces, till we have done something to be asham'd of; and then we'll blush once for all.

Enter Tattle, *and* Angelica.

Jeremy. I'll take care, and—

Valentine. Whisper.

Angelica. Nay, Mr. *Tattle*, If you make Love to me, you spoil my design, for I intended to make you my Confident.

Tattle. But, Madam, to throw away your Person, such a Person! and such a Fortune, on a Madman!

Endymion and the Moon—The Latmian shepherd of Spenser's *Epithalamium*, 1.380; cf. also his Gloss. to *Shep. Cal.* Julye, 276.

Juno's peacock—Ovid, *Metamorphoses* I, 1000, which Dryden had just translated thus: "Argus hundred Eyes . . . /These Juno takes, that they no more may fail, /And spreads them in her Peacock's gaudy tail."

Angelica. I never lov'd him till he was Mad; but don't tell any body so.

Scandal. How's this! *Tattle* making Love to *Angelica*!

Tattle. Tell, Madam! alas you don't know me———I have much ado to tell your Ladyship, how long I have been in Love with you———but encourag'd by the impossibility of *Valentine*'s making any more Addresses to you, I have ventur'd to declare the very inmost Passion of my Heart. Oh, Madam, look upon us both. There you see the ruins of a poor decay'd Creature—Here, a compleat and lively Figure, with Youth and Health, and all his five Senses in perfection, Madam, and to all this, the most passionate Lover—

Angelica. O fie for shame, hold your Tongue, A passionate Lover, and five Senses in perfection! when you are as Mad as *Valentine*, I'll believe you love me, and the maddest shall take me.

Valentine. It is enough. Ha! Who's here?

Mrs. Frail (*to* Jeremy). O Lord, her coming will spoil all.

Jeremy. No, no, Madam, he won't know her, if he shou'd, I can perswade him.

Valentine (*whispers*). *Scandal*, who are all these? Foreigners? If they are, I'll tell you what I think—get away all the Company but *Angelica*, that I may discover my design to her.

Scandal. I will,—I have discover'd something of *Tattle*, that is of a piece with Mrs. *Frail*. He Courts *Angelica*, if we cou'd contrive to couple 'em together———Heark'ee———.
Whisper.

Mrs. Foresight. He won't know you, Cousin, he knows no body.

Foresight. But he knows more than any body,———Oh Neice, he knows things past and to come, and all the profound Secrets of Time.

Tattle. Look you, Mr. *Foresight*, It is not my way to make many words of Matters, and so I shan't say much,——— But in short, de'e see, I will hold you a Hundred Pound now, that I know more Secrets than he.

Foresight. How! I cannot Read that knowledge in your Face, Mr. *Tattle*———Pray, what do you know?

Tattle. Why de'e think I'll tell you, Sir! Read it in my Face? No, Sir, 'tis written in my Heart. And safer there, Sir, than Letters writ in Juice of Lemon, for no Fire can fetch it out. I am no blab, Sir.

Valentine. Acquaint *Jeremy* with it, he may easily bring it about,—They are welcome, and I'll tell 'em so my self. (*To* Scandal) What, do you look strange upon me?———Then I must be plain. (*Coming up to them.*) I am Truth, and hate an Old Acquaintance with a new Face.

Scandal *goes aside with* Jeremy.

Tattle. Do you know me, *Valentine*?

Valentine. You? Who are you? No, I hope not.

Tattle. I am *Jack Tattle*, your Friend.

Valentine. My Friend, what to do? I am no Married Man, and thou can'st not lie with my Wife? I am very poor, and thou can'st not borrow Money of me; Then what Employment have I for a Friend.

Tattle. Hah! A good open Speaker, and not to be trusted with a Secret.

Angelica. Do you know me, *Valentine*?

Valentine. Oh very well.

Angelica. Who am I?

Valentine. You're a Woman,———One to whom Heav'n gave Beauty, when it grafted Roses on a Briar. You are the reflection of Heav'n in a Pond, and he that leaps at you is sunk. You are all white, a sheet of lovely spotless Paper, when you first are Born; but you are to be scrawl'd and blotted by every Goose's Quill. I know you; for I lov'd a Woman, and lov'd her so long, that I found out a strange thing: I found out what a Woman was good for.

Tattle. Aye, prithee, what's that?

Valentine. Why to keep a Secret.

Tattle. O Lord!

Valentine. O exceeding good to keep a Secret: For tho' she should tell, yet she is not to be believ'd.

Tattle. Hah! good again, faith.

Valentine. I would have Musick—Sing me the Song that I like—

SONG.

Set by Mr. *Finger*.

I tell thee, *Charmion*, could I Time retrieve,
And could again begin to Love and Live,
To you I should my earliest Off'ring give;
I know my Eyes would lead my Heart to you,
And I should all my Vows and Oaths renew,
But to be plain, I never would be true.

2.

For by our weak and weary Truth, I find,
Love hates to center in a Point assign'd,
But runs with Joy the Circle of the Mind.
Then never let us chain what should be free,
But for relief of either Sex agree,
Since Women love to change, and so do we.

No more, for I am melancholly.

Walks musing.

Jeremy (*to* Scandal). I'll do't, Sir.

Scandal. Mr. *Foresight*, we had best leave him. He may grow outragious, and do mischief.

Foresight. I will be directed by you.

Jeremy (*to* Mrs. Frail). You'll meet, Madam;———I'll take care every thing shall be ready.

Mrs. Frail. Thou shalt do what thou wilt, have what thou wilt, in short, I will deny thee nothing.

Tattle (*to* Angelica). Madam, shall I wait upon you?

Angelica. No, I'll stay with him—Mr. *Scandal* will protect me. Aunt, Mr. *Tattle* desires you would give him leave to wait on you.

Tattle. Pox on't, there's no coming off, now she has said that———Madam, will you do me the Honour?

Mrs. Foresight. Mr. *Tattle* might have us'd less Ceremony.

Scandal. Jeremy, follow *Tattle*.

Exeunt Foresight, Mrs. Foresight, Tattle, Mrs. Frail, *and* Jeremy.

Angelica. Mr. *Scandal*, I only stay till my Maid comes, and because I had a Mind to be rid of Mr. *Tattle*.

Scandal. Madam, I am very glad that I overheard a better Reason, which you gave to Mr. *Tattle*; for his impertinence forc'd you to acknowledge a Kindness for *Valentine*, which you deny'd to all his Sufferings and my Sollicitations. So I'll leave him to make use of the Discovery; and your Ladyship to the free Confession of your Inclinations.

Angelica. Oh Heavens! You wont leave me alone with a Madman?

Scandal. No, Madam; I only leave a Madman to his Remedy.
Exit Scandal.

Valentine. Madam, you need not be very much afraid, for I fancy I begin to come to my self.

Angelica (*aside*). Aye, but if I don't fit you, I'll be hang'd.

Valentine. You see what disguises Love makes us put on; Gods have been in counterfeited Shapes for the same Reason; and the Divine Part of me, my Mind, has worn this Mask of Madness, and this motly Livery, only as the Slave of Love, and Menial Creature of your Beauty.

Angelica. Mercy on me, how he talks! poor *Valentine*!

Valentine. Nay faith, now let us understand one another, Hypocrisie apart,———The Comedy draws toward an end, and let us think of leaving acting, and be our selves; and since you have lov'd me, you must own I have at length deserv'd you shou'd confess it.

Angelica (*sighs*). I would I had lov'd you———for Heaven knows I pitie you; and could I have foreseen the sad Effects, I wou'd have striven; but that's too late.
Sighs.

Valentine. What sad Effects?—What's too late? my seeming Madness has deceiv'd my Father, and procur'd me time to think of means to reconcile me to him; and preserve the right of my Inheritance to his Estate; which otherwise by Articles, I must this Morning have resign'd: And this I had inform'd you of to Day, but you were gone, before I knew you had been here.

Angelica. How! I thought your love of me had caus'd this Transport in your Soul; which, it seems, you only counterfeited, for mercenary Ends and sordid Interest.

fit you—punish, find a fit penalty.

Valentine. Nay, now you do me Wrong; for if any Interest was considered, it was yours; since I thought I wanted more than Love, to make me worthy of you.

Angelica. Then you thought me mercenary———But how am I deluded by this Interval of Sense, to reason with a Madman?

Valentine. Oh, 'tis barbarous to misunderstand me longer.

Enter Jeremy.

Angelica. Oh here's a reasonable Creature———sure he will not have the Impudence to persevere———Come, *Jeremy*, acknowledge your Trick, and confess your Master's Madness counterfeit.

Jeremy. Counterfeit, Madam! I'll maintain him to be as absolutely and substantially Mad, as any Freeholder in *Bethlehem*; Nay, he's as Mad as any Projector, Fanatick, Chymist, Lover, or Poet in *Europe*.

Valentine. Sirrah, you lie; I am not Mad.

Angelica. Ha, ha, ha, you see he denies it.

Jeremy. O Lord, Madam, did you ever know any Madman Mad enough to own it?

Valentine. Sot, can't you apprehend?

Angelica. Why he talk'd very sensibly just now.

Jeremy. Yes, Madam; He has Intervals: But you see he begins to look wild again now.

Valentine. Why you Thick-Skull'd Rascal, I tell you the Farce is done, and I will be Mad no longer.

Beats him.

Angelica. Ha, ha, ha, is he mad, or no, *Jeremy*?

Jeremy. Partly I think———for he does not know his Mind Two Hours———I'm sure I left him just now, in a Humour to be mad: And I think I have not found him very quiet at this present.

One Knocks.

Who's there?

Valentine. Go see, you Sot. I'm very glad that I can move your Mirth, tho' not your Compassion.

Exit Jeremy.

Freeholder in Bethelem—A lunatic in Bedlam.

Angelica. I did not think you had Apprehension enough to be exceptious: But Madmen shew themselves most, by over pretending to a sound Understanding; as Drunken men do by over acting Sobriety; I was half inclining to believe you, till I accidentally touch'd upon your tender Part: But now you have restor'd me to my former Opinion and Compassion.

Enter Jeremy.

Jeremy. Sir, your Father has sent to know if you are any better yet——Will you please to be Mad, Sir, or how?

Valentine. Stupidity! You know the Penalty of all I'm worth must pay for the Confession of my Senses; I'm Mad, and will be Mad to every Body but this Lady.

Jeremy. So——Just the very backside of Truth,——But lying is a Figure in Speech, that interlards the greatest part of my Conversation——Madam, your Ladyships Woman.

Goes to the Door.

Enter Jenny.

Angelica. Well, have you been there?——Come hither.

Jenny (*aside to* Angelica). Yes, Madam, Sir *Sampson* will wait upon you presently.

Valentine. You are not leaving me in this Uncertainty?

Angelica. Wou'd any thing, but a Madman complain of Uncertainty? Uncertainty and Expectation are the Joys of Life. Security is an insipid thing, and the overtaking and possessing of a Wish, discovers the Folly of the Chase. Never let us know one another better; for the Pleasure of a Masquerade is done, when we come to shew Faces; But I'll tell you two things before I leave you; I am not the Fool you take me for; and you are Mad and don't know it.

Exeunt Angelica *and* Jenny.

Valentine. From a Riddle, you can expect nothing but a Riddle. There's my Instruction, and the Moral of my Lesson.

Re-enter Jeremy.

Jeremy. What, is the Lady gone again, Sir? I hope you understood one another before she went.

Valentine. Understood! She is harder to be understood than a Piece of *Ægyptian* Antiquity, or an *Irish* Manuscript; you may pore till you spoil your Eyes, and not improve your Knowledge.

Jeremy. I have heard 'em say, Sir, they read hard *Hebrew* Books backwards; may be you begin to read at the wrong End.

Valentine. They say so of a Witches Pray'r, and Dreams and *Dutch* Almanacks are to be understood by contraries. But there's Regularity and Method in that; she is a Medal without a Reverse or Inscription; for Indifference has both sides alike. Yet while she does not seem to hate me, I will pursue her, and know her if it be possible, in spight of the Opinion of my Satirical Friend, *Scandal*, who says,

> That Women are like Tricks by slight of Hand,
> Which, to admire, we should not understand.

Exeunt.

The End of the Fourth Act.

ACT V. Scene I.

A Room in Foresight's *House.*

Enter Angelica *and* Jenny.

Angelica. Where is Sir *Sampson*? Did you not tell me, he would be here before me?

Jenny. He's at the great Glass in the Dining-Room, Madam, setting his Cravat and Wig.

Angelica. How! I'm glad on't——If he has a mind I should like him, it's a sign he likes me; and that's more than half my Design.

Jenny. I hear him, Madam.

Angelica. Leave me, and d'ye hear, if *Valentine* shou'd come, or send, I am not to be spoken with.

Exit Jenny.

Enter Sir Sampson.

Sir Sampson. I have not been honour'd with the Commands of a fair Lady, a great while———Odd, Madam, you have reviv'd me———Not since I was Five and Thirty.

Angelica. Why you have no great reason to complain, Sir *Sampson*, that is not long ago.

Sir Sampson. Zooks, but it is, Madam, a very great while; to a Man that admires a fine Woman, as much as I do.

Angelica. You're an absolute Courtier, Sir *Sampson.*

Sir Sampson. Not at all, Madam: Odsbud you wrong me; I am not so old neither, to be a bare Courtier, only a Man of Words. Odd, I have warm Blood about me yet, I can serve a Lady any way———Come, come, let me tell you, you Women think a Man old too soon, faith and troth you do ———Come, don't despise Fifty; odd Fifty, in a hale Constitution, is no such contemptible Age.

Angelica. Fifty a contemptible Age! Not at all, a very fashionable Age I think———I assure you I know very considerable Beaus, that set a good Face upon Fifty, Fifty! I have seen Fifty in a side Box by Candle-light, out-blossom Five and Twenty.

Sir Sampson. O Pox, outsides, outsides; a pize take 'em, meer outsides. Hang your side-Box Beaus; no, I'm none of those, none of your forc'd Trees, that pretend to Blossom in the Fall; and Bud when they should bring forth Fruit. I am of a long liv'd Race, and inherit Vigour, none of my Family married till Fifty; yet they begot Sons and Daughters till Fourscore. I am of your Patriarchs, I, a Branch of one of your *Antideluvian* Families, Fellows, that the Flood could not wash away. Well, Madam, what are your Commands? Has any young Rogue affronted you, and shall I cut his Throat? or—

Angelica. No, Sir *Sampson*, I have no Quarrel upon my Hands —I have more Occasion for your Conduct than your Courage at this time. To tell you the Truth, I'm weary of living single, and want a Husband.

Sir Sampson. Odsbud, and 'tis pity you should—(*Aside.*) Odd, wou'd she wou'd like me, then I shou'd hamper my young Rogues: Odd, wou'd she wou'd; faith and troth she's devilish Handsom.———Madam, you deserve a good Husband, and 'twere pity you shou'd be thrown away upon any

a pize—probably a substitute for "pox"; cf. Sir Sampson's other modified expressions, used here; "odd," "odsbud," "odso."

of these young idle Rogues about the Town. Odd, there's ne're a young Fellow worth hanging———that is a very young Fellow———Pize on 'em, they never think before-hand of any thing;———And if they commit Matrimony, 'tis as they commit Murder; out of a Frolick: And are ready to hang themselves, or to be hang'd by the Law, the next Morning.———Odso, have a care, Madam.

Angelica. Therefore I ask your Advice, Sir *Sampson*: I have Fortune enough to make any Man easie that I can like; If there were such a thing as a young agreeable Man, with a reasonable Stock of good Nature and Sense———For I would neither have an absolute Wit, nor a Fool.

Sir Sampson. Odd, you are hard to please, Madam; to find a young Fellow that is neither a Wit in his own Eye, nor a Fool in the Eye of the World, is a very hard Task. But, faith and troth you speak very discreetly; For I hate both a Wit and a Fool.

Angelica. She that marries a Fool, Sir *Sampson*, commits the Reputation of her Honesty or Understanding to the Censure of the World: And she that marries a very Witty Man, submits both to the Severity and insolent Conduct of her Husband. I should like a Man of Wit for a Lover, because I would have such an one in my Power; but I would no more be his Wife, than his Enemy. For his Malice is not a more terrible Consequence of his Aversion, than his Jealousie is of his Love.

Sir Sampson. None of old *Foresight*'s *Sybills* ever utter'd such a Truth. Odsbud, you have won my Heart: I hate a Wit; I had a Son that was spoil'd among 'em; a good hopeful Lad, till he learn'd to be a Wit———And might have risen in the State———But, a pox on't, his Wit run him out of his Money, and now his Poverty has run him out of his Wits.

Angelica. Sir *Sampson*, as your Friend, I must tell you, you are very much abus'd in that Matter; He's no more Mad than you are.

Sir Sampson. How, Madam! Wou'd I cou'd prove it.

Angelica. I can tell you how that may be done———But it is a thing that wou'd make me appear to be too much concern'd in your Affairs.

Sir Sampson (*aside*). Odsbud I believe she likes me———Ah, Madam, all my Affairs are scarce worthy to be laid at your Feet; And I wish, Madam, they stood in a better Posture, that I might make a more becoming Offer to a Lady of your incomparable Beauty and Merit.———If I had *Peru* in one Hand, and *Mexico* in t'other, and the *Eastern* Empire under my Feet; it would make me only a more glorious Victim to be offer'd at the Shrine of your Beauty.

Angelica. Bless me, Sir *Sampson*, what's the matter?

Sir Sampson. Odd, Madam, I love you———And if you wou'd take my Advice in a Husband—

Angelica. Hold, hold, Sir *Sampson*. I ask'd your Advice for a Husband, and you are giving me your Consent———I was indeed thinking to propose something like it in a Jest, to satisfie you about *Valentine*: For if a Match were seemingly carried on, between you and me, it would oblige him to throw off his Disguise of Madness, in Apprehension of losing me: For you know he has long pretended a Passion for me.

Sir Sampson. Gadzooks, a most ingenious Contrivance——— If we were to go through with it. But why must the Match only be seemingly carried on?———Odd, let it be a real Contract.

Angelica. O fie, Sir *Sampson*, what would the World say?

Sir Sampson. Say, they would say, you were a wise Woman, and I a happy Man. Odd, Madam, I'll love you as long as I live; and leave you a good Jointure when I die.

Angelica. Aye; But that is not in your Power, Sir *Sampson*; for when *Valentine* confesses himself in his Senses; he must make over his Inheritance to his younger Brother.

Sir Sampson. Odd, you're cunning, a wary Baggage! Faith and Troth I like you the better———But, I warrant you, I have a Proviso in the Obligation in favour of my self ———Body o'me, I have a Trick to turn the Settlement upon the Issue Male of our Two Bodies begotten. Odsbud, let us find Children, and I'll find an Estate.

Angelica. Will you? well, do you find the Estate, and leave the t'other to me—

Sir Sampson. O Rogue! But I'll trust you. And will you consent? Is it a Match then?

Angelica. Let me consult my Lawyer concerning this Obligation; and if I find what you propose practicable; I'll give you my Answer.

Sir Sampson. With all my Heart;———Come in with me, and I'll lend you the Bond,———You shall consult your Lawyer, and I'll consult a Parson; Odzooks I'm a Young Man: Odzooks I'm a young Man, and I'll make it appear——— Odd, you're devilish Handsom; Faith and Troth, you're very Handsom, and I'm very Young, and very Lusty——— Odsbud, Hussy, you know how to chuse, and so do I; ———Odd, I think we are very well met;———Give me your Hand, Odd let me kiss it; 'tis as warm and as soft ———as what?———Odd, as t'other Hand—give me t'other Hand, and I'll mumble 'em, and kiss 'em till they melt in my Mouth.

Angelica. Hold, Sir *Sampson*———You're profuse of your Vigour before your time: You'll spend your Estate before you come to it.

Sir Sampson. No, no, only give you a Rent-roll of my Possessions———Ah! Baggage———I warrant you for little *Sampson*: Odd, *Sampson*'s a very good Name for an able Fellow: Your *Sampsons* were strong Dogs from the Beginning.

Angelica. Have a care, and don't over-act your Part———If you remember, the strongest *Sampson* of your Name, pull'd an old House over his Head at last.

Sir Sampson. Say you so, Hussy?———Come lets go then; Odd, I long to be pulling down too, come away——— Odso, here's some body coming.

Exeunt.

Enter Tattle *and* Jeremy.

Tattle. Is not that she, gone out just now?

Jeremy. Aye, Sir, she's just going to the Place of appointment. Ah Sir, if you are not very faithful and close in this Business, you'll certainly be the Death of a Person that has a most extraordinary Passion for your Honour's Service.

Tattle. Aye, who's that?

Jeremy. Even my unworthy self, Sir———Sir, I have had an Appetite to be fed with your Commands a great while; ———And now, Sir, my former Master, having much troubled the Fountain of his Understanding; it is a very plausible Occasion for me to quench my Thirst at the Spring of your Bounty———I thought I could not recommend my self better to you, Sir, than by the delivery of a great Beauty and Fortune into your Arms, whom I have heard you Sigh for.

Tattle. I'll make thy Fortune; say no more———Thou art a pretty Fellow, and can'st carry a Message to a Lady, in a pretty soft kind of Phrase, and with a good perswading Accent.

Jeremy. Sir, I have the Seeds of Rhetorick and Oratory in my Head———I have been at *Cambridge*.

Tattle. Ay; 'tis well enough for a Servant to be bred at an University: But the Education is a little too pedantick for a Gentleman. I hope you are secret in your Nature, private, close, ha?

Jeremy. O Sir, for that Sir, 'tis my chief Talent; I'm as secret as the Head of *Nilus*.

Tattle. Aye? Who's he, tho? A Privy Counsellor?

Jeremy. O Ignorance! (*aside*). A cunning *Ægyptian*, Sir, that with his Arms would over-run the Country, yet no body could ever find out his Head-Quarters.

Tattle. Close Dog! A good Whoremaster, I warrant him ———the time draws nigh, *Jeremy*. *Angelica* will be veil'd like a Nun; and I must be hooded like a Friar; ha, *Jeremy*?

Jeremy. Aye, Sir, hooded like a Hawk, to seize at first sight upon the Quarry. It is the Whim of my Master's Madness to be so dress'd; and she is so in Love with him, she'll comply with any thing to please him. Poor Lady, I'm sure she'll have reason to pray for me, when she finds what a happy Exchange she has made, between a Madman and so Accomplish'd a Gentleman.

Tattle. Ay faith, so she will, *Jeremy*: You're a good Friend to her, poor Creature———I swear I do it hardly so much in consideration of my self, as Compassion to her.

Jeremy. 'Tis an Act of Charity, Sir, to save a fine Woman with Thirty Thousand Pound, from throwing her self away.

Head of Nilus—The source of the Nile was then still unknown.

Tattle. So 'tis, faith———I might have sav'd several others in my time; but i'Gad I could never find in my Heart to Marry any body before.

Jeremy. Well, Sir, I'll go and tell her my Master's coming; and meet you in half a quarter of an hour, with your Disguise, at your own Lodgings. You must talk a little madly, she won't distinguish the Tone of your Voice.

Tattle. No, no, let me alone for a Counterfeit;———I'll be ready for you.

Enter Miss Prue.

Miss Prue. O Mr. *Tattle*, are you here! I'm glad I have found you; I have been looking up and down for you like any thing, till I'm as tired as any thing in the World.

Tattle (aside). O Pox, how shall I get rid of this foolish Girl?

Miss Prue. O I have pure News, I can tell you pure News—I must not marry the Seaman now—my Father says so. Why won't you be my Husband? You say you love me, and you won't be my Husband. And I know you may be my Husband now if you please.

Tattle. O fie, Miss: Who told you so, Child?

Miss Prue. Why, my Father—I told him that you lov'd me.

Tattle. O fie, Miss, why did you do so? and who told you so, Child?

Miss Prue. Who? Why you did; did not you?

Tattle. O Pox, that was Yesterday, Miss, that was a great while ago, Child. I have been asleep since; slept a whole Night, and did not so much as dream of the matter.

Miss Prue. Pshaw, O but I dream't that it was so tho.

Tattle. Ay, but your Father will tell you that Dreams come by Contraries, Child———O fie; what, we must not love one another now———Pshaw, that would be a foolish thing indeed———Fie, fie, you're a Woman now, and must think of a new Man every Morning, and forget him every Night———No, no, to marry, is to be a Child again, and play with the same Rattle always: O fie, marrying is a paw thing.

paw—Slang term for "improper, obscene."

Miss Prue. Well, but don't you love me as well as you did last Night then?

Tattle. No, no, Child, you would not have me.

Miss Prue. No? Yes but I would tho.

Tattle. Pshaw, but I tell you, you would not—You forget you're a Woman, and don't know your own mind.

Miss Prue. But here's my Father, and he knows my Mind.

Enter Foresight.

Foresight. O, Mr. *Tattle*, your Servant, you are a close Man; but methinks your Love to my Daughter was a Secret I might have been trusted with,———Or had you a mind to try if I could discover it by my Art———hum, ha! I think there is something in your Physiognomy, that has a resemblance of her; and the Girl is like me.

Tattle. And so you wou'd infer, that you and I are alike—(*aside*) what do's the Old Prig mean? I'll banter him, and laugh at him, and leave him.
I fancy you have a wrong Notion of Faces.

Foresight. How? What? A wrong Notion! How so?

Tattle. In the way of Art: I have some taking Features, not obvious to Vulgar Eyes; that are Indications of a sudden turn of good Fortune, in the Lottery of Wives; and promise a great Beauty and great Fortune reserved alone for me, by a private Intriegue of Destiny, kept secret from the piercing Eye of Perspicuity; from all Astrologers, and the Stars themselves.

Foresight. How! I will make it appear that what you say is impossible.

Tattle. Sir, I beg your Pardon, I'm in haste—

Foresight. For what?

Tattle. To be married, Sir, married.

Foresight. Aye, but pray take me along with you, Sir—

Tattle. No, Sir; 'tis to be done Privately———I never make Confidents.

Foresight. Well; but my Consent I mean———You won't marry my Daughter without my Consent?

Tattle. Who I, Sir? I'm an absolute Stranger to you and your Daughter, Sir.

Foresight. Hey day! What time of the Moon is this?

Tattle. Very true, Sir, and desire to continue so. I have no more love for your Daughter, than I have likeness of you; and I have a Secret in my Heart, which you wou'd be glad to know, and shan't know; and yet you shall know it too, and be sorry for't afterwards. I'd have you to know, Sir, that I am as knowing as the Stars, and as secret as the Night. ———And I'm going to be Married just now, yet did not know of it half an Hour ago; and the Lady stays for me, and does not know of it yet———There's a Mystery for you,———I know you love to untie Difficulties———Or if you can't solve this; stay here a Quarter of an Hour, and I'll come and explain it to you.

Exit.

Miss Prue. O Father, why will you let him go? Won't you make him be my Husband?

Foresight. Mercy on us, what do these Lunacies portend? Alas! he's Mad, Child, stark Wild.

Miss Prue. What, and must not I have e're a Husband then? What, must I go to Bed to Nurse again, and be a Child as long as she's an Old Woman? Indeed but I won't: For now my Mind is set upon a Man, I will have a Man some way or other. Oh! methinks I'm sick when I think of a Man; and if I can't have one, I wou'd go to sleep all my Life: For when I'm awake, it makes me wish and long, and I don't know for what—And I'd rather be always a sleeping, than sick with thinking.

Foresight. O fearful! I think the Girl's influenc'd too,——— Hussy you shall have a Rod.

Miss Prue. A Fiddle of a Rod, I'll have a Husband; and if you won't get me one, I'll get one for my self: I'll marry our *Robbin* the Butler, he says he loves me, and he's a Handsome Man, and shall be my Husband: I warrant he'll be my Husband and thank me too, for he told me so.

Enter Scandal, Mrs. Foresight, *and* Nurse.

Foresight. Did he so———I'll dispatch him for't presently; Rogue! Oh, Nurse, come hither.

Nurse. What is your Worship's Pleasure?

Foresight. Here, take your young Mistress, and lock her up presently, till farther Orders from me———not a Word Hussy———Do what I bid you, no Reply, away. And bid *Robin* make ready to give an Account of his Plate and Linnen, d'ee hear, begone when I bid you.

Exeunt Nurse *and* Miss Prue.

Mrs. Foresight. What's the Matter, Husband?

Foresight. 'Tis not convenient to tell you now———Mr. *Scandal,* Heav'n keep us all in our Senses———I fear there is a contagious Frenzy abroad. How does *Valentine*?

Scandal. O I hope he will do well again———I have a Message from him to your Niece *Angelica.*

Foresight. I think she has not return'd, since she went abroad with Sir *Sampson.*

Enter Ben.

Mrs. Foresight. Here's Mr. *Benjamin,* he can tell us if his Father be come Home.

Ben. Who, Father? ay, he's come home with a Vengeance.

Mrs. Foresight. Why, What's the Matter?

Ben. Matter! Why he's Mad.

Foresight. Mercy on us, I was afraid of this.

Ben. And there's the handsome young Woman, she, as they say, Brother *Val.* went mad for, she's mad too, I think.

Foresight. O my poor Niece, my poor Niece, is she gone too? Well, I shall run mad next.

Mrs. Foresight. Well, but how mad? how d'ee mean?

Ben. Nay, I'll give you leave to guess—I'll undertake to make a Voyage to *Antegoa*———No, hold, I maynt say so neither———But I'll sail as far as *Ligorn,* and back again, before you shall guess at the matter, and do nothing else; Mess you may take in all the Points of the Compass, and not hit Right.

Mrs. Foresight. Your Experiment will take up a little too much time.

Antegoa—Presumably the island of Antigua, in the West Indies.
Ligorn—Livorno, a port of Tuscany.

Ben. Why then I'll tell you, There's a new wedding upon the Stocks; and they two are a going to be married to rights.

Scandal. Who?

Ben. Why Father and———the Young Woman. I can't hit of her Name.

Scandal. Angelica?

Ben. Aye, the same.

Mrs. Foresight. Sir *Sampson* and *Angelica*, impossible!

Ben. That may be———but I'm sure it is as I tell you.

Scandal. 'S'death it's a Jest. I can't believe it.

Ben. Look you, Friend, it's nothing to me, whether you believe it or no. What I say is true; d'ee see, they are married, or just going to be married, I know not which.

Foresight. Well, but they are not Mad, that is, not Lunatick?

Ben. I don't know what you may call Madness———But she's mad for a Husband, and he's Horn-mad, I think, or they'd ne're make a Match together———Here they come.

Enter Sir Sampson, Angelica, *with* Buckram.

Sir Sampson. Where is this old Soothsayer? This Uncle of mine elect? a ha, Old *Foresight*, Uncle *Foresight*, wish me Joy Uncle *Foresight*, double Joy, both as Uncle and Astrologer; here's a Conjunction that was not foretold in all your *Ephemeris*—The brightest Star in the blew Firmament ———is shot from above, in a Jelly of Love, and so forth; and I'm Lord of the Ascendant. Odd, you're an old Fellow, *Foresight*; Uncle I mean, a very old Fellow, Uncle *Foresight*; and yet you shall live to dance at my Wedding; faith and troth you shall. Odd we'll have the Musick of the Spheres for thee, old *Lilly*, that we will, and thou shalt lead up a Dance in *via Lactea.*

Foresight. I'm Thunder-strook! You are not married to my Niece?

Sir Sampson. Not absolutely married, Uncle; but very near it, within a Kiss of the matter, as you see.

Kisses Angelica.

Jelly of Love—Summers quotes Dryden, *Tyrannic Love*, IV, i, *Nakar.* "And drop from above/ In a Gelly of Love!" Revived at the Theatre Royal in 1694, it would be familiar to actors and audience (Nonesuch ed., II, 269).

Angelica. 'Tis very true indeed, Uncle; I hope you'll be my Father, and give me.

Sir Sampson. That he shall, or I'll burn his Globes———Body o'me, he shall be thy Father, I'll make him thy Father, and thou shalt make me a Father, and I'll make thee a Mother, and we'll beget Sons and Daughters enough to put the Weekly Bills out of Countenance.

Scandal. Death and Hell! Where's *Valentine*?

Exit Scandal.

Mrs. Foresight. This is so surprising—

Sir Sampson. How! What does my Aunt say? Surprizing, Aunt? Not at all, for a young Couple to make a Match in Winter? Not at all———It's a Plot to undermine Cold Weather; and destroy that Usurper of a Bed call'd a Warming-Pan.

Mrs. Foresight. I'm glad to hear you have so much Fire in you, Sir *Sampson*.

Ben. Mess, I fear his Fire's little better than Tinder; may hap it will only serve to light up a Match for some body else. The Young Woman's a Handsom Young Woman, I can't deny it: But, Father, if I might be your Pilot in this Case, you should not marry her. It's just the same thing, as if so be you should sail so far as the *Streights* without Provision.

Sir Sampson. Who gave you Authority to speak, Sirrah? To your Element, Fish, be mute, Fish, and to Sea, rule your Helm, Sirrah, don't direct me.

Ben. Well, well, take you care of your own Helm, or you mayn't keep your own Vessel steddy.

Sir Sampson. Why you impudent Tarpaulin! Sirrah, do you bring your Fore-castle Jests upon your Father? But I shall be even with you, I won't give you a Groat. Mr. *Buckram* is the Conveyance so worded, that nothing can possibly descend to this Scoundrel? I would not so much as have him have the Prospect of an Estate; tho' there were no way to come to it, but by the *North-East* Passage.

Buckram. Sir, it is drawn according to your Directions; there is not the least Cranny of the Law unstopt.

Streights—In this period, it usually means Straits of Gibraltar.
North-East Passage—The impossible route to the East.

Ben. Lawyer, I believe there's many a Cranny and Leak unstopt in your Conscience———If so be that one had a Pump to your Bosom, I believe we shou'd discover a foul Hold. They say a Witch will sail in a Sieve———But I believe the Devil wou'd not venture aboard o' your Conscience. And that's for you.

Sir Sampson. Hold your Tongue, Sirrah. How now, who's there?

Enter Tattle *and* Mrs. Frail.

Mrs. Frail. O, Sister, the most unlucky Accident!

Mrs. Foresight. What's the Matter?

Tattle. O, the Two most unfortunate poor Creatures in the World we are.

Foresight. Bless us! How so?

Mrs. Frail. Ah Mr. *Tattle* and I, poor Mr. *Tattle* and I are— I can't speak it out.

Tattle. Nor I———But poor Mrs. *Frail* and I are—

Mrs. Frail. Married.

Mrs. Foresight. Married! How?

Tattle. Suddainly———before we knew where we were— that Villain *Jeremy*, by the help of Disguises, trickt us into one another.

Foresight. Why, you told me just now, you went hence in haste to be married.

Angelica. But I believe Mr. *Tattle* meant the Favour to me, I thank him.

Tattle. I did, as I hope to be sav'd, Madam, my Intentions were good———But this is the most cruel thing, to marry one does not know how, nor why, nor wherefore——— The Devil take me if ever I was so much concern'd at any thing in my Life.

Angelica. 'Tis very unhappy, if you don't care for one another.

Tattle. The least in the World———That is for my Part, I speak for my self. Gad, I never had the least thought of serious Kindness—I never lik'd any body less in my Life. Poor Woman! Gad I'm sorry for her too; for I have no reason to hate her neither; but I believe I shall lead her a damn'd sort of a Life.

Mrs. Foresight (*aside to* Mrs. Frail). He's better than no Husband at all———tho he's a Coxcomb.

Mrs. Frail (*to her*). Aye, aye, it's well it's no worse—Nay, for my part I always despised Mr. *Tattle* of all things; nothing but his being my Husband could have made me like him less.

Tattle. Look you there, I thought as much———pox on't, I wish we could keep it secret, why I don't believe any of this Company wou'd speak of it.

Mrs. Frail. But, my Dear, that's impossible; the Parson and that Rogue *Jeremy* will publish it.

Tattle. Aye, my Dear, so they will as you say.

Angelica. O you'll agree very well in a little time; Custom will make it easie to you.

Tattle. Easie! Pox on't, I don't believe I shall sleep to Night.

Sir Sampson. Sleep Quotha! No, why you would not sleep o' your Wedding Night? I'm an older Fellow than you, and don't mean to sleep.

Ben. Why there's another Match now, as tho'f a couple of Privateers were looking for a Prize, and should fall foul of one another. I'm sorry for the Young Man with all my Heart. Look you, Friend, if I may advise you, when she's going, for that you must expect, I have Experience of her, when she's going, let her go. For no *Matrimony* is tough enough to hold her, and if she can't drag her Anchor along with her, she'll break her Cable, I can tell you that. Who's here? the Madman?

Enter Valentine *dress'd*, Scandal, *and* Jeremy.

Valentine. No; here's the Fool; and if occasion be, I'll give it under my hand.

Sir Sampson. How now?

Valentine. Sir, I'm come to acknowledge my Errors, and ask your Pardon.

Sir Sampson. What, have you found your Senses at last then? In good time, Sir.

Valentine. You were abus'd, Sir, I never was Distracted.

Foresight. How! Not Mad! Mr. *Scandal.*

Scandal. No really, Sir; I'm his Witness, it was all Counterfeit.

Valentine. I thought I had Reasons———But it was a poor Contrivance, the Effect has shewn it such.

Sir Sampson. Contrivance, what to cheat me? to cheat your Father! Sirrah, could you hope to prosper?

Valentine. Indeed, I thought, Sir, when the Father endeavoured to undo the Son, it was a reasonable return of Nature.

Sir Sampson. Very good, Sir———Mr. *Buckram*, are you ready?———Come, Sir, will you sign and seal?

Valentine. If you please, Sir; but first I would ask this Lady one Question.

Sir Sampson. Sir, you must ask my leave first; that Lady, No, Sir; you shall ask that Lady no Questions, till you have ask'd her Blessing, Sir; that Lady is to be my Wife.

Valentine. I have heard as much, Sir; but I wou'd have it from her own Mouth.

Sir Sampson. That's as much as to say, I lie, Sir, and you don't believe what I say.

Valentine. Pardon me, Sir. But I reflect that I very lately counterfeited Madness; I don't know but the Frolick may go round.

Sir Sampson. Come, Chuck, satisfie him, answer him;———Come, come, Mr. *Buckram*, the Pen and Ink.

Buckram. Here it is, Sir, with the Deed, all is ready.

Valentine *goes to* Angelica.

Angelica. 'Tis true, you have a great while pretended Love to me; nay, what if you were sincere? still you must pardon me, if I think my own Inclinations have a better Right to dispose of my Person, than yours.

Sir Sampson. Are you answer'd now, Sir?

Valentine. Yes, Sir.

Sir Sampson. Where's your Plot, Sir? and your Contrivance now, Sir? Will you sign, Sir? Come, will you sign and seal?

Valentine. With all my Heart, Sir.

Scandal. 'S'death, you are not mad indeed, to ruine your self?

Valentine. I have been disappointed of my only Hope; and he that loses hope may part with any thing. I never valu'd Fortune, but as it was subservient to my Pleasure; and my only Pleasure was to please this Lady: I have made many vain Attempts, and find at last, that nothing but my Ruine can effect it: Which, for that Reason, I will sign to——— Give me the Paper.

Angelica (*aside*). Generous *Valentine*!

Buckram. Here is the Deed, Sir.

Valentine. But where is the Bond, by which I am oblig'd to sign this?

Buckram. Sir *Sampson* you have it.

Angelica. No, I have it; and I'll use it, as I would every thing that is an Enemy to *Valentine*.

Tears the Paper.

Sir Sampson. How now!

Valentine. Ha!

Angelica (*to* Valentine). Had I the World to give you, it cou'd not make me worthy of so generous and faithful a Passion: Here's my Hand, my Heart was always yours, and struggl'd very hard to make this utmost Tryal of your Virtue.

Valentine. Between Pleasure and Amazement, I am lost——— But on my Knees I take the Blessing.

Sir Sampson. Oons, what is the meaning of this?

Ben. Mess, here's the Wind chang'd again. Father, you and I may make a Voyage together now.

Angelica. Well, Sir *Sampson*, since I have plaid you a Trick, I'll advise you, how you may avoid such another. Learn to be a good Father, or you'll never get a second Wife. I always lov'd your Son, and hated your unforgiving Nature. I was resolv'd to try him to the utmost; I have try'd you too, and know you both. You have not more Faults than he has Virtues; and 'tis hardly more Pleasure to me, that I can make him and my self happy, than that I can punish you.

Valentine. If my happiness cou'd receive Addition, this Kind surprize would make it double.

Sir Sampson. Oons you're a *Crocodile*.

Foresight. Really, Sir *Sampson*, this is a sudden Eclipse—

Sir Sampson. You're an illiterate Fool, and I'm another, and the Stars are Lyars; and if I had Breath enough, I'd curse them and you, my self and every Body—Oons, Cully'd, Bubbl'd, Jilted, Woman-bobb'd at last—I have not Patience.

Exit Sir Sampson.

Tattle. If the Gentleman is in this disorder for want of a Wife, I can spare him mine. (*to* Jeremy) Oh are you there, Sir? I'm indebted to you for my Happiness.

Jeremy. Sir, I ask you Ten Thousand Pardons, 'twas an errant mistake———You see, Sir, my Master was never mad, nor any thing like it———Then how could it be otherwise?

Valentine. *Tattle*, I thank you, you would have interposed between me and Heav'n; but Providence laid Purgatory in your way—You have but Justice.

Scandal. I hear the Fiddles that Sir *Sampson* provided for his own Wedding; methinks 'tis pity they should not be employ'd when the Match is so much mended. *Valentine*, tho' it be Morning, we may have a Dance.

Valentine. Any thing, my Friend, every thing that looks like Joy and Transport.

Scandal. Call 'em, *Jeremy*.

Angelica. I have done dissembling now, *Valentine*; and if that Coldness which I have always worn before you, should turn to an extream Fondness, you must not suspect it.

Valentine. I'll prevent that suspicion———For I intend to doat on at that immoderate rate, that your Fondness shall never distinguish it self enough, to be taken notice of. If ever you seem to love too much, it must be only when I can't love enough.

Angelica. Have a care of large Promises; You know you are apt to run more in Debt than you are able to pay.

Valentine. Therefore I yield my Body as your Prisoner, and make your best on't.

Scandal. The Musick stays for you.

Dance.

Scandal. Well, Madam, You have done Exemplary Justice, in punishing an inhumane Father, and rewarding a Faithful

Lover: But there is a Third good Work, which I, in particular, must thank you for; I was an Infidel to your Sex; and you have converted me———For now I am convinc'd that all Women are not like Fortune, blind in bestowing Favours, either on those who do not merit, or who do not want 'em.

Angelica. 'Tis an unreasonable Accusation, that you lay upon our Sex: You tax us with Injustice, only to cover your own want of Merit. You would all have the Reward of Love; but few have the Constancy to stay till it becomes your due. Men are generally Hypocrites and Infidels, they pretend to Worship, but have neither Zeal nor Faith: How few, like *Valentine*, would persevere even unto Martyrdom, and sacrifice their Interest to their Constancy! In admiring me, you misplace the Novelty.

The Miracle to Day is, that we find
A Lover true: Not that a Woman's Kind.

Exeunt Omnes.

FINIS.

Epilogue

Spoken at the opening of the New House,

By Mrs. *Bracegirdle.*

Sure Providence at first, design'd this Place
To be the Player's Refuge in distress;
For still in every Storm, they all run hither,
As to a Shed, that shields 'em from the Weather.
But thinking of this change which last befel us,
It's like what I have heard our Poets tell us:
For when behind our Scenes their Suits are pleading,
To help their Love, sometimes they show their Reading;
And wanting ready Cash to pay for Hearts,
They top their Learning on us, and their Parts.
Once of Philosophers they told us Stories,
Whom, as I think they call'd—*Py—Pythagories,*
I'm sure 'tis some such *Latin* Name they give 'em,
And we, who know no better, must believe 'em.
Now to these Men (say they) such Souls were given,
That after Death, ne're went to Hell, nor Heaven,
But liv'd, I know not how, in Beasts; and then
When many Years were past, in Men again.
Methinks, we *Players* resemble such a Soul,
That, does from Bodies, we from Houses strole.
Thus *Aristotle*'s Soul, of old that was,
May now be damn'd to animate an Ass;
Or in this very House, for ought we know,
Is doing painful Penance in some *Beau,*
And this our Audience, which did once resort
To shining Theatres to see our Sport,
Now find us toss'd into a Tennis-Court.
These Walls but t'other Day were fill'd with Noise
Of Roaring Gamesters, and your *Damme Boys.*
Then bounding Balls and Rackets they encompass'd,
And now they're fill'd with Jests, and Flights, and Bombast!
I vow, I don't much like this Transmigration,
Stroling from Place to Place, by Circulation.
Grant Heaven, we don't return to our first Station.
I know not what these think, but for my Part,
I can't reflect without an aking Heart,
How we shou'd end in our Original, a Cart.
But we can't fear, since you're so good to save us,

That you have only set us up, to leave us.
Thus from the past, we hope for future Grace,
I beg it—
And some here know I have a begging Face.
Then pray continue this your kind behaviour,
For a clear Stage won't do, without your Favour.

5

The Mourning Bride

INTRODUCTORY NOTE

If Congreve were to accept the position to which all his friends seemed to assume that he had a right after the success of his first play—as Dryden's acknowledged successor—it would clearly be necessary for him to try his hand at heroic tragedy. And there is reason to think that already in 1693 he may have been looking for a subject. However unreliable the source, Swift refers in his lines to Congreve, written probably in the latter part of 1693, to

> A late report your friends had vex'd,
> Who heard you meant to write heroics next;

It had come from a young spark who had returned during the summer from London;

> Stock'd with the freshest gibberish of the town
> . . . .
> For, tragedy, he knew, would lose you quite,
> And told you so at Will's but t'other night.[1]

It is referred to again two years later in a letter to Congreve from Walter Moyle, dated October 7, 1695, asking for news of the stage and of "what Progress you have made in your Tragedy."[2] A year later it was ready, and in February, 1697, it was another triumph for the company at Lincolns Inn Fields, where it had a run of thirteen days with crowded houses.

Congreve had again achieved a remarkable success with his first tragedy, written in the current fashion in competition with Dryden and Lee and Shadwell, and he obviously was not deterred by the devastating and amusing satire of the heroic mode that he must have enjoyed in *The Rehearsal*. True, he follows his master Dryden in abandoning rhyme and adopts the same sort of irregular blank verse, which

[1] Sir Harold Williams, *The Poems of Jonathan Swift*, 1937, I, 47.
[2] John Hodges, *Letters and Documents*, p. 192.

Dryden had used in *Don Sebastian*, 1690, and *Cleomenes*, which Southerne had helped to complete in 1692.[3]

Congreve was also certainly not unaware of what Dryden had written in his Preface to *Don Sebastian*:

> As for the story or plot of the Tragedy, 'tis purely fiction; for I take it up where the History has laid it down. . . . This ground work the History afforded me, and I desire no better to build a Play upon it: For where the Event of a great action is left doubtful, there the Poet is left Master: He may raise what he pleases on that foundation, provided he makes it of a piece, and according to the rule of probability.

For, in *The Mourning Bride*, the plot is "purely fiction" and the historical foundation is slight. The action takes place in Granada, in the south of Spain made familiar to the theater audience by Dryden's *Conquest of Granada*, which had frequently been acted since its first performance in 1670, and had appeared in a fifth edition in 1695. The plot is based on the earlier conflicts between Granada and Valencia, a city on the coast opposite the island of Majorca; and on the part played in this struggle by Moorish expeditions from the north coast of Africa. But the characters and the names of the characters are drawn from earlier heroic plays rather than from history. Parallels have been suggested with Dryden's *Indian Emperour* and *Indian Queen*; and Davies points out[4] echoes of Orestes' speeches to his sister in the talk of Osmyn and Almeria, without, however, remembering that it was probably André Dacier's version, 1692, of the *Electra*, in French, with which Congreve was immediately familiar. Sir Walter Scott noticed also some echoes from Dryden's *Cleomenes*, which had been first played in April, 1692, and which was also included in the third volume of Dryden's *Works*, 1695.

Dryden also referred, in the Preface to *Don Sebastian*, to his careful provision of language suitable to the loftiness of his subject, and to "some secret Beauties in the decorum of parts, and uniformity of Design" that would only be discovered by careful reading. Congreve had both these things in mind; and he would certainly have admitted that he had Dryden's example before him, in *Cleomenes*, "to write upon a single Plott, unmix'd with Comedy; which though it be

[3] They were both included in *The Works of John Dryden*, (London: Jacob Tonson, 1695), Vol. III (no. 166 in Congreve's library).

[4] Thomas Davies, *Dramatic Miscellanies*, 1784 III, 348.

the natural and true way, yet is not to the Genius of the Nation."[5] Congreve must have seen this play as it was superbly acted by his own company—the Bettertons, Mountford, who was then still living, Mrs. Bracegirdle, and Mrs. Barry, of whom Dryden wrote in the Preface:

> ... none of them will be offended, if I say what the Town has generally granted, that Mrs Barry, always Excellent, has, in this Tragedy, excell'd Herself, and gained a Reputation beyond any Woman whom I have ever seen on the Theatre.

It was, I think, these plays of Dryden that provided Congreve with the inspiration to write a heroic tragedy, which must have satisfied him sufficiently that he deemed it worthy to be offered to Her Royal Highness, the Princess Anne. Giles Jacob even goes so far as to say that it met with "Encouragement inferior to no Dramatick Piece, that has at any time appear'd on the *English* Stage."[6]

Even the Epilogue, written for Mrs. Bracegirdle, which seems to be so completely lacking in decorum, so needless a concession to the current fashion, is not quite so inexplicable after reading the Epilogue which Dryden had written for Mrs. Bracegirdle to speak at the end of *Cleomenes*:

> This Day, the Poet bloodily inclin'd,
> Has made me die, full sore against my Mind!
> Some of you naughty Men, I fear, will cry,
> Poor Rogue! would I might teach thee how to die!
> Thanks for your Love; but I sincerely say,
> I never mean to die, your wicked way.

In spite of the growing tendency to dismiss *The Mourning Bride* on account of the "rant and bombast," the "strained, unnatural sentiments," it continued to be played with great success in the theater throughout the eighteenth century; and in the time of Kemble and Mrs. Siddons, who always drew a crowded house when she played Zara, it was more frequently seen than the comedies.[7]

[5] John Dryden, *Preface to Cleomenes* ("Dramatic Works," ed. Montagu Summers [London: Nonesuch Press, 1932]), VI, 300.

[6] Giles Jacob, *Poetical Register* (1719), p. 43.

[7] Emmett L. Avery, *Congreve on the Eighteenth-century Stage*, 1951, esp. pp. 146, 166–67.

THE

Mourning Bride,

A

TRAGEDY.

As it is ACTED AT THE

Theatre in *Lincoln's-Inn-Fields*,

BY

His Majesty's Servants.

Written by Mr. *CONGREVE*.

——— *Neque enim lex æquior ulla,*
Quàm necis artifices arte perire sua.
Ovid. de Arte Am.

LONDON,

Printed for *Jacob Tonson* at the *Judge's-Head* near the *Inner-Temple-Gate*, in *Fleet-street*, 1697.

Neque . . . Amoris—"A rightful Doom, the Laws of Nature cry,/'Tis, the Artificers of Death should die." (Ovid, *Art of Love*, I, 655–56 [Dryden's translation].)

To
Her Royal Highness,
The
PRINCESS.

MADAM,

That high Station, which by Your Birth You hold above the People, exacts from every one, as a Duty, whatever Honours they are capable of paying to Your Royal Highness: But that more exalted Place, to which Your Vertues have rais'd You, above the rest of Princes, makes the Tribute of our Admiration and Praise, rather a choice more immediately preventing that Duty.

The Publick Gratitude is ever founded on a Publick Benefit; and what is universally bless'd, is always an universal Blessing. Thus from Your self, we derive the Offerings which we bring; and that Incense which arises to Your Name, only returns to its Original, and but naturally requires the Parent of its Being.

From hence it is that this Poem, constituted on a Moral, whose End is to recommend and to encourage Vertue, of consequence has recourse to Your Royal Highness's Patronage; aspiring to cast it self beneath Your Feet, and declining Approbation, till You shall condescend to own it, and vouchsafe to shine upon it as on a Creature of Your Influence.

'Tis from the Example of Princes, that Vertue becomes a Fashion in the People, for even they who are averse to Instruction, will yet be fond of Imitation.

But there are Multitudes, who never can have Means, nor Opportunities of so near an Access, as to partake of the Benefit of such Examples. And to these, Tragedy, which distinguishes it self from the Vulgar Poetry, by the Dignity of its Characters, may be of Use and Information. For they who are at that distance from Original Greatness, as to be depriv'd of the Happiness of Contemplating the Perfections and real Excellencies of Your Royal Highness's Person, in Your Court; may yet behold some small Sketches and Imagings of the Vertues of Your Mind, abstracted, and represented in the Theatre.

Thus Poets are instructed, and instruct; not alone by Precepts which persuade, but also by Examples which illustrate. Thus is Delight interwoven with Instruction; when not only Vertue is prescrib'd, but also represented.

But if we are delighted with the Livelyness of a feign'd Representation of Great and Good Persons and their Actions; how must we be charm'd with beholding the Persons themselves? If one or two excelling Qualities, barely touch'd in the single Action, and small Compass of a Play, can warm an Audience, with a Concern and Regard even for the seeming Success and Prosperity of the Actor: With what Zeal must the Hearts of all be fill'd, for the continued and encreasing Happiness of those, who are the true and living Instances of Elevated and Persisting Vertue? Even the Vicious themselves must have a secret Veneration for those peculiar Graces and Endowments, which are daily so eminently conspicuous in Your Royal Highness; and though repining, feel a Pleasure which in spite of Envy they per-force approve.

If in this Piece, humbly offer'd to Your Royal Highness, there shall appear the Resemblance of any one of those many Excellencies which You so promiscuously possess, to be drawn so as to merit Your least Approbation, it has the End and Accomplishment of its Design. And however imperfect it may be in the Whole, through the Inexperience or Incapacity of the Author, yet, if there is so much as to convince Your Royal Highness, that a Play may be with Industry so dispos'd (in spight of the licentious Practice of the Modern Theatre) as to become sometimes an innocent, and not unprofitable Entertainment; it will abundantly gratifie the Ambition and recompence the Endeavours of,

Your Royal Highness's
Most Obedient, and
most humbly Devoted Servant,

William Congreve.

Prologue.

Spoken by Mr. *Betterton*.

The Time has been when Plays were not so plenty,
And a less Number New, would well content ye.
New Plays did then like Almanacks appear;
And One was thought sufficient for a Year:
Tho' they are more like Almanacks of late;
For in One Year, I think they're out of Date.
Nor were they without Reason join'd together;
For just as one prognosticates the Weather,
How plentiful the Crop, or scarce the Grain,
What Peals of Thunder, and what Show'rs of Rain;
So t'other can foretel by certain Rules
What Crops of Coxcombs, or what Flouds of Fools.
In such like Prophecies were Poets skill'd,
Which now they find in their own Tribe fulfill'd:
The Dearth of Wit they did so long presage,
Is fall'n on us, and almost starves the Stage.
Were you not griev'd, as often as you saw
Poor Actors thresh such empty Sheafs of Straw?
Toiling and lab'ring at their Lungs Expence,
To start a Jest, or force a little Sence.
Hard Fate for us! still harder in th' Event;
Our Authors Sin, but we alone repent.
Still they proceed, and, at our Charge, write worse;
'Twere some Amends if they could reimburse:
But there's the Devil, tho' their Cause is lost,
There's no recov'ring Damages or Cost.
  Good Wits, forgive this Liberty we take,
Since Custome gives the Losers leave to speak.
But if, provok'd, your dreadful Wrath remains,
Take your Revenge upon the coming Scenes:
For that damn'd Poet's spar'd who dams a Brother,
As one Thief scapes, that executes another.
Thus far, alone does to the Wits relate;
But from the rest, we hope a better Fate.
To please and move, has been our Poets Theme,

empty Sheafs of Straw—Cf. Tom Brown, *Letters from the Dead* (1702) p. 37: "Inundations of Plays lately . . . The generality . . . dye the first day . . . or by meer dint of Acting, hold out to the third." In 1696 many first plays by Mrs. Manley, Mrs. Trotter, Mrs. Pix, Motteux, etc. had died.

Art may direct, but Nature is his aim;
And Nature miss'd, in vain he boasts his Art,
For only Nature can affect the Heart.
Then freely judge the Scenes that shall ensue,
But as with Freedom, judge with Candour too.
He wou'd not lose thro' Prejudice his Cause;
Nor wou'd obtain precariously Applause.
Impartial Censure, he requests from all,
Prepar'd, by just Decrees to stand, or fall.

Dramatis Personæ.

MEN

Manuel, the King of *Granada*	Mr. Verbruggen.
Gonsalez, his Favourite	Mr. Sanford.
Garcia, Son to *Gonsalez*	Mr. Scudamour.
Perez, Captain of the Guards	Mr. Freeman.
Alonzo, an Officer, Creature to *Gonsalez*	Mr. Arnold.
Osmyn, a Noble Prisoner	Mr. Betterton.
Heli, a Prisoner, his Friend	Mr. Bowman.
Selim, an Eunuch	Mr. Baily.

WOMEN

Almeria, the Princess of *Granada*	Mrs. Bracegirdle.
Zara, a Captive Queen	Mrs. Barry.
Leonora, chief Attendant on the Princess	Mrs. Bowman.

Women, Eunuchs, and Mutes attending Zara. *Guards*, &c.

The Scene *GRANADA*.

The Mourning Bride.

ACT I. Scene I.

A Room of State.

The Curtain rising slowly to soft Musick, discovers Almeria *in Mourning*, Leonora *waiting in Mourning.*

After the Musick Almeria *rises from her Chair, and comes forward.*

Almeria. Musick has Charms to sooth a savage Breast,
To soften Rocks, or bend a knotted Oak.
I've read, that things inanimate have mov'd,
And, as with living Souls, have been inform'd,
By Magick Numbers and persuasive Sound.
What then am I? Am I more senseless grown
Than Trees, or Flint? O Force of constant Woe!
'Tis not in Harmony to calm my Griefs.
Anselmo sleeps, and is at Peace; last Night,
The silent Tomb receiv'd the good old King;
He and his Sorrows now are safely lodg'd
Within its cold, but hospitable Bosom.
Why am not I at Peace?

Weeps.

Leonora. For Heaven's sake, dear Madam, moderate
Your Griefs, there is no Cause—

Almeria. Peace———No Cause! yes, there is Eternal Cause.
And Misery Eternal will succeed.
Thou canst not tell———thou hast indeed no Cause.

Leonora. Believe me, Madam, I lament *Anselmo*,
And always did compassionate his Fortune;
Have often wept, to see how cruelly
Your Father kept in Chains his Fellow-King:
And oft at Night, when all have been retir'd,
Have stoll'n from Bed, and to his Prison crept:
Where, while his Gaoler slept, I thro' the Grate

Curtain rising to Music—Written by Gottfried Finger, one of the four composers who later competed to set the music for Congreve's masque, *The Judgment of Paris*, 1700.

Have softly whisper'd, and enquir'd his Health;
Sent in my Sighs and Pray'rs for his Deliv'rance;
For Sighs and Pray'rs were all that I could offer.

Almeria. Indeed thou hast a soft and gentle Nature,
That thus couldst melt to see a Stranger's Wrongs.
O *Leonora*, hadst thou known *Anselmo*,
How would thy Heart have bled to see his Suff'rings!
Thou hadst no Cause, but general Compassion.

Leonora. My Love of you, my Royal Mistress, gave me Cause,
My Love of you begot my Grief for him,
For I had heard, that when the Chance of War
Had bless'd *Anselmo's* Arms with Victory,
And the rich Spoil of all the Field, and you
The Glory of the whole, were made the Prey
Of his Success; that then, in spite of Hate,
Revenge, and that Hereditary Feud
Entail'd between *Valentia*'s and *Granada*'s Kings;
He did endear himself to your Affection,
By all the worthy and indulgent ways,
His most industrious Goodness could invent;
Proposing by a Match between *Alphonso*
His Son, the brave *Valentia* Prince, and you,
To end the long Dissention, and unite
The Jarring Crowns.

Almeria. O *Alphonso*, *Alphonso*! thou art too
At Peace; Father and Son are now no more—
Then why am I? O when shall I have Rest?
Why do I live to say you are no more?
Why are all these things thus?—
Is there necessity I must be miserable?
Is it of Moment to the Peace of Heav'n
That I should be afflicted thus?———if not,
Why is it thus contriv'd? Why are things laid
By some unseen Hand, so, as of consequence
They must to me bring Curses, Grief of Heart,
The last Distress of Life, and sure Despair.

Leonora. Alas you search too far, and think too deeply.

Almeria. Why was I carried to *Anselmo's* Court?
Or, when there, why was I us'd so tenderly?
Why did he not use me like an Enemy?

Valentia's and Granada's Kings—This reference to historical places and feuds seems deliberately to be kept as vague and general as possible.

For so my Father would have us'd his Child.
O *Alphonso, Alphonso*!
Devouring Seas have wash'd thee from my sight,
But there's no time shall rase thee from my Memory.
No, I will live to be thy Monument;
The cruel Ocean would deprive thee of a Tomb,
But in my Heart thou art interr'd, there, there,
Thy dear Resemblance is for ever fixt;
My Love, my Lord, my Husband still, though lost.

Leonora. Husband! O heav'ns!

Almeria. What have I said?
My Grief has hurry'd me beyond all Thought.
I would have kept that Secret; though I know
Thy Love and Faith to me, deserve all Confidence.
But 'tis the Wretches Comfort still to have
Some small reserve of near and inward Woe,
Some unsuspected hoard of darling Grief,
Which they unseen, may wail, and weep, and mourn,
And Glutton-like alone devour.

Leonora. Indeed I knew not this.

Almeria. O no, thou know'st not half——thou know'st nothing
——If thou didst!—
If I should tell thee, wouldst thou pity me?
Tell me? I know thou wouldst, thou art compassionate.

Leonora. Witness these Tears—

Almeria. I thank thee——indeed I do—
I thank thee, that thou'lt pity thy sad Mistress;
For 'tis the poor Prerogative of Greatness,
To be wretched and unpitied—
But I did promise I would tell thee——What?
My Griefs? Thou dost already know 'em:
And when I said thou didst know nothing,
It was because thou didst not know *Alphonso*:
For to have known my Loss, thou must have known
His Worth, his Truth, and Tenderness of Love.

Leonora. The Memory of that brave Prince stands fair
In all Report—
And I have heard imperfectly his Loss;
But fearful to renew your Troubles past,
I never did presume to ask the Story.

Almeria. If for my swelling Heart I can, I'll tell thee.
I was a welcome Captive in *Valentia*,
Ev'n on the Day when *Manuel*, my Father,
Led on his conqu'ring Troops, high as the Gates
Of King *Anselmo*'s Pallace; which in Rage
And Heat of War, and dire Revenge, he fir'd.
Whilst the good King, to shun approaching Flames,
Started amidst his Foes, and made Captivity his Refuge;
Would I had perish'd in those Flames—
But 'twas not so decreed.
Alphonso, who foresaw my Father's Cruelty,
Had born the Queen and me, on board a Ship
Ready to sail, and when this News was brought,
We put to Sea; but being betray'd by some
Who knew our Flight, we closely were pursu'd,
And almost taken; when a sudden Storm,
Drove us and those that follow'd, on the Coast
Of *Africk*: There our Vessel struck the Shore,
And bulging 'gainst a Rock, was dash'd in pieces.
But Heav'n spared me for yet more Affliction!
Conducting them who follow'd us, to shun
The Shoal, and save me floating on the Waves,
While the good Queen and my *Alphonso* perish'd.

Leonora. Alas! were you then wedded to *Alphonso*?

Almeria. That Day, that fatal Day, our Hands were joyn'd:
For when my Lord beheld the Ship pursuing,
And saw her Rate so far exceeding ours;
He came to me, and beg'd me by my Love,
I would consent the Priest might make us one;
That whether Death, or Victory ensu'd,
I might be his, beyond the Power of future Fate:
The Queen too, did assist his Suit———I granted,
And in one Day, was wedded, and a Widow.

Leonora. Indeed 'twas mournful—

Almeria. 'Twas that,
For which I mourn, and will for ever mourn;
Nor will I change these black and dismal Robes,
Or ever dry these swoll'n, and watry Eyes;
Or, ever taste content, or peace of Heart,
While I have Life, or Memory of my *Alphonso*.

Leonora. Look down good Heav'n, with Pity on her Sorrows,
And grant, that Time may bring her some Relief.

Almeria. O no! Time gives Encrease to my Afflictions.
The circling Hours, that gather all the Woes,
Which are diffus'd thro' the revolving Year,
Come, heavy-laden with the oppressing Weight
To me; with me, successively, they leave
The Sighs, the Tears, the Groans, the restless Cares,
And all the Damps of Grief, that did retard their Flight;
They shake their downy Wings, and scatter all
The dire collected Dews, on my poor Head;
Then fly with Joy and Swiftness from me.

Leonora. Heark!
The distant Shouts, proclaim your Fathers Triumph;
Shouts at a Distance.
O cease, for Heaven's Sake, asswage a little,
This Torrent of your Grief; for, much I fear
It will incense him, thus to see you drown'd
In Tears, when Joy appears in every other Face.

Almeria. And Joy he brings to every other Heart,
But double, double Weight of Woe to mine;
For with him *Garcia* comes———*Garcia*, to whom
I must be sacrific'd, and all the Faith
And Vows I gave my Dear *Alphonso*, basely
Violated—
No, it shall never be; for I will die first,
Die ten thousand Deaths———Look down, look down
Kneels.
Alphonso, hear the Sacred Vow I make;
Leave for a Moment to behold Eternal Bliss,
And bend thy Glorious Eyes to Earth and me;
And thou *Anselmo*, if yet thou art arriv'd
Thro' all Impediments, of purging Fire,
To that bright Heav'n, where my *Alphonso* reigns,
Behold thou also, and attend my Vow.
If ever I do yield, or give consent,
By any Action, Word or Thought, to wed
Another Lord; may then just Heav'n show'r down
Unheard of Curses on me, greater far
(If such there be in angry Heav'ns Vengeance)
Than any I have yet endur'd———and now
Rising.
Methinks my Heart has some Relief: Having
Discharg'd this Debt, incumbent on my Love.
Yet, one Thing more, I would engage from thee.

Leonora. My Heart, my Life and Will, are only yours.

Almeria. I thank thee. 'Tis but this; anon, when all
Are busied in the General Joy, that thou
Wilt privately with me,
Steal forth, and visit good *Anselmo*'s Tomb.

Leonora. Alas! I fear some fatal Resolution.

Almeria. No, on my Life, my Faith, I mean no Violence.
I feel I'm more at large,
Since I have made this Vow:
Perhaps I would repeat it there more solemnly.
'Tis that, or some such Melancholy Thought,
Upon my Word no more,

Leonora. I will attend you.

Enter Alonzo.

Alonzo. The Lord *Gonsalez* comes to tell your Highness
Of the Kings approach.

Almeria. Conduct him in.

Exit Alonzo.

That's his Pretence. I know his Errand is
To fill my Ears, with *Garcia*'s valiant Deeds;
And with his Artful Tongue, to gild and magnifie
His Son's Exploits.
But I am arm'd, with Ice around my Heart,
Not to be warm'd with Words, nor idle Eloquence.

Enter Gonsalez, *Bowing very humbly.*

Gonsalez. Be every Day of your long Life like this.
The Sun, bright Conquest, and your brighter Eyes,
Have all conspir'd, to blaze promiscuous Light,
And bless this Day with most unequal Lustre.
Your Royal Father, my Victorious Lord,
Loaden with Spoils, and ever-living Lawrel,
Is entring now, in Martial Pomp the Pallace.
Five Hundred Mules, precede his solemn March,
Which groan beneath the Weight of *Moorish* Wealth.
Chariots of War, adorn'd with glittering Gems,
Succeed; and next, a Hundred neighing Steeds,
White as the fleecy Rain on *Alpine* Hills;
That bound, and foam, and champ the Golden Bit,
As they disdain'd the Victory they grace.
Prisoners of War in shining Fetters, follow;
And Captains of the Noblest Blood of *Affrick*,

Sweat by his Chariot Wheel, and lick, and grind
With gnashing Teeth, the Dust his Tryumphs raise.
The swarming Populace, spread every Wall,
And cling, as if with Claws they did enforce
Their Hold, thro' clifted Stones; stretching, and staring,
As they were all of Eyes, and every Limb
Would feed his Faculty of Admiration.
While you alone retire, and shun this Sight;
This Sight, which is indeed not seen (tho' twice
The Multitude should gaze) in Absence of your Eyes.

Almeria. My Lord, my Eyes ungratefully behold
The gilded Trophies of exterior Honours.
Nor will my Ears be charm'd with sounding Words,
Or pompous Phrase; the Pageantry of Souls.
But that my Father is return'd in Safety,
I bend to Heav'n with Thanks and Humble Praise.

Gonsalez. Excellent Princess!
But 'tis a Task unfit for my weak Age,
With dying Words, to offer at your Praise.
Garcia, my Son, your Beauties lowest Slave,
Has better done;
In proving with his Sword, upon your Foes
The Force and Influence of your matchless Charms.

Almeria. I doubt not of the Worth of *Garcia*'s Deeds,
Which had been brave, tho' I had ne'er been born.

Leonora. Madam, the King.

Flourish.

Almeria. My Women. I would meet him.

Attendants to Almeria *enter in Mourning.*

Symphony of Warlike Musick. Enter the King, attended by Garcia *and several Officers. Files of Prisoners in Chains, and Guards, who are ranged in Order, round the Stage.* Almeria *meets the King and kneels: afterwards* Gonsalez *kneels and kisses the King's Hand, while* Garcia *does the same to the Princess.*

King. Almeria, rise———My best *Gonsalez* rise.
What Tears! my good old Friend.—

Gonsalez. But Tears of Joy. To see you thus, has fill'd
My Eyes with more Delight, than they can hold.

clifted Stones—A vivid description of the Albaycin, at the heart of the old Moorish city, built on the steep hill, rising up from the river, and the neighboring Alhambra.

King. By Heav'n thou lov'st me, and I'm pleas'd thou do'st:
Take it for Thanks, Old Man, that I rejoice
To see thee weep on this Occasion———But some
Here are who seem to mourn at our Success!
How is it *Almeria*, that you meet our Eyes
Upon this solemn Day, in these sad Weeds?
You, and yours, are all, in opposition
To my Brightness, like Daughters of Affliction.

Almeria. Forgive me, Sir, if I offend.
The Year, which I have vow'd to pay to Heav'n,
In Mourning, and strict Life, for my Deliverance
From Death, and Wreck of the tempestuous Sea,
Wants yet to be expired.

King. Your Zeal to Heav'n is great; so is your Debt:
Yet something too is due to me, who gave
That Life, which Heav'n preserv'd. A Day bestow'd
In Filial Duty, had aton'd and giv'n
A Dispensation to your Vow———No more.
'Twas weak and wilful———and a Woman's Errour.
Yet———upon thought, it doubly wounds my sight,
To see that Sable worn upon the Day
Succeeding that, in which our deadliest Foe,
Hated *Anselmo*, was interr'd———By Heav'n,
It looks as thou didst mourn for him: Just as
Thy senseless Vow appear'd to bear its Date,
Not from that Hour, wherein thou wert preserv'd,
But that, wherein the curs'd *Alphonso* perish'd.
Ha! what? thou dost not weep to think of that?

Gonsalez. Have patience, Royal Sir, the Princess weeps
To have offended you. If Fate decreed,
One 'pointed Hour should be *Alphonso*'s Loss,
And her Deliverance; Is she to blame?

King. I tell thee she's to blame, not to have feasted
When my first Foe was laid in Earth, such Enmity,
Such Detestation, bears my Blood to his;
My Daughter should have revell'd at his Death.
She should have made these Pallace Walls to shake,
And all this high and ample Roof to ring
With her Rejoicings. What, to mourn, and weep;
Then, then, to weep, and pray, and grieve? By Heav'n,
There's not a Slave, a shackled Slave of mine,
But should have smil'd that Hour, through all his Care,
And shook his Chains in Transport, and rude Harmony.

Gonsalez. What she has done, was in excess of Goodness:
Betray'd by too much Piety, to seem
As if she had offended.

King. To seem is to commit, at this Conjuncture.
I wonnot have the seeming of a Sorrow seen
To day——Retire, divest your self with speed
Of that offensive black; on me be all
The Violation of your Vow.
You stand excused that I command it.

Garcia (kneeling). Your Pardon, Sir, if I presume so far,
As to remind you of your gracious Promise.

King. Rise, *Garcia*——I forgot. Yet stay, *Almeria.*

Almeria. O my boding Heart——What is your Pleasure,
Sir?

King. Draw near, and give your hand; and, *Garcia*, yours:
Receive this Lord, as one whom I have found
Worthy to be your Husband, and my Son.

Garcia. Thus let me kneel to take——O not to take,
But to devote, and yield my self for ever
The Slave and Creature of my Royal Mistress.

Gonsalez. O let me prostrate, pay my worthless Thanks
For this high Honour.

King. No more; my Promise long since pass'd, thy Loyalty,
And *Garcia*'s well-try'd Valour, all oblige me.
This Day we triumph; but to morrow's Sun
Shall shine on *Garcia*'s Nuptials.

Almeria. Oh!—

Faints.

Garcia. Alas, she faints! help to support her.

Gonsalez. She recovers.

King. A Bridal Qualm; soon off. How is't, *Almeria*?

Almeria. A sudden Chilness seizes on my Spirits.
Your Leave, Sir, to retire.

King. Garcia, conduct her.

Garcia *leads* Almeria *to the Door, and returns.*

This idle Vow hangs on her Woman's Fears.
I'll have a Priest shall preach her from her Faith,
And make it Sin, not to renounce that Vow,
Which I'd have broken.

Trumpets.

Enter Alonzo.

Alonzo. The beauteous Captive, *Zara*, is arriv'd,
And with a Train, as if she still were Wife
To *Albucacim*; and the *Moor* had conquer'd.

King. It is our Will she should be so attended.
Bear hence these Prisoners. *Garcia*, which is he,
Of whose mute Valour you relate such Wonders?
Prisoners led off.

Garcia. Osmyn, who led the *Moorish* Horse; he does,
Great Sir, at her Request, attend on *Zara*.

King. He is your Prisoner, as you please dispose him.

Garcia. I would oblige him, but he shuns my Kindness;
And with a haughty Mien, and stern Civility
Dumbly declines all Offers: if he speak
'Tis scarce above a word; as he were born
Alone to do, and did disdain to talk;
At least, to talk where he must not command.

King. Such sullenness, and in a Man so brave,
Must have some other Cause than his Captivity.
Did *Zara*, then, request he might attend her?

Garcia. My Lord, she did.

King. That join'd with his Behaviour,
Begets a Doubt. I'd have 'em watch'd: perhaps
Her Chains hang heavier on him than his own.

Flourish; and Enter Zara *and* Osmyn *bound; conducted by* Perez *and a Guard, and attended by* Selim, *and several Mutes and Eunuchs in a Train.*

King. What Welcome, and what Honours, beauteous *Zara*,
A King and Conquerour can give, are yours.
A Conquerour indeed, where you are won;
Who with such Lustre, strike admiring Eyes,
That had our Pomp, been with your Presence grac'd,
Th' expecting Crowd had been deceiv'd; and seen
Their Monarch enter not Triumphant, but
In Triumph led; your Beauty's Slave.

Zara. If I on any Terms could condescend
To like Captivity, or think those Honours,
Which Conquerours in Courtesie bestow,
Of equal Value, with unborrow'd Rule,

And Native Right to Arbitrary Sway;
I might be pleas'd when I behold this Train
With usual Homage wait. But when I feel
These Bonds, I look with loathing on my self;
And scorn vile Slavery, tho' doubly hid
Beneath Mock-Praises, and dissembled State.

King. Those Bonds! 'twas my Command you should be free:
How durst you, *Perez*, disobey me?

Perez. Great Sir.
Your Order was, she should not wait your Triumph;
But at some distance follow, thus attended.

King. 'Tis false; 'twas more; I bad she should be free:
If not in Words, I bad it by my Eyes.
Her Eyes, did more than bid———free her and hers,
With speed———yet stay———my Hands alone can make
Fit restitution here———Thus, I release you,
And by releasing you enslave my self.

Zara. Favours conferr'd, tho' when unsought, deserve
Acknowledgment from Noble Minds. Such Thanks
As one hating to be oblig'd—
Yet hating more, Ingratitude, can pay,
I offer.

King. Born to excel, and to command!
As by transcendent Beauty to attract
All Eyes, so by Preheminence of Soul
To rule all Hearts.
Garcia, what's he, who with contracted Brow,
Beholding Osmyn *as they unbind him.*
And sullen Port, glooms downward with his Eyes;
At once regardless of his Chains, or Liberty?

Garcia. That, Sir, is *Osmyn*.

King. He answers well, the Character you gave him.
Whence comes it, valiant *Osmyn*, that a Man
So great in Arms, as thou art said to be,
So ill can brook Captivity;
The common Chance of War?

Osmyn. Because Captivity has robb'd me of a just Revenge.

King. I understand not that.

Osmyn. I would not have you.

Zara. That Gallant *Moor*, in Battle lost a Friend
Whom more than Life he lov'd; and the Regret,
Of not revenging on his Foes, that Loss,
Has caus'd this Melancholy and Despair.

King. She does excuse him; 'tis as I suspected.
To Gonsalez.

Gonsalez. That Friend may be her self; show no Resentment
Of his Arrogance yet; she looks concern'd.

King. I'll have Enquiry made; his Friend may be
A Prisoner. His Name?

Zara. *Heli*.

King. *Garcia*, be it your Care to make that search.
It shall be mine to pay Devotion here;
At this fair Shrine, to lay my Laurels down,
And raise Love's Altar on the Spoils of War.
Conquest and Triumph, now, are mine no more;
Nor will I Victory in Camps adore:
For, ling'ring there, in long suspence she stands,
Shifting the Prize in unresolving Hands:
Unus'd to wait, I broke through her Delay,
Fix'd her by Force, and snatch'd the doubtful Day.
But late, I find, that War is but her Sport;
In Love the Goddess keeps her awful Court:
Fickle in Fields, unsteadily she flyes,
But rules with settled Sway in *Zara*'s Eyes.
Exeunt Omnes.

The End of the First Act.

ACT II. Scene I.

Representing the Ile of a Temple.

Enter Garcia, Heli *and* Perez.

Garcia. This Way, we're told, *Osmyn* was seen to walk;
Choosing this lonely Mansion of the Dead,
To mourn, brave *Heli*, thy mistaken Fate.

Heli. Let Heav'n with Thunder to the Centre strike me,
If to arise in very deed from Death,
And to revisit with my long-clos'd Eyes

This living Light, could to my Soul, or Sense
Afford a Thought, or Glimpse of Joy,
In least Proportion to the vast Delight
I feel, to hear of *Osmyn*'s Name; to hear
That *Osmyn* lives, and I again shall see him.

Garcia. Unparalell'd Fidelity!
I've heard with Admiration, of your Friendship;
And could with equal Joy and Envy, view
The transports of your meeting.

Perez. Yonder, my Lord, behold the Noble *Moor*.

Heli. Where, where?

Garcia. I see him not.

Perez. I saw him when I spoke, thwarting my View,
And striding with distemper'd Haste: his Eyes
Seem'd Flame, and flash'd upon me with a Glance;
Then forward shot their Fires, which he pursu'd,
As to some Object frightful, yet not fear'd.

Garcia. Let's haste to follow him, and know the Cause.

Heli. My Lord, let me entreat you to forbear:
Leave me alone, to find and cure the Cause.
I know his Melancholy, and such Starts
Are usual to his Temper. It might raise him
To act some Violence upon himself,
So to be caught in an unguarded Hour,
And when his Soul gives all her Passions Way,
Secure and loose in friendly Solitude.
I know his Noble Heart would burst with Shame
To be surpriz'd by Strangers in its Frailty.

Garcia. Go Gen'rous *Heli*, and relieve your Friend.
Far be it from me, officiously to pry
Or Press upon the Privacies of others.

Heli. Y'are truly Noble.

Exit.

Garcia. Perez, the King expects from our return,
To have his Jealousie confirm'd or clear'd
Of that appearing Love, which *Zara* bears
To *Osmyn*; but some other Opportunity
Must make that plain.

Perez. To me 'twas long since plain.
And every Look of his and hers confess it.

Garcia. If so, Unhappiness attends their Love
And I cou'd pity 'em. I hear some coming,
The Friends perhaps are met; let us avoid 'em.
Exeunt.

Enter Almeria *and* Leonora.

Almeria. It was a fancy'd Noise; for all is hush'd.

Leonora. It bore the Accent of a Humane Voice.

Almeria. It was thy Fear; or else some transient Wind
Whistling thro' Hollows of this vaulted Isle.
We'll listen—

Leonora. Hark!

Almeria. No, all is hush'd, and still as Death—'Tis dreadful!
How rev'rend is the Face of this tall Pile,
Whose antient Pillars rear their Marble Heads,
To bear aloft its arch'd and pond'rous Roof,
By its own Weight, made stedfast, and immoveable,
Looking Tranquility. It strikes an Awe
And Terror on my aking Sight; the Tombs
And Monumental Caves of Death, look Cold,
And shoot a Chilness to my trembling Heart.
Give me thy Hand, and speak to me, nay, speak,
And let me hear thy Voice;
My own affrights me with its Echo's.

Leonora. Let us return; the Horrour of this Place
And Silence, will encrease your Melancholy.

Almeria. It may my Fears, but cannot add to that.
No, I will on: shew me *Anselmo*'s Tomb,
Lead me o'er Bones and Skulls, and mouldring Earth
Of Humane Bodies; for I'll mix with them,
Or wind me in the Shroud of some pale Coarse
Yet green in Earth, rather than be the Bride
Of *Garcia*'s more detested Bed. That Thought,
Exerts my Spirits; and my present Fears
Are lost in dread of greater Ill. Shew me,
Lead me, for I am bolder grown: Lead me
Where I may kneel and pay my Vows again
To him, to Heav'n and my *Alphonso*'s Soul.

Leonora. I go; but Heav'n can tell with what Regret.
Exeunt.

[SCENE II]

The Scene opening discovers a Place of Tombs. One Monument fronting the View, greater than the rest.

Enter Heli.

Heli. I wander thro' this Maze of Monuments,
Yet cannot find him—Hark! sure 'tis the Voice
Of one complaining—There it sounds—I'll follow it.
Exit.

Re-Enter, Almeria *and* Leonora.

Leonora. Behold the Sacred Vault, within whose Womb,
The poor Remains of good *Anselmo* rest;
Yet fresh and unconsum'd by Time, or Worms.
What do I see? O Heav'n! either my Eyes
Are false, or still the Marble Door remains
Unclos'd; the Iron Grates that lead to Death
Beneath, are still wide stretch'd upon their Hinge,
And staring on us with unfolded Leaves.

Almeria. Sure, 'tis the Friendly Yawn of Death for me;
And that dumb Mouth, significant in Show,
Invites me to the Bed, where I alone
Shall rest; shews me the Grave where Nature wearied,
And long oppress'd with Woes and bending Cares,
May lay the Burden down, and sink in Slumbers
Of Eternal Peace. Death, grim Death, will fold
Me in his leaden Arms, and press me close
To his cold clayie Breast: my Father then,
Will cease his Tyranny; and *Garcia* too
Will fly my pale Deformity with loathing.
My Soul, enlarg'd from its vile Bonds will mount,
And range the Starry Orbs, and Milky Ways,
Of that refulgent World, where I shall swim
In liquid Light, and float on Seas of Bliss
To my *Alphonso*'s Soul. O Joy too great!
O Exstacy of Thought! help me *Anselmo*:
Help me *Alphonso*, take me, reach thy Hand;
To thee, to thee I call, to thee *Alphonso*.
O *Alphonso*.

Osmyn *ascending from the Tomb.*

Osmyn. Who calls that wretched thing, that was *Alphonso*?

Almeria. Angels, and all the Host of heaven support me!

Angels and all the Host of heaven—Cf. *Hamlet*, I, iv, 39: "Angels and Ministers of Grace defend us;" and I, v, 92: "O all you host of Heaven."

Osmyn. Whence is that Voice whose Shrilness from the Grave,
And growing to his dead Father's Shrowd, roots up *Alphonso*?

Almeria. Mercy and Providence! O speak to it,
Speak to it quickly, quickly, speak to me.
Comfort me, help me, hold me, hide me, hide me,
Leonora, in thy Bosome, from the Light,
And from my Eyes.

Osmyn. Amazement and Illusion! Rivet me
To Earth, and nail me, where I stand, ye Powers;
Coming forward.
That motionless, I may be still deceiv'd.
Let me not stir, nor breath, lest I disolve
That tender, lovely Form of painted Air
So like *Almeria.* Ha! it sinks, it falls,
I'll catch it 'ere it goes, and grasp her Shade.
'Tis Life! 'tis warm! 'tis she! 'tis she her self!
Nor Dead, nor Shade, but breathing and alive!
It is *Almeria*! 'tis my Wife!

Enter Heli.

Leonora. O Heav'n unfold these Wonders!
Alas, she stirs not yet, nor lifts her Eyes;
He too is fainting———help me, help me, Stranger,
Who 'ere thou art, and lend thy Hand to raise
These Bodies.

Heli. By Heav'n 'tis he, and with———ha! *Almeria*!
Almeria! O Miracle of Happiness!
O Joy unhop'd for, does *Almeria* live!

Osmyn. Where is she?
Let me behold and touch her, and be sure
'Tis she; shew me her Face, and let me feel
Her Lips with mine———'Tis she, I'm not deceiv'd;
I taste her Breath, I warm'd her and am warm'd.
Look up *Almeria,* bless me with thy Eyes;
Look on thy Love, thy Lover, and thy Husband,
Look on *Alphonso.*

Almeria. I've sworn I'll not wed *Garcia*; why d'ye force me?
Is this a Father?

Osmyn. Thy Father is not here, nor *Garcia*: I am
Neither, nor what I seem, but thy *Alphonso.*

Wilt thou not know me? Hast thou then forgot me?
Hast thou thy Eyes, yet can'st not see *Alphonso*?
Am I so alter'd, or, art thou so chang'd,
That seeing my Disguise, thou seest not me?

Almeria. It is, it is *Alphonso*, 'tis his Face,
His Voice, I know him now, I know him all.
O take me to thy Arms, and bear me hence,
Back to the Bottom of the boundless Deep,
To Seas beneath, where thou so long hast dwelt.
O how hast thou return'd? How hast thou charm'd
The Wildness of the Waves and Rocks to this?
That thus relenting, they have giv'n thee back
To Earth, to Light and Life, to Love and me.

Osmyn. O I'll not ask, nor answer how, or why,
We both have backward trod the paths of Fate,
To meet again in Life, to know I have thee,
Is knowing more than any Circumstance,
Or Means by which I have thee—
To fold thee thus, to press thy balmy Lips,
And gaze upon thy Eyes, is so much Joy;
I have not Leisure to reflect, or know,
Or trifle time in thinking.

Almeria. Let me look on thee, yet a little more.

Osmyn. What would'st thou? thou dost put me from thee.

Almeria. Yes.

Osmyn. Why? what dost thou mean? why dost thou gaze so?

Almeria. I know not, 'tis to see thy Face I think—
It is too much! too much to bear and live!
To see him thus again, is such profusion
Of delight, I cannot bear it———I shall
Be mad———I cannot be transported thus.

Osmyn. Thou Excellence, thou Joy, thou Heav'n of Love!

Almeria. Where hast thou been? and how art thou alive?
How is all this? All-powerful Heav'n, what are we!
O my strain'd Heart———let me behold thee,
For I weep to see thee———Art thou not paler,
Much, much, alas; how, thou art chang'd!

Osmyn. Not in my Love.

Almeria. No, no, thy Griefs have done this to thee.
Thou hast wept much *Alphonso*; and I fear,
Too much lamented me.

Osmyn. Wrong not my Love, to say too much.
No more, my Life; talk not of Tears or Grief;
Affliction is no more, now thou art found.
Why dost thou weep, and hold thee from my Arms,
My Arms which ake to fold thee fast, and grow
To thee with twining? Come, come to my Heart.

Almeria. I will, for I should never look enough.
They wou'd have marry'd me; but I had sworn
To Heav'n and thee; and sooner wou'd have dy'd—

Osmyn. Perfection of all Truth!

Almeria. Indeed I wou'd——Nay, I wou'd tell thee all
If I cou'd speak; how I have mourn'd and pray'd,
For I have pray'd to thee as to a Saint:
And thou hast heard my Prayer; for thou art come
To my Distress, to my Despair, which Heav'n
Without thee cou'd not cure.

Osmyn. Grant me but Life, good Heaven, but length of Days,
To pay some Part, some little of this Debt;
This countless Summ of Tenderness and Love,
For which I stand engag'd to this All-excellence:
Then, bear me in a Whirl-wind to my Fate;
Snatch me from Life, and cut me short unwarn'd:
Then, then 'twill be enough——I shall be Old.
I shall have liv'd beyond all *Æra*'s then,
Of yet unmeasur'd Time; when I have made
This exquisite, amazing Goodness,
Some Recompence of Love and matchless Truth.

Almeria. 'Tis more than Recompence, to see thy Face:
If Heaven is greater Joy, it is no Happiness,
For 'tis not to be born—What shall I say?
I have a thousand Things to know, and ask,
And speak—That thou art here, beyond all Hope,
All Thought; that all at once, thou art before me,
And with such Suddenness, hast hit my Sight;
Is such Surprize, such Mystery, such Exstacy,
As hurries all my Soul, and dozes my weak Sense.
Sure, from thy Father's Tomb, thou didst arise!

Osmyn. I did, and thou didst call me.

Almeria. How camest thou there? wert thou alone?

Osmyn. I was, and lying on my Father's Lead;
When broken Echoes of a distant Voice,

Disturb'd the Sacred Silence of the Vault,
In Murmurs round my Head. I rose and listened;
And thought, I heard thy Spirit call *Alphonso.*
I thought I saw thee too; but O, I thought not
I indeed shou'd see thee—

Almeria. But still, how camest thee hither? how thus?—Ha!
What's he, that like thy self, is started here
Ere seen?

Osmyn. Where? ha! what do I see? *Antonio* here!
My Friend too safe!

Heli. Most happily, in finding you thus bless'd.

Almeria. More Miracles! *Antonio* too escap'd!

Osmyn. And twice escap'd, both from the Wreck of Seas,
And Rage of War: For in the Fight, I saw
Him fall.

Heli. But fell unhurt, a Prisoner as your self;
And as your self made free, hither I came
To seek you, where, I knew your Grief would lead you,
To lament *Anselmo*—

Osmyn. There are no Wonders, or else all is Wonder.

Heli. I saw you on the Ground, and rais'd you up.
I saw *Almeria*—

Osmyn. I saw her too, and therefore saw not thee.

Almeria. Nor I, nor could I, for my Eyes were yours.

Osmyn. What means the Bounty of All-gracious Heav'n,
That thus with open Hand it scatters good,
As in a Waste of Mercy?
Where will this end! but Heav'n is Infinite
In all, and can continue to bestow,
When scanty Numbers shall be spent in telling.

Leonora. Or I'm deceiv'd, or I beheld the Glimpse
Of two in shining Habits, cross the Ile,
And bending this way.

Almeria. Sure I have dreamt, if we must part so soon.

Osmyn. I wish our Parting were a Dream; or we
Could sleep till we again were met.

Heli. Zara with *Selim*, Sir, I saw and know 'em:
You must be quick, for Love will lend her Wings.

Almeria. What Love? Who is she?

Osmyn. She's the Reverse of thee; she's my Unhappiness.
Harbour no Thought, that may disturb thy Peace;
But gently take thy self away, lest she
Should come and see the straining of my Eyes
To follow thee. I'll think, how we may meet
To part no more; my Friend will tell thee all;
How I escap'd, how I am here, and thus;
How I'm not call'd *Alphonso*, now, but *Osmyn*;
And he *Heli*. All, all he will unfold.

Almeria. Sure we shall meet again.

Osmyn. We shall; we part not but to meet again.
Gladness, and Warmth of ever-kindling Love,
Dwell with thee, and revive thy Heart in Absence.
Exit Almeria, Leonora, *and* Heli.
Yet I behold her———Now no more.
Turn your Lights inward, Eyes, and look
Upon my Thought; so, shall you still behold her.
It wonnot be; O, impotence of Sight!
Mechanick Sense, which to exteriour Objects,
Owest thy Faculty—
Not seeing of Election, but Necessity.
Thus, do our Eyes, like common Mirrours
Successively reflect succeeding Images;
Not what they would, but must; a Star, or Toad:
Just as the Hand of Chance administers.
Not so the Mind, whose undetermin'd View
Revolves, and to the present adds the past:
Essaying further to Futurity;
But that in vain. I have *Almeria* here.
At once, as I have seen her often;
I'll muse on that, lest I exceed in thinking.

Enter Zara *attended by* Selim.

Zara. See, where he stands, folded and fix'd to Earth,
Stiff'ning in Thought; a Statue amongst Statues.
Why, cruel *Osmyn*, dost thou fly me thus?
Is it well done? Is this then the Return
For Fame, for Honour, and for Empire lost?
But what is Loss of Honour, Fame and Empire?
Is this the Recompence of Love?
Why dost thou leave my Eyes, and fly my Arms,
To find this Place of Horrour and Obscurity?
Am I more loathsome to thee, than the Grave?

That thou dost seek to shield thee there, and shun
My Love. But to the Grave I'll follow thee—
He Looks not, minds not, hears not; barbarous Man!
Am I neglected thus? Am I despised?
Not heard! Ungrateful *Osmyn*.

Osmyn. Ha, *Zara*!

Zara. Yes, Traytor, *Zara*; lost, abandon'd *Zara*,
Is a regardless Suppliant, now, to *Osmyn*.
The Slave, the Wretch that she redeem'd from Death,
Disdains to listen now, or look on *Zara*.

Osmyn. Far be the Guilt of such Reproaches, from me;
Lost in my self, and blinded by my Thoughts,
I saw you not.

Zara. Now, then you see me—
But with such dumb, and thankless Eyes you look;
Better I was unseen, than seen thus coldly.

Osmyn. What would you from a Wretch, that came to mourn;
And only for his Sorrows chose this Solitude?
Look round; Joy is not here, nor Cheerfulness.
You have pursu'd Misfortune, to its Dwelling;
Yet look for Gaiety and Gladness there.

Zara. Inhumane! why, why dost thou wrack me thus?
And with Perverseness, from the Purpose, answer?
What is't to me, this House of Misery?
What Joy do I require? if thou dost mourn,
I come to mourn with thee; to share thy Griefs,
And give thee in Exchange, my Love.

Osmyn. O that's the greatest Grief———I am so poor,
I have not wherewithal to give again.

Zara. Thou hast a Heart, though 'tis a savage one;
Give it me as it is; I ask no more
For all I've done, and all I have endur'd,
For saving thee, when I beheld thee first,
Driv'n by the Tide upon my Country's Coast,
Pale and expiring, drench'd in briny Waves
Thou and thy Friend; till my Compassion found thee,
Compassion, scarce will it own that Name, so soon,
So quickly was it Love; for thou wert Godlike
Ev'n then. Kneeling on Earth, I loos'd my Hair,
And with it dry'd thy wat'ry Cheeks; chafing
Thy Temples, till reviving Blood arose,

And like the Morn vermilion'd o'er thy Face.
O Heav'n! how did my Heart rejoice and ake,
When I beheld the Day-break of thy Eyes,
And felt the Balm of thy respiring Lips!

Osmyn. O call not to my Mind what you have done,
It sets a Debt of that Account before me,
Which shews me Bankrupt even in my Hopes.

Zara. The faithful *Selim*, and my Women know
The Dangers which I 'tempted to conceal you.
You know how I abus'd the credulous King;
What Arts I us'd to make you pass on him,
When he receiv'd you as the Prince of *Fez*;
And as my Kinsman, honour'd and advanc'd you.
O, why do I relate what I have done?
What did I not? Was't not for you, this War
Commenc'd? not knowing who you were, nor why
You hated *Manuel*, I urg'd my Husband
On to this Invasion; where he was lost,
Where all is lost, and I am made a Slave.
Look on me now, from Empire fall'n to Slavery;
Think on my Suff'ring first, then, look on me;
Think on the Cause of all, then, view thy self:
Reflect on *Osmyn*, and then look on *Zara*,
The fall'n, the lost, the Captive *Zara*.
What then is *Osmyn*?

Osmyn. A fatal Wretch———a huge stupendous Ruine,
That tumbling on its Prop, crush'd all beneath,
And bore contiguous Pallaces to Earth.

Zara. Yet thus, thus fall'n, thus levell'd with the vilest;
If I have gain'd thy Love, 'tis Glorious Ruine;
Ruine, 'tis still to reign, and to be more
A Queen; for what are Riches, Empire, Power,
But larger Means to gratifie the Will?
The Steps on which we tread, to rise and reach
Our Wish; and that obtain'd, down with the Scaffolding
Of Sceptres, Crowns, and Thrones; they've serv'd their
    End,
And are like Lumber, to be left and scorn'd.

Osmyn. Why was I made the Instrument, to throw
In Bonds, the Frame of this exalted Mind?

Fez—The northern kingdom of Morocco, immediately south of the Straits of Gibraltar.

Zara. We may be free; the Conquerour is mine;
In Chains unseen, I hold him by the Heart,
And can unwind, or strain him as I please.
Give me thy Love, I'll give thee Liberty.

Osmyn. In vain you offer, and in vain require
What neither can bestow. Set free your self,
And leave a Slave the Wretch that would be so.

Zara. Thou canst not mean so poorly, as thou talk'st.

Osmyn. Alas, you know me not.

Zara. Not who thou art.
But what, this last Ingratitude declares,
This groveling Baseness———Thou say'st true, I know
Thee not, for what thou art, yet wants a Name:
But something so unworthy, and so vile,
That to have lov'd thee, makes me yet more lost
Than all the Malice of my other Fate.
Traytour, Monster, cold and perfidious Slave;
A Slave, not daring to be free! nor dares
To love above him, for 'tis dangerous:
'Tis that, I know; for thou dost look, with Eyes
Sparkling Desire, and trembling to possess.
I know, my Charms have reach'd thy very Soul,
And thrill'd thee through with darted Fires; but thou
Dost fear so much, thou dar'st not wish. The King!
There, there's the dreadful Sound, the King's thy Rival!

Selim. Madam, the King is here.

Zara. As I could wish; by Heav'n I'll be reveng'd.

Enter the King, Perez, *and Attendants.*

King. Why does the Fairest of her Kind, withdraw
Her shining from the Day, to gild this Scene
Of Death and Night? Ha! what Disorder's this?
Somewhat I heard of King and Rival mention'd.
What's he that dares be Rival to the King?
Or lift his Eyes to like, where I adore?

Zara. There, he; your Prisoner, and that was my Slave.

King (*aside*). How? better than my Hopes; does she accuse him?

Zara. Am I become so low, by my Captivity;
And do your Arms so lessen, what they conquer,
That *Zara* must be made the Sport of Slaves?

And shall the Wretch, whom yester Sun, beheld
Waiting my Nod, the Creature of my Lord,
And me; presume to day to plead audacious Love,
And build bold Hopes, on my dejected Fate?

King. Better for him, to tempt the Rage of Heav'n,
And wrench the Bolt red-hissing, from the Hand
Of him that thunders, than but think that Insolence.
'Tis daring for a God. Hence, to the Wheel
With that *Ixion*, who aspires to hold
Divinity embrac'd; to Whips and Prisons,
Drag him with speed, and rid me of his Face.
Guards carry off Osmyn.

Zara. Compassion led me to bemoan his State,
Whose former Faith had merited much more:
And through my Hopes in you, I promis'd Freedom
From his Chains; thence sprung his Insolence,
And what was Charity, he constru'd Love.

King. Enough; his Punishment be what you please.
But let me lead you from this Place of Sorrow,
To one, where young Delights attend; and Joys
Yet new, unborn and blooming in the Bud,
That wait to be full-blown at your Approach,
And spread like Roses to the Morning Sun.
Where, ev'ry Hour shall roll in circling Joys;
And Love, shall wing the tedious-wasting Day.
Life without Love is Load; and Time stands still:
What we refuse to him, to Death we give;
And then, then only, when we love, we live.
Exeunt Omnes.

The End of the Second Act.

ACT III. Scene I.

A Prison.

Enter Osmyn *alone, with a Paper.*

Osmyn. But now, and I was clos'd within the Tomb
That holds my Father's Ashes; and but now,
Where he was Pris'ner, I am too imprison'd.

Ixion—Who had made love to Hera, the Queen of Heaven, and was bound to the wheel for punishment.

Sure 'tis the Hand of Heav'n, that leads me thus,
And for some Purpose points out these Remembrances.
In a dark Corner of my Cell, I found
This Paper; what it is, this Light will show.

Reading.
If my Alphonso———Ha!
If my Alphonso *live, restore him, Heav'n,*
Give me more Weight, crush my declining Years
With Bolts, with Chains, Imprisonment and Want;
But bless my Son, visit not him for me.

It is his Hand; this was his Pray'r———yet more.

Reading.
Let ev'ry Hair, which Sorrow by the Roots,
Tears from my hoary and devoted Head;
Be doubled in thy Mercies to my Son:
Not for my self, but him, hear me, all-gracious—

'Tis wanting what should follow—Heav'n, Heav'n shou'd follow.
But 'tis torn off—why should that Word alone
Be torn from his Petition? 'Twas to Heav'n.
But Heav'n was deaf, Heav'n heard him not; but thus,
Thus as the Name of Heav'n from this is torn,
So did it tear the Ears of Mercy, from
His Voice; shutting the Gates of Pray'r against him.
If Piety be thus debarr'd Access
On high; and of good Men, the very best
Is singled out to bleed, and bear the Scourge;
What is Reward? or, what is Punishment?
But who shall dare to tax Eternal Justice!
Yet I may think———I may? I must; for Thought
Precedes the Will to think; and Errour lives
Ere Reason can be born: Reason, the Power
To guess at Right and Wrong; the twinkling Lamp
Of wand'ring Life, that winks and wakes by turns,
Fooling the Follower, betwixt Shade and Shining.
What Noise! Who's there? My Friend, how cam'st thou hither?

Enter Heli.

Reason—Cf. Dryden and Lee, *Oedipus*, III, i, 33:

Tiresias. Reason! alas it does not know itself!
Yet Man, vain Man wou'd with this short-lin'd Plummet
Fathom the vast Abysse of Heav'nly Justice.

Heli. The time's too precious to be spent in telling;
The Captain influenc'd by *Almeria*'s Power,
Gave order to the Guards for my Admittance.

Osmyn. How does *Almeria*? But I know; she is
As I am. Tell me, may I hope to see her?

Heli. You may; anon, at Midnight, when the King
Is gone to rest, and *Garcia* is retir'd,
(Who takes the Privilege to visit late,
Presuming on a Bridegroom's Right—) she'll come.

Osmyn. She'll come; 'tis what I wish, yet what I fear.
She'll come, but whither, and to whom? O Heav'n!
To a vile Prison, and a captiv'd Wretch;
To one, whom had she never known, she had
Been happy; why, why was that Heav'nly Creature
Abandon'd o'er to love what Heav'n forsakes?
Why does she follow with unwearied Steps,
One, who has tir'd Misfortune with pursuing?
One, driv'n about the World like blasted Leaves
And Chaff, the Sport of adverse Winds; till late
At length, imprison'd in some Cleft of Rock,
Or Earth, it rests, and rots to silent Dust.

Heli. Have Hopes, and hear the Voice of better Fate.
I've learn'd, there are Disorders ripe for Mutiny
Among the Troops who thought to share the Plunder,
Which *Manuel* to his own Use and Avarice,
Converts. This News has reach'd *Valentia*'s Frontiers;
Where many of your Subjects long oppress'd
With Tyranny and grievous Impositions,
Are risen in Arms, and call for Chiefs to head
And lead 'em, to regain their Liberty
And Native Rights.

Osmyn. By Heav'n thou'st rous'd me from my Lethargy.
The Spirit which was deaf to my own Wrongs,
Deaf to revenge, and the loud Crys of my
Dead Father's Blood; Nay, which refus'd to hear
The Piercing Sighs, and Murmurs of my Love
Yet unenjoy'd; what not *Almeria* could
Revive, or raise, my Peoples Voice has wak'ned.
O my *Antonio*, I am all on Fire,
My Soul is up in Arms, ready to charge
And bear amidst the Foe, with conqu'ring Troops.
I hear 'em call to lead 'em on to Liberty,
To Victory; their Shouts and Clamours rend

My Ears, and reach the Heav'ns; where is the King?
Where is *Alphonso*? ha! where? where indeed?
O I could tear and burst the Strings of Life,
To break these Chains. Off, off, ye Stains of Royalty.
Off Slavery. O curse! that I alone
Can beat and flutter in my Cage, when I
Would soar, and stoop at Victory beneath.

Heli. Our Posture of Affairs and scanty Time,
My Lord, require you should compose your self,
And think on what we may reduce to Practise.
Zara the Cause of your restraint, may be
The Means of Liberty restor'd. That, gain'd;
Occasion will not fail to point out Ways
For your Escape. Mean time, I've thought already
With Speed and Safety, to convey my self
Where not far off some Male-Contents hold Counsel
Nightly; hating this Tyrant; some, who love
Anselmo's Memory, and will, no doubt,
When they shall know you live, assist your Cause.

Osmyn. My Friend and Counsellour; as thou thinks't fit,
So do. I will with Patience wait my Fortune.

Heli. When *Zara* comes, abate of your Aversion.

Osmyn. I hate her not, nor can dissemble Love:
But as I may, I'll do. I have a Paper
Which I would shew thee Friend, but that the Sight
Would hold thee here, and clog thy Expedition.
Within I found it, by my Father's Hand
'Twas writ; a Prayer for me, wherein appears
Paternal Love prevailing o'er his Sorrows;
Such Sanctity, such Tenderness, so mix'd
With Grief, as wou'd draw Tears from Inhumanity.

Heli. The Care of Providence, sure left it there,
To arm your Mind with Hope. Such Piety
Was never heard in vain: Heav'n has in Store
For you, those Blessings it with-held from him.
In that Assurance live; which Time, I hope,
And our next meeting will confirm.

Osmyn. Farewell,
My Friend, the Good thou dost deserve attend thee.
Exit Heli.

I've been to blame, and question'd with Impiety
The Care of Heav'n. Not so, my Father bore

More Anxious Grief. This shou'd have better taught me;
This Lesson, in some Hour of Inspiration,
By him set down; when his pure Thoughts were born
Like Fumes of Sacred Incense, o'er the Clouds,
And wafted thence, on Angels Wings, thro' Ways
Of Light, to the bright Source of all. There, in
The Book of Prescience, he beheld this Day;
And waking to the World and mortal Sense,
Left this Example of his Resignation,
This his last Legacy to me, which I
Will treasure here; more worth than Diadems,
Or all extended Rule of regal Pow'r.

Enter Zara *veil'd.*

What Brightness, breaks upon me, thus thro' Shades,
And promises a Day to this dark Dwelling!
Is it my Love?—

Zara. O that thy Heart, had taught

Lifting her Veil.

Thy Tongue that Saying.

Osmyn. Zara! I'm betray'd
By my surprize.

Zara. What, does my Face displease thee?
That having seen it, thou do'st turn thy Eyes
Away, as from Deformity and Horrour.
If so, this Sable Curtain shall again
Be drawn, and I will stand before thee seeing,
And unseen. Is it my Love? ask again
That Question, speak again in that soft Voice,
And Look again, with Wishes in thy Eyes.
O no, thou canst not, for thou seest me now,
As she, whose savage Breast has been the Cause
Of these thy Wrongs; as she, whose barbarous Rage
Has loaden thee with Chains and galling Irons:
Well, dost thou scorn me, and upbraid my Falseness;
Cou'd one that lov'd, thus torture what she lov'd?
No, no, it must be Hatred, dire Revenge,
And Detestation, that cou'd use thee thus.
So thou dost think; then, do but tell me so;
Tell me, and thou shall see how I'll revenge
Thee on this false one, how I'll stab and tear
This Heart of Flint, 'till it shall bleed; and thou
Shalt weep for mine, forgetting thy own Miseries.

Osmyn. You wrong me, beauteous *Zara*, to believe
I bear my Fortunes with so low a Mind,
As still to meditate Revenge on all
Whom Chance, or Fate working by secret Causes,
Has made perforce subservient to that End
The Heav'nly Powers allot me; no, not you,
But Destiny and inauspicious Stars
Have cast me down to this low Being: or,
Granting you had, from you I have deserv'd it.

Zara. Can'st thou forgive me then! wilt thou believe
So kindly of my Fault, to call it Madness;
O, give that Madness yet a milder Name,
And call it Passion; then, be still more kind,
And call that Passion Love.

Osmyn. Give it a Name,
Or Being as you please, such I will think it.

Zara. O thou dost wound me now, with this thy Goodness,
Than e'er thou could'st with bitterest Reproaches;
Thy Anger cou'd not pierce thus, to my Heart.

Osmyn. Yet I could wish—

Zara. Haste me to know it, what?

Osmyn. That at this Time, I had not been this Thing.

Zara. What Thing?

Osmyn. This Slave.

Zara. O Heav'n! my Fears interpret
This thy Silence; somewhat of high Concern,
Long fashioning within thy labouring Mind,
And now just ripe for Birth, my Rage has ruin'd.
Have I done this? tell me, am I so curs'd?

Osmyn. Time may have still one fated Hour to come,
Which wing'd with Liberty, might overtake
Occasion past.

Zara. Swift as Occasion, I
My self will fly; and earlier than the Morn,
Wake thee to Freedom. Now, 'tis late; and yet
Some News, few Minutes past arriv'd, which seem'd
To shake the Temper of the King———who knows
What racking Cares disease a Monarch's Bed?
Or Love, that late at Night still lights his Camp,
And strikes his Rays thro' dusk, and folded Lids,

Forbidding rest; may stretch his Eyes awake
And force their Balls abroad, at this dead Hour.
I'll try.

Osmyn. I have not merited this Grace;
Nor, should my secret Purpose take Effect,
Can I repay, as you require, such Benefits.

Zara. Thou canst not owe me more, nor have I more
To give, than I've already lost. But as
The present Form of our Engagements rests,
Thou hast the Wrong, 'till I redeem thee hence;
That done, I leave thy Justice to return
My Love. Adieu.

Exit Zara.

Osmyn. This Woman has a Soul,
Of God-like Mould, intrepid and commanding,
And challenges in spight of me my best
Esteem; to this she's fair, few more can boast
Of Personal Charms, or with less Vanity
Might hope to captivate the Hearts of Kings.
But she has Passions which out-strip the Wind,
And tear her Virtues up, as Tempests root
The Sea. I fear when she shall know the truth,
Some swift and dire event, of her blind Rage,
Will make all fatal. But behold, she comes
For whom I fear, to shield me from my Fears.

Enter Almeria.

The Cause and Comfort of my boding Heart.
My Life, my Health, my Liberty, my All.
How shall I welcome thee, to this sad Place?
How speak to thee the Words of Joy and Transport?
How run into thy Arms with-held by Fetters,
Or take thee into mine, thus manacled
And pinion'd like a Thief or Murderer?
Shall I not hurt and bruise thy tender Body,
And stain thy Bosom with the Rust of these
Rude Irons? Must I meet thee thus, *Almeria*?

Almeria. Thus, thus; we parted, thus to meet again.
Thou told'st me thou would'st think how we might meet
To part no more—Now we will part no more,
For these thy Chains, or Death shall join us ever.

Osmyn. Hard Means, to ratifie that Word!—O Cruelty!
That ever I should think, beholding thee,

A Torture———yet, such is the bleeding Anguish
Of my Heart, to see thy Sufferings—O Heav'n!
That I cou'd almost turn my Eyes away,
Or wish thee from my Sight.

Almeria. O say not so;
Tho' 'tis because thou lov'st me. Do not say
On any Terms, that thou dost wish me from thee.
No, no, 'tis better thus, that we together
Feed on each others Heart, devour our Woes
With mutual Appetite; and mingling in
One Cup, the common Stream of both our Eyes,
Drink bitter Draughts, with never-slacking Thirst.
Thus, better, than for any Cause to part.
What dost thou think? Look not so tenderly
Upon me———speak, and take me in thy Arms—
Thou canst not! thy poor Arms are bound and strive
In vain with the remorseless Chains, which gnaw
And eat into thy Flesh, festring thy Limbs
With rancling Rust.

Osmyn. Oh! O—

Almeria. Give me that Sigh.
Why do'st thou heave, and stifle in thy Griefs?
Thy Heart will burst, thy Eyes look red and start;
Give thy Soul Way, and tell me thy dark Thought.

Osmyn. For this World's Rule, I wou'd not wound thy
Breast,
With such a Dagger, as then stuck my Heart.

Almeria. Why? why? to know it, cannot wound me more,
Then knowing thou hast felt it. Tell it me.
———Thou giv'st me Pain, with too much Tenderness!

Osmyn. And thy excessive Love distracts my Sense!
O could'st thou be less killing, soft or kind,
Grief wou'd not double thus, his Darts against me.

Almeria. Thou dost me Wrong, and Grief too robs my
Heart,
If there, he shoot not ev'ry other Shaft;
Thy second self should feel each other Wound,
And Woe shou'd be in equal Portions dealt.
I am thy Wife—

Osmyn. O thou hast search'd too deep.
There, there, I bleed; there pull the cruel Cords,
That strain my cracking Nerves; Engines and Wheels

That Piece-meal grind, are Beds of Down and Balm
To that soul-racking Thought.

Almeria. Then, I am curs'd
Indeed; if that be so, if I'm thy Torment,
Kill me, kill me then, dash me with thy Chains;
Tread on me, spurn me, am I the bosom Snake
That sucks thy warm Life-Blood, and gnaws thy Heart?
O that thy Words had force to break those Bonds,
As they have Strength to tear this Heart in sunder;
So should'st thou be at large from all Oppression.
Am I, am I of all thy Woes the worst?

Osmyn. My All of Bliss, my everlasting Life,
Soul of my Soul, and End of all my Wishes.
Why dost thou thus unman me with thy Words,
And melt me down to mingle with thy Weepings?
What dost thou ask? why dost thou talk thus piercingly?
Thy Sorrows have disturb'd thy Peace of Mind,
And thou dost speak of Miseries impossible.

Almeria. Did'st thou not say, that Racks and Wheels were Balm,
And Beds of Ease, to thinking me thy Wife?

Osmyn. No no, nor should the subtlest Pains that Hell,
Or hell-born Malice can invent; extort
A wish or Thought from me, to have thee other.
But thou wilt know, what harrows up my Heart.
Thou art my Wife—nay, thou art yet my Bride!
The Sacred Union of Connubial Love,
Yet unaccomplish'd; his mysterious Rites
Delay'd: nor has our Hymenial Torch
Yet lighted up, his last most grateful Sacrifice;
But dash'd with Rain from Eyes, and swail'd with Sighs,
Burns dim, and glimmers with expiring Light.
Is this dark Cell, a Temple for that God?
Or this vile Earth, an Altar for such Off'rings?
This Den for Slaves, this Dungeon damp'd with Woes;
Is this our Marriage Bed! are these our Joys!
Is this to call thee mine? O hold my Heart;
To call thee mine? yes, thus, ev'n thus, to call
Thee mine, were Comfort, Joy, extremest Exstacy.
But O thou art not mine, not ev'n in misery;
And 'tis deny'd to me, to be so bless'd,
As to be wretched with thee.

swail'd—Wasted away like a guttering candle (OED).

Almeria. No; not that,
The extremest Malice of our Fate can hinder:
That still is left us, and on that we'll feed,
As on Leavings of Calamity.
There, we will feast; and smile on past Distress,
And hug in scorn of it, our mutual Ruine.

Osmyn. O—thou dost talk, my Love, as one resolv'd,
Because not knowing Danger. But look forward;
Think on to Morrow, when thou shalt be torn
From these weak, strugling, unextended Arms;
Think how my Heart will heave, and Eyes will strain
To grasp and reach what is deny'd my Hands;
Think how the Blood will start, and Tears will gush
To follow thee my separating Soul.
Think how I am, when thou shalt wed with *Garcia*!
Then will I smear these Walls with Blood, dash my
Disfigur'd Face, and rive my clotted Hair,
Break on the flinty Ground my throbbing Breast,
And grovel with gash'd Hands to scratch a Grave,
Stripping my Nails, to tear this Pavement up
And bury me alive; where I will bite the Ground
'Till gorg'd with suffocating Earth.

Almeria. O dismal Cruelty! heart-breaking Horrour!

Osmyn. Then *Garcia* shall lie panting on thy Bosom,
Luxurious, revelling amidst thy Charms;
And thou perforce must yield, and aid his Transport,
Hell, Hell! have I not Cause to rage and rave?
What are all Racks, and Wheels, and Whips to this?
Are they not soothing Softness, sinking Ease,
And wafting Air to this? O my *Almeria*,
What do the Damn'd endure, but to despair,
But knowing Heav'n, to know it lost for ever.

Almeria. O, I am struck; thy Words are Bolts of Ice,
Which shot into my Breast, now melt and chill me.
I chatter, shake, and faint with thrilling Fears.
No, hold me not—O, let us not support,
But sink each other, lower yet, down, down,
Where levell'd low, no more we'll lift our Eyes,
But prone, and dumb, rot the firm Face of Earth
With Rivers of incessant scalding Rain.

Enter Zara, Perez, *and* Selim.

Zara. Somewhat of weight to me, requires his Freedom.

Dare you dispute the King's Command? Behold
The Royal Signet.

Perez. I obey; yet beg
Your Majesty one Moment to defer
Your entring, till the Princess is return'd,
From visiting the Noble Prisoner.

Exit Perez.

Zara. Ha!
What saist thou?

Osmyn. We are lost! undone! discover'd!
Retire, my Life, with speed—Alas, we're seen!
Speak of Compassion, let her hear you speak
Of interceding for me with the King;
Say somewhat quickly to conceal our Loves,
If possible—

Almeria. —I cannot speak.

Osmyn. Let me
Conduct you forth, as not perceiving her.
But till she's gone; then bless me thus again.

Zara. Trembling and weeping as he leads her forth!
Confusion in his Face, and Grief in hers!
'Tis plain, I've been abus'd—Death and Destruction!
How shall I search into this Mystery?
The bluest Blast of Pestilential Air,
Strike, damp, deaden her Charms, and kill his Eyes;
Perdition catch 'em both, and Ruine part 'em.

Osmyn. This Charity to one unknown, and in
Distress, Heav'n will repay; all Thanks are poor.

Exit Almeria.

Zara (*aside*). Damn'd, damn'd Dissembler! Yet I will be calm,
Choak in my Rage, and know the utmost depth
Of this Deceiver———you seem much surpriz'd.

Osmyn. At your return so soon and unexpected!

Zara. And so unwish'd, unwanted too it seems.
(*Aside.*) Confusion! yet I will contain my self.
You're grown a Favourite since last we parted;
Perhaps I'm sawcy and Intruding—

Osmyn. —Madam!

Zara. I did not know the Princess Favourite;
Your Pardon, Sir———mistake me not; you think

I'm angry: you're deceiv'd. I came to set
You free: But shall return much better pleas'd,
To find you have an Interest superiour.

Osmyn. You do not come to mock my Miseries?

Zara. I do.

Osmyn. I could at this time spare your Mirth.

Zara. I know thou could'st; but I'm not often pleas'd,
And will indulge it now. What Miseries?
Who would not be thus happily confin'd,
To be the Care of weeping Majesty?
To have contending Queens, at dead of Night
Forsake their down, to wake with wat'ry Eyes,
And watch like Tapers o'er your Hours of Rest.
O Curse! I cannot hold—

Osmyn. Come, 'tis much.

Zara. Villain!

Osmyn. How, Madam!

Zara. Thou shalt die.

Osmyn. I thank you.

Zara. Thou ly'st; for now I know for whom thou'dst live.

Osmyn. Then you may know for whom I'd die.

Zara. Hell ! Hell!
Yet I'll be calm—Dark and unknown Betrayer!
But now the Dawn begins, and the slow Hand
Of Fate, is stretch'd to draw the Veil, and leave
Thee bare, the naked Mark of Publick View.

Osmyn. You may be still deceiv'd; 'tis in my Power.

Zara. Ha!
Who waits there?

Enter Perez.

As you'll answer it, take heed
This Slave commit no Violence upon
Himself. I've been deceiv'd. The publick Safety
Requires he should be more confin'd; and none,
No not the Princess self, permitted to
Confer with him. I'll quit you to the King.
Vile and ingrate! too late thou shalt repent

The base Injustice thou hast done my Love.
Yes, thou shalt know, spite of thy past Distress,
And all those Ills, which thou so long hast mourn'd;
Heav'n has no Rage, like Love to Hatred turn'd,
Nor Hell a Fury, like a Woman scorn'd.

Exeunt Omnes.

The End of the Third Act.

ACT IV. Scene I.

A Room of State.

Enter Zara, *and* Selim.

Zara. Thou hast already rack'd me with thy stay;
Therefore require me not to ask thee twice;
Reply at once to all. What is concluded?

Selim. Your Accusation highly has incens'd
The King, and were alone enough to urge
The Fate of *Osmyn*: but to that, fresh News
Is since arrived, of more revolted Troops.
'Tis certain *Heli* too is fled, and with him
(Which breeds Amazement and Distraction) some
Who bore high Offices of Weight and Trust,
Both in the State and Army. This confirms
The King, in full belief of all you told him,
Concerning *Osmyn*'s corresponding with
The Heads of those who first began the Mutiny.
Wherefore a Warrant for his Death is sign'd;
And Order given for publick Execution.

Zara. Ha! haste thee! fly, prevent his Fate and mine;
Find out the King, tell him I have of Weight
More than his Crown, t'impart 'ere *Osmyn* die.

Selim. It needs not, for the King will strait be here,
And as to your Revenge, not his own Int'rest,
Pretend to sacrifice the Life of *Osmyn*.

Zara. What shall I say? Invent, contrive, advise
Somewhat, to blind the King, and save his Life
In whom I live. Spite of my Rage, and Pride,
I am a Woman, and a Lover still.

O 'tis more Grief but to suppose his Death,
Than still to meet the Rigour of his Scorn.
From my Despair, my Anger had its source;
When he is dead, I must despair for ever.
For ever! that's Despair———it was Distrust
Before; Distrust will ever be in Love,
And Anger in Distrust, both short-liv'd Pains.
But in Despair, and ever-during Death,
No Term, no Bound, but Infinite of Woe.
O Torment, but to think! what then to bear?
Not to be born—devise the means to shun it,
Quick; or, by Heav'n, this Dagger drinks thy Blood.

Selim. My Life is yours, nor wish I to preserve it,
But to serve you. I have already thought.

Zara. Forgive my Rage; I know thy Love and Truth.
But say, what's to be done? or when, or how
Shall I prevent, or stop th'approaching Danger?

Selim. You must still seem most resolute and fix'd
On *Osmyn*'s Death; too quick a Change of Mercy,
Might breed Suspicion of the Cause. Advise,
That Execution may be done in private.

Zara. On what Pretence?

Selim. Your own Request's enough.
However, for a Colour, tell him, you
Have Cause to fear his Guards may be corrupted,
And some of them bought off to *Osmyn*'s Int'rest,
Who at the Place of Execution, will
Attempt to force his way for an Escape.
The State of things will countenance all Suspicions.
Then offer to the King to have him strangl'd
In secret, by your Mutes; and get an Order,
That none but Mutes may have Admittance to him.
I can no more, the King is here. Obtain
This Grant—and I'll acquaint you with the rest.

Enter King, Gonsalez, Garcia, Perez.

King. Bear to the Dungeon, those Rebellious Slaves;
Th' ignoble Currs, that yelp to fill the Cry,
And spend their Mouths in barking Tyranny.
But for their Leaders, *Sancho*, and *Ramirez*,
Let 'em be led away to present Death.
Perez, see it perform'd.

Gonsalez. Might I presume;
Their Execution better were deferr'd,
Till *Osmyn* die. Mean time we may learn more
Of this Conspiracy.

King. Then be it so.
Stay, Soldier; they shall suffer with the *Moor*.
Are none return'd of those who follow'd *Heli*?

Gonsalez. None, Sir. Some Papers have been since discover'd,
In *Roderigo*'s House, who fled with him.
Which seem to intimate, as if *Alphonso*,
Still alive, were arming in *Valentia*:
Which wears indeed this Colour of a Truth;
They who are fled have that way bent their course.
Of the same Nature, divers Notes have been
Dispers'd, t'amuze the People; whereupon
Some ready of Belief, have rais'd this Rumour:
That being sav'd upon the Coast of *Africk*,
He there disclos'd himself to *Albucacim*,
And by a secret Compact made with him,
Open'd the Way to this Invasion;
While he himself, returning to *Valentia*
In private, undertook to raise this Tumult.

Zara (*aside to* Selim). Ha! hear'st thou that? Is *Osmyn* then *Alphonso*!
O Heav'n! a thousand things occur
To my Remembrance now, that make it plain.
O certain Death for him, as sure Despair
For me, if it be known—If not, what Hope
Have I? Yet 'twere the lowest Baseness, now,
To yield him up—No, I will still conceal him,
And try the Force of yet more Obligations.

Gonsalez. 'Tis not impossible. Yet, it may be,
That some Impostor has usurp'd his Name.
Your beauteous Captive, *Zara*, can inform,
If such a one, so 'scaping, was receiv'd
At any time, in *Albucacim*'s Court.

King. Pardon, fair Excellence, this long Neglect:
An unforeseen, unwelcome Hour of Business,
Has thrust between us and our while of Love;

amuze—Cheat. Cf. also ll. 401 and Act V, 211: "amuz'd mean time with Hopes."

Albucacim—The "credulous King" whom Zara had urged to make the invasion.

But wearing now a-pace with ebbing Sand,
Will quickly waste, and give again the Day.

Zara. You're too secure: The Danger is more imminent
Than your high Courage suffers you to see;
While *Osmyn* lives, you are not safe.

King. His Doom
Is pass'd; if you revoke it not, he dies.

Zara. 'Tis well. By what I heard upon your Entrance,
I find I can unfold what yet concerns
You more. One that did call himself *Alphonso*,
Was cast upon my Coast, as is reported;
And oft had private Conference with the King;
To what Effect I knew not then: But that
Alphonso, privately departed, just
About the time our Arms embark'd for *Spain*.
What I know more, is, That a tripple League
Of strictest Friendship, was profess'd between
Alphonso, *Heli*, and the Traytour *Osmyn*.

King. Publick Report, is ratify'd in this.

Zara. And *Osmyn*'s Death requir'd of strong necessity.

King. Give Order strait, that all the Pris'ners die,
We will our self behold the Execution.

Zara. Forbear a Moment; somewhat more I have
Worthy your private Ear, and this your Minister.

King. Let all else void the Room. *Garcia*, give Order
For doubling all our Guards; Command that our
Militia are in Arms: We will anon
Ride forth, and view the Order of our Troops.
Exeunt Garcia, Perez, *and Attendants.*

Zara. I am your Captive, and you've us'd me Nobly;
And in return of that, though otherwise
Your Enemy; I have discover'd *Osmyn*,
His private Practice and Conspiracy
Against your State: and fully to discharge
My self of what I've undertaken; now,
I think it fit to tell you that your Guards
Are tainted; some among 'em have resolv'd
To rescue *Osmyn* at the Place of Death.

King. Is Treason then so near us as our Guards!

Zara. Most certain; though my Knowledge is not yet
So ripe, to point at the particular Men.

King. What's to be done?

Zara. That too I will advise.
I have remaining in my Train, some Mutes,
A Present once, from the *Sultana* Queen,
In the *Grand Signior*'s Court. These from their Infancy
Are practis'd in the Trade of Death; and shall
(As there the Custom is) in private strangle
Osmyn.

Gonsalez. My Lord, the Queen advises well.

King. What Off'ring, or what Recompence remains
In me, that can be worthy so great Services?
To cast beneath your Feet the Crown you've sav'd,
Though on the Head that wears it, were too little.

Zara. Of that hereafter; but, mean time, 'tis fit
You order none may have Admittance to
The Pris'ner, but such Messengers, as I
Shall send.

King. Who waits there?

Enter Perez.

On your Life take heed,
That only *Zara*'s Mutes, or such who bring
Her Warrant, have Admittance to the *Moor*.

Zara. They and no other; not the Princess self.

Perez. Your Majesty shall be obey'd.

King. Retire.

Exit Perez.

Gonsalez. That Interdiction so particular,
Pronounc'd with Vehemence against the Princess,
Should have more Meaning than appears bare-fac'd.
The King is blinded by his Love, and heeds
It not. Your Majesty sure, might have spared
That last restraint; you hardly can suspect
The Princess is Confederate with the *Moor*.

Zara. I've heard, her Charity did once extend
So far to visit him, at his request.

Gonsalez. Ha!

King. How? she visit *Osmyn*! What, my Daughter?

Sultana Queen—The Queen of Turkey.

Selim. Madam, take heed; or you have ruin'd all.

Zara. And after did solicite you, on his
behalf—

King. Never. You have been mis-inform'd.

Zara. Indeed? Then 'twas a Whisper spread by some
Who wish'd it so: a common Art in Courts.
I will retire, and instantly prepare
Instruction, for my Ministers of Death.
Exeunt Zara *and* Selim.

Gonsalez. There's somewhat yet of Mystery in this;
Her Words and Actions are obscure and double,
Sometimes concur, and sometime disagree;
I like it not.

King. What dost thou think, *Gonsalez*;
Are we not much indebted to this fair one.

Gonsalez. I am a little slow of Credit, Sir,
In the Sincerity of Womens Actions.
Methinks this Lady's Hatred to the *Moor*,
Disquiets her too much; which makes it seem
As if she'd rather that she did not hate him.
I wish her Mutes are meant to be employ'd
As she pretends—I doubt it now—Your Guards
Corrupted; how? by whom? who told her so?
I'th' Evening *Osmyn* was to die; at Mid-night
She beg'd the Royal Signet to release him;
I'th' Morning he must die again; e're Noon
Her Mutes alone must strangle him or he'll
Escape. This put together, suits not well.

King. Yet, that there's Truth in what she has discover'd,
Is manifest from every Circumstance.
This Tumult, and the Lords who fled with *Heli*,
Are Confirmation.———That *Alphonso* lives,
Agrees expressly too with her Report.

Gonsalez. I grant it, Sir, and doubt not, but in Rage
Of Jealousie, she has discover'd what
She now repents. It may be I'm deceiv'd.
But why that needless Caution of the Princess?
What if she had seen *Osmyn*? tho' 'twere strange.
But if she had, what was't to her? unless
She fear'd her stronger Charms, might cause the *Moor*'s
Affection to revolt.

King. I thank thee Friend.
There's Reason in thy Doubt, and I am warn'd.
But think'st thou that my Daughter saw this *Moor*?

Gonsalez. If *Osmyn* be, as *Zara* has related,
Alphonso's Friend; 'tis not impossible,
But she might wish on his Account to see him.

King. Say'st thou? by Heav'n thou hast arous'd a Thought,
That like a sudden Earth-quake, shakes my Frame;
Confusion! then my Daughter's an Accomplice,
And plots in Private with this hellish *Moor*.

Gonsalez. That were too hard a Thought—but see she comes.
'Twere not amiss to question her a little,
And try howe'er, if I've divin'd aright.
If what I fear be true, she'll be concern'd
For *Osmyn*'s Death, as he's *Alphonso*'s Friend.
Urge that, to try if she'll sollicite for him.

Enter Almeria *and* Leonora.

King. Your coming has prevented me *Almeria*;
I had determin'd to have sent for you.
Let your Attendant be dismiss'd; I have
Exit Leonora.
To talk with you. Come near, why dost thou shake?
What mean those swollen and redfleck'd Eyes, that look
As they had wept in Blood, and worn the Night
In waking Anguish? why this, on the Day
Which was design'd to celebrate thy Nuptials?
But that the Beams of Light, are to be stain'd
With reeking Gore, from Traytors on the Rack:
Wherefore I have deferr'd the Mariage Rites,
Nor shall the guilty Horrours of this Day
Prophane that Jubilee.

Almeria. All Days, to me,
Henceforth are equal; this the Day of Death,
To Morrow, and the next, and each that follows,
Will undistinguish'd roll, and but prolong
One hated Line of more extended Woe.

King. Whence is thy Grief? give me to know the Cause,
And look thou answer me with truth: for know,
I am not unacquainted with thy Falshood.
Why art thou mute? base and degenerate Maid!

Gonsalez. Dear Madam, speak, or you'll incense the King.

Almeria. What is to speak? or wherefore should I speak?
What means these Tears, but Grief unutterable?

King. Yes, Guilt; they are the dumb Confessions of
Thy guilty Mind; and say thou wert Confederate
With damn'd Conspirators, to take my Life.
O Impious Parricide! now canst thou speak?

Almeria. O Earth, behold, I kneel upon thy Bosom,
And bend my flowing Eyes, to stream upon
Thy Face, imploring thee that thou wilt yield;
Open thy Bowels of Compassion, take
Into thy Womb the last and most forlorn
Of all thy Race. Hear me, thou common Parent;
——I have no Parent else——be thou a Mother,
And step between me and the Curse of him,
That was—that was, but is no more a Father.
But brands my Innocence with horrid Crimes,
And for the tender Names of Child and Daughter,
Now calls me Murderer, and Parricide.

King. Rise, I command thee rise—and if thou would'st
Acquit thy self of those detested Names,
Swear thou hast never seen that foreign Dog,
Now doom'd to die, that most accursed *Osmyn*.

Almeria. Never, but as with Innocence, I might,
And free of all bad Purposes. So Heav'ns
My Witness.

King. Vile equivocating Wretch!
With Innocence? Death and Perdition, she
Confesses it. By Heav'n I'll have him rack'd,
Torn, mangl'd, flay'd, impal'd——all Pains and Tortures
That Wit of Man, and dire Revenge can think,
Shall he accumulated under-bear.

Almeria. Oh I am lost——there, Fate begins to wound.

King. Hear me; then, if thou canst, reply, know Traitress,
I'm not to learn that curs'd *Alphonso* lives;
Nor am I Ignorant what *Osmyn* is—

Almeria. Then all is ended, and we both must die
Since thour't reveal'd, alone thou shalt not die.
And yet alone would I have dy'd, Heav'n knows,
Repeated Deaths, rather than have revealed thee.
Yes, all my Father's wounding Wrath, tho' each

Reproach cuts deeper than the keenest Sword,
And cleaves my Heart; I would have born it all,
Nay, all the Pains that are prepar'd for thee:
To the remorsless Rack I would have given
This weak and tender Flesh, to have been bruis'd
And torn, rather than have reveal'd thy being.

King. Hell, Hell! do I hear this, and yet endure!
What dar'st thou to my Face avow thy Guilt?
Hence, e'er I curse——fly my just Rage with speed;
Lest I forget us both, and spurn thee from me.

Almeria. And yet a Father! think I am your Child.
Turn not your Eyes away——look on me kneeling;
Now curse me if you can, now spurn me off.
Did ever Father curse his kneeling Child!
Never: For always Blessings crown that Posture.
Nature inclines, and half-way meets that Duty,
Stooping to raise from Earth the filial Reverence;
For bended Knees, returning folding Arms,
With Prayers and Blessings, and paternal Love.
O hear me then, thus crawling on the Earth—

King. Be thou advis'd, and let me go while yet
The light Impression thou hast made, remains.

Almeria. No, never will I rise, nor loose this Hold,
'Till you are mov'd, and grant that he may live.

King. Ha! who may live? take heed, no more of that.
For on my Soul he dies, tho' thou, and I,
And all should follow to partake his Doom.
Away, off, let me go,—Call her Attendants.

Enter Leonora *and Attendants.*

Almeria. Drag me, harrow the Earth with my bare Bosom.
I'll not let go, 'till you have spar'd my Husband.

King. Ha! what say'st thou? Husband! Husband!
Damnation!
What Husband? which? who?

Almeria. He, he is my Husband.

King. Poyson and Daggers! who?

Almeria. O—

Faints.

Gonsalez. Help, support her.

Almeria. Let me go, let me fall, sink deep———I'll dig,
I'll dig a Grave, and tear up Death; I will;
I'll scrape 'till I collect his rotten Bones,
And cloath their Nakedness with my own Flesh;
Yes, I will strip off Life, and we will change:
I will be Death; then tho' you kill my Husband,
He shall be mine, still and for ever mine.

King. What Husband? who? whom do'st thou mean?

Gonsalez. Alas, she raves!

Almeria. O that I did, *Osmyn*, he is my Husband.

King. Osmyn!

Almeria. Not *Osmyn*, but *Alphonso* is my Dear,
And wedded Husband———Heav'n, and Air, and Seas;
Ye Winds and Waves, I call ye all to witness.

King. Wilder than Winds or Waves thy self do'st rave.
Should I hear more; I too should catch thy Madness.
Yet somewhat she must mean of dire Import,
Which I'll not hear, 'till I am more at peace.
Watch her returning Sense, and bring me Word:
And look that she attempt not on her Life.

Exit King.

Almeria. O stay, yet stay, hear me, I am not mad.
I would to Heav'n I were———he's gone!

Gonsalez. Have Comfort.

Almeria. Curst be that Tongue, that bids me be of Comfort;
Curst my own Tongue, that cou'd not move his Pity.
Curst these weak Hands, that cou'd not hold him here;
For he is gone to doom *Alphonso*'s Death.

Gonsalez. Your too excessive Grief, works on your Fancy,
And deludes your Sense. *Alphonso*, if living,
Is far from hence, beyond your Father's Power.

Almeria. Hence, thou detested, ill-tim'd Flatterer;
Source of my Woes: thou and thy Race be curs'd;
But doubly thou, who could'st alone have Policy,
And Fraud, to find the fatal Secret out,
And know that *Osmyn* was *Alphonso*.

Gonsalez. Ha!

Almeria. Why dost thou start? what dost thou see, or hear?
Was it the doleful Bell, toling for Death?

Or dying Groans from my *Alphonso*'s Breast?
See, see, look yonder! where a grizled, pale
And ghastly Head, glares by, all smear'd with Blood,
Gasping as it would speak: and after it,
Behold a damp, dead Hand has drop'd a Dagger;
I'll catch it—hark! a Voice cries Murder! 'tis
My Father's Voice; hollow it sounds, and from
The Tomb it calls———I'll follow it, for there
I shall again behold my dear *Alphonso*.
Exit with attendants.

Gonsalez. She's greatly griev'd; nor am I less surpriz'd.
Osmyn Alphonso! no; she over-rates
My Policy, I ne'er suspected it:
Nor now had known it, but from her mistake.
Her husband too! Ha! where is *Garcia* then?
And where the Crown that shou'd descend on him,
To grace the Line of my Posterity?
Hold, let me think—if I shou'd tell the King—
Things come to this Extremety? his Daughter
Wedded already—what if he should yield?
Knowing no Remedy, for what is past;
And urg'd by Nature pleading for his Child,
With which he seems to be already shaken.
And tho' I know he hates beyond the Grave
Anselmo's Race; yet if———that If concludes me.
To doubt, when I may be assur'd, is Folly.
But how prevent the Captive Queen, who means
To set him free? Ay, now 'tis plain; O well
Invented Tale! he was *Alphonso*'s Friend.
This subtle Woman will amuze the King,
If I delay———'twill do———or better so.
One to my Wish. *Alonzo*, thou art welcome.

Enter Alonzo.

Alonzo. The King expects your Lordship.

Gonsalez. 'Tis no matter.
I'm not i'th' Way at Present, good *Alonzo*.

Alonzo. If't please your Lordship, I'll return, and say
I have not seen you.

Gonsalez. Do, my best *Alonzo*.
Yet stay, I would—but go; anon will serve—
Yet I have that, requires thy speedy help.
I think thou would'st not stop to do me Service.

Alonzo. I am your Creature.

Gonsalez. Say thou art my Friend.
I've seen thy Sword do noble Execution.

Alonzo. All that it can, your Lordship shall command.

Gonsalez. Thanks; and I take thee at thy Word. Thou'st seen
Among the followers of the Captive Queen,
Dumb Men, that make their Meaning known by Signs.

Alonzo. I have, my Lord.

Gonsalez. Could'st thou procure with speed,
And privacy, the wearing Garb of one
Of those, tho' purchas'd by his Death; I'd give
Thee such Reward, as should exceed thy Wish.

Alonzo. Conclude it done. Where shall I wait your Lordship?

Gonsalez. At my Appartment. Use thy utmost Diligence;
Away, I've not been seen—haste good *Alonzo.*
Exit Alonzo.
So, this can hardly fail. *Alphonso* slain,
The greatest Obstacle is then remov'd.
Almeria widow'd, yet again may wed;
And I yet fix the Crown on *Garcia*'s Head.
Exit.

The End of the Fourth Act.

ACT V. SCENE I.

A Room of State.

Enter King, Perez, *and* Alonzo.

King. Not to be found? in an ill hour he's absent.
None, say you, none? what not the Fav'rite Eunuch?
Nor she her self, nor any of her Mutes
Have yet required admittance?

Perez. None, my Lord.

King. Is *Osmyn* so dispos'd, as I commanded?

Perez. Fast bound in double chains, and at full length
He lies supine on earth; as easily
She might remove the fix'd foundation, as
Unlock the rivets of his bonds.

King. 'Tis well.

A Mute appears, and seeing the King retires.

Ha! seize that *Mute*; *Alonzo*, follow him.

Exit Alonzo.

Entring he met my Eyes, and started back,
Frighted, and fumbling one hand in his Bosom,
As to conceal th' Importance of his Errand.

Alonzo *re-enters with a Paper.*

Alonzo. O bloody Proof, of obstinate Fidelity!

King. What dost thou mean?

Alonzo. Soon as I seiz'd the Man,
He snatch'd from out his Bosom this———and strove
With rash and greedy haste, at once to cram
The Morsel down his throat. I catch'd his Arm,
And hardly wrench'd his Hand to wring it from him;
Which done, he drew a Ponyard from his side,
And on the instant, plung'd it in his Breast.

King. Remove the Body thence, 'ere *Zara* see it.

Alonzo. I'll be so bold to borrow his Attire;
'Twill quit me of my Promise to *Gonsalez*.

Exit.

Perez. Whate'er it is the King's Complexion turns.

King. How's this? my mortal Foe beneath my Roof!

Having read the Letter.

O, give me Patience, all ye Powers! no, rather,
Give me Rage, Rage, implacable Revenge,
And treble Fury———Ha! who's there?

Perez. My Lord.

King. Hence, Slave, how dar'st thou bide, to watch and pry
Into how poor and mean a thing, a King descends;
How like thy self when Passion treads him down?
Ha! stir not, on thy Life: For thou wert fix'd,
And planted here to see me gorge this Bait,
And lash against the Hook———by Heav'n you're all
Rank Traytors; thou art with the rest combin'd;
Thou knew'st that *Osmyn* was *Alphonso*, knew'st
My Daughter privately conferr'd with him,
And wert the Spy and Pander to their Meeting.

Perez. By all that's holy, I'm amaz'd—

King. Thou lyest.
Thou art Accomplice too much with *Zara*; here

Where she sets down———(*reading*) *still will I set thee free*—
That somewhere is repeated———*I have power*
O'er them that are thy Guards———Mark that thou Traytor.

Perez. It was your Majesty's Command, I should
Obey her Order—

King (*reading*). ———*And still will I set*
Thee free, Alphonso———Hell! curs'd, curs'd *Alphonso*!
False perfidious *Zara*! Strumpet Daughter!
Away begon thou feeble Boy, fond Love,
All Nature, Softness, Pity and Compassion,
This hour I throw ye off, and entertain
Fell hate, within my breast, Revenge and Gall.
By Heav'n I'll meet, and counterwork this Treachery.
Hark thee, Villain, Traitor—answer me Slave..

Perez. My Service has not merited those Titles.

King. Dar'st thou reply? Take that—thy Service? thine?
Strikes him.
What's thy whole Life, thy Soul, thy All, to my
One moment's Ease? Hear my Command; and look
That thou obey, or Horrour on thy Head.
Drench me thy Dagger in *Alphonso*'s Heart.
Why dost thou start? Resolve to do't, or else—

Perez. My Lord, I will.

King. 'Tis well———that when she comes to set him free,
His Teeth may grin, and mock at her Remorse.
Perez *going.*
—Stay thee———I've farther thought———I'll add to this,
And give her Eyes yet greater Disappointment.
When thou hast ended him, bring me his Robe;
And let the Cell where she'll expect to see him,
Be dark'ned, so as to amuze the Sight.
I'll be conducted thither—
But see she comes; I'll shun th'Encounter; do
Thou follow, and give heed to my Directon.
Exeunt.

Enter Zara, *and* Selim.

Zara. The *Mute* not yet return'd! 'tis strange. Ha! 'twas
The King that parted hence; frowning he went;
His Eyes like Meteors roll'd, then darted down

Their red and angry Beams; as if his Sight
Would, like the raging Dog-star, scorch the Earth,
And kindle Ruine in its Course. Think'st thou
He saw me not?

Selim. He did: But then as if
His Eyes had err'd, he hastily recall'd
Th' imperfect Look, and sternly turn'd away.

Zara. Shun me when seen! I fear thou hast undone me.
Thy shallow Artifice begets Suspicion,
And, like a Cobweb-Veil, but thinly shades
The Face of thy Design; alone disguising
What should have ne'er been seen; imperfect Mischief!
Thou like the Adder, venomous and deaf,
Hast stung the Traveller; and, after, hear'st
Not his pursuing Voice: ev'n where thou think'st
To hide, the rustling Leaves, and bended Grass
Confess, and point the Path which thou hast crept.
O Fate of Fools! officious in Contriving;
In executing, puzzled, lame and lost.

Selim. Avert it, Heav'n, that you should ever suffer
For my Defect; or that the Means which I
Devis'd to serve, should ruine your Design!
Prescience is Heav'ns alone, not giv'n to Man.
If I have fail'd in what, as being a Man,
I needs must fail; impute not as a Crime,
My Nature's want; but punish Nature in me:
I plead not for a Pardon, and to live,
But to be punish'd and forgiven. Here, strike;
I bare my Breast to meet your just Revenge.

Zara. I have not leisure, now, to take so poor
A Forfeit as thy Life: Somewhat of high
And more important Fate, requires my Thought.
When I've concluded on my self, if I
Think fit, I'll leave thee my Command to die.
Regard me well; and dare not to reply
To what I give in Charge: for I'm resolv'd.
Instruct the two remaining *Mutes*, that they
Attend me instantly, with each a Bowl
Of those Ingredients mix'd, as will with speed
Benumn the living Faculties, and give
Most easie and inevitable Death.

the raging Dog-star—Sirius, supposed the cause of excessive heat, when rising with the sun.

Yes, *Osmyn*, yes; be *Osmyn* or *Alphonso*,
I'll give thee Freedom, if thou dar'st be free:
Such Liberty as I embrace my self,
Thou shalt partake. Since Fates no more afford;
I can but die with thee to keep my Word.

Exeunt.

[Scene II]

Scene changes to the Prison.

Enter Gonsalez, *disguis'd like a Mute, with a Dagger.*

Gonsalez. Nor Centinel, nor Guard! the Doors unbarr'd!
And all as still, as at the Noon of Night!
Sure Death already has been busie here.
There lies my way, that Door is too unlock'd.

Looks in.

Ha! sure he sleeps———all's dark within, save what
A Lamp that feebly lifts a sickly Flame,
By fits reveals———his Face seems turn'd to favour
Th' Attempt: I'll steal, and do it unperceiv'd.
What Noise! some body coming? 'st, *Alonzo*?
No body? sure he'll wait without———I would
'Twere done———I'll crawl and sting him to the Heart;
Then cast my Skin, and leave it there to answer it.

Goes in.

Enter Garcia *and* Alonzo.

Garcia. Where? where? *Alonzo*, where's my Father? where
The King? Confusion, all is on the Rout!
All's lost, all ruin'd by Surprize and Treachery.
Where, where is he? Why dost thou thus mislead me?

Alonzo. My Lord, he enter'd, but a moment since,
And could not pass me unperceiv'd———What, hoa?
My Lord, My Lord, what, hoa? My Lord *Gonsalez*?

Enter Gonsalez, *bloody.*

Gonsalez. Perdition choak your Clamours—whence this
Rudeness?
Garcia!

Garcia. Perdition, Slavery, and Death,
Are entring now our Doors. Where is the King?
What means this Blood? and why this Face of Horrour?

Gonsalez. No matter———give me first to know the Cause
Of these your rash and ill-tim'd Exclamations.

Garcia. The Eastern Gate is to the Foe betray'd,
Who but for heaps of Slain, that choak the Passage,
Had enter'd long 'ere now, and born down all
Before 'em, to the Pallace Walls. Unless
The King in Person animate our Men,
Granada's lost; and to confirm this Fear,
The Traytor *Perez*, and the Captive *Moor*,
Are through a Postern fled, and join the Foe.

Gonsalez. Would all were false as that; for whom you call
The *Moor*, is dead. That *Osmyn* was *Alphonso*;
In whose Hearts Blood this Ponyard yet is warm.

Garcia. Impossible; for *Osmyn* flying, was
Proclaim'd aloud by *Perez*, for *Alphonso*.

Gonsalez. Enter that Chamber, and convince your Eyes,
How much Report has wrong'd your easie Faith.

Garcia *goes in*.

Alonzo. My Lord, for certain truth, *Perez* is fled;
And has declar'd the Cause of his Revolt,
Was to Revenge a Blow the King had giv'n him.

Garcia (*returning*). Ruine and Horrour! O heart-wounding sight!

Gonsalez. What says my Son? what Ruine? ha? what Horrour?

Garcia. Blasted my Eyes, and speechless be my Tongue,
Rather than or to see, or to relate
This Deed———O dire Mistake! O fatal Blow!
The King—

Gonsalez., *Alonzo.* The King!

Garcia. Dead, welt'ring, drown'd in Blood.
See, see, attir'd like *Osmyn*, where he lies.

They go in.

O whence, or how, or wherefore was this done?
But what imports the Manner, or the Cause?
Nothing remains to do, or to require,

But that we all should turn our Swords, against
Our selves, and expiate with our own his Blood.

Gonsalez. O Wretch! O curs'd, and rash, deluded Fool!
On me, on me, turn your avenging Sword.
I who have spilt my Royal Master's Blood,
Should make atonement by a Death as horrid;
And fall beneath the Hand of my own Son.

Garcia. Ha! what? atone this Murther with a greater!
The Horrour of that Thought, has damp'd my Rage.
The Earth already groans to bear this Deed;
Oppress her not, nor think to stain her Face
With more unnatural Blood. Murder my Father!
Better with this to rip up my own Bowels,
And bathe it to the Hilt, in far less damnable
Self-Murder.

Gonsalez. O my Son, from the blind Dotage
Of a Father's Fondness, these Ills arose;
For thee I've been ambitious, base, and bloody:
For thee I've plung'd into this Sea of Sin;
Stemming the Tide, with one weak Hand, and bearing
With the other, the Crown, to wreath thy Brow,
Whose weight has sunk me 'ere I reach'd the Shore.

Garcia. Fatal Ambition! Hark! the Foe is enter'd:
Shout.
The shrilness of that Shout speaks 'em at hand.
We have no time to search into the Cause
Of this surprizing and most fatal Errour.
What's to be done? the King's Death known, will strike
The few remaining Soldiers with Despair,
And make 'em yield to Mercy of the Conquerour.

Alonzo. My Lord, I've thought how to conceal the Body;
Require me not to tell the Means, till done,
Lest you forbid; what then you may approve.
Goes in.

Gonsalez. They shout again! Whate'er he means to do
Shout.
'Twere fit the Soldiers were amuz'd, mean time,
With Hopes, and fed with Expectation of
The King's immediate Presence at their Head.

curs'd, and rash, deluded Fool!—Cf. *Hamlet*, III, iv, 31: "Thou wretched, rash, intruding fool." Gonzales, with his fighting son and his clever plot, brings to mind Polonius.

Garcia. Were it a Truth, I fear 'tis now too late.
But I'll omit no Care, nor Haste; and try
Or to repell their Force, or bravely die.

Exit.

Gonsalez. What hast thou done, *Alonzo*?

Alonzo. Such a Deed,
As but an hour ago, I'd not have done,
Tho' for the Crown of Universal Empire.
But what are Kings reduc'd to common Clay?
Or who can wound the Dead?—I've from the Body,
Sever'd the Head; and in a Corner of
The Room, dispos'd it muffled in the *Mute*'s
Attire; leaving alone to View, the bloody
And undistinguishable Trunk:
Which may be still mistaken by the Guards,
For *Osmyn*, if in seeking for the King,
They chance to find it.

Gonsalez. 'Twas an Act of Horrour;
And of a piece with this Day's dire Misdeeds.
But 'tis not yet the time to ponder, or
Repent. Haste thee, *Alonzo*, hence, with speed,
To aid my Son. I'll follow with the last
Reserve, to re-inforce his Arms: at least
I shall make good, and shelter his Retreat.

Exeunt.

Enter Zara, *follow'd by* Selim, *and Two Mutes bearing the Bowls.*

Zara. Silence and Solitude are ev'ry where!
Thro' all the Gloomy Ways, and Iron Doors
That hither lead, nor Humane Face, nor Voice
Is seen, or heard. A dreadful Din was wont
To grate the Sense, when entred here; from Groans,
And Howls of Slaves condemn'd; from Clink of Chains,
And Crash of rusty Bars, and creeking Hinges:
And ever and anon, the Sight was dash'd
With frightful Faces, and the meagre Looks
Of grim and gashly Executioners.
Yet, more, this Stilness terrifies my Soul,
Than did that Scene of complicated Horrors.
It may be, that the Cause, and Purpose of
My Errand, being chang'd from Life to Death,
Has also wrought this chilling Change of Temper.

gashly—Dialect form of ghastly, perhaps by association with *gash*.

Or does my Heart bode more? what can it more
Than Death?—
Let 'em set down the Bowls, and warn *Alphonso*
That I am here———so. You return and find

Mutes go in.

The King; tell him, what he requir'd, I've done:
And wait his coming to approve the Deed.

Exit Selim.

What have you seen? Ha! wherefore stare you thus,

The Mutes return and look affrighted.

With haggar'd Eyes? why are your Arms a-cross
Your heavy and desponding Heads hung down?
Why is't you more than speak in these sad Signs?
Give me more ample Knowledge of this Mourning.

They go to the Scene which opens and shews the Body.

Ha! prostrate! bloody! headless! O———start Eyes,
Split Heart, burst ev'ry Vein, at this dire Object:
At once dissolve and flow; meet Blood with Blood;
Dash your encountering Streams, with mutual Violence,
'Till Surges roll, and foaming Billows rise,
And curl their Crimson Heads, to kiss the Clouds!
—Rain, rain ye Stars, spout from your burning Orbs
Precipitated Fires, and pour in sheets,
The blazing Torrent on the Tyrant's Head;
Scorch and consume the curst perfidious King.

Enter Selim.

Selim. I've sought in vain, the King is no where, to
Be found—

Zara. Get thee to Hell, and seek him there.

Stabs him.

His hellish Rage had wanted Means to act,
But for thy fatal and pernicious Counsel.

Selim. You thought it better then———but I'm rewarded.
The Mute you sent, by some Mischance was seen,
And forc'd to yield your Letter with his Life:
I found the dead and bloody Body strip'd—
My Tongue faulters, and my Voice fails—
Drink not the Poyson—for *Alphonso* is—

Dies.

Zara. As thou art now———And I shall quickly be.
'Tis not that he is dead; for 'twas decreed
We both should die. Nor is't that I survive;

I have a Remedy for that. But Oh,
He dy'd unknowing in my Heart.
He knew I lov'd, but knew not to what height:
Nor that I meant to fall before his Eyes,
A Martyr and a victim to my Vows:
Insensible of this last Proof he's gone.
Yet Fate, alone can rob his mortal Part
Of Sense: His Soul still sees, and knows each Purpose,
And fix'd event of my persisting Faith.
Then, wherefore do I pause?———give me the Bowl.

A Mute kneels and gives one of the Bowls.

Hover a Moment, yet, thou gentle Spirit,
Soul of my Love, and I will wait thy flight.
This, to our mutual Bliss when joyn'd above.

Drinks.

O friendly Draught, already in my Heart!
Cold, cold; my Veins are Icicles and Frost.
I'll creep into his Bosom, lay me there;
Cover us close———or I shall chill his Breast,
And fright him from my Arms———See, see, he slides
Still further from me; look, he hides his Face,
I cannot feel it—quite beyond my reach.
O now he's gone, and all is dark—

Dies.

The Mutes kneel and mourn over her.

Enter Almeria *and* Leonora.

Almeria. O let me seek him in this horrid Cell;
For in the Tomb or Prison, I alone
Must hope to find him.

Leonora. Heav'ns! what dismal Scene
Of Death, is this? The Eunuch *Selim* slain!

Almeria. Shew me, for I am come in search of Death;
But want a Guide: for Tears have dim'd my Sight.

Leonora. Alas, a little farther, and behold
Zara all pale and dead! two frightful Men,
Who seem the Murderers, kneel weeping by:
Feeling Remorse too late, for what they've done.
But O forbear———lift up your Eyes no more;
But haste away, fly from this Fatal Place,
Where Miseries are multiply'd; return
And look not on; for there's a Dagger that
Will stab the Sight, and make your Eyes rain Blood.

Almeria. O I fore-see that Object in my Mind.
Is it at last then so? is he then dead?
What dead at last, quite, quite, for ever dead?
There, there I see him; there he lies, the Blood
Yet bubling from his Wounds—O more than savage!
Had they or Hearts, or Eyes, that did this Deed?
Could Eyes endure to guide such cruel Hands?
Are not my Eyes guilty alike with theirs,
That thus can gaze, and yet not turn to Stone?
—I do not weep! The Springs of Tears are dry'd;
And of a suddain I am calm, as if
All things were well: and yet my Husband's murder'd!
Yes, yes, I know to mourn; I'll sluce this Heart,
The Source of Woe, and let the Torrent loose.
—Those Men have left to weep; and look on me!
I hope they murder all on whom they look.
Behold me well; your bloody Hands have err'd,
And wrongfully have put to Death those Innocents:
I am the Sacrifice design'd to bleed;
And come prepar'd to yield my Throat———they shake
Their Heads in Sign of Grief and Innocence!
They point at the Bowl on the Ground.
And point! what mean they; Ha! a Cup. O well
I understand what Medicine has been here.
O noble Thirst! and yet too greedy to
Drink all———O for another Draught of Death,
They point to the other Cup.
Ha! point again? 'tis there, and full I hope.
O thanks the liberal Hand that fill'd thee thus;
I'll drink my glad Acknowledgment—

Leonora. O hold
For Mercy's sake; upon my Knees—forbear—

Almeria. With Thee, the kneeling World should beg in vain
Seest thou not there, who prostrate lies;
And pleads against thee? who shall then prevail?
Yet I will take a cold and parting Leave,
From his pale Lips; I'll kiss him e'er I drink,
Lest the rank Juice should blister on my Mouth,
And stain the Colour of my last Adieu.
Horrour! a headless Trunk! nor Lips nor Face,
Coming nearer the Body, starts and lets fall the Cup.
But spouting Veins, and mangled Flesh! O, O.

Enter Alphonso, Heli, Perez, *with* Garcia *Prisoner, Guards and Attendants.*

Alphonso. Away, stand off, where is she? let me fly,
Save her from Death, and snatch her to my Heart.

Almeria. Oh—

Alphonso. Forbear; my Arms alone shall hold her up:
Warm her to Life, and wake her into Gladness.
O let me talk to thy reviving Sense,
The Words of Joy and Peace; warm thy cold Beauties,
With the new-flushing Ardour of my Cheek;
Into thy Lips, pour the soft trickling Balm
Of cordial Sighs; and re-inspire thy Bosom
With the Breath of Love. Shine, awake, *Almeria*,
Give a new Birth to thy long-shaded Eyes,
Then double on the Day reflected Light.

Almeria. Where am I? Heav'n! what does this Dream intend?

Alphonso. O may'st thou never dream of less Delight;
Nor ever wake to less substantial Joys.

Almeria. Giv'n me again from Death! O all ye Powers
Confirm this Miracle! can I believe
My Sight, against my Sight? and shall I trust
That Sense, which in one Instant shews him dead
And living? yes, I will; I've been abus'd
With Apparitions and affrighting Fantoms:
This is my Lord, my Life, my only Husband;
I have him now, and we no more will part.
My Father too shall have Compassion—

Alphonso. O my Heart's Comfort; 'tis not given to this
Frail Life, to be entirely bless'd. Even now,
In this extreamest Joy my Soul can taste,
Yet am I dash'd to think that thou must weep;
Thy Father fell, where he design'd my Death.
Gonsalez and *Alonzo*, both of Wounds
Expiring, have with their last Breath, confess'd
The just Decrees of Heav'n, in turning on
Themselves, their own most bloody Purposes.
Nay, I must grant, 'tis fit you shou'd be thus—
She weeps.
Let 'em remove the Body from her Sight.
Ill-fated *Zara*! Ha! a Cup? alas!
Thy Errour then is plain: but I were Flint
Not to o'er-flow in Tribute to thy Memory.
She shall be Royally interr'd. O *Garcia*,
Whose Virtue has renounc'd thy Father's Crimes,
Seest thou, how just the Hand of Heav'n has been?

Let us that thro' our Innocence survive,
Still in the Paths of Honour persevere;
And not from past or present Ills Despair:
For Blessings ever wait on vertuous Deeds;
And tho' a late, a sure Reward succeeds.

Exeunt Omnes.

Epilogue,

Spoken by Mrs. *Bracegirdle*.

The Tragedy thus done, I am, you know,
No more a Princess, but *in statu quo*:
And now as unconcern'd this Mourning wear,
As if indeed a Widow, or an Heir.
I've leisure, now, to mark your sev'ral Faces,
And know each Critick by his sowre Grimaces.
To poison Plays, I see some where they sit,
Scatter'd, like Rats-bane, up and down the Pit;
While others watch like Parish-Searchers, hir'd
To tell of what Disease the Play expir'd.
O with what Joy they run, to spread the News
Of a damn'd Poet, and departed Muse!
But if he 'scape, with what Regret they're seiz'd!
And how they're disappointed if they're pleas'd!
Criticks to Plays for the same end resort,
That Surgeons wait on Tryals in a Court;
For Innocence condemn'd they've no Respect,
Provided they've a Body to dissect.
As *Sussex Men*, that dwell upon the Shoar,
Look out when Storms arise, and Billows roar,
Devoutly praying, with up-lifted Hands,
That some well-laden Ship may strike the Sands;
To whose Rich Cargo, they may make Pretence,
And fatten on the Spoils of Providence:
So Criticks throng to see a New Play split,
And thrive and prosper on the Wrecks of Wit.
Small Hope our Poet from these Prospects draws;
And therefore to the Fair commends his Cause.
Your tender Hearts to Mercy are inclin'd,
With whom, he hopes, this Play will Favour find,
Which was an Off'ring to the Sex design'd.

FINIS.

Sussex Men—Seacoast nearest to London, where the storms blowing up the Channel cast many wrecks.

6

The Way of the World

INTRODUCTORY NOTE

In 1698, Congreve had been disturbed by Collier's attack upon him in his *Short View of the Immorality and Profaneness of the English Stage*, and had immediately answered him with *Amendments of Mr. Collier's False and Imperfect Citations* from his plays. In the following year he set out to provide a better answer in the form of another play, in which he proposed to vindicate himself by producing something of which no one would need to be ashamed. In his Prologue, it is true, he adopts the usual attitude of submission to the verdict of the theater audience; he professes to be "a Passive Poet, Who to your Judgments yields all Resignation." But, when he came to write the dedication of the printed play to the Earl of Montagu, we cannot fail to recognize beneath his flattering compliments that he regards this play as something on which he had lavished great pains and care to make it different from anything he had done before. He tells us that he had written it in the latter part of 1699, after a long summer visit as guest of the Earl of Montagu in the country, presumably at Boughton House, Northants, where King William had been splendidly entertained a few years earlier. Perhaps not only the dialogue, as he admitted, but even the characters of the play owe something to the other guests he met there. At least in these scenes, "abstracted" on the theater, we are given a very brilliant, sharply focused study of the way of the world in 1700. If, in the course of the comedy, some knaves and fools should be exposed, we need not be very much surprised; for Swift had called their host, with some reason, "as arrant a knave as any in his time."

Indeed, some of the gossip about Montagu and his first marriage seems almost to lend reality to the surprising intrigues so often used in Restoration comedy. For example, in a letter from Henry Ball written from Whitehall, dated October 10, 1673, to Sir Joseph Williamson, we find this lurid piece of gossip:

> My Lady of Northumberland and her new husband, Mr. Montague, have already begun to differ upon a

report risen from him, as shee sayes, that he bought her of her mayd for 500*l.* per annum, and the Towne talke of parting them.[1]

That was of course a long time ago; and in fact they had stayed together, and she bore him several children, and died in childbirth in 1690.

That was the kind of world in which the play took shape. By the end of the year it was still not finished. In a letter written at Christmas, 1699, Vanbrugh mentioned it, but said that nobody had seen it yet. It was first performed early in March, perhaps on March 4, 1700, if we accept the suggestion that James Brydges, afterwards Duke of Chandos, who records his visits to Lincoln's Inn Fields theater on March 4, 9, and 11 without mentioning the play, was probably drawn there by the distinguished audience that would be expected for a new play by Congreve.[2] It had what Dryden calls "but moderate success," although Congreve in the Dedication professes himself satisfied: "That it succeeded on the Stage, was almost beyond my Expectation; for but little of it was prepar'd for that general Taste which seems now to be predominant in the Pallats of our Audience."

The plot is contrived to illustrate the theme stated on the title page in the lines from Horace's *Satires*:[3] the fate of adulterers and the fears of a guilty woman for the loss of her dowry. The manners and morals of the characters are taken from that world to which the poet and his audience alike belong, as if to indicate that in spite of the recent reformation of manners, there is still ample material for comedy for anyone who has been taught by the Roman satirists to observe the way of the world. Perhaps the most important source is, therefore, this satire of Horace to which our attention is drawn.[4]

It is still difficult to explain why it did not have a longer run, since the performance of the company was highly praised; Mrs. Bracegirdle's Millamant "gained the applause of Court and City," and Mrs. Leigh as Lady Wishfort was highly appreciated. But Avery finds records of only two performances during the next fifteen years, although a second edition of the play was called for in 1706, which

[1] Camden Soc. new [2d] ser. vol. IX (2), 35, 1874.

[2] See Lucyle Hook, *James Brydges drops in at the Theatre*, *HLQ*, VIII, 1944–45, 306–11.

[3] I. ii, 37, 131.

[4] See Paul and Miriam Mueschke, *A New View of Congreve's Way of the World* (Ann Arbor: University of Michigan Press, 1958).

gave Congreve the opportunity to introduce some revisions.[5] During the nineteenth century, it was only played with considerable cuts and alterations to suit the taste of the times, but since its revival in 1904, it has gradually taken its place again and has even been triumphantly successful in the theater.

[5] See E. L. Avery, *Congreve on the Eighteenth-century Stage*, 1951, pp. 33–34.

THE

Way of the World,

A

COMEDY.

As it is ACTED AT THE

Theatre in *Lincoln's-Inn-Fields*,

BY

His Majesty's Servants.

Written by Mr. *CONGREVE*.

Audire est Operæ pretium, procedere recte
Qui mæchis non vultis —— Hor. Sat. 2. l. 1.
——*Metuat doti deprensa.*—— Ibid.

LONDON,

Printed for *Jacob Tonson*, within *Gray's-Inn-Gate* next *Gray's-Inn-Lane*. 1700.

Audire est . . .—

All you, who think the City ne'er can thrive,
Till ev'ry Cuckold-maker's flea'd alive;
Attend, while I their Miseries explain, . . .
Seized in the Fact, . . .
She kneels, she weeps, and worse! resigns her Dow'r.

(Horace, Satire I, ii: Pope's *Imitation* ll. 47–48, 172.)

To the Right Honourable

RALPH

Earl of Mountague, &c.

My LORD,

Whether the World will arraign me of Vanity, or not, that I have presum'd to Dedicate this Comedy to your Lordship, I am yet in doubt: Tho' it may be it is some degree of Vanity even to doubt of it. One who has at any time had the Honour of your Lordship's Conversation, cannot be suppos'd to think very meanly of that which he would prefer to your Persual: Yet it were to incur the Imputation of too much Sufficiency, to pretend to such a Merit as might abide the Test of your Lordship's Censure.

Whatever Value may be wanting to this Play while yet it is mine, will be sufficiently made up to it, when it is once become your Lordship's; and it is my Security, that I cannot have overrated it more by my Dedication, than your Lordship will dignifie it by your Patronage.

That it succeeded on the Stage, was almost beyond my Expectation; for but little of it was prepar'd for that general Taste which seems now to be predominant in the Pallats of our Audience.

Those Characters which are meant to be ridiculous in most of our Comedies, are of Fools so gross, that in my humble Opinion, they should rather disturb than divert the well-natur'd and reflecting part of an Audience; they are rather Objects of Charity than Contempt; and instead of moving our Mirth, they ought very often to excite our Compassion.

This Reflection mov'd me to design some Characters, which should appear ridiculous not so much thro' a natural Folly (which is incorrigible, and therefore not proper for the Stage) as thro' an affected Wit; a Wit, which at the same time that it is affected, is also false. As there is some Difficulty in the formation of a Character of this Nature, so there is some Hazard which attends the progress of its Success, upon the Stage: For many come to a Play, so over-charg'd with Criticism, that they very often let fly their Censure, when through their rashness they have mistaken their Aim. This I had occasion lately to observe: For this Play had been Acted two or three Days, before some of these hasty Judges cou'd find the leisure to distinguish betwixt the Character of a *Witwoud* and a *Truewit.*

I must beg your Lordship's Pardon for this Digression from the true Course of this Epistle; but that it may not seem altogether impertinent, I beg, that I may plead the occasion of it, in part of that Excuse of which I stand in need, for recommending this Comedy to your Protection. It is only by the Countenance of your Lordship, and the *Few* so qualified, that such who write with Care and Pains can hope to be distinguish'd: For the Prostituted Name of *Poet* promiscuously levels all that bear it.

Terence, the most correct Writer in the World, had a *Scipio* and a *Lelius* if not to assist him, at least to support him in his Reputation: And notwithstanding his extraordinary Merit, it may be, their Countenance was not more than necessary.

The Purity of his Stile, the Delicacy of his Turns, and the Justness of his Characters, were all of them Beauties, which the greater part of his Audience were incapable of Tasting: Some of the coursest Strokes of *Plautus*, so severely censured by *Horace*, were more likely to affect the Multitude; such, who come with expectation to Laugh out the last Act of a Play, and are better entertained with two or three unseasonable Jests, than with the artful Solution of the *Fable*.

As *Terence* excell'd in his Performances, so had he great Advantages to encourage his Undertakings; for he built most on the Foundations of *Menander*: His Plots were generally modell'd, and his Characters ready drawn to his Hand. He copied *Menander*; and *Menander* had no less Light in the Formation of his Characters, from the Observations of *Theophrastus*, of whom he was a Disciple; and *Theophrastus* it is known was not only the Disciple, but the immediate Successor of *Aristotle*, the first and greatest Judge of Poetry. These were great Models to design by; and the further Advantage which *Terence* possess'd, towards giving his Plays the due Ornaments of Purity of Stile, and Justness of Manners, was not less considerable, from the freedom of Conversation, which was permitted him with *Lelius* and *Scipio*, two of the greatest and most polite Men of his Age. And indeed, the Privilege of such a Conversation, is the only certain Means of attaining to the Perfection of Dialogue.

If it has hapned in any part of this Comedy, that I have gain'd a Turn of Stile, or Expression more Correct, or at least more Corrigible than in those which I have formerly written, I must, with equal Pride and Gratitude, ascribe it to the Honour of your Lordship's admitting me into your Conversation, and that of a Society where every-body else was so well worthy of you, in your Retirement last Summer from the Town: For it was immediately after, that this Comedy was written. If I have fail'd in my Performance, it is only to be regretted, where there were so many, not inferiour either to a *Scipio* or a *Lelius*, that there should be one wanting equal to the Capacity of a *Terence*.

If I am not mistaken, Poetry is almost the only Art, which has not yet laid claim to your Lordship's Patronage. Architecture, and Painting, to the great Honour of our Country, have flourish'd under your Influence and Protection. In the mean time, Poetry, the eldest Sister of all Arts, and Parent of most, seems to have resign'd her Birth-right, by having neglected to pay her Duty to your Lordship; and by permitting others of a later Extraction, to prepossess that Place in your Esteem, to which none can pretend a better Title. Poetry, in its Nature, is sacred to the Good and Great; the relation between them is reciprocal, and they are ever propitious to it. It is the Privilege of Poetry to address to them, and it is their Prerogative alone to give it Protection.

This receiv'd Maxim is a general Apology for all Writers who Consecrate their Labours to great Men: But I could wish at this time, that this Address were exempted from the common pretence of all Dedications; and that as I can distinguish your Lordship even among the most Deserving, so this Offering might become remarkable by some particular Instance of Respect, which shou'd assure your Lordship, that I am, with all due Sense of your extream Worthiness and Humanity,

My LORD,
Your Lordship's most obedient
and most oblig'd humble Servant,

Will. Congreve.

Prologue,

Spoken by Mr. *Betterton*.

Of those few Fools, who with ill Stars are curs'd,
Sure scribbling Fools, call'd Poets, fare the worst.
For they're a sort of Fools which *Fortune* makes,
And after she has made 'em Fools, forsakes.
With *Nature*'s Oafs 'tis quite a diff'rent Case,
For *Fortune* favours all her *Idiot-Race*:
In her own Nest the *Cuckow-Eggs* we find,
O'er which she broods to hatch the *Changling-Kind*.
No Portion for her own she has to spare,
So much she doats on her adopted Care.
  Poets are Bubbles, by the Town drawn in,
Suffer'd at first some trifling Stakes to win:
But what unequal Hazards do they run!
Each time they write, they venture all they've won:
The 'Squire that's butter'd still, is sure to be undone.
This Author, heretofore, has found your Favour,
But pleads no Merit from his past Behaviour.
To build on that might prove a vain Presumption,
Should Grants to Poets made, admit Resumption:
And in *Parnassus* he must lose his Seat,
If that be found a forfeited Estate.
  He owns, with Toil, he wrought the following Scenes,
But if they're naught ne're spare him for his Pains:
Damn him the more; have no Commiseration
For Dulness on mature Deliberation.
He swears he'll not resent one hiss'd-off Scene,
Nor, like those peevish Wits, his Play maintain,
Who, to assert their Sense, your Taste arraign.
Some Plot we think he has, and some new Thought;
Some Humour too, no Farce; but that's a Fault.
Satire, he thinks, you ought not to expect,
For so Reform'd a Town, who dares Correct?
To please, this time, has been his sole Pretence,
He'll not instruct, lest it should give Offence.
Should he by chance a Knave or Fool expose,
That hurts none here, sure here are none of those.
In short, our Play, shall (with your leave to shew it)
Give you one Instance of a Passive Poet.
Who to your Judgments yields all Resignation;
So Save or Damn, after your own Discretion.

Bubbles . . . butter'd—Gamesters' slang: "cheated" and "led to double his wager to recover his losses."

Dramatis Personæ

MEN.

Fainall, In Love with *Mrs. Marwood*	Mr. Betterton.
Mirabell, In Love with *Mrs. Millamant*	Mr. Verbrugen.
Witwoud, } Followers of *Mrs. Millamant*	Mr. Bowen.
Petulant, } Followers of *Mrs. Millamant*	Mr. Bowman.
Sir Wilfull Witwoud, Half Brother to *Witwoud,* and Nephew to *Lady Wishfort*	Mr. Underhill.
Waitwell, Servant to *Mirabell*	Mr. Bright.

WOMEN.

Lady Wishfort, Enemy to *Mirabell,* for having falsely pretended Love to her	Mrs. Leigh.
Mrs. Millamant, A fine Lady, Niece to *Lady Wishfort,* and loves *Mirabell*	Mrs. Bracegirdle.
Mrs. Marwood, Friend to *Mr. Fainall,* and likes *Mirabell*	Mrs. Barry.
Mrs. Fainall, Daughter to *Lady Wishfort,* and Wife to *Fainall,* formerly Friend to *Mirabell*	Mrs. Bowman.
Foible, Woman to *Lady Wishfort*	Mrs. Willis.
Mincing, Woman to *Mrs. Millamant*	Mrs. Prince.

Dancers, Footmen, *and* Attendants.

SCENE *LONDON.*

The Time equal to that of the Presentation.

The Way of the World.
A Comedy.

ACT I. Scene I.

A Chocolate-house.

Mirabell *and* Fainall *Rising from Cards.* Betty *waiting.*

Mirabell. You are a fortunate Man, Mr. *Fainall.*

Fainall. Have we done?

Mirabell. What you please. I'll play on to entertain you.

Fainall. No, I'll give you your Revenge another time, when you are not so indifferent; you are thinking of something else now, and play too negligently; the Coldness of a losing Gamester lessens the Pleasure of the Winner: I'd no more play with a Man that slighted his ill Fortune, than I'd make Love to a Woman who undervalu'd the Loss of her Reputation.

Mirabell. You have a Taste extreamly delicate, and are for refining on your Pleasures.

Fainall. Prithee, why so reserv'd? Something has put you out of Humour.

Mirabell. Not at all: I happen to be grave to day; and you are gay; that's all.

Fainall. Confess, *Millamant* and you quarrell'd last Night, after I left you; my fair Cousin has some Humours, that wou'd tempt the patience of a Stoick. What, some Coxcomb came in, and was well receiv'd by her, while you were by.

Mirabell. *Witwoud* and *Petulant*; and what was worse, her Aunt, your Wife's Mother, my evil Genius; or to sum up all in her own Name, my old Lady *Wishfort* came in.—

Fainall. O there it is then———She has a lasting Passion for you, and with Reason.———What, then my Wife was there?

Mirabell. Yes, and Mrs. *Marwood* and three or four more, whom I never saw before; seeing me, they all put on their grave Faces, whisper'd one another; then complain'd aloud of the Vapours, and after fell into a profound Silence.

Fainall. They had a mind to be rid of you.

Mirabell. For which Reason I resolv'd not to stir. At last the good old Lady broke thro' her painful Taciturnity, with an Invective against long Visits. I would not have understood her, but *Millamant* joining in the Argument, I rose and with a constrain'd Smile told her, I thought nothing was so easie as to know when a Visit began to be troublesome; she redned and I withdrew, without expecting her Reply.

Fainall. You were to blame to resent what she spoke only in Compliance with her Aunt.

Mirabell. She is more Mistress of her self, than to be under the necessity of such a resignation.

Fainall. What? tho' half her Fortune depends upon her marrying with my Lady's Approbation?

Mirabell. I was then in such a Humour, that I shou'd have been better pleas'd if she had been less discreet.

Fainall. Now I remember, I wonder not they were weary of you; last Night was one of their Cabal-nights; they have 'em three times a Week, and meet by turns, at one another's Apartments, where they come together like the Coroner's Inquest, to sit upon the murder'd Reputations of the Week. You and I are excluded; and it was once propos'd that all the Male Sex shou'd be excepted; but somebody mov'd that to avoid Scandal there might be one Man of the Community; upon which Motion *Witwoud* and *Petulant* were enroll'd Members.

Mirabell. And who may have been the Foundress of this Sect? My Lady *Wishfort*, I warrant, who publishes her Detestation of Mankind; and full of the Vigour of Fifty

expecting—Waiting for.

Cabal—A french term applied to a group of ministers intriguing together, popularized by its political use after the Restoration.

five, declares for a Friend and *Ratifia*; and let Posterity shift for it self, she'll breed no more.

Fainall. The discovery of your sham Addresses to her, to conceal your Love to her Niece, has provok'd this Separation: Had you dissembl'd better, Things might have continu'd in the state of Nature.

Mirabell. I did as much as Man cou'd, with any reasonable Conscience; I proceeded to the very last Act of Flattery with her, and was guilty of a Song in her Commendation: Nay, I got a Friend to put her into a Lampoon, and complement her with the Imputation of an Affair with a young Fellow, which I carry'd so far, that I told her the malicious Town took notice that she was grown fat of a suddain; and when she lay in of a Dropsie, persuaded her she was reported to be in Labour. The Devil's in't, if an old woman is to be flatter'd further, unless a Man shou'd endeavour downright personally to debauch her; and that my Virtue forbad me. But for the discovery of that Amour, I am Indebted to your Friend, or your Wife's Friend, Mrs. *Marwood.*

Fainall. What should provoke her to be your Enemy, without she has made you Advances, which you have slighted? Women do not easily forgive Omissions of that Nature.

Mirabell. She was always civil to me, till of late; I confess I am not one of those Coxcombs who are apt to interpret a Woman's good Manners to her Prejudice; and think that she who does not refuse 'em every thing, can refuse 'em nothing.

Fainall. You are a gallant Man, *Mirabell*; and tho' you may have Cruelty enough, not to satisfie a Lady's longing; you have too much Generosity, not to be tender of her Honour. Yet you speak with an Indifference which seems to be affected; and confesses you are conscious of a Negligence.

Mirabell. You pursue the Argument with a distrust that seems to be unaffected, and confesses you are conscious of a Concern for which the Lady is more indebted to you, than your Wife.

Fainall. Fie, fie Friend, if you grow Censorious I must leave you;———I'll look upon the Gamesters in the next Room.

Mirabell. Who are they?

Ratifia—A liqueur, rather like cherry brandy.

Fainall. Petulant and *Witwoud.*———Bring me some Chocolate.

Exit.

Mirabell. Betty, what says your Clock?

Betty. Turn'd of the last Canonical Hour, Sir.

Exit.

Mirabell. How pertinently the Jade answers me! Ha? almost One a Clock! (*Looking at his Watch*) O, y'are come—

Enter a Servant.

Well, is the grand Affair over? You have been something tedious.

Servant. Sir, there's such Coupling at *Pancras*, that they stand behind one another, as 'twere in a Country Dance. Ours was the last Couple to lead up; and no hopes appearing of dispatch, besides, the Parson growing hoarse, we were afraid his Lungs would have fail'd before it came to our turn; so we drove round to *Duke's Place*; and there they were riveted in a trice.

Mirabell. So, so, you are sure they are Married.

Servant. Married and Bedded, Sir: I am Witness.

Mirabell. Have you the Certificate?

Servant. Here it is, Sir.

Mirabell. Has the Taylor brought *Waitwell's* Cloaths home, and the new Liveries?

Servant. Yes, Sir.

Mirabell. That's well. Do you go home again, d'ee hear, and adjourn the Consummation till farther Order; bid *Waitwell* shake his Ears, and Dame *Partlet* rustle up her Feathers, and meet me at One a Clock by *Rosamond's* Pond. That I may see her before she returns to her Lady; and as you tender your Ears be secret.

Exit Servant.

Re-Enter Fainall.

Canonical Hour—The hours for a legal marriage in church.

Pancras—St. Pancras, then outside the city on the road to Highgate, where marriages were performed—for a fee—without a license and at any time.

Duke's Place—St. James Church, in Duke Place, Aldgate.

Dame Partlet—The wife of Chanticleer in the fable.

Rosamond's Pond—In St. James' Park, a favorite trysting place.

Fainall. Joy of your Success, *Mirabell*; you look pleas'd.

Mirabell. Ay; I have been engag'd in a Matter of some sort of Mirth, which is not yet ripe for discovery. I am glad this is not a Cabal-night. I wonder, *Fainall*, that you who are Married, and of Consequence should be discreet, will suffer your Wife to be of such a Party.

Fainall. Faith, I am not Jealous. Besides, most who are engag'd are Women and Relations; and for the Men, they are of a Kind too Contemptible to give Scandal.

Mirabell. I am of another Opinion. The greater the Coxcomb, always the more the Scandal: For a Woman who is not a Fool, can have but one Reason for associating with a Man that is.

Fainall. Are you Jealous as often as you see *Witwoud* entertain'd by *Millamant*?

Mirabell. Of her Understanding I am, if not of her Person.

Fainall. You do her wrong; for to give her her Due, she has Wit.

Mirabell. She has Beauty enough to make any Man think so; and Complaisance enough not to contradict him who shall tell her so.

Fainall. For a passionate Lover, methinks you are a Man somewhat too discerning in the Failings of your Mistress.

Mirabell. And for a discerning Man, somewhat too passionate a Lover; for I like her with all her Faults; nay, like her for her Faults. Her Follies are so natural, or so artful, that they become her; and those Affectations which in another Woman wou'd be odious, serve but to make her more agreeable. I'll tell thee, *Fainall*, she once us'd me with that Insolence, that in Revenge I took her to pieces; sifted her and separated her Failings; I study'd 'em, and got 'em by rote. The Catalogue was so large, that I was not without hopes, one Day or other to hate her heartily: To which end I so us'd my self to think of 'em, that at length, contrary to my Design and Expectation, they gave me every Hour less and less disturbance; 'till in a few Days it became habitual to me, to remember 'em without being displeas'd. They are now grown as familiar to me as my own Frailties; and in all probability in a little time longer I shall like 'em as well.

Fainall. Marry her, marry her; be half as well acquainted with her Charms, as you are with her Defects, and my Life on't, you are your own Man again.

Mirabell. Say you so?

Fainall. I, I, I have Experience: I have a Wife, and so forth.

Enter Messenger.

Messenger. Is one Squire *Witwoud* here?

Betty. Yes; what's your Business?

Messenger. I have a Letter for him, from his Brother Sir *Wilfull*, which I am charg'd to deliver into his own Hands.

Betty. He's in the next Room, Friend———That way.

Exit Messenger.

Mirabell. What, is the Chief of that noble Family in Town, Sir *Wilfull Witwoud*?

Fainall. He is expected to Day. Do you know him?

Mirabell. I have seen him, he promises to be an extraordinary Person; I think you have the Honour to be related to him.

Fainall. Yes; he is half Brother to this *Witwoud* by a former Wife, who was Sister to my Lady *Wishfort*, my Wife's Mother. If you marry *Millamant* you must call Cousins too.

Mirabell. I had rather be his Relation than his Acquaintance.

Fainall. He comes to Town in order to Equip himself for Travel.

Mirabell. For Travel! Why the Man that I mean is above Forty.

Fainall. No matter for that; 'tis for the Honour of *England*, that all *Europe* should know we have Blockheads of all Ages.

Mirabell. I wonder there is not an Act of Parliament to save the Credit of the Nation, and prohibit the Exportation of Fools.

Fainall. By no means, 'tis better as 'tis; 'tis better to Trade with a little Loss, than to be quite eaten up, with being overstock'd.

Mirabell. Pray, are the Follies of this Knight-Errant, and those of the Squire his Brother, any thing related?

Fainall. Not at all; *Witwoud* grows by the Knight, like a Medlar grafted on a Crab. One will melt in your Mouth, and t'other set your Teeth on edge; one is all Pulp, and the other all Core.

Mirabell. So one will be rotten before he be ripe, and the other will be rotten without ever being ripe at all.

Fainall. Sir *Wilfull* is an odd mixture of Bashfulness and Obstinacy———But when he's drunk, he's as loving as the Monster in the Tempest; and much after the same manner. To give the t'other his due; he has something of good Nature, and does not always want Wit.

Mirabell. Not always; but as often as his Memory fails him, and his common place of Comparisons. He is a Fool with a good Memory, and some few Scraps of other Folks Wit. He is one whose Conversation can never be approv'd, yet it is now and then to be endur'd. He has indeed one good Quality, he is not Exceptious; for he so passionately affects the Reputation of understanding Raillery; that he will construe an Affront into a Jest; and call downright Rudeness and ill Language, Satyr and Fire.

Fainall. If you have a mind to finish his Picture, you have an opportunity to do it at full length. Behold the Original.

Enter Witwoud.

Witwoud. Afford me your Compassion, my Dears; pity me, *Fainall*, *Mirabell*, pity me.

Mirabell. I do from my Soul.

Fainall. Why, what's the Matter?

Witwoud. No Letters for me, *Betty*?

Betty. Did not the Messenger bring you one but now, Sir?

Witwoud. Ay, but no other?

Betty. No, Sir.

Witwoud. That's hard, that's very hard;———A Messenger, a Mule, a Beast of Burden, he has brought me a Letter from the Fool my Brother, as heavy as a Panegyrick in a Funeral Sermon, or a Copy of Commendatory Verses from one Poet to another. And what's worse, 'tis as sure a forerunner of the Author, as an Epistle Dedicatory.

Monster in the Tempest—Referring to the immensely popular opera, made out of the Dryden-Davenant version of the *Tempest*, 1674 reset with Purcell's music in 1690.

Mirabell. A Fool, and your Brother, *Witwoud*!

Witwoud. Ay, ay, my half Brother. My half Brother he is, no nearer, upon Honour.

Mirabell. Then 'tis possible he may be but half a Fool.

Witwoud. Good, good *Mirabell, le Drole*! Good, good, hang him, don't let's talk of him:———*Fainall*, how does your Lady? Gad, I say any thing in the World to get this Fellow out of my Head. I beg Pardon that I shou'd ask a Man of Pleasure, and the Town, a Question at once so Foreign and Domestick. But I talk like an old Maid at a Marriage, I don't know what I say: But she's the best Woman in the World.

Fainall. 'Tis well you don't know what you say, or else your Commendation wou'd go near to make me either Vain or Jealous.

Witwoud. No Man in Town lives well with a Wife but *Fainall*: Your Judgment *Mirabell.*

Mirabell. You had better step and ask his Wife; if you wou'd be credibly inform'd.

Witwoud. Mirabell.

Mirabell. Ay.

Witwoud. My Dear, I ask ten thousand Pardons;—Gad I have forgot what I was going to say to you.

Mirabell. I thank you heartily, heartily.

Witwoud. No, but prithee excuse me,———my Memory is such a Memory.

Mirabell. Have a care of such Apologies, *Witwoud*;———for I never knew a Fool but he affected to complain, either of the Spleen or his Memory.

Fainall. What have you done with *Petulant*?

Witwoud. He's reckoning his Mony,———my Mony it was, ———I have no Luck to Day.

Fainall. You may allow him to win of you at Play;——— for you are sure to be too hard for him at Repartee: since you monopolize the Wit that is between you, the Fortune must be his of Course.

Mirabell. I don't find that *Petulant* confesses the Superiority of Wit to be your Talent, *Witwoud.*

Witwoud. Come, come, you are malicious now, and wou'd breed Debates.———*Petulant*'s my Friend, and a very honest Fellow, and a very pretty Fellow, and has a smattering—Faith and Troth a pretty deal of an odd sort of a small Wit: Nay, I'll do him Justice. I'm his Friend, I won't wrong him neither———And if he had but any Judgment in the World,———he wou'd not be altogether contemptible. Come come, don't detract from the Merits of my Friend.

Fainall. You don't take your Friend to be overnicely bred.

Witwoud. No, no, hang him, the Rogue has no Manners at all, that I must own———No more breeding than a Bum-baily, that I grant you,———'Tis Pity faith; the Fellow has Fire and Life.

Mirabell. What, Courage?

Witwoud. Hum, faith I don't know as to that,—I can't say as to that.———Yes, Faith, in a Controversie he'll contradict any Body.

Mirabell. Tho' 'twere a Man whom he fear'd, or a Woman whom he lov'd.

Witwoud. Well, well, he does not always think before he speaks;———We have all our Failings; you're too hard upon him, you are, faith. Let me excuse him;—I can defend most of his Faults, except one or two; one he has, that's the Truth on't, if he were my Brother, I cou'd not acquit him———That indeed I cou'd wish were otherwise.

Mirabell. Ay marry, what's that, *Witwoud*?

Witwoud. O pardon me———Expose the Infirmities of my Friend.———No, my Dear, excuse me there.

Fainall. What I warrant he's unsincere, or 'tis some such Trifle.

Witwoud. No, no, what if he be? 'Tis no matter for that, his Wit will excuse that: A Wit shou'd no more be sincere, than a Woman constant; one argues a decay of Parts, as t'other of Beauty.

Mirabell. May be you think him too positive?

Witwoud. No, no, his being positive is an Incentive to Argument, and keeps up Conversation.

Bum-baily—"A bailiff of the meanest kind; one employed in arrests" (Johnson's *Dictionary*).

Fainall. Too Illiterate.

Witwoud. That! that's his Happiness——His want of Learning, gives him the more opportunities to shew his natural Parts.

Mirabell. He wants Words.

Witwoud. Ay; but I like him for that now; for his want of Words gives me the pleasure very often to explain his meaning.

Fainall. He's Impudent.

Witwoud. No; that's not it.

Mirabell. Vain.

Witwoud. No.

Mirabell. What, he speaks unseasonable Truths sometimes, because he has not Wit enough to invent an Evasion.

Witwoud. Truths! Ha, ha, ha! No, no, since you will have it, —I mean he never speaks Truth at all,——that's all. He will lie like a Chambermaid, or a Woman of Quality's Porter. Now that is a Fault.

Enter Coachman.

Coachman. Is Master *Petulant* here, Mistress?

Betty. Yes.

Coachman. Three Gentlewomen in the Coach would speak with him.

Fainall. O brave *Petulant*, three!

Betty. I'll tell him.

Coachman. You must bring two Dishes of Chocolate and a Glass of Cinnamon-water.

Exit Betty, *and Coachman.*

Witwoud. That should be for two fasting Strumpets, and a Bawd troubl'd with Wind. Now you may know what the three are.

Mirabell. You are very free with your Friends Acquaintance.

Witwoud. Ay, ay, Friendship without Freedom is as dull as Love without Enjoyment, or Wine without Toasting; but

Cinnamon-water—A strong drink, flavored with cinnamon, a cure for vapors.

to tell you a Secret, these are Trulls that he allows Coach-hire, and something more by the Week, to call on him once a Day at publick Places.

Mirabell. How!

Witwoud. You shall see he won't go to 'em because there's no more Company here to take notice of him———Why this is nothing to what he us'd to do;———Before he found out this way, I have known him call for himself———

Fainall. Call for himself? What dost thou mean?

Witwoud. Mean, why he wou'd slip you out of this Chocolate-house, just when you had been talking to him———As soon as your Back was turn'd———Whip he was gone; ———Then trip to his Lodging, clap on a Hood and Scarf, and Mask, slap into a Hackney-Coach, and drive hither to the Door again in a trice; where he wou'd send in for himself, that I mean, call for himself, wait for himself, nay and what's more, not finding himself, sometimes leave a Letter for himself.

Mirabell. I confess this is something extraordinary—I believe he waits for himself now, he is so long a coming; O I ask his Pardon.

Enter Petulant.

Betty. Sir, the Coach stays.

Petulant. Well, well; I come———Sbud, a Man had as good be a profess'd Midwife as a profest Whoremaster, at this rate; to be knock'd up and rais'd at all Hours, and in all Places. Pox on 'em I won't come.———Dee hear, tell 'em I won't come.———Let 'em snivel and cry their Hearts out.

Fainall. You are very cruel, *Petulant.*

Petulant. All's one, let it pass———I have a Humour to be cruel.

Mirabell. I hope they are not Persons of Condition that you use at this rate.

Petulant. Condition, Condition's a dry'd Fig, if I am not in Humour—By this Hand, if they were your—a—a—your What-dee-call-'ems themselves, they must wait or rub off, if I want Appetite.

Mirabell. What-dee-call-'ems! What are they, *Witwoud*?

Witwoud. Empresses, my Dear———By your What-dee-call-'ems he means Sultana Queens.

Petulant. Ay, *Roxolana*'s.

Mirabell. Cry you Mercy.

Fainall. *Witwoud* says they are—

Petulant. What does he say th' are?

Witwoud. I; fine Ladies I say.

Petulant. Pass on, *Witwoud*———Hearkee, by this Light his Relations———Two Coheiresses his Cousins, and an old Aunt, that loves Catterwauling better than a Conventicle.

Witwoud. Ha, ha, ha; I had a Mind to see how the Rogue wou'd come off———Ha, ha, ha; Gad I can't be angry with him; if he said they were my Mother and my Sisters.

Mirabell. No!

Witwoud. No; the Rogue's Wit and Readiness of Invention charm me, dear *Petulant.*

Betty. They are gone Sir, in great Anger.

Petulant. Enough, let 'em trundle. Anger helps Complexion, saves Paint.

Fainall. This Continence is all dissembled; this is in order to have something to brag of the next time he makes Court to *Millamant*, and swear he has abandon'd the whole Sex for her Sake.

Mirabell. Have you not left off your impudent Pretensions there yet? I shall cut your Throat, sometime or other, *Petulant*, about that Business.

Petulant. Ay, ay, let that pass———There are other Throats to be cut—

Mirabell. Meaning mine, Sir?

Petulant. Not I———I mean no Body———I know nothing ———But there are Uncles and Nephews in the World ———And they may be Rivals———What then? All's one for that———

Mirabell. How! hearkee *Petulant*, come hither———Explain, or I shall call your Interpreter.

Roxolana's—The Sultana in Davenant's *Siege of Rhodes.*

Petulant. Explain, I know nothing———Why you have an Uncle, have you not, lately come to Town, and lodges by my Lady *Wishfort*'s?

Mirabell. True.

Petulant. Why that's enough———You and he are not Friends; and if he shou'd marry and have a Child, you may be disinherited, ha?

Mirabell. Where hast thou stumbled upon all this Truth?

Petulant. All's one for that; why then say I know something.

Mirabell. Come, thou art an honest Fellow, *Petulant*, and shalt make Love to my Mistress, thou sha't, Faith. What hast thou heard of my Uncle?

Petulant. I, nothing I. If Throats are to be cut, let Swords clash; snugs the Word, I shrug and am silent.

Mirabell. O Raillery, Raillery. Come, I know thou art in the Women's Secrets———What you're a Cabalist, I know you staid at *Millamant*'s last Night, after I went. Was there any mention made of my Uncle, or me? Tell me; if thou hadst but good Nature equal to thy Wit *Petulant, Tony Witwoud*, who is now thy Competitor in Fame, wou'd shew as dim by thee as a dead Whiting's Eye, by a Pearl of Orient; he wou'd no more be seen by thee, then *Mercury* is by the Sun: Come, I'm sure thou wo't tell me.

Petulant. If I do, will you grant me common Sense then, for the future?

Mirabell. Faith I'll do what I can for thee; and I'll pray that Heav'n may grant it thee in the mean time.

Petulant. Well, hearkee.

Fainall. Petulant and you both will find *Mirabell* as warm a Rival as a Lover.

Witwoud. Pshaw, pshaw, that she laughs at *Petulant* is plain. And for my part—But that it is almost a Fashion to admire her, I shou'd—Hearkee—To tell you a Secret, but let it go no further———Between Friends, I shall never break my Heart for her.

Fainall. How!

Witwoud. She's handsome; but she's a sort of an uncertain Woman.

Fainall. I thought you had dy'd for her.

Witwoud. Umh—No—

Fainall. She has Wit.

Witwoud. 'Tis what she will hardly allow any Body else;—Now, Demme, I shou'd hate that, if she were as handsome as *Cleopatra*. *Mirabell* is not so sure of her as he thinks for.

Fainall. Why do you think so?

Witwoud. We staid pretty late there last Night; and heard something of an Uncle to *Mirabell*, who is lately come to Town,—and is between him and the best part of his Estate; *Mirabell* and he are at some distance, as my Lady *Wishfort* has been told; and you know she hates *Mirabell*, worse than a Quaker hates a Parrot, or than a Fishmonger hates a hard Frost. Whether this Uncle has seen Mrs. *Millamant* or not, I cannot say; but there were Items of such a Treaty being in Embrio; and if it shou'd come to Life; poor *Mirabell* wou'd be in some sort unfortunately fobb'd i'faith.

Fainall. 'Tis impossible *Millamant* should hearken to it.

Witwoud. Faith, my Dear, I can't tell; she's a Woman and a kind of a Humorist.

Mirabell. And this is the Sum of what you cou'd collect last Night.

Petulant. The Quintessence. May be *Witwoud* knows more, he stay'd longer———Besides they never mind him; they say any thing before him.

Mirabell. I thought you had been the greatest Favourite.

Petulant. Ay *teste a teste*; But not in publick, because I make Remarks.

Mirabell. Do you.

Petulant. Ay, ay, pox I'm malicious, Man. Now he's soft you know, they are not in awe of him———The Fellow's well bred, he's what you call a———What-dee-call-'em. A fine Gentleman, but he's silly withal.

Humorist—Perhaps in the sense of one who indulges her own humors or fancies.

Mirabell. I thank you, I know as much as my Curiosity requires. *Fainall,* are you for the *Mall?*

Fainall. Ay, I'll take a turn before Dinner.

Witwoud. Ay, we'll all walk in the Park, the Ladies talk'd of being there.

Mirabell. I thought you were oblig'd to watch for your Brother Sir *Wilfull*'s arrival.

Witwoud. No, no, he comes to his Aunts, my Lady *Wishfort;* pox on him, I shall be troubled with him too; what shall I do with the Fool?

Petulant. Beg him for his Estate; that I may beg you afterwards; and so have but one Trouble with you both.

Witwoud. O rare *Petulant;* thou art as quick as a Fire in a frosty Morning; thou shalt to the *Mall* with us; and we'll be very severe.

Petulant. Enough, I'm in a Humour to be severe.

Mirabell. Are you? Pray then walk by your selves,——Let not us be accessary to your putting the Ladies out of Countenance, with your senseless Ribaldry; which you roar out aloud as often as they pass by you; and when you have made a handsome Woman blush, then you think you have been severe.

Petulant. What, what? Then let 'em either shew their Innocence by not understanding what they hear, or else shew their Discretion by not hearing what they would not be thought to understand.

Mirabell. But hast not thou then Sense enough to know that thou ought'st to be most asham'd thy Self, when thou hast put another out of Countenance.

Petulant. Not I, by this Hand——I always take blushing either for a Sign of Guilt, or ill Breeding.

Mirabell. I confess you ought to think so. You are in the right, that you may plead the error of your Judgment in defence of your Practice.

Where Modesty's ill Manners, 'tis but fit
That Impudence and Malice, pass for Wit.

Exeunt.

ACT II. SCENE I.

St. James's Park.

Enter Mrs. Fainall *and* Mrs. Marwood.

Mrs. Fainall. Ay, ay, dear *Marwood*, if we will be happy, we must find the means in our selves, and among our selves. Men are ever in Extreams; either doating or averse. While they are Lovers, if they have Fire and Sense, their Jealousies are insupportable: And when they cease to Love, (we ought to think at least) they loath; they look upon us with Horror and Distaste; they meet us like the Ghosts of what we were, and as such fly from us.

Mrs. Marwood. True, 'tis an unhappy Circumstance of Life, that Love shou'd ever die before us; and that the Man so often shou'd out-live the Lover. But say what you will, 'tis better to be left, than never to have been lov'd. To pass our Youth in dull Indifference, to refuse the Sweets of Life because they once must leave us; is as preposterous, as to wish to have been born Old, because we one Day must be Old. For my part, my Youth may wear and waste, but it shall never rust in my Possession.

Mrs. Fainall. Then it seems you dissemble an Aversion to Mankind, only in compliance with my Mothers Humour.

Mrs. Marwood. Certainly. To be free; I have no Taste of those insipid dry Discourses, with which our Sex of force must entertain themselves, apart from Men. We may affect Endearments to each other, profess eternal Friendships, and seem to doat like Lovers; but 'tis not in our Natures long to persevere. Love will resume his Empire in our Breasts, and every Heart, or soon or late, receive and readmit him as its lawful Tyrant.

Mrs. Fainall. Bless me, how have I been deceiv'd! Why you profess a Libertine.

Mrs. Marwood. You see my Friendship by my Freedom. Come, be as sincere, acknowledge that your Sentiments agree with mine.

Mrs. Fainall. Never.

Mrs. Marwood. You hate Mankind?

Mrs. Fainall. Heartily, Inveterately.

Mrs. Marwood. Your Husband?

Mrs. Fainall. Most transcendantly; ay, tho' I say it, meritoriously.

Mrs. Marwood. Give me your Hand upon it.

Mrs. Fainall. There.

Mrs. Marwood. I join with you; what I have said, has been to try you.

Mrs. Fainall. Is it possible? Dost thou hate those Vipers Men?

Mrs. Marwood. I have done hating 'em; and am now come to despise 'em; the next thing I have to do, is eternally to forget 'em.

Mrs. Fainall. There spoke the Spirit of an *Amazon*, a *Penthesilea.*

Mrs. Marwood. And yet I am thinking sometimes, to carry my Aversion further.

Mrs. Fainall. How?

Mrs. Marwood. Faith by Marrying; if I cou'd but find one that lov'd me very well, and would be throughly sensible of ill usage; I think I shou'd do my self the violence of undergoing the Ceremony.

Mrs. Fainall. You would not make him a Cuckold?

Mrs. Marwood. No; but I'd make him believe I did, and that's as bad.

Mrs. Fainall. Why, had not you as good do it?

Mrs. Marwood. O if he shou'd ever discover it, he wou'd then know the worst; and be out of his Pain; but I wou'd have him ever to continue upon the Rack of Fear and Jealousy.

Mrs. Fainall. Ingenious Mischief! Wou'd thou wert married to *Mirabell.*

Mrs. Marwood. Wou'd I were.

Mrs. Fainall. You change Colour.

Mrs. Marwood. Because I hate him.

Mrs. Fainall. So do I; but I can hear him nam'd. But what Reason have you to hate him in particular?

Penthesilea—Queen of the Amazons; see *Aeneid*, I, 491.

Mrs. Marwood. I never lov'd him; he is, and always was insufferably proud.

Mrs. Fainall. By the Reason you give for your Aversion, one wou'd think it dissembl'd; for you have laid a Fault to his Charge, of which his Enemies must acquit him.

Mrs. Marwood. O then it seems you are one of his favourable Enemies. Methinks you look a little pale, and now you flush again.

Mrs. Fainall. Do I? I think I am a little sick o' the suddain.

Mrs. Marwood. What ails you?

Mrs. Fainall. My Husband. Don't you see him? He turn'd short upon me unawares, and has almost overcome me.

Enter Fainall *and* Mirabell.

Mrs. Marwood. Ha, ha, ha; he comes opportunely for you.

Mrs. Fainall. For you, for he has brought *Mirabell* with him.

Fainall. My Dear.

Mrs. Fainall. My Soul.

Fainall. You don't look well to Day, Child.

Mrs. Fainall. Dee think so?

Mirabell. He is the only Man that do's, Madam.

Mrs. Fainall. The only Man that would tell me so at least; and the only Man from whom I could hear it without Mortification.

Fainall. O my Dear I am satisfy'd of your Tenderness; I know you cannot resent any thing from me; especially what is an effect of my Concern.

Mrs. Fainall. Mr. *Mirabell*; my Mother interrupted you in a pleasant Relation last Night: I wou'd fain hear it out.

Mirabell. The Persons concern'd in that Affair, have yet a tollerable Reputation———I am afraid Mr. *Fainall* will be Censorious.

Mrs. Fainall. He has a Humour more prevailing than his Curiosity, and will willingly dispence with the hearing of one scandalous Story, to avoid giving an occasion to make another by being seen to walk with his Wife. This way Mr. *Mirabell*, and I dare promise you will oblige us both.

Exeunt Mrs. Fainall *and* Mirabell.

Fainall. Excellent Creature! Well sure if I shou'd live to be rid of my Wife, I shou'd be a miserable Man.

Mrs. Marwood. Ay!

Fainall. For having only that one Hope, the accomplishment of it, of Consequence must put an end to all my hopes; and what a Wretch is he who must survive his hopes! Nothing remains when that Day comes, but to sit down and weep like *Alexander*, when he wanted other Worlds to conquer.

Mrs. Marwood. Will you not follow 'em?

Fainall. Faith, I think not.

Mrs. Marwood. Pray let us; I have a Reason.

Fainall. You are not Jealous?

Mrs. Marwood. Of whom?

Fainall. Of *Mirabell.*

Mrs. Marwood. If I am, is it inconsistent with my Love to you that I am tender of your Honour?

Fainall. You wou'd intimate then, as if there were a *fellow-feeling* between my Wife and Him.

Mrs. Marwood. I think she do's not hate him to that degree she wou'd be thought.

Fainall. But he, I fear, is too Insensible.

Mrs. Marwood. It may be you are deceiv'd.

Fainall. It may be so. I do now begin to apprehend it.

Mrs. Marwood. What?

Fainall. That I have been deceiv'd Madam, and you are false.

Mrs. Marwood. That I am false! What mean you?

Fainall. To let you know I see through all your little Arts— Come, you both love him; and both have equally dissembl'd your Aversion. Your mutual Jealousies of one another, have made you clash till you have both struck Fire. I have seen the warm Confession red'ning on your Cheeks, and sparkling from your Eyes.

Mrs. Marwood. You do me wrong.

Fainall. I do not———'Twas for my ease to oversee and wilfully neglect the gross advances made him by my Wife;

that by permitting her to be engag'd, I might continue unsuspected in my Pleasures; and take you oftner to my Arms in full Security. But cou'd you think because the nodding Husband would not wake, that e'er the watchful Lover slept!

Mrs. Marwood. And wherewithal can you reproach me?

Fainall. With Infidelity, with loving of another, with love of *Mirabell.*

Mrs. Marwood. 'Tis false. I challenge you to shew an Instance that can confirm your groundless Accusation. I hate him.

Fainall. And wherefore do you hate him? He is Insensible, and your Resentment follows his Neglect. An Instance? The Injuries you have done him are a proof: Your interposing in his Love. What cause had you to make Discoveries of his pretended Passion? To undeceive the credulous Aunt, and be the officious Obstacle of his Match with *Millamant*?

Mrs. Marwood. My Obligations to my Lady urg'd me: I had profess'd a Friendship to her; and could not see her easie Nature so abus'd by that Dissembler.

Fainall. What, was it Conscience then! profess'd a Friendship! O the pious Friendships of the Female Sex!

Mrs. Marwood. More tender, more sincere, and more enduring, than all the vain and empty Vows of Men, whether professing Love to us, or mutual Faith to one another.

Fainall. Ha, ha, ha; you are my Wife's Friend too.

Mrs. Marwood. Shame and Ingratitude! Do you reproach me? You, you upbraid me! Have I been false to her, thro' strict Fidelity to you, and sacrific'd my Friendship to keep my Love inviolate? And have you the baseness to charge me with the Guilt, unmindful of the Merit! To you it shou'd be meritorious, that I have been vicious. And do you reflect that Guilt upon me, which should lie buried in your Bosom?

Fainall. You misinterpret my Reproof. I meant but to remind you of the slight Account you once could make of strictest Ties, when set in Competition with your Love to me.

Mrs. Marwood. 'Tis false, you urg'd it with deliberate Malice—'Twas spoke in scorn, and I never will forgive it.

Fainall. Your Guilt, not your Resentment, begets your Rage. If yet you lov'd, you could forgive a Jealousy: But you are stung to find you are discover'd.

Mrs. Marwood. It shall be all discover'd. You too shall be discover'd; be sure you shall. I can but be expos'd—If I do it my self I shall prevent your Baseness.

Fainall. Why, what will you do?

Mrs. Marwood. Disclose it to your Wife; own what has past between us.

Fainall. Frenzy!

Mrs. Marwood. By all my Wrongs I'll do't—I'll publish to the World the Injuries you have done me, both in my Fame and Fortune: With both I trusted you, you Bankrupt in Honour, as indigent of Wealth.

Fainall. Your Fame I have preserv'd. Your Fortune has been bestow'd as the prodigality of your Love would have it, in Pleasures which we both have shar'd. Yet had not you been false, I had e'er this repaid it—'Tis true—Had you permitted *Mirabell* with *Millamant* to have stoll'n their Marriage, my Lady had been incens'd beyond all means of reconcilement: *Millamant* had forfeited the Moiety of her Fortune; which then wou'd have descended to my Wife;—And wherefore did I marry, but to make lawful Prize of a rich Widow's Wealth, and squander it on Love and you?

Mrs. Marwood. Deceit and frivolous Pretence.

Fainall. Death, am I not married? what's pretence? Am I not Imprison'd, Fetter'd? Have I not a Wife? Nay a Wife that was a Widow, a young Widow, a handsome Widow; and would be again a Widow, but that I have a Heart of Proof, and something of a Constitution to bustle thro' the ways of Wedlock and this World. Will you yet be reconcil'd to Truth and me?

Mrs. Marwood. Impossible. Truth and you are inconsistent ———I hate you, and shall for ever.

Fainall. For loving you?

Mrs. Marwood. I loath the name of Love after such usage; and next to the Guilt with which you wou'd asperse me, I scorn you most. Farewell.

Fainall. Nay, we must not part thus.

Mrs. Marwood. Let me go.

Fainall. Come, I'm sorry.

Mrs. Marwood. I care not———Let me go———Break my Hands, do———I'd leave 'em to get loose.

Fainall. I would not hurt you for the World. Have I no other Hold to keep you here?

Mrs. Marwood. Well, I have deserv'd it all.

Fainall. You know I love you.

Mrs. Marwood. Poor dissembling!———O that———Well, it is not yet———

Fainall. What? what is it not? What is it not yet? It is not yet too late—

Mrs. Marwood. No, it is not yet too late—I have that Comfort.

Fainall. It is to love another.

Mrs. Marwood. But not to loath, detest, abhor Mankind, my self and the whole treacherous World.

Fainall. Nay, this is Extravagance———Come I ask your Pardon———No Tears———I was to blame, I cou'd not love you and be easie in my Doubts———Pray forbear ———I believe you; I'm convinc'd I've done you wrong; and any way, every way will make amends;———I'll hate my Wife yet more, Dam her, I'll part with her, rob her of all she's worth, and we'll retire somewhere, any where to another World. I'll marry thee———Be pacify'd ———'Sdeath they come, hide your Face, your Tears— You have a Mask, wear it a Moment. This way, this way, be persuaded.

Exeunt.

Enter Mirabell *and* Mrs. Fainall.

Mrs. Fainall. They are here yet.

Mirabell. They are turning into the other Walk.

Mrs. Fainall. While I only hated my Husband, I could bear to see him; but since I have despis'd him, he's too offensive.

Mirabell. O you should Hate with Prudence.

Mrs. Fainall. Yes, for I have Lov'd with Indiscretion.

Mirabell. You shou'd have just so much disgust for your Husband, as may be sufficient to make you relish your Lover.

Mrs. Fainall. You have been the cause that I have lov'd without Bounds, and wou'd you set Limits to that Aversion, of which you have been the occasion? Why did you make me marry this Man?

Mirabell. Why do we daily commit disagreeable and dangerous Actions? To save that Idol Reputation. If the familiarities of our Loves had produc'd that Consequence, of which you were apprehensive, where could you have fix'd a Father's Name with Credit, but on a Husband? I knew *Fainall* to be a Man lavish of his Morals, an interested and professing Friend, a false and a designing Lover; yet one whose Wit and outward fair Behaviour have gain'd a Reputation with the Town, enough to make that Woman stand excus'd, who has suffer'd herself to be won by his Addresses. A better Man ought not to have been sacrific'd to the Occasion; a worse had not answer'd to the Purpose. When you are weary of him, you know your Remedy.

Mrs. Fainall. I ought to stand in some degree of Credit with you, *Mirabell.*

Mirabell. In Justice to you, I have made you privy to my whole Design, and put it in your Power to ruin or advance my Fortune.

Mrs. Fainall. Whom have you instructed to represent your pretended Uncle?

Mirabell. Waitwell, my Servant.

Mrs. Fainall. He is an humble Servant to *Foible* my Mothers Woman; and may win her to your Interest.

Mirabell. Care is taken for that———She is won and worn by this time. They were married this morning.

Mrs. Fainall. Who?

Mirabell. Waitwell and *Foible.* I wou'd not tempt my Servant to betray me by trusting him too far. If your Mother, in hopes to ruin me, shou'd consent to marry my pretended Uncle, he might like *Mosca* in the *Fox*, stand upon Terms; so I made him sure before-hand.

Mrs. Fainall. So, if my poor Mother is caught in a Contract, you will discover the Imposture betimes; and release her by producing a Certificate of her Gallants former Marriage.

humble Servant to—Courting.
Mosca in the Fox—See Ben Jonson, *Volpone*, Act. V, sc. xii.

Mirabell. Yes, upon Condition she consent to my Marriage with her Niece, and surrender the Moiety of her Fortune in her Possession.

Mrs. Fainall. She talk'd last Night of endeavouring at a Match between *Millamant* and your Uncle.

Mirabell. That was by *Foible's* Direction, and my Instruction, that she might seem to carry it more privately.

Mrs. Fainall. Well, I have an Opinion of your Success; for I believe my Lady will do any thing to get a Husband; and when she has this, which you have provided for her, I suppose she will submit to any thing to get rid of him.

Mirabell. Yes, I think the good Lady wou'd marry any Thing that resembl'd a Man, tho' 'twere no more than what a Butler cou'd pinch out of a Napkin.

Mrs. Fainall. Female Frailty! We must all come to it, if we live to be Old and feel the craving of a false Appetite when the true is decay'd.

Mirabell. An old Woman's Appetite is deprav'd like that of a Girl———'Tis the Green Sickness of a second Childhood; and like the faint Offer of a latter Spring, serves but to usher in the Fall; and withers in an affected Bloom.

Mrs. Fainall. Here's your Mistress.

Enter Mrs. Millamant, Witwoud, *and* Mincing.

Mirabell. Here she comes i'faith full sail, with her Fan spread and her Streamers out, and a shoal of Fools for Tenders ———Ha, no, I cry her Mercy.

Mrs. Fainall. I see but one poor empty Sculler; and he tows her Woman after him.

Mirabell. You seem to be unattended, Madam———You us'd to have the *Beau-mond* Throng after you; and a Flock of gay fine Perrukes hovering round you.

Witwoud. Like Moths about a Candle———I had like to have lost my Comparison for want of Breath.

Millimant. O I have deny'd my self Airs to Day. I have walk'd as fast through the Crowd—

Witwoud. As a Favourite in disgrace; and with as few Followers.

Millamant. Dear Mr. *Witwoud*, truce with your Similitudes: For I am as sick of 'em—

Witwoud. As a Phisician of a good Air———I cannot help it Madam, tho' 'tis against my self.

Millamant. Yet again! *Mincing*, stand between me and his Wit.

Witwoud. Do Mrs. *Mincing*, like a Skreen before a great Fire. I confess I do blaze to Day, I am too bright.

Mrs. Fainall. But dear *Millamant*, why were you so long?

Millamant. Long! Lord, have I not made violent haste? I have ask'd every living Thing I met for you; I have enquir'd after you, as after a new Fashion.

Witwoud. Madam, truce with your Similitudes———No, you met her Husband and did not ask him for her.

Mirabell. By your leave *Witwoud*, that were like enquiring after an old Fashion, to ask a Husband for his Wife.

Witwoud. Hum, a hit, a hit, a palpable hit, I confess it.

Mrs. Fainall. You were dress'd before I came abroad.

Millamant. Ay, that's true———O but then I had——— *Mincing* what had I? Why was I so long?

Mincing. O Mem, your Laship staid to peruse a Pecquet of Letters.

Millamant. O ay, Letters———I had Letters———I am persecuted with Letters—I hate Letters—No Body knows how to write Letters; and yet one has 'em, one does not know why———They serve one to pin up one's Hair.

Witwoud. Is that the way? Pray Madam, do you pin up your Hair with all your Letters? I find I must keep Copies.

Millamant. Only with those in Verse, Mr. *Witwoud*. I never pin up my Hair with Prose. I fancy ones Hair wou'd not curl if it were pinn'd up with Prose. I think I try'd once *Mincing*.

Mincing. O Mem, I shall never forget it.

Millamant. Ay, poor *Mincing* tift and tift all the morning.

Mincing. 'Till I had the Cremp in my Fingers I'll vow Mem. And all to no purpose. But when your Laship pins it up

tift—Dress, arrange.

with Poetry, it sits so pleasant the next Day as any Thing, and is so pure and so crips.

Witwoud. Indeed, so crips?

Mincing. You're such a Critick, Mr. *Witwoud.*

Millimant. Mirabell, Did not you take Exceptions last Night? O ay, and went away———Now I think on't I'm angry ———No, now I think on't I'm pleas'd———For I believe I gave you some Pain.

Mirabell. Do's that please you?

Millamant. Infinitely; I love to give Pain.

Mirabell. You wou'd affect a Cruelty which is not in your Nature; your true Vanity is in the power of pleasing.

Millamant. O I ask your Pardon for that———One's Cruelty is one's Power, and when one parts with one's Cruelty, one parts with one's Power; and when one has parted with that, I fancy one's Old and Ugly.

Mirabell. Ay, ay, suffer your Cruelty to ruin the object of your Power, to destroy your Lover———And then how vain how lost a Thing you'll be! Nay, 'tis true: You are no longer handsome when you've lost your Lover; your Beauty dies upon the Instant: For Beauty is the Lover's Gift; 'tis he bestows your Charms—Your Glass is all a Cheat. The Ugly and the Old, whom the Looking-glass mortifies, yet after Commendation can be flatter'd by it, and discover Beauties in it: For that reflects our Praises, rather than your Face.

Millamant. O the Vanity of these Men! *Fainall,* dee hear him? If they did not commend us, we were not handsome! Now you must know they could not commend one, if one was not handsome. Beauty the Lover's Gift——— Lord, what is a Lover, that it can give? Why one makes Lovers as fast as one pleases, and they live as long as one pleases, and they die as soon as one pleases: And then if one pleases, one makes more.

Witwoud. Very pretty. Why you make no more of making of Lovers, Madam, than of making so many Card-matches.

Millamant. One no more owes one's Beauty to a Lover, than one's Wit to an Eccho: They can but reflect what we look and say; vain empty Things if we are silent or unseen, and want a being.

Mirabell. Yet to those two vain empty Things, you owe two the greatest Pleasures of your Life.

Millamant. How so?

Mirabell. To your Lover you owe the pleasure of hearing your selves prais'd; and to an Eccho the pleasure of hearing your selves talk.

Witwoud. But I know a Lady that loves talking so incessantly, she won't give an Eccho fair play; she has that everlasting Rotation of Tongue, that an Eccho must wait till she dies, before it can catch her last Words.

Millamant. O Fiction; *Fainall*, let us leave these Men.

Mirabell (*aside to* Mrs. Fainall). Draw off *Witwoud.*

Mrs. Fainall. Immediately; I have a Word or two for Mr. *Witwoud.*

Mirabell. I wou'd beg a little private Audience too—

Exit Witwoud *and* Mrs. Fainall.

You had the Tyranny to deny me last Night; tho' you knew I came to impart a Secret to you, that concern'd my Love.

Millamant. You saw I was engag'd.

Mirabell. Unkind. You had the leisure to entertain a Herd of Fools; Things who visit you from their excessive Idleness; bestowing on your easiness that time, which is the incumbrance of their Lives. How can you find delight in such Society? It is impossible they should admire you, they are not capable: Or if they were, it shou'd be to you as a Mortification; for sure to please a Fool is some degree of Folly.

Millamant. I please my self———Besides sometimes to converse with Fools, is for my Health.

Mirabell. Your Health! Is there a worse Disease than the Conversation of Fools?

Millamant. Yes, the Vapours; Fools are Physicks for it, next to *Assa-fœtida.*

Mirabell. You are not in a Course of Fools?

Assa-fœtida—A kind of smelling salts.

Millamant. Mirabell, If you persist in this offensive Freedom ——You'll displease me——I think I must resolve after all, not to have you——We shan't agree.

Mirabell. Not in our Physick it may be.

Millamant. And yet our Distemper in all likelihood will be the same; for we shall be sick of one another. I shan't endure to be reprimanded, nor instructed; 'tis so dull to act always by Advice, and so tedious to be told of ones Faults——I can't bear it. Well, I won't have you *Mirabell* ——I'm resolv'd——I think——You may go—— Ha, ha, ha. What wou'd you give, that you cou'd help loving me?

Mirabell. I would give something that you did not know, I cou'd not help it.

Millamant. Come, don't look grave then. Well, what do you say to me?

Mirabell. I say that a Man may as soon make a Friend by his Wit, or a Fortune by his Honesty, as win a Woman with plain Dealing and Sincerity.

Millamant. Sententious *Mirabell*! Prithee don't look with that violent and inflexible wise Face, like *Solomon* at the dividing of the Child in an old Tapestry-hanging.

Mirabell. You are merry, Madam, but I wou'd perswade you for one Moment to be serious.

Millamant. What, with that Face? No, if you keep your Countenance, 'tis impossible I shou'd hold mine. Well, after all, there is something very moving in a love-sick Face. Ha, ha, ha——Well I won't laugh, don't be peevish——Heigho! Now I'll be melancholly, as melancholly as a Watch-light. Well *Mirabell*, If ever you will win me woe me now——Nay, if you are so tedious, fare you well;——I see they are walking away.

Mirabell. Can you not find in the variety of your Disposition one Moment—

Millamant. To hear you tell me that *Foible's* married, and your Plot like to speed——No.

Mirabell. But how you came to know it—

Solomon . . . in an old Tapestry-hanging—A story often illustrated: see I Kings 3.

Millamant. Unless by the help of the Devil you can't imagine; unless she shou'd tell me her self. Which of the two it may have been, I will leave you to consider; and when you have done thinking of that; think of me.

Exit.

Mirabell. I have something more———Gone———Think of you! To think of a Whirlwind, tho' 'twere in a Whirlwind, were a Case of more steady Contemplation; a very tranquility of Mind and Mansion. A Fellow that lives in a Windmill, has not a more whimsical Dwelling than the Heart of a Man that is lodg'd in a Woman. There is no Point of the Compass to which they cannot turn, and by which they are not turn'd; and by one as well as another; for Motion not Method is their Occupation. To know this, and yet continue to be in Love, is to be made wise from the Dictates of Reason, and yet persevere to play the Fool by the force of Instinct———O here come my pair of Turtles —What, billing so sweetly! Is not *Valentine's* Day over with you yet?

Enter Waitwell *and* Foible.

Sirrah, *Waitwell*, why sure you think you were married for your own Recreation, and not for my Conveniency.

Waitwell. Your Pardon, Sir. With Submission, we have indeed been solacing in lawful Delights; but still with an Eye to Business, Sir. I have instructed her as well as I cou'd. If she can take your Directions as readily as my Instructions, Sir, your Affairs are in a prosperous way.

Mirabell. Give you Joy, Mrs. *Foible*.

Foible. O las Sir, I'm so asham'd———I'm afraid my Lady has been in a thousand Inquietudes for me. But I protest, Sir, I made as much haste as I could.

Waitwell. That she did indeed, Sir. It was my Fault that she did not make more.

Mirabell. That I believe.

Foible. But I told my Lady as you instructed me, Sir. That I had a prospect of seeing Sir *Rowland* your Uncle; and that I wou'd put her Ladyship's Picture in my Pocket to shew him; which I'll be sure to say has made him so enamour'd of her Beauty, that he burns with Impatience to lie at her Ladyship's Feet and worship the Original.

Mirabell. Excellent *Foible*! Matrimony has made you eloquent in Love.

Waitwell. I think she has profited, Sir. I think so.

Foible. You have seen Madam *Millamant*, Sir?

Mirabell. Yes.

Foible. I told her Sir, because I did not know that you might find an Opportunity; she had so much Company last Night.

Mirabell. Your Diligence will merit more———In the mean time—

Gives Mony.

Foible. O dear Sir, your humble Servant.

Waitwell. Spouse.

Mirabell. Stand off Sir, not a Penny———Go on and prosper, *Foible*———The Lease shall be made good and the Farm stock'd, if we succeed.

Foible. I don't question your Generosity, Sir: And you need not doubt of Success. If you have no more Commands Sir, I'll be gone; I'm sure my Lady is at her Toilet, and can't dress till I come———(*Looking out.*) O Dear, I'm sure that was Mrs. *Marwood* that went by in a Mask; if she has seen me with you I'm sure she'll tell my Lady. I'll make haste home and prevent her. Your Servant Sir. B'w'y *Waitwell.*

Exit Foible.

Waitwell. Sir *Rowland* if you please. The Jade's so pert upon her Preferment she forgets her self.

Mirabell. Come Sir, will you endeavour to forget your self ———And transform into Sir *Rowland.*

Waitwell. Why Sir; it will be impossible I shou'd remember my self———Married, Knighted and attended all in one Day! 'Tis enough to make any Man forget himself. The Difficulty will be how to recover my Acquaintance and Familiarity with my former self; and fall from my Transformation to a Reformation into *Waitwell.* Nay, I shan't be quite the same *Waitwell* neither—For now I remember me, I am married, and can't be my own Man again.

Ay there's the Grief; that's the sad change of Life;
To lose my Title, and yet keep my Wife.

Exeunt.

ACT III. SCENE I.

A Room in Lady Wishfort's *House.*

Lady Wishfort *at her Toilet,* Peg *waiting.*

Lady Wishfort. Merciful, no News of *Foible* yet?

Peg. No, Madam.

Lady Wishfort. I have no more patience—If I have not fretted my self till I am pale again, there's no Veracity in me. Fetch me the Red—The Red, do you hear, Sweet-heart? An errant Ash colour, as I'm a Person. Look you how this Wench stirs! Why dost thou not fetch me a little Red? Did'st thou not hear me, Mopus?

Peg. The red *Ratifia* does your Ladyship mean, or the Cherry Brandy?

Lady Wishfort. Ratifia, Fool? No Fool. Not the *Ratifia* Fool—Grant me patience! I mean the *Spanish* Paper Idiot, Complexion Darling. Paint, Paint, Paint, dost thou understand that, Changeling, dangling thy Hands like Bobbins before thee. Why dost thou not stir Puppet? thou wooden Thing upon Wires.

Peg. Lord, Madam, your Ladyship is so impatient—I cannot come at the Paint, Madam; Mrs. *Foible* has lock'd it up, and carry'd the Key with her.

Lady Wishfort. A Pox take you both—Fetch me the Cherry-Brandy then—(*Exit* Peg). I'm as pale and as faint, I look like Mrs. Qualmsick the Curate's Wife, that's always breeding—Wench, come, come, Wench, what art thou doing, Sipping? Tasting? Save thee, dost thou not know the Bottle?

Enter Peg *with a Bottle and* China-*cup.*

Peg. Madam, I was looking for a Cup.

Lady Wishfort. A Cup, save thee, and what a Cup hast thou brought! Dost thou take me for a *Fairy,* to drink out of an *Acorn*? Why didst thou not bring thy Thimble? Hast thou ne'er a Brass-Thimble clinking in thy Pocket with a bit of Nutmeg? I warrant thee. Come, fill, fill.—So—again See who that is———(*One knocks.*) Set down the Bottle

Mopus—Current slang for a dullard.
Spanish Paper—For applying rouge, in which it was saturated.

first. Here, here, under the Table———What wou'dst thou go with the Bottle in thy Hand like a Tapster. As I'm a Person, this Wench has liv'd in an Inn upon the Road, before she came to me, like *Maritornes* the *Asturian* in *Don Quixote*. No *Foible* yet?

Peg. No Madam, Mrs. *Marwood.*

Lady Wishfort. O *Marwood*, let her come in. Come in good *Marwood.*

Enter Mrs. Marwood.

Mrs. Marwood. I'm surpriz'd to find your Ladyship in *dishabilie* at this time of day.

Lady Wishfort. Foible's a lost Thing; has been abroad since Morning, and never heard of since.

Mrs. Marwood. I saw her but now, as I came mask'd through the Park, in Conference with *Mirabell.*

Lady Wishfort. With *Mirabell*! You call my Blood into my Face, with mentioning that Traytor. She durst not have the Confidence. I sent her to Negotiate an Affair, in which if I'm detected I'm undone. If that wheadling Villain has wrought upon *Foible* to detect me, I'm ruin'd. Oh my dear Friend, I'm a Wretch of Wretches if I'm detected.

Mrs. Marwood. O Madam, you cannot suspect Mrs. *Foible's* Integrity.

Lady Wishfort. O, he carries Poyson in his Tongue that wou'd corrupt Integrity it self. If she has given him an Opportunity, she has as good as put her Integrity into his Hands. Ah dear *Marwood*, what's Integrity to an Opportunity? ———Hark! I hear her———Go you Thing and send her in. (*Exit* Peg.) Dear Friend retire into my Closet, that I may examine her with more freedom———You'll pardon me dear Friend, I can make bold with you———There are Books over the Chimney—*Quarles* and *Pryn*, and the *Short View of the Stage*, with *Bunyan*'s Works to entertain you.

Exit Marwood.

Maritornes—The innkeeper's daughter, who takes part in the scene where Don Quixote is made a knight. Lady Wishfort would more likely remember it from D'Urfey's popular play. Pt. I, Act II, sc. i.

Short View of the Stage—A contemptuous reference to Collier's book, in which he had attacked Congreve for contributing to the "Immorality and Profaneness of the English Stage" by putting it in fit company with the most popular books of Puritan piety.

Enter Foible.

O *Foible*, where hast thou been? What hast thou been doing?

Foible. Madam, I have seen the Party.

Lady Wishfort. But what hast thou done?

Foible. Nay, 'tis your Ladyship has done, and are to do; I have only promis'd. But a Man so enamour'd———So transported! Well, here it is, all that is left; all that is not kiss'd away—Well, if worshipping of Pictures be a Sin ———Poor Sir *Rowland*, I say.

Lady Wishfort. The Miniature has been counted like———But hast thou not betray'd me, *Foible*? Hast thou not detected me to that faithless *Mirabell*?———What had'st thou to do with him in the Park? Answer me, has he got nothing out of thee?

Foible (*aside*). So, the Devil has been before hand with me, what shall I say?———Alas, Madam, cou'd I help it, if I met that confident Thing? Was I in Fault? If you had heard how he us'd me, and all upon your Ladyship's Account, I'm sure you wou'd not suspect my Fidelity. Nay, if that had been the worst I cou'd have born: But he had a Fling at your Ladyship too; and then I could not hold; But i'faith I gave him his own.

Lady Wishfort. Me? What did the filthy Fellow say?

Foible. O Madam; 'tis a shame to say what he said——— With his Taunts and his Fleers, tossing up his Nose. Humh (says he) what you are a hatching some Plot (says he) you are so early abroad, or Catering (says he) ferreting for some disbanded Officer I warrant———Half Pay is but thin Subsistance (says he)———Well, what Pension does your Lady propose? Let me see (says he) what she must come down pretty deep now, she's super-annuated (says he) and—

Lady Wishfort. Ods my Life, I'll have him, I'll have him murder'd. I'll have him poyson'd. Where does he eat? I'll marry a Drawer to have him poyson'd in his Wine. I'll send for *Robin* from *Lockets*———Immediately.

Foible. Poyson him? Poysoning's too good for him. Starve him Madam, starve him, marry Sir *Rowland* and get him

Lockets—The famous eating house at Charing Cross.

disinherited. O you would bless your self, to hear what he said.

Lady Wishfort. A Villain, superannuated!

Foible. Humh (says he) I hear you are laying Designs against me too (says he), and Mrs. *Millamant* is to marry my Uncle; (he does not suspect a Word of your Ladyship;) but (says he) I'll fit you for that, I warrant you (says he) I'll hamper you for that (says he) you and your old Frippery too (says he) I'll handle you—

Lady Wishfort. Audacious Villain! handle me, wou'd he durst ———Frippery? old Frippery! Was there ever such a foul-mouth'd Fellow? I'll be married to Morrow, I'll be contracted to Night.

Foible. The sooner the better, Madam.

Lady Wishfort. Will Sir *Rowland* be here, say'st thou? when *Foible*?

Foible. Incontinently, Madam. No new Sheriff's Wife expects the return of her Husband after Knighthood, with that Impatience in which Sir *Rowland* burns for the dear hour of kissing your Ladyship's Hands after Dinner.

Lady Wishfort. Frippery? Superannuated Frippery! I'll Frippery the Villain; I'll reduce him to Frippery and Rags. A Tatterdemallion———I hope to see him hung with Tatters, like a long Lane Pent-house, or a Gibbet-thief. A slander-mouth'd Railer: I warrant the Spendthrift Prodigal's in Debt as much as the Million Lottery, or the whole Court upon a Birth day. I'll spoil his Credit with his Taylor. Yes, he shall have my Niece with her Fortune, he shall.

Foible. He! I hope to see him lodge in *Ludgate* first, and Angle into *Black Friers* for Brass Farthings, with an old Mitten.

Lady Wishfort. Ay dear *Foible*; thank thee for that dear *Foible*. He has put me out of all patience. I shall never recompose my Features, to receive Sir *Rowland* with any Oeconomy of Face. This Wretch has fretted me that I am absolutely decay'd. Look *Foible*.

Frippery—Worn out finery.

long Lane Pent-house—A stall under an overhanging roof where old clothes were sold. See Tom Brown, *Amusements serious and Comical* (1700), p. 37, the Impudent *Ragsellers* of *Long-Lane*.

Million Lottery—A government lottery of 1694.

Ludgate—The Fleet prison for debtors; Black Friars ran down from Ludgate to the river.

Foible. Your Ladyship has frown'd a little too rashly, indeed Madam. There are some Cracks discernable in the white Vernish.

Lady Wishfort. Let me see the Glass———Cracks, say'st thou? Why I am arrantly flea'd—I look like an old peel'd Wall. Thou must repair me *Foible*, before Sir *Rowland* comes; or I shall never keep up to my Picture.

Foible. I warrant you, Madam; a little Art once made your Picture like you; and now a little of the same Art, must make you like your Picture. Your Picture must sit for you, Madam.

Lady Wishfort. But art thou sure Sir *Rowland* will not fail to come? Or will a not fail when he does come? Will he be Importunate *Foible*, and push? For if he shou'd not be Importunate———I shall never break Decorums———I shall die with Confusion, if I am forc'd to advance———Oh no, I can never advance———I shall swoon if he shou'd expect advances. No, I hope Sir *Rowland* is better bred, than to put a Lady to the necessity of breaking her Forms. I won't be too coy neither.———I won't give him despair ———But a little Disdain is not amiss; a little Scorn is alluring.

Foible. A little Scorn becomes your Ladyship.

Lady Wishfort. Yes, but Tenderness becomes me best———A sort of a dyingness———You see that Picture has a sort of a———Ha *Foible*? A swimminess in the Eyes—Yes, I'll look so—My Niece affects it; but she wants Features. Is Sir *Rowland* handsome? Let my Toilet be remov'd—I'll dress above. I'll receive Sir *Rowland* here. Is he handsome? Don't answer me. I won't know: I'll be surpriz'd. I'll be taken by Surprize.

Foible. By Storm, Madam. Sir *Rowland's* a brisk Man.

Lady Wishfort. Is he! O then he'll Importune, if he's a brisk Man. I shall save Decorums if Sir *Rowland* importunes. I have a mortal Terror at the apprehension of offending against Decorums. Nothing but Importunity can surmount Decorums. O I'm glad he's a brisk Man. Let my Things be remov'd, good *Foible*.

Exit.

Enter Mrs. Fainall.

Mrs. Fainall. O *Foible*, I have been in a Fright, least I shou'd come too late. That Devil *Marwood* saw you in the Park with *Mirabell*, and I'm afraid will discover it to my Lady.

Foible. Discover what, Madam?

Mrs. Fainall. Nay, nay, put not on that strange Face. I am privy to the whole Design, and know that *Waitwell*, to whom thou wert this morning Married, is to personate *Mirabell's* Uncle, and as such winning my Lady, to involve her in those Difficulties, from which *Mirabell* only must release her, by his making his Conditions to have my Cousin and her Fortune left to her own disposal.

Foible. O dear Madam, I beg your Pardon. It was not my Confidence in your Ladyship that was deficient; but I thought the former good Correspondence between your Ladyship and Mr. *Mirabell*, might have hinder'd his communicating this Secret.

Mrs. Fainall. Dear *Foible* forget that.

Foible. O dear Madam, Mr. *Mirabell* is such a sweet winning Gentleman———But your Ladyship is the Pattern of Generosity.———Sweet Lady, to be so good! Mr. *Mirabell* cannot chuse but be grateful. I find your Ladyship has his Heart still. Now, Madam, I can safely tell your Ladyship our success, Mrs. *Marwood* had told my Lady; but I warrant I manag'd my self. I turn'd it all for the better. I told my Lady that Mr. *Mirabell* rail'd at her. I laid horrid Things to his charge, I'll vow; and my Lady is so incens'd, that she'll be contracted to Sir *Rowland* to Night, she says;—I warrant I work'd her up, that he may have her for asking for, as they say of a *Welch* Maiden-head.

Mrs. Fainall. O rare *Foible*!

Foible. Madam, I beg your Ladyship to acquaint Mr. *Mirabell* of his success. I wou'd be seen as little as possible to speak to him,———besides, I believe Madam *Marwood* watches me.———She has a Month's mind; but I know Mr. *Mirabell* can't abide her.———*(Enter Footman.) John*———remove my Lady's Toilet, Madam your Servant. My Lady is so impatient, I fear she'll come for me, if I stay.

Mrs. Fainall. I'll go with you up the back Stairs, lest I shou'd meet her.

Exeunt.

Month's mind—A strong inclination.

Enter Mrs. Marwood.

Mrs. Marwood. Indeed Mrs. Engine, is it thus with you? Are you become a go-between of this Importance? Yes, I shall watch you. Why this Wench is the *Pass-par-tout*, a very Master-Key to every Bodies strong Box. My Friend *Fainall*, have you carried it so swimmingly? I thought there was something in it; but it seems it's over with you. Your loathing is not from a want of Appetite then, but from a Surfeit. Else you could never be so cool to fall from a Principal to be an Assistant; to procure for him! A Pattern of Generosity, that I confess. Well, Mr. *Fainall*, you have met with your Match.———O Man, Man! Woman, Woman! The Devil's an Ass: If I were a Painter, I wou'd draw him like an Idiot, a Driveler, with a Bib and Bells. Man shou'd have his Head and Horns, and Woman the rest of him. Poor simple Fiend! Madam *Marwood* has a Months Mind, but he can't abide her———'Twere better for him you had not been his Confessor in that Affair; without you cou'd have kept his Counsel closer. I shall not prove another Pattern of Generosity; and stalk for him, till he takes his Stand to aim at a Fortune, he has not oblig'd me to that, with those Excesses of himself; and now I'll have none of him. Here comes the good Lady, panting ripe; with a Heart full of Hope, and a Head full of Care, like any Chymist upon the Day of Projection.

Enter Lady Wishfort.

Lady Wishfort. O dear *Marwood* what shall I say, for this rude forgetfulness———But my dear Friend is all Goodness.

Mrs. Marwood. No Apologies, dear Madam. I have been very well entertained.

Lady Wishfort. As I'm a Person I am in a very Chaos to think I shou'd so forget my self———But I have such an Olio of Affairs really I know not what to do—(*Calls*)—*Foible*—I expect my Nephew Sir *Wilfull* every moment too—Why *Foible*—He means to Travel for Improvement.

Mrs. Marwood. Methinks Sir *Wilfull* should rather think of Marrying than Travelling at his Years. I hear he is turn'd of Forty.

Lady Wishfort. O he's in less Danger of being spoil'd by his Travels———I am against my Nephews marrying too

Day of Projection—When the alchemist finally transmutes his base metal into gold.

young. It will be time enough when he comes back, and has acquir'd Discretion to choose for himself.

Mrs. Marwood. Methinks Mrs. *Millamant* and he wou'd make a very fit Match. He may Travel afterwards. 'Tis a Thing very usual with young Gentlemen.

Lady Wishfort. I promise you I have thought on't——And since 'tis your Judgment, I'll think on't again. I assure you I will; I value your Judgment extreamly. On my Word I'll propose it.

Enter Foible.

Come, come *Foible*——I had forgot my Nephew will be here before Dinner——I must make haste.

Foible. Mr. *Witwoud* and Mr. *Petulant*, are come to Dine with your Ladyship.

Lady Wishford. O Dear, I can't appear till I'm dress'd. Dear *Marwood* shall I be free with you again, and beg you to entertain 'em. I'll make all imaginable haste. Dear Friend excuse me.

Exit Lady *and* Foible.

Enter Mrs. Millamant *and* Mincing.

Millamant. Sure never any thing was so Unbred as that odious Man——*Marwood*, your Servant.

Mrs. Marwood. You have a Colour, what's the matter?

Millamant. That horrid Fellow *Petulant*, has provok'd me into a Flame—I have broke my Fan—*Mincing*, lend me yours; —Is not all the Powder out of my Hair?

Mrs. Marwood. No, What has he done?

Millamant. Nay, he has done nothing; he has only talk'd—Nay, he has said nothing neither; but he has contradicted every Thing that has been said. For my part, I thought *Witwoud* and he wou'd have quarrell'd.

Mincing. I vow Mem, I thought once they wou'd have fit.

Millamant. Well, 'tis a lamentable thing I'll swear, that one has not the liberty of choosing one's Acquaintance, as one does one's Cloaths.

Mrs. Marwood. If we had the liberty, we shou'd be as weary of one Set of Acquaintance, tho' never so good, as we are of one Suit, tho' never so fine. A Fool and a *Doily* Stuff wou'd now and then find Days of Grace, and be worn for variety.

Millamant. I could consent to wear 'em, if they wou'd wear alike; but Fools never wear out—they are such *Drap-du-berry* Things! without one cou'd give 'em to one's Chamber-maid after a day or two.

Mrs. Marwood. 'Twere better so indeed. Or what think you of the Play-house? A fine gay glossy Fool, shou'd be given there, like a new masking Habit, after the Masquerade is over, and we have done with the Disguise. For a Fool's Visit is always a Disguise; and never admitted by a Woman of Wit, but to blind her Affair with a Lover of Sense. If you wou'd but appear bare fac'd now, and own *Mirabell*; you might as easily put off *Petulant* and *Witwoud*, as your Hood and Scarf. And indeed 'tis time, for the Town has found it: The secret is grown too big for the Pretence: 'Tis like Mrs. *Primly's* great Belly; she may lace it down before, but it burnishes on her Hips. Indeed, *Millamant*, you can no more conceal it, than my Lady *Strammel* can her Face, that goodly Face, which in defiance of her Rhenish-wine Tea, will not be comprehended in a Mask.

Millamant. I'll take my Death, *Marwood*, you are more Censorious, than a decay'd Beauty, or a discarded Tost; *Mincing*, tell the Men they may come up. My Aunt is not dressing; their Folly is less provoking than your Mallice, the Town has found it. (*Exit* Mincing.) What has it found? That *Mirabell* loves me is no more a Secret, than it is a Secret that you discover'd it to my Aunt, or than the Reason why you discover'd it is a Secret.

Mrs. Marwood. You are nettl'd.

Millamant. You're mistaken. Ridiculous!

Mrs. Marwood. Indeed my Dear, you'll tear another Fan, if you don't mitigate those violent Airs.

Millamant. O silly! Ha, ha, ha. I cou'd laugh immoderately. Poor *Mirabell*! his Constancy to me has quite destroy'd his Complaisance for all the World beside. I swear, I never enjoin'd it him, to be so coy———If I had the Vanity to think he wou'd obey me; I wou'd command him to shew

Doily Stuff—A cheap fabric, recently introduced.
Drap-du-berry—Heavy wool cloth.
Rhenish-wine Tea—Perhaps thin tea, the color of hock.

more Gallantry———'Tis hardly well bred to be so particular on one Hand, and so insensible on the other. But I despair to prevail, and so let him follow his own way. Ha, ha, ha. Pardon me, dear Creature, I must laugh, Ha, ha, ha; tho' I grant you 'tis a little barbarous, Ha, ha, ha.

Mrs. Marwood. What pity 'tis, so much fine Raillery, and deliver'd with so significant Gesture, shou'd be so unhappily directed to miscarry.

Millamant. Hæ? Dear Creature I ask your Pardon———I swear I did not mind you.

Mrs. Marwood. Mr. *Mirabell* and you both, may think it a Thing impossible, when I shall tell him, by telling you—

Millamant. O Dear, what? for it is the same thing, if I hear it—Ha, ha, ha.

Mrs. Marwood. That I detest him, hate him, Madam.

Millamant. O Madam, why so do I—And yet the Creature loves me, Ha, ha, ha. How can one forbear laughing to think of it———I am a Sybil if I am not amaz'd to think what he can see in me. I'll take my Death, I think you are handsomer———And within a Year or two as young. ———If you cou'd but stay for me, I shou'd overtake you ———But that cannot be———Well, that Thought makes me Melancholly———Now I'll be sad.

Mrs. Marwood. Your merry Note may be chang'd sooner than you think.

Millamant. Dee say so? Then I'm resolv'd I'll have a Song to keep up my Spirits.

Enter Mincing.

Mincing. The Gentlemen stay but to Comb, Madam; and will wait on you.

Millamant. Desire Mrs.———that is in the next Room to sing the Song, I wou'd have learnt Yesterday. You shall hear it Madam———Not that there's any great matter in it———But 'tis agreeable to my Humour.

Set by Mr. John Eccles, *and Sung by* Mrs. Hodgson.

John Eccles—Who is said to have written also the incidental music for this play.

SONG.

I.

Love's but the frailty of the Mind,
When 'tis not with Ambition join'd;
A sickly Flame, which if not fed expires;
And feeding, wasts in Self-consuming Fires.

II.

'Tis not to wound a wanton Boy
Or am'rous Youth, that gives the Joy;
But 'tis the Glory to have pierc'd a Swain,
For whom inferiour Beauties sigh'd in vain.

III.

Then I alone the Conquest prize
When I insult a Rival's Eyes:
If there's Delight in Love, 'tis when I see
That Heart which others bleed for, bleed for me.

Enter Petulant *and* Witwoud.

Millamant. Is your Animosity compos'd, Gentlemen?

Witwoud. Raillery, Raillery, Madam, we have no Animosity—We hit off a little Wit now and then, but no Animosity———The falling out of Wits is like the falling out of Lovers———We agree in the main, like Treble and Base. Ha, *Petulant*!

Petulant. Ay in the main———But when I have a Humour to contradict.

Witwoud. Ay, when he has a Humour to contradict, then I contradict too. What, I know my Cue. Then we contradict one another like two Battle-dores: For Contradictions beget one another like *Jews*.

Petulant. If he says Black's Black———If I have a Humour to say 'tis Blue———Let that pass———All's one for that. If I have a Humour to prove it, it must be granted.

Witwoud. Not positively must—But it may—It may.

Petulant. Yes, it positively must, upon Proof positive.

Witwoud. Ay, upon Proof positive it must; but upon Proof presumptive it only may. That's a Logical Distinction now, Madam.

Mrs. Marwood. I perceive your Debates are of Importance and very learnedly handl'd.

Petulant. Importance is one Thing, and Learning's another; but a Debate's a Debate, that I assert.

Witwoud. Petulant's an Enemy to Learning; he relies altogether on his Parts.

Petulant. No, I'm no Enemy to Learning; it hurts not me.

Mrs. Marwood. That's a Sign indeed its no Enemy to you.

Petulant. No, no, it's no Enemy to any Body, but them that have it.

Millamant. Well, an illiterate Man's my Aversion. I wonder at the Impudence of any Illiterate Man, to offer to make Love.

Witwoud. That I confess I wonder at too.

Millamant. Ah! to marry an Ignorant! that can hardly Read or Write.

Petulant. Why shou'd a Man be ever the further from being married tho' he can't Read, any more than he is from being Hang'd. The Ordinary's paid for setting the *Psalm*, and the Parish-Priest for reading the Ceremony. And for the rest which is to follow in both Cases, a Man may do it without Book———So all's one for that.

Millamant. Dee hear the Creature? Lord, here's Company, I'll be gone.

Exeunt Millamant *and* Mincing.

Witwoud. In the Name of *Bartlemew* and his Fair, what have we here?

Mrs. Marwood. 'Tis your Brother, I fancy. Don't you know him?

Witwoud. Not I———Yes, I think it is he———I've almost forgot him; I have not seen him since the Revolution.

Enter Sir Wilfull Witwoud *in a Country Riding Habit, and Servant to* Lady Wishfort.

The Ordinary—The Newgate chaplain, who accompanied prisoners to execution.

Bartlemew—The Smithfield Fair at the Feast of St. Bartholomew, which was full of strange sights.

the Revolution—Of 1688, twelve years before.

Servant. Sir, my Lady's dressing. Here's Company; if you please to walk in, in the mean time.

Sir Wilfull. Dressing! What it's but Morning here I warrant with you in *London*; we shou'd count it towards Afternoon in our Parts, down in *Shropshire*———Why then belike my Aunt han't din'd yet———Ha, Friend?

Servant. Your Aunt, Sir?

Sir Wilfull. My Aunt Sir, yes my Aunt Sir, and your Lady Sir; your Lady is my Aunt, Sir———Why, what do'st thou not know me, Friend? Why then send Somebody here that does. How long hast thou liv'd with thy Lady, Fellow, ha!

Servant. A Week, Sir; longer than any Body in the House, except my Lady's Woman.

Sir Wilfull. Why then belike thou dost not know thy Lady, if thou see'st her, ha Friend?

Servant. Why truly Sir, I cannot safely swear to her Face in a Morning, before she is dress'd. 'Tis like I may give a shrew'd guess at her by this time.

Sir Wilfull. Well prithee try what thou can'st do; if thou can'st not guess, enquire her out, do'st hear Fellow? And tell her, her Nephew, *Sir Wilfull Witwoud* is in the House.

Servant. I shall, Sir.

Sir Wilfull. Hold ye, hear me Friend; a Word with you in your Ear, prithee who are these Gallants?

Servant. Really Sir, I can't tell; here come so many here, 'tis hard to know 'em all.

Exit Servant.

Sir Wilfull. Oons this Fellow knows less than a Starling; I don't think a' knows his own Name.

Mrs. Marwood. Mr. *Witwoud*, your Brother is not behind Hand in forgetfulness———I fancy he has forgot you too.

Witwoud. I hope so———The Devil take him that remembers first, I say.

Sir Wilfull. Save you Gentlemen and Lady.

Mrs. Marwood. For shame Mr. *Witwoud*; why won't you speak to him?———And you, Sir.

Witwoud. Petulant speak.

Petulant. And you, Sir.

Sir Wilfull. No Offence, I hope.

Salutes Mrs. Marwood.

Mrs. Marwood. No sure, Sir.

Witwoud. This is a vile Dog, I see that already. No Offence! Ha, ha, ha, to him; to him *Petulant*, smoke him.

Petulant. It seems as if you had come a Journey, Sir; hem, hem.

Surveying him round.

Sir Wilfull. Very likely, Sir, that it may seem so.

Petulant. No Offence, I hope, Sir.

Witwoud. Smoke the Boots, the Boots; *Petulant*, the Boots; Ha, ha, ha.

Sir Wilfull. May be not, Sir; thereafter as 'tis meant, Sir.

Petulant. Sir, I presume upon the Information of your Boots.

Sir Wilfull. Why, 'tis like you may, Sir: If you are not satisfy'd with the Information of my Boots, Sir, if you will step to the Stable, you may enquire further of my Horse, Sir.

Petulant. Your Horse, Sir! Your Horse is an Ass, Sir!

Sir Wilfull. Do you speak by way of Offence, Sir?

Mrs. Marwood. The Gentleman's merry, that's all, Sir——— S'life, we shall have a Quarrel betwixt an Horse and an Ass, before they find one another out. You must not take any Thing amiss from your Friends, Sir. You are among your Friends here, tho' it may be you don't know it———If I am not mistaken, you are Sir *Wilfull Witwoud.*

Sir Wilfull. Right Lady; I am Sir *Wilfull Witwoud*, so I write my self; no offence to any Body, I hope; and Nephew to the Lady *Wishfort*, of this Mansion.

Mrs. Marwood. Don't you know this Gentleman, Sir?

Sir Wilfull. Hum! What sure 'tis not———Yea by'r Lady, but 'tis———'Sheart I know not whether 'tis or no——— Yea but 'tis, by the *Rekin*. Brother *Anthony*! What *Tony*

smoke him—Make fun of him.
Rekin—The Wrekin, a hill that was the most prominent landmark in Shropshire.

i'faith! What do'st thou not know me? By'r Lady nor I thee, thou art so Becravated, and Beperriwig'd——— 'Sheart why do'st not speak? Art thou o'er-joy'd?

Witwoud. Odso Brother, is it you? Your Servant Brother.

Sir Wilfull. Your Servant! Why yours, Sir. Your Servant again———'Sheart, and your Friend and Servant to that— And a———(*puff*) and a flap Dragon for your Service, Sir: And a Hare's Foot, and a Hare's Scut for your Service, Sir; an you be so cold and so courtly!

Witwoud. No offence, I hope, Brother.

Sir Wilfull. 'Sheart, Sir, but there is, and much offence.— A pox, is this your Inns o' Court breeding, not to know your Friends and your Relations, your Elders, and your Betters?

Witwoud. Why Brother *Wilfull* of *Salop*, you may be as short as a *Shrewsbury* Cake, if you please. But I tell you, 'tis not modish to know Relations in Town. You think you're in the Country, where great lubberly Brothers slabber and kiss one another when they meet, like a Call of Serjeants———'Tis not the fashion here; 'tis not indeed, dear Brother.

Sir Wilful. The Fashion's a Fool; and you're a Fop, dear Brother. 'Sheart, I've suspected this———By'r Lady I conjectur'd you were a Fop, since you began to change the Stile of your Letters, and write in a scrap of Paper gilt round the Edges, no broader than a *Subpœna.* I might expect this, when you left off Honour'd Brother; and hoping you are in good Health, and so forth———To begin with a Rat me, Knight, I'm so sick of a last Nights debauch ———O'ds heart, and then tell a familiar Tale of a Cock and a Bull, and a Whore and a Bottle, and so conclude ———You cou'd write News before you were out of your Time, when you liv'd with honest *Pumple Nose* the Attorney of *Furnival's* Inn—You cou'd intreat to be remember'd then to your Friends round the *Rekin.* We cou'd have

flap Dragon—A raisin (in the game of snap-dragon); clap or a pox, (*Dictionary of the Canting Crew*).

Salop—Shropshire.

Shrewsbury Cake—a small round shortcake, made there.

Call of Serjeants—Probably the ceremonies when called to the Bar; cf. Pope, *Dunciad*, IV, 591: "The Judge to dance his brother Sergeant call;"

Gazetts then, and *Dawks*'s Letter, and the weekly Bill, 'till of late Days.

Petulant. S'life, *Witwoud,* were you ever an Attorney's Clerk? Of the Family of the *Furnivals.* Ha, ha, ha!

Witwoud. Ay, ay, but that was for a while. Not long, not long; pshaw, I was not in my own Power then. An Orphan, and this Fellow was my Guardian; ay, ay, I was glad to consent to that, Man, to come to *London.* He had the disposal of me then. If I had not agreed to that, I might have been bound Prentice to a Felt maker in *Shrewsbury*; this Fellow wou'd have bound me to a Maker of Felts.

Sir Wilfull. 'Sheart, and better than to be bound to a Maker of Fops; where, I suppose, you have serv'd your Time; and now you may set up for your self.

Mrs. Marwood. You intend to Travel, Sir, as I'm inform'd.

Sir Wilfull. Belike I may Madam. I may chance to sail upon the salt Seas, if my Mind hold.

Petulant. And the Wind serve.

Sir Wilfull. Serve or not serve, I shant ask License of you, Sir; nor the Weather-Cock your Companion. I direct my Discourse to the Lady, Sir: 'Tis like my Aunt may have told you, Madam———Yes, I have settl'd my Concerns, I may say now, and am minded to see Foreign Parts. If an how that the Peace holds, whereby that is, Taxes abate.

Mrs. Marwood. I thought you had design'd for *France* at all Adventures.

Sir Wilfull. I can't tell that; 'tis like I may, and 'tis like I may not. I am somewhat dainty in making a Resolution,—because when I make it I keep it. I don't stand shill I, shall I, then; if I say't, I'll do't: But I have Thoughts to tarry a small matter in Town, to learn somewhat of your *Lingo* first, before I cross the Seas. I'd gladly have a spice of your *French* as they say, whereby to hold discourse in Foreign Countries.

Mrs. Marwood. Here is an Academy in Town for that use.

Sir Wilfull. There is? 'Tis like there may.

Mrs. Marwood. No doubt you will return very much improv'd.

Dawks's Letter—A weekly paper, started in 1696.
the weekly Bill—"Of Mortality," notices of deaths.

Witwoud. Yes, refin'd, like a *Dutch* Skipper from a Whale-fishing.

Enter Lady Wishfort *and* Fainall.

Lady Wishfort. Nephew, you are welcome.

Sir Wilfull. Aunt, your Servant.

Fainall. Sir *Wilfull*, your most faithful Servant.

Sir Wilfull. Cousin *Fainall*, give me your Hand.

Lady Wishfort. Cousin *Witwoud*, your Servant; Mr. *Petulant*, your Servant.———Nephew, you are welcome again. Will you drink any Thing after your Journey, Nephew, before you eat? Dinner's almost ready.

Sir Wilfull. I'm very well I thank you Aunt———However, I thank you for your courteous Offer. 'Sheart, I was afraid you wou'd have been in the fashion too, and have remember'd to have forgot your Relations. Here's your Cousin *Tony*, belike, I may'nt call him Brother for fear of offence.

Lady Wishfort. O he's a Rallier, Nephew—My Cousin's a Wit. And your great Wits always rally their best Friends to chuse. When you have been abroad, Nephew, you'll understand Raillery better.

Fainall *and* Mrs. Marwood *talk a-part.*

Sir Wilfull. Why then let him hold his Tongue in the mean time; and rail when that day comes.

Enter Mincing.

Mincing. Mem, I come to acquaint your Layship that Dinner is impatient.

Sir Wilfull. Impatient? Why then belike it won't stay, 'till I pull off my Boots. Sweet-heart, can you help me to a pair of Slippers?———My Man's with his Horses, I warrant.

Lady Wishfort. Fie, fie, Nephew, you wou'd not pull off your Boots here———Go down into the Hall———Dinner shall stay for you———My Nephew's a little unbred, you'll pardon him, Madam———Gentlemen will you walk? *Marwood*—

Mrs. Marwood. I'll follow you, Madam—Before Sir *Wilfull* is ready.

Manent Mrs. Marwood *and* Fainall.

Fainall. Why then *Foible's* a Bawd, an Errant, Rank, Match-making Bawd, And I it seems am a Husband, a Rank-Husband; and my Wife a very Errant, Rank-Wife,—all in the Way of the *World.* 'S death to be an Anticipated Cuckold, a Cuckold in Embrio? Sure I was born with budding Antlers like a young Satyre, or a Citizens Child. 'S death to be Out-Witted, to be Out-Jilted———Out-Matrimony'd,———If I had kept my speed like a Stag, 'twere somewhat,———but to crawl after, with my Horns like a Snail, and out-strip'd by my Wife—'tis Scurvy Wedlock.

Mrs. Marwood. Then shake it off, You have often wish'd for an opportunity to part;—and now you have it. But first prevent their Plot,———the half of *Millamant's* Fortune is too Considerable to be parted with, to a Foe, to *Mirabell.*

Fainall. Dam him, that had been mine—had you not made that fond discovery—that had been forfeited, had they been Married. My Wife had added Lustre to my Horns, by that Encrease of fortune,—I cou'd have worn 'em tipt with Gold, tho' my forehead had been furnish'd like a Deputy-Lieutenant's Hall.

Mrs. Marwood. They may prove a Cap of Maintenance to you still, if you can away with your Wife. And she's no worse than when you had her—I dare swear she had given up her Game, before she was Marry'd.

Fainall. Hum! That may be—She might throw up her Cards; but I'le be hang'd if she did not put Pam in her Pocket.

Mrs. Marwood. You Married her to keep you; and if you can contrive to have her keep you better than you expected; why should you not keep her longer than you intended?

Fainall. The means, the means.

Mrs. Marwood. Discover to my Lady your Wife's conduct; threaten to part with her———My Lady loves her, and will come to any Composition to save her reputation, take the opportunity of breaking it, just upon the discovery of this imposture. My Lady will be enraged beyond bounds, and Sacrifice Neice, and Fortune, and all at that Con-

Deputy-Lieutenant's Hall—With the walls covered in antlers.
Cap of Maintenance—Heraldic; a cap with two horns behind, but worn as a symbol of dignity.
away with—Tolerate.
Pam—Knave of clubs, highest trump card in Loo.

juncture. And let me alone to keep her warm, if she should Flag in her part, I will not fail to prompt her.

Fainall. Faith this has an appearance.

Mrs. Marwood. I'm sorry I hinted to my Lady to endeavour a match between *Millamant* and Sir *Wilfull*, that may be an Obstacle.

Fainall. O, for that matter leave me to manage him; I'll disable him for that, he will drink like a *Dane*: after dinner, I'll set his hand in.

Mrs. Marwood. Well, how do you stand affected towards your Lady?

Fainall. Why faith I'm thinking of it.———Let me see——— I am married already; so that's over,———my Wife has plaid the Jade with me———Well, that's over too———I never lov'd her, or if I had, why that wou'd have been over too by this time—Jealous of her I cannot be, for I am certain; so there's an end of Jealousie. Weary of her, I am, and shall be—No, there's no end of that; No, no, that were too much to hope. Thus far concerning my repose. Now for my Reputation,—As to my own, I married not for it; so that's out of the Question,—And as to my part in my Wife's—Why she had parted with hers before; so bringing none to me, she can take none from me, 'tis against all rule of Play, that I should lose to one, who has not wherewithal to stake.

Mrs. Marwood. Besides you forget, Marriage is honourable.

Fainall. Hum! Faith and that's well thought on; Marriage is honourable as you say; and if so, Wherefore should Cuckoldom be a discredit, being deriv'd from so honourable a root?

Mrs. Marwood. Nay I know not; if the root be Honourable, why not the Branches?

Faihall. So, so, why this point's clear,———Well how do we proceed?

Mrs. Marwood. I will contrive a Letter which shall be deliver'd to my Lady at the time when that Rascal who is to act Sir *Rowland* is with her. It shall come as from an unknown hand—for the less I appear to know of the truth—the better I can play the Incendiary. Besides I would not have *Foible* provok'd if I cou'd help it,—because you know she knows some passages—Nay I expect all will come out —But let the Mine be sprung first, and then I care not if I'm discover'd.

Fainall. If the worst come to the worst,—I'll turn my Wife to Grass—I have already a deed of Settlement of the best part of her Estate; which I wheadl'd out of her; And that you shall partake at least.

Mrs. Marwood. I hope you are convinc'd that I hate *Mirabell*, now you'll be no more Jealous.

Fainall. Jealous no,—by this Kiss—let Husbands be Jealous; But let the Lover still believe. Or if he doubt, let it be only to endear his pleasure, and prepare the Joy that follows, when he proves his Mistress true; but let Husbands doubts Convert to endless Jealousie; or if they have belief, let it Corrupt to Superstition, and blind Credulity. I am single; and will herd no more with 'em. True, I wear the badge; but I'll disown the Order. And since I take my leave of 'em, I care not if I leave 'em a common Motto, to their common Crest.

All Husbands must, or pain, or shame, endure;
The Wise too Jealous are, Fools too secure.

Exeunt.

ACT IV. Scene I.

Scene Continues.

Enter Lady Wishfort *and* Foible.

Lady Wishfort. Is Sir *Rowland* coming say'st thou, *Foible*? and are things in Order?

Foible. Yes, *Madam.* I have put Wax-Lights in the Sconces; and plac'd the Foot-men in a Row in the Hall, in their best Liveries, with the Coach-man and Postilion to fill up the Equipage.

Lady Wishfort. Have you pullvill'd the Coach-man and Postilion, that they may not stink of the Stable, when Sir *Rowland* comes by?

pullvill'd—Pulvilio, a fragrant powder for periwigs.

Foible. Yes, *Madam.*

Lady Wishfort. And are the Dancers and the Musick ready, that he may be entertain'd in all points with Correspondence to his Passion?

Foible. All is ready, *Madam.*

Lady Wishfort. And—well—and how do I look, *Foible*?

Foible. Most killing well, *Madam.*

Lady Wishfort. Well, and how shall I receive him? In what figure shall I give his Heart the first Impression? There is a great deal in the first Impression. Shall I sit?———No I won't sit—I'll walk—aye I'll walk from the door upon his entrance; and then turn full upon him———No, that will be too sudden. I'll lie———aye, I'll lie down———I'll receive him in my little dressing Room, there's a Couch—Yes, yes, I'll give the first Impression on a Couch—I wont lie neither but loll and lean upon one Elbow; with one Foot a little dangling off, Jogging in a thoughtful way—Yes—and then as soon as he appears, start, ay, start and be surpriz'd, and rise to meet him in a pretty disorder—Yes—O, nothing is more alluring than a Levee from a Couch in some Confusion.———It shows the Foot to advantage, and furnishes with Blushes, and re-composing Airs beyond Comparison. Hark! There's a Coach.

Foible. 'Tis he, *Madam.*

Lady Wishfort. O dear, has my *Nephew* made his Addresses to *Millamant*? I order'd him.

Foible. Sir *Wilfull* is set in to Drinking, *Madam*, in the Parlour.

Lady Wishfort. Ods my life, I'll send him to her. Call her down, *Foible*; bring her hither. I'll send him as I go———When they are together, then come to me *Foible*, that I may not be too long alone with Sir *Rowland.*

Exit.

Enter Mrs. Millamant, *and* Mrs. Fainall.

Foible. Madam, I stay'd here, to tell your Ladyship that Mr. *Mirabell* has waited this half hour for an Opportunity to talk with you. Tho' my Lady's Orders were to leave you and Sir *Wilfull* together. Shall I tell Mr. *Mirabell* that you are at leisure?

Millamant. No———What would the Dear man have? I am thoughtfull and would amuse my self,———bid him come another time.

Repeating and Walking about.

There never yet was Woman made,
Nor shall but to be curs'd.

That's hard!

Mrs. Fainall. You are very fond of Sir *John Suckling* to day, *Millamant*, and the *Poets.*

Millimant. He? Ay, and filthy Verses—So I am.

Foible. Sir *Wilfull* is coming, *Madam.* Shall I send Mr. *Mirabell* away?

Millimant. Ay, if you please *Foible*, send him away,—Or send him hither,—just as you will Dear *Foible.*—I think I'll see him—Shall I? Ay, let the Wretch come.

(*Repeating.*) *Thyrsis a Youth of the Inspir'd train—*

Dear *Fainall*, Entertain Sir *Wilfull*—Thou hast Philosophy to undergo a Fool, thou art Married and hast Patience—I would confer with my own Thoughts.

Mrs. Fainall. I am oblig'd to you, that you would make me your Proxy in this Affair; but I have business of my own.

Enter Sir Wilfull.

O *Sir Wilfull*; you are come at the Critical Instant. There's your Mistress up to the Ears in Love and Contemplation, pursue your Point, now or never.

Sir Wilfull. Yes; my Aunt would have it so,—I would gladly have been encouraged with a Bottle or two, because I'm somewhat wary at first, before I am acquainted;—But I hope after a time, I shall break my mind—that is upon further acquaintance,—So for the present Cozen, I'll take my leave—If so be you'll be so kind to make my Excuse, I'll return to my Company—

This while Millamant *walks about Repeating to her self.*

Mrs. Fainall. O fie Sir *Wilfull*! What, you must not be Daunted.

There never yet, etc.—See Suckling, *Works* (1648), p. 20.
Thyrsis, etc.—See Waller, "The Story of Phoebus and Daphne applied," in *Poems* (1694), p. 29.

Sir Wilfull. Daunted, No, that's not it, it is not so much for that—for if so be that I set on't, I'll do't. But only for the present, 'tis sufficient till further acquaintance, that's all—your Servant.

Mrs. Fainall. Nay, I'll swear you shall never lose so favourable an opportunity, if I can help it. I'll leave you together and lock the Door.

Exit.

Sir Wilfull. Nay, nay Cozen,—I have forgot my Gloves,—What dee do? 'Shart a'has lock'd the Door indeed I think—Nay Cozen *Fainall*, open the Door—Pshaw What a Vixon trick is this?—Nay, now a'has seen me too—Cozen, I made bold to pass thro' as it were,—I think this Door's inchanted—.

Millamant (*Repeating*).

I prithee spare me gentle Boy,
Press me no more for that slight Toy.

Sir Wilfull. Anan? Cozen, your Servant.

Millamant. —*That foolish trifle of a heart*—Sir *Wilfull*!

Sir Wilfull. Yes,—your Servant. No offence I hope, Cozen.

Millamant (*Repeating.*)

I swear it will not do its part,
Tho' thou do'st thine, employ'st the Power and Art.

Natural, easie *Suckling*!

Sir Wilfull. Anan? *Suckling*? No such Suckling neither, Cozen, nor Stripling: I thank Heav'n, I'm no Minor.

Millamant. Ah Rustick! ruder than *Gothick*.

Sir Wilfull. Well, Well, I shall understand your *Lingo* one of these days, Cozen, in the mean while, I must answer in plain *English*.

Millamant. Have you any business with me, Sir *Wilfull*?

Sir Wilfull. Not at present Cozen,———Yes, I made bold to see, to come and know if that how you were dispos'd to

I prithee spare me. etc.—See Suckling, *ibid.*, p. 25.

easie Suckling—"Suckling's easie Pen"; cf. Earl of Rochester, *Satyr* (1685), in *The Collected Works of John Wilmot, Earl of Rochester*, ed. John Hayward (1926), p. 79 (hereafter referred to as *The Collected Works*).

fetch a walk this Evening, if so be that I might not be troublesome, I wou'd have sought a walk with you.

Millamant. A walk? What then?

Sir Wilfull. Nay nothing———Only for the walks sake, that's all—

Millimant. I Nauseate walking; 'tis a Country diversion, I loath the Country and every thing that relates to it.

Sir Wilfull. Indeed! Hah! Look ye, look ye, you do? Nay, 'tis like you may———Here are choice of Pastimes here in Town, as Plays and the like that must be confess'd indeed.

Millamant. Ah l' etourdie! I hate the Town too.

Sir Wilfull. Dear Heart, that's much———Hah! that you shou'd hate 'em both! Hah 'tis like you may; there are some can't relish the Town, and others can't away with the Country,———'tis like you may be one of those, Cozen.

Millamant. Ha, ha, ha. Yes, 'tis like I may.—You have nothing further to say to me?

Sir Wilful. Not at present, Cozen.———'tis like when I have an Opportunity to be more private,—I may break my mind in some measure,—I conjecture you partly guess—However that's as time shall try,—But spare to speak and spare to speed, as they say.

Millamant. If it is of no great Importance, Sir *Wilfull*, you will oblige me to leave me: I have just now a little business.—

Sir Wilfull. Enough, enough, Cozen, Yes, yes, all a case—When you're dispos'd, when you're dispos'd. Now's as well as another time; and another time as well as now. All's one for that,—yes, yes, if your Concerns call you, there's no hast; it will keep cold as they say,—Cozen, your Servant—I think this door's lock'd.

Millamant. You may go this way Sir.

Sir Wilfull. Your Servant, then with your leave I'll return to my Company.

Exit.

Millamant. Ay, ay, ha, ha, ha.

Like Phœbus *sung the no less am'rous Boy.*

Enter Mirabell.

Mirabell. ———*Like* Daphne *she as lovely and as Coy*. Do you lock your self up from me, to make my search more Curious? Or is this pretty Artifice Contriv'd, to Signifie that here the Chase must end, and my pursuit be Crown'd, for you can fly no further.—

Millamant. Vanity! No———I'll fly and be follow'd to the last moment, tho' I am upon the very Verge of Matrimony, I expect you shou'd solicite me as much as if I were wavering at the grate of a Monastery, with one foot over the threshold. I'll be solicited to the very last, nay and afterwards.

Mirabell. What, after the last?

Millamant. O, I should think I was poor and had nothing to bestow, if I were reduc'd to an Inglorious ease; and free'd from the Agreeable fatigues of sollicitation.

Mirabell. But do not you know, that when favours are conferr'd upon Instant and tedious Sollicitation, that they diminish in their value, and that both the giver loses the grace, and the receiver lessens his Pleasure?

Millamant. It may be in things of common Application; but never sure in Love. O, I hate a Lover, that can dare to think, he draws a moments air, Independent on the Bounty of his Mistress. There is not so Impudent a thing in Nature, as the sawcy look of an assured man, Confident of Success. The Pedantick arrogance of a very Husband, has not so Pragmatical an Air. Ah! I'll never marry, unless I am first made sure of my will and pleasure.

Mirabell. Wou'd you have 'em both before Marriage? Or will you be contented with the first now, and stay for the other till after grace?

Millamant. Ah don't be Impertinent———My dear Liberty, shall I leave thee? My faithful Solitude, my darling Contemplation, must I bid you then Adieu? ay-h adieu.—my morning thoughts, agreeable wakings, indolent slumbers, all ye *douceurs*, ye *Someils du Matin*, adieu—I can't do't, 'tis more than Impossible—positively *Mirabell*, I'll lie a Bed in a morning as long as I please.

Mirabell. Then I'll get up in a morning as early as I please.

douceurs, ye Someils du Matin—These luxurious delights can only be fully expressed in French.

Millamant. Ah! Idle Creature, get up when you will——— and dee hear, I won't be call'd names after I'm Married; positively I won't be call'd Names.

Mirabell. Names!

Millamant. Ay as Wife, Spouse, My dear, Joy, Jewel, Love, Sweet heart and the rest of that Nauseous Cant, in which Men and their Wives are so fulsomely familiar,———I shall never bear that,———Good *Mirabell* don't let us be familiar or fond, nor kiss before folks, like my Lady *Fadler* and Sr. *Francis*: Nor goe to *Hide-Park* together the first *Sunday* in a New Chariot, to provoke Eyes and Whispers; And then never to be seen there together again; as if we were proud of one another the first Week, and asham'd of one another for ever After. Let us never Visit together, nor go to a Play together, But let us be very strange and well bred: let us be as strange as if we had been married a great while; and as well bred as if we were not marri'd at all.

Mirabell. Have you any more Conditions to offer? Hitherto your demands are pretty reasonable.

Millamant. Trifles,———As liberty to pay and receive visits to and from whom I please, to write and receive Letters, without Interrogatories or wry Faces on your part. To wear what I please; and choose Conversation with regard only to my own taste; to have no obligation upon me to converse with Wits that I don't like, because they are your acquaintance; or to be intimate with Fools, because they may be your Relations. Come to Dinner when I please, dine in my dressing room when I'm out of humour without giving a reason. To have my Closet Inviolate; to be sole Empress of my Tea-table, which you must never presume to approach without first asking leave. And lastly, where ever I am, you shall always knock at the door before you come in. These Articles subscrib'd, If I continue to endure you a little longer, I may by degrees dwindle into a Wife.

Mirabell. Your bill of fare is something advanc'd in this latter account. Well, have I Liberty to offer Conditions—that when you are dwindl'd into a Wife, I may not be beyond Measure enlarg'd into a Husband?

Millamant. You have free leave; propose your utmost, speak and spare not.

Mirabell. I thank you. *Inprimis* then, I Covenant that your acquaintance be General; that you admit no sworn Confident, or Intimate of your own Sex; No she friend to skreen her affairs under your Countenance and tempt you to make tryal of a Mutual Secresie. No Decoy-Duck to wheadle you a *fop*———*scrambling* to the Play in a Mask———then bring you home in a pretended fright, when you think you shall be found out.———And rail at me for missing the Play, and disappointing the Frolick which you had to pick me up and prove my Constancy.

Millamant. Detestable *Inprimis*! I go to the Play in a Mask!

Mirabell. Item, I Article, that you continue to like your own Face, as long as I shall. And while it passes Current with me, that you endeavour not to new Coin it. To which end, together with all Vizards for the day, I prohibit all Masks for the Night, made of oil'd skins and I know not what ———Hog's-bones, Hare's-gall, Pig-water, and the marrow of a roasted Cat. In short, I forbid all Commerce with the Gentlewoman in *what-de-call-it*-Court. *Item,* I shut my doors against all Bauds with Baskets, and penny-worths of *Muslin, China, Fans, Atlases,* &c.—*Item* when you shall be Breeding—

Millamant. Ah! Name it not.

Mirabell. Which may be presum'd, with a blessing on our endeavours—

Millamant. Odious endeavours!

Mirabell. I denounce against all strait-Laceing, Squeezing for a Shape, till you mold my boy's head like a Sugar-loaf; and instead of a Man-child, make me the Father to a Crooked-billet. Lastly to the Dominion of the *Tea-Table,* I submit.—But with *proviso,* that you exceed not in your province; but restrain your self to Native and Simple *Tea-Table* drinks, as *Tea, Chocolate* and *Coffee.* As likewise to Genuine and, Authoriz'd *Tea-Table* talk,———such as mending of Fashions, spoiling Reputations, railing at absent Friends, and so forth—but that on no account you encroach upon the mens prerogative, and presume to drink healths, or toste fellows; for prevention of which; I banish all *Foreign Forces,* all Auxiliaries to the *Tea-Table,* as *Orange-Brandy,* all *Anniseed, Cinamon, Citron* and *Barbado's-Waters,* together with *Ratifia* and the most noble Spirit of *Clary,*———but

Atlases—"Satins flowered with gold or silver" (obs.; OED).
Anniseed . . . Barbado's-Waters . . . Clary—All "filthy strong waters."

for *Couslip-Wine*, *Poppy-Water* and all *Dormitives*, those I allow,———these *proviso*'s admitted, in other things I may prove a tractable and complying Husband.

Millamant. O horrid *proviso*'s! filthy strong Waters! I toste fellows, Odious Men! I hate your Odious proviso's.

Mirabell. Then wee're agreed. Shall I kiss your hand upon the Contract? and here comes one to be a witness to the Sealing of the Deed.

Enter Mrs. Fainall.

Millamant. *Fainall*, what shall I do? shall I have him? I think I must have him.

Mrs. Fainall. Ay, ay, take him, take him, what shou'd you do?

Millamant. Well then———I'll take my death I'm in a horrid fright———*Fainall*, I shall never say it—well—I think—I'll endure you.

Mrs. Fainall. Fy, fy, have him, have him, and tell him so in plain terms: For I am sure you have a mind to him.

Millamant. Are you? I think I have———and the horrid Man looks as if he thought so too———Well, you ridiculous thing you, I'll have you,—I won't be kiss'd, nor I won't be thank'd—here kiss my hand tho'—so hold your tongue now, and don't say a word.

Mrs. Fainall. *Mirabell*, there's a Necessity for your obedience, ———You have neither time to talk nor stay. My Mother is coming; and in my Conscience if she should see you, wou'd fall into fits, and maybe not recover time enough to return to Sir *Rowland*, who as *Foible* tells me is in a fair way to succeed. Therefore spare your Extacies for another occasion, and slip down the back-stairs, where *Foible* waits to consult you.

Millamant. Ay, go, go. In the mean time I suppose you have said something to please me.

Mirabell. I am all Obedience.

Exit Mirabell.

Mrs. Fainall. Yonder Sir *Wilfull's* Drunk; and so noisy that my Mother has been forc'd to leave Sir *Rowland* to appease him; But he answers her only with Singing and Drinking —what they have done by this time I know not. But *Petulant* and he were upon quarrelling as I came by.

Millamant. Well, If *Mirabell* shou'd not make a good Husband, I am a lost thing;———for I find I love him violently.

Mrs. Fainall. So it seems, when you mind not what's said to you,—If you doubt him, you had best take up with Sir *Wilfull*.

Millamant. How can you name that super-annuated Lubber, foh!

Enter Witwoud *from drinking*.

Mrs. Fainall. So, Is the fray made up, that you have left 'em?

Witwoud. Left 'em? I cou'd stay no longer—I have laugh'd like ten Christnings—I am tipsy with laughing—If I had staid any longer I shou'd have burst,—I must have been let out and piec'd in the sides like an unsiz'd Camlet,—Yes, yes the fray is compos'd; my Lady came in like a *Noli prosequi* and stop't their proceedings.

Millamant. What was the dispute?

Witwoud. That's the Jest, there was no dispute, they cou'd neither of 'em speak for rage; And so fell a sputt'ring at one another like two roasting Apples.

Enter Petulant *Drunk*.

Now *Petulant*, all's over, all's well; Gad my head begins to whim it about—Why dost thou not speak? thou art both as drunk and as mute as a Fish.

Petulant. Look you Mrs. *Millamant*,—If you can love me dear Nymph—say it—and that's the Conclusion—pass on, or pass off,—that's all.

Witwoud. Thou hast utter'd *Volumes*, *Folio's*, in less than *Decimo Sexto*, my Dear *Lacedemonian*, Sirrah *Petulant*, thou art an Epitomizer of words.

Petulant. *Witwoud*———You are an anihilator of sense.

Witwoud. Thou art a retailer of Phrases; and dost deal in Remnants of Remnants, like a maker of Pincushions—thou art in truth (Metaphorically speaking) A speaker of short-hand.

Noli prosequi—Putting an end to legal proceedings.
Lacedemonian—Spartan, given to few words.

Petulant. Thou art (without a figure) Just one half of an Ass; and *Baldwin* yonder, thy half Brother is the rest—A *gemini* of Asses split, would make just four of you.

Witwoud. Thou dost bite my dear Mustard-seed; kiss me for that.

Petulant. Stand off———I'll kiss no more Males,———I have kiss'd your *twin* yonder in a humour of reconciliation, till he (*hiccup*) rises upon my stomack like a Radish.

Millamant. Eh! filthy creature—what was the quarrel?

Petulant. There was no quarrel—there might have been a quarrel.

Witwoud. If there had been words enow between 'em to have express'd provocation; they had gone together by the Ears like a pair of Castanets.

Petulant. You were the Quarrel.

Millamant. Me!

Petulant. If I have a humour to Quarrel, I can make less matters conclude Premises,———If you are not handsom, what then? If I have a humour to prove it.———If I shall have my Reward, say so; if not, fight for your Face the next time your self———I'll go sleep.

Witwoud. Do, rap thy self up like a *Wood-louse* and dream Revenge———and hear me, if thou canst learn to write by to morrow Morning, Pen me a Challenge—I'll carry it for thee.

Petulant. Carry your Mistresses *Monkey* a *Spider,*———go flea Dogs, and read Romances———I'll go to bed to my Maid.

Exit.

Mrs. Fainall. He's horridly drunk———how came you all in this pickle?—

Witwoud. A plot, a plot, to get rid of the Knight,———your Husband's advice; but he sneak'd off.

Enter Lady Wishfort *and* Sir Wilfull *drunk.*

Baldwin—The ass, in the well-known fable of *Reynard the Fox,* reprinted in 1694.

Mistresses Monkey—Fashionable pets after the Restoration; cf. Earl of Rochester, "Letter from Artemisia," in *The Collected Works,* p. 30: "Her much-esteem'd, dear Friend, the Monkey . . . / The dirty, chattering Monster she embrac'd."

Lady Wishfort. Out upon't, out upon't, at years of Discretion, and Comport your self at this Rantipole rate.

Sir Wilfull. No Offence Aunt.

Lady Wishfort. Offence? As I'm a Person, I'm asham'd of you, —Fogh! how you stink of Wine! Dee think my Neice will ever endure such a *Borachio*! you're an absolute *Borachio.*

Sir Wilfull. Borachio!

Lady Wishfort. At a time when you shou'd commence an Amour and put your best foot foremost—

Sir Wilfull. 'Sheart, an you grutch me your Liquor, make a Bill—Give me more drink and take my Purse.

(*Sings,*)

Prithee fill me the Glass
Till it laugh in my Face,
With Ale that is Potent and Mellow;
He that Whines for a Lass,
Is an Ignorant Ass,
For a *Bumper* has not its Fellow.

but if you wou'd have me Marry my Cozen,—say the Word, and I'll do't—*Wilfull* will do't, that's the Word—*Wilfull* will do't, that's my Crest—my Motto I have forgot.

Lady Wishfort. My Nephew's a little overtaken Cozen—but 'tis with drinking your Health—O' my Word you are oblig'd to him.

Sir Wilfull. In vino veritas Aunt,—If I drunk your Health to day Cozen—I am a *Borachio.* But if you have a mind to be Marry'd, say the Word, and send for the Piper, *Wilfull* will do't. If not, dust it away, and let's have tother round—*Tony*, Ods heart where's *Tony*—*Tony*'s an honest fellow, but he spits after a Bumper, and that's a Fault.

(*Sings,*)

We'll drink and we'll never ha' done Boys
Put the glass then around with the Sun Boys;
Let *Apollo*'s Example invite us;
For he's drunk every Night,
And that makes him so bright,
That he's able next Morning to light us.

Rantipole—Disorderly (obs.).
Borachio—Goatskin for wine; thus, drunkard.
grutch—A touch of dialect for "grudge."

the Sun's a good Pimple, an honest Soaker, he has a Cellar at your *Antipodes*. If I travel Aunt, I touch at your *Antipodes* ———your *Antipodes* are a good rascally sort of topsy-turvy Fellows———If I had a Bumper I'd stand upon my Head and drink a Health to 'em—A Match or no Match, Cozen, with the hard Name,—Aunt, *Wilfull* will do't, If she has her Maidenhead let her look to't,—is she has not, let her keep her own Counsel in the mean time, and cry out at the nine Months end.

Millamant. Your Pardon Madam, I can stay no longer—Sir *Wilfull* grows very powerful, Egh! how he smells! I shall be overcome if I stay.

Exeunt Millamant *and* Mrs. Fainall.

Come, Cozen.

Lady Wishfort. Smells! he would poison a Tallow-Chandler and his Family. Beastly Creature, I know not what to do with him—Travel quoth a; Ay travel, travel, get thee gone, get thee but far enough, to the *Saracens* or the *Tartars*, or the *Turks*—for thou are not fit to live in a Christian Commonwealth, thou beastly Pagan.

Sir Wilfull. Turks, no; no *Turks*, Aunt: Your *Turks* are Infidels, and believe not in the Grape. Your *Mahometan*, your *Mussulman* is a dry Stinkard—No Offence, Aunt. My Map says that your *Turk* is not so honest a Man as your Christian—I cannot find by the Map that your *Mufti* is Orthodox—Whereby it is a plain Case, that Orthodox is a hard Word, Aunt, and (*hiccup*) Greek for Claret.

(*Sings*,)

To drink is a Christian Diversion,
Unknown to the *Turk* and the *Persian*:
Let *Mahometan* Fools
Live by Heathenish Rules,
And be damn'd over Tea-Cups and Coffee.
But let British Lads sing,
Crown a Health to the King,
And a Fig for your *Sultan* and *Sophy*.

Ah *Tony*!

Enter Foible, *and whispers* Lady Wishfort.

pimple—Slang for "a boon companion" (see J. S. Farmer, *Slang and its Analogues* [1890]).
Mufti—A Mohammedan priest.
Sophy—The family name of the Persian dynasty, Sufi.

Lady Wishfort. Sir *Rowland* impatient? Good lack! what shall I do with this beastly Tumbril?———Go lie down and sleep, you Sot—Or as I'm a person, I'll have you bastinado'd with Broom-sticks. Call up the Wenches.

Exit Foible.

Sir Wilfull. Ahey! Wenches, where are the Wenches?

Lady Wishfort. Dear Cozen *Witwoud,* get him away, and you will bind me to you inviolably. I have an Affair of moment that invades me with some precipitation—You will oblige me to all Futurity.

Witwoud. Come Knight—Pox on him. I don't know what to say to him—will you go to a Cock-match?

Sir Wilfull. With a Wench, *Tony*? Is she a shake-bag Sirrah? let me bite your Cheek for that.

Witwoud. Horrible! He has a breath like a *Bagpipe*—ay, ay, come will you March my *Salopian*?

Sir Wilfull. Lead on little *Tony*—I'll follow thee my *Anthony,* My *Tantony,* Sirrah thou sha't be my *Tantony*; and I'll be thy *Pig.*

—and a fig for your *Sultan* and *Sophy.*

Exit Singing with Witwoud.

Lady Wishfort. This will never do. It will never make a Match. —At least before he has been abroad.

Enter Waitwell, *disguis'd as for* Sir Rowland.

Dear Sir *Rowland,* I am Confounded with Confusion at the Retrospection of my own rudenes,———I have more pardons to ask than the *Pope* distributes in the Year of *Jubilee.* But I hope where there is likely to be so near an alliance,———We may unbend the severity of *Decorum* ———and dispence with a little Ceremony.

Waitwell. My Impatience *Madam,* is the effect of my transport; —and till I have the possession of your adoreable Person, I am tantaliz'd on a rack; And do but hang *Madam,* on the tenter of Expectation.

Anthony—Patron saint of swineheards.

Year of Jubilee—Normally celebrated every twenty-five years with special Papal Indulgences, but Pope Innocent XII, when elected in 1691, had proclaimed a Year of Jubilee, which had attracted many to Rome. Farquhar's immensely popular play, *The Constant Couple, or A Trip to the Jubilee,* is full of it.

Lady Wishfort. You have Excess of gallantry Sir *Rowland*; and press things to a Conclusion, with a most prevailing Vehemence.———But a day or two for decency of Marriage—

Waitwell. For decency of Funeral, *Madam.* The delay will break my heart———or if that should fail, I shall be Poyson'd. My *Nephew* will get an inkling of my Designs and Poison me,———and I wou'd willingly starve him before I die———I wou'd gladly go out of the World with that Satisfaction.———That wou'd be some Comfort to me, If I cou'd but live so long as to be reveng'd on that Unnatural *Viper.*

Lady Wishfort. Is he so Unnatural say you? truely I wou'd Contribute much both to the saving of your Life; and the accomplishment of your revenge———Not that I respect my self; tho' he has been a perfidious wretch to me.

Waitwell. Perfidious to you!

Lady Wishfort. O Sir *Rowland*, the hours that he has dy'd away at my Feet, the Tears that he has shed, the Oaths that he has sworn, the Palpitations that he has felt, the Trances, and the Tremblings, the Ardors and the Ecstacies, the Kneelings and the Riseings, the Heart-heavings, and the hand-Gripings, the Pangs and the Pathetick Regards of his protesting Eyes! Oh no memory can Register.

Waitwell. What, my Rival! is the Rebell my Rival? a'dies.

Lady Wishfort. No, don't kill him at once Sir *Rowland*, starve him gradually inch by inch.

Waitwell. I'll do't. In three weeks he shall be bare-foot; in a month out at knees with begging an *Alms*,———he shall starve upward and upward, till he has nothing living but his head, and then go out in a stink like a Candle's end upon a Save-all.

Lady Wishfort. Well, Sir *Rowland*, you have the way,——— You are no Novice in the Labyrinth of Love———You have the Clue———But as I am a person, Sir *Rowland*, You must not attribute my yielding to any sinister appetite, or Indigestion of Widdow-hood; Nor Impute my Complacency, to any Lethargy of Continence———I hope you do not think me prone to any iteration of Nuptials.—

Waitwell. Far be it from me—

Save-all—Small holder, with a pin to hold candle-ends.

Lady Wishfort. If you do, I protest I must recede———or think that I have made a prostitution of decorums, but in the Vehemence of Compassion, and to save the life of a Person of so much Importance—

Waitwell. I esteem it so—

Lady Wishfort. Or else you wrong my Condescension—

Waitwell. I do not, I do not—

Lady Wishfort. Indeed you do.

Waitwell. I do not, fair shrine of Vertue.

Lady Wishfort. If you think the least scruple of Carnality was an Ingredient—

Waitwell. Dear *Madam*, no. You are all *Camphire* and *Frankincense*, all *Chastity* and *Odour*.

Lady Wishfort. Or that—

Enter Foible.

Foible. Madam, the Dancers are ready, and there's one with a Letter, who must deliver it into your own hands.

Lady Wishfort, Sir *Rowland*, will you give me leave? think favourably, Judge Candidly and conclude you have found a Person who wou'd suffer racks in honour's cause, dear Sir *Rowland*, and will wait on you Incessantly.

Exit.

Waitwell. Fie, fie!—What a Slavery have I undergone; Spouse, hast thou any *Cordial*———I want *Spirits*.

Foible. What a washy Rogue art thou, to pant thus for a quarter of an hours lying and swearing to a fine Lady?

Waitwell. O, she is the *Antidote* to desire. Spouse, thou will't fare the worse for't———I shall have no appetite to iteration of Nuptials———this eight and fourty Hours ———by this hand I'd rather be a *Chair-man* in the *Dog-days*———than Act Sir *Rowland*, till this time to morrow.

Enter Lady Wishfort *with a Letter.*

Lady Wishfort. Call in the *Dancers*;———Sir *Rowland*, we'll sit if you please, and see the Entertainment.

Dance.

Now with your permission Sir *Rowland* I will peruse my Letter———I wou'd open it in your presence, because I wou'd not make you Uneasie. If it shou'd make you Uneasie I wou'd burn it———speak if it do's———but you may see by the Superscription it is like a Woman's hand.

Foible (*to him*). By Heaven! Mrs. *Marwood*'s, I know it,——— my heart akes—get it from her—.

Waitwell. A Woman's hand? No *Madam*, that's no Woman's hand I see that already. That's some body whose throat must be cut.

Lady Wishfort. Nay Sir *Rowland*, since you give me a proof of your Passion by your Jealousie, I promise you I'll make you a return, by a frank Communication———You shall see it—wee'll open it together—look you here.

Reads—Madam, *tho' unknown to you* (Look you there 'tis from no body that I know)—*I have that honour for your Character, that I think my self oblig'd to let you know you are abus'd. He who pretends to be Sir* Rowland *is a cheat and a Rascal.*—

Oh Heavens! what's this?

Foible. Unfortunate, all's ruin'd.

Waitwell. How, how, Let me see, let me see—(*reading*) *A Rascal and disguis'd and subborn'd for that imposture,*—O villany, O villany!—*by the Contrivance of*—

Lady Wishfort. I shall faint, I shall die, I shall die, oh!

Foible (*to him*). Say 'tis your Nephew's hand.—quickly, his plot, swear, swear it.—

Waitwell. Here's a Villain! *Madam*, don't you perceive it, don't you see it?

Lady Wishfort. Too well, too well. I have seen too much.

Waitwell. I told you at first I knew the hand———A Womans hand? the Rascal writes a sort of a large hand; your *Roman* hand—I saw there was a throat to be cut presently. If he were my Son as he is my Nephew I'd Pistoll him—

Foible. O Treachery! But are you sure Sir *Rowland*, it is his writing?

Waitwell. Sure? am I here? do I live? do I love this Pearl of *India*? I have twenty Letters in my Pocket from him, in the same Character.

Lady Wishfort. How!

Foible. O what luck it is Sir *Rowland*, that you were present at this Juncture! this was the business that brought Mr. *Mirabell* disguis'd to *Madam Millamant* this Afternoon. I thought something was contriving, when he stole by me and would have hid his face.

Lady Wishfort. How, how!—I heard the Villain was in the house indeed, and now I remember, my *Niece* went away abruptly, when Sir *Wilfull* was to have made his addresses.

Foible. Then, then *Madam*, Mr. *Mirabell* waited for her in her Chamber, but I wou'd not tell your Lady-ship to discompose you when you were to receive Sir *Rowland.*

Waitwell. Enough, his date is short.

Foible. No, good Sir *Rowland*, don't incurr the Law.

Waitwell. Law? I care not for Law. I can but die, and 'tis in a good cause———my Lady shall be satisfied of my Truth and Innocence, tho' it cost me my life.

Lady Wishfort. No, dear Sir *Rowland*, don't fight, if you shou'd be kill'd I must never shew my face; or hang'd,—O Consider my Reputation Sir *Rowland*—No you shan't fight,—I'll go in and Examine my *Niece*; I'll make her Confess. I conjure you Sir *Rowland* by all your love not to fight.

Waitwell. I am Charm'd *Madam*, I obey. But some proof you must let me give you;—I'll go for a black box, which Contains the Writings of my whole Estate, and deliver that into your hands.

Lady Wishfort. Ay dear Sir *Rowland*, that will be some Comfort; bring the Black-box.

Waitwell. And may I presume to bring a Contract to be sign'd this Night? May I hope so farr?

Lady Wishfort. Bring what you will; but come alive, pray come alive. O this is a happy discovery.

Waitwell. Dead or Alive I'll come—and married we will be in spight of treachery; Ay and get an Heir that shall defeat the last remaining glimpse of hope in my abandon'd *Nephew*. Come my Buxom Widdow.

Ere long you shall Substantial proof receive
That I'm an Arrant Knight—

Foible. Or arrant Knave.

Exeunt.

ACT V. Scene I.

Scene Continues.

Lady Wishfort *and* Foible.

Lady Wishfort. Out of my house, out of my house, thou *Viper*, thou *Serpent*, that I have foster'd, thou bosome traytress, that I rais'd from nothing—begon, begon, begon, go, go,—that I took from Washing of old Gause and Weaving of dead Hair, with a bleak blew Nose, over a Chafeing-dish of starv'd Embers and Dining behind a Traverse Rag, in a shop no bigger than a Bird-cage,——— go, go, starve again, do, do.

Foible. Dear *Madam*, I'll beg pardon on my knees.

Lady Wishfort. Away, out, out, go set up for your self again ———do, drive a Trade, do, with your three penny-worth of small Ware, flaunting upon a Packthread, under a Brandy-sellers Bulk, or against a dead Wall by a Ballad-monger. Go hang out an old *Frisoneer-gorget*, with a yard of Yellow *Colberteen* again; do; an old gnaw'd *Mask*, two rowes of *Pins* and a *Childs Fiddle*; A *Glass Necklace* with the Beads broken, and a *Quilted Night-cap* with one Ear. Go, go, drive a trade,———these were your *Commodities* you treacherous Trull, this was your *Merchandize* you dealt in when I took you into my house, plac'd you next my self, and made you Governante of my whole Family. You have forgot this, have you, now you have feather'd your Nest?

Foible. No, no, dear *Madam*. Do but hear me, have but a Moment's patience—I'll Confess all. Mr. *Mirabell* seduc'd

Arrant—A play on the two meanings, wandering and outlawed criminal.

Frisoneer-gorget—Stiff neckpiece, made of Friesland stuff.

Colberteen—Coarse French lace, named after Colbert who introduced it from Italy.

me; I am not the first that he has wheadl'd with his dissembling Tongue; Your Lady-ship's own Wisdom has been deluded by him, then how shou'd I a poor Ignorant, defend my self? O *Madam*, if you knew but what he promis'd me; and how he assur'd me your Ladyship shou'd come to no damage———Or else the Wealth of the *Indies* shou'd not have brib'd me to conspire against so Good, so Sweet, so kind a Lady as you have been to me.

Lady Wishfort. No damage? What to Betray me, to Marry me to a Cast-serving-man; to make me a receptacle, an Hospital for a decay'd Pimp? No damage? O thou frontless Impudence, more than a big-Belly'd Actress.

Foible. Pray do but hear me *Madam*, he cou'd not marry your Lady-ship, *Madam*———No indeed his Marriage was to have been void in Law; for he was married to me first, to secure your Lady-ship. He cou'd not have bedded your Lady-ship: for if he had Consummated with your Ladyship, he must have run the risque of the Law, and been put upon his *Clergy*———Yes indeed, I enquir'd of the Law in that case before I wou'd meddle or make.

Lady Wishfort. What, then I have been your Property, have I? I have been convenient to you it seems,———while you were Catering for *Mirabell*; I have been broaker for you? What, have you made a passive Bawd of me?——— this Exceeds all precedent; I am brought to fine uses, to become a botcher of second hand Marriages, between *Abigails* and *Andrews*! I'll couple you, Yes, I'll baste you together, you and your *Philander*. I'll *Dukes-Place* you, as I'm a Person. Your Turtle is in Custody already; You shall Coo in the same Cage, if there be Constable or warrant in the Parish.

Exit.

Foible. O that ever I was Born, O that I was ever Married, ———a Bride, ay I shall be a *Bridewell*-Bride. Oh!

Enter Mrs. Fainall.

Mrs. Fainall. Poor *Foible*, what's the matter?

Foible. O *Madam*, my Lady's gone for a Constable; I shall be had to a Justice, and put to *Bridewell* to beat Hemp, poor *Waitwell*'s gone to prison already.

meddle or make—Interfere (proverbial).
Dukes-Place—The place where they had been coupled for a fee.
Bridewell—A prison and house of correction for women.

Mrs. Fainall. Have a good heart *Foible, Mirabell*'s gone to give security for him. This is all *Marwood*'s and my Husband's doing.

Foible. Yes, yes; I know it *Madam*; she was in my Lady's Closet, and over-heard all that you said to me before Dinner. She sent the Letter to my Lady, and that missing Effect, Mr. *Fainall* laid this Plot to arrest *Waitwell*, when he pretended to go for the Papers; and in the mean time Mrs. *Marwood* declar'd all to my Lady.

Mrs. Fainall. Was there no mention made of me in the Letter?—My Mother do's not suspect my being in the Confederacy? I fancy *Marwood* has not told her, tho' she has told my husband.

Foible. Yes *Madam*; but my Lady did not see that part; We stifl'd the Letter before she read so far. Has that mischeivous Devil told Mr. *Fainall* of your Ladyship then?

Mrs. Fainall. Ay, all's out, My affair with *Mirabell*, every thing discover'd. This is the last day of our living together, that's my Comfort.

Foible. Indeed *Madam*, and so 'tis a Comfort if you knew all, ———he has been even with your Ladyship; which I cou'd have told you-long enough since, but I love to keep Peace and Quietness by my good will: I had rather bring friends together, than set 'em at distance. But Mrs. *Marwood* and He are nearer related than ever their Parents thought for.

Mrs. Fainall. Say'st thou so *Foible*? Canst thou prove this?

Foible. I can take my Oath of it *Madam*, so can Mrs. *Mincing*; we have had many a fair word from *Madam Marwood*, to conceal something that pass'd in our Chamber one Evening when you were at *Hide-Park*;—And we were thought to have gone a Walking: But we went up unawares,—tho' we were sworn to secresie too; *Madam Marwood* took a Book and swore us upon it: But it was but a Book of Verses and Poems,—So as long as it was not a Bible-Oath, we may break it with a safe Conscience.

Mrs. Fainall. This discovery is the most opportune thing I cou'd wish. Now *Mincing*?

Enter Mincing.

Mincing. My Lady wou'd speak with Mrs. *Foible*, *Mem*. Mr. *Mirabell* is with her, he has set your Spouse at liberty Mrs.

Foible; and wou'd have you hide your self in my Lady's Closet, till my old Lady's anger is abated. O, my old Lady is in a perilous passion, at something Mr. *Fainall* has said. He swears, and my old Lady cry's. There's a fearful Hurricane I vow. He says *Mem*, how that he'll have my Lady's Fortune made over to him, or he'll be divorc'd.

Mrs. Fainall. Do's your Lady and *Mirabell* know that?

Mincing. Yes *Mem*, they have sent me to see if Sir *Wilfull* be sober, and to bring him to them. My Lady is resolv'd to have him I think, rather than loose such a vast Summ as six thousand Pound. O, come Mrs. *Foible*, I hear my old Lady.

Mrs. Fainall. Foible, you must tell *Mincing*, that she must prepare to vouch when I call her.

Foible. Yes, yes *Madam.*

Mincing. O yes *Mem*, I'll vouch any thing for your Ladyship's service, be what it will.

Exeunt Mincing *and* Foible.

Enter Lady Wishfort *and* Marwood.

Lady Wishfort. O my dear Friend, how can I Enumerate the benefits that I have receiv'd from your goodness? To you I owe the timely discovery of the false vows of *Mirabell*; To you the Detection of the Imposter Sir *Rowland*. And now you are become an Intercessor with my Son-in-Law, to save the Honour of my House, and Compound for the frailties of my Daughter. Well Friend, you are enough to reconcile me to the bad World, or else I wou'd retire to Desarts and Solitudes; and feed harmless Sheep by *Groves* and *Purling Streams*. Dear *Marwood*, let us leave the World, and retire by our selves and be *Shepherdesses.*

Mrs. Marwood. Let us first dispatch the affair in hand *Madam*, we shall have leisure to think of Retirement afterwards. Here is one who is concern'd in the treaty.

Lady Wishfort. O Daughter, Daughter, Is it possible thou shoud'st be my Child, Bone of my Bone, and Flesh of my Flesh, and as I may say, another Me, and yet transgress the most minute Particle of severe Vertue? Is it possible you should lean aside to Iniquity who have been Cast in the direct Mold of Vertue? I have not only been a Mold but a Pattern for you, and a Model for you, after you were brought into the World.

Mrs. Fainall. I don't understand your Ladyship.

Lady Wishfort. Not understand? Why have you not been Naught? Have you not been Sophisticated? Not understand? Here I am ruin'd to Compound for your *Caprices* and your *Cuckoldomes.* I must pawn my *Plate*, and my *Jewells* and ruine my *Neice*, and all little enough—

Mrs. Fainall. I am wrong'd and abus'd, and so are you. 'Tis a false accusation, as false as *Hell*, as false as your Friend there, ay or your Friend's Friend, my false Husband.

Mrs. Marwood. My Friend, Mrs. *Fainall*? Your Husband my Friend, what do you mean?

Mrs. Fainall. I know what I mean *Madam*, and so do you; and so shall the World at a time Convenient.

Mrs. Marwood. I am sorry to see you so passionate, *Madam.* More Temper wou'd look more like Innocence. But I have done. I am sorry my Zeal to serve your Ladyship and Family, shou'd admit of Misconstruction, or make me liable to affronts. You will pardon me, *Madam*, If I meddle no more with an affair, in which I am not Personally concern'd.

Lady Wishfort. O dear Friend; I am so asham'd that you should meet with such returns;———you ought to ask Pardon on your Knees, Ungratefull Creature; she deserves more from you than all your life can accomplish—O don't leave me destitute in this Perplexity;—No, stick to me my good Genius.

Mrs. Fainall. I tell you *Madam* you're abus'd———stick to you? ay, like a *Leach*, to suck your best Blood———she'll drop off when she's full. *Madam* you sha'not pawn a *Bodkin*, nor part with a *Brass Counter* in Composition for me. I defie 'em all. Let 'em prove their aspersions: I know my own Innocence, and dare stand a tryall.

Exit.

Lady Wishfort. Why, If she shou'd be Innocent, If she shou'd be wrong'd after all, ha? I don't know what to think,—and I promise you, her Education has been unexceptionable—I may say it; for I chiefly made it my own Care to Initiate her very Infancy in the Rudiments of Vertue, and to Impress upon her tender Years, a Young *Odium* and *Aversion* to the very sight of Men,———ay Friend, she wou'd ha' shriek'd, If she had but seen a Man, till she was in her Teens. As I'm a Person 'tis true———She was never suffer'd to play with a Male-Child, tho' but in Coats; Nay her very Babies were of the *Feminine Gender*, ———O, she never look'd a Man in the Face but her own Father, or the Chaplain, and him we made a shift to put upon her for a Woman, by the help of his long Garments, and his Sleek-face; till she was going in her fifteen.

Mrs. Marwood. Twas much she shou'd be deceiv'd so long.

Lady Wishfort. I warrant you, or she wou'd never have born to have been Catechis'd by him; and have heard his long lectures, against Singing and Dancing, and such Debaucheries; and going to filthy *Plays*; and Profane *Musick-meetings*, where the Leud Trebles squeek nothing but Bawdy, and the Bases roar *Blasphemy*. O, she wou'd have swooned at the sight or name of an obscene Play-Book—and can I think after all this, that my Daughter can be Naught? What, a Whore? And thought it excommunication to set her foot within the door of a Play-house. O my dear friend, I can't believe it, No, no; as she says, let him prove it, let him prove it.

Mrs. Marwood. Prove it *Madam*? What, and have your name prostituted in a publick Court; Yours and your Daughters reputation worry'd at the Barr by a pack of Bawling Lawyers? To be usherd in with an *O Yez* of Scandal; and have your Case open'd by an old fumbling Leacher in a Quoif like a Man Midwife to bring your Daughter's Infamy to light, to be a Theme for legal Punsters, and Quiblers by the Statute; and become a Jest, against a Rule of Court, where there is no precedent for a Jest in any record; not even in *Dooms-day-Book*: to discompose the gravity of the Bench, and provoke Naughty Interrogatories, in more Naughty *Law Latin*; while the good Judge tickl'd with the proceeding, Simpers under a Grey beard, and fidges off and on his Cushion as if he had swallow'd *Cantharides*, or sat upon *Cow-Itch*.

Lady Wishfort. O, 'tis very hard!

Mrs. Marwood. And then to have my Young *Revellers* of the *Temple*, take Notes like Prentices at a *Conventicle*; and after, talk it all over again in Commons, or before Drawers in an *Eating-house*.

cantharides—A diuretic, or aphrodisiac.
Cow-Itch—Or cowage, the pods of a tropical plant with stiff bristles which cause intolerable itching.
in Commons—Dining in hall.

Lady Wishfort. Worse and Worse.

Mrs. Marwood. Nay this is nothing; if it wou'd end here, 'twere well. But it must after this be consign'd by the Short-hand Writers to the publick Press; and from thence be transferr'd to the hands, nay into the Throats and Lungs of Hawkers, with Voices more Licentious than the loud *Flounder-man's* or the *Woman* that crys *Grey-pease*; and this you must hear till you are stunn'd; Nay you must hear nothing else for some days.

Lady Wishfort. O, 'tis Insupportable. No, no, dear Friend make it up, make it up; ay, ay, I'll Compound. I'll give up all, my self and my all, my *Neice* and her all,—any thing, everything for Composition.

Mrs. Marwod. Nay *Madam*, I advise nothing, I only lay before you as a Friend the Inconveniencies which perhaps you have Overseen. Here comes Mr. *Fainall.* If he will be satisfi'd to huddle up all in Silence, I shall be glad. You must think I would rather Congratulate, than Condole with you.

Enter Fainall.

Lady Wishfort. Ay, ay, I do not doubt it, dear *Marwood*: No, no, I do not doubt it.

Fainall. Well Madam; I have suffer'd my self to be overcome by the Importunity of this Lady your Friend; and am content you shall enjoy your own proper Estate during Life; on condition you oblige your self never to Marry, under such penalty as I think convenient.

Lady Wishfort. Never to Marry?

Fainall. No more Sir *Rowlands*,———the next Imposture may not be so timely detected.

Mrs. Marwood. That condition I dare answer, my Lady will consent to, without difficulty; she has already but too much experienc'd the perfidiousness of Men. Besides Madam, when we retire to our pastoral Solitude we shall bid adieu to all other Thoughts.

Lady Wishfort. Aye that's true; but in Case of Necessity; as of Health, or some such Emergency—

Fainall. O, if you are prescrib'd Marriage, you shall be consider'd; I will only reserve to my self the Power to chuse for you. If your Physick be wholsome, it matters not who is your Apothecary. Next, my Wife shall settle on me the remainder of her Fortune, not made over already; And for her Maintenance depend entirely on my Discretion.

Lady Wishfort. This is most inhumanly Savage; exceeding the Barbarity of a *Muscovite* Husband.

Fainall. I learn'd it from his *Czarish* Majestie's Retinue, in a Winter Evenings Conference over Brandy and Pepper, a-mongst other secrets of Matrimony and Policy, as they are at present Practis'd in the *Northern* Hemisphere. But this must be agreed unto, and that positively. Lastly, I will be endow'd in right of my Wife, with that six thousand Pound, which is the Moiety of Mrs. *Millamant's* Fortune in your Possession: And which she has forfeited (as will appear by the last Will and Testament of your deceas'd Husband Sir *Jonathan Wishfort*) by her disobedience in Contracting her self against your Consent or Knowledge; and by refusing the offer'd Match with Sir *Wilfull Witwoud*, which you like a careful Aunt had provided for her.

Lady Wishfort. My Nephew was *non Compos*; and cou'd not make his Addresses.

Fainall. I come to make demands,———I'll hear no objections.

Lady Wishfort. You will grant me time to Consider.

Fainall. Yes, while the Instrument is drawing, to which you must set your Hand till more sufficient Deeds can be perfected, which I will take care shall be done with all possible speed. In the mean while, I will go for the said Instrument, and till my return, you may Ballance this Matter in your own Discretion.

Exit Fainall.

Lady Wishfort. This Insolence is beyond all Precedent, all Parallel, must I be subject to this merciless Villain?

Mrs. Marwood. 'Tis severe indeed *Madam*, that you shou'd smart for your Daughters wantonness.

Lady Wishfort. 'Twas against my Consent that she Married this Barbarian, But she wou'd have him, tho' her Year was not out.———Ah! her first Husband my Son *Languish*, would not have carry'd it thus. Well, that was my Choice,

Czarish Majestie's Retinue—Recent visit of Peter the Great to London, in 1697, which had prompted books about Muscovy and its people.

this is her's; she is match'd now with a Witness——I shall be mad, Dear Friend is there no Comfort for me? Must I live to be confiscated at this Rebel-rate?——Here come two more of my *Egyptian* Plagues too.

Enter Millamant *and* Sir Wilfull.

Sir Wilfull. Aunt, your Servant.

Lady Wishfort. Out *Caterpillar,* Call not me Aunt, I know thee not.

Sir Wilfull. I confess I have been a little in disguise as they say, —S'heart! and I'm sorry for't. What wou'd you have? I hope I committed no Offence Aunt——and if I did I am willing to make satisfaction; and what can a man say fairer? If I have broke any thing, I'll pay for't, an it cost a Pound. And so let that content for what's past, and make no more words. For what's to come to pleasure you I'm willing to marry my Cozen. So pray lets all be Friends, she and I are agreed upon the matter, before a Witness.

Lady Wishfort. How's this dear *Neice*? Have I any comfort? Can this be true?

Millamant. I am content to be a Sacrifice to your repose *Madam,* and to Convince you that I had no hand in the Plot, as you were misinform'd; I have laid my commands on *Mirabell* to come in Person, and be a Witness that I give my hand to this flower of *Knight-hood*; and for the Contract that past between *Mirabell* and me, I have oblig'd him to make a Resignation of it, in your Lady-ship's presence; ——He is without and waits your leave for admittance.

Lady Wishfort. Well, I'll swear I am something reviv'd at this Testimony of your Obedience; but I cannot admit that Traytor,—I fear I cannot fortifie my self to support his appearance. He is as terrible to me as a *Gorgon*; if I see him, I fear I shall turn to Stone, petrifie Incessantly.

Millamant. If you disoblige him he may resent your refusal and insist upon the contract still. Then 'tis the last time he will be offensive to you.

Lady Wishfort. Are you sure it will be the last time?——if I were sure of that——shall I never see him again?

Millamant. Sir *Wilfull,* you and he are to Travel together, are you not?

Sir Wilfull. 'Sheart the Gentleman's a civil Gentleman, Aunt, let him come in; why we are sworn Brothers and fellow Travellers.—We are to be *Pylades* and *Orestes*, he and I—He is to be my Interpreter in foreign Parts. He has been Over-sea's once already; and with proviso that I Marry my Cozen, will cross 'em once again, only to bear me Company,———'Sheart, I'll call him in,———an I set on't once, he shall come in; and see who'll hinder him.

Exit.

Mrs. Marwood. This is precious Fooling, if it wou'd pass, but I'll know the bottom of it.

Lady Wishfort. O dear *Marwood*, you are not going?

Marwood. Not far Madam; I'll return immediately.

Exit.

Re-enter Sir Wilfull *and* Mirabell.

Sir Wilfull. Look up Man, I'll stand by you, 'sbud an she do frown, she can't kill you;—besides—Hearkee she dare not frown desperately, because her face is none of her own; 'Sheart an she shou'd her forehead wou'd wrinkle like the Coat of a Cream-cheese, but mum for that, fellow Traveller.

Mirabell. If a deep sense of the many Injuries I have offer'd to so good a Lady, with a sincere remorse, and a hearty Contrition, can but obtain the least glance of Compassion I am too Happy,—Ah *Madam*, there was a time—but let it be forgotten—I confess I have deservedly forfeited the high Place I once held, of sighing at your Feet; nay kill me not, by turning from me in disdain,—I come not to plead for favour;———Nay not for Pardon, I am a Suppliant only for your pity———I am going where I never shall behold you more—

Sir Wilfull. How, fellow Traveller!—You shall go by your self then.

Mirabell. Let me be pitied first; and afterwards forgotten, —I ask no more.

Sir Wilfull. By'r Lady a very reasonable request; and will cost you nothing, Aunt—Come, come, Forgive and Forget Aunt, why you must an you are a Christian.

Pylades and Orestes—Whose faithful friendship had become proverbial. See the story in Ovid, *De Ponto*, iii, 65.

Mirabell. Consider *Madam*, in reality; You cou'd not receive much prejudice; it was an Innocent device; tho' I confess it had a Face of guiltiness,—it was at most an Artifice which Love Contriv'd—and errours which Love produces have ever been accounted *Venial.* At least think it is Punishment enough, that I have lost what in my heart I hold most dear, that to your cruel Indignation, I have offer'd up this Beauty, and with her my Peace and Quiet; Nay all my hopes of future Comfort.

Sir Wilfull. An he do's not move me, wou'd I might never be *O' the Quorum*—an it were not as good a deed as to drink, to give her to him again,—I wou'd I might never take Shipping—Aunt, if you don't forgive quickly; I shall melt, I can tell you that. My contract went no further than a little Mouth-Glew, and that's hardly dry;—One dolefull Sigh more from my fellow Traveller and 'tis dissolv'd.

Lady Wishfort. Well *Nephew*, upon your account———ah, he has a false Insinuating Tongue—Well Sir, I will stifle my just resentment at my *Nephew's* request. —I will endeavour what I can to forget,—but on *proviso* that you resign the Contract with my *Neice* Immediately.

Mirabell. It is in Writing and with Papers of Concern; but I have sent my Servant for it, and will deliver it to you, with all acknowledgments for your transcendent goodness.

Lady Wishfort (*apart*). Oh, he has *Witch-craft* in his Eyes and Tongue;———When I did not see him I cou'd have brib'd a Villain to his Assassination; but his appearance rakes the *Embers* which have so long layn smother'd in my Breast.—

Enter Fainall *and* Mrs. Marwood.

Fainall. Your date of deliberation *Madam*, is expir'd. Here is the Instrument, are you prepar'd to sign?

Lady Wishfort. If I were prepar'd; I am not Impowr'd. My *Neice* exerts a lawfull claim, having Match'd her self by my direction to Sir *Wilfull.*

Fainall. That sham is too gross to pass on me,———tho 'tis Impos'd on you, *Madam.*

O' the Quorum—Refers to his commission as a country Justice of the Peace.

Millamant. Sir, I have given my consent.

Mirabell. And Sir, I have resign'd my pretensions.

Sir Wilfull. And Sir, I assert my right; and will maintain it in defiance of you Sir, and of your Instrument. S'heart an you talk of an Instrument Sir, I have an old *Fox* by my Thigh shall hack your Instrument of *Ram Vellum* to shreds, Sir. It shall not be sufficient for a *Mittimus* or a *Taylor's* measure; therefore withdraw your Instrument Sir, or by'r Lady I shall draw mine.

Lady Wishfort. Hold *Nephew*, hold.

Millamant. Good Sir *Wilfull*, respite your valour.

Fainall. Indeed? are you provided of a Guard, with your single Beef-eater there? but I'm prepar'd for you; and Insist upon my first proposal. You shall submit your own Estate to my management, And absolutely make over my Wife's to my sole use; As pursuant to the Purport and Tenor of this other Covenant,—I suppose *Madam*, your Consent is not requisite in this Case; nor Mr. *Mirabell*, your resignation; nor Sir *Wilfull*, your right—You may draw your *Fox* if you please Sir, and make a *Bear-Garden* flourish somewhere else; For here it will not avail. This, my Lady *Wishfort*, must be subscrib'd, or your Darling Daughter's turn'd a drift, like a Leaky hulk to Sink or Swim, as she and the Current of this Lewd Town can agree.

Lady Wishfort. Is there no means, no Remedy, to stop my ruine? Ungrateful Wretch! dost thou not owe thy being, thy subsistance to my Daughter's Fortune?

Fainall. I'll answer you when I have the rest of it in my possession.

Mirabell. But that you wou'd not accept of a Remedy from my hands———I own I have not deserv'd you shou'd owe any Obligation to me; or else perhaps I cou'd advise.—

Lady Wishfort. O what? what? to save me and my Child from Ruine, from Want, I'll forgive all that's past; Nay I'll consent to any thing to come, to be deliver'd from this Tyranny.

Mirabell. Ay *Madam*; but that is too late, my reward is intercepted. You have dispos'd of her, who only cou'd have

Mittimus—A warrant for imprisonment.
Taylor's measure—Often made out of old parchment.

made me a Compensation for all my Services;———But be it as it may. I am resolv'd I'll serve you, you shall not be wrong'd in this *Savage* manner.

Lady Wishfort. How! dear Mr. *Mirabell,* can you be so generous at last! But it is not possible. *Hearkee.* I'll break my *Nephews* Match, you shall have my *Niece* yet, and all her fortune; if you can but save me from this imminent danger.

Mirabell. Will you? I take you at your word. I ask no more. I must have leave for two Criminals to appear.

Lady Wishfort. Ay, ay, any Body, any body.

Mirabell. Foible is one and a Penitent.

Enter Mrs. Fainall, Foible, *and* Mincing.

Mrs. Marwood (*to* Fainall) O my shame! (Mirabell *and* Lady Wishfort *go to* Mrs. Fainall *and* Foible). These Corrupt things are bought and brought hither to expose me—

Fainall. If it must all come out, why let 'em know it, 'tis but *the way of the World.* That shall not urge me to relinquish or abate one tittle of my Terms, no, I will insist the more.

Foible. Yes indeed *Madam*; I'll take my Bible-oath of it.

Mincing. And so will I, *Mem.*

Lady Wishfort. O *Marwood, Marwood* art thou false? my friend deceive me? hast thou been a wicked accomplice with that profligate man?

Mrs. Marwood. Have you so much Ingratitude and Injustice, to give credit against your Friend, to the Aspersions of two such Mercenary Truls?

Mincing. Mercenary, *Mem*? I scorn your words. 'Tis true we found you and Mr. *Fainall* in the Blew garret; by the same token, you swore us to Secresie upon *Messalinas*'s Poems. Mercenary? No, if we wou'd have been Mercenary, we shou'd have held our Tongues; You wou'd have brib'd us sufficiently.

Messalinas's Poems—As Bonamy Dobrée suggests, Mincing probably means "miscellany poems." *The Collection of Miscellany Poems by Mr. Brown,* which had just appeared in 1699, would have spoiled the sacredness of any oath.

Fainall. Go, you are an Insignificant thing,———Well, what are you the better for this? Is this Mr. *Mirabell*'s Expedient? I'll be put off no longer———You thing that was a Wife, shall smart for this. I will not leave thee wherewithall to hide thy Shame; Your Body shall be Naked as your Reputation.

Mrs. Fainall. I despise you and defie your Malice———You have aspers'd me wrongfully———I have prov'd your falsehood———Go you and your treacherous———I will not name it, but starve together—perish.

Fainall. Not while you are worth a Groat, indeed my dear. *Madam*, I'll be fool'd no longer.

Lady Wishfort. Ah Mr. *Mirabell*, this is small comfort, the detection of this affair.

Mirabell. O in good time—Your leave for the other Offender and Penitent to appear, *Madam*.

Enter Waitwell *with a Box of Writings.*

Lady Wishfort. O Sir *Rowland*———well Rascal.

Waitwell. What your Ladyship pleases.—I have brought the Black box at last, *Madam*.

Mirabell. Give it me. *Madam*, you remember your promise.

Lady Wishfort. I, dear Sir!

Mirabell. Where are the Gentlemen?

Waitwell. At hand Sir, rubbing their Eyes,———Just risen from Sleep.

Fainall. S'death what's this to me? I'll not wait your private concerns.

Enter Petulant *and* Witwoud.

Petulant. How now? what's the matter? who's hand's out?

Witwoud. Hey day! what are you all got together like Players at the end of the last Act?

Mirabell. You may remember Gentlemen, I once requested your hands as Witnesses to a certain Parchment.

Witwoud. Ay I do, my hand I remember———*Petulant* set his Mark.

Mirabell. You wrong him, his name is fairly written as shall appear—you do not remember Gentlemen, any thing of what that Parchment contain'd———(*undoing the Box.*)

Witwoud. No.

Petulant. Not I. I writ. I read nothing.

Mirabell. Very well, now you shall know—*Madam*, your promise.

Lady Wishfort. Ay, ay, Sir, upon my honour.

Mirabell. Mr. *Fainall*, it is now time that you shou'd know, that your Lady while she was at her own disposal, and before you had by your Insinuations wheadl'd her out of a pretended Settlement of the greatest part of her fortune—

Fainall. Sir! pretended!

Mirabell. Yes Sir. I say that this Lady while a Widdow, having it seems receiv'd some Cautions respecting your Inconstancy and Tyranny of temper, which from her own partial Opinion and fondness of you, she cou'd never have suspected—she did I say by the wholesome advice of Friends and of Sages learned in the Laws of this Land, deliver this same as her Act and Deed to me in trust, and to the uses within mention'd. You may read if you please ———(*holding out the Parchment.*) tho perhaps what is inscrib'd on the back may serve your occasions.

Fainall. Very likely Sir, What's here? Damnation! (*Reads*) *A deed of Conveyance of the whole Estate real of* Arabella Languish *Widdow in trust to* Edward Mirabell. Confusion!

Mirabell. Even so Sir, 'tis *the way of the World*, Sir: of the Widdows of the World. I suppose this Deed may bear an Elder Date than what you have obtain'd from your Lady.

Fainall. Perfidious Fiend! then thus I'll be reveng'd.—(*offers to run at Mrs.* Fainall.)

Sir. Wilfull. Hold Sir, now you may make your *Bear-Garden* flourish somewhere else Sir.

Fainall. Mirabell, You shall hear of this Sir, be sure you shall, let me pass *Oafe*.

Exit.

Mrs. Fainall. Madam, you seem to stifle your Resentment: You had better give it Vent.

Mrs. Marwood. Yes it shall have Vent———and to your Confusion, or I'll perish in the attempt.

Exit.

Lady Wishfort. O Daughter, Daughter, 'tis plain thou hast inherited thy Mother's prudence.

Mrs. Fainall. Thank Mr. *Mirabell*, a Cautious Friend, to whose advice all is owing.

Lady Wishford. Well Mr. *Mirabell*, you have kept your promise,—and I must perform mine.———First I pardon for your sake, Sir *Rowland* there and *Foible*,———The next thing is to break the Matter to my *Nephew*———and how to do that—

Mirabell. For that *Madam*, give your self no trouble———let me have your Consent———Sir *Wilfull* is my Friend; he has had compassion upon Lovers and generously engag'd a Volunteer in this Action, for our Service, and now designs to prosecute his Travells.

Sir Wilfull. S'heart Aunt, I have no mind to marry. My Cozen's a Fine Lady, and the Gentleman loves her and she loves him, and they deserve one another; my resolution is to see Foreign Parts—I have set on't—And when I'm set on't, I must do't. And if these two Gentlemen wou'd Travel too, I think they may be spar'd.

Petulant. For my part, I say little———I think things are best off or on.

Witwoud. I Gad I understand nothing of the matter,———I'm in a maze yet, like a *Dog* in a *Dancing School.*

Lady Wishfort. Well Sir, take her, and with her all the Joy I can give you.

Millamant. Why do's not the man take me? wou'd you have me give my self to you over again.

Mirabell. Ay, and over and over again; for I wou'd have you as often as possibly I can. (*Kisses her hand*). Well, heav'n grant I love you not too well, that's all my fear.

Sir Wilfull. S'heart you'll have him time enough to toy after you're married; or if you will toy now; Let us have a Dance in the mean time, that we who are not Lovers, may have some other employment, besides looking on.

Mirabell. With all my heart dear Sir *Wilfull*, what shall we do for Musick?

Foible. O Sir, Some that were provided for Sir *Rowland*'s Entertainment are yet within Call.

A Dance.

Lady Wishfort. As I am a person I can hold out no longer;—I have wasted my spirits so to day already; that I am ready to sink under the fatigue; and I cannot but have some fears upon me yet, that my Son *Fainall* will pursue some desperate Course.

Mirabell. Madam, disquiet not your self on that account, to my knowledge his Circumstances are such, he must of force comply. For my part I will Contribute all that in me lies to a Reunion, (*To Mrs.* Fainall) in the mean time, *Madam*, let me before these Witnesses, restore to you this deed of trust. It may be a means well manag'd to make you live Easily together.

From hence let those be warn'd, who mean to wed;
Lest mutual falsehood stain the Bridal-Bed:
For each deceiver to his cost may find,
That marriage frauds too oft are paid in kind.

Exeunt Omnes.

Epilogue.

Spoken by Mrs. *Bracegirdle*.

After our *Epilogue* this Crowd dismisses,
I'm thinking how this Play'll be pull'd to Pieces.
But pray consider, ere you doom its fall,
How hard a thing 'twould be, to please you all.
There are some Criticks so with Spleen diseas'd,
They scarcely come inclining to be Pleas'd:
And sure he must have more than mortal Skill,
Who pleases any one against his Will.
Then, all bad Poets we are sure are Foes,
And how their Number's swell'd the Town well knows:
In shoals, I've mark'd 'em judging in the Pit;
Tho' they're on no pretence for Judgment fit
But that they have been Damn'd for want of wit.
Since when, they by their own offences taught
Set up for Spys on Plays and finding Fault.
Others there are whose Malice we'd prevent;
Such, who watch Plays, with scurrilous intent
To mark out who by *Characters* are meant.
And tho' no perfect likeness they can Trace;
Yet each pretends to know the *Copy'd Face*.
These with false Glosses, feed their own Ill-nature,
And turn to *Libel*, what was meant a *Satire*.
May such malicious *Fops* this Fortune find,
To think themselves alone the *Fools* design'd:
If any are so arrogantly Vain,
To think they *singly* can support a *Scene*,
And furnish *Fool* enough to entertain.
For well the Learn'd and the Judicious know,
That *Satire* scorns to stoop so meanly low,
As any *one abstracted Fop* to shew.
For, as when Painters form a matchless Face,
They from each *Fair One* catch some different Grace,
And shining Features in one Portrait blend,
To which no single Beauty must pretend:
So Poets oft, do in one Piece expose
Whole *Belles Assemblées* of *Cocquetts* and *Beaux*.

FINIS.

Textual Notes

This simple textual apparatus has been designed to show wherever it has been necessary to introduce any substantive emendation into the reading of the copytext, and to give the source of the emendation; and further by giving collations with the later editions printed during Congreve's life to record all the substantive corrections and alterations for which he was responsible or that he at least accepted in the final texts printed under his supervision. Thus, for instance, many changes have been made in the accidentals of the copytext of *The Old Batchelour* that are not recorded here. The first edition was set up very hurriedly and contains many minor literal errors which were corrected in the second edition. It is enough to give some examples here: *wos* for *was*; *Tha's* for *That's*; *trnth* for *truth*; *your* for *you're*; *trival* for *trivial*; *Faver* for *Fever*; *pepare* for *prepare*. There are frequent omissions of hyphens and apostrophes; commas are left out or inserted in the wrong places. All such errors have been corrected and are given in the form in which they appeared in the early quartos. In the other plays, printed for Tonson, the first quartos were set more carefully, and few emendations have been required except in minor matters of punctuation. Although a considerable number of copies of the first quartos have been examined and compared with the photocopies of the Harvard copies which have been used as copytext, no record of press variants is given here; the text of the corrected state has been followed, as well as the corrections that have been made by cancels.

THE OLD BATCHELOUR

EMENDATIONS OF COPYTEXT

p. 34 *Prologue intended for the Old Batchelour*

Written by the Lord *FALKLAND*] W; *sent to the Author, by an unknown Hand* Qq.

p. 36 Dramatis Personæ] W; Personæ Dramatis Qq.
MEN] W; Men By Qq.
Boy and Footmen] W; *Footmen* Qq.

I, i

52 in] Q3; An Q1–2.
267 Lady's] Q3; Ladies Q1–2
340 *Wittol*] Q6; *Wittal* Q1–5

II, i

24 lost] Q2; cost Q1
206 name] Q2; am Q1, 5
218 eat] Q3; let Q1, 2, 5

II, ii

125 a Dun] Q2; have done Q1, 5

III, i

85 lose] Q5; loose Q1–4
160 interrupt] Q5; intempt Q1–4

IV, iii

11 unhewn] Q4; unknown Q1–3, 5
185 mystically] W, *Errata*; mystically, Qq., W.

V, ii

86 *Wittol*] W; *Wittal* Qq.
109 Wife's] Q3; Wive's Q1, 2, 5, 6

COLLATIONS OF EARLY EDITIONS

The present text has been collated with the seven quarto editions and with the collected editions of Congreve's works, as listed below:

First edition, printed for Peter Buck, 1693, Q1
Second, third, fourth editions, 1693, Q2–4
Fifth edition (Knapton), 1694, Q5
Sixth edition, 1697, Q6
Seventh edition, 1707, Q7

Collected Works, first edition, 8vo., 1710, W1; third edition, corrected, 12mo., 1719, W2.

Dedication

The Epistle Dedicatory] *Dedication* Ww.
p. 29, l. 33 Vertues] Qualities Ww.
p. 30, l. 9 of Action] of the Action Ww.
l. 17 need] needed Ww.

To Mr. Congreve, by J. Marsh

5 Spight would] Spirit Ww.

To Mr. Congreve by Bevil Higgons

15 our Clapping does you Justice do] with Clapping, we are just to you Ww.

20 give] giv'st Q6, 7, Ww.

p. 34 Prologue intended for the Old Batchelour

Written by the Lord FALKLAND] *sent to the Author, by an unknown Hand* Qq.

p. 36 Dramatis Personæ] Personæ Dramatis Qq.

MEN] Men By Qq.

Alexander] Verbruggen Q7, Ww.

Boy and Footmen] *Footmen* Qq.

The Scene] SCENE, Ww.

I, i

p. 37 The Street.] SCENE, *The Street.* Ww.

3 a'] h' Q6; he Ww.

9 Pox o' Business] Business! Ww.

19 Ay, ay Pox] Ay, ay, Ww.

25 earthy] earthly Q5–7, Ww.

46 enjoy'd] had Ww.

52 in] An Q1–2

61 For she only stalks under him to take Aim at her Husband] *om.* Ww.

128 on't] of it Ww.

132 Service] Services Ww.

133 seeing] having seen Ww.

148 Soliloques] Soliloquys Q6, W1; Soliloquies Q7, W2

266 when it may be the means of getting into a fair Lady's Books] *om.* Ww.

270 even this may] even, that, may Ww.

323 a'] h' Q6; he Ww.

338 here he comes,] stand close, let 'em pass.] 'tis Sir *Joseph Wittoll* with his Friend; Ww.

(Sir *Joseph Wittoll* and Capt. *Bluffe*, cross the Stage.)] but I see he has turn'd the Corner and goes another way. Ww.

364 help'd] had help'd Ww.

II, i

5 devour'd my Members] devour'd &c. Ww.

24 lost] cost Q1

35 sorry] very sorry Q5–7, Ww.

54 must] most Q3, 4, Ww.

89 refunding] paying Ww.

123 God bless us] bless us Ww.

141 How, how,] How now Q6, 7, Ww.

200 am] name Q2–4, 6, Ww.

218 eat] let Q1, 2, 5

II, ii

6 you] you've Ww.
125 a Dun] have done Q1, 5
185 standing] most prevailing Q3–4, 6–7, Ww.
185 depress'd] express'd Q6–7, Ww.
207 in the] into the Q3–4

III, i

1 a'] h' Q6–7; he Ww.
31 meet his Lust] meet his Ww.
34 itches] kindles Ww.
72 Hust] Hush Ww.
74 Foregod] Foregad Ww.
85 lose] loose Q1–4
93 betwixt] between Q5–7, Ww.
101 easie] easily Ww.
142 but the tother] but the other Q2–4; but t'other Q6–7; t'other Ww.
160 interrupt] intempt Q1–4
197 as a Clap is to the Pox] *om.* Ww.
204 Mistress mine] Mistress of Mine Q5–7, Ww.
211 *Cries.*] *om.* Ww.
245 *Fondle-wife*] *Fumblewife* Q1
328 without] unless Ww.

III, ii

1–24 SONG] *Verses ii and iii om.* Ww.
42 in] with Q5–7, Ww.
55 Pox] Death Ww.
78 Melancholy] Melancholick Ww.
79 you . . . you] thee . . . thee Ww.
112 be naught] naught Q5–7
129 her sight] sight Q5–7, Ww.
134 she kisses] her kiss is Q6–7, Ww.
135 Resolve] Resolves Ww.
163 do] both Ww.

IV, i

17 *Varlet*] *Valet* Q1, 2, 5
38 affair so!] Affair, Sir! Ww.
45 Go in] Go Ww.
84 You will have it some where else] *om.* Ww.
102 terrible] terribly Q2–7, Ww.
177 ore] over Q5–7, Ww.

IV, ii

2 I'll call my Mistress] My Mistress is coming, Sir. Ww.

IV, iii

10 put] have put Ww.
11 unhewn] unknown Q1–3, 5
40 Courtesies] Curtsies Q6–7, Ww.
54 Kid] Kid-leather Ww.
99 a Distance] some Distance Ww.
154 have] has Ww.
156 the t'other] t'other Ww.
178 here is] here's Ww.
185 mystically] mystically, Qq., W (*uncorr.*)

IV, iv

97 a warm] some warm Ww.
165 I wish he had lain upon no-bodies stomach but his own.] *om.* Ww.
166 me that,] me, Ww.
168 excuse] to excuse Q4, 7
243 coming] come Q5–7, Ww.
251 Philistines have been upon thee] Philistines—Ww.

V, i

17 Pox] ay Ww.
49 stop] make Ww.
51 It is] is it Q5–7, Ww.
63 have you know] have you to know Q6–7, Ww.
90 so musty] musty Ww.
183 fit] fitting Q5–7, Ww.
187 his extremity] Extremity Q6–7, Ww.
232 foolish as] foolish a thing as Ww.
261 Ladies favours] ladies favour Q5–7; Lady's favour Ww.
342 succeeding] succeeded Q5–7, Ww.
369 flattering] fluttering Ww.
392 I'm in haste now, but I'll come in at the Catastrophe.] *om.* Ww.

V, ii

7 Leave me.] *om.* Ww.
31 *Jesus,* how] How Ww.
67, 69 Whore . . . Whore] Mistress . . . Mistress Ww.
172 *To* Araminta.] *om.* Q5–7, Ww.

Epilogue

last line; End] Ends Ww.

THE DOUBLE-DEALER

EMENDATIONS OF COPYTEXT

To my Dear Friend Mr. Congreve

32 Nor] W; Now Qq.

Prologue

16 too] W; to Qq.
126 Dramatis Personæ] W; Personæ Dramatis Qq.
MEN] W; Men By Qq. WOMEN] W; Women by Qq.

I

101 put it] Q2; put Q1
192 Lady's] W; Ladies Qq.

II

25 nor] Q2; and Q1
328 not] Q2; no Q1
416 ay] Q2; I Q1
427 if I accomplish] Q2; if accomplish Q1

III

196 and I] Q2; I Q1
256 awe] Q2; one Q1
430 you—my] W; you why my Q1; you my Q2

IV, i

208 and kiss *Papa*] Q2; kiss and *Papa* Q1
209 in such] Q2; such Q1
252 did; all] W; did. All Q1
430 have a] Q2; have Q1

IV, ii

17 to] Q2; too Q1
77 was] Q2; ways Q1
130 Furies] Q2; Funes Q1

Epilogue

29 Poor Poets thus] W2; Thus poor Poets Qq. W1.

COLLATIONS OF EARLY EDITIONS

The present text has been collated with the two quarto editions of 1694 (Q1) and 1706 (Q2) and the collected editions of 1710 and 1719.

N.B. The title page of the second quarto contained after the lines from Horace the following addition:

Huic equidem Consilio palmam do: his me magnifice effero, qui vim tantam in me & potestatem habeam tantæ astutiæ, vera dicendo ut eos ambos fallam. Syr. in Terent. Heaut.

Dedication

p. 118, l. 9 are] is Ww.
13–30 And give me leave . . . unnecessary expence] *om.* Q2, Ww.
32 and ready to own 'em; but it shall be to those who are able to find 'em out] *om.* Q2, Ww.

last l. perfect] regular Ww.
p. 119, 9–13 which I have visibly done... every Character. However,] *om.* Ww.
18 in me] for me Q2, Ww.
20 kind] very kind Q2, Ww.
21 you have injoy'd her, and... fruitful in] and... fruitful to you in Ww.
30 their] the Ww.
34–56 Some little snarling... opened at all.] *om.* Q2, Ww.
p. 120, l. 17 Person's] Q2, Persons Q1
44 have 'em again look] beg 'em again to look Q2, Ww.
46 any Body] *Mellefont* Q2, Ww.
p. 121, l. 1 find they have only] it may be found they have Q2, Ww.
11 Sexes that I know, viz.] Sexes, Male and Female, Q2, Ww.
17 I'm sure cannot] can hardly be Q2; should not Ww.
24–31 I have heard some whispering... before the *Plain-Dealer*] *om.* Ww. *and altered in* Q2.
36–40 I hear a great many of the Fools... owning the *Character*] *om.* Q2., Ww.
last l. Charity] Humanity Q2, Ww.

To my Dear Friend Mr. Congreve

21 had not] had no Q2, Ww.
32 Now] Nor Ww.

p. 126 Dramatis Personæ] Personæ Dramatis Qq.
MEN] Men By Qq.
WOMEN] Women By Qq.
Mr. *Alexander*] Mr. *Verbruggen* Ww.

I

3 Pox I'm] I'm Ww.
9 the more] more Ww.
11 that end] the end Q2, Ww.
14 of following] to follow Ww.
28 Pox, Man] Pshaw, Man Ww.
96 of her Revenge] of Revenge Q2, Ww.
101 put it] put Q1
118 she had] they had Ww.
124 that you] you Q2, Ww.
137 any Suspicion] a Suspicion Q2
154 For all] Notwithstanding Ww.
179 would have been] would be Q2
199 Jesu, 'tis] 'tis Q2, Ww.
203 him] one Q2, Ww.
219 you're going to joke] you joke Ww.
238 particular and novel] particular Q2, Ww.
255 would bepiss yourself—] would—well— Ww.
273 allow] allows Ww.
296 *allons*] allons, here is Company coming Ww.
324 Vice] a Vice Q2, Ww.

329–32 one who . . . hideous form] *om.* Ww.
378 nought] none Q2, Ww.
384 your self] you your self Q2, Ww.
402 Enjoy and ruin] possess and ruin Qq.

II

25 nor . . . ever] and . . . ever Q1; nor . . . never Q2
49 *bel air*] *Belle-air* Qq.
60 my dear *Cynthia*] *Cynthia* Q2, Ww.
89 O Lord] dear Q2, Ww.
91 Jesu] Heav'ns Q2, Ww.
144 all] that Q2, Ww.
150 that tho'] tho' Q2, Ww.
156 Wits] Wit Ww.
171 Shared between us] laid out in an Entertainment Ww.
189 *does*] *must* Ww.
207 inspiration] Inflation Ww.
230 because I won't be headstrong] *om.* W2.
248 in] is in Ww.
255 this three year] these three years Q2, Ww.
257 impenetrable] invincible Ww.
263 speak] say Ww.
283 any Child . . . were] a Child . . . was Q2, Ww.
291 lov'd] loves Ww.
308 procure] to procure Q2, Ww.
323 sure, is it] Is it Ww.
328 or not] or no Q1
365 melancholly] melancholick Ww.
397 my being] being Q2
401 and to—] and to—and to— W2
405 I see] see Q2, Ww.
416 ay] I Q1
427 if I accomplish] if accomplish Q1
469 *The End*] *End* Ww.

III

56 rest] to rest Ww.
89 on his] of his W2
160 of another] another Q2, Ww.
161 To cheat you] To you W2 (misprint)
176 and I lov'd] I lov'd Q1
205 discover all] discover 'em all W1, discover them all W2
219 I shall do] I do Q2, Ww.
256 in awe] in one Q1
270 Pox I can't] I can't Q2, Ww.
283 *Signior*'s] *Signior* Ww.
288 his Wife] a Wife Ww.
327 Jesu, Sir] Sir Q2, Ww.
331 Pray . . . you about you to] Pray . . . you to Ww.
363 so boon mein] *bonnemine* Ww.
381 her Sex] her own Sex Ww.

414 beholding] beholden Ww.
430 you—my] you why my Q1; you my Q2
451 your next] the next Ww.
470 Conversation there?] Conversation? Ww.
510 beholding] beholden Ww.
533 well.] well. *More or less.* Ww.
549 Was that he then] Was he Ww.
550 into . . . Criticisms] in . . . Criticism Q2, Ww.
569 'tis *Eringo*'s] *Eringo*'s Ww.
579 in exposing] by exposing Ww.
636 *The End*] *End* W.

IV, i

12 so willing] willing Q2, Ww.
24 why have you] you have Ww.
39 this moment] this very moment Ww.
93 aking] *om.* Q2, Ww.
136 Heaven] Heav'ns Q2, Ww.
153 this Match] the Match Q2, Ww.
201 doings] doing Q2, Ww.
208 and kiss Papa] kiss and Papa Q1
209 am in such] and such Q1
252 did; all] did. All Q1
255 being] living Q2, Ww.
259 and he talks charmingly] *om.* Ww.
265 the Accounts] Accounts Ww.
277 Fiddles] Fiddlers Q2, Ww.
310 Break Heart] Break my Heart W2
327 represent] present W2
344 self, neither, ha] self, ha Q2, Ww.
345 have a violent] have violent Q1
420 a Cuckold] Cuckold Q2
425 even been] been even Q2, Ww.
426 and render'd . . . benefits of Nature] *om.* Ww.
457 there has . . . us, and] *om.* Ww.
481 Well remember for this . . . come to Bed] Oh! he comes, the Tarquin comes; I cannot bear his Sight. Ww.
515 down from] into Q2, Ww.
521 she's but gone to make] she's gone to make Q2; after she has made Ww.
523 and will] she'll retire Ww.
552 can make you no] can't make you an Q2, Ww.
553 so silent] silent Ww.

IV, ii

6 *Hanging*] Hangings Q2, W1
17 to blame] too blame Q1
24 had made] has made Q2, Ww.
72 it is] 'tis Ww.
77 was] ways Q1

99 e'er I be] e'er I'll be Q2, Ww.
113 he is] he's Q1
124 Though she can . . . in the dark] *om.* Ww.
130 Furies] Funes Q1
144 grown] grow Ww.

V

133 I told you] I tell you Ww.
143 damn'd Villain!] Villain! Ww.
144 Hell and Fire, it] It Ww.
147 to stay his Stomach in the road to her] *om.* Ww.
148 Destruction] Distraction Ww.
152 to a Hell . . . his Element] *om.* Ww.
164 all your Sex] your Sex Q2
176 or not] or nor Q2
192 your own] your Q2
193 and pimp for your Living] *om.* Ww.
195 She's] You're Ww.
230 (*aside*) You may be deceived—] *om.* Ww.
236 but that thou'rt] but thou art Q2, Ww.
255 leads] leading Ww.
269 'em have] 'em has Q2; them has Ww.
281 pleasure] a pleasure Ww.
319 should] shall Ww.
345 that I] I Q2, Ww.
372 Hellish Traitor] Traitor Ww.
387 by Heav'n, this] this Ww.
431 wide Circle] rich Circle Ww.
451 Death] Heart Ww.
456 there want] there wants Q2; it wants Ww.
530 comparable] comparably Ww.
534 O Jesu! Madam] Madam Q2, Ww.
560 and Plagues, and Curses seize you all] *om.* Ww.
566 *lugging in* Maskwell . . . Mellefont *like a Parson*] *disguis'd in a Parson's Habit and pulling in* Maskwell Ww.
577 *They carry out* Maskwell . . . *head*] *Servants seize him.* Ww.

Epilogue

29 Poor Poets thus] Thus poor Poets Qq., W1

LOVE FOR LOVE

EMENDATIONS OF COPYTEXT

p. 215 Dramatis Personæ] Personæ Dramatis Q1
MEN] Men By Q1
WOMEN] Women By Q1
Bowman] W; *Boman* Q1

I

527 you] W; Your Q
577 has] Q2; hast Q1 (*uncorr.*)

II

79 did] Q2; hid Q1 (*uncorr.*)

III

190 don't] Q3; doubt on't Q1, 2
225 me] Q3; one Q1–2
552 Stars] Q3; Science Q1, 2
705 you're] Q2; your Q1

V

501 *Room*] Q2; *Rome* Q1
54 that is] Q2; that's Q1
614 able to pay] Q2; able pay Q1

p. 315 *Epilogue printed her eat the end*] W2; *follows Prologue in* Qq. *and* W1

COLLATIONS OF EARLY EDITIONS

The present text has been collated with the second edition of 1695, the third of 1697, and the fourth of 1704, and with the collected editions of 1710 and 1719.

p. 209 Dedication

9 that smiles [who smiles Ww.
10 that looks] who looks Ww.
11 are each of] are both of Ww.
WILL. CONGREVE] *William Congreve* Ww.
p. 211 PROLOGUE for the Opening of the new Play-House &c.; *om.* Ww.

p. 213 Prologue

8 upon the ungrateful] upon ungratefull Ww.
15 And plant] Well plant Ww.
25 this our] thus our Ww.
p. 215 Dramatis Personæ] Personæ Dramatis Qq.
MEN] Men By Qq. WOMEN] Women By Qq.

I

36 Men in all Ages; these Poets and] *om.* W2
55 that Love] the Love Q3, 4, Ww.
56 I'm sure I'm] I'm sure I am Ww.
141 you won't] you shan't Ww.
157 What do] What does Ww.

159 used] uses Ww.
194 intend] intended Ww.
214 and my] with my W1,
308 *Enter Steward and Whispers*] Steward *who whispers* Ww.
314 drank] drunk Ww.
394 Reputation] Reputations Ww.
467 Lips] Hips Ww.
510 Have you] Is there Ww.
527 you] Ww.; your Qq.
546 Hey day!] *om.* Ww.
558 he have] he has Ww.
574 bode no] bodes me no Q3, 4, Ww.
614 she is obliged] she's obliged Ww.
639 burning of Brandy] burning Brandy Ww.
659 be only to] be but to Ww.
668 a tender for] a Tendre for W2
673 making] to make Q4

II

15 tell, Sir, and] tell and Ww.
70 Jealous when] Jealous of her when Ww.
89 Apostle's Spoons] Apostle Spoons Ww.
125 or any Teats, . . . Years] *om.* Ww.
170 said—] said—he's here already Ww.
228 Wives] Wife's Ww.
251 sent home] brought home Ww.
280 is too] be too Ww.
331 beat up for you . . . and] *om.* Ww.
340 deprive] divest Ww.
393 his Entrails] his own Entrails Ww.
441 these] those Ww.
453 Impudence] Confidence Ww.
477 that] what Ww.
500 for] to be Ww.
503 liking of you] liking you Ww.
509 are not you] are you not Q3, 4, Ww.

III

3 has not locked] has locked Ww.
14 Tattle *and* Miss Prue *at the Door.*] *om. at the Door* Ww.
30 or no] or not Ww.
45 for *Valentine*] to *Valentine* Ww.
152 pox] *om.* Ww.
155 Porters of] Porters at Ww.
190 No don't] No doubt on't Q1, 2
225 press me] press one Q1, 2.
280 Forsooth an you] Forsooth if you Ww.
426 selling of] selling Ww.
486 and the] or the Ww.
487 Without Popery] Unless Popery Ww.

498 yet says] yet he says Ww.
534 of Art] of the Art Q4
552 Stars] Science Q1, 2
631 taking] take W2
677 the t'other] with t'other Q3, 4, Ww.
690 yet I] but I Ww.
752 was marry'd] marry'd W2
805 beholding] beholden Ww.

IV

34 was poor for] was for Q1, 2
44 me truth] me the truth W2
59 tell me, tell me, for] tell me, for W2
83 sorry for him as] sorry as Q3, 4, Ww.
131 a most] almost Ww.
158 this is honest] this honest W2
200 sit you] sit thee Ww.
280 use to be] us'd to be W2
296 unconvertible] unconverted Qq.
331 with that face] with what Face W2
336 denying favours] denying that she had done favours Ww.
350 in to him] to him Ww.
425 have good] have a good Ww.
484 make sport] make us sport Ww.
489 I tell] I'll tell Ww.
505 Wives and Husbands] Husbands and Wives W2
569 intended] intend Q3, 4, Ww.
581 compleat and lively] compleat, lively W2
593 are all these?] are these Q3, 4, Ww.
673 have what thou wilt] *om.* Ww.
712 sad Effects] bad Effects Q3, 4, Ww.
724 for mercenary] for by, mercinary Q1, 2; for by mercenary Q3, 4, W1
753 his Mind] his own Mind Ww.
754 in a Humour] in the Humour Ww.
790 shew Faces] shew our Faces Ww.

V

Sc. 1 *Room*] *Rome* Q1
23 I can] and can Q3, 4, Ww.
33 O Pox] *om.* Ww.
37 Family] Ancestors Ww.
52 'twere pity] 'twere a pity Q4
54 that is] that's Q1, 2
70 commits . . . to the Censure of the World] forfeits Ww.
73 submits both] is a Slave Ww.
95 stood] were Ww.
130 the t'other] the other W2
158 the strongest *Sampson* of your Name] *Sampson,* the strongest of the Name Ww.

161 pulling down] pulling Ww.
269 promise a] promise of Q2–4
301 him be] him to be Q3, 4, Ww.
311 always a sleeping] always asleep Q3, 4, Ww.
329 *Exeunt* Nurse *and* Miss.] *om.* Ww. (*But add at the end of the scene:* Nurse, why are you not gone?)
351 No, hold, I] No, I W2
421 your own Vessel] your new Vessel Q3, 4, Ww.
438 there?] here? Ww.
517 ask my leave] ask me leave Q3, 4, Ww.
528 Come, come Mr.] Come, Mr. W2
583 illiterate Fool] illiterate old Fool W2
584 and the Stars are Lyars; and . . . I have not Patience] *om.* Ww.
589 in this Disorder] in Disorder W2
609 on at that immoderate rate] to that immoderate Degree Ww.
613 of large Promises] of Promises Q3, 4, Ww.
614 able to pay] able pay Q1
633 unto Martyrdom] to Martyrdom Ww.

THE MOURNING BRIDE

EMENDATIONS OF COPYTEXT

When the emendation is taken from one of the three quartos or from the text of the collected editions, the earliest source is given, followed by rejected reading of the copytext.

Prologue

29 if, provok'd] W2; if provok'd Q1–3, W1
41 lose] Q3; loose Q1–2
42 precariously] Q3; percariously Q1–2
p. 325 Dramatis Personæ] W1; Personæ Dramatis Q1–3
MEN] *om.* Qq.
Bowman] Q3; *Boman* Q1–2

I

5 Numbers] Q3; Numbers, Q1–2
23 Chains] Q3; Chains, Q1–2
144 which] Q3; which, Q1–2

II, ii

21 Me in] Q3; Me, in Q1–2
37 Whence is that Voice, whose Shrilness,] Q3; Whence, is that Voice whose Shrilness Q1–2
47 stand, ye] Q3; stand ye Q1–2

III

129 Thoughts] Q3; Thoughts, Q1–2
350 Then] Q2; Then; Q1

IV

1 hast] Hadst
25 Pride,] Q3; Pride. Q1–2
234 then] Q2; than Q1
273 thy] Q2; the Q1
277 thy] Q2; the Q1
315 fly] Q2; fly, Q1
351 off] W2; of Q1–3, W1
412 how prevent] Q3; how, prevent Q1–2
424 Do, my] Q3; Do my Q1–2

V

5 None, my Lord.] Q3; None, my Lord. Q1–2

COLLATIONS OF EARLY EDITIONS

The text is printed from the Harvard copy of the first quarto of 1697. This has been collated with the second quarto of 1697 (Q2) and the third quarto of 1703 (Q3) and the collected works of 1710 (W1) and 1719 (W2).

I

15–17 For Heaven's sake . . . yes,] Dear Madam, cease / Or moderate your Griefs; there is no Cause— / No Cause! Peace, peace; Ww.
35 My Love of you, my] Love of my Ww.
44 Entail'd between] Between Ww.
52–53 O *Alphonso*, *Alphonso*! thou art too / At Peace;] *Alphonso!* O *Alphonso*! / Thou too art quiet—long hast been at Peace— / Both, both— Ww.
56–57 thus?— /] thus— Is it of Force? / Ww.
65 of consequence] of sure consequence Ww.
66 Or, when there,] Or there, Ww.
67 Why did he not use me] Why not ill treated, Ww.
71 But there's no time] No Time Ww.
73 would deprive thee of a] is no more thy Ww.
78 What] Alas! What Ww.
80 I know] I knew Q2
89–90 Indeed I knew not this . . . —If thou didst—] Indeed / I knew not this. *Alm.* O no, thou know'st not half, / Know'st nothing of my Sorrows—if thou didst— Ww.
94–95 indeed I do——— / I thank thee, that thou'lt pity] Leonora, / Indeed, I do, for pitying Ww.
96 'tis] 'tis, alas, Ww.
96–97 Greatness, To] Prerogative / Of Greatness Ww.
99 Griefs] Miseries Ww.
100 said thou didst know nothing,] told thee thou didst nothing know, Ww.

115–17 Whilst . . . perish'd in] The good King flying to avoid the Flames, / Started amidst his Foes, and made Captivity / His fatal Refuge—Wou'd that I had fall'n / Amid Ww.
137 might] shou'd Ww.
143 'Twas that,] 'Twas—as I have told thee— Ww.
148 or Memory] and Thought Ww.
167 It will incense him, thus to . . . drown'd / In Tears, when] 'Twill urge his Wrath, to . . . Tears, / When Ww.
172 Faith / And Vows] Vows / I Ww.
basely / Violated] basely broken. / Ww.
175–76 die first, / Die ten] die; / First, die ten Ww.
179 Leave for a Moment to behold Eternal Bliss] One Moment, cease to gaze on perfect Bliss, Ww.
192 Methinks my . . . Having] My . . . having so well Ww.
197–99 Are busied in the General Joy, . . . and visit] Are wrap'd and busied in the general Joy, / Thou wilt withdraw, and privately with me / Steal forth, to visit Ww.
201–3 no Violence. . . . this Vow:] no Ill, / Nor Violence.———I feel my self more light, / And more at large, since I have made this Vow. Ww.
210 Of the Kings approach.] The King is just arriv'd Ww.
213 . . . I know, his Errand is] his Errand is, I know, Ww.
215 And with his Artful Tongue, to gild] And gild Ww.
218 nor] or Ww.
223 unequal] unequal'd Ww.
241 As they were all of] As if they were all of Q3; As if they were all Ww.
242 his] its Ww.
251 and Humble Praise.] *om.* Ww.
256–57 Has better done; / In proving with his Sword, upon your Foes] Has better done; in proving with his Sword Ww.
273 Joy. To] Joy. Believe me, Sir, to Ww.
277 —But some] —some Ww.
279 How is it] Why is't, Ww.
281–82 You, and yours, . . . Affliction] In opposition to my Brightness, you / And yours are all like Daughters of Affliction. Ww.
283 I offend] I in this offend. Ww.
286–87 From Death . . . expired.] From Wreck and Death, wants yet to be expired. Ww.
320 offended.] offended.—Sure, no more, Ww.
325–26 Vow. / You stand excused] Vow: For you, / It shall be your Excuse Ww.
330 O my] My Ww.
339 For this high Honour.] *om.* Ww.
340 Loyalty] Services Ww.
343 Shall shine on *Garcia*'s Nuptials] *Garcia*, shall shine to grace thy Nuptials— Ww.
346 Alas,] *om.* Ww.
348 A Bridal Qualm; soon off.] A Fit of Bridal Fear; W1; —Fear: W2.

356 *Trumpets.* Enter Alonzo.] Now, what would *Alonzo*? Ww.
359 Alonzo.] Officer Qq.
The] Your Ww.
366 he does] but he Ww.
367 attend] attends Ww.
392 In Triumph] In pleasing Triumph Ww.
404 disobey me?] disobey? Ww.
408–9 bad ... bad] bid ... bid Ww.
415 Favours conferr'd] Such Favours so conferr'd Ww.
416 deserve / ... Thanks /] unsought / ... Minds / Ww.
428 is *Osmyn*] is he of whom I spoke, that's W1;—spoke; that's W2
432 So ill can brook] So hardly can endure Ww.
443 show no Resentment] seem not to heed
444 Of his Arrogance yet] His arrogant Reply
445 his Friend may be] perhaps his Friend / Yet lives, and is Ww.
448 be it your Care to make that search] that Search shall be your Care: Ww.
458 But] Now Ww.
The End] *End* Ww.

II, i

8 or Glimpse] or show a Glimpse Ww.
12 Unparalell'd Fidelity!] *om.* Ww.
14–15 And could ... Meeting] *om.* Ww.
18 I see him not.] I saw him not, nor any like him Ww.
38 *Heli.* Y'are truly Noble.] *om.* Ww.
46 of his and hers confess it] from him and her confirms it Ww.
67 speak to me, nay, speak,] let me hear thy Voice; Ww.
68 And let me hear thy Voice; / My own] Nay, quickly speak to me, and let me hear / Thy Voice—my own Ww.
80 Shew] Then shew Ww.
81 Lead me] Lead on Ww.

II, ii

14 *Almeria.*] *om.* Q1.
17 wearied] weary Ww.
20 Eternal Peace] Peace Eternal Ww.
39 his dead] his Ww.
41 Mercy and Providence! O speak to it] Mercy! Providence! O speak Ww.
46 ... rivet me To Earth, and] Rivet me, and W1; Rivet and W2
56 'tis my] 'tis, it is, my Ww.
57 O Heav'n unfold these Wonders!] *om.* Ww.
63 By Heav'n———*Almeria*!] Ha! 'tis he! and with———*Almeria!* Ww.
64 *Almeria!*] *om.* Ww.
64–65 Happiness! / O Joy] Happiness! O Joy / Ww.
73 Look on *Alphonso.*] *om.* Ww.
76 Thy Father is not here ... nor] Look on thy *Alphonso.* / Thy Father is not here, my Love, nor *Garcia*: Nor am I Ww.

100 Let] Stay a while— / Let Ww.
103 Why] And why Ww.
107 Of Delight, I cannot bear it—I shall] Of Joy, of Bliss—I cannot bear—I must Ww.
112 me behold] me again behold Ww.
114 much, alas; how] much; how Ww.
116 Griefs have] Griefs, I know, have Ww.
118 much lamented] much, too tenderly lamented Ww.
119 too much] too tenderly Ww.
128 Truth] Faithfulness and Love! Ww.
134 Without thee cou'd not cure.] Could only by restoring thee have cur'd. Ww.
145 exquisite, amazing] exquisite, this most amazing Ww.
155 As . . . dozes my weak Sense] It . . . stuns my Sense Ww.
157 thou didst call me] thou, my Love, didst call me; thou Ww.
158 How camest] True; but how cam'st Ww.
165 I indeed shou'd see thee—] That I indeed shou'd be so blest to see thee Ww.
166 thee] thou Ww.
167 that] who Ww.
169 *Antonio* here! / My . . . Wreck of Seas] *Antonio* / I'm fortunate indeed—my . . . Rage of Seas Ww.
174–75 And Rage of War: . . . saw / Him fall.] And War: For in the Fight I saw him fall. / Ww.
178 to seek . . .] Impatiently to seek Ww.
179 lead you, / To] knew / Your Grief Ww.
181 I saw] When with Astonishment I saw Ww.
186 That thus . . . good / As] That persevering still . . . Hand, / It . . . as Ww.
193 And bending this way.] Who by their pointing seem to mark this Place Ww.
195 wish our . . . we / Could] wish at least . . . Dream, / Or we Ww.
199 she?] she? Why are you alarm'd? Ww.
208 unfold.] unfold, / E'er next we meet——— Ww.
214 her—Now] her—yet—And now Ww.
215f. and look / Upon my Thought . . . Faculty] and view my Thought, / So shall you still behold her———'twill not be. / O impotence of Sight! Mechanick Sense, / Which to exterior Objects ow'st thy Faculty, Ww.
221 like] as do all Ww.
229 I have] I before have Ww.
230 I'll muse on that, lest I exceed in thinking.] *om.* Ww.
238 of Love?] reserv'd for Love? Ww.
247 Ha, Zara!] Ha, 'tis Zara! Ww.
254 not.] not, 'till now.
258 that] who Ww.
269 thee in] thee, for 'em, in Ww.
279 will it] will't Ww.
282 chafing] then chaf'd Ww.
290 Bankrupt even in my Hopes.] Bankrupt even in Hopes Q2, 3; / poor and Bankrupt even in Hopes. Ww.

301 On to . . . he was lost] To . . . he late was lost Ww.
307 lost, the] lost, and now the Ww.
308 What] And now abandon'd—say, what Ww.
349 here] here, and entring now. Ww.
365 Lord] Pow'r Ww.
366 And me; presume] Presume Ww.
378–79 promis'd Freedom / From his Chains] undertook / He should be set at large Ww.

III

20 Heav'n, Heav'n] *Heav'n* Q2, 3; Ww.
71–72 Liberty And Native Rights] Rights and Liberty. Ww.
75–76 Deaf to Revenge . . . Nay,] And the loud Cries of my dead Father's Blood / Deaf to Revenge—nay, Ww.
100 Counsel] Council Q3, Ww.
101 hating] who hate W2
102 no doubt] for certain Ww.
132 There, in] For there Ww.
133 The . . . he beheld] He in the . . . saw Ww.
136–37 which I / Will treasure here] which here / I'll treasure as Ww.
161 that . . . what] who . . . whom Ww.
165 thou shall] thou shalt Q3, Ww.
216–17 as / The present . . . rests] now / So does the . . . rest Ww.
240 mine, thus] mine, while I'm thus Ww.
242 and bruise] or bruise Q2, 3; W1
279 Then] Than Q3, Ww.
282–83 could'st . . . wou'd] would'st . . . cou'd Ww.
296 Indeed; . . . so,] Indeed, . . . so; Q3, Ww.
297 kill me then,] then kill me W2
298 me, spurn me,] me: What, Ww.
308 What] Why Ww.
350 dash my / Disfigur'd Face] disfigure / And dash my Face Ww.
352 the flinty Ground] the Ground Q2, 3; the flinty Floor Ww.
355–57 where I will bite . . . Cruelty] *om.* Ww.
371 lower] deeper Ww.
403–4 and in / Distress] and thus / Distress'd Ww.
431 'tis much] 'tis too much Ww.
444 Ha!] *om.* Ww.
447 take heed . . . Himself.] look, this Slave / Attempt no Means to make himself away; Ww.
449 Safety] Safety now Ww.
451–52 Princess self, permitted to / Confer] Princess suffer'd or to see / Or speak Ww.

IV

1 hast] hadst Q1, 2
13–14 corresponding with / The Heads of those] and his Correspondence / With them Ww.
77–78 Alphonso, / Still alive, were] Alphonso / Were still alive, and Ww.

87 Open'd the] Open'd and urg'd the Ww.
92 occur] occur at once Ww.
116 that] who Ww.
119–20 that / *Alphonso*, privately] he, / *Alphonso*, secretly Ww.
128 We will our self behold the Execution.] *om.* Ww.
131 all else void] except *Gonsalez* leave Ww.
131–34 *Garcia*, give Order . . . Troops.] *om.* Ww.
162 You order none may have Admittance to] You give strict Charge, that none may be admitted Ww.
163 The Pris'ner, . . . Messengers] To see the Pris'ner, . . . Mutes Ww.
269–70 Yes, Guilt: . . . Thy Guilty Mind;] They are the dumb Confessions of thy Mind;] They mean thy Guilt; Ww.
281 That was—that was] Who was—who was Ww.
293 Death and Perdition, she] O Patience, hear—she owns it! Ww.
355 Alas, she raves!] She raves! Ww.
389 after it,] after, see! Ww.
391 'tis] ah! Ww.
392–93 from / The Tomb it calls—] calls / Me from the Tomb—Ww.
434 that] who Ww.
443 Away,] And say Ww.

V, i

8 as easily] with as much ease Ww.
9–10 fix'd foundation, as / Unlock] Centre of this Earth, / As loose Ww.
13 Ha! seize] Ha! stop and seize Ww.
18 Alonzo *re-enters with a Paper.*] Alonzo *follows him, and returns with a Paper.* Ww.
26 a Ponyard] his Ponyard W2.
36 Rage, Rage] new Rage Ww.
37 treble Fury] trebled Fury Q2, 3, Ww.
40 poor and mean] poor Ww.
47 conferr'd with him] with him conferr'd; Ww.
75 Resolve to do't, or else—] Resolve, or Ww.
76 My Lord] Sir Ww.
86–87 thither———] thither—mark me well— / There with his Turbant, and his Robe array'd / And laid along as he now lies supine, / I shall convict her to her Face of Falshood. / When for Alphonso's she shall take my Hand, / And breath her Sighs upon my Lips for his, / Sudden I'll start, and dash her with her Guilt. Ww.
88 do / Thou follow,] thou / Follow me, Ww.
91 'tis strange. Ha! 'twas / ha! 'twas the King! Ww.
96–97 Think'st thou / He saw me not?] Dost think / He saw me?
98 He did: But then as if] Yes: But then, as if he thought Ww.
130 Instruct . . . that they] Give Order, that Ww.
132 those; such Ww.

V, ii

Scene changes to the Prison. *Scene opening shews the Prison.* *Enter* Gonsalez,] Gonsalez *alone*, Ww.

4 is too unlock'd] too is unlock'd W2.
43–44 flying, was / Proclaim'd] was, while flying / Pronounc'd Ww.
85–86 with one weak Hand, and bearing / With the other,] with only one weak Hand, / While t'other bore Ww.
102–03 amuz'd, mean time, . . . Presence] amus'd with Hopes; / And in the meantime fed with Expectation / To see the King in Person Ww.
115–18 a Corner of / The Room . . . Trunk] an obscure Corner / Dispos'd it, muffled in the Mute's Attire, / Leaving to view of them that enter next, / Alone the undistinguishable Trunk: Ww.
124 not yet the] no Ww.
125 Repent. Haste thee, *Alonzo*, hence] Haste thee, *Alonzo*, haste thee hence Ww.
144 Cause, and Purpose of] Cause of this my Errand Ww.
145 My Errand,] And Purpose, Ww.
162–71 O——start Eyes, . . . perfidious King] O——I'm lost, / O Osmyn! O Alphonso! Cruel Fate! / Cruel, cruel, O more than killing Object! / I came prepar'd to die, and see thee die— / Nay, came prepar'd my self to give thee Death— / But cannot bear to find thee thus, my Osmyn—/ O this accurs'd, this base, this treach'rous King! Ww.
173 the King is no where, to] for no where can the King Ww.
183 fails—] fails—I sink— Ww.
189 a Remedy . . . But Oh, / He] a certain Remedy . . . / But Oh, Ww.
229–30 And look not on; . . . rain Blood.] Return and look not on; for there's a Dagger / Ready to stab the Sight, and make your Eyes / Rain Blood.— Ww.
231 O I foresee that Object in my Mind.] O I foreknow, foresee that Object. Ww.
245 and look] they look Ww.
248 put to Death] slain Ww.
255–56 and yet too greedy . . . of Death] yet greedy, to drink all— / —Oh, for another Draught of Death—What mean they? Ww.
259 O thanks] Thanks to Ww,
262 Knees—forbear.—] Knee I beg—— Ww.
264 there, who prostrate lies;] there? behold who prostrate lyes, Ww.
307 in turning on] which on themselves Ww.
308 Themselves] Has turn'd Ww.
315 She shall be Royally interr'd.] *om.* Ww.
318 that] who Ww.

Epilogue

7 some] them W2
14 if they're] when they're Ww.

THE WAY OF THE WORLD

EMENDATIONS OF COPYTEXT

p. 394 Dramatis Personæ] Personæ Dramatis Qq.
MEN] W; MEN By Qq.

I

485 Parrot, or than] Q2; Parrot: Or then Q1

II

245 we'll] W; will Qq.
443 than the] Q2; then the Q1

III

393 have] Q2; have have Q1

IV

117 sought] fought Qq., Ww. (*misprint uncorrected*)
492 on the rack] Q2; on a rack Q1

V

24 hear] Q2; here Q1
131 frailties] Q2; frailty's Q1
178 a tryall] Q; by a tryall Q1

Epilogue

l. 2 I'm thinking] Q2; In thinking Q1

COLLATIONS OF EARLY EDITIONS

The present text has been collated with the second quarto of 1706 and the editions of the collected works, 1710 and 1719.

p. 390 Dedication

p. 390, 23 ridiculous] ridicul'd Q2, Ww.
391, 26 Laugh out] laugh at Q2, Ww.
392, 5 wanting equal to the Capacity of] wanting, equal in Capacity to Ww.
p. 394 Dramatis Personæ] Personæ Dramatis Qq.
MEN] MEN . . . By Q1

I

79 that Amour] this Amour Q2, Ww.
82 without she] unless she Ww.
97 than your] than is your Ww.
147 Man that is] Man who is one Ww.

221 the t'other] t'other Ww.
240 the Messenger] a Messenger Ww.
259 But she's] she's W2
289 honest Fellow, and a very pretty] pretty Fellow, and a very honest W2
292 him neither— . . . had but any] him— . . . had any Ww.
299 Pity faith] Pity Ww.
346 the Coach] a Coach Ww.
359 Trulls that] Trulls whom Ww.
408 that loves] who loves Ww.
485 Parrot, or than] Parrot: Or then Q1
502 Do you.] You do? Ww.
519 a Fire] Fire Ww.

II

8 as such] as from such Ww.
19 compliance with] compliance to Ww.
151 loving of another] loving another Ww.
242 I've done] I have done Q2
245 we'll retire] will retire Q1, 2
300 Condition she] Condition that she Ww.
324 her Streamers] Streamers Ww.
335 in Disgrace] just disgrac'd Ww.
366 I fancy ones Hair wou'd not curl if it were pinn'd up with Prose;] *om.* Q2, Ww.
443 than the] Q2, then the Q1
471 one Moment] a Moment W2
482 that *Foible*'s] *Foible*'s Ww.
561 I am married] I'm married Q2, Ww.

III

61 Go you Thing and send her in.] (*Moved to the end of the scene*) Ww.
76 Well here it is, all that is left; all that is not kiss'd away—] *om.* Q2, Ww.
127 Hands] Hand Q2, Ww.
156 Will a not] Will he not W2
169 swimminess] swimmingness Q2, Ww.
179 Nothing but Importunity can surmount Decorums] *om.* Q2, Ww.
227 *Pass-par-tout*] *Pass-par-toute* Ww.
243 and stalk for him, till he takes his Stand to aim at a Fortune] *om.* Ww.
296 I'll swear] I swear Q2, Ww.
299 the Liberty] that Liberty Ww.
374 *And sung by Mrs.* Hodgson] *om.* Ww.
429 Read, any more than] read, than Ww.
454 Somebody here that] some Body hither that Ww.
457 any Body in] any in W2
614 I come] I am come W2
631 an Anticipated Cuckold] a Cuckold by Anticipation Ww.
637 and outstrip'd] and be outstripp'd Q2, Ww.

653 She might throw up her Cards; but Ile be hang'd if she did not put Pam in her Pocket.] *om.* Ww.
712 *Mirabell,* now] *Mirabell.* now Q1; *Mirabell* now; You'll Ww.

IV

73 would have] will have Q2, Ww.
117 sought] fought (*misprint*) Qq. Ww.
143 when you're dispos'd.] *om.* W2
206 for ever after] ever after Q2, Ww.
262 me the Father] me Father Ww.
317 when you] for you Ww.
330 their proceedings] the Proceedings Ww.
463 Wenches.] Wenches with broom-sticks. Ww.
492 on the rack] on a rack Q1.
573 see by the Superscription it is like] see, the Superscription is like Ww.

V

19 your *Merchandize*] the Merchandize Ww.
24 hear] here Q1
55 be Constable] be a Constable W2
99 of Verses and Poems] of Poems Ww.
178 stand] stand by Q1
205 O my dear] O dear Ww.
234 *Flounder-man*'s or the *Woman* that crys *Grey-pease*] Flounder-man's Ww.
245 Congratulate, than] Q2, Congratulate then Q1
363 an she] and she Q2, Ww.
374 for your pity] for Pity Ww.
392 wou'd I might] wou'd I may Ww.
408 *apart*] *Aside* Ww.
474 bought and brought] brought Ww.
549 inscrib'd] written Ww.
596 again; for I] again; I Q2, Ww.

Epilogue

l. 2 I'm thinking] In thinking Q1